HANDBOOK OF CRITICAL POLICY STUDIES

HANDBOOKS OF RESEARCH ON PUBLIC POLICY

Series Editor: Frank Fischer, *Rutgers University, New Jersey, USA*

The objective of this series is to publish *Handbooks* that offer comprehensive overviews of the very latest research within the key areas in the field of public policy. Under the guidance of the Series Editor, Frank Fischer, the aim is to produce prestigious high-quality works of lasting significance. Each *Handbook* will consist of original, peer-reviewed contributions by leading authorities, selected by an editor who is a recognized leader in the field. The emphasis is on the most important concepts and research as well as expanding debate and indicating the likely research agenda for the future. The *Handbooks* will aim to give a comprehensive overview of the debates and research positions in each key area of focus.

Titles in the series include:

International Handbook on Ageing and Public Policy
Edited by Sarah Harper and Kate Hamblin

Handbook on Complexity and Public Policy
Edited by Robert Geyer and Paul Cairney

Handbook of Critical Policy Studies
Edited by Frank Fischer, Douglas Torgerson, Anna Durnová and Michael Orsini

Handbook of Critical Policy Studies

Edited by

Frank Fischer

Rutgers University, New Jersey, USA

Douglas Torgerson

Trent University, Canada

Anna Durnová

University of Vienna, Austria

Michael Orsini

University of Ottawa, Canada

HANDBOOKS OF RESEARCH ON PUBLIC POLICY

Cheltenham, UK • Northampton, MA, USA

Published by
Edward Elgar Publishing Limited
The Lypiatts
15 Lansdown Road
Cheltenham
Glos GL50 2JA
UK

Edward Elgar Publishing, Inc.
William Pratt House
9 Dewey Court
Northampton
Massachusetts 01060
USA

A catalogue record for this book
is available from the British Library

Library of Congress Control Number: 2015943169

This book is available electronically in the **Elgar**online
Social and Political Science subject collection
DOI 10.4337/9781783472352

ISBN 978 1 78347 234 5 (cased)
ISBN 978 1 78347 235 2 (eBook)

Typeset by Servis Filmsetting Ltd, Stockport, Cheshire
Printed and bound by CPI Group (UK) Ltd, Croydon, CR0 4YY

Contents

Contributors

Heidrun Åm is a Researcher at the Centre for Technology and Society, Department of Interdisciplinary Studies of Culture, NTNU in Trondheim, Norway. Heidrun is interested in the governance of new and emerging technologies and in the sociomaterial production of evidence for policy-making. She has looked at themes such as nanotechnology, integrated research, and responsible research and innovation (RRI). Her analysis combines poststructuralist policy analysis and Science and Technology Studies (STS).

Mani R. Banjade is Postdoctoral Research Fellow at the Center for International Forestry Research (CIFOR). His current research engagement is on emergence, processes and outcomes of land and forest tenure reforms in developing countries across Latin America, Africa and Asia. His research interests include deliberative governance, community forestry and multi-level governance.

Marlon Barbehön is a Research Fellow at the Institute of Political Science at Heidelberg University, Germany. His current work focuses on discourse-analytical approaches within urban studies and welfare state research.

Kathrin Braun is Professor for Comparative Politics and Policy Analysis at the University of Vienna, Austria. Her main research areas are science and technology policy, governance and biomedicine, biopolitics and politics of historic justice and memory.

Vincent Dubois is Professor of Sociology and Political Science at the University of Strasbourg, France, where he is a member at the SAGE research unit and at the Institute for Advanced Study. His research fields include cultural policy and social welfare.

Anna Durnová is Hertha-Firnberg Assistant Professor at the Department of Political Science at the University of Vienna, Austria. She researches the role of emotions in policy process using examples from health care policies. She is also Book Review Editor of *Critical Policy Studies*.

Laureen Elgert is Assistant Professor of International Development and Environmental Politics at Worcester Polytechnic Institute, Massachusetts, USA. Her research involves the politics of expertise, evidence and metrics of sustainability and how critical analysis can contribute to improving deliberative environmental policy. Laureen's geographical interests include Latin America and, more recently, China.

Selen A. Ercan is a Postdoctoral Research Fellow at the Institute for Governance and Policy Analysis, University of Canberra, Australia. She works in the area of deliberative democracy focusing particularly on the capacity of this approach in addressing irreconcilable value conflicts in contemporary democracies. Aside from the theory and practice of deliberative democracy, Selen's current research interests include alternative forms of political participation, protest movements and interpretivist approaches to policy analysis.

Susan S. Fainstein is a Senior Research Fellow in the Department of Urban Planning and Design at the Harvard University Graduate School of Design, where she was a professor until 2012. She is also a Visiting Professor at the Lee Kuan Yew School of Public Policy of the National University of Singapore. She previously taught at Columbia and Rutgers universities. She is a recipient of the Distinguished Educator Award for lifetime contributions and of the Davidoff Award for her book *The Just City*, both from the Association of Collegiate Schools of Planning (ACSP). She is the co-author of *Restructuring the City* (Longman) and *Urban Political Movements* (Prentice Hall) and has edited books on gender and planning, urban tourism, urban theory and planning theory. Her areas of research are comparative public policy, urban redevelopment and planning theory.

Frank Fischer is Senior Research Associate at the Environmental Policy Research Centre at the Free University of Berlin, Germany and Rutgers University, New Jersey, USA. His most recent publications include *Democracy and Expertise: Reorienting Policy Inquiry* (Oxford) and *The Argumentative Turn Revisited: Public Policy as Communicative Practice* (Duke University Press), co-edited with Herbert Gottweis. Currently he is completing *Climate Change and the Democratic Prospect* (Oxford). He is also co-editor of the journal of *Critical Policy Studies* (Routledge).

Steven Griggs is Professor of Public Policy at De Montfort University, UK. His research interests are in political discourse theory and its contribution to our understanding of policy-making. He has recently published *The Politics of Airport Expansion in the UK* (Manchester University Press) (with David Howarth) and the edited collection, *Practices of Freedom* (Cambridge University Press) (with Aletta J. Norval and Hendrik Wagenaar).

David Howarth is Professor in Social and Political Theory at the University of Essex, UK. His research interests are in poststructuralist theories of society, politics and policy-making. His publications include *Discourse* (Open University Press), *Logics of Critical Explanation in Social and Political Theory* (Routledge) (with Jason Glynos) and *The Politics of Airport Expansion in the UK* (Manchester University Press) (with Steven Griggs). He has recently published the research monograph *Poststructuralism and After* (Palgrave Macmillan).

Helen Ingram is a Research Fellow at the Southwest Center, University of Arizona, USA. She previously retired from the University of California at Irvine. In addition to her much cited work with Anne Schneider continued in the chapter included in this volume, she has written widely in both public policy and water policy. She is a co-author of the book *The Power of Narratives in Environmental Networks* (The MIT Press, 2013).

Bob Jessop is Distinguished Professor of Sociology and Co-Director of the Cultural Political Economy Research Centre at Lancaster University, UK. He developed the strategic-relational approach in the social sciences and is well known for his contributions to state theory, critical political economy and, most recently, cultural political economy. His most recent book is *The State: Past, Present, Future* (Polity, 2015).

Wolfram Lamping is an Associate Professor at the Technische Universität Darmstadt, Germany. He works on comparative public policy, policy analysis and political systems in a comparative perspective.

Raul P. Lejano is Associate Professor of Environmental Education at New York University, USA and conducts research on relational approaches to environmental policy and institutions. He is the author of *Frameworks for Policy Analysis: Merging Text and Context* (Routledge) and is co-author of *The Power of Narrative in Environmental Networks* (The MIT Press).

Eva Lövbrand is Associate Professor at the Department of Thematic Studies: Environmental Change at Linköping University, Sweden. Much of Eva's work has focused on the ideas, knowledge claims and expert practices that inform environmental politics and policy-making. She is also co-editor of the forthcoming *Research Handbook on Climate Governance* (Edward Elgar Publishing, 2015).

Timothy W. Luke is University Distinguished Professor of Political Science at Virginia Polytechnic Institute and State University in Blacksburg, Virginia, USA. He also serves as the Program Chair for Government and International Affairs in the School of Public and International Affairs, and founded the Alliance for Social, Political, Ethical, and Social Theory (ASPECT) doctoral program in the College of Liberal Arts and Human Sciences at Virginia Tech.

Ricardo Fabrino Mendonça is Assistant Professor in the Department of Political Science, Federal University of Minas Gerais, Brazil and one of the coordinators of the Research Group on Democracy and Justice (Margem). He works on democratic theory, critical theory, social movements and political communication. Some of his recent publications have appeared in *Policy Studies*; *Constellations*; *Political Studies*; *Policy & Society*; *Critical Policy Studies*; and *Brazilian Political Science Review*.

Sybille Münch is Assistant Professor of Theory of Public Policy at the Center for the Study of Democracy at Leuphana University Lüneburg, Germany. Her research focuses on interpretive approaches to policy analysis as well as urban and migration research.

Hemant R. Ojha is currently a Research Fellow at the School of Social Sciences at UNSW, Australia. He is also a Senior Fellow (honorary) at the University of Melbourne. For more than 15 years he has worked in Nepal on critical action research and policy analysis in forestry, natural resource management and rural development. He is a founder of ForestAction Nepal (2000) for which he served as the Executive Coordinator and the Chair of the board. He is also the founding Chair of the Southasia Institute of Advanced Studies (2011) based in Nepal.

Michael Orsini is Full Professor in the School of Political Studies and currently Director of the Institute of Feminist and Gender Studies at the University of Ottawa, Canada. He is the co-editor of *Critical Policy Studies* (University of British Columbia Press, 2007) and *Worlds of Autism: Across the Spectrum of Neurological Difference* (University of Minnesota Press, 2013).

Sung Jin Park is a Senior Consultant in Samsung SDS's Smart Town Consulting Group, Seoul, Republic of Korea. She has a PhD in urban and regional planning, and her work has focused on the relationship between implementation and so-called middle-level bureaucrats. Related to this is much work conducted by her on the digital empowerment of rural communities.

Stephanie Paterson is an Associate Professor in the Department of Political Science at Concordia University in Montreal, Canada. Her research interests include gender and public policy, feminist policy analysis and reproductive politics.

Dieter Plehwe, PhD, political scientist, works as Senior Fellow at the Social Policy and Inequality Department of the Berlin Social Science Research Centre, Germany. He is best known for his work on think-tanks, transnational expertise, consulting and lobby/advocacy networks and the history and transformation of neoliberalism.

Thomas Saretzki is Professor of Political Theory and Public Policy at the Institute of Political Science and head of the research area on participation and public policy at the Center for the Study of Democracy, Leuphana University of Lüneburg, Germany.

Francesca Scala is an Associate Professor of Political Science at Concordia University in Montreal, Canada. Her research focuses on issues related to gender, policy analysis and the politics of knowledge and expertise.

Vivien A. Schmidt is Jean Monnet Professor of European Integration, Professor of International Relations in the Frederick S. Pardee School of Global Studies and Professor of Political Science at Boston University, where she is also Founding Director of BU's Center for the Study of Europe. Her recent books include *Resilient Liberalism in Europe's Political Economy* (co-edited, Cambridge, 2013), *Debating Political Identity and Legitimacy in the European Union* (co-edited, Routledge, 2011), *Democracy in Europe* (Oxford, 2006) and *The Futures of European Capitalism* (Oxford, 2002). She is currently working on a book entitled *Discursive Institutionalism: Ideas and Discourse in Political Analysis* (Oxford, forthcoming).

Anne L. Schneider has had a long-time interest in the question of how public policy can (should) serve democracy but so often fails to do so. She and her colleague Helen Ingram are the authors of *Policy Design for Democracy* (University of Kansas Press) and *Deserving and Entitled: Social Constructions and Public Policy* (SUNY Press). She is now retired but active in tracking legislation and advocating for socially just public policy in Arizona.

Krishna K. Shrestha is Senior Lecturer in Development Studies at the University of New South Wales, Australia. His core research interest encompasses political ecology, climate change adaptation, development studies and urban planning, and in particular the intersection of the four with the work on environmental and climate justice in Nepal, India and Australia.

Holger Strassheim is Assistant Professor at the Humboldt-University of Berlin and guest researcher at the Berlin Social Science Center, Germany. His publications include works on public policy and governance, expertise and evidence-based policy, welfare change, consumer policy and behavioural economics.

Johannes Stripple is Associate Professor in Political Science, Lund University, Sweden. He explores and develops critical climate studies at the intersection between critical political theory and emerging practices of a rapidly warming and carbon constrained world. Johannes has recently edited (with Harriet Bulkeley) *Governing the Climate: New Approaches to Rationality, Power and Politics* (Cambridge University Press, 2014).

Ngai-Ling Sum is Reader in Cultural Political Economy and Co-director of the Cultural Political Economy Research Centre at Lancaster University, UK. She has made pioneering theoretical contributions to cultural political economy and applied these to China/Hong Kong and East Asia more generally. She is the senior author, with Bob Jessop, of *Towards a Cultural Political Economy: Putting Culture in its Place in Political Economy* (Edward Elgar Publishing, 2013).

Douglas Torgerson is Professor Emeritus of Politics at Trent University in Canada. A past Editor of *Policy Sciences* and a current Forum Editor for *Critical Policy Studies*, he focuses his work on theoretical aspects of policy studies and environmentalism.

Hendrik Wagenaar is Professor in the Department of Urban Studies and Planning and Associate Director of the Crick Centre for Understanding Politics at the University of Sheffield, UK. He is author of *Meaning in Action: Interpretation and Dialogue in Policy Analysis* (M.E. Sharpe, 2011) and co-editor of *Practices of Freedom: Decentered Governance, Conflict and Democratic Participation* (Cambridge University Press, 2014).

Dvora Yanow is Guest Professor in Wageningen University's Department of Social Sciences, Communication, Philosophy and Technology Sub-Department, the Netherlands. Her research/teaching explores the generation and communication of knowing and meaning in organizational and policy settings. Her most recent book, *Interpretive Research Design: Concepts and Processes*, written with Peregrine Schwartz-Shea, is the first volume in their co-edited Routledge Series on Interpretive Methods; their co-edited *Interpretation and Method: Empirical Research Methods and the Interpretive Turn* (M.E. Sharpe) is now out in a second edition.

In memory of Herbert Gottweis, 1958–2014

1 Introduction to critical policy studies
Frank Fischer, Douglas Torgerson,
Anna Durnová and Michael Orsini

1. EMERGENCE AND THEORETICAL EVOLUTION

Critical policy studies, like policy studies generally, focuses on the policymaking process. That focus includes two key concerns: one involves
how policies are decided in a political setting and the other is focused
on the practices of policy analysis, specifically on how they address the
formulation and assessment of particular policies and their outcomes. As
such, critical policy studies has emerged as an effort to understand policy
processes not only in terms of apparent inputs and outputs, but more
importantly in terms of the interests, values and normative assumptions –
political and social – that shape and inform these processes (see Barbehön
et al., Chapter 13, this volume; Lejano and Park, Chapter 15, this volume;
and Åm, Chapter 16, this volume). Rejecting the assumption that analysis
can be neutral, entirely uncommitted to and removed from interests and
values, critical policy studies seeks to identify and examine existing commitments against normative criteria such as social justice, democracy and
empowerment (see Fainstein, Chapter 10, this volume).[1]

Basic to policy analysis generally are two very old ideas – namely, the
ideas that government decisions should be based on sound knowledge,
and that such knowledge should rise above politics. Although these ideas
have their roots in the ancient notion of rule by philosopher kings, in the
modern world these ideas point instead to the conception of a governing
elite of technical experts – or technocracy – working as a neutral instrument on behalf of human progress. Critical policy studies throws the
ideas of 'expertocracy' and technical governance into question, regarding
them as advancing both an unrealistic promise and a threat to practical
knowledge and democratic governance.

One of the most important issues for critical policy studies, then, has to
do with the nature of knowledge, both the knowledge used to shape policy
and the kinds of knowledge and assumptions that guide the implementation of policy decisions. Basic to this approach has been a critique of the
positivist conception of knowledge that has long informed the theory
and practice of policy studies and policy analysis in particular. Critical

policy studies, drawing on studies of the cultural and historical context of knowledge, largely adopts an interpretive, culturally and historically constructivist understanding of knowledge and its creation.

With regard to knowledge of the policy process, critical policy studies examines the implications of the social construction of knowledge for policy decision-making (see Ingram and Schneider, Chapter 14, this volume; and Paterson and Scala, Chapter 25, this volume). It seeks to reveal the ways in which particular kinds of policy analysis – together with their findings and recommendations – have different sorts of impacts on the political and policy processes. This is the case whether analysis projects an image of neutrality that leaves unexamined and unchallenged the context of power relationships in which it is undertaken (see Luke, Chapter 8, this volume); or whether, in contrast, inquiry is explicitly undertaken with normative criteria that follow an emancipatory interest seeking to empower participation and enhance democracy.

In the decades following World War II, Harold Lasswell introduced the 'policy orientation' and a call for the 'policy sciences of democracy' (see Torgerson, Chapter 2, this volume). But the approach that actually emerged in the political and social sciences was inspired by a technocratic notion of social engineering and political steering. The idea of technocracy itself goes back to nineteenth-century positivism in Europe, and France in particular, a school of thought that influenced progressivism in the United States during the early twentieth century.[2] After World War II, the accent on social engineering in the United States came with an expansion of the role of policy analysis in government, associated with the War on Poverty and the Vietnam War (see Fischer, Chapter 3, this volume). But these experiences were not without problems, giving rise to skeptical responses from various quarters of society. These responses arose in part due to concern about the growing prominence of unelected and largely unknown policy experts in governmental decision processes and in part as a consequence of the failure of policy analysts and expert advisors to provide the promised results. One important strand of response by the later 1970s was reflected in a new orientation in policy inquiry – variously called post-positivist, interpretive, or critical.

Critical policy studies, and critical policy analysis in particular, were an academic response to the social and political turmoil of a particular period, roughly from the middle of the 1960s into the 1970s and beyond. During those years Western societies, and especially the United States, experienced a sustained period of turmoil resulting from a wide spectrum of political unrest. Beset with tensions – created by the civil rights struggle, the War on Poverty, the Vietnam War, the threat of nuclear holocaust, student unrest, the emergence of the women's movement, health and safety problems, recognition of the environmental crisis, and more – society seemed to be unraveling at the seams. At the time, the social sciences appeared to many to be irrelevant to these pressing issues. Seen as being focused on abstract issues pursued from the ivory tower, the social sciences faced criticism by increasing numbers of students and professors in the United States and Europe. The critics, of whom there were many, began to call for a different sort of social and political research, a kind that was socially relevant to the issues in the streets. The call for relevance led to epistemological turmoil in the social sciences, even for a while taking the form in the disciplines of social science as a politics of methodology between empiricist and the normative theorists.

Fundamental to this call for new methods was a challenge to the 'rational' model of positivist policy analysis and its fact–value dichotomy. Critics argued that the problems confronting society were lodged in under-lying value conflicts that were not readily accessible to empiricist methods; this shortcoming blocked the deliberate and sustained interpretation of the common understandings through which these conflicts appeared. Martin Rein (1976) in policy analysis and Richard Bernstein (1971, 1976) in the philosophy of the social sciences maintained in the 1970s that the failure to adequately address the relationship between facts and values was a major barrier to a social science capable of understanding, and thus effectively contributing to, the solution of policy problems (Fischer 1980, p. 10).

To a growing number of political theorists and policy scholars, the sharp separation of facts and values and the value neutrality that positiv-ists insisted upon obscured the role of norms and values and the ways they need to be approached (e.g., Taylor 1967). This insistence placed severe limitations on efforts to design a discipline to assist in addressing the important issues confronting decision-makers – issues concerned as much, or more, with appraising and proposing goals and ends. That is, a discipline that would move beyond narrow technical issues about how to efficiently achieve pre-given, unexamined ends to broader questions about how ends are actually instituted and how they might be established through participatory processes. As one writer put it at the time, 'it seems unfortunate to have rational procedures available for the relatively less important decisions of life and to have none for dealing with the most important decisions' (Diesing 1962, p. 1; Fischer 1980).

As social and political pressures intensified, some leaders in the social sciences, especially in political science, recognized the need to respond and called for the study of public policy in a way that addressed questions of relevance (e.g., Easton 1969). The study of public policy, as such, came to be seen as a way both to understand the conflicts in society and to bring the social sciences to bear on the effort to find solutions. The only caveat was that such research should be conducted with rigorous empiricist methods of the social sciences, aided by a relatively new systems approach to problem solving and by the emerging promise of computers to handle large bodies of data. Indeed, this came to be and still remains the primary methodological orientation in policy studies. The emphasis has been particularly clear, both theoretically and methodologically, in the work of leading figures such as the late Paul Sabatier. In his highly influential work on advocacy coalitions, Sabatier (1988; also see Weimer and Vining 2010) called for a rigorous empirical search for causal relationships as the essence of valid policy research.

This development of this field of inquiry appeared attractive to many, as it offered a way to do social science research and be socially useful at the same time. The appeal was reflected in the rapid expansion of the sub-field of public policy, especially in political science. Within a very short period of time, the policy focus became one of the leading specializations in the discipline, perhaps even the leading specialty in political science. At the same time, however, the insistence on rigorous empiricist investigation failed to actually address the concerns that had been raised by critics, particularly by social and political theorists focused on problems of norms, values and practice (see, e.g., Bernstein 1976). For them, the crisis in society could not be comprehended from an objectivist orientation to social reality that failed to understand the subjective and intersubjective human dimensions of the crisis. The crisis in society fundamentally involved a 'crisis of values' that could be approached only through the common understandings among different social actors interacting with one another. Rather than seeing a promise of solutions through the formulation of policies based on the explanation of political behavior in terms of causal relations, these critics saw the answer to be more deeply connected to intersubjective understandings, with the consequent need for methods of '*verstehen*' in order to develop forms of practice able to respond effectively to social problems (e.g., Taylor 1971).

The intellectual crisis in the social sciences only intensified as it became clear into the 1970s that the great outpouring of policy research – thanks in particular to monies made available by the struggle to end poverty – was unable to solve the many pressing problems confronting society. In frustration, leading policy scholars, such as Charles Lindblom, came to ask, what is 'usable knowledge'? That concern opened up deeper epistemological questions about the nature of knowledge and its relationship to the political and social organization of society (see Fischer, Chapter 3, this volume).

Indeed, a group of young policy scholars, initially North American but increasingly European, began in the 1980s to look for alternatives that built on the epistemological critique advanced earlier by philosophers and political theorists. Bringing theoretical questions of knowledge to bear on the more practical concerns of policy problems, these scholars set out to develop a critical perspective on public policy. Of crucial importance to this effort was the critical theory of the German philosopher Jürgen Habermas – whose work had begun appearing in English translation during the early 1970s – particularly his critique of scientism and the legitimation crisis in modern society (see Saretzki, Chapter 4, this volume). Drawing on his early turn to language and communication, for example, writers such as Fischer and Forester (1993; also see 1987) outlined the 'argumentative turn' in planning and policy analysis. Although there were many other influences, this work helped to promote a turn away from a purely empiricist approach to include an understanding as well of the assumptions informing – and the communicative processes mediating – the formulation and implementation of policy.

The critical orientation has since expanded to include theoretical and empirical work on discourse analysis, policy deliberation, deliberative democracy, citizen juries and consensus conferences, participatory governance, and the politics of expertise, as well as participatory policy analysis and collaborative planning, local and tacit ways of knowing, interpretive and ethnographic methods (see Dubois, Chapter 24, this volume). Such lines of investigation were also further developed by the emergence of a feminist approach to critical policy studies (see Paterson and Scala, Chapter 25, this volume). Even though, as Fischer and Gottweis (2012, pp. 1–2) point out, these research foci of critical policy studies 'are hardly synonymous, they share the special attention they give to communication and argumentation, in particular the processes of utilizing, mobilizing and assessing communicative practices in the interpretation and praxis of policymaking and analysis'.

2. CONTEMPORARY ISSUES IN CRITICAL POLICY STUDIES

Emerging from such developments, critical policy studies today has moved beyond an initial concern with criticizing technocracy and positivism to a sharpened focus on effectively enhancing both practical knowledge and democracy. Central to the policy turn in the social sciences, as we have noted, was the ideal of a dominant, if not exclusive, reliance upon scientific knowledge. Indeed, this still remains the prevailing orientation in policy analysis, as reflected in the use of evidence-based policymaking and the prominence of cost–benefit analysis as a decision-making methodology (see Strassheim, Chapter 17, this volume; and Elgert, Chapter 18, this volume). It is obvious in engineering, for instance, that scientific knowledge can be successfully applied even though detached from the context of application. That is far from obvious, however, in the case of technocratic social engineering. Indeed, from the perspective of critical policy studies, the idea is simply misbegotten.

Critical policy studies, as such, emphasizes the importance of contextual understanding, ordinary knowledge, narrative storytelling, emotional expression and communicative practices generally. This emphasis has especially resonated with critical policy approaches emerging from political science – a discipline in which many political theorists have continued to stress the importance of political understanding for inquiry as well as practical judgment and action.[3] Political understanding, so understood, is by no means the exclusive province of experts; it belongs even more fundamentally to the domain of citizens. A focus on political understanding (as opposed to political *explanation* as formally understood in the social sciences) thus helps open the door to a participatory orientation in the relationship between experts and citizens, breaking with the technocratic conception (see Dubois, Chapter 24, this volume). That reorientation favors democratization through approaches such as deliberative democracy and participatory governance.[4]

In the critical approach, the goals of enhancing both practical knowledge and democracy are connected by a focus on the idea of democratizing policy inquiry – a link that has become especially apparent with the 'argumentative turn'. With that turn, there is a shift in focus from empirical analysis to the communicative practices of argumentation and discourse, including discourse coalitions (Hajer 1995). Hence we see efforts at designing and employing means to encourage debate, deliberation and participation in policy inquiry (see Durnová, Chapter 12, this volume).

Such efforts to democratize inquiry are part of the larger project to 'democratize democracy' (Santos 2007; also see Fung and Wright 2003, on 'deepening democracy'), in contrast to the famous contention arising from the Trilateral Commission that there is a 'crisis of democracy' because emerging social movements overburden the democratic political system with demands, resulting in 'system overload'. The crisis of democracy, then, was 'too much' democracy (Crozier et al. 1975). Indeed, such rhetoric continues to be heard as journalists, scholars and politicians speak of the 'crisis of representative government'. The rationale for developing democratic designs in inquiry is, in contrast, that effective practical knowledge often requires such movements. Democratizing inquiry, of course, cannot democratize society and governance on its own, but it has to be an important component of genuine democratization, particularly in helping to develop cognitive and deliberative capacities among citizens and institutions. The agenda of critical policy studies thus is influenced by, and supportive of, social movements with agendas supporting democratization (see Mendonça and Ercan, Chapter 11, this volume).

The concern to enhance democracy largely follows from the conviction that a 'democratic deficit' is typical of not only nominally democratic countries, but the more advanced Western democracies as well. Critics of elitist, technocratic liberalism have often focused on the specter of an oligarchy of experts while proponents have imagined a benign elite. Both views now seem naive. Experts, as Foucault has made clear, are indispensable in societies that are technologically advanced or advancing, but experts always operate within structures and relations of power (see Lövbrand and Stripple, Chapter 5, this volume). Although critical policy studies remains concerned about a ruling elite of experts, it is even more interested in the role experts play in serving or challenging established elites, whose power is at the root of democratic deficits.

A significant problem here is that the technical mystique can obscure actual power dynamics by enveloping experts with a misleading aura of objective rationality. The concern in critical policy studies that elites dominate existing democracies has, as we have noted, coincided with the rise of a host of new social movements. These movements have directly challenged technocratic governance with the fact that their voices are routinely discounted or ignored by the political powers that be. In contrast to those who take such movements to be problematic, especially as they threaten existing power relationships, the critical policy perspective embraces them not only as an opportunity to develop the focus of investigation, but also as an opportunity to advance democratic governance and the democratization of policy inquiry.

Democratizing inquiry can be understood as part of the politics of expertise. Because it depends on a notion of unequivocal, objective knowledge, the ideals of 'expertocracy' do not recognize or face up to the problem of persistent disagreements among experts. This issue is particularly reflected in the rise of 'think-tanks' and their discourse coalitions, often gravitating toward opposing ideological commitments in a way that clearly undermines an otherwise unquestioned objectivity of experts (see Plehwe, Chapter 19, this volume). This concern has been underscored by the fact that social movements have themselves entered directly into the politics of expertise, often employing their own movement experts – as 'counter-experts' – and giving explicit attention to language as they work to reframe and redefine policy problems (see Ojha et al., Chapter 20, this volume; and Braun, Chapter 23, this volume).

Aiming to enhance practical knowledge together with democratic politics, critical policy studies takes a special interest in the concept of practice. The earlier term 'critical policy analysis' indicated a focus on the inadequacies of conventional policy analysis in providing applied knowledge. That focus is maintained in critical policy studies, but attention also clearly moves beyond it to encourage perspectives that have less direct interest in application than in understanding the institutional, cultural, historical, political and philosophical contexts and implications of policy inquiry (e.g., Orsini and Smith 2007).

From the above sketch it is not difficult to note that this critical approach has not developed into a unified field that can be categorically defined or reduced to a single theoretical perspective. Rather it is marked by differences and contentions, which may well be inherent aspects of its agonistic nature. Theoretical issues and controversies will remain important for future developments, however concrete they may become. Although different theoretical approaches indeed continue to emerge, there are three that stand out: interpretive, critical and poststructuralist. These approaches – while sharing a common point of departure in language and communicative practices – differ to the extent that they stress, or acknowledge, an interest in political emancipation. Nonetheless, such an interest appears as implicitly or explicitly involved in each. Rejecting the prevailing model of an elitist, technocratic liberal democracy, all offer support for projects designed to further the processes of democratization.

Interpretive policy analysis proceeds from the advent of interpretation in the social sciences more generally (Jennings 1983). Departing from the positivist insistence that social science must depend on objectively given 'hard data', the interpretive approach has maintained that the necessary source of access to evidence in social science is a grasp of the common understandings in a cultural context (Taylor 1971). The conduct of interpretation proceeds from these understandings, but by no means necessarily remains 'common' – often offering uncommon insights by throwing into question what is normally taken for granted. Such insights can follow from a self-reflective acknowledgment of the 'world' as a human artifice or of the 'social construction of reality' (Arendt 1958; Berger and Luckmann 1967). In a policy context, that acknowledgment can prompt a 'defamiliarization' or 'denaturalization' of conventional categories, typifications and procedures that would otherwise simply be taken for granted. With the conventional thrown sharply into question, attention can turn to examining the contingent processes of its construction and impact in specific circumstances of the policy process. Reflexivity of this kind can become particularly potent and illuminating when policy analysts focus attention on the 'framing' and 'reframing' of policy problems (Schön and Rein 1994). An interpretation, however, does not necessarily embrace an emancipatory interest and can in fact serve to reinforce traditional authority – as is evident, for example, from the history of hermeneutics, which has influenced the interpretive approach. Nonetheless, interpretive policy analysis (see Yanow, Chapter 21, this volume; Wagenaar, Chapter 22, this volume; also see Wagenaar 2011) clearly indicates an emancipatory interest in its critique of contemporary techno-empirical policy analysis, as in the case of evidence-based policymaking. With its methodological orientation, moreover, interpretive inquiry also poses a direct challenge to policy elites in contemporary society by calling into question taken-for-granted assumptions.

Closely related to interpretive analysis has been the turn to stories and narratives, which do not exist outside of the political, cultural and social environment in which they are constituted. Narrative policy analysis tends to focus on the issue-oriented stories told by policy actors. The goal, as Yanow (2000, p. 8) puts it, is to use 'such analysis to clarify policy positions and perhaps mediate among them'. Such investigation 'analyzes the structure either of the policy and agency stories told by various actors or of their content, allowing comparisons across different versions'. With some exceptions, narrative approaches tend to analyze storytelling from the perspective of actors seeking to influence or shape policy and politics with their version of events. As with interpretation generally, a focus on narrative is not inherently critical. But, as with interpretive analysis, the approach of narrative policy analysis can be practiced in a critical manner.

A standard reference in the development of a critical perspective was Bernstein's *The Restructuring of Social and Political Theory* (1976). Offering a powerful critique of positivism and 'technocratic consciousness', this book took up an interpretive perspective, but culminated with a focus on the potentialities of Habermas's approach to critical theory. For Habermas, indeed, interpretation is necessary as a point of departure, but is insufficient for critical inquiry without an analysis of the forces shaping the context of common understandings and interactions – in other words, without an examination of the established 'power structure' (1970a, p. 111) that constitutes the *'objective context'* (1988, p. 174, emphasis in original). It is not clear whether Habermas's objectifying move here must ultimately involve a shift to a standpoint beyond a cultural context of interpretation.[5] Nonetheless, his account of the 'ideal speech situation' is based upon the conception of a general structure of language use – or 'universal pragmatics' – focused on the very presuppositions of communication (Habermas 1970b, 1979). Habermas here offers the image of an idealized argument as a norm by which to identify and assess distorted patterns of communication.

When John Drzyek used the term 'critical policy analysis' early on, he distanced himself from a strictly interpretive posture and explicitly invoked Habermas's ideal speech situation: 'Critical policy analysis devotes itself to the elimination of distortion, which can occur through suppression, debasement, or deception' (Bobrow and Dryzek 1987, p. 169; also see Dryzek 1990, chapter 6). Habermas's move to posit a transcendental standard by which to assess actual language practices has met many objections and may, indeed, ultimately fall prey to its own formalism (Morris 1996). However, his image of argument under the conditions of a level playing field remains relevant to practical efforts to design settings for a reasonably fair debate. Here an emancipatory interest remains obvious but a practical problem potentially arises if emancipation is to support democratization. This is because – as Habermas himself acknowledges (1974, p. 40) – a project to emancipate and enlighten society introduces the specter of elitism resulting from the very distinction between those who are enlightened and those who are not.

In his seminal critique of technocratic policy discourse during the early 1970s, Laurence Tribe (1971, 1972, 1973) invoked Foucault to demonstrate an 'elemental fallacy' in the objectivist contention that there could be neutrality in 'naming categories' because discourse 'imposes its own categories and paradigms on the world of experience' (1972, pp. 98, 72). Although the influence of poststructuralism in critical policy studies has been relatively recent, it is now one of the key theoretical orientations in the field (see Howarth and Griggs, Chapter 6, this volume). Foucault, in particular, has emerged as a unique focus of attention (see Lövbrand and Stripple, Chapter 5, this volume).[6] There is often a particular emphasis on his analysis of power as a 'multiplicity of force relations' (Foucault 1980b, p. 92) that is immanent to a field, in which comprehensive categories – such as 'state' or 'society' – are decomposed in favor of indeterminate networks examined at minute and interstitial levels. Foucault's famous notion of 'power/knowledge' (Foucault 1979) also clearly disrupts the technocratic presupposition that knowledge can be neutral. The question of power is further pursued in critical policy studies with attention to his problematization of 'discipline' (1980a) and 'governmentality' (1991a). Foucault is typically understood to be critical, implicitly in any case, especially in regard to his approach to power. As with poststructuralism generally, however, he tended to be equivocal, ambiguous or coy about an emancipatory interest. Nonetheless, in explicitly associating his late turn to the question of 'enlightenment' with the critique of enlightenment in early Frankfurt critical theory, Foucault (1991c, pp. 116–124; 2007, pp. 51–55; also see Horkheimer and Adorno 2002) came to a similar point of ambivalence. Although he questioned whether the 'critical task' still requires a 'faith in Enlightenment', Foucault nonetheless left no ambiguity that his effort was animated by an interest in emancipation. As he put it, 'this task requires work on our limits, that is, a patient labor giving form to our impatience for liberty' (1984, p. 50). If we can find no explicit political project in Foucault (e.g., 1991b), such a project nonetheless becomes central to Laclau and Mouffe's influential effort (1985) to combine features of Foucault's discourse theory with Gramsci's accent on hegemony (see Howarth and Griggs, Chapter 6, this volume; Sum and Jessop, Chapter 7, this volume). Laclau and Mouffe explicitly advance a strategy for a 'radical democracy' that accentuates antagonism as opposed to consensus and thus rejects a common tendency in deliberative democracy. As such, they sharply distance themselves from the prevailing model of liberal democracy.

With an accent on contexts of shared understandings, those who adopt an interpretive approach are sometimes troubled by the tendencies they detect in the critical orientation, insofar as it can suggest a potential distancing from the common world. This concern is not only methodological but also political, identifying a propensity in critical inquiry toward an elitist posture of enlightenment. Strikingly, Habermas expresses much the same concern, saying that although the 'superiority of those who do the enlightening over those who are to be enlightened is theoretically unavoidable', it is also 'fictive' and needs to be corrected: 'in a process of enlightenment there can only be participants' (1974, p. 40). The 'theoretically unavoidable' problem that arises here points back, however, to a practical context of common understandings among participants – to a return, that is, to an interpretive domain and to the 'action oriented self-understanding' that Habermas himself has praised in Gadamer's hermeneutics (1988, p. 162).

When interpretive social science was beginning to have an effect on policy analysis, Bruce Jennings (1983) ironically likened policy analysts to the famous bourgeois gentleman in Molière's play who was pleasantly surprised to learn that he had been speaking prose all his life: policy analysts were surprised to learn that they were doing 'hermeneutics'. They thus learned the obvious: that, contrary to what their training and professional status might suggest, they were part of a common world where everyone found their way through the interpretation and understanding of one another. With that came the recognition that a focus on interpretation basically only made explicit much of what they were already doing. It was a short step from that realization, according to Jennings, to an appreciation of the inescapable relevance of political understanding and judgment, as these had come to be associated with the Aristotelian conception of *phronēsis*.[7] Indeed, if critical policy studies is to be relevant for projects of democratization, it appears that debates involving political understanding and judgment – in contrast to the narrower emphasis on political explanation that has long informed mainstream social science – offer an indispensable reference point in linking theory with practice.

3.   THE *HANDBOOK*

With this volume, we hope to further advance the development of critical policy studies. To that end, we begin with essays that give a clearer definition to the field by examining its emergence both in a practical context and in connection with the varied theoretical influences and initiatives that make for its continuing commonalities and differences. This focus is meant both to inform readers of the *Handbook* and to stimulate debate among those who are interested in shaping the orientation and issues that are to guide the project of critical policy studies in the future. The essays in the book thus range from those that are more theoretical in focus to those that are distinctly concerned with practice. The significance of power is a topic that runs through many of the essays, together with concerns about justice, democracy, deliberation, discourse and empowerment. Policy processes, from agenda-setting, problem definition and formulation to implementation are viewed from critical perspectives. Attention also turns to the politics of expertise, including think-tanks and participatory research, while methodological and epistemological problems arising from social construction, gender, ethnography, emotions and interpretation are all given explicit treatment as part of the critical project. With that, we can briefly introduce the six parts of the volume and the particular essays in each, together with their importance for critical policy studies.

Part I   Origins and Theoretical Development: From Lasswell to Habermas and Foucault

Focused on the origins and evolution of critical policy studies, the first part of the volume opens with an essay by Douglas Torgerson, 'Harold D. Lasswell and critical policy studies: the threats and temptations of power', that offers an account of Lasswell's early project for 'the policy sciences of democracy' in terms of both its advances and limitations. Torgerson argues that, despite common misunderstandings of his work, Lasswell anticipated many aspects of what now seems new with critical policy studies. Nonetheless, Lasswell's commitment to a critical project advancing the democratization of society ultimately embroiled him in perplexing problems, particularly in connection with what he called 'the threats and temptations of power'. Focusing on these problems in Lasswell allows us to see more clearly how similar difficulties now also confront critical policy studies.

Frank Fischer's chapter, 'In pursuit of usable knowledge: critical policy analysis and the argumentative turn', examines the history of the critical orientation in policy analysis while introducing the argumentative turn, which was influential in paving a new way for policy analysis based on communication. Along the way, this chapter explains what the argumentative turn has meant for standard models of policy analysis, and in particular what makes it critical. The perspective, Fischer argues, has evolved over two decades, moving from a focus on argumentation to include deliberation, discourse, citizens panels, participatory expertise, interpretation, transformative learning, a recognition of the importance of emotions in policy deliberative processes, among other topics. A four-level model of policy discourse is presented, with particular reference to the limitations of the advocacy coalition framework. It concludes with a discussion of the relationship of argumentation and discourse to politics, with an emphasis on policy change.

As the argumentative turn took its initial impulse from the work of German philosopher Jürgen Habermas, the third essay by Thomas Saretzki, 'Habermas, critical theory and public policy', focuses on this foundational contribution to the study of language and deliberation. Habermas influenced the development of critical policy studies by stimulating insights on epistemological and methodological issues and on the relation of theory to practice. The chapter starts with a short recollection of the program for the policy sciences of democracy and the conceptual problems it presents concerning the relationship between scientific objectivity and democracy. Recalling Habermas's interventions in the positivist dispute, the technocracy debate and the controversy on the relation of hermeneutics and critical theory, the chapter then explains why policy scholars committed to democratizing policy deliberation took an interest in Habermas and how his theoretical perspectives and concepts played a role in policy evaluation. The chapter ends with a critical reflection that considers some of the problems that have been experienced by those who have recommended his concepts for democratizing processes of policy analysis and policymaking.

Next comes a discussion of the seminal contribution of Michel Foucault by Eva Lövbrand and Johannes Stripple, 'Foucault and critical policy studies'. They argue that Foucault's work paves the way for a decentered form of policy analysis by asking how we govern and are governed in micro-settings, including at the level of the individual subject. The focus on the 'how of governing' stems from Foucault's rejection of any *a priori* understanding of the distribution of power or location of government, turning instead to an interest in – and awareness of – the historically situated practices, rationalities and identities by which governing operates. Viewed in this manner, Foucault-inspired policy studies neither offers us a substantive theory about the forces that shape public policy (e.g., actors, interests, structures) nor does it tell us what constitutes public policy. The primary role of the critical analyst is instead to interrogate how these political spaces come about, how power – including disciplinary power – operates through them and, ultimately, how they could be different.

Part II   Theoretical Perspectives: Critical Reflexivity, Hegemony and Power

In 'Poststructuralist discourse theory and critical policy studies: interests, identities and policy change', David Howarth and Steven Griggs argue that the explanation of policy change need not be caught in a stand-off between those who privilege interests or those who advance ideas, or those who foreground either agency or structure. Rejecting these oppositions, the chapter demonstrates how poststructuralist discourse theory offers a novel articulation of the role of ideas, interests, agency and structures in accounts of policy change. Moreover, it recognizes the centrality of politics and power in the forging of policy frames and discourses in particular social and historical contexts. This involves the articulation of the concepts of hegemony, rhetoric and Lacan's concept of fantasy to account for the emergence and formation of policy discourses.

The chapter by Ngai-Ling Sum and Bob Jessop, 'Cultural political economy and critical policy studies: developing a critique of domination', advances their theory of cultural political economy and its contribution to critical policy studies. The chapter introduces cultural political economy to explore the interconnected semiotic and structural aspects of social life. Their approach offers a preliminary set of basic sensitizing concepts and positive guidelines that are relevant to historical description, hermeneutic interpretation and causal explanation. It aims thereby to overcome the often compartmentalized analysis of semiosis/culture and structuration/institutions by integrating semiosis into political economy and applying evolutionary and institutional analyses to semiosis. This has important implications for understanding the limits of constructivist and structuralist analyses, lived experience and lesson-drawing, the relations among polity and policy, and specific fields of public policy. Finally, drawing on the work of Antonio Gramsci, they show the ways in which their theoretical framework can also provide the basis for critiques of ideology and domination in political and policy processes.

The final chapter in this part is by Timothy Luke, titled 'The interpretation of power'. When it comes to the discussion of policy decision-making, or adoption and legitimation, policy studies has typically borrowed from theoretical work in political science and sociology on pluralism and the power elite, including structured pluralism and its account of the business bias in liberal capitalist systems. In this essay, borrowing from more contemporary theoretical work, Foucault in particular, Luke demonstrates the limits of those perspectives under modern circumstances. The chapter explores how critical policy studies could productively approach the challenges of interpreting power as an object of political analysis by re-evaluating the sites and settings in which power typically is studied by policy analysis. Luke makes a case for interpreting power as a set of directive relations, which is co-evolving and co-constituting in agent-structure interactions with knowledge. He encourages critical policy analysis to contest technocratic uses of power in policymaking, and endorses the acceptance of more flexible and fluid interpretations of power at work in multiple sites and settings at all levels of governance.

Part III   Discursive Politics: Deliberation, Justice, Protest and Emotion

Policy discourse and deliberation constitute a primary focus in critical policy studies, having emerged early with the impetus given by Habermas's theories of ideal speech and communicative ethics. A different emphasis on discourse followed as the contribution of Foucault entered political and social theory and began to influence the policy field.

Part III leads off with Vivien Schmidt's chapter on 'Discursive institutionalism: understanding policy in context'. Schmidt offers her prominent theory of discursive institutionalism as an umbrella concept for approaches concerned with the substantive content of ideas, their social construction and the interactive processes of discourse in institutional contexts. The chapter illustrates the relevance of discursive institutionalism to critical policy studies by considering both the wide range of ideas in policy discourse and the ways in which political and policy actors articulate such ideas in policy construction and attempt to politically legitimate them. Along the way, she theorizes about the nature of the power of ideas, particularly as they are played out through discourse.

The second chapter, by Susan Fainstein, 'Social justice and urban policy deliberation: balancing the discourses of democracy, diversity and equity', puts the focus on the discourse of social justice in urban policy politics. Although the identification of social injustices has always been part of urban policy, politics and planning, there has been all-too-little effort to specify what constitute 'just' policies. Choosing justice as the norm for urban policy, she explains that it is a response to the growing inequality and social exclusion resulting from the application of neo-liberalism to public policy and its insistence on the normative criterion of efficiency. Instead, she uses the three general principles of democracy, diversity and equity to define justice and, with the assistance of case illustrations, derives from them more specific metrics by which to judge the policymaking processes and outcomes of particular policies.

Ricardo Mendonça and Selen Ercan take up a central topic in contemporary political theory, deliberative democracy. By questioning one of the basic tenets of most work devoted to the topic – the fundamental role of consensus as the goal of deliberation – they illustrate in their chapter, 'Deliberation and protest: revealing the deliberative potential of protest movements in Turkey and Brazil', that political conflict can actually facilitate rather than hinder the processes of deliberation. Taking into consideration the important fact that protest movements have become primary events across the globe since the beginning of the century, they pose as problematic the dichotomy of a consensus-oriented deliberative democracy versus an agonistic politics that emphasizes opposition and conflict. They argue, in contrast to such a dichotomy, that the adversarial nature of the protests can promote rather than hinder the prospects for deliberation. Drawing particularly on experiences related to protest movements in Brazil and Turkey in 2013, the authors present them as important illustrations of the centrality of agonistic politics to political deliberation and deliberative democracy.

Finally, Anna Durnová's chapter, 'Lost in translation: expressing emotions in policy deliberation', turns to one of the crucially important topics to emerge in policy studies in recent years, namely the role of emotion. Once seen as the enemy of rationality, emotion now is increasingly portrayed as more closely linked to rationality than previously believed. Indeed, there is research showing that they are dependent on one another. As an important theorist in opening up this line of investigation in policy studies, Durnová draws attention to recent research on policy discourse and deliberation to show that emotions represent a crucial point of intersection between the individual and the collective dimensions of discourse, one that structures deliberation. Emotions are portrayed as affecting the nature of the knowledge at stake in deliberation and as shaping both the social configuration and attitudes of actors who take part in these processes and the ways in which they participate.

IV   Policy Processes: Problem Definitions, Evidence and Social Construction

Although policy studies has long been organized around the 'stages model' of the policy process, this approach has also been criticized as lacking empirical rigor and causal connections. Nonetheless, the model still remains a useful heuristic in addressing various aspects of the policymaking process. As such, the model represents policy as moving through a series of stages, from agenda-setting and policy formulation to policy adoption, implementation and evaluation. The authors in this part examine various stages from critical perspectives to illustrate the political, discursive and constructivist character of the policy process.

The opening piece by Marlon Barbehön, Sybille Münch and Wolfram Lamping, 'Problem definition and agenda-setting in critical perspective', delineates the crucial nature of the politics of problem definition in the agenda-setting process. Arguing that agenda-setting cannot be explained by rationalistic, positivist models, they show problem definition in agenda-setting to be a discursive process – part of the social construction of a political world – that attributes responsibility to political actors or institutions. Problem definition and agenda-setting are constructions of reality that can be identified within the larger policymaking process.

The discussion then turns to policy formulation, which in contemporary practice is largely dominated by cost–benefit analysis. Knowledge of costs and benefits, as well as other forms of evidence-based information, is important to decision-making. But when it is utilized independently of the social and political context to which it applies, it tends to serve an ideological role by simply accepting, and thus implicitly legitimating, the given set of governing arrangements. Critical policy analysis seeks to set such data in political context and explicate its implications. In their chapter, Helen Ingram and Anne Schneider offer an important illustration. In 'Making distinctions: the social construction of target populations', they demonstrate the socially constructed character of the target populations as they become delineated in the policy formulation process. As a pathbreaking contribution to policy studies generally, they show how political actors assign particular social definitions to the populations to be served by a policy in ways that give meaning to the distribution of costs and benefits. The definitions, as they show, attribute the status of deserving or underserving to different members of the public. The process, they argue, often works insidiously to undercut possibilities of democratic governance.

Raul Lejano and Sung Jin Park follow next with 'The autopoietic text' to show the ways in which policy texts, as narratives, often mediate between the crafting of a policy and its implementation. Such texts can serve as boundary objects that afford close interaction among policy actors. At the same time, strongly textualist policy domains can rigidly disempower these same actors, leading to shallow, rather than deep, approaches to implementation. At the most extreme, 'autopoietic texts' function as vehicles furthering ideological systems of thought.

Finally, Heidrun Åm in 'Co-production and public policy: evidence, uncertainty and socio-materiality' draws on the theory of co-production in science and technology studies to enhance the explanatory power of a poststructuralist approach. Examining the construction of newly emerging technologies, she rejects rational-choice approaches as unable to explain negotiations of regulatory policies in a context of uncertainty. Specifically, Åm shows that technoscientific developments, such as nanotechnology, confound evidence-based policymaking efforts. In the face of an 'institutional void', she argues that a combination of poststructuralist and co-productionist approaches helps to illustrate how proactive regulatory frameworks have become the authoritative mode of regulation in the nanotechnology field.

Part V   The Politics of Policy Expertise: Knowledge, Think-Tanks and Action Research

The relationship of expert knowledge to society is underscored in this part as a central concern of critical policy studies. The key questions are these: Who is considered to have such knowledge and who is not? What forms does such knowledge take? What are its social and political implications? Part V begins with Holger Strassheim's chapter on 'Politics and policy expertise: towards a political epistemology'. Strassheim acknowledges a need for educated advice from specialists in a world confronting complex problems such as global warming and food insecurities. Nonetheless, he points to the fact – paradoxical for some – that, along with this need, citizens are today questioning the role of expertise in society more than ever. In that regard, he points to tendencies toward both the expertization of democracy and the democratization of expertise. Critically exploring these relationships among science, policy and society, he asks how policy expertise is generated, communicated and justified. How do cultural contexts shape and constrain the politics of policy expertise, and how do we explain changes in that regard? To answer these questions, Strassheim conceptualizes expertise as a nexus of authority attributions embedded in discursive and institutional cultures. With an emphasis on 'political epistemologies', he seeks to open up opportunities for a critical re-examination of the production of public knowledge.

Continuing with a further exploration of the politics of expert knowledge, Laureen Elgert focuses on the construction and use of sustainability indicators in contemporary global governance. In 'Global governance and sustainability indicators: the politics of expert knowledge', she argues that conventional approaches to the relationship between knowledge and policy employ expert indicators as a means of packaging and presenting knowledge in objective and universally valid ways for transparent and democratic policy analysis. Toward this end, she employs the case of 'responsible soy' certification standards to analyze the political role of indicators in the knowledge-policy interface, both as technologies of knowledge production and technologies of governance. She concludes that indicators are better understood as a way of disseminating norms and values than as mechanisms of transparent and efficient global governance.

In the third chapter, 'The politics of policy think-tanks: organizing expertise, legitimacy and counter-expertise in policy networks', Dieter Plehwe explores the role of policy think-tanks, which have become prominent organizations in political processes at national and international levels. He examines two competing perspectives. One of these praises think-tanks for their capacity to conduct policy-relevant research, for their ability to innovate, and for their capacity to reach out to practicing politicians. The other is a more critical perspective that points to the fact that many think-tanks not only fail to significantly contribute to research, but also form discourse coalitions that mainly serve elite, government or business interests far removed from any conception of the public interest. Although the two perspectives are clearly at odds, the contradiction can be resolved by recognizing different types of think-tanks, together with their diverse roles in particular policy communities at various stages in policy processes. A necessary part of such recognition is to sort out the political dimension of the knowledge and expertise produced and processed by think-tanks. A social network approach, Plehwe contends, can identify and clarify resources relevant to think-tank knowledge production, with respect for example to specific academic, political, corporate or ideological backgrounds. Gaining a critical understanding of the political character of think-tank knowledge, he argues, helps to improve policy deliberation and decision-making through the greater transparency and accountability of policy actors.

The final chapter of Part V, 'Critical action research and social movements: revitalizing participation and deliberation for democratic empowerment' by Hemant Ojha, Mani Banjade and Krishna Shrestha, deals with two additional points of reference for critical policy analysis: social movements and participatory policy expertise. The authors outline a critical action research approach designed to enhance the interplay among policy research, social movement practices and democratic governance. Their concern is a general lack of effective deliberation in the policy processes. Drawing on three cases from Nepal, India and Australia, the authors demonstrate that interactive learning is crucial for revitalizing democratic empowerment across multi-scalar engagements. They conclude that there is enormous scope for revitalizing democratic empowerment in participatory policy processes, which can be facilitated by strengthening the ways in which researchers interact with communities and policy actors and by balancing epistemic and action objectives in specific contexts of application.

VI   Methodological Issues: Interpretation, Framing and Social Constructions

The methodological implications of critical approaches to policy studies are closely related to reflection on the ways to think and analyze the complexity of policy processes and the forms of knowledge that support them from the very beginning. While these canons of thought cannot be unified under one single approach, they nonetheless share common ground by opposing a positivist view of social science in favor of a 'post-positivist', interpretive perspective. As Dvora Yanow (1996, p. 5) states in her pathbreaking book, *How Does a Policy Mean?*, 'We act; we have intentions about our actions; we interpret others' action. We make sense of the world: we are meaning making creatures.' Her chapter, 'Making sense of policy practices: interpretation and meaning', which opens Part VI of this volume with a detailed account of the beginning of interpretive analysis, is anchored both in a critique of mainstream policy analysis and in broader reflections about meaning and language in the social sciences. The author lays the ground for interpretive practice in policy studies and defines its guiding principles. Yanow tackles the methodological implications that arise once we take seriously the issue of the power dimensions of knowledge claims. She invites us to search for meaning-focused analytical practice that might be useful for both academics and practitioners in the field.

Such reflection then continues with another prominent figure of the interpretive policy approach, Hendrik Wagenaar, with his contribution, 'Transforming perspectives: the critical functions of interpretive policy analysis'. Wagenaar sees interpretive policy analysis as providing a kind of knowledge with a better fit with society than conventional empiricist policy analysis. Although the latter takes an unreflexive, objectivist view of the categories of analysis and is oblivious to the meaning of the data that interpretation promises, interpretive policy analysis performs a variety of critical functions, explained by the author in terms of three main categories of interpretive practice: hermeneutic, discursive and dialogical.

All these practices, he maintains, are critical enterprises that contribute to a deepening of democracy.

Kathrin Braun, in 'Between representation and narration: analysing policy frames', acknowledges the heterogeneous character of the methodological approaches in critical policy studies by highlighting the points that concepts of frame and framing have multiple meanings, and that doing frame analysis may mean very different things. Frames can be seen as having a narrative nature or a representational nature, or they can be regarded as ideological constructs that call for critical interventions into relations of power. The aim of the author is to explain the epistemological background of these differences and to guide us through possibilities and limitations of each of the classifications.

In his chapter 'Critical policy ethnography', Vincent Dubois presents a comprehensive review of the various orientations of policy ethnography, and defines four features of critical policy ethnography: to challenge mainstream positivist approaches to public policy; to confront common-sense and official views on policy; to conceive individual experiences and micro-observations from the broader perspective of power and inequality structures; and, last but not least, to unveil processes of social, economic, symbolic and political domination operating in and through policy processes.

The volume closes with a chapter by Stephanie Paterson and Francesca Scala, titled 'Making gender visible: exploring feminist perspectives through the case of anti-smoking policy'. With a feminist approach to the critical practice of policy analysis, Paterson and Scala seek to go beyond common expectations and thereby bring attention to crucial dimensions of feminist policy studies that can enhance critical approaches by making gender visible, even in regard to policies where it may not immediately appear to be a concern. In their discussion of anti-smoking policy, the authors find a relevant case to show how policy analysis often ignores or marginalizes women's voices and experiences. While women and girls tend to be the subjects of anti-smoking media campaigns, intervention strategies often rely on androcentric assumptions. By structuring their analysis around questions of power and difference, Paterson and Scala show how feminist perspectives can join forces with other critical approaches to advance the emancipatory potential of policy studies.

NOTES

1. In the context of policy evaluation, these can be understood as higher-order normative criteria (see Fischer 1995).

2. In the 1920s Thorstein Veblen (1963) was a key American proponent of technocracy who stressed the role of engineering. On technocracy generally, see Fischer (1990).
3. 'Political life does not yield its significance to terse hypotheses but is elusive, and hence meaningful statements about it often have to be allusive and intimative. Context becomes supremely important, for actions and events occur in no other setting. Knowledge of this type tends, therefore, to be suggestive and illuminative rather than explicit and determinate' (Wolin 1969, p. 1070; cf. Beiner 1983).
4. The theory and practice of governance is closely related to policy studies, but we do not treat it here as necessarily a part of critical policy studies. One reason is that much of it is not critical, as Davies (2011) makes clear. We do, however, see participatory governance as part of the critical perspective.
5. Habermas (1984, pp. 109–111), in this respect, connects Giddens's account of the 'double hermeneutic' of the social sciences to the pragmatist concept, from Peirce to Dewey, of a community of inquirers (cf. Habermas 1971, pp. 101–102, 137–139; Bernstein 1971, pp. 176, 190, 201).
6. A large stream of thought in both philosophy and the social sciences, poststructuralism has launched an investigation of the transformative potentials of knowledge (Howarth 2000; Gottweis 2003; Braidotti 2006; Glynos and Howarth 2008). Towards that end, poststructuralist political theory has developed a set of instruments to identify both how knowledge is shaped by discourses and, in turn, also shapes them – and the way in which institutions thereby legitimize their agendas.
7. On the relationship of *phronēsis* to the development of policy analysis, see Torgerson (1995). For a recent example, see Flyvbjerg (2001).

REFERENCES

Arendt, Hannah (1958), *The Human Condition*, Chicago: University of Chicago Press.
Beiner, Ronald (1983), *Political Judgement*, London: Methuen.
Berger, Peter and Thomas Luckmann (1967), *The Social Construction of Reality: A Treatise in the Sociology of Knowledge*, Garden City, NY: Anchor Books.
Bernstein, Richard J. (1971), *Praxis and Action*, Philadelphia: Pennsylvania University Press.
Bernstein, Richard J. (1976), *The Restructuring of Social and Political Theory*, New York: Harcourt Brace Jovanovich.
Bobrow, Davis B. and John S. Dryzek (1987), *Policy Analysis by Design*, Pittsburgh, PA: University of Pittsburgh Press.
Braidotti, Rosi (2006), *Transpositions: On Nomadic Ethics*, Cambridge: Polity.
Crozier, Michel J., Samuel P. Huntington and Joji Watanuki (1975), *The Crisis of Democracy: Report on the Governability of Democracies to the Trilateral Commission*, New York: New York University Press.
Davies, Jonathan S. (2011), *Challenging Governance: From Networks to Hegemony*, Bristol: Polity.
Diesing, Paul (1962), *Reason in Society*, Urbana, IL: University of Illinois Press.
Dryzek, John S. (1990), *Discursive Democracy*, Cambridge: Cambridge University Press.
Easton, David (1969), 'The new revolution in political science', *American Political Science Review*, **63** (4), 1051–1061.
Fischer, Frank (1980), *Politics, Values and Public Policy: The Problem of Methodology*, Boulder, CO: Westview Press.
Fischer, Frank (1990), *Technocracy and the Politics of Expertise*, Newbury Park, CA: Sage.
Fischer, Frank (1995), *Evaluating Public Policy*, Chicago: Nelson-Hall.
Fischer, Frank and John Forester (eds) (1987), *Confronting Values in Policy Analysis: The Politics of Criteria*, Newbury Park, CA: Sage.
Fischer, Frank and John Forester (eds) (1993), *The Argumentative Turn in Policy Analysis and Planning*, Durham, NC: Duke University Press.

Fischer, Frank and Herbert Gottweis (2012), *The Argumentative Turn Revisited: Public Policy as Communicative Practice*, Durham, NC: Duke University Press.

Flyvbjerg, Bent (2001), *Making Social Science Matter*, Cambridge: Cambridge University Press.

Foucault, Michel (1979), *Power/Knowledge*, New York: Pantheon Books.

Foucault, Michel (1980a), *Discipline and Punish: The Birth of the Prison*, A. Sheridan (trans.), New York: Vintage Books.

Foucault, Michel (1980b), *The History of Sexuality, Vol. 1: An Introduction*, Richard Hurley (trans.), New York, Vintage Books.

Foucault, Michel (1984), 'What is enlightenment?', in Paul Rabinow (ed.), *The Foucault Reader*, New York, Pantheon Books, pp. 32–50.

Foucault, Michel (1991a) 'Governmentality', in Graham Burchell, Colin Gordon and Peter Miller (eds), *The Foucault Effect*, Chicago: University of Chicago Press, pp. 87–104.

Foucault, Michel (1991b) 'Politics and the study of discourse', in Gordon Burchell, Colin Gordon and Peter Miller (eds), *The Foucault Effect*, Chicago: University of Chicago Press, pp. 53–72.

Foucault, Michel (1991c), *Remarks on Marx*, New York: Semiotext(e).

Foucault, Michel (2007), 'What is critique?', in *The Politics of Truth*, Lysa Hochroth and Catherine Porter (trans.), Los Angeles: Semiotext(e), pp. 41–81.

Fung, Archon and Erik Olin Wright (2003), *Deepening Democracy: Institutional Innovations in Empowered Participatory Governance*, London: Verso Books.

Glynos, Jason and David Howarth (2008), 'Structure, agency and power in political analysis: beyond contextualized self-interpretations', *Political Studies Review*, **6** (2), 155–169.

Gottweis, Herbert (2003), 'Theoretical strategies of poststructuralist policy analysis: towards an analytics of government', in Maarten Hajer and Hendrick Wagenaar (eds), *Deliberative Policy Analysis: Understanding Governance in the Network Society*, Cambridge: Cambridge University Press, pp. 247–265.

Habermas, Jürgen (1970a), *Toward a Rational Society*, Jeremy J. Shapiro (trans.), Boston: Beacon Press.

Habermas, Jürgen (1970b), 'Toward a theory of communicative competence', *Inquiry*, **13**, 360–375.

Habermas, Jürgen (1971), *Knowledge and Human Interests*, Jeremy J. Shapiro (trans.), Boston: Beacon Press.

Habermas, Jürgen (1974), *Theory and Practice*, John Viertel (trans.), Boston: Beacon Press.

Habermas, Jürgen (1984), *The Theory of Communicative Action*, Vol. 1, Thomas McCarthy (trans.), Boston: Beacon Press.

Habermas, Jürgen (1988), *On the Logic of the Social Sciences*, Shierry Weber Nicholsen and Jerry A. Stark (trans.), Cambridge, MA: The MIT Press (German publication 1970).

Habermas, Jürgen (1979), 'What is universal pragmatics?', in *Communication and the Evolution of Society*, Thomas McCarthy (trans.), Boston: Beacon Press, pp. 1–68.

Hajer, Maarten (1995), *The Politics of Environmental Discourse: Ecological Modernisation and the Policy Process*, Oxford: Oxford University Press.

Horkheimer, Max and Theodor Adorno (2002), *Dialectic of Enlightenment*, Edmund Jephcott (trans.), Stanford: Stanford University Press (German publication 1947).

Howarth, David (2000), *Discourse*, Buckingham, UK: Open University Press.

Jennings, Bruce (1983), 'Interpretive social science and policy analysis', in Daniel Callahan and Bruce Jennings (eds), *Ethics, the Social Sciences and Policy Analysis*, New York: Plenum Press, pp. 3–35.

Laclau, Ernesto and Chantal Mouffe (1985), *Hegemony and Socialist Strategy: Towards a Radical Democratic Politics*, London: Verso.

Morris, Martin (1996), 'On the logic of the performative contradiction: Habermas and the radical critique of reason', *Review of Politics*, **58** (4), 735–760.

Orsini, Michael and Miriam Smith (eds) (2007), *Critical Policy Studies*, Vancouver: University of British Columbia Press.

Rein, Martin (1976), *Social Science and Public Policy*, New York: Penguin.

Sabatier, Paul (1988), 'An advocacy coalition model of policy change and the role of policy-oriented learning therein', *Policy Sciences*, **21**, 129–168.

Santos, B.D. (ed.) (2007), *Democratizing Democracy: Beyond the Liberal Democratic Canon*, London: Verso.

Schön, Donald A. and Martin Rein (1994), *Frame Reflection*, New York: Basic Books.

Taylor, Charles (1967), 'Neutrality in political science', in Peter Laslett and W.G. Runcimann (eds), *Philosophy, Politics and Society* (Third Series), Oxford: Blackwell, pp. 25–57.

Taylor, Charles (1971), 'Interpretation and the sciences of man', *Review of Metaphysics*, **25** (3), 3–51.

Torgerson, Douglas (1995), 'Policy analysis and public life: the restoration of *phronēsis*?', in James Farr, John S. Dryzek and Stephen T. Leonard (eds), *Political Science in History: Research Programs and Political Traditions*, Cambridge: Cambridge University Press, pp. 225–252.

Tribe, Laurence H. (1971), 'Trial by mathematics: precision and ritual in the legal process', *Harvard Law Review*, **84** (6), 1329–1393.

Tribe, Laurence H. (1972), 'Policy science: analysis or ideology?', *Philosophy and Public Affairs*, **2** (1), 66–110.

Tribe, Laurence H. (1973), 'Technology assessment and the fourth discontinuity: the limits of instrumental rationality', *Southern California Law Review*, **46** (3), 617–660.

Veblen, Thorstein (1963), *The Engineers and the Price System*, New York: Harcourt, Brace & World (original publication 1921).

Wagenaar, Hendrik (2011), *Meaning in Action: Interpretation and Dialogue in Policy Analysis*, New York: M.E. Sharpe.

Weimer, David L. and Aidan R. Vining (2010), *Policy Analysis: Concepts and Practice*, 5th edition, Boston: Pearson.

Wolin, Sheldon (1969), 'Political theory as a vocation', *American Political Science Review*, **63** (4), 1062–1082.

Yanow, Dvora (1996), *How Does a Policy Mean? Interpreting Policy and Organizational Actions*, Washington, DC: Georgetown University Press.

Yanow, Dvora (2000), *Conducting Interpretive Policy Analysis*, Thousand Oaks, CA: Sage.

PART I

ORIGINS AND THEORETICAL DEVELOPMENT: FROM LASSWELL TO HABERMAS AND FOUCAULT

2 Harold D. Lasswell and critical policy studies: the threats and temptations of power
Douglas Torgerson

1. THE CRITICAL ORIENTATION AND THE LASSWELL PARADOX

Critical policy studies looks like it might be something new under the sun. It has come onto the scene in sharp opposition to technocracy. It has rejected the technocratic guise of neutrality while instead advancing a distinctly political agenda, committed to democracy and democratization. In that way, the critical orientation in policy studies has, in recent decades, issued a direct political challenge to the technocratic orientation.

We often associate that orientation with the term 'policy sciences'. Despite the connotations of the term, however, there is more than a little irony in associating it with a narrow, technocratic rationalism. That is because Harold D. Lasswell, the figure who invented and promoted it, cannot appropriately be understood as a technocrat. Those active in advancing a critical focus were, in fact, largely aware that Lasswell was much more complex and sophisticated than commonly acknowledged. That seemed especially so given his explicit and sustained advocacy for a profession dedicated to 'the policy sciences of democracy' (Lasswell 1948, pp. 118ff., 1951b).[1]

Here we come to a striking paradox: Lasswell, the founder of the policy sciences, appears to have anticipated many aspects of what now seems new with critical policy studies. He especially offers an approach to the problem of context that remains unmatched in its importance. Thought through seriously, Lasswell's posture can help to illuminate both the nature of critical policy studies and the challenges facing it, especially in a political connection. With that in mind, we will here focus at a conceptual level on the relationship between Lasswell and critical policy studies.

We will find less difference, and more similarity, between Lasswell and critical policy studies with respect to the ideas of advancing democratization and promoting a critical stance. The chief difference pertains to matters of political judgment, especially concerning the question of the appropriate relationship between policy inquiry and political interventions into controversial issues. It is at this juncture, as we will see, that the logic of Lasswell's position becomes embroiled in contradictions that point our attention to the structures and dynamics of power. Yet, critical policy studies occupies no happily privileged position. The complex questions involved in confronting power remain crucial and unresolved for any critical approach.

One of the most influential – as well as intellectually innovative and wide- ranging – political scientists of the twentieth century, Lasswell did exhibit elitist and technocratic inclinations in his early work. However, his later 'contextual, problem-oriented, multi-method' (1971, p. xiii) framework for the policy sciences is expressly committed to democracy and is clearly critical. A critical focus, already obvious in his early work, is in fact a principal feature of some of his most important works. Its importance has, however, often been obscured by the fact that Lasswell was clearly a proponent of the scientific 'mood' characterizing the 1950s' behavioral revolution in American political science (Dahl 1961, pp. 763, 768).

The behavioral revolution, which was primarily positivist in inclination, generally resisted an agenda of application, at least in the immediate or near term, instead pursuing the development of a science of politics that might one day be sufficiently advanced for application. In response to later objections about a lack of 'relevance' in the discipline, the 'policy turn' of the 1970s encouraged a greater focus on application. Nonetheless, the positivist spirit – heedless of the methodological need for critical reflection – carried on as part of the increased focus on policy (Torgerson 1995, pp. 228–230). To understand Lasswell's much earlier proposal for the policy sciences of democracy, however, we must look to his distinct intellectual development, which clearly sets him apart from the positivist spirit.

As the outstanding representative of Charles Merriam's Chicago school of political science during the 1920s and 1930s, Lasswell was long a staunch advocate of empirical inquiry. He was not a positivist, though, but a pragmatist – whose work also displayed clear critical features (Torgerson 2007b, pp. 15–17).[2] Principally inspired by John Dewey's pragmatist conception of social science as a mode of social problem solving, Lasswell exhibited no vacillation in pursuing a problem orientation (Torgerson 1995, pp. 235–240). Already clear from unpublished texts of the mid- to late 1920s (Torgerson 1987, 1990), Lasswell's problem orientation becomes publicly obvious in 1930 with his *Psychopathology and Politics* (especially pp. 196–203). His position, moreover, remained at a clear distance from the typically reductive positivist conception of science: 'No useful purpose is served by trying to establish uniformity of usage for a word of such importance in modern civilization as "science"' (Lasswell 1950, p. 422). That distance is also suggested by the particular science that first attracted his serious attention during his early teens (Rotsen 1969, p. 6) and that was later of major importance to his conception of the policy sciences – i.e., psychoanalysis. Indeed, not only Freud, but also Marx, was of extraordinary importance for Lasswell in his conceptualization and elaboration of a distinctly critical approach.

The crucial feature of critical inquiry is that it is guided by an emancipatory interest (cf. Habermas 1971, pp. 197–198), and in that regard Lasswell's conception of the policy sciences is connected to the emancipatory logic of psychoanalysis. In 1928, he underwent a didactic analysis in Berlin by Theodore Reik (Lasswell 1928; Smith 1969, p. 57), one of Freud's first and most outstanding students. Soon afterwards, Lasswell would go on to practice as a lay psychoanalyst in the course of research on 'political types' in *Psychopathology and Politics* (1930, p. 273; cf. Torgerson 1985, pp. 256–257n. 7). In that book he offered this portrayal of the 'prolonged interview' of the psychoanalytic process (p. 215):

> Back and forth, bit by bit, there is reconstructed the subjective history of a life. To put it metaphorically, old sores run anew, smoldering embers of jealousy and lust flame once more, and ancient wounds yawn again. Reminiscence reguilds the faded tapestries of the past, and restores to the full glare of consciousness the cobwebs of the mind that house the spiders of malevolence and lechery.

The process prepares the way for 'liberation and understanding' (ibid., p. 210) and culminates, according to Lasswell, at a point where '[p]rimitive meanings, once appropriate to a situation and later projected unintentionally into the adult world' are exposed to conscious attention so that they might be 'criticized' (ibid., p. 215).[3] Indeed, Lasswell would later offer a blunt response to the view, typical of positivism, that the point of the scientific study of human affairs is 'prediction': he emphasized that the 'role' of social science is instead the promotion of 'freedom' – freedom, in particular, from unconscious compulsions that constrain choice (1951a, p. 524). Beyond the depth psychological level, as we shall see, Lasswell also advocated an adaptation of the logic of psychoanalysis to the level of culture and society (1971, p. 158), where the emancipatory logic becomes manifest as, in effect, a critique of ideology (1948, p. 220).

An emancipatory interest draws the focus of attention to forces that, both overtly and surreptitiously, serve to shape and sustain structures and dynamics of power. From the perspective advanced by critical policy studies, indeed, technocracy needs to be understood not simply in terms of an oligarchy of experts, but also in terms of the support given by experts to oligarchic forces in the power structures and dynamics of advanced industrial societies (Fischer 1990). In light of these oligarchic forces, a critical focus on power relations supports an agenda favoring the advance of democratization. The critical perspective, moreover, typically challenges the conventionally sanguine view of power relations under established liberal democracy. In terms of democratic theory, critical policy studies thus exhibits an affinity to more participatory alternatives, usually conceived as some type of deliberative democracy. Lasswell's conception of democracy actually shows the same kind of affinity, despite his common reputation as a liberal democrat advancing nothing but democratic elitism.

In the course of our discussion, we will see that Lasswell's critical orientation focused on the problem of context. We will also see that his promotion of 'the policy sciences of democracy' depended upon seeing the policy sciences in context. Lasswell's turn away from elitist and technocratic inclinations to an unequivocal embrace of democracy came well after he had adopted a critical stance. That shows that there is no necessary connection between a critical orientation and democracy. As we will see, a critical stance is not even necessarily inconsistent with elitism. That is a point that is significant not just in understanding Lasswell's development, but also in recognizing the complexities that face the project of critical policy studies.

Lasswell's affirmation of democracy was not an endorsement of established liberal democratic government. He posed the daunting challenge, rather, of advancing the *democratization of society*. By taking on that challenge, Lasswell's policy sciences of democracy come with a definite political commitment that is bound to be controversial. Such a commitment poses a perplexity for Lasswell, however, in that he follows a reformist inclination and does not encourage the direct involvement of the policy sciences in politically controversial matters.

That is a perplexity that cannot be adequately addressed without going beyond the conventional ambit of social science and venturing into the realm of political judgment. It may well be that critical policy studies is better equipped to deliberately undertake the tasks of political judgment than Lasswell's policy sciences profession might be. Yet, that would not lessen the difficulties facing any democratically inclined critical perspective in reaching judgments about political intervention. It is thus that serious attention to Lasswell's critical approach may help us to understand – with a clarity otherwise not possible – the questions that arise for critical policy studies in a political connection.

2.   POLICY SCIENCES IN CONTEXT

'We must, as part of our study, expose ourselves to ourselves' (Atkins and Lasswell 1924, p. 7). This reflexive principle, announced in the introduction to Lasswell's first book, suggested already the influence of psychoanalysis and was to be a guiding feature throughout his work. He would address psychoanalysis most directly and extensively in *Psychopathology and Politics* (1930) and would later link Freud with Marx in *World Politics and Personal Insecurity* (1935), as he initiated the elaboration of his reflexive principle by laying stress on the importance of context. Although Lasswell's early work exhibited technocratic features, his approach nonetheless always stood well apart from common technocratic conventions by virtue of the reflexive principle guiding it (Torgerson 2013, pp. 3–6). The need for contextual orientation would be a central feature of the overview of his framework presented in his late work *A Pre-View of Policy Sciences*, in which Lasswell advanced a proposal for a project of 'contextual mapping' (1971, chapter 1, pp. 63–67).

No one, according to Lasswell, can 'escape an *implicit* map of self-in-context' (ibid., p. 155, emphasis in original), and the conduct of inquiry depends upon making such implicit maps *explicit*, exposing them to systematic criticism through a project of 'contextual mapping' so that inquirers are enabled to use their 'capacities for imagination and judgment' (ibid., pp. 155–156; cf. pp. 54, 63ff.). For Lasswell, moreover, the mapping of 'self-in-context' involves the levels of both depth psychology and world history.

In the first chapter of *World Politics and Personal Insecurity*, Lasswell indicates the relevance of psychoanalysis to 'the symbolic aspects of historical development' (1935, p. 19; cf. Torgerson 1985), but the form – if not the content – of Marx's thought here represents his key point of departure, particularly through the Hegelian-Marxist 'exposition of the dialectical method' offered by Georg Lukács in *History and Class Consciousness* (Lasswell 1935, p. 18n). What inquiry demands is 'an act of creative orientation' (ibid., p. 13) in regard to an 'all-encompassing totality' (ibid., p. 12), including 'the continuum which embraces past, present, and future' (ibid., p. 4). What becomes evident here is a dialectic of part and whole, as Lasswell emphasizes the importance of 'the gradual creation of a sense of wholeness' (ibid., p. 16; cf. Lasswell 1948, p. 218) while indicating that the significance of details will be misconstrued if they are not properly located in relationship to their context. However, on Lasswell's own terms, no image of the whole can be other than provisional and incomplete – a point that becomes particularly obvious in regard to the historical dimension of contextual orientation.

Lasswell explicitly acknowledges the influence of Marx in advancing the concept of the 'developmental construct' to address the historical aspect of contextual orientation. Yet he clearly distances himself from Marx (as Lasswell interprets him) by disavowing any sense of historical determinism or inevitability (Torgerson 2013, pp. 5–6). In attempting to grasp the 'continuum' of past, present and future, Lasswell maintains, inquirers must accept the unavoidability of future events being 'partly probable and partly chance' (1971, p. 11). It is thus that Lasswell recommends the elaboration of a plurality of developmental constructs, which may vary as to whether they are deemed likely or desirable, but which must be disciplined by intensive and extensive attention to conditions and trends, together with the 'crucial test' of emerging events (1935, p. 13). In other words, as Lasswell emphatically insists, such constructs are not to be an expression of mere wishful thinking (1962, p. 80). There is a further complexity that Lasswell adds to his account, reinforcing his rejection of historical determinism or inevitability. That is the significance of self-fulfilling or self-denying prophecies: 'The act of considering the shape of things to come is itself an event that is not without effect on the ensuing events' (1980, p. 518).

Central to Lasswell's take on historical development is what he calls 'the world revolution of our time' (1965), which exhibits 'the rise to power of the intellectual class' and a 'permanent revolution of modernizing intellectuals' (1968, p. 185). Lasswell's promotion of the policy sciences follows from this view, and here the key issue that arises is that of democracy versus oligarchy – 'whether the overriding aim of policy should be the realization of human dignity of the many, or the dignity of the few (and the indignity of the many)' (1971, p. 41). For Lasswell, human dignity is equivalent to human freedom, and he suggests that in political terms the goal of freedom and dignity 'unmistakably includes democracy, or the sharing of power in the community decision process' (Rubenstein and Lasswell 1966, p. 8).

Threatened by the twin dangers of 'oligarchy' and 'bureaucratism' (1971, p. 119), democratization depends for Lasswell on theorists and practitioners of the policy sciences achieving and maintaining a professional identity committed to its realization. The advance of democratization can, for him, hardly be taken for granted, particularly because his principal contribution to the elaboration of developmental constructs focused on the rise of 'specialists on violence' in fostering an oligarchic 'garrison state' (Lasswell 1941b) – an idea that would later influence President Dwight Eisenhower's famous warning of the 'military-industrial complex' (Friedberg 2000, pp. 56–58). For Lasswell, the very point of the garrison state construct was to help forestall 'the unspeakable contingencies latent in tendencies already more than faintly discernable' (1965, p. 96).

Achieving a creative orientation to context is an emancipatory project necessarily involving individuals, but Lasswell also stresses that it is 'no private act' (1974, p. 183) – 'no one individual can hope to have an exhaustive map of the whole' (1958b, p. 210). It is a collective enterprise focused on achieving a 'distinctive' professional identity (1971, p. 120). Lasswell portrays the policy sciences profession as being guided by the 'principal value goal' of 'truth in the sense of *enlightenment* about the policy process and its interaction with the social context . . .' (1974, p. 181, emphasis in original; cf. 1971, pp. 155–156). To be sustained, the commitment to enlightenment requires reflexivity, particularly in the face of pressures arising from 'the threats and temptations of power' (1974, p. 177). The challenge of shaping a professional identity capable of consistently adhering to the goal of enlightenment, however, goes beyond overt threats and temptations.

'The world about us', Lasswell once remarked, 'is much richer in meanings than we consciously see' (1930, p. 36). Contextual mapping includes an elucidation of such meanings, by virtue of which 'established relationships' can be changed (1956, p. 115). The relationships are 'subject to change with notice' – that is to say, to change 'with insight' (1965, p. 33) into the way human interactions have been established and maintained. Lasswell here follows Freud in insisting upon 'the efficacy of insight' (1956, p. 114). The mapping of self-in-context depends upon 'insight into the Self' (1958a, p. 96) in order to uncover features of the personality 'ordinarily excluded from the focus of full waking attention by the smooth working mechanisms of "resistance" and "repression"' (ibid., p. 97). The goal is emancipation, 'freedom from obsession and compulsivity' (ibid., p. 92).

Although the emancipatory logic of psychoanalysis is Lasswell's touchstone, he nonetheless introduces a key qualification. 'Traditional psychoanalysis laid so much emphasis on the "deeper" motivations that it failed', he argues, 'to provide for proportionate, contextual insight into social reality at different levels' (1971, p. 158). Accordingly he proposes 'critique' at levels of society and culture, capable of achieving 'contextual insight' (ibid.) able to counter resistance in social scientific circles, for example, to ideas at odds with conventional 'ideology' (Lasswell 1961, p. 112). It is thus that Lasswell suggests using 'the contextual principle to remove the ideological blinders from our eyes . . .' (1948, p. 220).

Lasswell's account of the historical importance of 'modernizing intellectuals' – that, in particular, of a policy sciences profession – could well be viewed as overstated and as neglecting other forces of historical development. However, this emphasis has a rationale, minimally, in that policy experts – together with their education and their commitments – seem sure to be at least important in any plausible future. Critical policy studies, in fact, also clearly presupposes that the orientation of policy professionals is important for the future. Lasswell hoped that the future would be democratic, and he believed such a future was at least possible. However, even with the undesirable advent of a garrison state, Lasswell maintained, policy professionals favoring democracy could nonetheless play a role in attempting to preserve at least some vestiges of democratic values (1941b, p. 467).

From his early period, when elitist and technocratic tendencies were most salient in his thought, through to his later promotion of the policy sciences of democracy, Lasswell maintained the importance of enlightening of experts. To what extent, however, was this enlightenment supposed to inform the larger populace? In the early period, with *Psychopathology and Politics* as the key point of reference, he placed emphasis more on immunizing the populace than on enlightening it, even deploying propaganda to forestall the agitation of social tensions and irrationalities (cf. Horwitz 1962). However, his later democratic tendency emphasized the sharing of power (Lasswell 1971, p. 44), the 'encouragement of continuous general participation' (ibid., p. 117), the promotion of 'all the rationality of which individuals and groups are capable' (ibid., p. 120), and – as we shall see – the widespread fostering of critical insight.

3.   THE PROGRESSIVE DEMOCRATIZATION OF SOCIETY

What is the relationship between a critical orientation in policy studies – including Lasswell's policy sciences – and the promotion of democracy? In a world marked by elitist or oligarchic tendencies, the emancipatory interest displayed by a critical orientation certainly tends to suggest an inclination in favor of democracy. Although Lasswell held a non-cognitivist position on normative questions, he still suggested that, in practice, his approach was connected to democracy. For he found it hard to understand how anyone seriously applying the contextual principle would not come to endorse democratic values (1968, p. 162). Critical policy studies also maintains a commitment to democracy, though with no clear consensus on the normative grounds. Is there any necessary connection between a critical orientation and a commitment to democracy? Could it even be that the reverse is the case? Could it be that a critical orientation might turn out to be, if not actually antithetical to democracy, at least somehow at odds with it?

Lasswell's commitment to democracy has often been questioned. Critics have branded him as more an elitist than a democrat, portraying him as committed at best to conventional liberal democracy (e.g., Bachrach 1967). However, a well-observed shift in Lasswell moves from an early phase, characterized by an elitist tendency, to a later phase – beginning around 1940 – characterized by an emphatic endorsement of democracy (Easton 1950). His 'Garrison state' article, published in early 1941, is a clear indication of this shift (Lasswell 1941b). Yet, what kind of democracy does he advocate? What we need to recognize at the outset is that, when he first publicly advocated 'the policy sciences of democracy' in 1948, Lasswell explicitly connected this project not to the status quo of established power relations, but to 'the progressive democratization of society' (1948, p. 184).

The democratic commitment of critical policy studies is seldom questioned, but might it be that it too is potentially troubled by the problem of elitism? Does the emancipatory interest of critical inquiry even carry with it the inherent problem of an elitist tendency? That is a question that recalls the difference between interpretive and critical inquiry: an interpretive orientation gains access to its subject matter by virtue of being 'in on' common sense understandings (Taylor 1971, p. 13) whereas a critical orientation, although also dependent upon such understandings, requires the critical distance of an objective moment that provides insight into the limitations of common understandings.

Both interpretive and critical orientations gain access to their subject matter through a linguistic medium, but the objective moment of a critical approach reveals that language is not simply a medium of communication sustaining human relationships: 'Language is *also* a medium of domination and social power' (Habermas 1988, p. 172, emphasis in original). Rather than remaining at a level of common understandings that serves to legitimate 'relations of organized force' (ibid.), a critical approach thus needs to expose such relationships so that they may be appraised and possibly changed. The potentially 'elitist' character of such a critical posture has long been obvious. It is a potential that is clear enough in the psychoanalytic relationship of analyst and patient, as it also is in connection to the leadership of a revolutionary movement (see Habermas 1974, pp. 1–40).

Even with its commitment to democracy, the critically informed policy sciences profession that Lasswell promoted cannot escape this problem. Nor, it should be added, can critical policy studies. That does not mean that a critical standpoint is not relevant, even necessary, for a project of democratization. What it does indicate is that commitment to a democratic project cannot rely solely upon an emancipatory interest, but also depends upon a practical interest – interpretive in character – in interacting with others in a common world (cf. Habermas 1971, pp. 195–197; 1974, especially p. 40).

Elitist and technocratic accents in Lasswell's early work were animated by what he saw as the worrisome rise of irrationality in mass societies following World War I, particularly in Europe. His concerns are evident from unpublished writings of the 1920s (Torgerson 1987, 1990) and from his 1927 book on wartime propaganda (Lasswell 1927). They are amplified, moreover, in his psychoanalytically informed proposal in 1930 for a 'politics of prevention' to curb the irrationalities of politics: 'Our problem is to be ruled by the truth about the conditions of harmonious human relations, and the discovery of the truth is an object of specialized research; it is no monopoly of people as people, or of the ruler as ruler' (1930, p. 197). In his *World Politics and Personal Insecurity* of 1935, Lasswell supported a benevolent form of elitism, involving 'an elite which propagates itself by peaceful means and wields a monopoly of coercion which it is rarely necessary to apply to the uttermost' (1935, p. 181). Since his critical orientation was already well developed during his elitist phase, it is obvious that this critical focus *preceded* – and thus did not initially accompany – his later commitment to the progressive democratization of society.

It is notable that Lasswell's democratic turn came as he was advancing his developmental construct of the garrison state, portraying it as an anti-democratic historical prospect to be avoided. He first formulated the idea of the garrison state in 1937, with reference the Sino-Japanese War (Lasswell 1937), and his definitive statement – also a clear mark of his democratic turn – followed in 1941, prior to U.S. entry into World War II (Lasswell 1941b). It was in the same year that he published *Democracy through Public Opinion*, a book whose content and title are remarkable given the doubts about public opinion in progressive circles following World War I (Lasswell 1941a). Especially as debated by Walter Lippmann and John Dewey, these are doubts that Lasswell himself clearly expressed during the course of his early work (Torgerson 2007b, pp. 23–24).

The skepticism that critics have expressed about Lasswell's democratic commitment neglects the substance of his proposal. What they miss are the clearly participatory and, at times, radical features of his conception of democracy. These are already obvious in his first public statement of his proposal for 'the policy sciences of democracy' in his 1948 book *Power and Personality* (pp. 118ff.). Most notably, Lasswell's conception of democracy involves not simply a form of government – the typical focus of liberal democratic theory – but more generally a form of society.[4] It was in *Power and Personality*, indeed, that Lasswell proposed the 'progressive democratization of society' – calling for 'the continual reconstruction of whatever practices stand in the way of democratic personality and polity' (ibid., p. 148). This was a project of reconstruction that he would soon afterwards portray as requiring 'drastic' change (Lasswell 1951a, p. 513).

Despite Lasswell's clearly democratic turn, he obviously remained concerned with the potential irrationalities of politics, so that democratization – however drastic the change required – appears in his view as a project not of extreme conflict and social upheaval, but of progressive reform. Nonetheless, *Power and Personality* reversed his position in *Psychopathology and Politics* concerning the priority of expert versus public enlightenment. He moves to the view that the 'specialized training of the few' is not as important for democracy as 'elevating the level of . . . the whole community' (Lasswell 1948, p. 148; cf. 1930, p. 201). He also indicates a need 'to organize all institutions' (1948, p. 174) so as to support progressive democratization (ibid., p. 184). Nonetheless, Lasswell remains decidedly reformist in his orientation (e.g., ibid., pp. 130–131, 192–193), concerned about propagandistic agitation by political movements in promoting 'the dubious and dangerous expectation of democracy through mass revolution' (ibid., p. 212). There is thus an evident continuity with his earlier 'preventative politics', at least to the extent that he calls for a form of 'democratic leadership' (ibid., p. 108) that avoids the provocation of social conflict and, in fact, serves to reduce social anxiety. Notably, however, his call for democratic leadership to keep 'provocative crises . . . at a minimum' (ibid., p. 174) does not only involve enhanced democratic education (ibid., p. 221); also needed is a recognition that the values of a democratic society 'depend on a very considerable dispersion of wealth throughout the community' (ibid., p. 149).

Lasswell points to Keynesian interventions as a way to mollify the conflicts provoked by crises stemming from the 'structural defect' of underemployment in the market system (ibid., p. 175). Beyond the prevention of provocative crises, Lasswell also calls for a more 'affirmative' approach to institutional change for the democratization of society (ibid., p. 188). Here he stresses the common failure of 'even democratic regimes to adapt their procedures to the elementary need of giving everyone a voice in what seems to concern' them (ibid., p. 190). Lasswell particularly points to the problem of 'policing the market against monopoly' (ibid., p. 191). The point is not so much to protect an elusive free market, but to curb capitalist political power. Due to the failure to take 'measures essential to check the silent transformation of genuinely competitive markets (where such existed) into monopoly-political arenas . . .' (ibid., p. 213), he argues, capitalism had been 'transformed into a political organization' – one that conceals 'its nature by speaking the language of "business," "competition," "free enterprise" and the like' (ibid., p. 214). The consequence is 'that the competitive market has been subtly transformed into a political arena, since a few policy makers exert disproportionate influence upon the general supply of goods and services' (ibid., p. 191). When that is the case, Lasswell maintains, 'some means must be invented for representing those affected' (ibid., pp. 191–192):

> Policy choices which were formerly governed by calculations of economic advantage become transformed ... into power decisions, since they threaten severe deprivation by unilateral action, or are enforceable against dissenters by procedures that entail the application of severe sanctions. The corporation that decides to close down a given plant in the community may inflict severe deprivations upon workers who have invested in homes, paid taxes for municipal services, and developed community life.

Such 'undermining of democracy when people are subject to arbitrary exercises of power' is, he argues, a concern for 'the community'. However, Lasswell does not leave the matter as one only for the 'local community' as if it were 'the unit for organizing full participation in monopolistic-political controls' (ibid., p. 192). Although 'local controls' will at times be sufficient, more is needed when 'the scale' ascends 'to the regional, national or global level' (ibid., p. 192).

Notably, Lasswell's commitment to the progressive democratization of society included a striking comment on radical hopes for democracy and, indeed, on anarchist ideals (ibid., p. 110):

> It should not be denied that the long-run aim of societies aspiring toward human freedom is to get rid of power and to bring into existence a ... commonwealth in which coercion is neither threatened, applied or desired. This is the thread of the anarchist idealism that appears in all uncompromising applications of the key conception of human dignity.

Such, Lasswell argues, is 'the hope, though not necessarily the certainty, of the radical democrat'. 'In our day, however', he adds, 'the probability that we can reduce power to the vanishing point seems very remote indeed': 'The urgent task', consequently, 'is to chasten and subordinate power to the service of respect'. This task follows from what Lasswell sees as the relationship between power and democracy: 'In a democratic commonwealth, power is not only shared but subordinated to respect for the dignity of human personality' (ibid., p. 108).

The 'conception of democracy' that guides Lasswell's proposal for the policy sciences of democracy is one 'of a network of congenial and creative interpersonal relations' (ibid., p. 110). That goal calls for democratic education (ibid., pp. 171–173) and for 'the citizen' to 'maintain some degree of active and informed participation in public affairs' (ibid., p. 150). Maintaining that progressive democratization is an historical possibility, though far from a certainty, Lasswell stresses that it poses an immense challenge: 'The task is nothing less than the drastic and continuing reconstruction of ... civilization ...' (Lasswell 1951a, p. 513). Although he recognizes this challenge, Lasswell does not seek to enlist the policy sciences of democracy in anything as drastic as democratic struggle against anti-democratic alignments of power (see, e.g., ibid., p. 514). The policy sciences profession is thus portrayed as remaining primarily within the conventional domain of social science and as not venturing into that of direct political engagement.

4.   THE POLITICAL CONNECTION

Political commitment is clearly involved as soon as we place the promotion of democracy onto the agenda of inquiry and practice. We thus cannot escape the question of the appropriate role of inquirers in relation to political advocacy and engagement. Although Lasswell promoted a policy sciences profession committed to democracy, he was markedly reticent to have policy scientists engage in political intervention, particularly when it was controversial. The very term 'policy sciences', indeed, reflects a concern by Lasswell to avoid controversial associations with political engagement and intervention. He chose the term 'policy', as he explicitly indicates, in part to escape the connotations of narrow partisanship – and, no doubt, conflict – borne by the term 'politics' (Lasswell 1948, p. 124).

The conceptual rationale for this posture was the key distinction Lasswell made between two value goals, enlightenment and power. For him, the 'principal value goal' for the policy sciences profession – and thereby a rationale for invoking the term 'science' – was 'enlightenment', rather than 'power' (1974, p. 181; cf. 1971, p. 155). In his view, a commitment to enlightenment is susceptible to the pressure of the circumstances faced by policy scientists, particularly – as we have seen – the threats and temptations of power. Yet, to what extent can the distinction between enlightenment and power can be maintained in theory or in practice?[5] Does a commitment to progressive democratization not make political intervention and engagement in power relations inescapable for both Lasswell and critical policy studies? If so, the threats and temptations of power would not be eliminated simply by acknowledging them. Facing up to the inescapability of political engagement would by itself offer no simple solution. However, it would become clear that, in a quest for enlightenment, the conduct of inquiry depends upon political judgments about how best to deal with power.

In keeping with his critically informed commitment to progressive democratization, Lasswell looked to potentials for the sharing of power. He called in particular for 'the transformation of passive or episodic audiences into active and continuing participants in the policy processes, including the conduct of research analysis, and systematic appraisal' (1971, p. 117). Toward that end, he introduced a type of participatory exercise that he called 'prototyping'. Prototypes were not cases that policy scientists would simply study, but were power-sharing efforts they would actively develop as models for democratization. The prototype reported in Lasswell's book with psychiatrist Robert Rubenstein, *The Sharing of Power in a Psychiatric Hospital* (Rubenstein and Lasswell, 1966), has, in particular, been described by Henry Kariel as a 'dramatic illustration of how social science can creatively restructure a prevailing system of power' in order to establish 'a democratic forum for sharing power' (Kariel 1969, pp. 137–138).

Yet, there remains the key issue of how a prototype is related to its context. Lasswell emphasizes that prototyping is distinguished by its goal values, which feature '*subordination to enlightenment rather than power*' (1971, p. 70, emphasis in original). The development of a power-sharing prototype 'uses available power as a base for enlightenment' and can proceed only when there is 'no outside pressure of public controversy' (ibid.). The point with a prototype is to examine the potential for democratizing power relations in order to generate proposals to inform 'future strategists of power sharing' (ibid., p. 71). The prototype is thus largely detached from its context. Lasswell emphasizes that if and when a prototype becomes involved in the pressures and controversies of a larger context of power, it loses the character of a prototype and becomes 'direct political intervention' (ibid., p. 70). Here the work of policy scientists is conceived as maintaining a stance, in effect, of something approaching political neutrality.

Nothing like political neutrality is, by comparison, suggested by proposals from critical policy studies seeking to advance democratization, whether for example in Dryzek's account of 'discursive democracy' (1990, cf. 2000; Dryzek et al. 2003) or in Fischer's call for 'deliberative empowerment' and 'participatory expertise' (2009, chapter 9; 1992). Such proposals are obviously controversial and confront opposition in the established structures and dynamics of power. Viewed by themselves in contexts that are inimical to democratic power sharing, of course, even such proposals might themselves be seen as merely limited reforms, their democratic potential almost destined to be absorbed by the power structures and dynamics of an undemocratic context.

The picture changes, however, if the context is instead a site of active democratic struggle. Here the proposals exhibit the potential to expand in significance, especially when the broader historical context is animated by social movements and emergent publics committed to the cause of progressive democratization (cf. Torgerson 2007a). The proposals thus become more than techniques in a toolbox. They become political interventions that are themselves part of the context of historical development.

Lasswell's non-controversial and reformist inclinations fit with his emphasis on securing and maintaining the stability of democracy. That emphasis is clearly at odds with accounts of progressive democratization as demanding democratic struggle, let alone of democratic forces being necessarily disruptive to any established order (e.g., Rancière 1998). On Lasswell's own terms, though, how can reformism accord with a project of democratization requiring 'drastic and continuing reconstruction' (1951a, p. 513)?

Although democratically committed, Lasswell remained concerned about the danger that agitation could provoke political irrationalities. Here he maintained a continuity with his earlier view of 'belligerent crusades to change the world' as being both dangerous and self-defeating (1930, p. 194) and of politically engaged movements as being entangled with irrationality (ibid., p. 202). Nonetheless, if the context is one in which progressive democratization depends upon the controversial mobilization of democratic struggle, then Lasswell is in a quandary.

Still, a potential way out may be suggested by this observation concerning social movements, made during the mid-1960s in Lasswell's book with Robert Rubenstein (Rubenstein and Lasswell, 1966, p. 2): 'The great social movements of our time concern the demand for full participation as equals in the affairs of the community by the disadvantaged. Sermons and speeches have long acknowledged the justice of this demand, but the insistence that we take the democratic ideology seriously and live by it is revolutionary.' This passage suggests that it is advisable to consider the advent of social movements and emergent publics in terms other than simply the mobilization of irrational energies. That would suggest the possibility – as taken up by critical policy studies – that these developments might be considered, quite differently, in terms of their potential contribution to progressive democratization.

When Lasswell first publicly proposed the policy sciences of democracy, he spoke hopefully of 'the possible dissemination of insight on a vast scale to the adult population' (1948, p. 196; cf. 1941b, p. 332). If such insight exposes not only psychopathological constraints, but also ideological ones, an obvious example of a relevant insight would arise from Lasswell's critique of the failure, by supposedly democratic regimes, to 'give everyone a voice' – particularly with regard to the transformation of capitalism 'into a political organization' that conceals its own character (Lasswell 1948, p. 214). Yet such an insight could hardly be communicated widely and effectively without entering into controversial political intervention. Here the key question is how, on the grounds of Lasswell's own position, it would be possible for the policy sciences to advance the progressive democratization of society without making this highly controversial insight, as well as many others, widely shared among the public.

Since the 1920s and throughout nearly his whole career, Lasswell believed that social scientists could map the social and historical context in a consensual manner (Torgerson 1987, 1990). With his democratic turn, he came to advocate the sharing of such a map with the larger populace. His view of the importance of a consensual map clearly changed only toward the end of his career: 'The scholars from various cultural and ideological backgrounds currently differ in interpreting the dynamics of society' (1979, p. 63). He thus came to the view that greater illumination about the social and historical context would depend upon offering the populace 'alternative versions' (ibid.).

What Lasswell in effect recognizes here is 'the politics of expertise', as it has been called in the literature of critical policy studies (Fischer 1990). Yet, the politics of expertise involves not only difference, but also conflict and controversy. Disseminating insight in such a context unavoidably entails political intervention. Should policy professionals disseminate controversial insights? If so, how?

These are questions that call for political judgment. Clearly, such judgment cannot be compelled by the certainty commonly associated with scientific knowledge. Nonetheless, it may well involve the 'judicious exchange of opinion' that animates an illuminating debate (Arendt 1968, p. 222; cf. Beiner, 1983). As developed through debate, however, political judgment is itself a matter of political controversy. Controversial engagement thus becomes a perplexing challenge that cannot be escaped by critically oriented policy professionals who are committed to the progressive democratization of society.

NOTES

1. See, for example, the association of Lasswell with 'critical policy analysis' in Bobrow and Dryzek (1987, pp. 172–174). Dryzek (1990, p. 128) went so far as to venture the term 'critical policy science'; cf. Torgerson (1985). Although nominally about 'policy science', Tribe's (1972) seminal critique of technocratic policy discourse makes no reference to Lasswell.
2. Herbert Simon was a student at the University of Chicago when Lasswell was a faculty

member there. Unlike Lasswell, however, Simon deliberately distanced himself from pragmatism in favor of the greater formalism of neo-positivism, and he advanced an especially sophisticated technocratic perspective (see Torgerson 1995, pp. 240–242).

3. It should be noted that Lasswell here indicates criticism 'in the light of . . . appropriateness to society' (1930, p. 215), thereby suggesting an accent on normalization and the capability of the mature ego that would later become associated with Neo-Freudianism and that may be related to Lasswell's reformist disposition (see Birnbach 1961, chapter 7, pp. 177–186; cf. Lasswell 1951a, p. 524).

4. Easton (1950) astutely identified Lasswell's move from elitism to democracy. Easton's treatment was marred, however, in dating Lasswell's early phase as 1934–1940, thereby neglecting *Psychopathology and Politics* (1930) and its proposal for a 'politics of prevention' (chapter 10). With this oversight, Easton also claimed incorrectly that Lasswell's early elitist phase was devoted to a 'purely scientific, objective science of politics' (Easton 1950, p. 459). Easton's misconception of Lasswell as a kind of positivist (ibid., p. 454), moreover, ignores his pragmatism and evidently arises from mistakenly equating positivism with ethical non-cognitivism – the latter not being unique to positivism. Bachrach (1967) neglected both Easton's (1950) thesis of Lasswell's shift from elitism to democracy and Lasswell's most substantive conceptualization of democracy (1948). Farr et al. (2006, 2008; cf. Brunner 2008) have more recently voiced doubts about Lasswell's democracy. Their consideration culminates, however, in the striking suggestion that Lasswell might be construed as a precursor to current conceptions of democracy involving 'discussion, debate, and deliberation', if he is read 'selectively and programmatically' (Farr et al. 2008, p. 30; cf. Dryzek 1990, pp. 113–114). Reading Lasswell at a sustained conceptual level is necessary rather for an immanent critique, as is attempted in this chapter.

5. Lasswell's reliance on the distinction between the goals of 'enlightenment' and 'power' might be questioned, e.g., in light of Horkheimer and Adorno (2002) and Foucault (1980). Still, for Lasswell, enlightenment requires objectivity, but an objectivity of reflexive contextualization, rather than detachment. Indeed, the objectivity of 'a participant-observer of events who tries to see things as they are' is indispensable to the policy sciences (Lasswell 1971, p. 3; cf. pp. 58, 74–75). Notable, nonetheless, is Gramsci's rejection of the very possibility of a 'purely "objective" prediction', in favor of his contention that a strong effort of 'will' is needed 'to identify the elements that are necessary' for achieving specific goals – a view evidently owing more to Machiavelli than Marx (Gramsci 1971, p. 171).

REFERENCES

For chronological clarity, works (except translations) are listed and cited by the date of initial publication, which appears within square brackets. The date of the edition used follows within the parentheses.

Arendt, Hannah (1968), 'The crisis in culture', in Hannah Arendt, *Between Past and Future: Eight Exercises in Political Thought*, New York: Viking Press, pp. 197–226.

Atkins, Willard E. and Harold D. Lasswell (1924), *Labor Attitudes and Problems*, New York: Prentice-Hall.

Bachrach, Peter (1967), *The Theory of Democratic Elitism: A Critique*, Boston: Little, Brown.

Beiner, Ronald (1983), *Political Judgement*, London: Methuen.

Birnbach, Martin (1961), *Neo-Freudian Social Philosophy*, Stanford: Stanford University Press.

Bobrow, Davis and John S. Dryzek (1987), *Policy Analysis by Design*, Pittsburgh: University of Pittsburgh Press.

Brunner, Ronald D. (2008), 'The policy scientist of democracy revisited', *Policy Sciences*, **41**, 3–19.
Dahl, Robert (1961), 'The behavioral approach in political science: epitaph for a monument to a successful protest', *American Political Science Review*, **55** (4), 763–772.
Dryzek, John S. (1990), *Discursive Democracy*, Cambridge: Cambridge University Press.
Dryzek, John S. (2000), *Deliberative Democracy and Beyond*, Oxford: Oxford University Press.
Dryzek, John S., David Downes, Christian Hunold and David Schlosberg (2003), *Green States and Social Movements: Environmentalism in the United States, United Kingdom, Germany and Norway*, Oxford: Oxford University Press.
Easton, David (1950), 'Harold Lasswell: policy scientist for a democratic society', *The Journal of Politics*, **12** (3), 450–477.
Farr, James, Jacob S. Hacker and Nicole Kazee (2006), 'The policy scientist of democracy: the discipline of Harold D. Lasswell', *American Political Science Review*, **100** (4), 579–587.
Farr, James, Jacob S. Hacker and Nicole Kazee (2008), 'Revisiting Lasswell', *Policy Sciences*, **41** (1), 21–32.
Fischer, Frank (1990), *Technocracy and the Politics of Expertise*, Newbury Park, CA: Sage.
Fischer, Frank (1992), 'Participatory expertise: toward the democratization of policy science', in William N. Dunn and Rita M. Kelly (eds), *Advances in Policy Studies Since 1950*, New Brunswick, NJ: Transaction Press, pp. 351–376.
Fischer, Frank (2009), *Democracy and Expertise*, Oxford: Oxford University Press.
Foucault, Michel (1980), *The History of Sexuality*, Vol. 1, Richard Hurley (trans.), New York: Vintage Books (French publication, 1976).
Friedberg, A.L. (2000), *In the Shadow of the Garrison State*, Princeton: Princeton University Press.
Gramsci, Antonio (1971), *Selections from the Prison Notebooks*, Quintin Hoare and Geoffrey Nowell Smith (trans.), New York: International Publishers.
Habermas, Jürgen (1971), *Knowledge and Human Interests*, Jeremy J. Shapiro (trans.), Boston: Beacon Press (German publication, 1968).
Habermas, Jürgen (1974), *Theory and Practice*, John Viertel (trans.), Boston: Beacon Press.
Habermas, Jürgen (1988), *On the Logic of the Social Sciences*, Shierry Weber Nicholsen and Jerry A. Stark (trans.), Cambridge, MA: The MIT Press (German publication, 1970).
Horkheimer, Max and Theodor W. Adorno (2002), *Dialectic of Enlightenment*, Edmund Jephcott (trans.), Stanford: Stanford University Press (German publication, 1947).
Horwitz, Robert (1962), 'Scientific propaganda: Harold D. Lasswell', in Herbert J. Storing (ed.), *Essays on the Scientific Study of Politics*, New York: Holt, Rinehart and Winston, pp. 225–304.
Kariel, Henry S. (1969), *Open Systems: Arenas for Political Action*, Itasca, IL: F.E. Peacock Publishers.
Lasswell, Harold D. ([1927] 1971), *Propaganda Technique in World War I*, Cambridge, MA: The MIT Press.
Lasswell, Harold D. (1928), Letter to Anna P. and Linden Lasswell, 3 December. Harold D. Lasswell Papers (Box 56, Folder 784), Manuscripts and Archives, Yale University Library, New Haven, CT.
Lasswell, Harold D. ([1930] 1977), *Psychopathology and Politics*, Chicago: University of Chicago Press.
Lasswell, Harold D. ([1935] 1965), *World Politics and Personal Insecurity*, New York: The Free Press.
Lasswell, Harold D. ([1937] 1997). 'Sino-Japanese crisis: the garrison state versus the civilian state', in Jay Stanley (ed.), *Essays on the Garrison State*, New Brunswick, NJ: Transaction Publishers, pp. 43–54.
Lasswell, Harold D. (1941a), *Democracy through Public Opinion*, Menasha, WI: George Banta Publishing Company.
Lasswell, Harold D. (1941b), 'The garrison state', *American Journal of Sociology*, **46**, 455–468.

Lasswell, Harold D. ([1948] 1976), *Power and Personality*, New York: W.W. Norton.
Lasswell, Harold D. (1950), 'The semantics of political science: discussion', *American Political Science Review*, **44** (2), 422–425.
Lasswell, Harold D. (1951a), 'Democratic character', in *The Political Writings of Harold D. Lasswell*, Glencoe, IL: The Free Press, pp. 465–525.
Lasswell, Harold D. (1951b), 'The policy orientation', in Daniel Lerner and Harold D. Lasswell (eds), *The Policy Sciences*, Stanford: Stanford University Press, pp. 3–15.
Lasswell, Harold D. (1956), 'Impact of psychoanalytic thinking on the social sciences', in Leonard D. White (ed.), *The State of the Social Sciences*, Chicago: University of Chicago Press, pp. 84–115.
Lasswell, Harold D. (1958a), 'Clarifying value judgment: principles of content and procedure', *Inquiry*, **1**, 87–98.
Lasswell, Harold D. (1958b), Postscript to *Politics: Who Gets What, When, How* [1936], New York: Meridian Books, pp. 181–211.
Lasswell, Harold D. (1961), 'The qualitative and the quantitative in political and legal analysis', in Daniel Lerner (ed.), *Quantity and Quality*, New York: The Free Press of Glencoe, pp. 103–116.
Lasswell, Harold D. (1962), 'The garrison state hypothesis today', in Jay Stanley (ed.), *Essays on the Garrison State*, New Brunswick, NJ: Transactions Publishers, 1997, pp. 77–116.
Lasswell, Harold D. (1965), 'The world revolution of our time: a framework for basic policy research', in Harold D. Lasswell and Daniel Lerner (eds), *World Revolutionary Elites*, Cambridge, MA: The MIT Press, pp. 29–96.
Lasswell, Harold D. (1968), 'Policy sciences', *International Encyclopedia of the Social Sciences*, **12**, 181–189.
Lasswell, Harold D. (1971), *A Pre-View of Policy Sciences*, New York: American Elsevier.
Lasswell, Harold D. (1974), 'Some perplexities of policy theory', *Social Research*, **14**, 176–189.
Lasswell, Harold D. (1979), *The Signature of Power*, New Brunswick, NJ: Transaction Books.
Lasswell, Harold D. (1980), 'The future of world communication and propaganda', in Harold D. Lasswell, Daniel Lerner and Hans Speier (eds), *Propaganda and Communication in World History*, Vol. 3, Honolulu: University Press of Hawaii, pp. 516–534.
Lukács, Georg (1971), *History and Class Consciousness: Studies in Marxist Dialectics*, Rodney Livingstone (trans.), London: Merlin Press (German publication, 1923).
Rancière, Jacques (1998), *Disagreement: Politics and Philosophy*, Julie Rose (trans.), Minneapolis: University of Minnesota Press (French publication, 1995).
Rotsen, Leo (1969), 'Harold Lasswell: a memoir', in Arnold A. Rogow (ed.), *Politics, Personality, and Social Science in the Twentieth Century: Essays in Honor of Harold D. Lasswell*, Chicago: Chicago University Press, pp. 1–14.
Rubenstein, Robert and Harold D. Lasswell (1966), *The Sharing of Power in a Psychiatric Hospital*, New Haven: Yale University Press.
Smith, Bruce Lannes (1969), 'The mystifying intellectual history of Harold D. Lasswell', in Arnold A. Rogow (ed.), *Politics, Personality, and Social Science in the Twentieth Century: Essays in Honor of Harold D. Lasswell*, Chicago: Chicago University Press, pp. 41–105.
Taylor, Charles (1971), 'Interpretation and the sciences of man', *Review of Metaphysics*, **25** (3), 3–51.
Torgerson, Douglas (1985), 'Contextual orientation in policy analysis: the contribution of Harold D. Lasswell', *Policy Sciences*, **18**, 241–261.
Torgerson, Douglas (1987), 'Political vision and the policy orientation: Lasswell's early letters', paper presented at the Annual Meetings of the American Political Science Association, Chicago, 3–6 September.
Torgerson, Douglas (1990), 'Origins of the policy orientation: the aesthetic dimension in Lasswell's political vision', *History of Political Thought*, **11**, 339–351.
Torgerson, Douglas (1995), 'Policy analysis and public life: the restoration of *phronēsis*?', in James Farr, John S. Dryzek and Stephen T. Leonard (eds), *Political Science in History:*

Research Programs and Political Traditions, Cambridge: Cambridge University Press, pp. 225–252.

Torgerson, Douglas (2007a), 'Policy discourse as dialogue: emergent publics and the reflexive turn', *Critical Policy Analysis*, **1** (1), 1–17.

Torgerson, Douglas (2007b), 'Promoting the policy orientation: Lasswell in context', in Frank Fischer, Gerald J. Miller and Mara S. Sidney (eds), *Handbook of Public Policy Analysis*, London and New York: Taylor and Francis, pp. 15–28.

Torgerson, Douglas (2013), 'Reflexivity and developmental constructs: the case of sustainable futures', *Journal of Environmental Policy and Planning*, **15**, 1–15 (online).

Tribe, Laurence H. (1972), 'Policy science: analysis or ideology?', *Philosophy and Public Affairs*, **2**, 66–110.

3   In pursuit of usable knowledge: critical policy analysis and the argumentative turn
Frank Fischer

A basic question that initiated critical policy analysis and the argumentative turn was the concern that much or most of policy analysis research and advice was either useless to policy decision-makers or of questionable value. By the late 1970s and into the 1980s it became clear that there was a substantial gap between social science and real-world public policymaking, a problem of essential importance for an applied discipline. Insofar as the policy analysis emerged to inform decision-making, it was difficult to overlook this gap. How to explain this became an important question in the discipline generally, but especially for critical policy studies, as it gave this emerging perspective an opening to demonstrate its contribution in practical terms.

The chapter begins with a general outline of some of the main considerations in the history of the effort to provide a professional discipline capable of providing policy advice for political decision-making. The discussion then turns to problems encountered in the initial phase of the development of policy analysis by the empirical social-scientific approach to policy problem-solving. It then examines the two approaches for dealing with these problems during the 1970s and 1980s, one political and one epistemological. The emphasis in the next section turns to the epistemological approach, particularly as spelled out in the 'argumentative turn' toward a critical policy analysis. After outlining a logic for critical policy argumentation, the chapter concludes with a discussion of the relation of citizens to policy experts, the need for a focus on 'policy epistemics,' and the implications of critical policy analysis more generally.

POLICY KNOWLEDGE: FROM PLATO TO LASSWELL

The role of political and policy advice is hardly a new topic in governance and politics. The significance of politically relevant counsel, together with the question of who should supply it, is found in the earliest treatises on political wisdom and statecraft. It is a prominent theme in the phi-losophy of Plato, in Machiavelli's discussion of the role of the Prince, St Simon and August Comte's theory of technocracy, the 'Brain Trust' of Franklin Roosevelt's New Deal, the writings of the U.S. policy intellectu-als during the Great Society of the 1960s, and modern-day think-tanks since Ronald Reagan and Margaret Thatcher, just to name a few of the more prominent instances (Fischer 1990). Today it is a prominent topic in the discourses of policy theory.

From the outset, a basic theme running through such writings has focused on replacing or minimizing political debate with more rigorous or systematic modes of thought. Within this tradition we find the recurring idea that those with knowledge should rule (Fischer 1990). By the time of St Simon and Comte such writings involved a call for a more 'positivist' epistemological form of knowledge emphasizing testable theory rather than the 'negativism' of earlier philosophers based on critique and specula-tive reason. Whereas philosophical critique was seen to provide no concrete foundation for 'social progress,' the accumulation of positivist knowledge provided the basis for the building of a harmonious, prosperous society.

Policy expertise is in the first instance an American story with roots in the Progressive Era of American politics around the turn into the twentieth century. During this period, there was an explicit call for tech-nocratic expertise in politics. Herbert Croly, a prominent Progressive thinker of the period, became a devotee of the theories of Comte (Levy 1985). Drawing on Comte's theory of technocracy, he promoted the role of policy expertise as an approach to political reform designed to deal with the pressing social and economic problems brought on by rapid urban industrialization. Specifically, he and other Progressives called for the adoption of the principles and practices of Taylorism and 'Scientific Management' to guide such reforms (Wiebe, 1967).[1] In short, a 'neutral' scientific method as opposed to political argumentation would show the way to the good society. It was a political orientation shared by two U.S. Presidents, Theodore Roosevelt and Woodrow Wilson, one Republican and the other Democrat (Fischer and Forester 1993; Fischer 2006).[2]

The emerging positivist or 'behavioral' orientation in the newly devel-oping social sciences was initially closely related to the problem-oriented political reform movements of the 1920s and 1930s (Fischer 2006). In fact, the goal of writers during this period was to substitute corrupt party politics and an 'irrational public' with technocratic planning and manage-ment based on tested knowledge from the newly emerging social sciences (Lippman 1922). In short, to replace the thinking of politicians with the analyses of professional experts (Fischer and Forester 1993; Fischer 2006).

A substantial extension of Progressive ideas followed with the New Deal 'Brain Trust' of the Roosevelt Administration during the Depression of the 1930s (Graham 1976). This development gave impetus to a large influx of economists and other social scientists to the Capitol engaged in policy planning, giving rise to the administrative state and what Karl (1975) called the New Deal 'Liberal Reform Strategy', designed to solve public problems and thus win political elections.

In the post-WWII period a public role for social science in policy advisement was formally advanced by Harold Lasswell, who called for the 'policy orientation' and the development of the 'policy sciences' in the later 1940s and the 1950s. Lasswell (1951) introduced the policy orientation as a multidisciplinary approach to assist policy decision-makers with policy problem-solving. Basic to his concern was the distance between academic social science and the world of policy problem-solving. This was grounded in particular in concerns about the rise of modern mass society and the dominant role of political elites in policy decision processes.

The worry here was about the fact that the public seemed to be disturbingly uninformed and often irrational in its thinking. A major manifestation of this was fascism in Europe during WWII. Another was the emergence of various studies in the United States that showed relatively high levels of ignorance on the part of the public, raising important questions about the viability of democratic politics in an increasingly complex society. It was a theme that resonated with Dewey's (1927) earlier apprehensions about the ability of the public to meaningfully engage issues in a technological society. In fact, Lasswell emerged from the context of Progressivism and was decisively influenced by American Pragmatism in the form of Dewey's approach to social problem-solving. To address Dewey's problem of the public, Lasswell outlined what he referred to as the 'policy sciences of democracy.' It was an orientation designed as an approach for providing politicians, policy decision-makers and the public with the relevant knowledge needed to render informed decisions.

Toward this end, Lasswell advanced a grand multidisciplinary approach that included qualitative disciplines like anthropology as well as economics and political science. The approach recognized that policy analysis requires two dimensions: it not only needs a contextual understanding of how policy processes work, but also a body of causal knowledge related to the particular problems at issue – poverty, environment, etc. Taken together, this has proven to be no small order.

FROM THEORY TO PRACTICE: THE TRIBULATIONS OF TECHNOCRATIC POLICY ANALYSIS

By and large, policy analysis neglected Lasswell's broader theoretical orientation. Taking roots in the United States the actual practice started out with a much narrower technical or technocratic perspective, influenced by WWII operations research in combination with postwar developments in systems analysis. The field, as we know it today, emerged with two U.S. wars in the 1960s – the War on Poverty and the Vietnam War – before traveling abroad.

The War on Poverty started out with a noble goal, namely to end poverty in American society. This was based on a straightforward theory of policy and policy analysis. It assumed a relatively direct connection between knowledge and decision-making; scientifically tested social-scientific findings would speak directly to the problems at hand. It assumed that facts and values could be neatly separated and therefore policy research could be largely value-free. And it assumed that better arguments based on such knowledge could diminish, if not eliminate, political disagreement. When politicians and the public possess empirically demonstrated facts and solutions, so went the contention, what was there left to argue about?

The approach also presumed, in theory, that we have adequate causal problem-oriented knowledge to intervene effectively. That is, we know the reasons why problems such as poverty exist and that such knowledge can be translated into action programs (Farmbry 2014). But experience rather quickly showed this to be a serious misjudgment. Much of the War on Poverty, based on research funded earlier by the Ford Foundation, tended to deal more with the consequences of poverty rather than attack its underlying causes. And the Vietnam War, as the Secretary of Defense Robert McNamara (1996) later admitted, was largely based on a misunderstanding of Vietnamese culture and political motivations, with disastrous results for both the Vietnamese and the United States.

In this early phase, there was a great flurry of activities devoted to policy formulation, using causal findings about poverty from various disciplines, packaged as a comprehensive program (Wood 1993). The simplicity of the policy thinking was captured by the 'Moon/Ghetto' metaphor, which assumed a straightforward equivalency between engineering and social engineering: if the country could put a man on the moon, it could eliminate poverty in an 'affluent' society. At the same time, the Vietnam War was pursued technocratically by the Pentagon, using elaborate systems-based planning methods and a reliance on empirical measures, such as body counts and kill ratios.

The enthusiasm for such methods established policy analysis as both an attractive academic specialty and an emerging job category (an interesting story unto itself). There was a 'policy analysis explosion,' as the editors of *Society* magazine titled a symposium on the subject (Nagel 1979). Moreover, this was academically contagious. Both policy theory and policy analysis started to travel across to various European countries, even if only slowly at first. The Netherlands, a land long known for its import/export industries, was one of the first to take up this literature and bring this enterprise to Holland, thanks in significant part to Robert Hoppe. And slowly other European countries began to follow suit, especially in northern Europe. This gave rise to ongoing exchanges between European and American policy scholars. Some Europeans even made their careers by more or less representing U.S. theories in their own countries. But many also began by making new contributions as well, especially in matters related to policy implementation and evaluation.

Policy-analytic theory, however, encountered some unexpected and very challenging questions along the way, particularly as they related to the promise of problem-solving. Early on the 'utilization' of knowledge proved to be more difficult than conventional policy theory suggested. Not only did the United States fail to solve the poverty problem, it flat out lost the Vietnam War, despite the policy roles of the 'best and brightest,' as the phrase went (Halberstram 1972).

The concern was captured by the Secretary of Defense, James Schlesinger (1969: 310), when he testified to Congress that 'everyone is, in principle, in favor of policy analysis but few are hopeful that its conclusions will be utilized in real-world-policy making.' And the Chairperson of the Council of Economic Advisors, Charles Schultz (1968: 89), concluded that 'What we can do best analytically, we find hardest to achieve politically.'

These concerns gave rise to a new specialization and journal in the field concerned with the question of utilization. The journal, *Knowledge*, explored both practical cases studies concerning the uses – successes and failures – of policy findings and broader discussions of the relation of knowledge in society more generally. Along the way, others such as Rittel and Webber (1973), spoke of 'wicked problems,' in which not only the solution is missing, but the definition of the problem as well is unknown or uncertain. Today, scholars also refer to 'messy problems,' to capture the uncertainty and risks associated with complex problems like climate change or global financial crises (Ney 2009).

TOWARD USABLE KNOWLEDGE: COMPETING RESPONSES

Broadly speaking there were two competing responses to these setbacks, one political and the other academic. On the political front, conservatives singled out the methods and practices of policy analysis as 'metaphysical madness,' an argument that picked up steam from the Nixon to the Reagan years. Send these 'so-called experts' back to the Ivory Tower, these conservatives argued: bring back lawyers and businessmen, viewed to be closer to the practical realities of Main Street.

However, these conservatives – both politicians and intellectuals – did not end up rejecting policy analysis; rather they turned it to conservative purposes. Instead of using policy analysis to create new social programs, they discovered that they could also use it to cut or eliminate the same programs. Counseled by conservative policy intellectuals, these administrations shifted first to 'evaluation research' directed to program outcomes rather than policy formulation inputs. Insofar as social programs often show mixed results, given the complexity of social problems, they discovered that they could use rigorous, empirical evaluations to provide arguments for cutting programs out of the budget.

It is not hard to challenge programs with either uncertain – or mixed – outcomes or on methodological grounds. Questions related to how the data were obtained, which definitions and assumptions were employed, the nature of the sample groups, what kinds of statistical tests were employed, and the like. Indeed, this gave rise to a kind of 'politics of methodology.'

To further facilitate this orientation, the economist's method of cost–benefit analysis was elevated by conservatives to serve as the test for all programs. Given the difficulties in monetizing social benefits as opposed to costs (most of which are much easier to identify than benefits), many liberal programs – especially social programs – have trouble surviving a cost–benefit test. A cost–benefit test can thus function to filter out deliberation on social-democratic issues by adding a business-friendly overlay on the decision process. This is particularly the case for programs justified in the name of the 'public interest' or the 'common good.'

It is not that deliberative argumentation vanishes; the decision-makers always deliberate among themselves. It is rather the scope of the deliberation that is at issue – in particular, who is excluded. In this regard, cost–benefit analysis and evidence-based decision-making tend to be used to justify political decisions made behind closed doors.

For conservatives, usable policy knowledge involves a mix of program performance data and comparisons of costs and benefits, presented as the essence of rationality in decision-making. This approach was further supported by ideas about 'evidence-based' policy analysis, which emerged in Britain during the Blair years, before spreading to other parts of the world. In short, empirical objectivity became the privileged mode of thinking, as regularly reflected in the rhetoric of politicians and policymakers. This orientation is not all that different from the earlier approaches the conservatives were criticizing. But this was about partisan politics, not usable knowledge per se.

The competing response to the problem of usable knowledge came mainly from academic policy scholars, who recognized the need to confront the fact that policy analysis – though widely commissioned as an approach to problem-solving – was not widely used. Research showed that some two-thirds of policy research was never used in one way or another by the decision-makers who paid for it. This led deLeon (1989) to ironically comment that policy analysis would not be able to pass a cost–benefit analysis.

One of the first efforts to put this problem in theoretical perspective came from Collingridge and Reeve (1989), two British researchers who referred in their book, *Science Speaks to Power*, to the 'unhappy marriage' between social science and policy. They developed a two-category model: one, an 'over-critical model' in which scientific contributions lead only to continuing technical debate and thus fuel political conflict; and the other, an 'under-critical model' in which analysis serves to legitimate predetermined political positions. These two models align with how conservatives – as well as many politicians generally – have used analysis: either to hamper programs they do not like with further expert debate (such as in the case of climate change) or to justify their existing positions (for example, fiscal austerity).

The problem led Lindblom and Cohen (1978) to ask: What is 'usable knowledge'? Insofar as giving up on policy analysis in a complex and uncertain world seemed unwise, the challenge was to discover what sort of knowledge might be used. The first consideration was the fairly obvious recognition that politicians, in whichever country we find them, are wired differently than professional policy analysts. While policy analysts seek to be problem-solvers, this is only a secondary concern of politicians. Uppermost in their minds is not whether their decisions will solve a particular policy problem, but rather what impact their actions will have on their ability to stay in office and/or to make further career gains. For this reason, politicians choose personally trusted advisors to ensure that only 'safe', information reaches them. Their advisors are not chosen for their policy-analytic expertise, but for their ability to protect their interests.

This tendency, of course, is not new, but we still tend to overlook its deeper implications. More typically, policy analysts look for ways to break through to decision-makers – to bridge the gap – than to fully acknowledge and confront the depth of the divide. Most mainstream practitioners – in the United States, Europe and elsewhere – still approach policy analysis as a form of rational – or at least 'semi-rational' – problem-solving. Even if the process is not entirely 'rational,' so the argument goes, positivist analysts should strive to make it more rational. But this has largely failed; we need to rethink our practices.

As a move in this direction, Lindblom and Cohen (1978) find the solution to the problem in turning away from an exclusive emphasis on professional-analytic inquiry to what they have called 'ordinary knowledge.' In this view, the idea would be to improve our 'ordinary' policy knowledge rather than further pursue – in vain – the effort to supply scientifically validated policy knowledge. This move would, at the same time, break down the divide between analysts and decision-makers (practitioners who communicate and trade in ordinary knowledge). It would, as such, help decision-makers on their own terms, rather than only those of academic social science (Fischer 2003).

Another approach that moved in a similar direction was advanced by Carol Weiss (1977). In response to the failures to produce usable knowledge, she called for a shift from the problem-solving focus to what she called an 'enlightenment function.' In this view, policy analysis is seen to play a less technical, more intellectual role. Rather than seeking technical solutions – which go wanting anyway – the task is more appropriately understood as helping decision-makers think about the problems they face – i.e., to improve their understanding with the help of relevant findings and analytical perspectives (Fischer 2009). This role might not be the direct one that policy analysts have sought, but it is not to be underestimated. For one thing, policy concepts have clearly penetrated political discourse; politicians speak of a 'culture of poverty,' a 'broken window theory of crime,' a clash of civilizations, etc. Indeed, how to think about and frame issues is what social scientists do well. Seen this way, social-scientific policy inquiry is scarcely a failure.

THE ARGUMENTATIVE TURN

Building upon earlier critiques of conventional policy analysis, an emerging breed of 'postpositivists' in the United States and Europe began raising deeper epistemological questions about the appropriateness of the standard social-scientific approach as a way of dealing with policy formulation. Starting with questions about what it means to evaluate something – following philosophers such as Michael Scriven (1987) – policy analysis was seen to require – like any mode of inquiry – its own contextually-based method of inquiry and advice-giving. Addressing this contextual issue was seen to be better served by shifting from the logic of science to the logic of argumentation, as suggested by the work of Stephen Toulmin (1958).

Added to this was the influence of the translated works of Habermas (see Saretzki, Chapter 4, this volume), especially on the nature of communicative interaction, and later the writings of Foucault on discourse (see Lövbrand and Stripple, Chapter 5, this volume). Habermas's work helped to stimulate the 'argumentative turn in policy and planning,' as identified and advanced by Fischer and Forester (1993). This drew attention to the fact that policymakers work and communicate contextually in the medium of ordinary language and argumentation. If science cannot supply sufficiently robust knowledge for the real world of decision-making, so it was suggested, then we could shift to the task of improving arguments. It was a position that directly and indirectly built on both the works of Lindblom and Cohen on ordinary language policy knowledge and Weiss on the enlightenment function of policy research (Fischer and Forester 1993).[3]

Fischer and Forester's book set out a new orientation in these two closely related fields that constituted a move away from the conventional empirical approach to problem-solving that was inherent to the field from the outset. It did this by introducing language and argumentation as fundamental dimensions of policy and planning theory and analysis. As an alternative approach the 'argumentative turn' combined developments in postpositivist epistemology with critical social and political theory in the pursuit of a relevant policy methodology.[4] At the start, the approach stressed practical argumentation, rhetorical analysis, frame analysis, narrative storytelling and policy judgment (Gottweis 2006). Maturing in the early part of the 1990s, the postpositivist conception of argumentative policy analysis emerged as a significant development in contemporary policy studies. As Peters (2004) put it, the approach had become one of competing theoretical perspectives.

Along the way, this argumentative approach expanded to embrace discourse analysis, deliberation and deliberative democracy, citizens' juries, consensus conferences, governance, participatory expertise, and local knowledge. All of these foci give attention to communication and argumentation, especially in utilization, mobilization, and assessment of communicative practices in policy analysis and policymaking (Fischer 2003; Gottweis 2006). Foremost, the argumentative approach to policy inquiry rejects the idea that policy analysis can be a value-free technical project (Fischer and Gottweis 2012: 2). As maintained by Fischer and Gottweis (2012), 'neopositivist approaches generally embrace a technically oriented rational approach to policymaking – an attempt to provide unequivocal, value-free answers to the major questions of policy making – the argumentative approach rejects the idea that policy analysis can be a straightforward application of scientific techniques.'[5] Rather than 'a narrow focus on empirical measurement of inputs and outputs, it takes the policy argument as the starting point of analysis.' In no way denying the role of empirical analysis, 'the argumentative turn seeks to understand the relationship between the empirical and the normative as they are configured in the processes of policy argumentation.' It therefore 'concerns itself with the validity of empirical and normative statements, but moves beyond the traditional empirical emphasis to examine the ways in which they are combined and employed in the political process.'

This approach is of special significance for an applied field such as policy analysis. Because the discipline exists to support real-world decision-makers, policy analysis has to be relevant to them. In this regard, the argumentative approach analyzes policy in an effort to inform the ordinary-language processes of policy argumentation, in particular as reflected in the talk and deliberation of politicians, policy experts and citizens (Lindblom and Cohen 1978). Rather than imposing theoretical frameworks on the processes of policy argumentation, frameworks designed to inform academic disciplines, policy analysis accepts the argument as the unit of analysis. It 'rejects the "rational" assumptions underlying many approaches in policy inquiry and embraces an understanding of human action as intermediated and embedded in symbolically rich social and cultural contexts' (Fischer and Gottweis 2012).

Understanding that policy is constituted by and mediated through communication, the argumentative turn first seeks to assess policymaking on its own terms before examining specific policies in the context of competing theoretical perspectives. In the process, the approach works to reconstruct what policy analysts do and when they do it, and to understand how their research findings are conveyed and how they are comprehended by the recipients. This necessitates close attention to the social construction of the policy arguments of those who struggle over power and policy, which introduces more specifically the critical-analytical perspective. We can better understand this by turning to the levels of policy argumentation (Fischer 1995).

THE LEVELS OF POLICY ARGUMENTATION: LINKING THE TECHNICAL TO THE CRITICAL

The turn to argumentation offers a useful alternative to the mainstream technocratic approach to policy analysis and its problems. But an argumentative approach is in itself not enough to qualify as critical policy analysis. The defining characteristic of critical policy analysis is the task of assessing standard techno-empirical policy findings against higher level norms and values. Such an approach requires that policy arguments be submitted to a higher-level normative critique. To clarify this task we can start by outlining a logic of policy argumentation.

Following Majone (1989: 63) we can understand a policy argument to involve a complex mix of empirical findings and normative interpretations linked together by an 'argumentative thread.' Whereas conventional policy analysis typically focuses on the statistical analysis of the empirical elements, the goal of a critical policy analysis is reflexive deliberation. To be reflexive means to not only focus on the problems and decisions designed to deal with them, but also to examine the normative assumption upon which they are based. Toward this end, the aim is to explore and establish the full range of components that the argumentative thread draws together. This includes 'the empirical data, normative assumptions, that structure our understandings of the social world, the interpretive judgments involved in the data collection process, the particular circumstances of a situational context (in which the findings are generated or the prescriptions applied), and the specific conclusions' (Fischer 2003: 191). Beyond technical issues, the acceptability of the policy conclusion in such an analysis depends on this full range of interconnections, including tacit elements withheld from easy scrutiny. Whereas it is commonplace for empiricists to maintain that their empirical-analytical orientation is more rigorous and therefore superior to less empirical, more normative based methods, 'this model of critical policy argumentation actually makes the task more demanding and complex.' The policy researcher 'still collects the data, but now has to situate or include them in the interpretive framework that gives them meaning' (Fischer 2003:191).

In *Evaluating Public Policy* (Fischer 1995; also see Fischer 2012) the author has presented a multi-methodological scheme for integrating these levels of analysis along concrete case illustration. Drawing on Toulmin's informal logic of argumentation, the approach offers a four-level logic of interrelated discourses that move analysis from concrete questions concerning programmatic efficiency or effectiveness up through the relevant situational context of the program, through an assessment of the programmatic implications for the societal system to the abstract normative issues concerning the impact of the policy on a particular way of life. More specifically, they range from questions of whether a policy program works, whether or not it is relevant to the particular situation to which it is to be applied, and how it fits into the structure and process of the existing society system, to a critique of this system in terms of the basic normative ideals that do or do not undergird it (Fischer 1995, 2003). Such a critique, from a Habermasian perspective, is motivated by the 'emancipatory interest' inherent to human inquiry. It is this additional set of deliberations – contextual, societal and normative critique – that defines critical policy inquiry.

Such deliberations across these four levels offer the critical policy analyst a framework for organizing a dialectic communication between policy analysts and the participants involved in a deliberation. It is the case, to be sure, that many of the dominant policy players will not be interested in engaging in such an extended deliberation, as it would run the risk of exposing basic ideological beliefs to discussion and criticism. But this in no way renders the perspective irrelevant. Critical policy analysis is advanced to serve a larger public, not just the immediate decision-makers and stakeholders. It can be used, in this regard, as a probe for testing opposing arguments, thus permitting other parties to a deliberative struggle – particularly affected parties – to construct better arguments that both enrich the quality of the communicative exchanges and, in the process, increase the chances of more effective and legitimate outcomes.

With this approach, good policy advice depends not only on empirical evidence but also on establishing understandings that can help to forge consensus. Here the best decision is frequently not the most efficient one. Rather, it is the one that has been deferred until all disagreements have either been discursively resolved or placated, at least enough to be accepted in specific circumstances. Even though apparently less-than-optimally efficient, such decisions have a greater chance of being politically usable and thus implementable. Because deliberation can eliminate or diminish the counter-reactions of those who otherwise seek to block a particular decision, it also serves to keep the political unit together. The trust and good faith that results from such deliberation carries forward to future policy decision-making.

The policy argument then is never an objective category per se. It is instead a politically negotiated social construction. As such, we can understand policy knowledge to be a 'hybrid' fusion, a kind of 'co-production,' of empirical and normative elements (Jasanoff 2006; Fischer 2009). More than just a matter of efficiency, policy statements are fundamentally normative constructs about why and how an action should be done. As Schram and Neisser (1997) have demonstrated, a policy also conveys directly and indirectly a deeper narrative about the particular society of which it is part. This is a point clearly illustrated by Ingram and Schneider's discussion of the social construction of a policy's target population (see Chapter 14, this volume). In particular, they lay out the ways in which such constructions – for instance, who are the deserving and undeserving recipients of public monies – are typically employed by political actors to manipulate public opinion in order to gain electoral advantage.

CRITICAL POLICY INQUIRY AS DIALECTICAL ARGUMENTATION

Some will ask what can we do with this perspective? How can it be 'operationalized' (Landemore 2014)? But this question misses the point. The goal of critical policy analysis is not to replace one operational methodology with another. Instead, it more fundamentally concerns a mode of thinking; it is a way of grasping a deeper intellectual understanding of the problem at hand by examining what it is a part of. Whereas a method such as cost–benefit analysis treats its numbers as if they speak for themselves, critical policy analysis connects those numbers to the debates about context, social system and ideological principles that give them social meaning. To the degree that critical policy analysis does involve a methodology, it is a question of developing and employing an alternative inquiry system based on dialectical argumentation.

From this theoretical orientation, critical policy analysts can start to think about designing alternative inquiry systems for policy argumentation and deliberation. The place to begin is the adoption of a dialectical understanding of argumentation and the fact that the most essential dimension of inquiry is the identification of 'ways of seeing' (Guba and Lincoln 1989; Guba 1990; Fischer 2003). Although the technical aspects of problem-solving remain important considerations in policy analysis, as we saw in the discussion of the levels of policy argumentation, equally important in dialectical argumentation are the ways in which political actors and members of the public understand and frame a problem. Framing, as such, predetermines the use of the techno-empirical analysis that subsequently comes into play (see Braun, Chapter 23, this volume). By including the higher-level questions of critical policy inquiry the argumentative approach assumes a more comprehensive enlightenment role than in the standard conception of policy analysis.

With the recognition of different ways of seeing as essential to the enlightenment of policy argumentation, we can relatively quickly grasp the dialectical role of conflict in deliberation, as opposed to the more typical search for consensus. Although consensus is not to be altogether discarded, it largely operates within existing normative frameworks rather than opening them up to scrutiny. It is the confrontation of beliefs that can potentially lead to a deeper understanding that can be the basis for an enduring political or policy consensus. Such discursive conflict takes the inquirers beyond easy consensus grounded in a given set of discursive constructs and the power relations that undergird them (Mouffe 1999).

The argumentative approach, then, starts with the normative rather than the empirical assignment. 'Instead of fitting the norms and values into the empirical framework,' as Fischer and Gottweis (2012) put it, the task critical task 'is to test empirical findings within normative frameworks.' In this view, critical analysis 'can be facilitated by an organized deliberation among competing normative positions,' especially as they pertain to larger societal concerns and the normative frameworks around which they are organized. Designed 'to both identify potential conflicts or create consensus, the model emphasizes the interactive and productive role of communication in cognitive processes.'

In this scheme, a formalized process of argumentation and deliberation can be a very instructive aspect of the analytical process. Designed to clarify normative and empirical assumptions that underlie competing policy positions, such an approach facilitates the processes of judgment and decision-making. Even when policy analysts are unable to agree, deliberative argumentation offers a method for 'probing the normative implications of recommendations and for indicating potentially consensual conclusions that can offer productive ways to move forward.' Along the way, it also helps to clarify points of disagreement that impede the path to consensual agreement.

The primary advantage of this approach is that it provides policy decision-makers and other political actors with a better spectrum of relevant information than does conventional empirical policy analysis. Moreover, it better reflects the way in which policy deliberation works in practice. In the political world, politicians and policymakers put forward proposals about courses of action anchored to normative arguments. In this process, empirical questions and findings seldom drive or determine the debate (Fischer and Forester 1993, 2006). In general, actors tend to hang onto their normative orientations in the face of conflicting or problematic facts, only altering or changing their views when literally forced to by circumstances. Empirical information comes into play but generally when specific factual aspects come into question.

These concerns, it is important to emphasize, assume particular significance in a turbulent world. The policy problems, and thus the argumentative policy processes, facing today's governments are found to be more complex, uncertain, and very often riskier than they were when policy analysis was first put forward. Frequently poorly defined, contemporary policy issues are far 'messier' than they were in earlier periods, lacking clear-cut solutions – technical solutions in particular (Ney 2009). Under these circumstances, conventional argumentation – often technocratic – has proven insufficient. Indeed, as Fischer and Gottweis (2012) note, scientific inquiry and knowledge have often tended to confound problem-solving, themselves contributing to ambiguity or uncertainty. Rather than solving such problems they can even counter-productively generate further conflict. Only through critical argumentation can these ambiguities, uncertainties and conflicts be effectively sorted out, discussed and sometimes even decided.

DIALECTICAL INQUIRING SYSTEMS FOR POLICY ARGUMENTATION

There have been a number of deliberative innovations that introduce such argumentation. One approach is the now neglected work on dialectical inquiring systems developed by C. West Churchman (1971) and his associates designed for managerial decision-making. George (1972) and Porter (1980) have also focused on expert deliberation in national security policy and economic policymaking respectively. Although none of these approaches could be described as exercises in critical policy analysis, they nonetheless represent important steps toward the development of a dynamic methodology designed to facilitate complex dialectical exploration of facts and values, empirical and normative inquiry, throughout the policy decision process (Mitroff 1971). Despite the fact that most of these schemes focus on public and private managerial deliberation, such approaches could also be extended to viewpoints drawn from the wider policy environment, including stakeholders and the public (Fischer 2009). As such, an expansion of these models could easily encompass the requirements of a critical policy deliberation.

Another useful example is the approach developed by the National Research Council (NRC), an agency of the U.S. Academy of Science (Fischer 2009). The NRC developed an 'analytic-deliberative' method for bringing together citizens and experts. Even though this method was initially advanced some time ago, it remains one of the most detailed schemes for such deliberation. While mainly focused on issues pertaining to science, technology and environmental policy, the method is largely applicable to deliberation on policy issues generally. It remains an approach well worth returning to and building upon.

Understood as a method capable of bringing experts and citizens into closer contact, it provides guidelines for organizing a participatory process capable of 'broadly formulating the decision problem, guiding analysis to improve decision participants' understanding, seeking the meaning of analytic findings and uncertainties, and improving the ability of interested and affected parties to participate effectively in the risk decision process' (National Research Council 1996). As such, the approach spells out the need for a diverse range of participants from across the spectrum of affected parties, interested groups, experts and policy decision-makers, all of whom should be involved at each stage of the deliberative process, especially the early phases of problem identification and formulation. Deliberation is foreseen as a crucial step to inform decision-making in each phase of the process that informs decision-making, from determining the problems to be analyzed to finding ways to characterize scientific uncertainty and negotiate disagreements about goals and strategies. As the NRC puts it, 'deliberation frames analysis, analysis informs deliberation, and the process benefits from the feedback from the two.'

Deliberation, as the NRC makes clear, does not end all disputes. But controversies are seen as helpful in identifying problems, especially normative problems, that can otherwise block or impede efforts to reach agreements that permit forward movement. 'Not only do controversies encourage in-depth analysis to identify and explicate the social implications of a policy solution, they can also surface partly conflicting assessments of programs and policies that can then be further articulated and consolidated in the course of a controversy' (Fischer 2012). And it is here that such deliberation can be extended to the higher levels of deliberation, if they don't surface in the process on their own.

A challenge from the perspective of critical policy analysis is to make sure that a division of labor that privileges the experts does not emerge (Ojha et al., Chapter 20, this volume).[6] Specifically, the question is whether analytic work and normative deliberation are kept separate or are treated as complementary processes. The challenge of the critical argumentative approach is to bring them into closer interaction with one another. The contribution from the critical perspective is to minimize, if not transcend, the division between citizens and experts. This can be done by taking a more direct look at scientific practices, policy science in particular (see Strassheim, Chapter 17, this volume). The key task is to illustrate how normative assumptions are embedded in both the research designs and the conduct of empirical policy investigation which, in turn, involve judgments that need to be interpretively identified and submitted to deliberation. A critical postpositivist orientation recognizes that the inquiry process and its research outcomes are infused with social meanings, often in the form of social and political assumptions, that are interpreted by different actors – expert communities, social groups or the public more generally – and that these meanings and assumptions have important implications for policy decision-making. Such meanings are lodged in the very understandings of the objects and relationships under investigation. As a consequence, the social constructions of the objects or entities to be empirically analyzed have to be interrogated.

For this reason, empirical and normative argumentation need to be understood as continuous processes that are located across a deliberative continuum. It is important to acknowledge here that critical policy analysis enters rather uncharted terrain, particularly in matters related to the participatory nature of such investigation. Participatory experiments make clear that citizens are capable of engaging in such deliberative processes. However, numerous questions remain about the extent of participation, as well as when and where it is appropriate or necessary. Such questions involve practical concerns that require further attention, or what might be called 'policy epistemics' (Fischer 2009). Policy epistemics focus, among other things, on 'the ways people communicate across differences, the flow and transformation of ideas across borders of different fields, how different professional groups and local communities see and inquire differently, and the ways in which differences become disputes' (Fischer 2009). Here the processes of argumentation are the medium through which experts, citizens and policymakers engage one another.

CONCLUSION

We began with a recognition that policy analysis has failed to fulfill its initial promise of problem-solving, mainly understood as a scientific, largely technocratic task. Indeed, we have seen the various ways that policy failures are the result of technocratic assumptions about the relation of knowledge to policy decision-making. Although policy analysts do not need to devote all of their time and energy to policy epistemics, the discipline should establish it as a new specialty devoted to exploring these critical issues and concerns. It would be an important step toward making policy analysis more relevant and thus useful to the practical needs and interests of both policymakers and the public citizen. Beyond the conventional concern that greater citizen participation poses a threat to rationality, indeed, attention in policy epistemics should now focus on the extent to which rationality may actually depend upon enhanced participation.

Why, then, does this argumentative approach remain on the margins of policy analysis and real-world policy advice-giving? The answer has to do with power and the politics of policy analysis that emerged with conservative politics. Conservative administrations have imposed cost–benefit analysis and evidence-based policymaking as ways to discourage rather than promote public deliberation. Based on the specious notion that the facts speak for themselves, these methods are chosen and promoted as privileged techniques – wittingly and unwittingly – to rule out the very kinds of deliberation about social meanings and values that a deliberative approach would foster. To the degree that they fail to quash such deliberation, they can alternatively facilitate the 'overly-critical model' of policy analysis by producing counter policy arguments that can both mystify the public and, when necessary, delay unwanted decisions. Here, policy argumentation has openly and unapologetically become a strategic game. As such, these methodologies have become part of an anti-political ideological strategy. For this reason, critical policy analysis has emerged itself as part of a counter-strategy designed to contribute to the struggle for a more open, deliberative democratic society.

NOTES

1. In line with the enthusiasm of the era, leading University of Chicago sociologist Lester Ward even argued that legislators should have training in the social sciences to be qualified for office, if not be social scientists themselves.
2. Their elections and the politics surrounding them reflected the would-be 'value-free' nature of scientific management and the 'nonideological' approach to good government through expertise that it prescribed. Indeed, Wilson, himself a political scientist (and often considered one of the founders of the American discipline of public administration), called for scientifically explicating the efficient practices of Prussian bureaucracy and applying them – independently of culture or context – to American government. In the process, this emerging field of investigation and its practices would substitute the traditional emphasis on legal-rational bureaucratic authority with social-scientific theories and principles of management and organization (Weber 1947; Fischer 1990).
3. Around the same time Giandomenico Majone (1989) also called for a shift of attention from analysis to argument. Although his work was influential, he did not later further pursue this line of investigation.
4. Postpositivism refers here to a tradition in the social sciences that approaches the social world as uniquely constructed around social meanings inherent to social and political action. Explanation cannot meaningfully proceed as context-independent or value-free. Thus the pursuit of methods based on the epistemologies of the 'hard science' lead to a misrepresentation and thus misunderstanding of the social objects under investigation. For a theoretical discussion of the postpositivist perspective in policy analysis, and empirical applications, see Bernstein (1976), Hawkesworth (1988), Fischer and Forester (1993), Fischer (2003), Hajer and Wagenaar (2003) and Gottweis (2006).
5. Like all concepts, the concepts of 'positivism' and 'neo-postivism' have their limitations. Nonetheless, these concepts have a long tradition in epistemological discussions in the social sciences. The use of the term 'neo-positivist' is employed to acknowledge that there have been a number of reforms in the 'positivist' tradition that recognize the limitations of earlier conceptions of the approach, taken to refer to the pursuit of an empirically rigorous, value-free, causal science of society. That is, there is no one neo-positivist approach. The term is employed as a general concept to denote an orientation that continues to strive for empirically rigorous causal explanations that can transcend the social context to which they apply, but recognizes the difficulties encountered in achieving such explanations. Neo-positivist policy analysts (Sabatier, for example) typically argue that while policy research cannot be fully rational or value-free, the analysis should nonetheless adopt these standards and strive toward their fulfillment.

For general references to these debates see Bernstein (1976), Hawkesworth (1988) and Fischer (2009).
6. The NRC advocates offering technical assistance to inexperienced and unorganized groups. In this regard, the NRC Council proposes that policy experts serve as facilitators along the way.

REFERENCES

Bernstein, R. (1976), *The Restructuring of Social and Political Theory*, New York: Harcourt Brace Jovanovich.
Churchman, C.W. (1971), *The Design of Inquiring Systems*, New York: Basic Books.
Collingridge, D. and Reeve, C. (1989), *Science Speaks to Power: The Role of Experts in Policy Making*, London: Frances Pinter.
deLeon, P. (1989), *Advice and Consent: The Development of the Policy Sciences*, New York: Russell Sage Foundation.
Dewey, J. (1927), *The Public and its Problems*, New York: Swallow.
Farmbry, K. (ed.) (2014), *The War on Poverty: A Retrospective*, Lexington, MA: Lexington Books.
Fischer, F. (1990), *Technocracy and the Politics of Expertise*, Newbury Park, CA: Sage Publications.
Fischer, F. (1995), *Evaluating Public Policy*, Belmont, CA: Wadsworth.
Fischer, F. (2003), *Reframing Public Policy: Discursive Politics and Deliberative Practices*, Oxford: Oxford University Press.
Fischer, F. (2006), 'The Argumentative Turn in Policy Expertise: Deliberation as Postpositivist Practice', available at: http://fau.edu/spa/pdf/Fischer_argumentative_turn_Florida.pdf.
Fischer, F. (2009), *Democracy and Expertise: Reorienting Policy Inquiry*, Oxford: Oxford University Press.
Fischer, F. (2012), 'Debating the Head Start Program: The Westinghouse Reading Scores in Normative Perspective', in P. Hupe and M. Hill (eds), *Public Policy*, Vol. 1, London: Sage Publications.
Fischer, F. and Forester, J. (1993), *The Argumentative Turn in Policy Analysis and Planning*, Durham, NC: Duke University Press.
Fischer, F. and Gottweis, H. (2012), *The Argumentative Turn Revisited: Public Policy as Communicative Practice*, Durham, NC: Duke University Press.
George, A. (1972), 'The Case of Multiple Advocacy in Making Foreign Policy', *American Political Science Review*, **66**, 761–785.
Gottweis, H. (2006), 'Argumentative Policy Analysis', in J. Pierre and B.G. Peters (eds), *Handbook of Public Policy*, Thousand Oaks, CA: Sage Publications, pp. 461–480.
Graham, O.L. (1976), *Toward a Planned Society: From Roosevelt to Nixon*, New York: Oxford University Press.
Guba, E.G. and Lincoln, Y. (1989), *Fourth Generation Evaluation*, Newbury Park, CA: Sage Publications.
Guba, E.G. (1990), *The Paradigm Dialog*, Newbury Park, CA: Sage Publications.
Hajer, M.A. and Wagenaar, H. (eds) (2003), *Deliberative Policy Analysis*, Cambridge: Cambridge University Press.
Halberstram, D. (1972), *The Best and the Brightest*, New York: Random House.
Hawkesworth, M.E. (1988), *Theoretical Issues in Policy Analysis*, Albany, NY: SUNY Press.
Jasanoff, S. (2006), 'Ordering Knowledge, Ordering Society', in S. Jasanoff (ed.), *States of Knowledge. The Co-production of Science and Social Order*, London: Routledge, pp. 13–45.
Karl, B. (1975), 'Presidential Planning and Social Science Research', in *Perspectives in America History*, Vol. 3, Cambridge, MA: Charles Warren Center for Studies in American History.

Landemore, H. (2014), 'Review of "The Argumentative Turn Revisited: Public Policy as Communicative Practice"', *Perspective on Politics*, **12** (2), 522–523.

Lasswell, H. (1951), 'The Policy Orientation', in H. Lasswell and D. Lerner (eds), *The Policy Sciences*, Stanford, CA: Stanford University Press.

Levy, D. (1985), *Herbert Croly of the New Republic: The Life and Thought of an American Progressive*, Princeton, NJ: Princeton University Press.

Lindblom, C.E. and Cohen, D. (1978), *Usable Knowledge: Social Science and Social Problem Solving*, New Haven, CT: Yale University Press.

Lippman, W. (1922), *Public Opinion*, New York: Macmillan.

McNamara, R. (1996), *In Retrospect: The Tragedy and Lessons of Vietnam*, New York: Vintage Books.

Majone, G. (1989), *Evidence, Argument and Persuasion in the Policy Process*, New Haven, CT: Yale University Press.

Mitroff, I.I. (1971), 'A Communications Model of Dialectical Inquiring Systems: A Strategy for Strategic Planning', *Management Science*, **1**, B634–B648.

Mouffe, C. (1999), 'Deliberative Democracy or Agonistic Pluralism?', *Social Research*, **66**, 745–758.

Nagel, S. (1979), 'Policy Analysis Explosion', *Transaction*, **16** (6), 9–10.

National Research Council (1996), *Understanding Risk: Informing Decisions in a Democratic Society*, Washington, DC: National Academy Press.

Ney, S. (2009), *Resolving Messy Problems: Handling Conflict in Environment, Transport, Health and Aging Policy*, London: Earthscan.

Peters, B.G. (2004), 'Review of "Reframing Public Policy: Discursive Politics and Deliberative Practices"', *Political Science Quarterly*, **119** (3), 566–567.

Porter, R.B. (1980), *Presidential Decision Making: The Economic Policy Board*, Cambridge: Cambridge University Press.

Rittel, H.W. and Webber, M.D. (1973), 'Dilemmas in a General Theory of Planning', *Policy Sciences*, **4**, 155–169.

Schlesinger, J. (1969), Testimony to US Congress, Senate Subcommittee on National Security and International Operations, Planning-Programming-Budgeting Hearings, 91st Congress, 1st session.

Schram, S. and Neisser, P.T. (eds) (1997), *Tales of State: Narrative in Contemporary U.S. Politics and Public Policy*, New York: Rowman & Littlefield.

Schultz, C.L. (1968), *The Politics and Economics of Public Spending*, Washington, DC: Brookings, 1968.

Scriven, M. (1987), 'Probative Logic', in F.H. Van Eemeren et al. (eds), *Argumentation Across the Line of Discipline*, Amsterdam: Foris.

Toulmin, S. (1958), *The Uses of Argument*, Cambridge: Cambridge University Press.

Weber, M. (1947), *The Theory of Economic and Social Organization*, New York: Oxford University Press.

Weiss, C. (1977), 'Research for Policy's Sake: The Enlightenment Function of Social Research', *Policy Analysis*, **3** (4), 531–545.

Wiebe, R.H. (1967), *The Search for Order, 1877–1920*, New York: Hill and Wang.

Wood, R.C. (1993), *Whatever Possessed the President? Academic Experts and Presidential Policy, 1960–88*, Cambridge, MA: MIT Press.

4   Habermas, critical theory and public policy
Thomas Saretzki

1.   INTRODUCTION

As a philosopher and social scientist, Jürgen Habermas did not directly contribute to the field of policy studies by working substantially on specific public policies. Neither did he present a specific theory or methodology tailored to policy analysis and planning. Yet in his work he reformulated the tradition of critical social thought from Marx and the psychological concepts of Freud to the critical theory of the Frankfurt School and opened theoretical perspectives that strongly influenced policy studies indirectly. His critique of positivistic science and traditional approaches to hermeneutics inspired many policy scholars on their way from conventional policy analysis to post-positivist perspectives on public policy and to critical policy studies. Moreover, his models of policy advice, his theory of communicative action, his concepts of the public sphere, discourse ethic and deliberative democracy became reference points for many debates on practical perspectives for policy-making in modern democracies.

Why did some scholars in the field of policy studies find an interest in Habermas and critical theory? Which concepts and arguments have been of importance to critical policy studies? If we start with the 'policy orientation' and the program of the 'policy sciences of democracy' that Harold D. Lasswell formulated after the Second World War, then we can get a sense of why there is some kind of resonance between this program and the work of Habermas. And if we consider how the problems of this program unfolded over time, then we can also recognize some of the reasons why, about thirty years later, Habermas was taken to be helpful in conceptualizing these problems in the stream that came to understand itself as critical policy studies (section 2). What is characteristic about Habermas's work is systematically rooted in his understanding of the relation between philosophy and social science. The theoretical significance of Habermas for the development of critical policy studies can be traced back to the epistemological and methodological debate in the philosophy of science known as the 'positivist dispute' (section 3). Habermas exposed the implications of the positivist concept of knowledge for the relation of theory and practice in the 'technocracy debate' which in turn led to reflections about the understanding of policy analysis as science (section 4). He maintained the necessity of an interpretive approach, yet criticized the limits of hermeneutics in the so called 'interpretivist-criticist debate' with Gadamer (section 5). Based on his critique of the notion of value-freedom Habermas developed normative principles that have been used for the evaluation of policy processes (section 6). Finally, his understanding of democratization as a self-reflective learning process draws attention to some of the problems in participatory and deliberative projects in policy analysis and policy-making (section 7).

2.   THE POLICY ORIENTATION AND ITS PROBLEMS: BETWEEN SCIENTIFIC METHODS AND DEMOCRACY

After the Second World War, Harold D. Lasswell called for a reorientation of the sciences with a focus on policy. Although there are different sources for the intellectual origin of the policy orientation – such as providing contexts for more reflective critical readings (see Torgerson, Chapter 2, this volume) – Lasswell's introduction to the first edited volume on the 'policy sciences' became something like the standard reference for the reception of his program of the *policy sciences of democracy*. In this seminal text, Lasswell (1951, p. 10) outlined a program for problem-oriented inquiry that was, 'on the doctrinal level', explicitly based on 'the demand to achieve a world community in which the dignity of man is realized in theory and practise'. Different interpretations and justifications notwithstanding, this explicit emphasis on human dignity and democracy strongly resonates with the basic convictions and normative perspectives of Habermas.

With regard to conceptual problems of a *problem-oriented approach* with a practical intent, Lasswell outlined an agenda for the policy sciences that was explicitly sensitive to the social and political context of such inquiries (Torgerson 1985). Looking more closely, one could recognize also that this program entailed a number of internal tensions. With regard to the *different concerns* that the policy sciences should address, his agenda was ambivalent in many respects (Fischer 1990, pp. 341–346), raising questions about how these concerns could and should be integrated, on what level and by whom.

On the one hand, the policy sciences should not primarily be concerned with the systematic production of scientific knowledge per se. A policy scientist was not supposed to focus on developing and testing disciplinary scientific theories with a systematic intent. Policy sciences would differ from the classical notion of pure science searching for knowledge about general laws. Explaining his understanding of the policy orientation, Lasswell (1951, p. 7) referred to the question 'Knowledge for what?' and outlined a concept of problem-oriented sciences with a practical intent. As such, his policy sciences were neither confined to epistemic progress within the theoretical frameworks of established scientific disciplines nor could or should they simply provide objective and value-free knowledge about facts. With their emphasis upon problems and the search for their solution, policy sciences were supposed to proceed interdisciplinarily and, in order to provide an orientation for action, the 'policy sciences of democracy' should have an explicit normative foundation: human dignity and its fuller realization (Lasswell 1951, p. 10). Referring to 'An American Dilemma', he took this classical study on problems of ethnic relations in modern democracy from 1944 as an example to illustrate that a scientist who carries the awareness of problems of the time and accepts or even initiates opportunities for research with a policy orientation becomes '*value-orientated*'.

Such a clear value-orientation notwithstanding, however, Lasswell still saw no problem for a claim to the possibility of *objective knowledge*: 'It is not necessary for the scientist to sacrifice objectivity in the execution of a project.' He justified this claim by conceptualizing the involvement of the policy scientist as a linear process with two clearly separated stages. According to this notion, questions of value are a matter of decision, to be taken first, while maximizing objectivity is related to methods, to be discussed later: 'The place for nonobjectivity is in deciding what ultimate goals are to be implemented. Once this choice is made, the scholar proceeds with maximum objectivity and uses all available methods' (Lasswell 1951, p. 11).

How are these two concerns for 'the realization of human dignity in theory and fact' (Lasswell 1951, p. 15) and for 'maximum objectivity' based on all available scientific methods to be integrated in the practice of 'the policy sciences of democracy'? In his original outline, Lasswell seemed to suggest that these two concerns simply go together well without further problems or contradictions. Yet, speaking of 'the aims of a democratically oriented policy science', Lasswell (1951, p. 12) at least implicitly acknowledged that the 'problem attitude' he called for may also be developed in a framework for policy sciences with a different political orientation. In other words, in his model of basic value choices and objective analysis as two separate stages, there is *no compelling internal connection* between the policy sciences striving for maximum objectivity, on the one hand, and democracy aspiring to foster the fuller realization of human dignity, on the other hand. If the orientation toward democracy is but a matter of a contingent decision for the policy scientist, then we may also have to consider the conditions under which a program that was originally supposed to evolve as the 'policy sciences of democracy' might turn out to be a 'policy science of tyranny' (Torgerson 1985, p.252, cf. Dryzek 1990, pp.113–117). As critics basically sympathetic to the idea of 'policy sciences of democracy' pointed out, such unwelcome alternatives could emerge as a consequence of the institutional context of a democratic or autocratic political system in which a policy scientist is trying to practice according to the problem attitude (Torgerson 2007). Yet ambivalent normative implications might also emerge out of the analytic process itself. In his original outline, Lasswell seemed to presuppose that his emphasis on striving for 'maximum objectivity' in the analytic process and the use of whatever methods available would not produce effects and feedback loops that might contradict or even jeopardize the value choices and normative commitments that were made in the first place. In other words, Lasswell did not consider the possibility that some of the methods that he emphasized so strongly might not merely turn out as neutral tools to be safely employed for the purposes of democracy only.

In his own specific way, Lasswell outlined a program for the 'policy sciences of democracy' that embodied not one but two important albeit often *conflicting commitments* not uncommon for many approaches in American political science: the intent 'to serve American democracy and to be a true "science"' (Smith 1997, p.253). Thereby he reproduced a *dilemma* that can be identified in the development of American political science more broadly: 'efforts to assist American democracy via science have indeed played a large role in the discipline historically but have led the discipline to set an agenda that is often at war with itself' (Smith 1997, p.259). In the 1960s and 1970s, when policy-makers and bureaucrats raised their demand for policy advice and policy analysis became a 'growth industry', this dilemma gained in importance in the theory and practice of policy-making and policy analysis (deLeon 1997). The emphasis on certain scientific methods started to dominate over the commitment to democratic values. As these methods and their results were presented by experts claiming scientific authority in policy processes, policy analysis seemed to pre-empt democratic deliberation and decision-making. Since such implications did not pass by entirely unnoticed, the relation of these two concerns became an issue in academic and political debates. It is in the context of these debates that policy scholars referred to Habermas to articulate their feeling of unease and specify their critique about the dominant trends in conventional policy analysis and its understanding of the relation between science and democracy as well as its practice concerning the relation of knowledge and politics (Torgerson 1986a).

3. CRITIQUE OF POSITIVISM: POLICY ANALYSIS AS SCIENCE?

In the 1960s some social scientists believed and wanted the world to believe that at least the industrial countries had finally reached the '*end of ideology*' – a stage of the development of modern societies, when conflicts over competing ideas and interests would vanish and the remaining agenda would focus on questions concerning the most effective and efficient means. Technology seemed to matter much more than ideology. Moreover, in this perspective, even controversies over means–ends relationships could be reduced to the rational choice of efficient means to given ends with the help of analytical tools and scientific methods such as cost–benefit analysis, operations research, systems analysis and decision theory, among others. Thus, the '*technological fix*' prevailing at the time was extended from the level of direct technological problem-solving to include the level of making political choices by way of applying scientific methods and analytic tools to the decision-making process. Based on these scientific methods and analytical techniques, the mainstream of conventional policy sciences seemed to be striving for maximum objectivity and on these analytic grounds promised to provide an objective foundation for practical problem-solving and rational orientation for political decision-making. At least it could be seen or portrayed as providing such an objective and rational analysis by policy-makers who were trying to justify their decisions and actions by referring to the epistemic authority ascribed to science and the efficiency associated with technological expertise.

Whether driven by policy-makers looking for advice, by professional policy analysts offering their services or by some combination of political demand and professional supply, in the 1960s the policy sciences left the academic realm and actually tried to provide the knowledge that was supposed to 'improve the practise of democracy' (Lasswell 1951, p. 15). As a result, the promises of its providers and the expectations of its users were put to practical tests and, henceforth, to critical scrutiny. In an early influential article entitled 'Policy science: analysis or ideology?', Laurence Tribe (1972) questioned the belief that the analytical techniques used in conventional policy sciences intrinsically provide 'nothing beyond value-free devices for organizing thought in rational ways'. For Tribe (1972, p. 270), such a claim was but a 'myth', resting on the 'objectivist ideal' of social science striving towards the same kind of detached, impersonal and value-free analysis as the natural sciences were supposed to provide. If policy sciences would stick to such a claim, they would have to face the charge of presenting a study as neutral and value-free analysis that nonetheless was based on specific world views and loaded with values. Rather than delivering unbiased neutral scientific analysis, policy sciences would turn into an ideology seeking to 'masquerade as analysis, deriving a power it could never justly claim from the garb of neutrality it has at times contrived to wear'. In the 1960s this masquerade had reached 'new levels of sophistication and effectiveness' (Tribe 1972, p. 264). Yet raising these critical questions did not automatically lead to a total rejection or outright dismissal of these analytical tools and methods altogether. What Tribe (1972, p. 271) was aiming at, rather, was 'to investigate the ways in which a self-consciously objectivist ideal may substantially structure the characteristics and the conclusions of a given mode of thought'. To that end, his contribution was meant to initiate critical reflection on 'the ways in which the policy sciences structure our world, the gaps they leave and the distortions they promote in that world as we might otherwise perceive it, or as we might otherwise wish to approach it' (Tribe 1972, p. 270).

If they shared this interest in critical reflection on the theoretical assumptions and normative implications of mainstream policy analysis and its dominant methodologies and analytical techniques at the time, students of policy who had heard the call for a 'problem-attitude' for science in a democracy – yet worried about the ways it was put to practice in the mainstream – could find an illuminating source for their considerations in the work of Habermas. In his postscript to the so-called '*positivist dispute*' in German sociology, Habermas had explained the dialectical position of Adorno, one of the leading members of the Frankfurt School. Adorno (1969) had maintained a critical insight that positivism seemed to have lost, namely that the research process organized by subjects – through the very acts of knowing – is part of the objective context that is supposed to be recognized (Habermas 1969a, p. 156). Habermas had also clarified the issues in this somewhat puzzling controversy on the 'logic of the social sciences' that started with a debate between Adorno and Popper on a conference of the German Sociological Association in Tübingen in 1961.

While both Popper and Adorno claimed to follow a critical approach, the disagreement between them seemed to emerge prima facie from their differences with regard to the *object of critique*. Focusing on the tension between what we know and do not know, Popper (1969) saw the task of research in narrowing this gap on the epistemic level, i.e. to provide knowledge that could stand all tests to falsify specified empirical hypotheses. In order to provide knowledge of 'scientific value', the research process would have to strive for the objectivity of science. To that end, it would be the task of scientific criticism to keep extra-scientific value judgments away from questions of truth (Popper 1969, p. 114). Thus, Popper's critical rationalism seemed to focus and at the same time limit his critical method to the test of scientific hypotheses about the state of the world as it is. Adorno (1969), for his part, held on to a concept of society as a totality, extending the object domain of social research beyond confined and controlled experimental situations and isolated facts to include the dialectical relations in which they are embedded. As a consequence, the researcher was to realize also that he or she is part of the object domain that he or she is trying to recognize. Consequently, Adorno (1969, pp. 134–136) aimed at a dialectical theory including the critique of society as its final object.

Reconstructing the dispute as a controversy between 'analytic theory of science and dialectics', Habermas (1969a, pp. 155–191) differentiated the issues systematically by focusing on four basic questions: the relationship of theory to objects, to experience, to history and to practice. In addition, he focused on the notion of *value-freedom* by questioning Popper's dualism of facts and decisions. In Habermas's view, the notion of value-freedom is epistemologically misleading as it disregards rather than reflects the cognitive interest in the technical control of reified natural and social processes that guides empirical-analytical research. While Popper acknowledged that scientific experiments and their value for the empirical test of scientific hypotheses depend on conventions of the research communities, he treated these conventions as mere decisions of researchers, neglecting the communicative processes in the scientific community in which these conventions are formulated, criticized or approved. If even the description of observations of empirical phenomena by 'basic statements' depends on some kind of implicit pre-understanding or explicit agreements to be reached within the research community, then the 'facts' are not merely 'given' as such. Already the validity of observations, let alone their relation to theoretical concepts, is also constituted by communicative processes and inter-subjective agreements in the research community based on language. However, the meaning of this language used to describe and explain the observations cannot itself be adequately grasped within a positivistic model of science. To make sense in and of these communicative processes, different competences are required – competences that allow for mutual understanding and rational discussion. To understand the meaning of these communicative processes, different methodologies would be needed, methodologies that include interpretation and hermeneutic reflection. Thus, positivism rests on presumptions that it cannot explain within in its own epistemological framework.

In a subsequent polemical exchange to this dispute with Hans Albert, a German sociologist who defended Popper's position, Habermas (1969b) pointed out that his 'critique of empiricism' is not directed against the research practises of empirical social sciences, but, rather, against the positivistic interpretation of such research processes (Habermas 1969b, pp. 235, 261). In order to look through the pretence of a 'positivistically bisected rationalism' and gain access to the dimension of a 'comprehensive rationality', he proposed to trust in the power of self-reflection (Habermas 1969b, p. 236). Reflecting on the communicative conditions of research processes and their constitutive function for scientific knowledge and its rationality was the way to recognize the shortcomings of the prevailing new forms of positivism that tried to replace classical epistemology including its critical heritage from Kant to Hegel and Marx. As he argued in a short formula in his subsequent reconstruction of the pre-history of the new positivism: that we '*disavow reflection*' is the characteristic feature of positivism (Habermas 1973a, p. 9). Hence, it is not empirical research but this disavowal of reflection that needs to be criticized and overcome in order to regain an unrestricted understanding of knowledge and its possible meaning. From a critical philosophical perspective, empirical-analytical science as defined by an explication of certain methods is but one category of possible knowledge. To renounce epistemological reflection and make a dogma out of the sciences' belief in their exclusive validity, based on certain methodological rules and procedures, is 'scientism' (Habermas 1973a, p. 13). As such, that belief coincides with and reinforces the 'objectivistic illusion', the view 'according to which the world is conceived as a universe of facts independent of the knower, whose task is to describe them as they are in themselves' (McCarthy 1978, p. 59).

The central charge that a commitment to positivistic science and a strict compliance to its methodology imply an avoidance or even denial of self-reflection was a challenge not only to prevailing epistemological approaches in the philosophy of science. Rather, in terms of research practice, it was and still is a challenge also for the scientist who is limiting his or her thinking to the production of 'positive' knowledge about the world as it is, neglecting the fact that what we want to know about the world depends not only on the questions we are raising (ignoring what we do not want to see) but also on the categories and concepts we are using to describe the phenomena we want to observe, explain or predict. Moreover, the scientist strictly following the positivistic model disregards the fact that these concepts are based on language. And any concept-constituting *language* that a researcher uses is not only his or hers, but the prerequisite as well as the product of a communicating research community. Thus, an unrestricted self-reflection of science cannot be limited to the experimental activities of the individual researcher, but has to include the *communicative process* in the research communities in which these concepts are defined, interpreted and reformulated. Lastly, avoiding or reducing reflection on the context of initiating research and on the possible context of application for the positive knowledge to be produced is another critical aspect that played an important role in the critique of positivism. Even in scientific communities dedicated to seeking the truth, communicative processes might be distorted in one way or the other. Thus, the critical self-reflection of scientific communities needs to include the historical context of research in a given place and time to understand the interrelations of science and society – together with their implications for the kind of knowledge and the conditions of its production and application. To that end, Habermas (1973a) proposed to understand epistemology as social theory.

4. POLICY EXPERTISE BETWEEN SCIENCE AND POLITICS: CRITIQUE OF TECHNOCRACY AND DECISIONISM

From the perspective of dialectical critique, the 'positivist dispute' should not be confined to epistemological and methodological debates within philosophy and sociology. Consequently, Habermas was among those who started to discuss the preconditions and consequences of positivism not only for the concept of knowledge and self-understanding of the social sciences within the academic realm. He also engaged in public debates on the role of science in politics and in scientific advice. In the early 1960s, references to '*scientization*' as a major emerging trend in modern societies were quite common. In addition, the growing application of science via technology seemed to dominate, if not determine, social and political change. Concepts of a 'technological society' and a 'technical state' gained prominence, leading to the so-called '*technocracy debate*' (Weingart 2003, pp. 57–62).

Linking critical philosophical reflection and practical political perspectives, Habermas (1970, pp. 60–80) problematized the application of positivistic models of science in counseling and advising policy-makers. In an article on 'the scientization of politics and public opinion', originally published in 1964, Habermas (1970, pp. 62–80) distinguished three models of the relation of expertise and political practise: a 'technocratic' model, a 'decisionistic' model and a 'pragmatistic' model. These models soon became classical references in the debate. The first '*technocratic model*' was due to the thought-provoking discourse on scientization of the time, but had a longer history. In the wake of the debate on positivism this 'technocratic model' conceptualized the relation of scientific expertise to political practise following the scientistic tradition of Francis Bacon and

Saint-Simon. According to this model, politicians lose their personal space for voluntary political decisions based on their convictions and values. Instead, the politician becomes 'the mere agent of a scientific intelligentsia, which, in concrete circumstances, elaborates the objective implications and requirements of available technique and resources as well as of optimal strategies and rules of control'. Under the conditions of this model, 'the politician in the technical state is left with nothing but a fictitious decision-making power'. In any case, the initiative 'has passed to scientific analysis and technical planning. The state seems forced to abandon the substance of power in favour of an efficient way of applying available techniques in the framework of strategies that are objectively called for.' Yet this technocratic model is based on presumptions that do not stand critical scrutiny for at least two reasons: it 'assumes an immanent necessity of technical progress' and it 'presupposes a continuum of rationality in the treatment of technical and practical problems' (Habermas 1970, pp. 63–64).[1]

While this model provided the term and the reference point of the whole debate, Habermas did not overlook the countervailing attempts to re-establish the old political sovereignty of politicians over scientists in spite of a complex modern world and its increasing dependence on science and technology. According to the classical *'decisionistic model'*, which we find in Max Weber's work, there was and should be a strict separation of labor between scientific experts and political leadership. On the one hand, there were experts and administrators who may be scientifically informed and technically trained to give advice and to work efficiently in specialized bureaucracies. On the other hand, it took political leaders with a strong personal conviction based on certain interests and values, a power instinct and an intense will to actually make political decisions in accordance with their chosen values. The problem with this model, in Habermas's view, is that it rests on presumptions that limit the possibilities of rationalization to technical means and leave us with nothing but arbitrariness as far as norms and values are concerned.

> In the last analysis political action cannot rationally justify its own premises. Instead a decision is made between competing value orders and convictions, which escape compelling arguments and remain inaccessible to cogent discussion. As much as the objective knowledge of the expert may determine the techniques of rational administration and military security and thereby subject the means of political practice to scientific rules, practical decisions in concrete situations cannot be sufficiently legitimated through reason. Rationality in the choice of means accompanies avowed irrationality in orientation to values, goals, and needs. (Habermas 1970, p. 63)

Adherents of both models are unnecessarily limiting a possible rationalization in the sense of rationally enlightened will formation and decision-making. Decisionists are precluding such a perspective conceptually by excluding values categorically from rational consideration and discussion. Technocrats are neglecting the possibility of a reasoned choice de facto by reducing the range of alternative options to the 'best one way' that was supposed to be identified by scientific methods and calculations of technical efficiency.

In order to overcome the limitations of these two models on either the normative or the technical side of rational problem-solving and decision-making, Habermas (1970, p. 66) proposed a third *'pragmatistic model'* in which 'the strict separation between the function of the expert and the politician is replaced by a critical interaction'. While he explicitly referred to John Dewey as he introduced this model, it is still often falsely curtailed and cited as 'pragmatic', neglecting its conceptual origin in the context of pragmatism. Dewey had not only rejected the notion of a neutral or value-free science but had also criticized philosophical ideas of abstract values or concepts like an 'end-in-itself'. For him, abstract values or ends could not provide orientation for action if separated from concrete situations with their specific problems or conflicts and the means to solve them. As abstract entities, separated from the situated practices of problem-solving and conflict-regulation in concrete contexts, value convictions would not persist. Rather, they are likely to turn into ideologies of the powers that be if they lose intelligible connections to practical needs and the means for their satisfaction. Dewey provided an appropriate starting point to overcome the one-sidedness and the shortcomings of the two other models as 'he insisted on the pragmatic examination and consequently the rational discussion of the relation between available techniques and practical decisions' – a relation that had been 'ignored by the decisionists' viewpoint' (Habermas 1970, p. 66).

The 'technocracy debate' was and often still is being framed as a debate about the distribution of authority and power in a relationship between two groups of players: scientific experts and politicians. Consequently, the questions are formulated within this bilateral frame: Do science and technology dominate over politics like in a technocracy dominated by scientific and technical experts, or is it the other way round? Who has authority, who has power in this relationship?

With his contribution, Habermas proposed a conceptual alternative to this frame that allowed for interpretive contextualization and political perspectives. Contrary to the strict separation of power and responsibility inherent in both the technocratic and decisionistic view, the pragmatistic model provided the conceptual ground for his claim that 'reciprocal communication seems possible and necessary, through which scientific experts advise the decision-makers and politicians consult scientists in accordance with practical needs' (Habermas 1970, p. 67). Referring to Dewey and his understanding of intelligent problem-solving and cooperative conflict-regulation in a democratic community, Habermas's pragmatistic model brought a third reference point to the debate: *the public*. If we consider 'the three models of the relation of expertise and politics' with reference to 'the structure of modern mass democracy', Habermas (1970, p. 67) argued, then we come to realize: 'Only one of them, the pragmatistic, is necessarily related to democracy.'

5.   NECESSITY AND LIMITS OF HERMENEUTICS: POLICY INTERPRETATION AS CRITIQUE?

In his contributions to the positivist dispute, Habermas (1969a, p. 158) had already pointed out that communication within the research community about the relation of scientific theories to objects or experience requires the explication of meaning with reference to the hermeneutics of the social lifeworld. In his critique of both the technocratic and the deci-sionistic models in the technocracy debate, he reaffirmed the *necessity of hermeneutics* to understand the communication both within the research community between its various disciplines and between scientific experts and the public. In the context of scientization, the 'process of translation between science and politics is related to public opinion' and requires the 'confrontation of technical knowledge and capacity with tradition-bound self-understanding' (Habermas 1970, p. 74):

> The latter forms the horizon within which needs are interpreted as goals and goals are hypostatized as values. An element of anticipation is always contained in the integration of technical knowledge and the hermeneutical process of arriving at self-understanding. For it is set in motion by discussion among scientists isolated from the citizenry. The enlightenment of a scientifically instrumented political will according to standards of rationally binding discussion can proceed only from the horizon of communicating citizens themselves and must lead back to it.

The requirement of understanding meaning in communication processes confronts the expert with a specific hermeneutic task that cannot be realized from the classical scientific position of an external observer looking at his subject matter from the outside: 'The consultants who would like to find out what will is expressed by political organizations are equally subject to the hermeneutic constraint of participating in the historical self-understanding of a social group – in the last analysis, in the conversations of citizens. Such an explication is, of course, bound to the methods of the hermeneutic sciences.' Adopting this interpretive approach and bringing these methods into play, however, is a necessary, but not a sufficient, condition for the kind of enlightenment envisioned by critique with a practical intent. From the critical perspective of Habermas (1970, p. 75), *interpretative approaches* have their *limits*, too. The methods of the hermeneutic sciences 'do not destroy the dogmatic core of traditional, historically generated interpretations, they only clarify them'.

At this point, Habermas was already addressing the conceptual and methodological *difference between interpretation and critique* with a specific eye on their implications for an emancipatory political practice. These implications were openly discussed in his debate with Georg Gadamer that is, as noted earlier, sometimes labeled as the interpretivist–criticist controversy (Holub 1991, pp. 49–77). From the perspective of critical theory, interpreting a given tradition and explicating its meaning is necessary insofar as it is a prerequisite for understanding the background and the horizon with which people enter into communication with each other and may or may not reach a consensus. But interpretation of a given tradition and explication of its central concepts in and by itself does not allow one to take a critical stance towards this tradition and the assumed authority of its particular self-understanding or view of the world. Traditions may be loaded with a coercive or biased heritage and their horizons imply standpoints that limit possible visions. If there are prejudices or even a 'dogmatic core' within a given tradition, interpretation could allow us to understand their meaning. But it does not enable us to analyze and criticize them as ideologies. Ideologies, however, may produce the appearance of a consensus that is based on unrecognized and unjustified forms of power. In contradistinction to Gadamer, who took a skeptical stance towards the enlightenment, Habermas explicitly maintained that hermeneutic understanding needs to be complemented with critical reflection if it is supposed to open perspectives for emancipatory practice (Apel et al. 1971).

While the controversy between hermeneutics and critical theory was intensively discussed in philosophy, it did not attract so much attention in policy studies. The positivist dispute played a bigger role for policy studies and it saw both interpretative and critical approaches on the side of those who were criticizing the notion of policy analysis as science in the positivist sense. An interpretive approach to policy inquiry could highlight the limitations of 'the received view', as the conventional approach to policy based on a positivist model of science was called (Healy 1986). In relation to this view, both interpretivists and critical theorists were striving towards post-positivist concepts of policy studies. Yet on the way, the differences between them sometimes seemed to have been overlooked in the reception among policy scholars. As the controversy about the relation between hermeneutics and the critique of ideology (Apel et al. 1971) had revealed, however, these differences were not only differences in methodology. From the perspective of critical theory, purely interpretive approaches entailed limitations especially with respect to the critique of ideology and to the relation of theory and practice. The limitations of an interpretive or hermeneutic posture and its difference to a critical approach were pointed out by Torgerson (1986b) in a critique of approaches which included the work of Habermas, but presented themselves as 'interpretive policy inquiry' (Healy 1986) or as advocating a 'hermeneutic model of policy analysis' (Dryzek 1982). If it is more than an interpretive interest in under-standing, if it is an interest in enlightenment and emancipation: 'Why say *interpretive* when we mean *critical*?' (Torgerson 1986b, p. 40).

How can the *perspectives of critical theory* be included in the *pragmatistic model* of the relation between science and politics? If hermeneutic approaches are necessary, but not sufficient, what does this imply for the pragmatistic model and its appropriateness as a framework for a critical approach to processes of scientization? What else is required for the concept of a 'critical interaction' that 'not only strips the ideologically supported exercise of power of an unreliable basis of legitimation but makes it accessible *as a whole* to scientifically informed discussion, thereby changing it'? (Habermas 1970, p. 67). To guarantee that the explication of any given self-understanding or world view does not merely affirm the status quo or limit the search for new interpretations of social needs, then further conditions for the communication between scientists, politicians and citizens are required (Habermas 1970, p. 75):

> While integrating technology into the hermeneutically explicated self-understanding of a given situation, the process of the scientization of politics could be realized only if we had the guarantee that political will had obtained the enlightenment it wanted and simultaneously that enlightenment had permeated existing political will as much as it could under given, desired, and controllable circumstances. This could be guaranteed only by the ideal conditions of general communication extending to the entire public and free from domination.

These reflections point to *normative requirements* for *communicative processes* in the context of scientization that provide an orientation from the perspective of a critical theory with a practical intent. Habermas (1970, p. 75) leaves no doubt that these are 'considerations of principle'. As such, they provide normative principles for the critical evaluation of communicative practices, for judgments about policy processes and, ultimately, for judgments about policies. Yet they should not 'disguise the fact that empirical conditions for the application of the pragmatistic model are lacking'. To clarify whether and to what extent these *conditions* are given in a particular place at a particular time, empirical and historical studies are required. The general constraints of the existing political system had been the subject of his study on the transformation of the public sphere (Habermas 1962) which left no room for illusions in the early 1960s: 'The depoliticization of the mass of the population and the decline of the public realm as a political institution are components of a system of domination that tends to exclude practical [i.e., normative] questions from public discussion' (Habermas 1970, p. 75). While this diagnosis left not much hope for a public sphere without domination in the foreseeable future, it was and still is precisely this difference between what is required from a normative point of view and what is given in a particular situation that a critical theory is supposed to reveal and explain in order to stimulate thinking about ways to overcome distortions of a free public communication among equal citizens.

6. BEYOND THE FACT–VALUE DICHOTOMY: POLICY EVALUATION AS PRACTICAL DISCOURSE

The epistemological critique of the notion of value-freedom is of basic importance for any problem-oriented science, let alone for the original concept of policy sciences for democracy. If there are always already norms and values involved in any analysis of problems and the search for their possible solutions in policy processes, then a policy analysis that does not want to contribute to further depoliticization by keeping the relations of relevant facts to certain values away from the public's eyes would have to be openly *value-critical*, at least in the sense of making these normative implications explicit. Yet a policy analysis inspired by the critical theory of Habermas would go beyond the call for transparency.

As Habermas had already implied in his critical contributions to the positivist dispute and the technocracy debate – and explained in more detail later in his theory of communicative action and his discourse ethics (Habermas 1984, 1987) – a rational way to respond to practical problems in coordinating action would be to communicate about these problems in a reflexive manner by turning to a meta-level of communication, i.e. a *practical discourse*. To reach a mutual understanding about the problem and the situation, the communicative process on the level of a practical discourse should be free from domination. Communication on this level of reflection could be rational to the extent that it corresponds with certain requirements and formal conditions that Habermas tried to explain with the concept of an '*ideal speech situation*'. The purpose of this counterfactual idea was to propose a standard that could allow one to distinguish between a reasonable *consensus* and a false one. According to this critical measure, a factual consensus could be called into question by checking the conditions of the communicative process that brought it about. It could count as a reasonable consensus only to the extent that it was reached without constraints which could prevent, hinder or reduce the open discourse between free and equal participants. Ideally, there should be no external or internal force except for the force of the better argument. *Distortions* of a communicative process could be intentional or systematic. The latter type could be brought about by structural features of an unequal society, by forces resulting from the economic or bureaucratic dynamics and functional imperatives of capitalist markets or administrative states and by institutional restrictions of political processes. While depoliticization caused by intentional distortions of communication could often be overcome by efforts within reach of the actors involved, depoliticization of the public sphere under conditions of systematically distorted communication is much harder to come by as such a repoliticization demands a change of societal structures and political institutions.

Although the counterfactual concept of an 'ideal speech situation' was intensively criticized as being too idealistic or too demanding, it was nonetheless taken up to serve as a normative standard in a number of critical evaluations of policy processes related to controversial public policies. A first and often cited example is a study by Ray Kemp (1985) on the Windscale Inquiry, a *public hearing* on a planned thermal oxide reprocessing plant (THORP) for nuclear fuels in the late 1970s in England. The hearing was officially designated to include broader publics in the evaluation of this part of British nuclear policy. Based on Habermas's concept of an ideal speech situation, Kemp (1985, pp. 182–189) derived certain institutional requirements which he then used as normative standards in his evaluation of this public inquiry. He came to the conclusion that the communicative process of the Windscale Inquiry 'was in fact systematically distorted and that the subsequent decision to allow the construction of THORP did not reflect a genuine consensus on the issue' (Kemp 1985, p. 190).

Critical studies like these can produce knowledge for the *evaluation of the policy process* based on intelligible standards derived from the concept of an ideal speech situation. They can raise awareness for the political implications of procedural rules and social conditions of public policy processes and highlight constraints on open communication that can hinder mutual understanding between free and equal participants. Thus, they can provide important insights that help to explain why there is depoliticization related to important policy issues even in public arenas. Considering the focus of Kemp's and similar studies, one could get the impression that studies referring to Habermas's work are mainly related or even limited to the process dimension, while policy sciences originally had a broader concern for knowledge 'of' as well as 'in' the policy process (Lasswell 1951, pp. 3, 14). While Habermas certainly maintained a normative position according to which a modern society of free and equal citizens can govern itself only on the grounds of procedural legitimation principles and hence in the framework of a procedural democracy, he was not insensitive to the interrelations of form and content. In his early contributions to the positivist dispute, criticizing reduced versions of technical and instrumental rationality, he already pointed to the idea of a broader, more *comprehensive rationality*. Thus, it is no wonder that policy scholars referred to this idea when they approached the task of overcoming the fact-value dichotomy, as Habermas's theory seemed to have the 'ability to clarify both the boundaries and the interrelationships of technical and normative reason' (Fischer 1990, p. 234).

With regard to policy evaluation, a Habermasian perspective suggests that the task is to integrate empirical and normative knowledge without neglecting their categorical distinctiveness. This task is related to knowledge of as well as knowledge in the policy process. In addition, a Habermasian perspective suggests that policy analysts inspired by critical theory do not have to limit their contributions to critical ex post assessments of policy processes. The perspective provides space and concepts to develop a *critical* as well as a *constructive* approach to *policy evaluation* including an elaborate methodology for its practice: The reason for such an endeavour is very much in line with Habermas's general reflections on the old critical theory of the Frankfurt School and its limitations with regard to the relation of theory and practice: 'We must come to realize that at some point endless critique without the substitution of an alternative, teachable methodological framework serves only to perpetuate the marginalization of the critical theory project' (Fischer 1995, p. 239).

Based on the critical theory of Habermas, Frank Fischer (1980) has been engaged in the fact-value debate with the objective to address the problem of rational judgment by developing a methodology for the political evaluation of public policy. Over the last 35 years, this *methodological framework* has seen some reformulations and more applications in critical empirical case studies (Fischer 1995). But in spite of further elaborations, the basic elements of this 'dialectical model of policy analysis' (Fischer 2003, p. 202) remain unchanged. In contrast to positivistic models of policy analysis as science, policy inquiry is conceptualized as a form of practical discourse in the Habermasian sense. Communicating in the policy process, policy analysts are seen as making practical *argu-ments*. 'Practical arguments are, in this sense, propositions which seek to establish that particular acts are good and should have been performed. Practical reasoning takes in account, however, the conditions under which agents in real life accept these implied norms as meaningful and commit themselves to them personally' (Fischer 2003, p. 189). With this concep-tualization of the communicative practice in policy processes Fischer did not only initiate the 'argumentative turn' in policy analysis and planning (Fischer and Forester 1993) – he also referred to Habermas's basic category for bringing substance in rational form to processes of communication – argument – and used it to develop his methodology for arriving at rational judgments in processes of policy evaluation. Processes of argumentation are reconstructed in detail with the help of Toulmin's concept of an informal logic of argumentation, which also played a sig-nificant role in the development of Habermas's (1984, pp. 22–42) theory of argumentation.

Fischer's methodological framework for policy evaluation is con-structed to capture both empirical and normative concerns related, on a micro level, to the situation – involving the circumstances of the problem, the policy in question, and the participants – as well as, on the macro level, the possible impacts on the social system and the values of the social order as a whole (Fischer 1980, 1995). With this multi-method and multi-level approach, the framework conceptualizes policy evaluation as a practical discourse that proceeds on four different but interrelated levels which may be dealt with in phases or through other linkages. No matter how the inquiry might move through the discourses associated with these levels, as a whole an argumentative analysis based on this framework is supposed to come close to a full evaluation, addressing both empirical and normative questions. On each level, as well as between the levels, the methodology assumes *participation* of various actors and allows for a kind of commu-nication oriented towards mutual understanding. As such, it conceptual-izes a complex process for the task of integrating facts, values and their meaning for different actors.

7.   DEMOCRATIZING POLICY DELIBERATION: THEORY AND PRACTICE IN CRITICAL PERSPECTIVE

After 1989, with the breakdown of many autocratic regimes still in view, John Dryzek and Douglas Torgerson (1993, p. 127) began their 'progress report' on '*democracy and the policy sciences*' with a tribute to the general mood in the heyday of the last wave of democratization: 'Democracy appears victorious and, with it, so do the policy sciences of democracy.' At the beginning of the 1990s, Lasswell's post-war call for the policy sciences of democracy emerged in the moment 'without serious challenge in the sense that every policy scientist now seems to be a policy scientist of democracy'. Yet this democratic ascendency in terms of public justifications for policies and programs did not remove the controversies on 'issues involving the relationship between knowledge and power'. Scratching the surface of the symbolism, Dryzek and Torgerson (1993, p. 127) claimed that 'the actual content of many of the justifications labelled "democratic" soon appears problematic, in the policy sciences no less than elsewhere'. For Dryzek and Torgerson (1993, p. 128), in spite of the 'democratic victory' of the day, 'a basic question still confronts the policy sciences of democracy: is the tension between reason and democracy unavoidable? Or can it be reduced, even largely avoided, by the promotion of an educated, active public able to enter or create new relationships between citizens and experts?' In that self-critical perspective, Dryzek and Torgerson (1993, p. 136) reminded their readers that there was 'less an accomplishment now to be celebrated than a project to be pursued'.

More than 20 years later, a lot of conceptual work by policy scholars and many practical attempts by policy practitioners has been pursued to put that project on track and keep it going. Conceptually, some scholars argued that the legitimation problems of policy analysis vis-à-vis citizens and the public more broadly should and could be approached with a reflexive strategy, i.e. the *democratization of policy analysis* itself. Proposals included concepts like 'participatory policy analysis' (deLeon 1997, pp. 111–122), 'discursive designs' (Dryzek 1990, pp. 40–43), or some form of 'deliberative policy analysis' (Hajer and Wagenaar 2003) including the theoretical issues and practical challenges for the 'deliberative policy analyst' (Fischer 2003, pp. 221–237).

If we consider the spread of *participatory and deliberative projects* in many western democracies since the 1990s, 'in all sorts of policy areas' (Chambers 2003, p. 316), we could simply evaluate that diffusion of ideas and practices as a success story, as empirical proof that Habermasian (and other) approaches to bring participatory and deliberative democracy to policy analysis and policy-making have already successfully been put into practice. At least deliberative democracy, a model of democracy outlined and endorsed by Habermas (1996), among others, played a significant role in the 'deliberative turn' in democratic theory (Dryzek 2000, pp. 1–7) and subsequently also in attempts to democratize policy analysis and policy-making. As an often cited review states, deliberative democracy is no longer just a theoretical statement, but has turned out to be a 'working theory' (Chambers 2003, p. 307), especially in relation to policy evaluation and policy-making.

If an idea or a theory is working in the sense of being put into practice, its proceedings and impacts become phenomena in the world on the level of practices that can be observed, analyzed and explained in empirical studies. The participatory and deliberative experiments are empirical phenomena that in many cases policy analysts have designed, called for or used as examples in order to illustrate the practical relevance of their theoretical ideas. Thus, the evaluation of these participatory and deliberative experiments in policy analysis and policy-making requires some kind of *self-reflection* and *self-critique* by those who made theoretical arguments for those practices in the first place. These experiments raise a number of questions for the relation of theory and practice. Such reflections presuppose that we know what these practices actually look like. To acquire such knowledge, the practices become objects of some kind of empirical study – and that is where the question of positivist research and its critique comes in again.

A first problem worthy of critical reflection concerns the way in which empirical knowledge about these participatory and discursive practices is produced and presented. This problem refers to the epistemological and methodological questions of the relationship of theory and experience. As the discursive practises become objects of empirical studies undertaken within the frameworks of mainstream social science, they are often simply presented as the '*real world*' *of participation and deliberation* that is supposed to be different from the theoretical world that some normative political theorist had in mind. However, such juxtapositions of the 'real' vs. 'theoretical' (i.e. normative) world are often presented as if the state of the 'real world' is more or less self-evident and can be grasped before or beyond specific theoretical frameworks and methodological approaches come into play. Yet these frameworks and methodologies are themselves loaded with theoretical presuppositions, as we know and should not forget as a lesson from the positivist dispute. Critical reflection on this 'positive' knowledge about participatory and deliberative practises may often reveal that the 'real world' presented in these studies does not merely consist of observable data. Rather, it might turn out to be the 'real world' that is not only measured by indicators of some mainstream approach in empirical research on deliberation; it might also explicitly or implicitly be reconceptualized in theoretical frameworks which focus on the calculation of consequences including rational choice theory (Saretzki 2009).

Another problem that is worthy of critical consideration concerns the focus and the research interest that many empirical studies of participatory and deliberative designs bring to their subjects. Increasingly, these studies follow research questions of the management sciences, searching for '*best practice schemes*'. In such management oriented frameworks, the studies are driven by and nurture the illusion that there is or could be the 'one best way' for participatory and deliberative projects in policy analysis or policy-making. Such an illusion is well known from the critical debate on technocracy (Saretzki 2012, p. 13) but it nonetheless re-emerges in empirical evaluations of deliberative projects (Saretzki 2014, pp. 44–45).

A critical analysis of, and reflection on, the context of initiation and application is another prominent aspect of the critique of positivist science. It may shed more light on what many participants involved in deliberative projects feel and describe as some kind of instrumental use of their participation or of the project as a whole by governments or interest groups for given purposes. While such experiences refer to *instrumentalization* of participatory and deliberative projects from outside, the 'islands of deliberation' may also experience problems from the inside. These 'islands' are increasingly planned, organized and coordinated by professional experts from consulting companies or law firms specializing in mediation or other social techniques to manage different and conflicting stakeholder groups in informal settings. What has been labeled as a growing 'deliberative industry' requires further critical analysis and evaluation. Facilitation, generally regarded as a necessary prerequisite for successful implementation of participatory and deliberative designs in complex actor constellations with lay people, may not only be professionalized. It may also bring in consultants, planners and process managers – i.e. all kinds of scientifically trained experts in communication and process management – who may have economic and other interests of their own. Thus, it is the task of (self-)critical policy studies to reflect on the implications of these tendencies towards *commercialization* and *industrialization* of participatory and deliberative projects that sometimes are not experienced as being as self-governing by the participants as they are supposed to be (Saretzki 2008, pp. 44–51).

8. CONCLUSION

The epistemological critique of the positivistic conception of science and rationality as formulated by critical theory was, and still is, significant for policy studies in many respects. Habermas's contributions to the positivist dispute, his studies on the methodology of the social sciences and his reflections on the relation of theory and practice implied challenges and provided perspectives for policy scholars to rethink their model of knowledge. His interventions in the technocracy debate required a reconsideration of established models of politics and of policy advice in their historical context.

As Habermas's concept of deliberative democracy is basically a procedural one, one could at first glance suppose that his work is relevant for critical policy studies mainly with respect to 'knowledge of the policy process'. However, looking more closely we can realize that it is procedural, yet reflective, inducing policy analysts to consider carefully how substantial problems and issues could and should be related to what kind of methodology in terms of their analysis and evaluation and to what kind of procedure in terms of their public deliberation and decision-making. Thus, his pragmatistic model of policy advice and his deliberative concept of democracy point to mutual relations of procedural and substantial questions. Habermas offers principles that can help to formulate criteria for the critical evaluation of the methods and procedures that frame the process and influence how policies are made and put into effect.

Going one step further from evaluation to practice, Habermas's work also served as a point of reference for those who wanted to study public policy not only with a critical but also with a practical intent. His concepts provide principles for formulating proposals for the design of democratic public policy processes and the place of policy expertise therein that have been used in participatory projects and discursive experiments. Since Habermas understood the process of institutionalizing a democratic system of problem-solving and conflict regulation – and its possible reform – as a self-controlled learning process, his contribution for policy studies is critical in a self-reflective sense. As such, it also draws attention to the problems and contradictions that have been experienced by those who tried to use his concepts to design and implement strategies to democratize processes of policy analysis and policy-making.

NOTE

1.   There are different senses of 'practical' in Habermas's texts. Not all of them coincide with the usual understanding in everyday language, especially not in English (cf. translator's note that in English 'practice' has a different range of meaning compared to the German original 'Praxis' in Habermas 1973b, pp. viii–ix). In Habermas's texts, the term 'practical' gains its specific meaning in the context of specific explicit or implicit distinctions. In the passage quoted in the text, Habermas (1970, p. 64) makes a distinction of *technical vs. practical* to point out that there is no continuum of rationality, but a conceptual difference between 'technical' and 'practical' problems when we think of their rational treatment that should not be neglected. For him, 'practical problems' and the 'decision of practical issues' have specific normative implications that cannot be grasped or addressed adequately within a calculus of instrumental or technical rationality since that system of reference excludes questions concerning the rationality of values and norms. 'Within the framework of research operations that expand our power of technical

control we can make no cogent statements about "value systems", that is, about social needs and objective states of consciousness, about the dimensions of emancipation and regression' (Habermas 1970, p. 64). In his view, it would be a category mistake to neglect the difference between 'technical' and 'practical' when talking about the rationality of action. While it can be traced back to the classical Aristotelian distinction between *techne* and *praxis*, the difference gained new significance in relation to the public sphere of modern societies: 'Technical questions are posed with a view to the rationally goal-directed organization of means and the rational selection of instrumental alternatives, once the goals (values and maxims) are given. Practical questions, on the other hand, are posed with a view to the acceptance or rejection of norms, especially norms for action, the claims to validity of which we can support or oppose with reason' (Habermas 1973b, p. 3). While the distinction of technical vs. practical refers to different forms of rationality within the sphere of action, the term 'practical' also appears in contradistinction to 'theoretical'. This distinction of *theoretical vs. practical* appears in discussions of the relation between thinking and acting or theory and practise that Habermas (1970, 1973b, 1984) has approached repeatedly in his work. In his theory of communicative action, Habermas (1984) explicates his concept of communicative rationality and makes a distinction between different types of action and related types of discourses. Actors can deal with negative experiences in their efforts to coordinate their actions and try to reach an understanding by thematizing 'contested validity claims and attempt[ing] to vindicate or criticize them through argumentation' (Habermas 1984, p. 18). On this reflexive level of communicating about problems of communication and interaction, Habermas distinguishes between a *theoretical discourse* as 'the form of argumentation in which controversial truth claims are thematized' and a *practical discourse* as 'the form of argumentation in which claims to normative rightness are made thematic' (Habermas 1984, p. 19). Thus, the term 'practical' appears in Habermas's texts to characterize problems, issues, needs, questions, types of argumentation and discourses or forms of rationality that are directly or indirectly related to the sphere of action, indicating a normative rather than purely descriptive reference or perspective.

REFERENCES

Adorno, Theodor W. (1969), 'Zur Logik der Sozialwissenschaften', in Theodor W. Adorno et al. (eds), *Der Positivismusstreit in der deutschen Soziologie*, Neuwied and Berlin: Luchterhand, pp. 125–143.

Apel, Karl-Otto et al. (1971), *Hermeneutik und Ideologiekritik*, Frankfurt am Main: Suhrkamp.

Chambers, Simone (2003), 'Deliberative Democratic Theory', *Annual Review of Political Science* 6, 307–326.

deLeon, Peter (1997), *Democracy and the Policy Sciences*, Albany, NY: SUNY Press.

Dryzek, John S. (1982), 'Policy Analysis as a Hermeneutic Activity', *Policy Sciences* 14, 309–329.

Dryzek, John S. (1990), *Discursive Democracy. Politics, Policy, and Political Science*, Cambridge: Cambridge University Press.

Dryzek, John S. (2000), *Deliberative Democracy and Beyond. Liberals, Critics, Contestations*, Oxford: Oxford University Press.

Dryzek, John S. and Douglas Torgerson (1993), 'Democracy and the Policy Sciences', *Policy Sciences* 26, 127–137.

Fischer, Frank (1980), *Politics, Values and Public Policy: The Problem of Methodology*, Boulder, CO: Westview Press.

Fischer, Frank (1990), *Technocracy and the Politics of Expertise*, Newbury Park/London/New Delhi: Sage.

Fischer, Frank (1995), *Evaluating Public Policy*, Chicago: Nelson-Hall.

Fischer, Frank (2003), *Reframing Public Policy. Discursive Politics and Deliberative Practises*, Oxford: Oxford University Press.
Fischer, Frank and John Forester (eds) (1993), *The Argumentative Turn in Policy Analysis and Planning*, Durham, NC and London: Duke University Press.
Habermas, Jürgen (1962), *Strukturwandel der Öffentlichkeit. Untersuchungen zu einer Kategorie der bürgerlichen Gesellschaft*, Neuwied and Berlin: Luchterhand.
Habermas, Jürgen (1969a), 'Analytische Wissenschaftstheorie und Dialektik. Ein Nachtrag zur Kontroverse zwischen Popper und Adorno', in Theodor W. Adorno et al. (eds), *Der Positivismusstreit in der deutschen Soziologie*, Neuwied and Berlin: Luchterhand, pp. 155–191.
Habermas, Jürgen (1969b), 'Gegen einen positivistisch halbierten Rationalismus. Erwiderung eines Pamphlets', in Theodor W. Adorno et al. (eds), *Der Positivismusstreit in der deutschen Soziologie*, Neuwied and Berlin: Luchterhand, pp. 235–266.
Habermas, Jürgen (1970), *Toward a Rational Society. Student Protest, Science, and Politics*, Boston: Beacon Press.
Habermas, Jürgen (1973a), *Erkenntnis und Interesse. Mit einem neuen Nachwort*, Frankfurt am Main: Suhrkamp.
Habermas, Jürgen (1973b), *Theory and Practice*, Boston: Beacon Press.
Habermas, Jürgen (1984), *The Theory of Communicative Action, Vol. 1: Reason and the Rationalization of Society*, Boston: Beacon Press.
Habermas, Jürgen (1987), *The Theory of Communicative Action, Vol. 2: Lifeworld and System: A Critique of Functionalist Reason*, Boston: Beacon Press.
Habermas, Jürgen (1996), *Between Facts and Norms. Contributions to a Discourse Theory of Law and Democracy*, Cambridge: Polity Press.
Hajer, Maarten A. and Hendrik Wagenaar (eds) (2003), *Deliberative Policy Analysis. Understanding Governance in the Network Society*, Cambridge: Cambridge University Press.
Healy, Paul (1986), 'Interpretive Policy Inquiry: A Response to the Limitations of the Received View', *Policy Sciences* **19**, 381–396.
Holub, Robert C. (1991), *Jürgen Habermas. Critic in the Public Sphere*, London and New York: Routledge.
Kemp, Ray (1985), 'Planning, Public Hearing, and the Politics of Discourse', in John Forester (ed.), *Critical Theory and Public Life*, Cambridge, MA: The MIT Press, pp. 177–201.
Lasswell, Harold D. (1951), 'The Policy Orientation', in Daniel Lerner and Harold D. Lasswell (eds), *The Policy Sciences. Recent Developments in Scope and Method*, Stanford: Stanford University Press, pp. 3–15.
McCarthy, Thomas (1978), *The Critical Theory of Jürgen Habermas*, Cambridge, MA and London: The MIT Press.
Popper, Karl R. (1969), 'Die Logik der Sozialwissenschaften', in Theodor W. Adorno et al. (eds), *Der Positivismusstreit in der deutschen Soziologie*, Neuwied and Berlin: Luchterhand, pp. 103–123.
Saretzki, Thomas (2008), 'Policy-Analyse, Demokratie und Deliberation: Theorieentwicklung und Forschungsperspektiven der "Policy Sciences of Democracy"', in Frank Janning and Katrin Toens (eds), *Die Zukunft der Policy-Forschung. Theorien, Methoden, Anwendungen*, Wiesbaden: VS Verlag für Sozialwissenschaften, pp. 34–54.
Saretzki, Thomas (2009), 'From Bargaining to Arguing, from Strategic to Communicative Action? Analytical Distinctions and Methodological Problems in Empirical Studies of Deliberative Policy Processes', *Critical Policy Studies* **3**, 153–183.
Saretzki, Thomas (2012), 'Legitimation Problems in Participatory Processes in Technology Assessment and Technology Policy', *Poiesis & Praxis* **9**, 7–26.
Saretzki, Thomas (2014), 'Deliberative Politik und demokratische Legitimität: Perspektiven der Kritik zwischen empirischer Deliberationsforschung und reflexiver Demokratie', in Oliver Flügel-Martinsen, Daniel Gaus, Tanja Hitzel-Cassagnes and Franziska Martinsen (eds), *Deliberative Kritik – Kritik der Deliberation. Festschrift für Rainer Schmalz-Bruns*, Wiesbaden: Springer VS, pp. 24–48.

Smith, Rogers M. (1997), 'Still Blowing in the Wind: The American Quest for a Democratic, Scientific Political Science', *Daedalus* **126**, 253–287.

Torgerson, Douglas (1985), 'Contextual Orientation in Policy Analysis: The Contribution of Harold D. Lasswell', *Policy Sciences* **18** (3), 241–261.

Torgerson, Douglas (1986a), 'Between Knowledge and Politics: Three Faces of Policy Analysis', *Policy Sciences* **19**, 33–59.

Torgerson, Douglas (1986b), 'Interpretive Policy Inquiry: A Response to its Limitations', *Policy Sciences* **19**, 397–405.

Torgerson, Douglas (2007), 'Promoting the Policy Orientation: Lasswell in Context', in Frank Fischer, Gerald J. Miller and Mara S. Sidney (eds), *Handbook of Public Policy Analysis. Theory, Politics, and Methods*, Boca Raton, FL, London and New York: CRC Press, pp. 15–29.

Tribe, Laurence H. (1972), 'Policy Science: Analysis or Ideology?', *Philosophy and Public Affairs* **2**, 66–110.

Weingart, Peter (2003), 'Paradox of Scientific Advising', in Gotthard Bechmann and Imre Hronszky (eds), *Expertise and its Interface. The Tense Relationship of Science and Politics*, Berlin: edition sigma, pp. 53–89.

5 Foucault and critical policy studies
Eva Lövbrand and Johannes Stripple

INTRODUCTION

The post-positivist turn in policy studies has been well documented during the past years (cf. Fischer and Gottweis 2012; Fischer 2003; Hajer and Wagenaar 2003) and is often taken to denote a shift away from rationalist, empiricist and quantitative modes of policy analysis to more interpretative and qualitative lines of enquiry. What today is referred to as interpretative, deliberative or critical policy studies (Yanow 1999; Hajer and Wagenaar 2003; Fischer et al., Chapter 1, this volume) is a literature that has taken seriously the linguistic, ideational and normative dimensions of public policy, and hereby has drawn attention to the systems of meaning and frames of reference that underpin institutionalized policy practices. While important efforts have been made to distil the different theoretical traditions included in this 'post-positivist counter narrative' (Hajer and Wagenaar 2003), less attention has been paid to date to the various forms of critique it represents and projects. Given the many possible foundations, techniques and aims of social critique, we contend that critical policy studies cannot be approached in the singular but is likely to represent divergent, and possibly conflicting, analytical trajectories.

The basic question of what it means to be critical in social theory was asked already by Horkeimer ([1937] 1976) and Marcuse (1937) and, together with other members of the Frankfurt School, they have been a major source of inspiration for scholars who have tried to develop policy analysis in critical directions (Torgerson 1986). In this chapter we explore how Foucault-inspired policy studies may feed into this analytical exercise. While Michel Foucault almost never cited the early Frankfurt School, he recognized in various interviews the similarity between his work and that of the early Frankfurt scholars.[1] In fact, he wished that he had 'known them and studied them much earlier than was the case' (Foucault 1991a). But then again, Foucault was a thinker in perpetual motion. 'Like a kaleidoscope, elements and concepts rearrange or appear anew as he moves from one project to the next with the result that we see things differently each time' (Walters 2012, p. 8). With this 'mobile ethos' in mind, this chapter does not aspire to provide a comprehensive account of Foucault's academic oeuvre, neither to summarize the rich body of work that it has inspired. More modestly, we instead explore what kinds of critical policy studies may transpire from Foucault's analytics of power and government, and more specifically, what forms of critique such studies represent.

In a recent overview of Foucault's 'genealogy of the state', Lemke (2012) reminds us that Foucault never answered the question, 'What is critique'. Although his famous problematizations of the mad, the criminal and the sexually deviant (Foucault 1991b, 1998) were conducted in a time when the theoretical foundations and resources for social critique offered by classical Marxism were increasingly challenged, Foucault did not offer any new universal ground for critical social theorizing. Instead of looking for the essence of critique, his work raises questions such as: 'How does critique work? How is it performed? How is the practice of critique defined?' (Lemke 2012, p. 58). This shift from 'the what' to 'the how' of critique represents an important intellectual achievement that captures much of the novelty and potency of Foucault's approach to politics and government. From the nominalist worldview that Foucault cultivated throughout his academic life, there are no universals or prior forces that stand apart from history and the flux of all things. The key question to be asked about 'the state', 'politics' or 'power' is thus not what it is, but *how* – by what techniques – it is exercised and with what effects (Triantafillou 2012, p. 7). The aim of this nominalist approach is not to dispute that there are objects to which concepts such as 'the state' refer. The trick is rather, as Walters explains (2012, p. 18), to shift the study from objects as naturally given to the historically contingent practices that produce those objects as their *effects*.

In the following we explore in further detail what Foucault's 'effective historicism' entails and how it recasts traditional political theorizing. To that end the chapter begins with an introduction to Foucault's analytics of government. We here draw upon key texts from the burgeoning field of governmentality studies to outline how Foucault and his followers have approached and reworked central political concepts such as power, government and the state. The second section of the chapter is devoted to the critical effects of work in this field. We here introduce problematization and experimentation as two critical practices that scholars of public policy may employ to transgress the boundaries of conventional political thought and hereby free us from some of its constraints. We conclude that there is a particular 'critical attitude' emanating from Foucault's nominalist perspective on political power that invites us to draw attention to the historically situated practices, rationalities and identities by which particular policy issues become established as domains of politics and government. Foucault-inspired policy studies can help us to open up these political spaces to critical scrutiny by interrogating how they came about, how power operates through them, and, ultimately, how they could be different. The position of the analyst in this endeavour is not transcendent, but immanent;[2] it emerges from within the everyday experience of governing and being governed. As Foucault noted in an interview, 'critique is not a matter of saying that things are not right as they are. It is a matter of pointing out on what kind of assumptions, what kind of familiar, unchallenged, unconsidered modes of thought the practices that we accept rest' (Foucault 1988, p. 154).

FOUCAULT'S ANALYTICS OF GOVERNMENT

> Let's suppose that universals do not exist. And then I put the question to history and historians: How can you write history if you do not accept *a priori* the existence of things like the state, society, the sovereign, and subjects? (Foucault 2008, p. 3)

Michel Foucault was a scholar who devoted most of his academic life to problematizing the historically contingent nature of what philosophy has traditionally viewed as absolute and universal. In fact, to Foucault the very ideas of absolute and universal knowledge and moral values are themselves historical phenomena (Taylor 2011, p. 2). In order to advance this nominalist claim, Foucault developed a form of historical analysis that sought to identify the conditions out of which prevailing modes of thought and existence have come to be seen as given and necessary. However, rather than searching for origins in the sense of essential beginnings, Foucault's historical project turns attention to accidents, disparity and conflict to demonstrate the contingency of contemporary forms of knowledge, rationality and truth (Brown 1998). Foucault's 'effective history' – more commonly referred to as genealogy – differs from traditional history in being without constants. It is a mode of analysis that denaturalizes the present by examining, in empirical detail, how our time contingently came into being and how non-inevitable its existence is (Foucault 1984). As explained by Barry et al. (1996) our present 'is not presumed to be the bearer or culmination of some grand historical process, it has not inevitability, no spirit, no essence or underlying cause. The "present", in Foucault's work, is less an epoch than an array of questions . . . to be *acted upon* by historical investigation' (Barry et al. 1996, p. 5, italics in original).

Michel Foucault is perhaps most well-known for his historical investigations into the constitution of the modern subject. In famous volumes such as *Discipline and Punish: The Birth of the Prison* ([1977] 1991b) and *The History of Sexuality* ([1978] 1998) he enquires into the numerous technologies of categorization, normalization and control 'by which, in our culture, human beings are made subjects' (Foucault 1982, p. 208). Hence, rather than approaching the rational and autonomous subject as an immutable and inert given, Foucault's work breaks with most of modern philosophy by illustrating how subjectivity itself is a socio-historical phenomenon that is 'made up' in relation to a contingent set of norms, standards and techniques that shape our thoughts and actions (Taylor 2011, p. 8). This way of thinking of subjectification is closely related to Foucault's 'micro-physics of power' (Foucault 1991b). For Foucault 'power is not an institution, and not a structure; neither is it a certain strength we are endowed with; it is the name that one attributes to a complex strategic situation in a particular society' (Foucault 1998, p. 93). Rather than being something that a person, a state or an institution can possess, Foucault's micro-political analytics of power calls attention to its multiple, relational and pervasive *effects*. Through situated histori-cal analyses of the specific 'dispositions, manoeuvres, tactics, techniques, functionings' (Foucault 1991b, p. 26) through which power operates in singular institutions like the prison or the hospital, Foucault's work illustrates how the processes of human subjectification are bound up with disciplinary practices of subjugation and self-formation.

Whereas Foucault's rethinking of power in non-subjective, relational and productive terms represents a significant break with traditional theo-ries of power, it would take some time before his work had bearing on political philosophy and theorizing (Allen 1998). As observed by Brown (1998), most of Foucault's early interviews and writings bear an apoliti-cal tenor. '[T]he questions that occupy him – about Truth, power, body, soul, rationality, the subject, or ethics – while of obvious relevance to politics, are often posed in strikingly unpolitical fashion' (Brown 1998, pp. 33–34). It was only later in his academic life, when Foucault linked the micro-physics of power to the macro-political questions of the modern state, that the political significance of his genealogical analyses was fully recognized. The concept of *governmentality*, introduced during a lecture series at Collège de France in Paris in the late 1970s, plays a central role in this analytical effort.

In the course entitled *Security, Territory, Population*, held during spring 1978, Foucault outlines a research programme to trace the history of modern forms of government and statehood (Foucault 2008). The gov-ernmentality concept surfaces several times during this course, but its meaning is not straightforward. As suggested by Walters (2012, p. 11), we can identify three distinct emphases in Foucault's use of the governmen-tality concept throughout the lecture series. First, in its broadest sense, the concept denotes the exercise of power as the 'conduct of conduct'

(Foucault 2008, p. 186). As elaborated by Dean (2004, p. 10), this definition plays on several senses of the word 'conduct'. As a verb, 'to conduct'
means to lead, to direct and to guide. As a noun, conduct refers to our
behaviours, our actions or comportment. To analyse governmentality as
'the conduct of conduct' thus implies a study of government in the plural.
The word government is here not restricted to a conventional political
structure like the state, for the activity it names, observes Allen (1998,
p. 117): 'concerns nothing less than the entire spectrum of ways in which
conduct, individual or collective, can be directed'. To analyse government,
in this broad sense, thus entails an investigation into any 'form of activity
aiming to shape, guide or affect the conduct of some person or persons'
(Gordon 1991, p. 2).

   The second use of the governmentality concept is one more closely tied
to the modern state. In his 1978 lectures, Foucault examined in length
the political rationalities and forms of power that have been applied to,
and are found to be constitutive of, the set of institutions that we today
recognize as the modern state (Foucault 2008; Walters 2012, p. 20). When
Foucault addresses the state under the banner of governmentality it is not,
however, from the outlook of a *theory* of the state. In his lecture series
Foucault questioned the scholarly fascination with the state's genesis, its
history, its advance, its powers and abuses. '[T]he state, no more probably today than at any other time in history, does not have this unity, this
individuality, this rigorous functionality, no, to speak frankly, this importance, maybe, after all, the state is no more than a composite reality and
mythicized abstraction, whose importance is a lot more limited than many
of us think' (Foucault 1991c, p. 103). Following the nominalist mode
of enquiry cultivated during his academic life, Foucault instead paved
the way for a genealogy of the state at the level of definite practices and
techniques, arts and methods, programmes and strategies that produce
the modern state as their effect (Walters 2012). Rather than approaching the state as a historical constant, with a single origin and fixed identity, the governmentality concept is here invoked both to disassemble and
historicize the modern state by reflecting on its conditions of existence and
rules of transformation. As suggested by Lemke (2012, p. 26), this effort to
historically situate modern statehood gives rise to a set of *how* questions:
'How does the state come to act, if at all, as a coherent political force? How
is the imaginary unity of the state produced in practical terms? How does a
plurality of institutions and processes become "the state"?'

   During his governmentality lectures, Foucault answered these questions
by exploring how the idea of government is transformed from Ancient
Greek and Roman notions of political power and Christian religious
conceptions of pastoral power, to early modern 'reasons of the state' and

more recent liberal and neo-liberal rationalities of government (Foucault 2008; Bröckling et al. 2011, p. 3). This historical investigation into the 'arts of governing' that have produced the modern state as their contingent effect offers yet a third interpretation of the governmentality concept. As noted by Walters (2012, p. 13), Foucault at times uses the governmentality concept to denote to a liberal art of governing that emerged in the 18th century and concerned the administration of life, particularly as it appears at the level of populations (Foucault 1998). Instead of approaching liberalism as a theory, an ideology or a judicial philosophy of individual freedom, Foucault here regards liberalism (in its earlier and later forms) as a particular mentality of rule that draws upon techniques of freedom and self-correction to foster rational, responsible and calculating individuals (Burchell 1996; Foucault 2008). The governmentality concept hereby introduces a new dimension to Foucault's power analysis that allows him to study the co-evolution of modern statehood and modern subjectivity; macro-political techniques of rule and micro-physical 'technologies of the self' (Bröckling et al. 2011, p. 2).

Many observers have noted the unfinished and provisional nature of Foucault's 'genealogy of the state'. The 1978–9 lectures at Collège de France were not meant for publication and only limited parts were translated into English before Foucault's death in 1984. Nonetheless, Foucault's governmentality lectures inspired scholarly work across the social sciences and have given rise to a dispersed and heterogeneous field that we today may term governmentality studies. Scholars active within this field often hesitate to speak of governmentality studies as a coherent analytical tradition. As suggested by Walters (2012, p. 2) Foucault-inspired analytics of government should instead be approached as an analytical toolbox or a cluster of concepts that can be used to enhance the 'think-ability' and 'criticize-ability' of past and present forms of governance. While the field contains divergent interpretations of Foucault's notion of governmentality (cf. Denzelot and Gordon 2008), it converges around an empirical interest in government as a practical activity that can be studied, historicized and specified at the level of rationalities, techniques and subjectivities which underpin it and give it form and effect (Walters 2012, p. 2). The principled refusal to equate government with the state, understood as a centralized locus of rule, means that governmentality scholars seldom begin their analytics of government in the formal state apparatus. Focus is more often turned to the heterogeneous and dispersed ways by which practices of government are applied in micro-settings including at the level of the individual subject (Jessop 2011, p. 58). This decentred approach to government and statehood has important implications for how the study of public policy is undertaken.

FOUCAULT AND CRITICAL POLICY STUDIES

In recent years we have seen a wide uptake of Foucault's analytics of government across various policy 'areas' such as economic development (MacKinnon 2000), housing (Cheshire et al. 2009; Murdoch 2000), social policy (Mckee 2009), education (Triantafillou 2012), urban planning (Raco and Imrie 2000; Osborne and Rose 1999), waste (Bulkeley et al. 2007), natural resources (Lockwood and Davidson 2010), biodiversity (Bryant 2002), water supply (Kooy and Bakker 2008), and development (Li 2007), as well as in relation to specific policy practices typical for our times such as public participation (Roy 2009), auditing (Kipnis 2008), and privatization (Lipschutz and Rove 2005). While many of these studies share an interest in the processes of subjectification resulting from more or less formalized policy practices, they remain diverse and do not add up to any coherent theory of public policy. Neither do they offer critique in the traditional sense of the term. Inspired by Foucault's historical nominalism, work in this field typically rejects any universal ground for critical theorizing and instead exercises situated critique from within particular historic situations. In the following section we discuss the critical effects generated by this Foucauldian literature, and ask how it expands the register of critical policy studies. We do so by focusing on two analytical practices that capture central traits of Foucault's critical attitude: problematization and experimentation.

Problematization as Critical Practice

> The notion common to all the work I have done since Histoire de la folie is that of problematization, though it must be said that I never isolated this notion sufficiently. But one always finds what is essential after the event; the most general things are those that appear last. (Foucault 1988, p. 257)

The term problematization occurs frequently in Foucault's work, but like many of the concepts in his analytical ensemble it is not straightforwardly understood. Bacchi (2012, p.1) makes a distinction between two uses of the term. Firstly, problematization describes Foucault's mode of enquiry that he calls 'thinking problematically'. Secondly the term has an empirical meaning and denotes the historical processes by which things (human behaviour, phenomena) become problems of government (Bacchi 2012, p. 1). This dual meaning of problematization is central to many studies of governmentality. In order to understand how modern government is practised, Rose and Miller suggest that we have to approach it as a problematizing activity that is closely linked to 'the problems around which it circulates, the failings it seeks to rectify, the ills it seeks to cure' (Rose and Miller 1992, p. 182). Rather than seeing problems of government as something pre-given or self-evident, they suggest that students of governmentality should foster a problematizing form of enquiry that pays attention to the fragile and contingent processes by which things and persons are made visible as problems under labels such as madness and criminality (Miller and Rose 2008, p. 16). Through situated analyses of those moments and practices where our own conduct, and that of others, is called into question, Foucauldian analytics of government typically strive to open up such labels to critical forms of scrutiny (Dean 2004, p. 27). This critical practice is not derived from general principles or theories about, say, social movements, the working class or the bureaucratic state. Instead it is 'an exercise in clarifying and intensifying the problematizations which condition ourselves in the present' (Koopman 2009, p. 105).

Foucault-inspired policy students therefore typically begin their analyses in descriptions of particular policy problems. These could be, for example, the increased age of retirement, a new infrastructure model for high-speed trains, public reports on the uneven use of parental leave, the evaluation of a needle exchange programme for intravenous drug users or the mobilization against 'honour killing' in neighbourhoods dominated by 'immigrants'. In each of these sites, we can expect a circulation of knowledge (e.g. media reports, police investigations, academic research), experts being put to work, recommendations being suggested and particular policies perhaps being changed or new ones implemented. Walters (2012, p. 58) suggests that this material – the documents and reports, the proposals for revised practices and the politics, programmes and strategies that build on these or contest them – should be analysed with specific questions in mind: 'What kind of political subjects are being described or assumed in these documents?'; 'Within what kinds of moral and epistemic frames are the problems of government being imagined?' These questions lead to the specificity of governance being explored. Instead of offering an overarching account of a policy area, a Foucault-inspired analytics of government draws attention to the particular rationalities and practices that govern everyday life at particular times, each with a particular history.

For example, when Miller and Rose study 'welfare policy' as political rationality their analyses begin in specific problematizations: 'the declining birthrate; delinquency and anti-social behaviour; the problem family; the social consequences of ill health and the advantages conferred by a healthy population; and the integration of citizens into the community' (Miller and Rose 2008, p. 73). In order to study how these issues and concerns become problems of government, Miller and Rose follow the 'birth and the activities of many of these little engineers of the human soul, and their mundane knowledges, techniques and procedures – psychologists, psychiatrists, medics, accountants, social workers, factory managers, town planners and others' (Miller and Rose 2008, p. 5). They draw attention to the kind of conceptions of the human being that are a held at a particular time (as citizen, schoolchild, customer, worker, manager) and particularly how such conceptions are problematized and how interventions are devised in diverse sites such as the school, the home, the workplace, the courtroom (Miller and Rose 2008, p. 7). Rather than taking the problematizations that condition our lives for granted, Miller and Rose's work effectively illustrates how certain forms of conduct are turned problematic in different ways, in different sites, and involving different agents.

Another example can be found in the field of climate policy. In this emerging policy area, the individual citizen-consumer has in recent years become the target of numerous campaigns aimed at reducing that individual's 'carbon footprint' through changes in dietary preferences, travel patterns and household spending (e.g. workplace champion schemes, collective purchasing, meatless-Monday campaigns). A Foucauldian analytics of climate government would typically approach these initiatives as problematizing activities within which individual 'carbon conduct' is called into question and intervention is devised (Paterson and Stripple 2010). What counts as 'climate policy' is hereby opened up to encompass not just formal policies and measures but a wide range of 'initiatives' that govern individual or collective behaviour by bringing together 'a sufficient marriage of power and legitimacy to establish, operationalize, apply, enforce, interpret, or vitiate' (Conca 2005, p. 190) rationalities and practices intended to respond to climate change. Miller and Rose have coined the term 'programmes of government' to capture the manifold and diverse activities 'that seek to configure specific locales and relations in ways thought desirable' (Miller and Rose 2008, p. 63). To study climate policy in programmatic terms entails a close examination of the many initiatives devised to 'conduct carbon conduct' across territorially defined jurisdictions, systems and arenas. These initiatives may govern by advancing new frames and arguments, but also through practical and mundane techniques, such as redesigning refrigeration in supermarkets, smart energy meters in the household or lessons in fuel-efficient car driving. Envisioned in this way, critical climate policy studies become an enquiry not simply into the design of laws and regulations, but a close engagement with how these are taken up, worked through and reconfigured in the day-to-day practice and culture of everyday life.

When approached from the horizon of Foucauldian analytics of government, policy is a practical activity that can be 'historicized and specified at the level of the rationalities, programmes, techniques and subjectivities which underpin it and give it form and effect' (Walters 2012, p. 3). A

Foucauldian 'critical policy analyst' should thus refrain from trying to establish something like 'climate policy' as an abstract and general category that governs in a homogeneous way. To advance problematization as a mode of enquiry instead entails a close examination of particular articulations (e.g. 'climate campaigns'), rationalities (e.g. low-carbon lifestyles) and programmes (e.g. carbon accounting schemes) by which subjectivities are moulded and mobilized at certain times in history. As an approach within critical policy studies, governmentality is highly capable of registering even subtle shifts in these programmes and techniques. As highlighted by Walters, it is this sensitivity to the 'intricacies of contemporary governance and the nuances of political change' (2012, p. 3) that explains the wide uptake of governmentality across social science and the humanities.

Critique as a Mode of Experimentation

> Do not ask who I am and do not ask me to remain the same: leave it to our bureaucrats and our police to see that our papers are in order. At least spare us their morality when we write. (Foucault 1972, p. 17)

This famous, but intriguing, citation from *The Archaeology of Knowledge*, alludes to the question of critique in Foucault's work. A Foucauldian approach to policy is indeed critical, but it does not produce critique in the familiar sense of the term. Much of social theory assumes a particular ground from where critique can be leveraged. This assumed ground could be particular subjects of history (e.g. classes, civilizations), an ethics (e.g. Habermasian discourse ethics, Rawlsian veil of ignorance) or an ontological condition (e.g. utilitarian rationality, eternal anarchy). As is well known, 'the postmodern condition' and its declared 'end of meta-narratives' implies that this ground is nowhere to be found. Thus, Foucault's critique denotes 'the exposure and contestation of assumptions rather than to express a general oppositional stance to the putatively pathological character of a social or cultural totality' (Dean 1994, p. 119). This is a circumstance that has brought about criticisms and frustration from progressives and those on the left generally.

Much of this frustration is directed towards Foucault's genealogical method, influenced by Friedrich Nietzsche. In 'Nietzsche, genealogy, history', Foucault describes genealogy as a critical method and a diagnostic tool that differs from conventional history by challenging the belief in the purity of origins and the notion of linear, teleological development. Genealogy does not seek to 'capture the exact essence of things, their purest possibilities, and their carefully protected identities' (Foucault 1984, p. 78). Rather, to Foucault, the critical potential of genealogy is precisely that 'it disturbs what was previously considered immobile; it fragments what was thought unified; it shows the heterogeneity of what was imagined consistent with itself' (Foucault 1984, p. 82). In Foucault's hands genealogy reveals the present to be the consequence of a history fraught with accidents, conflicts and unrelated events. It is thus a mode of enquiry that seeks to illustrate how 'self-understandings that are taken as universal, eternal and necessary have a history, a beginning, and therefore, possibly, an end' (Hoy 1998, p. 31). This historical nominalism produces a particular critical attitude.

Dean describes Foucauldian analytics of government as a 'critical practice' that seeks to 'gain clarity about the conditions under which we think and act in the present' (Dean 2004, p. 36). By problematizing what is given to us as necessary to think and do, this analytical tradition sets out to open up new fields of experience that allow us to do things differently. The role of the analyst becomes one of destabilizing accustomed ways of thinking and clearing a space for thinking and being otherwise (Burchell 1996, p. 33). To challenge prevailing and narrowly defined terms of what it is possible and acceptable to do, is an important dimension of Foucault's notion of freedom. As explained by May (2011), Foucault does not defend any form of metaphysical freedom but approaches freedom as a historical and political concept. His critical project lies in exposing the specific constraints that are part of our historical legacy. Only by asking what they are, how they came to be that way, and what their effects are, can we begin to liberate ourselves from them (May 2011, p. 74). However, to Foucault, freedom does not stand in opposition to power relations. Freedom is not a state we occupy, but a practice that we undertake. By experimenting with other subject positions than those that our socio-historical context makes available to us, Foucault suggests that it is possible to navigate power relations in ways that both constitute and promote practices of freedom (Taylor 2011, p. 7).

However, Foucault does not tell us what to struggle for or against. The focus on singular experiences and specific regimes of government means that Foucauldian policy analysts must refrain from any claims to universality or necessity. As explained by Rose et al. (2006), studies of governmentality offer ways of asking questions that do not lay claims to totality – they do not seek to explain why things happened, but *how* they happened and how they differ from what has been going on before. This 'ethos of investigation' has, according to Walters, led many scholars to be 'sceptical commentators' instead of trying to play a more invested role in political debates (Walters 2012, p. 148). This distant role between the world of academic critique and that of everyday political life differs significantly from how Foucault himself viewed and practised critique. In the course *The Courage of Truth: The Government of Self and Others II*, held at the Collège de France in 1984, Foucault asks how free speech and truth-telling has been practised throughout the years and how people constitute themselves as someone who is telling the truth. By relating the Greek concept *epimeleia heatou* (care of the self) to the Socratic approach to the concept of *parrhesia* (free speech, the courage to tell the truth), Foucault here approaches critique as a particular 'technology of the self', a process through which we form ourselves (Foucault 2011). To Foucault, the project of critique involves exposing oneself as a subject from within a particular historical situation. As clarified by Lemke (2012, p. 73), critique is an integral part of ethical self-formation that seeks to make visible the limits of 'what we are' in order to transgress them. Social critique can therefore not be reduced to a theoretical concern or an epistemological exercise. To Foucault critique is, by Lemke's account, 'an attitude, an ethos, a philosophical life' driven by passion and political affect (Lemke 2012, p. 73).

What has troubled many of Foucault's critics is the uncertain position he leaves us in. Foucault's invitation to think and act differently does neither suggest any definite direction for resistance and change, nor does it guarantee that it lead us to a better situation. As noted by May (2011, p. 80):

> to open up a 'space for concrete freedom' is not to figure out who we might be and then go there; it is to try out different possibilities for our lives; different 'possible transformations' to see where they might lead. To live freely is to experiment with oneself, not always knowing if one is getting free of the forces that have moulded one, nor . . . being sure of the effects of one's experimentation.

Therefore, the critical enquiry which we might learn from Foucault should not be approached as a social theory with a strict methodological inventory at its disposal (Bröckling et al. 2011, p. 15). Many observers instead highlight the experimental dimension of Foucault's analytics of government. To Rabinow and Rose, it represents 'a movement of thought that invents, makes use of, and modifies conceptual tools as they are set into a relation with specific practices and problems. When we have done this work, with regret, they can be recycled or even discarded' (Rabinow and Rose 2003, p. xv). Walters (2012, p. 5) also sees Foucault's genealogical critique as an analytical toolbox that needs to be reimagined as a dynamic, transactional space. If we apply it as a fully formed perspective we run the risk of turning it into a self-contained theory and thereby diminish its diagnostic potential through repetition. When critique itself, rather than what is being criticized, becomes common sense, suggests Bröckling et al. (2011, p. 16), 'the gesture of critical unveiling becomes obsolete'.

CONCLUSIONS

In this chapter we have suggested that Michel Foucault's nominalist engagement with traditional political concepts such as power, government and the state has paved the way for a decentred form of policy analysis that asks how we govern in micro-settings including at the level of the individual subject. The focus on the 'how of governing' stems from a rejection of any *a priori* understanding of the distribution of power or location of government, and arises instead from an interest in, and awareness of, the historically situated practices, rationalities and identities by which governing operates. Viewed in this manner, Foucault-inspired policy studies neither offer us a substantive theory about the forces that shape public policy, nor do they tell us what constitutes public policy (e.g. actors, interests, structures). Rather, to problematize government in a Foucauldian sense involves a close examination of the 'regimes of truth, the practices and strategies that ontologise the world in the first place' (Walters 2012, p. 57).

We have argued that Foucault's nominalist analytics of government produce a distinct critical attitude that may help students of public policy to interrogate our particular historical constraints and to experiment with possible spaces of transformation. However, it is a form of critique that calls for analytical playfulness and experimentation. Scholars familiar with the work of Michel Foucault will know that it is a difficult, and, as argued in this chapter, far from desirable task to deduce a strict theoretical or methodological framework from his many and heterogeneous writings, lectures and interviews. As observed by Rabinow and Rose (2003, p. vii):

> Foucault would undoubtedly, have been wryly sceptical about the growth of 'Foucault studies' and the related attempt to discipline his thought and turn it into orthodoxy. His texts did not invite that kind of treatment . . . they set out to open things up, not close them down; to complicate, not simplify; not to police the boundary of an oeuvre but to multiply lines of investigation and possibilities for thought. They are not aspects of a single project, but fragmentary – experiments, interventions, provocations and reflections.

Rabinow and Rose (2003) describe how Foucault in his last years returned to basic questions about what it means to be a thinking person. He enquired into the possibility of critical thought that does not 'judge', that is not 'a quasi-judicial tribunal passing down verdicts of guilt or innocence on persons or events' (Rabinow and Rose 2003, p. xxiv). Foucault did not leave us with any firm answer to these questions. He did, however, urge us all to employ critical thought to revisit the assumptions, notions and ways of thinking upon which accepted and authorized practices of being critical are based. In an interview from 1984 (given the same year as he died at the age of 57), Foucault indicates where this critical attitude may lead students of public policy (Foucault 1988, p. 265):

> The work of an intellectual is not to shape others' political will; it is, through the analyses that he carries out in his own field, to question over and over again what is postulated as self-evident, to disturb people's mental habits, the way they do and think things, to dissipate what is familiar and accepted, to reexamine rules and institutions and on the basis of this re-problematization (in which he carries out his specific task as intellectual) to participate in the formation of a political will (in which he has a role as citizen to play).

Rather than telling us 'what critique is', Foucault is a scholar who invites us to interrogate how we constitute ourselves as scholars of 'critical policy studies' and to deploy these insights to create new options for thought, and new possibilities for action. Critique is here not set up as opposed to power, it does not claim to 'overcome' power to uncover our true selves. Since relations of power are ubiquitous and constitutive of society and ourselves, critique entails thinking through these relations 'with as little domination as possible' (Foucault 1997, p. 298). This invitation to try out different possibilities for our lives, to experiment with different possible transformations, remains equally relevant today. To us, it offers a compelling analytical challenge and a fruitful source of inspiration that sets the field and practice of critical policy studies into productive motion.

NOTES

1. For a more thorough treatment of the links between Foucault's work and critical theory, see Dean (1994). Dean's discussion runs through central themes in Foucault's work – truth, knowledge and rationality; power, domination and government; and the self and ethical practice – and shows both similarities and differences with the early Frankfurt scholars and the work of Habermas.
2. The 'immanent critique' that we refer to is also prominent in the early Frankfurt School, whose key figures were circumspect about the theoretical affirmation of a normative position. With Habermas came a move in critical theory towards a transcendent critique, which is at odds with Foucault's orientation and also marks a discontinuity within the Frankfurt School.

REFERENCES

Allen, B. (1998), 'Foucault and modern political philosophy', in Moss, J. (ed.), *The Later Foucault*, London, Thousand Oaks, CA and New Delhi: Sage Publications.
Bacchi, C. (2012), 'Why study problematizations? Making politics visible', *Open Journal of Political Science* **2** (1), 1–8.

Barry, A., Osborne, T. and Rose, N.S. (1996), *Foucault and Political Reason: Liberalism, Neo-liberalism, and Rationalities of Government*, Chicago: University of Chicago Press.
Bröckling, U., Krasmann, S. and Lemke, T. (eds) (2011), *Governmentality. Current Issues and Future Challenges*, New York, Oxford: Routledge.
Brown, W. (1998), 'Genealogical politics', in Moss, J. (ed.), *The Later Foucault*, London, Thousand Oaks and New Delhi: Sage Publications.
Bryant, R. (2002), 'Non-governmental organizations and governmentality: "consuming" biodiversity and indigenous people in the Philippines', *Political Studies* **50**, 268–292.
Bulkeley, H., Watson, M. and Hudson, R. (2007), 'Modes of governing municipal waste', *Environment and Planning A* **39** (11), 2733–2753.
Burchell, G. (1996), 'Liberal government and techniques of the self', in Barry, A., Osborne, T. and Rose, N. (eds), *Foucault and Political Reason: Liberalism, Neo-Liberalism and Rationalities of Government*, Chicago: University of Chicago Press.
Cheshire, L.A., Rosenblatt, T., Lawrence, G. and Walters, P. (2009), 'The governmentality of master planning: housing consumption, aesthetics and community on a new estate', *Housing Studies* **24** (5), 653–667.
Conca, K. (2005), 'Old states in new bottles? The hybridization of authority in global environmental governance', in Barry, J. and Eckersley, R. (eds), *The State and the Global Ecological Crisis*, Cambridge, MA: The MIT Press.
Dean, M. (1994), *Critical and Effective Histories: Foucault's Methods and Historical Sociology*, London, New York: Routledge.
Dean, M. (2004), *Governmentality: Rower and Rule in Modern Society*, 2nd edn, London, Thousand Oaks, CA: Sage Publications.
Denzelot, J. and Gordon, C. (2008), 'Governing liberal societies. The Foucault effect in the English speaking world', *Foucault Studies* **5**, 48–62.
Fischer, F. (2003), *Reframing Public Policy: Discursive Politics and Deliberative Practices*, Oxford: Oxford University Press.
Fischer, F. and Gottweis, H. (2012), *The Argumentative Turn Revisited. Public Policy as Communicative Practice*, Durham and London: Duke University Press.
Foucault, M. (1972), *The Archaeology of Knowledge*, New York: Pantheon Books.
Foucault, M. (1982), 'Afterword', in Dreyfus, H. and Rabinow, P. (eds), *Michel Foucault: Beyond Structuralism and Hermeneutics*, Chicago: University of Chicago Press.
Foucault, M. (1984), 'Nietzsche, genealogy, history', in Rabinow, P. (ed.), *The Foucault Reader*, New York: Pantheon Books.
Foucault, M. (1988), 'The concern for truth', in Kritzman, L.D. (ed.), *Politics, Philosophy, Culture, Interviews and Other Writings 1977–1984*, New York and London: Routledge.
Foucault, M. (1991a), *Remarks On Marx: Conversations with Duccio Trombadori*, trans. James Goldstein, R. and Cascaito, J., New York: Semiotext(e).
Foucault, M. (1991b), *Discipline and Punish. The Birth of the Prison* (this translation first published by Allen Lane in 1977), London: Penguin Books.
Foucault, M. (1991c), 'Governmentality', in Burchell, G., Gordon, C. and Miller, P. (eds), *The Foucault Effect: Studies in Governmentality*, Chicago: University of Chicago Press.
Foucault, M. (1997), 'What is critique?', in Lotringer, S. (ed.), *The Politics of Truth: Michel Foucault*, New York: Semiotext(e).
Foucault, M. (1998), *The History of Sexuality: Volume 1* (this translation first published in 1978), London: Penguin Books.
Foucault, M. (2008), *The Birth of Biopolitics, Lectures at Collège de France 1978–1979*, Basingstoke, UK, New York: Palgrave Macmillan.
Foucault, M. (2011), *The Courage of Truth: the Government of Self and Others II, Lectures at the Collège de France 1983–1984*, Basingstoke, UK, New York: Palgrave Macmillan.
Gordon, C. (1991), 'Governmental rationality: an introduction', in Burchell, G., Gordon, C. and Miller, P. (eds), *The Foucault Effect: Studies in Governmentality*, Chicago: University of Chicago Press.

Hajer, M. and Wagenaar, H. (eds) (2003), *Deliberative Policy Analysis: Understanding Governance in a Network Society*, Cambridge: Cambridge University Press.

Horkheimer, M. (1976), 'Traditional and critical theory', in Connerton, P. (ed.), *Critical Sociology: Selected Readings* (originally published in 1937), Harmondsworth, UK: Penguin.

Hoy, D.C. (1998), 'Genealogy and the scope of the political', in Moss, J. (ed.), *The Later Foucault*, London, Thousand Oaks and New Delhi: Sage Publications.

Jessop, B. (2011), 'Constituting another Foucault effect. Foucault on states and statecraft', in Bröckling, U., Krasmann, S. and Lemke, T. (eds), *Governmentality. Current Issues and Future Challenges*, New York and London: Routledge.

Kipnis, A.B. (2008), 'Audit cultures: neoliberal governmentality, socialist legacy, or technologies of governing?', *American Ethnologist* **35** (2), 275–289.

Koopman, C. (2009), 'Two uses of genealogy: Michel Foucault and Bernard Williams', in Prado, C.G. (ed.), *Foucault's Legacy*, London and New York: Continuum International Publishing Group.

Kooy, M. and Bakker, K. (2008), 'Technologies of government: constituting subjectivities, spaces, and infrastructures in colonial and contemporary Jakarta', *International Journal of Urban and Regional Research* **32** (2), 375–391.

Lemke, T. (2012), *Foucault, Governmentality, and Critique*, Boulder, CO: Paradigm Publishers.

Li, T. (2007), *The Will to Improve: Governmentality, Development, and the Practice of Politics*, Durham, NC: Duke University Press.

Lipschutz, R.D. and Rove, J.K. (2005), *Globalization, Governmentality and Global Politics: Regulation for the Rest of Us?*, New York: Routledge.

Lockwood, M. and Davidson, J. (2010), 'Environmental governance and the hybrid regime of Australian natural resource management', *Geoforum* **41** (3), 388–398.

Mckee, K. (2009), 'Post-Foucauldian governmentality: what does it offer critical social policy analysis?', *Critical Social Policy* **29** (3), 465–486.

MacKinnon, D. (2000), 'Managerialism, governmentality and the state: a neo-Foucauldian approach to local economic governance', *Political Geography* **19**, 293–314.

Marcuse, H. (1937), 'Philosophie und kritische theorie', *Zeitschrift für Sozialforschung* **VI** (3), 631–647.

May, T. (2011), 'Foucault's conception of freedom', in Taylor, D. (ed.), *Michel Foucault. Key Concepts*, Durham, UK: Acumen Publishing Limited.

Miller, P. and Rose, N. (2008), *Governing the Present*, Cambridge, Malden: Polity Press.

Murdoch, J. (2000), 'Space against time: competing rationalities in planning for housing', *Transactions of the Institute of British Geographers* **25** (4), 503–519.

Osborne, T. and Rose, N. (1999), 'Governing cities: notes on the spatialisation of virtue', *Environment and Planning D: Society and Space* **17** (6), 737–760.

Paterson, M. and Stripple, J. (2010), 'My space: governing individuals' carbon emissions', *Environment and Planning D: Society and Space* **28** (2), 341–362.

Rabinow, P. and Rose, N. (2003), *The Essential Foucault. Selections from the Essential Works of Foucault 1954–1984*, New York and London: The New Press.

Raco, M. and Imrie, R. (2000), 'Governmentality and rights and responsibilities in urban policy', *Environment and Planning A* **32**, 2187–2204.

Rose, N. and Miller, P. (1992), 'Political power beyond the state: problematics of government', *British Journal of Sociology* **42** (2), 173–205.

Rose, N., O'Malley, P. and Velverde, M. (2006), 'Governmentality', *Annual Review of Law and Social Science* **2**, 83–104.

Roy, A. (2009), 'Civic governmentality: the politics of inclusion in Beirut and Mumbai', *Antipode* **41** (1), 159–179.

Taylor, D. (2011), 'Introduction', in Taylor, D. (ed.), *Michel Foucault. Key Concepts*, Durham, UK: Acumen Publishing Limited.

Torgerson, D. (1986), 'Between knowledge and politics: three faces of policy analysis', *Policy Sciences* **19** (1), 33–59.

Triantafillou, P. (2012), *New Forms of Governing. A Foucauldian Inspired Analysis*, Basingstoke and New York: Palgrave Macmillan.

Walters, W. (2012), *Governmentality. Critical Encounters*, New York and London: Routledge.

Yanow, D. (1999), *Conducting Interpretative Policy Analysis*, Thousand Oaks, CA: Sage Publications.

PART II

THEORETICAL PERSPECTIVES: CRITICAL REFLEXIVITY, HEGEMONY AND POWER

6 Poststructuralist discourse theory and critical policy studies: interests, identities and policy change
David Howarth and Steven Griggs[1]

The issues of policy change and policy continuity have been the subject of much theoretical discussion. One perennial stand-off, involving intellectual giants as different as Marx, Weber and Keynes, pits the role of ideas against economic or material interests (Griggs and Howarth, 2002). Another dispute opposes those who, on the one hand, stress the importance of social structures as the key determinants of policy change, in which underlying systems of social relations strongly shape the emergence of new policy frameworks, and those, on the other hand, who emphasize the role of individual and collective agents. A third issue arises from those approaches that focus on the relative importance of exogenous shocks or events that dislocate existing policies, and thus make change possible, as against those perspectives that privilege the importance of endogenous factors of change, in which policies change as a result of internal pressures and adjustments.

In seeking to bring together these different elements in a synthetic account of economic policy reversals, Christopher Hood identifies four main types of explanation. These are (1) the role of climate-changing ideas, which introduce novel thinking into the policy process; (2) significant shifts of interests, which are engineered by alliances of forces or agents; (3) underlying changes of structures or institutions; and (4) the possibility of what he calls 'policy self-destructions', in which an 'internal self-destructive dynamic' is deemed responsible for the extinction of a 'policy dinosaur' (1994: 13).

In our view, such oppositions and elements can be properly integrated within a poststructuralist approach to critical policy studies. This approach highlights the centrality of politics and power in the forging, sustenance, and grip of various policy frames or discourses in particular social and historical contexts. In substantive theoretical terms, a poststructuralist perspective involves the articulation of a neo-Gramscian concept of hegemony in order to account for the emergence and formation of policy discourses, and the recognition of the constitutive character of rhetoric. It also draws upon Lacanian psychoanalysis and the category of fantasy to grapple with the way in which policies are stabilized and sedimented, and to account for their subjective grip. Such theoretical resources, we argue, offer an innovative way to integrate the role of ideas, interests, agents, and structures in explaining policy change and continuity.

We begin by setting out our approach to discourse and its implications for critical policy studies. We then consider the way in which the concept of hegemony and the affective dimension of policy-making can shed new light on the practices of policy change. In conclusion, we bring to the fore the different ways in which poststructuralism redefines the relationship between ideas and interests in the policy process.

POSTSTRUCTURALIST DISCOURSE THEORY

Let us first establish our particular approach to discourse. In contrast to minimal and purely ideational understandings of discourse, in which it is reduced to another empirical variable to be tested against others, we propose a 'thicker' conception of discourse, in which the latter does not just consist of an abstract cognitive system of beliefs and words, but is a constitutive dimension of social relations (Howarth and Griggs, 2012; Howarth, 2013). All objects and practices in this approach – natural things and physical processes, social and cultural phenomena – acquire their meaning and significance in specific discourses; they are 'discursively constructed' in multiple ways. Although such entities certainly 'exist' independently of any particular discourse, their peculiar import – and thus how they are engaged with by social actors – depends on their positioning and use within particular symbolic frameworks (Howarth, 2000; Laclau and Mouffe, 2001).

Put in a different way, discourse is a 'shared way of understanding the world' which 'enables those who subscribe to it to interpret bits of information and put them together into coherent stories or accounts' (Dryzek, 1997: 8). Yet, in bringing order to such complexities, discourse does not simply re-present or reflect a pre-existing or underlying reality. It serves, instead, to partially bring that reality into being, so that it has a *constitutive* function as well (cf. Gottweis, 2003: 252). As Laclau and Mouffe insist, 'a *discursive structure* is not a merely "cognitive" or "contemplative" entity; it *is an articulatory practice* which constitutes and organizes social relations' (Laclau and Mouffe, 1985: 96, our emphasis).

Think, for example, of a forest that blocks the path of a proposed road or airport runway. The significance of this object depends on the way it is perceived and constructed in different discourses by various subjects or groups. Amongst the latter, for example, is the construction company, which hopes to profit by building the transport infrastructure, or the government, which is endeavouring to resolve a policy problem. By contrast, for conservationists, environmentalists or scientists, the forest is constituted and represented in radically different ways. Discourses thus represent objects in different ways. But proponents of poststructuralist discourse theory also argue that the objects themselves are radically contingent entities that admit of different discursive articulations; the 'form' or 'essence' of something does not exhaust its being or existence. Similar considerations apply to all things, be it airports, health or urban austerity, and the discourses that constitute their meanings.

This understanding of discourse involves three conceptual steps. In the first instance, we enlarge the purview of traditional discourse theory – the analysis of 'texts and talk in contexts' – to incorporate the role of social practices and political activities. *All* objects and social practices are discursive because their meaning and position depend upon their articulation within socially constructed systems of rules and differences (Laclau and Mouffe, 1985; Howarth and Stavrakakis, 2000: 3). Secondly, we infuse this alternative understanding of discourse with the work of structural linguists, particularly that of Saussure (1983), in order to develop a relational and differential account of discourse. In this model, four particular kinds of entity – agents (or subjects), objects, words and actions – are individuated and rendered intelligible within the context of a particular practice. Each element acquires meaning only in relation to the others (Howarth, 2009: 311–12). Finally, drawing on poststructuralists like Jacques Derrida (1978, 1982), Michel Foucault (1972, 1981, 1984) and Jacques Lacan (2006), we stress the radical contingency and structural undecidability of things and discursive structures (Howarth, 2009: 312).

Such contingency or undecidability arises because we assume that all systems of meaning are, in a fundamental sense, incomplete. The incompletion of discourses does not just mean that they are simply missing something; it is not synonymous with the fact that a piece of a puzzle is missing from a jigsaw box, or that a cup of coffee is only half-full. Instead, from our perspective, the condition of incompletion denotes the presence of an absence or negativity that structurally prevents the completion of a discourse, thereby indicating its limits. Discourses are thus incomplete systems of meaningful practice, because they are predicated on the active exclusion of certain elements. Yet, at the same time, these excluded elements are required for the very identity of the discourse in question. This absence or negativity thus prevents the full constitution of a discursive structure, so that every structure is thus dislocated. This 'out of joint-ness' is evident in particular dislocations or events that show the incompletion of a discourse, whilst the construction of social antagonisms signifies the limits of any discourse or social order, that is, its contestation by competing political forces.

In our perspective, then, building on the work of Laclau and Mouffe, discourse is a kind of social practice that links together and modifies heterogeneous elements in changing historical formations (Laclau and Mouffe, 1985: 96). The outcomes of such practices are discursive formations, in which the linkages between the elements of these systems are relational and differential. Discursive formations are finite, uneven and incomplete. Both as a practice and as an incomplete system of related moments, discourse also presupposes a world of contingent elements – linguistic and non-linguistic, social and natural – that can be linked together in various ways. This perspective is consistent with a minimal realism that acknowledges the existence of the objects and processes that we think about, though our practices of reflection are never external to the lifeworlds into which we are thrown. Indeed, it is only within such symbolic orders that we encounter such objects.

Such ontological postulates can be expressed in a more technical idiom. To begin with, the elements or building blocks of a discourse are best conceived as 'floating signifiers', which can in certain circumstances be articulated by rival political projects that seek to fix their meaning and import, whereas moments are those elements whose identities have been assigned and positioned in a particular discourse. Nodal points are those privileged points of signification within a discourse that partially fix the meaning of a range of adjacent practices and institutional configurations. For example, the signifier 'free economy' in a neoliberal discourse confers meaning to a range of connected practices and policies, including liberalization, marketization, privatization, the reduction of state interventions, and so forth.

Empty signifiers, by contrast, provide the symbolic means to represent discourses, which in our view are essentially incomplete orders. Their function is to incarnate the 'absent fullness' of such discourses – to provide some means of signification for what is an impossible object. In short, then, floating signifiers are ideological elements that, not being securely fixed in a particular discourse, can be constructed in diverse ways, whereas empty signifiers are points of symbolic fixation, which provide the representational resources that can hold together multiple and even contradictory demands in a precarious unity (Laclau, 1990, 1995).

PROBLEMATIZING POLICY CHANGE

What does this understanding of discourse mean for the study of policy change? To begin with, poststructuralist traditions of enquiry provide an effective way of deconstructing the dominant theories of policy-making, which all tend to focus on the presumed existence of groups, movements or networks operating in a particular policy subsystem. In contrast, post-structuralist accounts adopt an anti-essentialist and anti-foundationalist orientation. This approach rejects accounts of policy-making which assume that objects, human subjects, or social formations have fixed essences. It also dismisses those totalizing narratives that impute some kind of inevitability to policy change and its direction of travel. Such presuppositions are most evident in the economic determinism and class reductionism of Marxist explanations of social and political change. But they also operate in some of the predominant narratives of governance networks, which understand governance networks to be a 'necessary' or 'inevitable' response to changing historical forces or shifts in the socio-economic structures, whether the latter take the form of globalization or increasing demands for democratization (Bevir, 2004).

Public policies, in our view, are political constructs. Here we foreground the contextualized meanings attributed to policy practices by 'situated subjects', whilst our analytical focus involves the critical explanation of the discourses that bring policies into being. Such perspectives necessitate an acceptance of the radical contingency of social life. In other words, when conceptualized as objects of discourse, public policies are radically contingent constructs which can be understood and re-understood in different ways. Invariably, they will take different forms in different political and historical contexts, whether this be across multiple spatial scales, shifting balances of political forces, predominant socio-economic processes, or social practices and cultural representations (Howarth and Griggs, 2012).

Take, for example, the mobilization of climate change policy coalitions or networks in the policy process. How do we explain the emergence of such phenomena? From our perspective, we should not impute to actors in such political formations ties of mutual dependency or shared identities, or assume that such ties emerge automatically from shared interests, institutional locations, or the constraining complexities of policy environments. We need instead to account for the political practices that produce and reproduce the shared identities that ultimately hold different formations together.

Poststructuralists thus challenge the tendency to emphasize either/or oppositions. They question, for example, the privileging of *either* the role of interests and material incentives, on the one hand, *or* the salience of identities and values in explaining the function and impact of groups and networks in the policy process on the other. They are sceptical, moreover, about a necessary and automatic connection between interests and agency. Sharing a common interest does not necessarily lead social actors to become agents who are intent on mobilizing others, or joining groups or networks. Such common interests or ties of mutual dependency are constructed politically via acts of power that draw boundaries between those within the networks and those who remain external to them. In other words, governance practices in any policy subsystem cannot be divorced from an inclusionary/exclusionary dynamic, which foregrounds the political and delimits the borders of political formations, not by pre-assumed patterns of resource dependency or shared interests, but by the political construction of social antagonisms and the opposition to an external 'other'.

Against this background, we conceptualize policy regimes as more or less sedimented systems of discourse. These regimes structure social practices, though in conditions of crisis and dislocation they can be reconstituted by political practices. As systems of discourse, they are partially fixed systems of rules, norms, resources, practices and subjectivities that are linked together in particular ways. In the form of the state, institutions and the personnel that occupy powerful positions in these structures, they can often shape the character and direction of policy; their institutional inertia often constitutes an important obstacle to policy change. Importantly, as we suggest above, their emergence and formation is based on the drawing of boundaries or frontiers between differently positioned social agents, and the discourses wherein their identities are constituted. Because no discourse *exhausts* the meaning of objectivity, as any identity or order is marked by a 'constitutive outside', the formation and reproduction of any policy regimes is ultimately entwined with the practice of drawing boundaries. In our perspective, this exemplary political practice involves the construction of social antagonisms and the creation of political frontiers between forces and subjects.

It follows that an important condition for policy change is the dislocation of existing discursive structures and the identities they confer. Not only are public policies subject to contingent events or crises, but they are also vulnerable to challenges from those forces that are excluded. During such moments of crisis, where there is a failure of 'normal politics', social actors may need to reconfigure and transform identities to address this new situation, and in such contexts new forms of political agency can come into being, as subjects construct and identify newly constituted and available discourses. Such change requires actors to articulate new mobilizing narratives and campaigns with new means of representation and signifiers to partially stabilize policy regimes (Griggs and Howarth, 2004). During these dislocatory moments of policy-making, the role of agency and individual actors, or policy entrepreneurs, much like Gramsci's (1971: 5–23) 'organic intellectuals' whose political and ideological task is to elaborate and inculcate the new 'common sense' that is to form the basis of a particular historical bloc, comes to the 'front of the stage' in explanations of policy change as actors (potentially) make decisions *about* structures rather than *within* structures.

This theoretical orientation means that our particular understanding of policy-making privileges the role of power and political processes. Policies will be the contingent outcomes of political struggles between competing discourses. Politics in this view cannot be reduced to a neutral terrain, but is better conceptualized as the contestation and institution of social relations and practices, which render apparent the contingent character of any practice or institution by showing the role of power and exclusion in its formation. It involves acts of power and the posing of antagonisms. Actors engage in hegemonic struggles to articulate political frontiers between 'insiders' and 'outsiders' by way of the definition of a 'core opposition' between 'friend' and 'enemy' (Howarth, 2000, 2013). As we argue above, every discursive structure is uneven, heterogeneous and hierarchical. Indeed, one of the challenges of poststructuralist policy analysis is to deconstruct 'taken for granted' regimes of policy practices and objects, whilst exposing their exclusionary logics and advancing alternatives (Gottweis, 2003: 49).

But how exactly are we to understand the politics of policy-making? How are particular policies constituted and reproduced? And how are they transformed or overthrown? We have already hinted at some responses to these questions, pointing to the construction of political frontiers and the masking over of differences by opposition to an 'other'. In the next section, we develop such insights further. By radicalizing the insights of the Marxist theorist Antonio Gramsci (1971), and by drawing on the work of Laclau and Mouffe, we argue that discourses are stabilized and challenged by multiple hegemonic operations, whose general structure consists of the logics of equivalence and difference. The concept of hegemony is thus central to the critical explanation of policy change that we put forward here. Change and inertia in policy practices will be the outcome of hegemonic struggles (Howarth, 2009, 2013; Howarth and Griggs, 2012).

HEGEMONIC POLITICS AND POLICY CHANGE

It is widely acknowledged that the concept of hegemony is complex and contested (see Howarth and Griggs, 2012). Here we draw upon the work of Gramsci and other neo-Gramscians, for whom the concept of hegemony is defined as that complex set of social and political practices through which the active and passive consent of key social actors in a particular historical bloc is secured, whilst at the same time ensuring the compliance of others, if necessary by force and coercion. Hegemony in this sense goes further than the simple accomplishment of political leadership (of one class, for example, over others as in the Leninist model), or the maintenance of political domination, because it entails the winning of 'ethical and intellectual leadership' by a dominant force (or alliance of forces) in society to its norms and values (Gramsci, 1971).

More specifically, we develop the approach of Ernesto Laclau, Chantal Mouffe, and other proponents of the Essex School of discourse analysis, who have taken Gramsci's work in a poststructuralist direction (Laclau and Mouffe, 1985; Howarth and Stavrakakis, 2000). In Chapter 7 of this volume, Ngai-Ling Sum and Bob Jessop take an alternative path, advancing neo-Gramscian theory in the elaboration of the strategic relational state, which they supplement with the insights of cultural political economy. By contrast, in our approach, the concept of hegemony is intimately connected to the operation of political logics, whose role is to cast light on the institution, contestation, and transformation of policy regimes and practices.

In developing our poststructuralist interpretation of Gramsci, we begin by delineating two aspects of the concept of hegemony, which we argue are vital in developing a viable approach to critical policy analysis (Howarth, 2009). First, hegemony is a type of rule or governance, which captures the way in which a regime, practice or policy actively or passively *holds sway* over a set of subjects by a particular entwining of consent, compliance and coercion. Second, hegemony is a practice of politics that involves the linking together of disparate demands to forge projects or 'discourse coalitions' (to use Hajer's (1995) phrase), which can actively *contest* a particular form of rule, practice or policy. These practices presuppose the existence of antagonisms and the presence of 'floating signifiers' that can be articulated by rival political forces in the struggle for power. In the context of policy change, let us turn first to this latter dimension of hegemony.

Hegemony as a practice of politics highlights the linking together of different demands and identities in efforts to challenge and even replace a given practice or social order (Howarth, 2009). Here hegemony is a type of political relation or practice that involves the drawing of equivalences between disparate elements via the construction of political frontiers that divide social fields into opposed camps. An alliance, in other words, is an identity that is partially stabilized as the differences within it are superseded in importance by what it shares in common with respect to an opposing force. The identities that compose such equivalential chains are, moreover, modified by this practice. For example, local campaigns to oppose particular airport expansions can be linked together into a broader political formation, which in turn may also be linked to wider adjacent social demands, such as environmental protection or planning reforms, by finding points of equivalence amongst these struggles. In this case, the very identities of local struggles will be modified to reflect their more universal character, whilst the content of the new demand will be given by a more general opposition to a government's overall national policy of airport expansion, and/or to its environmental consequences (Griggs and Howarth, 2013).

In terms of rhetorical tropes, this aspect of hegemony foregrounds the metonymical, or contiguous, dimension of political practices: the way in which a particular group or movement located in a particular sphere begins to take responsibility for tasks and activities in adjacent or connected spheres of social relations, thus seeking to hegemonize such demands (Howarth, 2009). Yet this emphasis on the metonymic does not preclude the metaphorical dimension of sameness or similarity. On the contrary, metaphor is essential because, if a group is to successfully hegemonize the demands and identity of others, it must create analogical relations – forms of resemblance – between such demands, whilst articulating empty signifiers that can partially fix or condense such demands into a more universal (if ultimately precarious) unity. As we shall argue below, the metaphorical dimension produces empty signifiers able to hold together differences by successfully establishing a contingent identity that draws frontiers against and excludes the other. Here again metaphorically accentuated difference will begin to assume a more universal function.

In our terms, therefore, the construction of political projects depends, on the one hand, on the capacities of policy actors or entrepreneurs to cover over the differences that exist between themselves and others in any policy subsystem. Policy actors will forge popular demands which construct equivalential linkages between previously dispersed social and political demands as they attempt to integrate hostile opponents into discourse coalitions through the negation of existing antagonisms. In fact, in order for social actors to succeed in hegemonizing different groups and sectors around their plans and projects, they have to universalize their narrow sectional demands and values, thus providing the symbolic means to unify other identities in a common political project. The construction of these equivalential chains requires the production of empty signifiers, a means of representation that can serve as points of subjective identification to hold together a diverse set of agencies in a precarious and contingent unity (see Howarth, 1997, 2000, 2013; Laclau, 1995).

Yet, on the other hand, the successful constitution of political projects or discourse coalitions will require not only the erasure of difference, but also the differentiation of the project from something other than itself.

This is accomplished through acts of exclusion and the production of a 'constitutive outside' (Laclau, 2005: 69–71). Exclusions of this nature are in our view predicated upon the negation of a common 'other,' such as the shared 'enemy' of a rival state or a stigmatized social group. Empty signifiers are thus understood as a means of representation, which enables the articulation of internal differences, whilst simultaneously showing the limits of a group's identity, and its dependence on the opposition to other groups (see Howarth, 1995, 2000). Depending on a common opposition to other groups and forces, policy practices or regimes of practices are thus inherently exclusionary, as individual actors are obliged to draw boundaries between different social groups and their demands.

Returning to the first dimension of hegemony as a form of rule leads us to question the way in which subjects accept and conform to a particular regime, practice or policy, even though they may have previously resisted or opposed it (Howarth, 2009). Of particular significance here are what have been termed logics of difference in which rival chains of demands are disarticulated, incorporated into existing regimes, or negated (Laclau and Mouffe, 1985). Each concrete form of governance in our picture thus consists of different mixtures of force and consent, but the rhetorical dimension of a hegemonic relation is the same: a particular set of demands and values comes to function as universal arguments about demands and values, thus representing a concrete 'totality' or order that exceeds them (Laclau, 2005: 72). Expressed in rhetorical terms, such a relation is best captured by the figure of synecdoche, whereby a part represents the whole. The relation between part and whole thus furnishes an important means to conceptualize the hegemonic relation within policy regimes, though a thorough empirical analysis will also require an account of the identifications and attachments through which subjects are gripped by such regimes and practices (as we discuss in the next section).

In exploring hegemony as a form of rule, it is possible for poststructuralists to borrow from Foucault's concept of governmentality as a means of characterizing and critically evaluating the social practices of policy regimes. Within this perspective, government is analysed in terms of the 'different modalities and possible ways that exist for guiding men, directing their conduct, constraining their actions and reactions, and so on' (Foucault, 2008: 1–2, cited in Howarth, 2013: 222). Turning our attention to the multiple technologies, instruments, rationalities and forms of knowledge through which government intervenes in society and the economy, this approach recognizes that government undertakes 'critical educative functions that shape cultural and social practices, though they in turn are "educated" and shaped by practices in other fields' (Howarth, 2013: 222). Typically, Swyngedouw (2005, 2010) thus argues

that in the field of urban politics the dialogical form of consensus formation, which has come to characterize governance practices, represents
a new 'Janus-faced' autocratic form of governmentality that, through
the technologies of self-management/self-responsibility and participation,
suggests empowerment but invokes particular forms of behaviour and
types of instruments that are fundamental to the strengthening of top-
down neoliberalism, whilst fuelling antagonisms but denying legitimate
channels for their expression (see also Mouffe, 2000, 2005).

THE AFFECTIVE DIMENSION OF POLICY PRACTICES

Whilst recognizing the hegemonic struggles that constitute actors, we have
said little about why and how they are gripped by, or fail to be attached
to, particular policies. We address this question by turning to the affective
dimension of actors' engagements in policy practices and by considering
the related notion of lack. Here we argue that an adequate approach to
critical policy studies must also take into consideration the unconscious
and affective investments of subjects in certain rhetorical devices, signifiers and images. For example, governance networks are 'communities that
narrate themselves into existence', with the emplotment of specific narratives binding actors into a 'coherent whole' (Lejano et al., 2013: 47). In
other words, the specific 'plot' of a narrative accounts for 'what is special,
motivational, compelling and affective about it' (Lejano et al., 2013: 40).
In fact, it is in this context that the Lacanian logic of fantasy, which has
been developed by theorists such as Slavoj Žižek, can focus our attention
on the enjoyment subjects procure from their identifications with certain
signifiers and figures or, in other words, certain fantasmatic narratives.

It is important to stress that fantasy is not an ideological illusion or a
form of false consciousness that comes between a subject and social reality
(e.g. Žižek, 1989). On the contrary, in this approach, fantasies partly
organize our perceptions of reality and structure our understanding of
social relations by covering over their radical contingency. Social relations
thus appear to subjects as natural and sedimented. Indeed, one of the indicators of the 'success' of a fantasy is its invisibility: the fact that it supports
social reality *without* our being conscious of it. On the other hand, the visibility of fantasmatic figures and devices – their disclosure and appearance
as fantasies – means that they cease to function properly in this regard. Of
course, there are different ways to come to terms with social fantasies and
their grip, ranging from their repression to their traversal.

The logic of fantasy thus operates to bring a form of ideological closure to the radical contingency of social relations, and to naturalize the different relations of domination within which a subject is enmeshed. It does this through a fantasmatic narrative or discourse that promises a fullness-to-come once a named or implied obstacle is overcome – the beatific dimension of fantasy – or which foretells of disaster if the obstacle proves insurmountable, which might be termed the horrific dimension of fantasy, though in any particular instance the two work hand-in-hand (Stavrakakis, 1999: 108–9, 2007). The beatific side, as Žižek puts it, has 'a *stabilizing* dimension, which is governed by the dream of a state without disturbances, out of reach of human depravity', whilst the horrific aspect possesses 'a *destabilizing* dimension', where the Other – a 'Jewish plot' or the lazy/overzealous immigrant – is presented as a threatening or irritating force that must be rooted out or destroyed (Žižek, 1998: 192). On the whole, then, fantasmatic logics capture the various way subjects organize their enjoyment by binding themselves to particular objects and representations so as 'to resolve some fundamental antagonism' (Žižek, 1997: 11).

The role of subjective desire and attachment adds further elements to the conceptual grammar of poststructuralist perspectives on how regimes of policy practices come into being and are reproduced over time. They provide the means to explore the way in which identities are stabilized and given direction, as well as the moments when such identifications begin to lose their adhesion or fail to resonate at all. Indeed, in our perspective, the critical assessment of policy practices rests on the discernment and description of those political and fantasmatic logics that enable us to show the contingency and undecidability of particular social relations and structures.

ARTICULATING IDEAS AND INTERESTS

The affective dimension of our analysis focuses attention on the way subjects are gripped by certain policy discourses as well as the identities which are constructed and come into play within the policy process. However, the importance of subjective identities also needs to be connected to the role of ideas and interests, so we shall now say a few words about how we can articulate such elements in an alternative account of policy change (for a fuller explanation, see Howarth, 2013). The role of novel ideas is important because they can help to dissolve existing coalitions and accepted patterns of policy-making, whilst inspiring social movements and groups seeking to bring about social and policy change. Indeed, we should also stress the importance of knowledge and scientific expertise in shaping policy debate, by often providing important ammunition for the forces engaged in shaping policy. In our view, especially in the world of politics and policy-making, therefore, ideas are often complex configurations that consist of multiple components, which can be interpreted and constructed in competing ways. Expressed more theoretically, they are best conceptualized as floating signifiers or contingent elements, whose meanings and political import depend on their articulation into various discourses via the operation of hegemonic practices.

However, despite various misconceptions about poststructuralist policy analysis, we also emphasize the role of interests. Interests are important in motivating actors, organizing alliances and channelling demands into political actions, but they are not given, nor are they unchanging. To begin with, it is important to stress that interests are always relative to historically positioned agents with sedimented forms of identity. As we have elaborated, poststructuralist theories of discourse, such as those developed by Michel Foucault, Ernesto Laclau and Chantal Mouffe, provide an important starting point for rethinking the concepts of identity and interest, and their interconnectedness (Foucault, 1972; Laclau and Mouffe, 1985). In these approaches, identities are contingent constructs, which are the products of social and political identifications with the roles and subject positions made available by historically produced discourses (Howarth, 2000). Typically, for instance, a prospective direct action protester might identify with the role of a 'radical environmentalist' or an 'eco-warrior', which has emerged as a specific subject position in contemporary environmental movements and their discourses. This subject position provides a place from which an individual can speak and act.

But even more strongly, the role of radical agency or subjectivity is to constitute these very points of identification, when in conditions where the dislocatory character of social structures is rendered visible, subjects are compelled to act or decide in a 'foundational fashion'. Identities are thus strategic constructs, but they are social constructions that are always more or less sedimented in any particular conjuncture. Varying degrees of sedimentation make possible the production of new identities, but do not allow all and every possible form of identification to be actualized. An important condition for the emergence of new identities, as we discuss above, is the dislocation of existing discursive structures and the identities they confer. In a situation where identities are threatened – the building of a new runway in a rural area for example – social actors may need to reconstruct and redefine their identities to deal with this new situation, and it is precisely in this context that new forms of political agency are likely to arise, as subjects construct and identify newly constructed and available discourses. Indeed, such conditions bring to the fore the role of agency and individual agents in bringing about policy change.

To define and constitute interests is thus a political project in two senses.

On the one hand, interests cannot be assumed to pre-exist social agents (whether as subjective preferences, or as real entities that are imputed on to agents by external observers), nor can they be assumed to exhibit a content that is wholly objective, in the sense that they are 'concerned with the matters of the world of things in which men move, which physically lies between them and out of which arise their specific, objective, worldly interests' (Arendt, 1958: 182). Instead, they are constructed politically and discursively via hegemonic projects; or, to put it in Arendt's terms, 'interests constitute, in the word's most literal significance, something which inter-est, which lies between people and therefore can relate and bind them together' (Arendt, 1958: 182). On the other hand, agents themselves are historical and political products whose identities are contingent upon their relation to other identities. It may seem obvious, then, but interests are always the interests of particular agents – and both the identities and the interests that are relative to them can never be assumed, but are contingent outcomes constituted through strategic relationships.

In short, interests are not reducible to unchanging sets of preferences, which can be simply attributed to social actors, or read-off underlying social structures. They are better understood as politically constructed guides to action and practice, which are contingent, contested and forged in practice. Interests are thus connected to social subjects and their identities, and the latter are related to the ideas and signifiers with which subjects identify in moments of dislocation, and to which they are attached. Identities and social structures are incomplete; they consist of multiple elements that can be rearranged and composed. In our perspective, these elements are linked through articulatory and hegemonic practices, and explained via our logics of critical explanation. Critical in this regard is the making and breaking of projects or discourse coalitions. Here the immediate focus is to explore the intersecting logics of equivalence and difference to characterize and explain the coupling or decoupling of heterogeneous social demands. But this focus also involves important rhetorical and strategic operations, in which social agents constitute the identities and interests of particular social subjects in historical contexts by reframing and redescribing social phenomena using various tropes and figures.

CONCLUSIONS

In this contribution, we have argued that most mainstream explanations of policy change have rested upon and provoked a series of perennial stand-offs. In response, predominant perspectives within policy analysis have at times tended to advocate 'multiple lens' approaches, which undertake different readings of the same case so as to offer a rounded explanation (Cairney, 2007: 46). Alternatively, the emphasis has been on the development of synthetic approaches, which attempt to integrate the insights from 'institutions, networks, socio-economic processes, choices and ideas' (John, 2003: 487). Indeed, some advocates of the synthetic approach have sought to combine the insights from the advocacy coalition, multiple streams, and punctuated equilibrium perspectives (Nowlin, 2011). In contrast, this chapter has sought to demonstrate how poststructuralist discourse theory offers an alternative articulation or synthesis of the role of ideas, interests, agency and structures in accounts of policy change.

In so doing, our approach positions politics and power at the heart of critical explanations of policy change and stability. Theoretically, through a novel reworking of the concept of hegemony, the recognition of the constitutive character of rhetoric, and an emphasis on the affective dimension of the Lacanian category of fantasy, we have sought to re-articulate the relationship between ideas and interests, whilst offering an innovative explanation for agency and institutions in the transformation, stabilization and reproduction of policies in particular historical contexts. Importantly, we have challenged misguided claims that poststructuralism ignores interests, offering instead an understanding of interests as politically constructed guides to action and practice, which are contingent, contested and forged in practice. We have also suggested how we might move beyond negative critique to the generation of positive alternatives for change. Indeed, the practice of critique can be tied to the discernment of political and fantasmatic logics, for their articulation foregrounds the contingency and undecidability of social relations and structures.

It is with this emphasis on the complexity of the different elements that need to be brought together in order to explain policy change that we hope to contribute to the field of critical policy studies and to trigger debates as to how we might begin to grasp and render comprehensible the 'messiness' of the policy process and the practices of policy-makers.

NOTE

1. This chapter draws upon and restates some of the arguments that we have advanced elsewhere, notably in our research monograph, *The Politics of Airport Expansion in the United Kingdom* (2013, Manchester University Press), and our contribution, 'Poststructuralist Policy Analysis: Discourse, Hegemony and Critical Explanation', in F. Fischer and H. Gottweis (eds), *The Argumentative Turn Revisited* (2012, Duke University Press).

REFERENCES

Arendt, Hannah (1958), *The Human Condition*, Chicago, IL: University of Chicago Press.
Bevir, Mark (2004), 'Governance and Interpretation: What are the Implications of Postfoundationalism?', *Public Administration* **82** (3), 605–25.
Cairney, Paul (2007), 'A "Multiple Lenses" Approach to Policy Change: The Case of Tobacco Policy in the UK', *British Politics* **2**, 45–68.
Derrida, Jacques (1978), *Writing and Difference*, trans. A. Bass, London: Routledge.
Derrida, Jacques (1982), *Margins of Philosophy*, Brighton: Harvester Press.
Dryzek, John (1997), *The Politics of the Earth*, Oxford: Oxford University Press.
Foucault, Michel (1972), *The Archaeology of Knowledge*, London: Tavistock.
Foucault, Michel (1981), 'The Order of Discourse', in Robert Young (ed.), *Untying the Text*, London: Routledge, pp. 48–79.
Foucault, Michel (1984), 'Nietzsche, Genealogy, History', in Paul Rabinow (ed.), *The Foucault Reader*, Harmondsworth: Penguin Books, pp. 76–100.
Foucault, Michel (2008), *The Birth of Biopolitics*, edited by Michel Senellart, Basingstoke: Palgrave Macmillan.
Gottweis, Herbert (2003), 'Theoretical Strategies of Poststructuralist Policy Analysis: Towards an Analytics of Government', in M. Hajer and H. Wagenaar (eds), *Deliberative Policy Analysis: Understanding Governance in the Network Society*, Cambridge: Cambridge University Press, pp. 247–65.
Gramsci, Antonio (1971), *Selections from the Prison Notebooks*, trans. Q. Hoare and G. Nowell Smith, New York: International Publishers.
Griggs, Steven and David Howarth (2002), 'The Work of Ideas and Interests in Public Policy', in Alan Finlayson and Jeremy Valentine (eds), *Politics and Post-Structuralism: An Introduction*, Edinburgh: Edinburgh University Press, pp. 97–112.
Griggs, Steven and David Howarth (2004), 'A Transformative Political Campaign? The New Rhetoric of Protest Against Airport Expansion in the UK', *Journal of Political Ideologies* **9** (2), 167–87.
Griggs, Steven and David Howarth (2013), *The Politics of Airport Expansion in the United Kingdom: Hegemony, Policy and the Rhetoric of 'Sustainable Aviation'*, Manchester: Manchester University Press.
Hajer, Maarten, A. (1995), *The Politics of Environmental Discourse: Ecological Modernisation and the Policy Process*, Oxford: Oxford University Press.
Hood, Christopher (1994), *Explaining Economic Policy Reversals*, Buckingham: Open University Press.
Howarth, David (1995), 'Discourse Theory', in D. Marsh and G. Stoker (eds), *Theory and Methods in Political Science*, London: Macmillan, pp. 115–33.
Howarth, David (1997), 'Complexities of Identity/Difference', *Journal of Political Ideologies* **2** (1), 51–78.
Howarth, David (2000), *Discourse*, Buckingham: Open University Press.
Howarth, David (2009), 'Discourse, Power and Policy: Articulating a Hegemony Approach to Critical Policy Studies', *Critical Policy Studies* **3** (3/4), 309–35.
Howarth, David (2013), *Poststructuralism and After. Structure, Subjectivity and Power*, Basingstoke: Palgrave Macmillan.
Howarth, David and Steven Griggs (2012), 'Poststructuralist Policy Analysis: Discourse, Hegemony and Critical Explanation', in Frank Fischer and Herbert Gottweis (eds), *The Argumentative Turn Revisited: Public Policy as Communicative Practice*, Durham, NC: Duke University Press, pp. 305–43.
Howarth, David and Yannis Stavrakakis (2000), 'Introducing Discourse Theory and Political Analysis', in David Howarth, Aletta J. Norval and Yannis Stavrakakis (eds), *Discourse Theory and Political Analysis*, Manchester: Manchester University Press, pp. 1–23.
John, Peter (2003), 'Is There Life After Policy Streams, Advocacy Coalitions and Punctuations: Using Evolutionary Theory to Explain Policy Change?', *Policy Studies Journal* **31** (4), 481–98.

Lacan, Jacques (2006), *Écrits*, New York: W.W. Norton.
Laclau, Ernesto (1990), *New Reflections on the Revolution of Our Time*, London: Verso.
Laclau, Ernesto (1995), 'Why do Empty Signifiers Matter to Politics?', in Jeffrey Weeks (ed.), *The Greater Evil and the Lesser Good*, London: River Oram, pp. 168–77.
Laclau, Ernesto (2005), *On Populist Reason*, London: Verso.
Laclau, Ernesto and Chantal Mouffe (1985), *Hegemony and Socialist Strategy: Towards a Radical Democratic Politics*, London: Verso.
Laclau, Ernesto and Chantal Mouffe (2001), *Hegemony and Socialist Strategy: Towards a Radical Democratic Politics*, 2nd edition, London: Verso.
Lejano, Raul, Mrill Ingram and Helen Ingram (2013), *The Power of Narrative in Environmental Networks*, Cambridge, MA: MIT Press.
Mouffe, Chantal (2000), *The Democratic Paradox*, London: Verso.
Mouffe, Chantal (2005), *On the Political*, London: Routledge.
Nowlin, Matthew C. (2011), 'Theories of the Policy Process: State of the Research and Emerging Trends', *Policy Studies Journal* **39** (s1), 41–60.
Saussure, Ferdinand de (1983), *Course in General Linguistics*, London: Duckworth.
Stavrakakis, Yannis (1999), *Lacan and the Political*, London: Routledge.
Stavrakakis, Yannis (2007), *The Lacanian Left*, Edinburgh: Edinburgh University Press.
Swyngedouw, Erik (2005), 'Governance Innovation and the Citizen: The Janus Face of Governance-beyond-the-State', *Urban Studies* **42** (11), 1991–2006.
Swyngedouw, Erik (2010), 'Apocalypse Forever? Post-political Populism and the Spectre of Climate Change', *Theory, Culture and Society* **27** (2–3), 213–32.
Žižek, Slavoj (1989), *The Sublime Object of Ideology*, London: Verso.
Žižek, Slavoj (1997), *Plague of Fantasies*, London: Verso.
Žižek, Slavoj (1998), 'The Seven Veils of Fantasy', in Dany Nobus (ed.), *Key Concepts of Lacanian Psychoanalysis*, London: Rebus Press, pp. 190–218.

7   Cultural political economy and critical policy studies: developing a critique of domination
Ngai-Ling Sum and Bob Jessop

Cultural political economy (CPE) is one among several recent approaches that explore the interconnected semiotic and structural aspects of social life.[1] It differs from other such paradigms in combining critical, historically sensitive, semiotic analyses with concepts from heterodox evolutionary and institutional political economy. It aims to overcome the compart-mentalized analysis of semiosis/culture and structuration/institutions by integrating semiosis into political economy and applying evolutionary and institutional analyses to semiosis. This has important implications for understanding the limits of constructivist and structuralist analyses; the relations among polity, politics, and policy; lived experience and lesson-drawing; and specific fields of public policy. We explore some of these issues below.

CPE AS GRAND THEORY AND EMPIRICAL ANALYSIS

Among approaches to policy analysis, CPE belongs in the camp of 'grand theories' insofar as it offers (1) a preliminary set of basic and sensitizing con-cepts and positive guidelines that are (2) relevant to historical description, hermeneutic interpretation, and causal explanation, (3) applicable to differ-ent scales of analysis without seeking to unify the micro-, meso- and macro-levels (however defined) within a single system, and that (4) recognize the importance of evolutionary mechanisms and contingent effects, without assuming these always have progressive and/or irreversible effects.

CPE has six features that, together, distinguish it from other approaches that aim to combine semiosis and political economy.

1. Its grounding of the cultural (or semiotic) turn in political economy (and beyond) in the existential necessity of complexity reduction.
2. Its emphasis on the role of evolutionary mechanisms in shaping the movement from social *construal* to social *construction* and their

implications for the production and reproduction of domination and hegemony.

3. Its concern with the interdependence and co-evolution of the semiotic and extra-semiotic and the diverse ways in this co-evolution is mediated.

4. Its integration of individual, organizational, and societal learning in response to 'problems' or 'crises' into the dialectic of semiosis and structuration and, by extension, of path-shaping and path-dependency.

5. The significance of four modes of strategic selectivity: structural, discursive, (Foucauldian) technological, and agential in the consolidation and contestation of domination and hegemony.

6. Its de-naturalization of economic and political imaginaries and their role in guiding strategies and policies and, hence, the role of CPE in advancing critical policy studies and the critique of ideology and forms of domination.

While CPE draws on various theoretical and empirical approaches for each aspect, it aims to produce a coherent account that avoids eclecticism. Moreover, to translate its 'grand theoretical' ambitions into empirical analyses, CPE makes two further theoretical and methodological steps. It draws strategically on critical discourse analysis and similar analytical methods in order to study semiosis and connect its arguments to various cultural turns; and it adopts appropriately scaled concepts from heterodox economic and political analysis to locate its enquiries in the field of political economy. Together these facilitate the critical 'attitude of mind' essential to developing critical policy studies.

CPE posits that the world is too complex to be grasped in all its complexity in real time (or ever) and that not all permutations of social relations can be realized in a given time-space. However, rather than seeking to theorize or model complexity as such (which, paradoxically, always involves complexity reduction), it explores how actors seek to reduce complexity (without thereby mastering it) through their efforts at sense- and meaning-making and setting limits to compossible social relations. We refer to the first as semiosis, the latter as structuration.

Sense-making refers to the cognitive, normative, or appreciative *apprehension of the natural and social world* and highlights the referential value of semiosis, even if this reference is to as yet unrealized possibilities, immaterial or virtual entities, or inexistent but culturally recognized entities (such as the Devil or 'Mr Market'). Reference to such 'irreal' possibilities is especially important for the pursuit of politics as the art of the possible, policy entrepreneurship, and policy-making as well as efforts to explain (away) policy failures. *Meaning-making* refers to processes of signification and meaningful communication, and includes non-linguistic (e.g., visual images) as well as linguistic modes thereof. Such practices not only reduce complexity for actors (and observers) but may also help to *constitute* as well as *construe* the natural and social worlds insofar as they guide a critical mass of self-confirming actions based on more or less correct diagnoses of unrealized potentials (on construal vs. construction, see Sayer 2000: 90–93). Construals thereby acquire 'material force', that is, have durable transformative effects in the world.

Structuration (or structure-building) sets limits (however achieved) on the articulation of social relations such that 'not everything that is *possible* is *compossible*'. For, in contrast to the immense variety of individual *elements* of a social formation that could occur at a given point in space-time when each is considered in isolation, there is a much smaller number of sets of elements that can be combined as articulated *moments* of relatively coherent and reproducible structures. There are many efforts at many scales to structure social relations and most fail to a greater or lesser extent. Moreover, if structural coherence and a strategic line do emerge, even in a partial, unstable way, this cannot be attributed to a single master subject but results from the contingent interaction of many factors (cf. Foucault 2008).

Because a complex world cannot be grasped in all its complexity, individuals, social movements, organizations, and institutions are forced to rely, wittingly or not, on specific social imaginaries that provide entry-points and standpoints for their social practices and projects. In this regard, the authors' previous work has focused largely, but not exclusively, on various economic imaginaries (e.g., Jessop 2004, 2009, 2012; Sum 2009, 2010; Sum and Jessop 2013). These involve more or less extensive construals of the boundaries, scope, forms, substance, and dynamics of the economic field and are often articulated to, or embedded in, other socially constructed sense- and meaning-making perspectives on the natural and social worlds, such as ecological, spatial, temporal, gendered, national, scientific, and religious worldviews, ideational systems, and discourses. Nonetheless, economic imaginaries comprise only one set of possible entry-points and standpoints regarding complexity reduction and are by no means the most suitable analytical starting point for critical policy analysis, let alone for all perceived circumstances and challenges arising in the wider world. To be sure, they are directly pertinent to economic policy and indirectly so to a wide range of economically relevant policies, especially where this relevance is acknowledged – as in debates about welfare and workfare, education and competitiveness, regional planning and uneven development, immigration and the 'war for talents', and so on. But this does not imply that other types of imaginary are irrelevant to the policy field (let alone more generally). A simple classification of actors involved in policy debates, formation, implementation, and contestation would suffice to indicate the importance of other types of imaginary. And, of course, political imaginaries of various kinds are crucial to the demarcation of the polity, the conduct of politics, and the design and implementation of policies. In this sense, the concepts and methods of cultural political economy have a much broader relevance than economic imaginaries and the critique of political economy.

We note in passing that a major inspiration for the elaboration of CPE comes from Antonio Gramsci's 'philosophy of praxis'. He avoided one-sided temptations and, in more or less equal measure, developed: (1) a philological (linguistic, semiotic, or discursive) interest in the *constitutive role of ideation*, ranging from abstract ideas to common sense and folklore; (2) a critical (and dialectical) interest in the *materiality and causal efficacy of social relations*; and (3) the *mutual conditioning, reciprocal action, and co-evolution of ideation and structuration*. Gramsci's innovative work has clear implications for *critical* policy studies (see Addendum below).

BEYOND DISCURSIVE INSTITUTIONALISM

Knowledgeable readers may have noted an affinity between CPE and the 'fourth institutionalism', namely, the rather heterogeneous set of constructivist, discursive or ideational variants of institutionalism. These claim that ideas mediate institutional effects; that institutions filter the role of discourses; and/or that they reflect, embody, or reproduce particular social imaginaries, discursive practices, and projects. In making the case for the 'newest "new institutionalism"', Vivien Schmidt argues that it:

> . . . lends insight into the role of ideas and discourse in politics while providing a more dynamic approach to institutional change than the older three new institutionalisms. Ideas are the substantive content of discourse. They exist at three levels – policies, programs, and philosophies – and can be categorized into two types, cognitive and normative. Discourse is the interactive process of conveying ideas. It comes in two forms: the coordinative discourse among policy actors and the communicative discourse between political actors and the public . . . The institutions [posited by] discursive institutionalism, moreover, are not external-rule-following structures but rather are simultaneously structures and constructs internal to agents whose 'background ideational abilities' within a given 'meaning context' explain how institutions are created and exist and whose 'foreground discursive abilities,' following a 'logic of communication,' explain how institutions change or persist. Interests are subjective ideas, which, though real, are neither objective nor material. Norms are dynamic,

intersubjective constructs rather than static structures. (Schmidt 2008: 303; cf. Schmidt 2012: 85–88)

This constructivist, discursive, or ideational research agenda includes: (1) the timing and speed of changes in ideas and discourses, theoretical and policy paradigms, political traditions, and broad philosophical outlooks; (2) different actors' 'background ideational abilities' – in our terms, sense- and meaning-making abilities – and 'foreground discursive abilities', which shape construals and construction; (3) the benefits of taking everyday experience or more abstract models of reality as an analytical entry-point; and (4) the influence of elite discourse coalitions and social movements in communicating and/or coordinating responses to discursively framed problems (Schmidt 2012: 88–108; see also Béland and Cox 2011).

Such themes are also part of the emerging CPE agenda. However, in contrast to the more open-textured, middle-range analyses offered by the rich and still-expanding body of work inspired by 'discursive institutionalism' *sensu latissimo*, CPE has a more explicit meta-theoretical framework and aims to put both semiotic and institutional analysis in their place within a broader critique of political economy. In particular, it builds directly on the heterodox critique of the political economy of capitalist social formations and deploys many concepts from this theoretical tradition, developing and re-specifying them in the light of the broader CPE agenda. Thus the two approaches have different strengths and our task in this chapter is to make a nuanced case for those of CPE.

CPE AND THE CRITIQUE OF POLITICAL ECONOMY

CPE was developed as a means of navigating between a purely constructivist approach that one-sidedly explores the power of discourse, ideation, and signification and a rigid structuralism that focuses one-sidedly on structural constraints, 'iron laws', and functional imperatives. Thus it regards semiosis and structuration as the principal modes through which social agents reduce complexity in order to 'go on' in the world and, on this basis, it explores possible disjunctions as well as complementarities between sense- and meaning-making and efforts to structure social relations. This requires sufficiently rich and elaborate concepts for both moments of complexity reduction combined with extensive work to make these concepts commensurable, without conflating them (for details, see Sum and Jessop 2013). This chapter is not the proper place to introduce the concepts that we use to develop our critique of market-oriented, profit-oriented accumulation as a defining feature of contemporary capitalist societies – especially as the overall focus of the *Handbook* is critical policy studies. So we will now introduce a key concept that has emerged from our work in CPE that bears more directly on this more restricted field of enquiry but can also be linked to wider issues.

This concept is the *dispositive*. This is not just an alternative *name* for institution, which would enable its absorption into mainstream and discursive institutionalisms. Rather, it is used *critically* to disclose how heterogeneous sets of instituted social practices (including their discursive as well as 'material' aspects) instantiate, reflect, and refract power relations. Dispositives are contingent 'discursive–material' fixes that emerge in response to specific (and specifically problematized) challenges to social order (with a referent in the 'real world') and that thereby create a strategic imperative to address and, if possible, solve the challenge. Drawing on the relevant Foucault-inspired literature, we suggest the following definition. A dispositive is a contingent, strategically-selective, problem-oriented assemblage that comprises: (1) a dispersed apparatus, comprising institutions, organizations, and networks; (2) an order of discourse, with corresponding thematizations and objectivations; (3) diverse devices and technologies involved in producing various forms of power/ knowledge that contribute to the realization of the strategic imperative; and (4) subject positions and subjectivation. In short, dispositive analysis focuses on how institutions aid the provisional stabilization (institutionalization) of patterns of domination and it provides a fruitful conceptual framework for a critical exploration of policy dynamics.

When examining dispositives, we can ask, with Foucault, how discursive tactics and strategies are generalized to create a specific strategic logic as a condition of effective action in response to an urgent problem; and, conversely but reciprocally, how a heterogeneous ensemble of diverse [structural] elements are articulated into an apparatus that supports a specific strategic logic. This is a complex process. The emerging general strategic line depends on the path-dependent contexts in which a dispositive is assembled; in turn, a dispositive emerges from the intersection of different, potentially path-shaping strategic lines. It is a response to urgent problems and, hence, involves not only discursive practices but also wider social practices developed to resolve the problem as interpreted and re-interpreted over time. In addressing dispositivization, CPE follows Foucault in scaling up the microphysics of power to macro-level questions of political economy and the state (2008: 186) and combines this with Gramscian interests in the forms and mechanisms of hegemony, passive revolution, and domination. At stake is how micro-technologies get assembled and articulated to form more encompassing and enduring sets of social relations that are embedded in everyday life but also provide the substratum of institutional orders and, in some cases, even broader patterns of social domination.

One approach to analysing the assembling and consolidation of dispositives in response to specific 'problematizations' is to study this evolutionary process in terms of the interaction of different modes of variation, selection, and retention. In addition to the semiotic and structural moments that provide the two principal alternative starting points of CPE analyses, there are two cross-cutting modes of selectivity: technological and agential. All four involve different modalities of variation, selection, and retention and their differential articulation, when condensed into diverse fixes or dispositives, shapes both the semiotic and 'material' moments of the dynamic of social relations. We now briefly introduce each mode.

Structural selectivity denotes the asymmetrical configuration of constraints and opportunities on social forces as they pursue particular projects. It exists only insofar as it is reproduced through social practices and can be transformed through time, through cumulative molecular changes and/or more deliberate attempts to transform the pattern of constraints and opportunities.

Discursive selectivity is also asymmetrical thanks to the constraints and opportunities inscribed in particular forms of discourse in terms of what can be enunciated, who is authorized to enunciate, and how enunciations enter more encompassing discursive fields. Semiotic resources set limits to what can be imagined, whether in terms of 'objects', possible statements within a discursive formation, themes that can be articulated within a given semantic field, or subject positions that can be adopted. A related set of selectivities concerns the extent and grounds that make some discursive forms more or less accessible to some agents rather than others because of their sense- and meaning-making competence (Schmidt's 'background ideational abilities') and/or their discursive competence (Schmidt's 'foreground discursive abilities'). This holds both for everyday interactions and for socialization into specialized discourses (e.g., law, medicine, and engineering). Regarding spatio-temporal selectivities, languages have different ways of expressing temporality and spatiality, privileging some spatio-temporal horizons over others and allowing for greater or lesser anticipation of as yet unrealized possibilities. Together, these aspects of discursive selectivity frame and filter specific appeals, arguments, recontextualizations, claims, and legitimations, making some more resonant than others. Discursive selectivity is not purely discursive, however; it has other moments too. For example, the asymmetries inscribed in a repertoire of discursive possibilities are overdetermined by the media of communication used in enunciations (its technological mediation and the biases these contain) and by the linguistic and communicative competences of particular agents (its agential mediation).

Technological selectivities have two referents. They can denote the selectivities entailed in material and intellectual forces of production and their associated technical and social relations of production. They can also denote the social technologies involved in constituting objects, creating subject positions and recruiting subjects, and, in particular, creating relations of power/knowledge and enabling governmentalization. The second referent involves the Foucauldian technologies of discipline, normalization, and governmentality and their role in power/knowledge relations, the governance of conduct, mediated through specific instruments of classification, registration, calculation, and so on. These technologies condition the production of hegemony and its sub-hegemonic or counter-hegemonic alternatives.

Agential selectivities refer to the capacities of specific social agents (or sets of agents) to 'make a difference' in particular conjunctures thanks to their idiosyncratic abilities to exploit structural, discursive, and technological selectivities. These include abilities to: (1) read conjunctures and identify potentials for action; (2) re-politicize sedimented discourses and re-articulate them; (3) invent new social technologies or recombine extant technologies; and (4) deploy strategies and tactics to shift the balance of forces in space-time.

Attention to all four aspects *and* their interaction is required to explain why and how some construals are selected, get embodied/embrained in individual agents or routinized in organizational operations, are facilitated or hindered by specific social technologies and affordances, and become embedded in specific social structures ranging from routine interactions via institutional orders to large-scale social formations. Taking policy formation and implementation as an example, a CPE approach could start from competing policy proposals (variation), consider why some proposals get translated into specific policies (selection), and investigate why some policies succeed and get consolidated (retention). All four modes of selectivity are relevant to such an enquiry.

Given the potential for enormous variation in the construals of social problems (*urgences*) and proposed solutions, CPE scholars explore how some construals and solutions are selected and retained in and through emergent, non-semiotic features of social structure as well as by inherently semiotic factors. This is essential to explain the movement from *construal* to *construction* and, on this basis, to explain the character of the dispositives that get consolidated around specific construals of a social problem and its corresponding set of policy solutions. Many construals and proposed solutions are arbitrary, irrational, and short-lived; but some are more plausible and stand a good chance of being selected. In this regard the plausibility of construals and their associated policy solutions (including taking no action) depends on their resonance (and hence capacity to reinterpret and mobilize) with the key forces able to translate them into policy.

Although many plausible narratives may be advanced, their narrators will not be equally effective in conveying their messages and securing support for the proposed solutions. Powerful resonance does not mean that these construals and solutions should be taken at face value. All narratives are selective, appropriate some arguments, and combine them in specific ways. So we must also consider what goes unstated or silent, repressed or suppressed, in specific discourses. Interpretive power depends on the 'web of interlocution' (Somers 1994) in different fields and its discursive selectivities, the organization and operation of the mass media, the role of intellectuals in public life, and the structural biases and strategically selective operations of various public and private apparatuses of economic, political, and ideological domination. This is mainly an issue of political contestation.

An important distinction here concerns interpretive power and interpretive authority (cf. Heinrich and Jessop 2014). The former refers to differences in the ability of social forces to identify and construe urgent social problems and translate these into policies, successful or not, intended to address, maintain, or transform the world. This is not so much a question of having the best scientific analyses and most persuasive arguments as it is one of having the capacities to act upon a given interpretation, which also involves access to key decision-making structures, the availability of appropriate governmental technologies, and the ability to mobilize sufficient support to make a difference in a particular conjuncture. Interpretive authority is narrower in scope but sometimes more significant in practice. It refers to the legal instance or authority with the legal right to interpret the law in a given juridico-political context and translate that interpretation into policy. This is especially important regarding the right to declare a state of emergency (e.g., military, political, or economic) and authorize exceptional crisis-management measures. More generally, of course, it shows the limits of a purely constructivist approach to policy studies that somehow manages to forget that institutions also matter.

An important CPE hypothesis is that the relative importance of semiosis declines from the stage of variation in policy proposals based on different (policy-relevant) imaginaries through the stage in policy development when they are selectively translated into specific material (policy) practices to the stage when they may become integrated into a strategically codified, structurally coherent, and mutually supportive (or, at least, negatively integrated, non-disruptive) set of dispositives within a given spatio-temporal envelope. Technologies have a key role in the selection and retention of specific imaginaries insofar as they provide reference points not only in meaning-making but also in the coordination of actions within and across specific personal interactions, organizations and networks, and institutional orders. Policies, policy decisions' techniques, policy instruments and policy evaluation are important technologies in this regard because each, in its own way, contributes to the selection and retention of its associated policy discourses, often transforming them at the same time. This is why one must look beyond agenda setting, policy discourses, and policy formulation to examine how policies actually get implemented and with what effects, whether intended or not. Success-failure in this regard also depends on how specific construals correspond to the properties of the 'raw materials' (including social phenomena such as actors and institutions) that provide the target and/or tools of attempts to construct social reality. Finally, the CPE approach posits that the relative weight of semiotic and extra-semiotic mechanisms varies across social fields and, *a fortiori*, policy fields. For example, the scope for semiosis to shape policy would be greater in the long run in fields such as education in the arts and humanities than it would be in infrastructure and technology policy.

It is through the interaction of all four modes of selectivity that particular dispositives and strategic logics are selected and consolidated in the face of contestation and resistance. And exploring this interaction contributes to an ideological critique that exposes the socially constructed nature of dispositives and their integration into patterns of domination and hegemony that legitimize the sectional interests of particular groups at the expense of others. We return to this point in our conclusions.

THEORETICAL PARADIGM, POLICY PARADIGM, AND KNOWLEDGE BRAND

In developing this policy-oriented CPE agenda, it is also useful to distinguish theoretical from policy paradigms. This distinction has been presented as follows: 'Policy paradigms derive from theoretical paradigms but possess much less sophisticated and rigorous evaluations of the intellectual underpinnings of their conceptual frameworks. In essence, policy advisers differentiate policy paradigms from theoretical paradigms by screening out the ambiguities and blurring the fine distinctions characteristic of theoretical paradigms' (Wallis and Dollery 1999: 5).

We might add that policy paradigm shifts are also influenced by intellectual fashion and, often, the latest fads in the business world. Thus, in contrast to the development of normal science and occasional ruptural paradigm shifts in the scientific world, policy paradigms occur more frequently and are subject to other kinds of selectivity (cf. Wallis and Dollery 1999).

Another useful concept is knowledge brand. This indicates how 'knowledge' enters into the assembling of dispositives and their associated forms of strategic calculation, policy formulation and implementation via 'knowledge brands' marketed as patent remedies for solving socially diagnosed problems. A knowledge brand can be defined as a resonant hegemonic meaning-making device advanced in various ways by 'world-class' guru-academic-consultants who claim unique knowledge of a relevant strategic or policy field and pragmatically translate this into policy symbols, recipes, and tool kits that address policy problems and dilemmas at different sites and scales and appeal to pride, threats, and anxieties about social change and major challenges. Knowledge can circulate as a knowledge brand in knowledge-consultancy-policy circuits and, as such, has key roles at multiple sites and scales in meeting the demand for quick fixes and fast policy in an era of space-time compression and acceleration. Knowledge brands are linked to various knowledging technologies and apparatuses (e.g., numbers, standards, programmes, guidelines, scorecards) and other common discursive stratagems (for example, naturalization, inevitabilization, otherization, and nominalization) (Sum 2009, 2010).

There are many complementary, competing and hybridized 'knowledge brands' that have resonance within and/or across different policy fields. Recent examples in the field of political economy are Harvard Business School's Michael Porter, whose approach to competitive advantage has travelled from corporate strategy to the state's role in promoting competitiveness (initially at the national level, then at urban, regional, inner-city, and European scales) and, later, to ethical and/or green competitiveness (cf. Sum 2009, 2010). Another celebrated example is Richard Florida's successful marketing of the 'creative class' in urban regeneration (for an incisive deconstruction and critique, see Peck 2010). A third case is the successful reinvention of Jeffrey Sachs, as he has transited from neo-liberal economist overseeing the post-socialist transition in Russia via various reincarnations to become a progressive evangelist of bottom-up poverty reduction in the Third World (Wilson 2014). While agential selectivities clearly matter in each case, these must also be related to shifts in discursive resonance, structural power, and knowledging technologies. And, of course, as each case vividly shows, the policies adopted on the basis of these knowledge brands are by no means certain to succeed.

A CPE APPROACH TO POLITY, POLITICS, AND POLICY

A basic distinction in political analysis is the three Ps: polity, politics, and policy (Heidenheimer 1986, and, for global politics, Lipschutz 2005). This distinction highlights the ontological depth of the political field and its tangled hierarchies. The constitution of the polity (constitutive politics) has asymmetrical effects on capacities to engage in politics (to influence, as Lasswell (1936) put it, 'who gets what, when, how') and this in turn constrains the range of policies that can feasibly be pursued in specific conjunctures (policy-making as the art of the possible). Yet some policies transform constitutive politics (witness the politicizing role of neo-liberal policies or the politicizing effects of the feminist claim that the personal is political) and reshape political practices (e.g., modifying the balance of forces and stimulating new political claims and movements). All three Ps have semiotic and structural features as well as obvious technological and agential selectivities.

Polity denotes that societal sphere in which political activities occur in contrast with other, non-political spheres, such as religion, the economy, law, education, science, or art. This concept covers the institutional archi-tecture of the political field, including the forms of its separation and modes of boundary-maintenance vis-à-vis non-political spheres, and the asymmetric effects of this architecture on political practice. Key issues include the institutional specificity of the political sphere (its disembed-ding from society and/or its particularization vis-à-vis other institutional orders), the separation of powers, the distinctiveness of political rational-ity and calculation, the structuring of the political field in normal states and exceptional regimes, differences among normal and exceptional politi-cal regimes, and issues of scale (e.g., parish government vs. global govern-ance). The identity of the polity involves material and discursive lines of demarcation between the state *qua* institutional ensemble and other insti-tutional orders or 'civil society'. At stake here is the constitutive moment of politics, i.e., the construction of the political sphere as the reference point for political projects and activities. The 'public-private' distinction is a key, socially-constituted dividing line here but is also problematic (e.g., the claim that the personal is political). Polities are nonetheless articulated to other institutional orders, civil society, and informal social practices. All of these issues are suited to a CPE approach that focuses on political imaginaries and the mechanisms in and through which the polity is demar-cated from society and/or from other spheres and how reproducing this demarcation is crucial to politics and policy (cf. Mitchell 1991).

Politics in turn refers to formally instituted, organized, or informal practices that are directly oriented to, or otherwise shape, the exercise of state power. Whereas the polity provides a rather static, spatial referent, politics comprises an inherently dynamic, open-ended, and heterogeneous ensemble of political practices that are directly oriented to, or otherwise shape, the exercise of state power. Politics can occur within the formal political sphere, on its margins, or well beyond it. The set of activities included within politics ranges from practices concerned to transform the scope of the political sphere, to define the nature and purposes of the state, to modify the institutional integration and operating unity of the state, to exercise direct control over the use of state powers, to shape the form and function of dispositives, to influence the balance of forces inside the state, to block or resist the exercise of state power from 'outside', or to modify the wider balance of forces that shapes politics as the art of the possible. Relevant issues concern: (1) the forms and stakes of normal and/or exceptional politics; (2) the thematization of issues as controversial, negotiable, or consensual; (3) the subjective identity as well as the material and ideal interests of political agents; (4) their location within, on the margins of, or at a distance from the state's institutional architecture; (5) who has the interpretive authority to declare a state of exception or emergency; (6) the positioning of themes in the front- or back-stage of the political scene; and (7) the political conjuncture that delimits feasible political action. All of these issues are implicated in competing political imaginaries and can be studied in terms of the CPE approach outlined here.

Finally, *policy* concerns a wide range of issues: the aims and content of particular decisions and non-decisions in particular policy fields, the appropriate modes and fields of state intervention and non-intervention, the changing responsibilities of different branches and scales of its apparatuses, and the overall strategic line of the state. CPE can illuminate the various modes (discursive, structural, technological, and agential) that are deployed and/or operate unwittingly to place specific policies, policy-making and policy-taking approaches, and detailed policy implementation within the field of open political contention or, conversely, to depoliticize them. Sedimentation is a key mechanism here because it removes many taken-for-granted themes from the political field, from the scope of contentious politics, or from policy considerations. Supplementing this is thematization of some issues as non-political and some policies as non-negotiable. Conversely, and paradoxically, the highlighting of a restricted set of policy choices can also serve as a means of depoliticalization (for further discussion, see Jessop 2014).

A CPE OF LESSON-DRAWING

A fourth feature of CPE, introduced in our opening remarks, is its concern with individual, organizational, and societal learning in response to 'problems' or 'crises'. This is clearly related to dispositivization insofar as dispositives emerge through a trial-and-error process of variation, selection, and retention that involves the social construction of 'urgent problems' (*urgences*) and the search for corresponding solutions. More generally, as a capacity to transform as well as rationalize social relations and structures, *learning* is crucial to social stabilization and transformation. This can be seen in contested efforts at crisis prevention, crisis-management, and crisis resolution and the uneven capacities to shape, impose, or ignore lessons.

In contrast to constructivism, which confines itself to the link between *signum* (sign) and *signans* (signifier) and brackets the *signatum* (referent), CPE argues that crisis symptoms are indexical signs that reflect an underlying reality grounded in a causal nexus that connects an initially invisible entity to the visible signs that it produces. This relation is not immediately transparent or self-evident but requires interpretation to connect the real (an invisible entity or entities), the actual (a crisis event or process), and the empirical (the visible sign). Just as a medical diagnosis requires knowledge based on careful observation, trial-and-error learning, and successful retroduction, so too does the construal of crisis symptoms (on the symptomatology of crises, see Jessop 2015). Indeed, crises are moments of profound cognitive and strategic disorientation. They disorient inherited expectations and practices; challenge past lessons and ways of learning; and open space for new lessons and ways of learning. In this context it is useful to distinguish learning in crisis, learning about crisis, and learning from crisis (Ji 2006; Sum and Jessop 2013; and, for a similar distinction, Boin et al. 2008).

Learning in crisis occurs in the immediacy of crisis and is oriented to its phenomenal forms. For those directly affected, learning occurs via direct experience of these forms. Lived experience will vary across persons, groups, and organizations. How someone experiences and understands his/her world(s) as real and meaningful depends on their subject positions and standpoint. For those not directly affected, learning in crisis occurs through real-time observation of its *phenomenal* forms. This is often mediated through diverse forms of representation (serious and tabloid journalism, statistics, charts, econometric models, reports, etc.) and is typically heavily dependent on how the media thematize the crisis. In neither case does such learning dig beneath surface phenomena to deeper causes, crisis-tendencies, etc.

Learning about crisis occurs with lags in real time as a crisis unfolds, often in unexpected ways, and as the routine crisis-management measures resorted to by actors prove, seem to be, or are held to be inadequate or inappropriate. Crisis construal and management are now more experimental as actors seek to make sense of the crisis not merely at the phenomenal level but also in terms of underlying mechanisms and crisis dynamics. For those directly affected, this occurs when attention turns from phenomenal forms to deeper causes and dynamics and their bearing on crisis management. For 'outside' observers, it occurs when they focus on real causes, dynamics, and effects, and monitor actors' trial-and-error attempts to solve a crisis and/or how other 'outsiders' seek to shape its course, costs, and outcome. Not all actors or observers move to this stage; it is typically highly selective, partial, and provisional as well as mediated and mediatized.

Learning from crisis occurs later, as crisis-management efforts succeed or recovery takes place for other reasons, and actors reflect on the crisis and its import for future crises and crisis management. Whether one has directly experienced the crisis or 'merely' observed it in real time, learning from a crisis occurs after 'it' ends. Learning from a crisis can also occur through institutionalized enquiries, based on reports from those who experienced it, observed it, and tried to describe, interpret, and explain it. This is an important mechanism of policy learning for future crisis prevention and crisis management. It may shape policy in two ways. First, lessons learnt by those directly affected can be conveyed in more or less codified terms to others who experience similar crises. This may lead to fast policy transfer, whether appropriate or not, especially when crises are acute and demand urgent action. Calls for quick action lead to shorter policy development cycles, fast-tracking decision-making, rapid programme roll-out, continuing policy experiments, institutional and policy Darwinism, constant revision of guidelines, and so on (on fast policy, see Peck and Theodore 2015). This affects the choice of policies, initial policy targets, sites where policy is implemented, and the criteria adopted for success. It also discourages proper evaluation of a policy's impact over various spatio-temporal horizons, including delayed and/or unintended consequences and feedback effects. Second, lessons drawn by 'outside' observers may be conveyed to those directly affected as more or less codified guidance for managing future crises. This can backfire where this is followed rigidly without regard to the tacit knowledge and improvisation that also shaped more or less successful crisis management, where false analogies are drawn, and/or where novel features of the next crisis are overlooked. Lessons from the past can also be invoked deliberately to steer crisis construal towards one rather than another set of crisis measures (on historical parallels, see Samman 2012).

TOWARDS CRITICAL POLICY STUDIES

Drawing on the CPE approach as outlined above and developed elsewhere in greater detail theoretically and empirically, we suggest that four steps are required to promote critical policy studies:

1. An immanent, reasoned critique of policy proposals based on deficiencies in their internal assumptions, categories, problematization, and argumentation, with a view to disclosing empirical inadequacies or anomalies and, perhaps, practical failings, and relating these to inconsistencies in the underlying theoretical paradigms, policy paradigms, or knowledge brands.
2. Identification of the ideal and material interests favoured by specific policy proposals or strategic lines in specific periods or conjunctures, whether this privileging of some interests over others is motivated by bad faith or results from the naturalization, reification, or fetishization of specific social facts.
3. An account of the role, if any, of the policies, policy paradigm, or overall strategic line in reproducing one or more durable, structured forms of social domination.
4. The proposal of alternative interpretations, policies, and strategies to facilitate the emancipation of subordinate social forces (and, perhaps, dominant forces too) from the harmful effects of the pattern of domination that is naturalized or legitimated by those subject to this critique.

All four steps are required to deliver a CPE critique that has *practical* policy relevance as well as *theoretical* appeal. Immanent critique shows the historicity of a given dispositive along with its policy discourses and practical implementation. It should also analyse the polity, politics, and policy in terms of how these reflect and refract the discursively- and institutionally-mediated condensation of a changing balance of forces. It examines struggles to shape the identities, subjectivities, and interests of the forces engaged in struggles to maintain or transform the political system, the forms of politics, and specific policies and their various modes of selectivity. Thus CPE goes beyond the critique of ideology to explore the semiotic and extra-semiotic mechanisms involved in selecting and consolidating the dominance and/or hegemony of some meaning systems and ideologies over others. This offers more solid foundations to understand forms of social domination, develop a critique of domination, and contribute thereby to critical policy studies.

CONCLUSIONS

As a 'grand-theoretical' project, many of the insights of CPE can be applied far beyond its original home domain in the critique of political economy. The challenge of avoiding both a voluntarist, idealist constructivism and a reified, mechanical structuralism are not confined to the analysis of differential capital accumulation and its régulation-cum-governance.[2] On the contrary, many types of social scientific enquiry could gain from a reflexive, critical engagement with the meta-theoretical assumptions that inform CPE, its emphasis on the equal foundational importance of sense- and meaning-making *and* efforts to limit compossible variation among social relations, and its attention to the articulation and interaction of discursive, structural, technological, and agential selectivities. Whether or not a scholar interested in the critique of the polity, politics, and policy approaches this task, as we have tended to do, in terms of their relevance to differential accumulation and class domination, s/he can still gain intellectual and critical value from an evolutionary approach to the movement from *construal* to *construction* in terms of the respective contributions of discursive, structural, technological, and agential selectivities in the transition from variation through selection to retention. The CPE approach developed by the present authors has not as yet elaborated an equivalent set of substantive concepts for social fields, institutions and institutional complexes, and system dynamics beyond the profit-oriented, market-mediated economy. This challenge to develop an appropriate 'conceptual dispositive' is one for us but also for all of those interested in CPE's potential in other fields.

ADDENDUM ON GRAMSCI AS A PRECURSOR OF CPE

The Italian communist intellectual and party leader Antonio Gramsci (1891–1937) sought to navigate a path between the equally inadequate, but then prevailing, alternatives of speculative idealism and mechanical materialism. His approach is a significant innovation in Marxist accounts of the relation between the so-called economic base and different layers of the superstructure, notably the juridico-political ensemble formed by what Gramsci called 'the state in its inclusive sense' (see below) and struggles over state power and, additionally, second- and higher-order reflections on the natural and social world as distinct from the practical consciousness that was an inevitable and integral aspect of all social practices. This approach was not directly motivated, however, by the desire to solve the hoary base–superstructure problem. Rather, it stems from his university studies in philology (especially historical and spatial linguistics), which were important substantively and methodologically. Indeed, Gramsci even described his method as philological. These studies were also the initial source of his interest in hegemony, before he met it in Lenin's work on class and party alliances (for a nuanced analysis of the relation between philology and politics in his work, see Carlucci 2015). Thus, in contrast to its conventional meaning in international relations and Marxist-Leninist political theory, Gramsci redefined hegemony to denote the formation and organization of consent.

As noted, he aimed to avoid the twin errors of idealist and positivist approaches to language and social order more generally. He emphasized that language permeates all social relations and that it secretes a particular view of the world into everyday life and special social fields. In this context, he argued that:

> All men are philosophers. Their philosophy is contained in: 1. *language itself*, which is a totality of determined notions and concepts and not just words grammatically devoid of content; 2. 'common sense' and 'good sense'; 3. popular religion and, therefore, also in the entire system of belief, superstitions, opinions, ways of seeing things and of acting which are collectively bundled together under the name of 'folklore'. (Gramsci 1971: 323)

In the same vein, Gramsci argued that everyone is an intellectual, but not everyone has the function of an intellectual (Gramsci 1971: 9). In this context, he paid particular attention to the role of intellectuals in mediating the relations between 'ideas' and social structure. These claims can be illustrated from Gramsci's analyses of the articulation of base and superstructure, relations between political and civil society, and intellectuals' vital role in establishing and reproducing these mediations in capitalist social order. They also have implications for critical policy studies (see below).

First, in place of the base-superstructure distinction, Gramsci redefined David Ricardo's notion of *mercato determinato* (determinate market) as 'equivalent to [a] determined relation of social forces in a determined structure of the productive apparatus, this relationship being guaranteed (that is, rendered permanent) by a determined political, moral and juridical superstructure' (Gramsci 1971: 410). This pointed to the need for an integral analysis of historically specific economic regimes, their modes of social regulation, and their contingent, tendential laws of motion. For example, in his famous notes on Americanism and Fordism, Gramsci showed the importance of new economic imaginaries and organic intellectuals in promoting 'Americanism' as a mode of growth in response to the crisis of liberal capitalism and also identified how new social and cultural practices helped to consolidate Fordism as a new mode of regulation and societal organization (1971: 310–13). Gramsci also noted that it would be hard to implant and consolidate Fordism in Europe. This is because of the deadweight of tradition, the incrustations of the past that must be swept away, and the presence of parasitic classes and strata (1971: 281, 285, 317). Such arguments put the struggle for political, intellectual, and moral leadership at the heart of efforts to establish new economic regimes and embed them in capitalist societies.

A second concept that Gramsci used to explore the imbrication of economic and non-economic relations was 'historical bloc'. He asked in what sense 'the complex, contradictory and discordant ensemble of the superstructures is the reflection of the ensemble of the social relations of production'. He answered that the historical bloc reflects 'the necessary reciprocity between structure and superstructure' (1971: 366). This reciprocity is realized through specific intellectual, moral, and political practices. These translate narrow sectoral, professional, or local (in his terms, 'economic-corporate') interests into wider 'ethico-political' ones. Agreement on the latter not only helps co-constitute economic structures (by providing a shared orientation) but also gives them their rationale and legitimacy. Analysing the historical bloc in this way also shows how 'material forces are the content and ideologies are the form, though this distinction between form and content has purely didactic value' (1971: 377).

Third, in his best known concept, Gramsci related hegemony (*egemonia*) to the capacity of dominant groups to establish and maintain political, intellectual, and moral leadership and secure the 'broad-based consent' of allied and subordinate groups to the prevailing relations of economic and political domination. Just as he studied the economy in its integral sense as a determined market, Gramsci studied the state in its integral sense. He defined it as 'political society + civil society' and examined state power, in liberal democracies based on mass politics, as 'hegemony protected by the armour of coercion' (1971: 263). His analysis of hegemony–consent–persuasion is not restricted to civil society but extends into what are conventionally regarded as economic and political spheres. Paraphrasing, effective hegemony depends on the capacity of dominant groups to suture the identities, interests, emotions, and values of key sectors of subordinate classes and other subaltern groups into a hegemonic vision and embed this in institutions and policies – leading in turn to their translation into 'good' common sense. At the same time, reflecting the 'material' as well as discursive moment of social practice, hegemony depends on material concessions to subaltern groups and this means that it must rest on 'a decisive economic nucleus'.

For Gramsci, just as the moment of force is institutionalized in a system of coercive apparatuses (that may not coincide with the state's formal juridico-political apparatuses), hegemony is crystallized and mediated through a complex system of ideological (or hegemonic) apparatuses located throughout the social formation. While present in the juridico-political apparatuses, hegemonic practices are largely concentrated in civil society (i.e., the 'ensemble of organisms commonly called "private"' (Gramsci 1971: 12). Relevant 'hegemonic apparatuses' include the Church, trade unions, schools, the mass media, or political parties (Gramsci 1971: 10–14, 155, 210, 243, 261, 267).

Fourth, Gramsci's interest in the determined market, historical blocs, and state power was closely related to his studies of intellectuals (also very broadly defined). He regarded them as the creators and mediators of hegemony, as crucial bridges between economic, political, and ideological domination, and as active agents in linking culture (especially common sense or everyday knowledge, passions, feelings, and customs) and subjectivity in the production of hegemony. Gramsci rejected an elitist or vanguard role for intellectuals, stressing the need for hegemony to be rooted in everyday practices and interests. He also highlighted how hegemony is anchored in the activities of traditional and/or organic intellectuals whose specialized function in the division of labour is to elaborate ideologies, educate the people, organize and unify social forces, and secure the hegemony of the dominant group (Gramsci 1971: 5–23; for an excellent review of intellectuals' role in this regard, especially in shaping historical blocs, see Portelli 1972). Thus the task of organic intellectuals is to promote and consolidate a conception of the world that gives homogeneity and awareness to a fundamental class in the economic, political, and social fields; and this, in turn, becomes the basis for efforts to create hegemony within the wider society (Gramsci 1971: 5). Whereas organic intellectuals identify with the dominant classes or, at least, have roles coeval with the historically specific forms of their economic, political, and ideological domination, traditional intellectuals have roles inherited from earlier modes of production or ways of life (e.g., priests) and appear to be less closely tied to the currently dominant classes.

A final set of comments concern the implications of Gramsci's analyses for *critical* policy studies. Gramsci was, of course, a political activist with a strong interest in the class relevance of the institutional architecture of the polity (in its inclusive sense), forms of political (including party) organization, strategies and tactics regarding politics as the art of the possible, and specific policies – that is, a strong interest in their potential and actual contribution to reproducing economic exploitation and class domination. This said, inspired in part by Machiavelli, he sought to develop an *autonomous science of the political* (1971: 136–44). He aimed thereby to avoid reducing the logic of politics and the content of policies to a crude reflection of the 'economic structure' and/or interpreting them simply as means to advance narrow economic-corporate interests. This concern with 'political science' was rooted in many theoretical and political motivations. These included: to explain the failure of Italian state formation and how it helped to create the conditions for the rise of fascism; to identify the specificity of political and ideological struggle on the terrain of the state in an age of mass politics (which he dated from the 1870s) where the institutions of civil society were as important as, if not more important than, the repressive state apparatus in securing the conditions for class rule; to work out the modalities of the exercise of political power, ranging from an inclusive hegemony through passive revolution and fraud-corruption to the resort to naked coercion in an open war of class struggle; to distinguish different kinds of political strategies and their articulation, notably long-term wars of position and short-term wars of manoeuvre; to identify successive political conjunctures in the context of permanent but shifting unstable equilibria of compromise, marked by offensive and defensive steps in class struggle; and to distinguish between political strategies, tactics, and policies that had some mid- to long-term structural significance and manoeuvres and policies that were concerned with sectarian or organizational questions or the preservation of the state apparatus as a condition of political life, or that even resulted just from sheer political miscalculation and policy errors that might be corrected in due course through normal politics (see especially Gramsci 1971: 141–5, 171, 178–80, 239, 373–7).

Regarding the last point, Gramsci cautioned against deriving specific policies from economic needs or interests – for the policy process depends on a specific dynamic of political struggles rather than on immediate economic circumstances. He noted:

> The claim, presented as an essential postulate of historical materialism, that every fluctuation of politics and ideology can be presented and expounded as an immediate expression of the [economic] structure, must be contested in theory as primitive infantilism, and combated in practice with the authentic testimony of Marx, the author of concrete political and historical works. (1971: 407)

In this context, Gramsci noted that: (1) the development of political regimes through, using our CPE terminology, variation, selection, and retention, makes real-time analysis of the longer-term significance of present tendencies and counter-tendencies difficult; (2) errors of strategic and tactical calculation are common, leading to trial-and-error learning, often steered by crises, and facilitated by the play of forces; and (3) many political actions derive from organizational necessities related to the preservation of state or party unity rather than to class interests (Gramsci 1971: 407–9). In short, politics cannot be read off directly from changing economic circumstances, economic crises, underlying contradictions, and the like.

Within this wide-ranging and conjuncturally sophisticated analytical (but also, for Gramsci, always deeply class-sensitive) framework, he compared different political arrangements (never just at the formal, constitutional level), political strategies across political regimes and conjunctures, the articulation of politics and policies within and across different fields, ranging from technology, agrarian, colonial, labour, economic, financial, public works, social and trade policies through issues of juridico-political and police-military policy to spheres such as education, culture, nationalities, science, religion, and philosophy (see Gramsci 1971 and 1995 passim). Politics and policies were rarely considered in narrow organizational, administrative, or legal-juridical terms – they were almost always related to the social forces that promoted or benefitted from them (or resisted them), how these advanced specific interests, a general strategic line, or overall hegemonic project, the conceptions of the world that they embodied or articulated, their theoretical, ideological, and practical limits, and their modification in and through the normal play of politics. These are all key questions in critical policy studies.

NOTES

1. For a survey of five other self-designated 'cultural political economy' or 'cultural economy' approaches plus eight projects that make a cultural turn to advance the critique of political economy and/or to identify significant shifts in capitalism, see Sum and Jessop (2013: 18–20).
2. There is a difference between regulation and régulation – the latter is borrowed from the French; in French, regulation is réglementation, i.e., top-down regulation; régulation denotes regularization.

REFERENCES

Béland, Daniel and Robert Henry Cox (eds) (2011) *Ideas and Politics in the Social Sciences*, Oxford: Oxford University Press.

Boin, Arjen, Allan McConnell and Paul 't Hart (eds) (2008) *Governing after Crisis. The Politics of Investigation, Accountability and Learning*, Cambridge: Cambridge University Press.

Carlucci, Alessandro (2015) 'Gramsci, language and pluralism', in Mark McNally (ed.), *Antonio Gramsci*, Basingstoke, UK: Palgrave Macmillan, 76–94.

Foucault, Michel (2008) *The Birth of Biopolitics: Lectures at the Collège de France, 1978–1979*, Basingstoke, UK: Palgrave.

Gramsci, Antonio (1971) *Selections from the Prison Notebooks*, London: Lawrence & Wishart.

Gramsci, Antonio (1995) *Further Selections from the Prison Notebooks*, London: Lawrence & Wishart.

Heidenheimer, Arnold J. (1986) 'Politics, policy and *policey* as concepts in English and Continental languages', *Review of Politics*, **48** (1), 1–26.

Heinrich, Mathis and Bob Jessop (2014) 'The crisis in the EU from a cultural political economy perspective: crisis interpretations and their translation into policy', in Bob Jessop, Brigitte Young and Christoph Scherrer (eds), *Cultures of Finance and Crisis Dynamics*, London: Routledge, 278–293.

Jessop, Bob (2004) 'Critical semiotic analysis and cultural political economy', *Critical Discourse Studies*, **1** (2), 159–74.

Jessop, Bob (2009) 'Cultural political economy and critical policy studies', *Critical Policy Studies*, **3** (3–4), 336–56.

Jessop, Bob (2012) 'Economic and ecological crises: Green New Deals and no-growth economies', *Development*, **55** (1), 17–24.

Jessop, Bob (2014) 'Repoliticising depoliticisation', *Policy & Politics*, **42** (2), 207–23.

Jessop, Bob (2015) 'The symptomatology of crises: reading crises and learning from them. Some critical realist reflections', *Journal of Critical Realism*, **14** (3), 238–71.

Ji, Joo-Hyoung (2006) *Learning from Crisis: Political Economy, Spatio-Temporality, and Crisis Management in South Korea, 1961–2002*, PhD thesis: Lancaster University.

Lasswell, Harold (1936) *Politics: Who Gets What, When, How*, New York: Meridian.

Lipschutz, Ronnie D. (2005) 'Global civil society and global governmentality', in Gideon Baker and David Chandler (eds), *Global Civil Society*, London: Routledge, 145–58.

Mitchell, Timothy J. (1991) 'The limits of the state: beyond statist approaches and their critics', *American Political Science Review*, **85** (1), 77–96.

Peck, Jamie A. (2010) *Constructions of Neoliberal Reason*, New York: Oxford University Press.

Peck, Jamie and Nik Theodore (2015) *Fast Policy*, Minneapolis: University of Minnesota Press.

Portelli, Hugues (1972) *Gramsci et le bloque historique*, Paris: Maspero.

Samman, Amin T. (2012) *Re-Imagining the Crises of Global Capitalism*, PhD thesis: University of Birmingham.

Sayer, Andrew (2000) *Realism and Social Science*, London: Sage Publications.

Schmidt, Vivien A. (2008) 'Discursive institutionalism: the explanatory power of ideas and discourse', *Annual Review of Political Science*, **11**, 303–26.

Schmidt, Vivien A. (2012) 'Discursive institutionalism: scope, dynamics, and philosophical underpinnings', in Frank Fischer and Herbert Gottweis (eds), *The Argumentative Turn Revisited*, Durham, NC: Duke University Press, 85–113.

Somers, Margaret (1994) 'The narrative constitution of identity: a relational and network approach', *Theory and Society*, **23** (5), 605–49.

Sum, Ngai-Ling (2009) 'The production of hegemonic policy discourses: "competitiveness" as a knowledge brand and its (re-)contextualization', *Critical Policy Studies*, **3** (2), 184–203.

Sum, Ngai-Ling (2010) 'The cultural political economy of transnational knowledge brands: Porterian competitiveness discourse and its recontextualization to Hong Kong/Pearl River Delta', *Journal of Language and Politics*, **9** (4), 184–203.

Sum, Ngai-Ling and Bob Jessop (2013) *Towards a Cultural Political Economy: Putting Culture in its Place in Political Economy*, Cheltenham, UK and Northampton, MA, USA: Edward Elgar.

Wallis, Joe and Brian E. Dollery (1999) *Market Failure, Government Failure, Leadership and Public Policy*, Basingstoke, UK: Macmillan.

Wilson, Japhy (2014) *Jeffrey Sachs: The Strange Case of Dr Shock and Mr Aid*, London: Verso.

8 The interpretation of power
Timothy W. Luke

Critical policy studies has developed as a cohesive tradition of political analysis by contesting, first, conventional technocratic dispositions toward 'power' that typically treat it as an unproblematic resource. All too often, authoritative policy experts can call upon these formulations of powers without impediment to implement what they regard as the rational, just and/or efficient deployment of technical expertise in governance. By calling upon argumentative, discursive or rhetorical grounds to contest this mode of governance, key works in critical policy studies have shown how these technocratic styles of administration undercut civic life and the democratic community (Hawkesworth, 1988; Fischer and Forester, 1993; Fischer, 1995; Fischer and Gottweis, 2012).

Such instrumentally rational constructions of expert knowledge, second, are challenged constantly in critical policy studies. Experts who present such programmatic visions of policy options to decision-makers and the public as implicitly legitimate, explicitly reasonable, and essentially pragmatic solutions to collective policy choices (Hajer, 1995; Rose, 1999; Torgerson, 1999; Flyvberg, 2001; Fischer, 2003) usually are one-sided in their practices and one-dimensional in their thinking. In the place of technocratic expertise, critical policy studies often turns to diffuse governance networks of citizens, experts, and governmental authorities (Fischer, 2000; Fischer and Gottweis, 2012), which are regarded by many as more adaptive, collaborative, and/or democratic means for governing than rule by technocratic bureaucracies. Here, one must ask if power as a phenomenon can be confronted more critically, and if critical policy studies should grapple with its constitutive qualities and complex articulations. These efforts cannot be definitely conclusive, but they can be initially suggestive.

The discussion, therefore, will begin by reconsidering the senses and settings associated with power as an object of political analysis. It then will examine the dual development of enlightenment/empowerment with modernity to set the stage for examining agency and structure (Habermas, 1987; Latour, 1993; Luke, 1989). Finally, it encourages critical policy analysis to more carefully assess power in contemporary policy-making environments.

1.   THE SETTINGS OF POWER

Often, the analytical challenges of defining power are entwined with political struggles for new freedoms in economies and societies experiencing the modernizations of urbanization, mechanization, industrialization, globalization, or commercialization toward both deeper empowerment and greater enlightenment (Alasuutari, 2011). These connections are crucial concerns, and they cannot be discounted. The contradictory demands of freedom also cannot be moved very far away from attentive reconsiderations of power/knowledge (Foucault, 1980b) as the core of what many analysts (Polsby, 1963; Gaventa, 1982; Boulding, 1990) crystallize as power's three dimensions/faces/modes expressed in the activities of agents, as Lukes (1974) or Bachrach and Baratz (1962) assert. Yet, in the disciplined production of specific forms of individual and collective subjectivity (Kern, 1983; Luke, 1995; Mumford, 1986), especially that unfolding out of modernity's opportunities for greater empowerment and enlightenment in urban-industrial societies (Giedion, 1948; Bourdieu, 1990; Nye 1990; Baudrillard, 1996), power is agency, structure, and their mutual co-constitution all at once.

To make this claim is not to stage a test of strength between approaches that favor agency over structure or vice versa. Most conventional depictions of power typically place either 'agency' or 'structure' factors in a more decisive, determinant, or dominant position in their models, theories, or process tracings. Either 'agents' or 'structures' are cast as the key operative 'inside' of most power dynamics, while the appositive factor is deemed to be less central, coherent, or crucial at the ancillary 'outside' of power practices. In actuality, the interpretation of power in critical policy studies must accept the indispensability of agency and structure, along with how they *coincide* as mutually decisive factors both inside and outside the workings of power dynamics.

Does what is regarded as 'power' arise openly from specific conjunctures of very complex new technics, social institutions, industrial processes, and organizational articulations that co-evolve with modernization as well as new logics of governmentality (Foucault, 1991)? Growing human populations, which now inhabit the spaces invaded by industrial marketing, machinic infrastructures, welfare agencies, factory production, or mechanized transport, essentially must endure greater governance by state formations. When and where such states exert growing command and control over territories and populations, one finds that a proliferation of new sites, systems, and structures for power also begin to simultaneously emerge (Mitchell, 2002), which provide the decision points where, how, and why some agents get other agents to do what they otherwise would not do (Dahl, 1957). Objective discourses of enlightenment merge with these institutions of empowerment, producing many textures to the milieux of modernity that afford more people some expanding power opportunities, deficits, blockages, surpluses in the pragmatic imperatives, and ascetic opportunities of modernizing cultures as they change in these conditions (Nickel, 2015: 1–3).

Plotting power's flow and capture is a search for the concretizations of modern milieux woven into each apparatus, attitude, and action for 'relating to contemporary reality; a voluntary choice made by certain people; in the end, a way of thinking and feeling; a way, too, of acting and behaving that at one and the same time marks a relation of belonging and presents itself as a task' (Foucault, 1984: 39). As this chapter suggests, power need not only appear as a determinate necessity; it also can be a chain of decisions in which being, or perhaps becoming, powerful and/or powerless are essentially presented as choices to specific individuals in many collectivities. These decisions are made, as ways of belonging, thinking, and feeling; and the power of agents to prompt others to do what they would not do otherwise is integral to the co-constitution of agents and structures.

The challenge for power interpretation is, however, recognizing how also exercising extensive state sovereignty and implementing intensive corporate productivity simultaneously creates greater domination and liberation in the multi-layered milieux of modernity (Perrow, 1984; Clegg, 1989; Luke, 1996; Nye, 1996). Without tracking down many such dark trails into these larger ecologies of order, social science researchers often overlook important counterintuitive or contradictory outcomes: more control creates new powers for almost everyone, but these crucial empowering developments rarely enhance critical vision. By tracing out various operational opportunity sets at play in the routines of governmentalization, industrialization, and urbanization, it becomes evident that modes of knowledge about subjectivity formation and social enforcement make endless series of new 'A' and 'B' agents to enact these collectives' own destiny to shape and steer mass society (Mumford, 1963). These changes are too frequently celebrated as mere 'democracy,' because they are mainly '*cratic*,' or regime rule-centered conjunctures of control giving fluid *demos* of 'A' agents the leave to get 'B' agents to do what they otherwise would not do. Their democratic qualities, however, are not as evident as their bureaucratic or technocratic possibilities.

Not surprisingly, the study of power in most political and policy studies communities –which tend to focus on discrete actors who are enlisted as individual officers, managers, leaders, or decision-makers in bigger social systems – favors theoretical frameworks in which power-as-agency is highlighted. This bias towards looking at 'deciders' – who must make decisions to administer, manage, or rule – runs throughout many policy-relevant literatures that try to gauge how and why actor/agent 'A' gets actor/agent 'B' and/or 'C' to do what 'A' wants done from taking the decision. The capability for exerting such powerful sway in determinate ways, in turn, is tied to actions that render the desired outcome visible, measurable and, most crucially, compliant. Here it is believed one sees power-to-act, power-in-action, and power-enacted by 'A' vis-à-vis 'B' and/or 'C.'

While these studies are worth doing, the foregrounding of agency elides power-as-structure. More focused attention on structure is needed, because actors are agents of, in, for, and/or against structures, but such analysis must surpass the recent efforts to reconcile the 'old' and the 'new' institutionalism by looking only at incentives, procedures, or rules (Peters, 2011). Structures are arguably prior decisions, and non-decisions, accumulated with such density and depth that they congeal into less visible background conditions. Yet, their force remains as decisions-once-taken, needing to be maintained, enforced, or again actuated by agents renewing, reinterpreting, and reactivating behaviors. Both settings of activity then co-constitute each other in co-evolutionary, collaborative, and conterminous manners. Critical policy studies then can add much to the understanding of power by adding to existing ethnographies of structure as processes, institutions, and ethics co-instantiating themselves in the actions of agents.

2.   EMPOWERMENT

Particularly in Cold War-era Anglo-American political science, it is arguably the case that many theories of power focus on the face of the agents that seem to exercise it. As Dahl (1957: 202–203) asserts, '*A* has power over *B* to the extent he can get *B* to something *B* otherwise would not do.' While Dahl admits this capacity is always relational and contingent, how this action is accomplished mystifies how power is always already there being manipulated, managed, or made in the structuring of such milieux. In turn, lazy philosophical and political analyses of power idly float their accounts of power on a misplaced faith in such changes adding up to potential zones of human liberation when, in fact, they also create denser material regimens for human domination in the many dimensions of power implementation (Lukes, 1974; Gaventa, 1982; Lasswell, 1990; Bourdieu, 1998). If politics can be reduced to the distributive-transactional logic of Lasswell's (1990) 'Who gets what, when, and how?' then understanding political processes of innumerable 'A' agents getting equally large numbers of 'B' agents to accept the how, when, where, and what of all that is 'gotten' and 'not-gotten' is a never-ending critical interpretive puzzle (Lasswell, 1974: 177).

Dissecting the tough questions of power in diffuse or concentrated, coercive or productive, normalizing or juridical modes against the horizon of modern governmentality is a core component of Foucault's 'critical ontology' of ourselves and structures that enable us to express a 'critique of what we are' along with 'the historical analysis of the limits imposed on us and an experiment with the possibility of going beyond them' (1984: 50). Limits imposed and unbreakable as well as those imposed upon us with these limits is central to power's operations. Foucault (1984: 39) appraises modernity as 'attitude' or 'ethos,' so it makes sense to explore these limits as attitudinal markers or ethos points in the milieux of modernity.

To explore how the limits in/of power alternate as possibilities and prohibitions within the articulation of technified governmentality (Law, 1991; Luke, 1998; Mitchell, 2002) one must recognize how fully democracy as government of/by/for the people entails this dual subjectivity of ruler/ruled created from/to/through government. A critical interpretation of power also should examine how much oligarchy, technocracy, or plutocracy mediates what ordinary decision-making routines for governance mediate government from/to/through the populace. How the governmentalization of populations sculpts, stabilizes, and then settles for this dual subjectivity is necessary for the rule of experts behind the veil of collaboration by the populace-as-ruler/-ruled in both liberal capitalist democracy as well as illiberal statist oligarchy (Rose, 1999). And, the empowerments of modern milieux bring new cadres of expert managers and technicians into authority. On the eve of the Second Industrial Revolution, empowerments proliferate in America's modern industrial formations, commercial culture, and national bureaucracies. They are the material substrates for sustaining new everyday practices in 'industrial democracy,' which is legitimated by personal consumerism and guided free enterprise that become recast as the *sine qua non* of liberty, equality, and fraternity.

The advent of enlightenment, if Foucault's vision of this shift holds, brings a proliferation of attitudes, apparatuses, and affinities in the economy and society, which enhance the ambit and effect of power (Foucault, 2000). Once 'power' affects the 'knowledge' regime, however, this shift builds up the less well-understood advent of empowerment both inside and outside of the state. Power/knowledge unfold together, but the nature of empowerment – via dominion, domination, or designation – is much less explored than the characteristics of enlightenment. The capacity for control embedded in design, and its technicities, is particularly occluded in too many studies of power. Hence, this nexus requires greater examination.

Without boxing the approach here into some questionable taxonomic system to define *what* it is, *how* interpretative analysis is done should be considered. Methodologically speaking, this interpretative approach to power is obviously riddled with assumptions and assertions about power and how to interpret it. Such realities are admittedly a limitation on this mode of analysis; but, within such limits, power and its working can be interpreted. By the same token, this analysis of power strives to avoid a foundationalist reading of knowledge and reality. Pre-categorical domains of events, materials, times, structures, or agents exist, but their dispositions and prior discursive treatments do not create them per se (Bourdieu, 1984). Categorical constructs of critique slip into these currents of what-exists before what-exists-is-appraised, and thus one tries to avoid endorsing any epistemic or ontic foundationalist systems as determinate in its analysis.

The Enlightenment, then, 'is defined by a modification of the pre-existing relation linking will, authority, and the use of reason' (Foucault, 1984: 35). As this modification manifests itself in new and different knowledge, it also by implication should involve new and different power. For those 'who dare to know,' it soon becomes obvious that they also now 'know how to dare' with audacious courage, resolve, or force. Foucault emphasizes 'the Enlightenment must be considered both as a process in which men participate collectively and as an act of courage to be accomplished personally' (Foucault, 1984: 32). If one regards the Enlightenment as a two-fold process of 'enlightening' and 'empowering' human beings, then the empowerment is enlightenment's occluded twin.

Here, can one also sense the co-constitutive qualities of power in the co-evolution of agency and structure mutually instantiating each other? Any 'process in which men participate collectively' is a structure, and an act of courageous, audacious knowing is 'accomplished personally' by an agent. With the emergence of enlightenment/empowerment in modernity's modified relations of will, authority, and use of reason, the structured agency/ agentifying structure of modern power ignites its cogenerative effects. The agent, structure, and co-constitution of power perhaps provisionally could be traced to the recognition that 'men are at once elements and agents of a single process. They may be actors in the process to the extent that they participate in it; and the process occurs to the extent that men decide to be voluntary actors' (Foucault, 1984: 33).

Clearly, as Yanow and Schwartz-Shea (2000) maintain, taking this critical interpretative approach toward power and operations will be a tentative, multi-modal exploration. And, such nuanced appraisals of power and its problematizations in the conduct of agents in structures, structures of agents, and milieux enveloping agents and structures with the material and temporal qualities or 'the exercise of power as a mode of action upon the actions of others' (Foucault, 1982: 221), will be demanding. Nonetheless, such careful ethnographic tracings would permit one to interpret their actions, structurations, and interrelation of mutual operations or dissonant conditions.

Such understandings of critical interpretation exceed the directions of simplistic methodological individualism or holism. These default positions in social analysis instead must be themselves problematized to enquire how individuals or collectives are methodically propounded with sufficient demarcation to be methodologically mobilized by explanations centered on the individual agent or a collective structure. Subject-biased epistemologies are always put into object-neglecting ontologies in modernity to explore the putative command of science and technology over society and nature. Yet, these self-same concepts activate certain senses of subjectivity and objectivity that an interpretation of power must watch warily.

Positivist epistemic regimes are the most prevalent, but their control over explanation often is incomplete, superficial, and underdetermined. Thicker, tighter, and tougher descriptions through careful interpretation often exceed the satisfaction of simplistic thin causal explanation. And, ironically, the unrelenting din of causal methods spinning up tough, tight or thick descriptions of what they aspire to achieve is all too often mistaken for their actual achievement. Interpretative analyses of power, like this one, must work to achieve their aspirations for testing out thicker, tighter, and tougher explorations of power in as many performative aspects of their expression as possible from direct dominance to discrete discourse (Bourdieu, 1990; Hajer, 1995; Flyvberg, 2001).

3. AGENTS AND STRUCTURES: THREE FACES AND BEYOND

Power, position, and privilege exist, and their structurations in discrete actions and enduring institutions by groups of agents are seen as 'self'-interested, 'self'-centered, and 'self'-serving. Hegemony forms at these conjunctures and the faces of power usually are best calm, collected, and content. Subservience from the subservient, who must accede to power's self-interested centers of self-service, works best when it sees contentment, and not caution, in the visages of those moving them to become and stay compliant. Hegemony circulates in common courtesies, humdrum compliance, and unchallenged convention, giving both the powerful and powerless their scripts to express in thought and deed. To be powerless is not to have lost all power, it only implies wielding or wheeling less power than those in more powerful places. And, a fullness of power is never boundless. Hegemony keeps these doubts and worries quiet in the clatter of complying to do what one otherwise would not, and having done what otherwise one could not enjoy without the getting of it. Interpretative mappings of the power manifest in domination, agenda setting, ideology, or institutional inertia all implicitly disclose how much interpretative discourse mediates the knowledges such power presumes, while explicitly retracing power effects cascading along with these analytical efforts.

C. Wright Mills presents a liberal notion of power, inasmuch as he presumes the government of people rests upon their explicit or implicit consent to be ruled, when he frets in *The Sociological Imagination* about how power actually operates in the present without much evidence of individual or collective consent. No one today should assume, he claims,

> that men must in the last resort be governed by their own consent. Among the means of power that now prevail is the power to manage and manipulate the consent of men. That we do not know the limits of such power – does not remove the fact that much power today is successfully employed without the sanction of the reason or the conscience of the obedient. (Mills, 1959: 40–41)

Such doubts about the legitimacy, limits, and/or legality of power in Mill are particularly curious in light of Robert Dahl's very political intuition of power as 'something like this: A has power over B to the extent that he can get B to do something that B would not otherwise do' (1957: 202–203). The focus of such accounts of power is action, and the evidence of power is made manifest in the behavior of agents A and B when B does something A commands or expects that B otherwise would not do. Nonetheless, the conditions shifting what, where, why, when, and how congeal in structures, and this 'to the extent' comes from as well as continues itself in the structural workings of power for agents.

Playing off Foucault, how does the notion of 'agent' come into being? As the privileged point of action as well as the actor experiencing other actions directed at one's points of privilege, one must find relationships between agent and structure that expose the problematic notions of act, acting, or action that efface persons in the positions of A and B. Even when an individual is regarded as an actor, one should ask if everything he or she did, imposed, or endured is part of their labor. Agent functions in such structures characterize the range of operation for certain discourses about domination/submission, controlling/controlled, and positioning/positioned in society.

The agent in theories of power, then, is the basis for explaining the unfolding of particular events in structures, and their transformation, stasis, effects. Agents institute institutions, configure structures, fabricate foundations, which become limits of agency to abide by or transgress. The 'agent function' is also already always to an extent a 'structure operation.' To exercise power there must be power exercises, and the decider who plays games of power means embracing technocratic games of power as material decision-making. A-getting-B-to-do-so, meaning B otherwise would not do so, also occludes the other things not done, the relationality of A possessing the capacity over B to make B do that which A would have done, and all of these co-constituted activities unfold in the context of so many other actions in operation.

Dahl's sense of power plainly expresses the relationality, contingency, potentiality, and operationality of agents exercising power from a perspective beyond liberal consent, but he leaves that flexibility largely silent in his analyses. Of course, Bachrach and Baratz (1962), like Dahl, have a more tactical and operational understanding of power to the degree that power has 'two faces.' Not only must power analysis look at how the powerful make the less powerful directly do their bidding, but so too will the powerful show a second face in their 'mobilization of bias' (1962: 947–952) that keeps many questions, issues, decisions, and actors out of political contests altogether. This is a matter of 'consent,' since the larger remits of authority behind the consciousness and conscience of all are also managed and manipulated to the point that many people are kept out beyond the pale of politics. As E.E. Schattschneider asserts, the study of power should concentrate 'both on who gets what, when and how and who gets left out and how' (1960: 105).

Lukes's third face of power looks beyond the first-dimensional exercise of power in decision-making as Polsby suggests by raising questions about 'who participates, who gains and loses, and who prevails in decision-making' (Polsby, 1963: 55). Here, Lukes looks past the second face of power where non-decision frequently trumps decision in managing and manipulating the outcomes of conflict. On this aspect of power, Schattschneider lays out the problem very clearly, 'whoever decides what the game is about also decides who gets in the game' (1960: 105). This coincidence of agency and structure reveals how power is productive as well as coercive.

Lukes's third-dimensional view of power also tries to pick up bits of this intuition in pushing past the positions taken by Mills, and Bachrach and Baratz, as well as Dahl. The third-dimension of power gestures at how power operates, in many ways, more productively, hegemonically, or diffusely. That is, 'A may exercise power over B by getting him to do what he does not want to do, but he also exercises power over him by influencing, shaping or determining his very wants' (Lukes, 1974: 23). This approach begins to subsume and supersede the more individual-oriented, conflict-driven, and interest-based views of the neo-elitists and pluralists by asking political analysts to consider something like structure to account for 'the prospect of a serious sociological and not merely personalized explanation of how political systems prevent demands from becoming political issues or even from being made' (1974: 38). Gramsci, indeed, points to this boundary condition for power and policy when he muses about political agents: 'only the man who wills something strongly can identify the elements which are necessary to the realization of his will' (1971: 171). Such elements often are identified as structure.

Lukes's purportedly radical view of power, nonetheless, remains in too many ways over the years (Lukes, 1974, 2005) an agent-based model. He seeks to explain how a 'who' does some 'what' at a specific 'where' in accord with some recognizable 'how' that then can manifest an important discernable 'why.' His genealogical analyses of power are largely distributive ethnographies, which endeavor to read the three faces, gauge the three dimensions or disclose the three operationalities of power. Like many other liberal individualist frameworks for explaining power, Lukes turns to the authorities, agents, and actors at work in what could be reduced to the institutions of executive, legislative, judicial, or managerial governance.

Therefore, power can be disclosed for Lukes in the unconsciously comfortable sense that most people enable or experience its effects. That is, how 'A' interacts with 'B' across three dimensions of power and is represented 'in terms of the ways of coding and defining or delimiting the proper apparatus of rule, the strategies and limits proper for rulers, and the relations between political rule and that executed by other authorities' (Barry et al., 1996: 13–14). Looking at agents – individual and collective – allows Lukes to track power across and around the fluid operations, shifting spaces, and changing boundaries of the personal and political, economic and social, ideational and institutional, ethical and technical, but structure is at work in the zones that agents wend across and around.

4.   A CRITICAL ANALYSIS OF POLICY STRUCTURES

Lukes's profile of power, then, is one fully cognizant that 'government not only has to deal with a territory, with a domain, and with its subjects, but that it also has to deal with a complex and independent reality that has its own laws and mechanisms of disturbance. This new reality is society' (Foucault, 1989: 261). Still, he tends to avoid structure. Lukes's ethical, legalistic, or moralist concerns with each actor's intentions behind, consequences of, and connections between the three dimensions of power at play initially fixated his attention upon agents rather than structures as well as the contexts of both at work together and at odds with each other. Here, critical policy analyses must, as Foucault would direct, push for a further elucidation, elaboration, or explication of agents acting together, since that perspective will demonstrate how necessary it is to accept these agent assemblages in/of/as 'society,' and 'reflect upon it, upon its specific characteristics, its constants and variables' (Foucault, 1989: 261).

Despite the promise posed in the original expression, Lukes's notion of power famously persists as 'an agent-centered notion of dominating power in three dimensions' (Hayward and Lukes, 2008: 7). It stresses the centrality of agency – individual and collective – to ascertain whose actions or inactions count in the sense of serving or disserving their interests, creating or evading the responsibility, helping or harming others. The nearly unconscious common-sensical notions of power Lukes presumes, as Foucault might argue, represent 'ways of thinking about power (based on legal models) that is: What legitimates power' (Foucault, 2000: 327) in stressing the interests, responsibilities and impact of agents. Against Lukes's famous three dimensions, or 'faces' as Boulding (1990) would characterize power, a strong focus on structure never gels in Lukes's narratives about (1) 'decision- and policy-making power,' (2) 'attempts to control agendas,' and (3) framing issues in a way that 'distorts or suppresses people's perceptions of their interests' (Hayward and Lukes, 2008: 7). The approach to power Lukes takes does not sufficiently check what Foucault calls 'the "conceptual needs"' (2000: 327) behind a theory of power. Ultimately, Lukes came to realize, his radical view of power, especially in its initial articulation, ignored what Foucault regarded as 'the historical conditions that motivate our conception' and displayed little 'historical awareness of our present circumstance' by simply founding his conceptualizations of power in 'a theory of the object' through which, in fact, 'the conceptualized object' more or less proves repeatedly it is affording the criteria needed for 'a good conceptualization' (Foucault, 2000: 327).

A critical interpretative policy analysis, then, shows that conventional interpretations of power distract attention from structural contexts, symbolic codes, and/or social capacities in which power flows. Liberal notions of power, in particular, are mired in presumptions about a state of nature, original condition or foundational time in which men can dominate women, the violent will cow the nonviolent, or claimants of exclusive dominion must suppress proponents for inclusive communalism. Yet, the liberal account also assures that agents will not eclipse structures, erase codes, or evade capacities wherein empowerments originate and operate, because such assumptions naturalize state functions, conditional-ize origins, and time foundations in ways that prevent one from observing empowerment co-construction or co-evolution with enlightenment.

Fixating upon originary moments and assertive agents frames power with chains of A-getting-B to do something they otherwise would not do; yet, sustaining structures, constructing codes, and constituting capacities typically require and/or enable B to do this for A. Moreover, empow-erment at the level of agency is both A getting, and B doing, what B otherwise would, should, or could not do as figures of activity. At the level of structure, however, context constructs the underpinning ground constituting the where-fors of powerful/powerless, power relations, and power capabilities of the actors in structures, following codes, and exert-ing capacities that evince empowered acts. The more urban-industrial, technified, or modern 'the context' is, the more these sites of operation are found. Power, then, is an essential knowledge to sustain an economy, governance, society, and the wherewithal they afford to those residing in their ambit. Power poses information, energy, and material in acts and artifacts, which are too narrowly reduced to the agent's 'will to power' even though these capacitating factors can force agents to exercise and experience power effects.

Lukes neglects these domains. He instead embeds his discussion in the conceptual bogs of 'the literature' from the mid-20th-century American political science studies of elitism, pluralism, and democracy as raised in discussions of public policy issues by Robert Dahl, Peter Bachrach, Morton S. Baratz, and Nelson Polsby. The endless debates there about 'decisions' versus 'non-decisions' and 'decision-making' versus 'agenda setting' seem today like artifacts of the moment intended to legitimate Cold War America's technocracy. Little effort consequently was spent checking 'the type of reality with which we are dealing' or 'the concep-tual needs' (Foucault, 2000: 327) behind those debates, because Lukes and those who celebrate his 'radical view' of power are trapped in their tiny hall of mirrors in 'the literature' of the time. C. Wright Mills would attribute these delicate deceptions as part and parcel of powerful elites pretending to be public servants, while systematically turning democratic proceduralism into the pragmatics of deception with games organized for non-decision-making. He warns critical policy analysts to be wary: 'we must expect fumbles when, without authority or official aid, we set out to investigate something which is in part organized for the purpose of causing fumbles among those who would understand it plainly' (Mills, 1956: 353).

Power remakes ordinary discursive principles. It assures the exclusion or inclusion of who shall dominate whom, what is used to determine what to survey, how to intervene, when to exclude some, where to include others, or why to continue conducting specific parameters of conduct. Yet, how these assurances unfold often cannot be pinned down precisely. Such variations in the governmentalization of power articulate 'a will to knowledge that is anonymous, polymorphous, susceptible to regular transformations, and determined by the play of identifiable dependencies' (Foucault, 1977: 200–201). Still, channels of authority flowing within the milieux of transnational corporate enterprise and modern nation-states also valorize strings of knowledge for self-mastery as another range of the power effects in modern social formations. Their power, as Foucault observes, 'traverses and produces things . . . It needs to be considered as a productive network which runs through the whole social body, much more than a negative instance whose function is repression' (Foucault, 1980a: 119). This insight also echoes Marcuse's psychosocial understandings of domination (1964). Specific sets of divided capacity and imposed limits on knowing underpin the reticulations of productive power to manage individual persons and collective populations.

In the prevailing regimes of truth in contemporary public administration and/or private technology, the sciences of governmentality reproduce those bodies of practice and types of discourse that the executives and experts managing contemporary state and corporate institutions would regard as 'objective,' 'valid,' or 'useful.' By reconsidering how these professional networks of experts discursively construct the 'ethos' of imposed limits, as Foucault suggests, one can attempt

> to define the way in which individuals or groups represent words to themselves, utilize their forms and meanings, compose real discourse, reveal and conceal in it what they are thinking or saying. Perhaps unknown to themselves, more or less than they wish, but in any case leave a mass of verbal traces of those thoughts, which must be deciphered and restored as far as possible to their representative vivacity. (Foucault, 1994: 353)

Nonetheless, at the junctions of life, labor, and language in governmentality discourses and practices, there are traces of a complex analytic of power/knowledge 'which shows how man, in his being, can be concerned with the things he knows, and know the things that, in positivity, determine his mode of being' (Foucault, 1994: 314), articulated through highly focalized professional-technical constructs of permissible 'freedoms,' which operationally structure knowing, deciding, and commanding. The 'freedom' given by the economy and society, if we follow Foucault's lines of reasoning, must not be understood either as the naturally given sphere of natural impulses which human powers try to keep under rein nor as a mysterious domain of obscure artificial events which human moral knowledge cannot adequately explain. Instead, it emerges as a historical artifact that is culturally constructed by governmentalizing interventions to attain both technical control and scientific explanation.

Out of this elaborate network of technical interventions into the working of society, a full spectrum of political challenges – ranging from the simulation of space, the intensification of resources, and the incitement of discoveries to the formation of special knowledge, the strengthening of controls, and the provocation of resistances – all are linked to one another as 'the empiricities' of structure that are at stake in moral and political discourses about both powerful and powerless agents who enable such structures (Foucault, 1994: 362–363).

For critical interpretative policy analysis, truths about power are not timeless objective verities; they are instead operational concords of various professional-technical practices, as they have been haltingly produced by the state and society, and then formalized in the decision, policy, and social sciences (Hawkesworth, 1988; Hajer, 1995; Fischer, 2003). The senses and settings of expert disciplines are where visions of 'truth,' or 'a system of ordered procedures for the production, regulation, distribution, circulation, and operation of statements' (Foucault, 1980b: 133), arise from knowledge formations largely generated of, for, and by professional-technical elites and their meritocratic oligarchy. Critical policy interpretations rightly observe those views are biased 'process tracings' of the reified decisions attributed to individual agents. To the extent that the embedded ordering capacities of those structures enveloping democratic subjects also build trust in expertise, and enflame faith in the ruler/ruled subject, these are default decisions to let those 'who know best' decide. The findings of such science far too often are simple. There are 'deciders,' and their attainments justify faith in capital-as-technology, but mystified as 'businesses,' 'corporations' or 'firms,' waiting the outcomes of policy processes to support the organization of markets to be regulated by technocratic managers.

Interpreting power in critical policy analysis, then, should direct its proponents and practitioners to push much harder and further. Plainly, the critical interpretive policy analysis of power must exemplify, if only provisionally, Foucault's awareness of how power is agency, structure, and their mutual co-constitution all at once. To that extent, they can become formidable forces in the economies of discourse tracking down truths in the workings of power/knowledge. Since the 'manifold relations of power which permeate, characterize and constitute the social body, and these relations of power cannot themselves be established, consolidated nor implemented without the production, accumulation, circulation and functioning of a discourse' (Foucault, 1980b: 95).

To conclude, critical interpretive policy studies of power assess power as this 'economy of discourses of truth which operates through and on the basic of this association' (Foucault, 1980b: 95). Trusting technocratic discourses as the pure use of friction-free power by agents in structures is not enough, as this brief overview of classic understandings of power has recounted. The occluded linkages of agency, structures, and their simultaneous co-instantiation must be studied more carefully. As they are explored, critical interpretations of power should find endless opportunities to account for the multiple folds of power relations, which permeate all social bodies and constitute their members in endless ongoing associations.

REFERENCES

Alasuutari, Pertti (2011) 'Modernization as a Tacit Concept used in Governance', *Journal of Political Power*, **4** (2), 217–235.

Bachrach, Peter and Baratz, Morton S. (1962) 'The Two Faces of Power', *American Political Science Review*, **56**, 947–952.

Barry, Andrew, Osborne, Thomas and Rose, Nikolas (eds) (1996) *Foucault and Political Reason: Liberalism, Neo-Liberalism and Rationalities of Government*, London: University of Chicago Press.

Baudrillard, Jean (1996) *The System of Objects*, London: Verso.

Boulding, Kenneth E. (1990) *Three Faces of Power*, Newbury Park, CA: Sage Publications.

Bourdieu, Pierre (1984) *Distinction: A Social Critique of the Judgement of Taste*, Cambridge, MA: Harvard University Press.

Bourdieu, Pierre (1990) *The Logic of Practice*, Stanford, CA: Stanford University Press.

Bourdieu, Pierre (1998) *Acts of Resistance: Against the Tyranny of the Market*, New York: The New Press.

Clegg, Stewart R. (1989) *Frameworks of Power*, London: Sage Publications.

Dahl, Robert (1957) 'The Concept of Power', *Behavioral Science*, **2** (3 (July)), 201–215.

Fischer, Frank (1995) *Evaluating Public Policy*, Florence, KY: Wadsworth.

Fischer, Frank (2000) *Citizens, Experts and the Environment*, Durham, NC: Duke University Press.

Fischer, Frank (2003) *Reframing Public Policy: Discursive Politics and Deliberative Practices*, Oxford: Oxford University Press.

Fischer, Frank and Forester, John (eds) (1993) *The Argumentative Turn in Policy Analysis*, Durham, NC: Duke University Press.

Fischer, Frank and Gottweis, Herbert (eds) (2012) *The Argumentative Turn Revisited: Public Policy as Communicative Practice*, Durham, NC: Duke University Press.

Flyvberg, Bent (2001) *Making Social Science Matter*, Cambridge: Cambridge University Press.

Foucault, Michel (1977) *Language, Counter-Memory, Practice: Selected Essays and Interview*, Ithaca, NY: Cornell University Press.

Foucault, Michel (1980a) *History of Sexuality: Vol. I*, New York: Vintage.

Foucault, Michel (1980b) *Power/Knowledge: Selected Interviews & Other Writings, 1972–1977*, New York: Pantheon.

Foucault, Michel (1982) 'Afterword: The Subject and Power', in *Beyond Structuralism and Hermeneutics*, eds Hubert L. Dreyfus and Paul Rabinow, 2nd edn, Chicago: University of Chicago Press, pp. 208–226.

Foucault, Michel (1984) 'What is Enlightenment', in *The Foucault Reader*, ed. Paul Rabinow, New York: Pantheon, pp. 32–50.

Foucault, Michel (1989b) 'An Ethics of Pleasure', in *Foucault Live*, ed. S. Loringer, New York: Semiotext(e), pp. 257–276.
Foucault, Michel (1991) *The Foucault Effect: Studies in Governmentality*, eds Graham Burchell, Colin Gordon and Peter Miller, Chicago: University of Chicago Press.
Foucault, Michel (1994) *The Order of Things: An Archaeology of the Human Sciences*, New York: Vintage.
Foucault, Michel (2000) 'The Subject and Power', in *Power*, ed. James Falbion, New York: New Press.
Gaventa, John (1982) *Power and Powerlessness: Quiescence and Rebellion in an Appalachian Valley*, Urbana, IL: University of Illinois Press.
Giedion, Sigfried (1948) *Mechanization Takes Command: A Contribution to Anonymous History*, New York: Norton.
Gramsci, Antonio (1971) *Selections from the Prison Notebooks*, New York: International Publishers.
Habermas, Jürgen (1987) *The Philosophical Discourse of Modernity*, Cambridge, MA: The MIT Press.
Hajer, Maarten (1995) *The Politics of Environmental Discourse: Ecological Modernization and the Policy Process*, Oxford: Oxford University Press.
Hawkesworth, Mary (1988) *Theoretical Issues in Policy Analysis*, Albany, NY: SUNY Press.
Hayward, Clarissa and Lukes, Steven (2008) 'Nobody to Shoot? Power, Structure and Agency: A Dialogue', *Journal of Power*, **1** (1 (April)), 5–20.
Kern, Stephen (1983) *The Culture of Time and Space: 1880–1918*, Cambridge, MA: Harvard University Press.
Lasswell, Harold (1974) 'Some Perplexities of Policy Theory', *Social Research*, **14**, 176–189.
Lasswell, Harold (1990) *Politics: Who Gets What When and How*, New York: Peter Smith.
Latour, Bruno (1993) *We Have Never Been Modern*, London: Harvester Wheatsheaf.
Law, John (ed.) (1991) *A Sociology of Monsters: Essays on Power, Technology, and Domination*, London: Routledge.
Luke, Timothy W. (1989) *Screens of Power: Ideology, Domination, and Resistance in Informational Society*, Urbana, IL: University of Illinois Press.
Luke, Timothy W. (1995) 'New World Order or Neo-World Orders: Power, Politics and Ideology in Informationalizing Glocalities', in *Global Modernities*, eds Mike Featherstone, Scott Lash and Roland Robertson, London: Sage Publications, pp. 91–107.
Luke, Timothy W. (1996) 'Identity, Meaning and Globalization: Space-Time Compression and the Political Economy of Everyday Life', in *Detraditionalization: Critical Reflections on Authority and Identity*, eds Scott Lash, Paul Heelas and Paul Morris, Oxford: Blackwell, pp. 109–133.
Luke, Timothy W. (1998) '"Moving at the Speed of Life?" A Cultural Kinematics of Telematic Times and Corporate Values', *Cultural Values*, **2** (2 and 3), 320–339.
Lukes, Steven (1974) *Power: A Radical View*, London: Macmillan.
Lukes, Steven (2005) *Power: A Radical View*, 2nd edn, New York: Palgrave Macmillan.
Marcuse, Herbert (1964) *One-Dimensional Man: Studies in the Ideology of Advanced Industrial Society*, Boston, MA: Beacon.
Mills, C. Wright (1956) *The Power Elite*, Oxford: Oxford University Press.
Mills, C. Wright (1959) *The Sociological Imagination*, Oxford: Oxford University Press.
Mitchell, Timothy (2002) *Rule of Experts: Egypt, Techno-Politics, Modernity*, Berkeley, CA: University of California Press.
Mumford, Lewis (1963) *Technics and Civilization*, New York: Harcourt Brace Jovanovich.
Mumford, Lewis (1986) *The Lewis Mumford Reader*, ed. Donald Miller, New York: Pantheon.
Nickel, Patricia (2015) *Culture, Politics and Governing: The Contemporary Ascetics of Knowledge Production*, New York: Palgrave Macmillan.
Nye, David E. (1990) *Electrifying America: Social Meanings of a New Technology*, Cambridge, MA: The MIT Press.
Nye, David E. (1996) *The Technological Sublime*, Cambridge, MA: The MIT Press.

Perrow, Charles (1984) *Normal Accidents: Living with High Risk Technologies*, New York: Basic Books.
Peters, Guy (2011) *Institutional Theory in Political Science: The New Institutionalism*, 3rd edn, New York: Bloomsbury Publishing.
Polsby, Nelson W. (1963) *Community Power and Political Theory*, New Haven, CT: Yale University Press.
Rose, Nikolas (1999) *Powers of Freedom: Reframing Political Thought*, Cambridge: Cambridge University Press.
Schattschneider, E.E. (1960) *The Semi-Sovereign People: A Realist's View of Democracy in America*, New York: Holt, Rinehart and Winston.
Torgerson, Douglas (1999) *The Promise of Green Politics: Environmentalism and the Public Sphere*, Durham, NC: Duke University Press.
Yanow, Dvora and Schwartz-Shea, Peregrine (eds) (2006) *Interpretation and Method: Empirical Research Methods and the Interpretive Turn*, Armonk, NY: M.E. Sharpe.

PART III

DISCURSIVE POLITICS: DELIBERATION, JUSTICE, PROTEST AND EMOTION

9 Discursive institutionalism: understanding policy in context
Vivien A. Schmidt

'Discursive institutionalism' gives a name to the very rich and diverse set of ways of explaining political and social reality that are focused on the substantive content of ideas and the interactive processes of discourse in institutional context. It represents a fourth 'new institutionalist' approach in political science, in contrast to the three older 'new institutionalisms' – rational choice, historical, and sociological.[1] As such, discursive institutionalism calls attention to the significance of approaches that theorize about ideas and discourse in their many different forms, types, and levels as well as in the interactive processes of policy coordination and communication by which ideas and discourse are generated, articulated, and contested by 'sentient' (thinking, speaking, and acting) agents. As an umbrella concept, it encompasses a wide range of approaches focused on ideas – as in the 'ideational turn' (Blyth 1997) or 'ideational constructivism' (Hay 2006) – as well as discourse. Discourse encompasses not just the representation or embodiment of ideas – as in discourse analysis (following, say, Foucault 2000, Bourdieu 1990, or Laclau and Mouffe 1985) but also the interactive processes by and through which ideas are generated in the policy sphere by discursive policy communities and entrepreneurs (e.g., Haas 1992; Hajer 1993; Sabatier 1993) and communicated, deliberated, and/or contested in the political sphere by political leaders, social movements, and the public (e.g., Habermas 1989; Zaller 1992; Mutz et al. 1996; Dryzek 2000; Wodak 2009).

The institutionalism in the name underlines the importance of considering ideas and discourse in institutional context – both in terms of the meaning contexts as well as the formal (or informal) institutional contexts that are the main objects of concern of the three older institutionalisms, as rationalist incentive structures, historical rules, or cultural frames that serve as external constraints to agents' action. In discursive institutionalism, these kinds of institutions may be treated either as unproblematic background information or they may themselves be the objects of inquiry. Agents' ideas, discourse, and actions in any institutional context, however, must also be seen as responses to the material (and not so material) realities which affect them – including material events and pressures, the unintended consequences of their own actions, the actions of others, the ideas and discourse that seek to make sense of any such actions, as well as the structural frameworks of power and position.

THE CONTENT OF IDEAS AND DISCOURSE

Discursive institutionalists tend to divide between those who concentrate on ideas and those who privilege discourse. The difference is primarily one of emphasis. Scholars concerned with ideas tend to focus on the substantive content of such ideas while leaving the interactive processes of discourse implicit. Scholars who prefer discourse themselves divide into those who also emphasize its substantive content as the representation or embodiment of ideas and those who are more concerned with the discursive interactions through which actors generate, argue about, and communicate ideas in given institutional contexts.

Among the scholars concerned most with the substantive content of ideas and discourse, differences abound with regard to the forms of ideas they identify, of which there are a vast array (see, e.g., Goodin and Tilly 2006, part 4). Such ideas may be cast as strategic weapons in the battle for 'hegemonic' control (Muller 1995; see also Blyth 2002); 'frames' that provide guideposts for knowledge, analysis, persuasion, and action through 'frame-reflective discourse' (Rein and Schön 1994); narratives or discourses that shape understandings of events (e.g., Roe 1994); 'frames of reference' that orient entire policy sectors or epochs (Jobert 1989; Muller 1995); 'storytelling' to clarify practical rationality (Forester 1993); 'collective memories' that frame action (Rothstein 2005); discursive 'practices' or fields of ideas that define the range of imaginable action (Bourdieu 1994; Torfing 1999; Howarth et al. 2000); 'argumentative practices' at the center of the policy process (Fischer and Forester 1993); or the results of 'discursive struggles' that set the criteria for social classification, establish problem definitions, frame problems, define ideas, and create the shared meanings on which people act (Stone 1988).

Scholars differ also with regard to the types of ideas and discourse they investigate. The comparative politics and comparative political economy literature tends to be more concerned with cognitive ideas and discourse that provide guidelines for political action and serve to justify programs through arguments focused on their interest-based logics and necessity (see Hall 1993; Muller 1995; Schmidt 2002a, 2008) than on normative ideas and discourse that attach values to political action and serve to legitimize the policies in a program through arguments based on their appropriateness, often with regard to underlying public philosophies (see

March and Olsen 1989; Schmidt 2000, 2002a: 213–17). By contrast, in international relations the focus is more on norms, defined as ideas about appropriate standards of behavior or desirable actions shared by members of a social entity (Finnemore 1996), and on the mechanisms by which ideas take hold and are diffused, such as learning, diffusion, transmission, and mimesis (Dobbin et al. 2007).

With regard to the timing of change in ideas and discourse, whether fast or slow, incremental or abrupt, differences among scholars have much to do with the level of generality they consider (see Schmidt 2008, 2010a). At the most immediate level, scholars have long tended to focus on policy ideas. They have tended to portray them as changing most rapidly when windows of opportunity open in the face of events, and as old policies no longer solve the problems or fit the politics for which they were designed (Kingdon 1984). But what remains unclear is whether events drive change in policy ideas or whether ideas open windows, creating new opportunities for policy change.

Scholars who focus instead on the intermediate level of policy programs mostly depict them as the objects of 'great transformations' in periods of uncertainty (Blyth 2002) or as 'paradigms' – often building on Kuhn's (1970) approach in the philosophy of science. These are characterized as having a single overarching set of ideas for which a 'paradigm-shift' produces incommensurable or revolutionary change (e.g., Jobert 1989; Hall 1993; Schmidt 2002a chapter 5, 2010b). Here, the problem is that although the concept of paradigm-shift serves nicely as a metaphor for radical ideational change, it offers little guidance as to how, when, or even why a shift takes place, and rules out the coexistence of rival paradigms or the possibility that paradigm change can occur even without a clear idea behind it, say, as the result of layering new policies onto the old in a given policy program (see Schmidt 2002a).

Finally, philosophical ideas are generally situated at the deepest level of ideas, and therefore the most long-lasting. They are also often seen as more based in the political sphere than in the policy sphere, as broad concepts tied to normative values and moral principles (Weir 1992: 169), whether seen as 'global frames of reference' (Muller 1995), structures of 'discourse' (Foucault 2000), 'hegemonic discourse' (Gramsci 1971), or ideologies that set an all-encompassing perspective on reality (Freeden 2003). Here, the danger is to assume that philosophical ideas never change at all, rather than looking to the ways in which public philosophies may be created and recreated over time, which is often the focus of more historically minded political scientists (e.g., Berman 1998: 21) or historians (e.g., Hunt 1984; Nora 1989).

As for scholarly analyses of change over time, most political scientists go directly to empirical studies, both quantitative as well as qualitative. Among qualitative studies, process-tracing methods are the most prevalent. These show how ideas and discourse are tied to action by serving as guides to public actors for what to do and as sources of justification and legitimation for what such actors do (see Berman 1998; Blyth 2002). In addition to tracing empirically the ideas and discourse central to the processes of transformation, such processes can also serve to demonstrate the causal influence of ideas. This could involve providing matched pairs of cases in which everything is controlled for except the discourse, as in demonstrating the success of neo-liberal discourse in economic reform (Schmidt 2002b) or in elucidating the ways in which ideas trap or capture agents, whether through rhetorical traps (Schimmelfennig 2001) or previous diplomatic agreements that agents find themselves bound to follow, like it or not (Parsons 2003).

Another approach that takes us deeper into the theorization of the content of ideational change – this time from public administration – is provided by Bevir and Rhodes (2003), whose theory of meaning focuses on the incremental changes around a 'web of beliefs' that over time constitute political traditions. These political traditions are (re)created through individuals' narratives, arguments, and storylines about how what they are doing fits with the tradition even as they alter it. Bevir (2010) argues that such an 'interpretive' social science should take the place of 'modernist' social science, and its concept of 'governance,' in order to develop 'decentered' narratives that make better sense of the meanings people give to their actions through their 'webs of belief' that develop historically as political traditions.

Yet another way of thinking about ideational continuity as well as change is through the concept of resilience. Schmidt and Thatcher (2013) use this concept to analyze the development of neo-liberalism in its many different forms at different levels over time, but in particular since the 1980s. They propose five lines of analysis to explain the resilience of neo-liberal ideas. First, the flexibility of neo-liberalism's core principles has made it highly adaptable and mutable across time, countries, and policy sectors – e.g., from the conservative roll-back of the state to free up the markets in the 1980s to the social-democratic roll-out of the state to enhance the markets in the 1990s and early 2000s, and then to the ramp-up of supranational 'stability' rules of the European Union in the Eurozone sovereign debt crisis. Second, the gaps between neo-liberal rhetoric and reality may actually promote neo-liberal resilience by serving the next generation of neo-liberal politicians as a rallying cry, say, when outsize promises to radically reduce the welfare state or cut taxes are not fulfilled. Third, the strength of neo-liberal discourse in debates – or the weakness of alternatives – is another source of resilience, often because neo-liberal ideas may appear more commonsensical than, say, neo-Keynesian ideas, even though they have proven economically disastrous time and again. Fourth, neo-liberal resilience also stems from the power of coalitions of interests in the strategic use of neo-liberal ideas to promote their own interests, whether they believe in neo-liberalism or not. And finally, the force of institutions in the embedding of neo-liberal ideas is also a source of neo-liberal strength, since once institutionalized such ideas are very difficult to dislodge.

For in-depth philosophical theorizing about how the content of the ideas themselves change, however, one generally needs to turn to more post-modernist or post-structuralist approaches to policy change following discourse analyses that build on the work of Bourdieu, Foucault, and Laclau and Mouffe. These theoretical concepts can provide great value to the analysis of the content of ideas and how they change (and continue) over time. For example, discourse analyses that build on Michel Foucault can offer insights into how to investigate the archaeology of what was acceptable in a given discursive formation over time, from one period's *episteme* to the next, through examination of networks of rules establishing what is meaningful at any given time (Foucault 2000; see also Pedersen 2011). Conversely, discourse analyses built on Laclau and Mouffe (1985) can point to different ways in which concepts may be employed, such as 'nodal points' from which all other ideas take their meanings in an ideological system, for example, how communism in Central and Eastern Europe served to distinguish between 'real' (communist) democracy and 'bourgeois' democracy (Howarth et al. 2000).

SENTIENT AGENTS AND DISCURSIVE PRACTICES

Ideas, naturally, do not 'float freely' (Risse-Kappen 1994). They need to be carried by agents. But even where agents are treated as carriers of ideas, the connection between ideas and collective action remains unclear. The missing link is discourse not as representation but as interaction, and the ways in which ideas conveyed through discursive argumentation lead to action. But discourse also cannot be considered on its own, since it requires agents who articulate and communicate their ideas through discourse in exchanges that may involve discussion, deliberation, negotiation, and contestation. These agents can be defined as sentient (thinking and speaking) beings who generate and deliberate about ideas through discursive interactions that lead to collective action.

Focusing on sentient agents is important, because it emphasizes the fact that 'who is speaking to whom about what where and why,' or the inter-active practices of discourse, makes a difference. It is not just that agents are thinking beings who have ideas and arguments but that they are also speaking beings who share their ideas through discursive interactions that can lead to collective action. What makes agents sentient is that they are possessed not only of 'background ideational abilities,' which underpin their ability to make sense of as well as act within a given meaning context, that is, in terms of the ideational rules or rationality of that setting. It is that they also have 'foreground discursive abilities' that enable them to communicate, argue, and deliberate about taking action collectively to change their institutions (see Schmidt 2008: 314–16; 2012: 92–5).

This means that institutions – or structures – are socially constructed. As Searle (1995) explains, although 'institutional facts' – such as property, money, marriage, governments, human rights, and cocktail parties – are consciously created by sentient agents through words and action, once they are constituted people lose sight of this not only because they are born into them but also because they use them as part of a whole hierar-chy of institutional facts, in which they may be conscious of this or that institution but not of the whole architecture. Moreover, as they use them in speech and practice, the institutions themselves may evolve, whether unconsciously, as people change how they use them, or consciously, as people decide to use them differently or not to use them at all.

But where then is agency? For Searle (1995: 140–45), the whole hierarchy of institutional facts makes up the structure of constitutive rules to which agents are sensitive as part of their 'background abilities' that enable them to speak, argue, and act without the conscious or unconscious following of rules external to the agent assumed by the older neo-institutionalists by way of rationalist calculations, historical path-dependencies, or normative appropriateness. This concept of background abilities is also present in Bourdieu's notion of the '*habitus*' (as Searle 1995: 127–32 acknowledges). Bourdieu sees human activity as neither constituted nor constitutive but both simultaneously, as human beings act 'following the intuitions of a "logic of practice" which is the product of a lasting exposure to conditions similar to those in which they are placed' (Bourdieu 1990: 11). In psychol-ogy, the theory of cognitive dissonance also comes close to what we are talking about here, since it shows that people generally act without think-ing of any rules they may be following, but then check what they are doing against the various rules that might apply, with consciousness about the rules coming into play mainly where cognitive dissonance occurs, that is, when the rules are contradictory (Harmon-Jones and Mills 1999).

But although the concept of such 'background ideational abilities' helps us to explain what goes on in individuals' minds as they come up with new ideas or follow old ones, it does not explain much about the processes by which institutions change, which is a collective endeavor. It also underemphasizes a key component in human interaction that helps explain such change: discourse.

We undersell discursive institutionalism if we equate the ontology of institutions with background ideational abilities alone, neglecting sentient agents' 'foreground discursive abilities.' This is peoples' ability to think and argue outside the institutions in which they continue to act, to talk about such institutions in a critical way, to communicate and deliberate about them, to persuade themselves as well as others to change their minds about their institutions, and then to take action to change them, individually or collectively. Discourse as an interactive process is what enables agents to consciously change institutions, because the deliberative nature of discourse allows them to have ideas of and talk about institutions as objects at a distance, and to dissociate themselves from them to critique them even as they continue to use them.

Calling this interactive externalization of agents' internal ideational processes 'foreground discursive abilities' offers a generic term close to Habermas's (1989) view of 'communicative action' (although without the normative prescriptions). It is also in line with much of the underlying assumptions of the literature on 'discursive democracy' and 'deliberative democracy' (e.g., Dryzek 2000), which is all about the importance of discourse and deliberative argumentation in breaking the elite monopoly on decision making while ensuring democratic access. These are the abilities that ensure that people are able to reason, argue, and change the structures they use – a point also brought out by Antonio Gramsci (1971), who emphasizes the role of intellectuals in breaking the hegemonic discourse. But the term also points to the importance of public debates in democratic societies in serving to expose the ideas which serve as vehicles for elite domination and power or, more simply, the 'bad' ideas, lies, and manipulations in the discourse of any given political actor or set of actors.

The epistemological questions raised by this ontological discussion of sentient agents' ideational and discursive abilities are mainly about, 'How can we be sure that we know what we know?' and 'What is reality in a world in which structure and agency are as one?' These questions often lead to accusations against those who come down on the agency side of the agency-structure debate that they cannot know anything for certain once they give up the independence of structures – or materialism – because they turn reality itself into a social construction, and that they therefore are on the slippery slope of relativism.

Fears of relativism have led some discursive institutionalists to stay on the materialist side of the materialist-constructivist divide, with a correspondence view of the world that assumes that material reality is out there for agents to see, and that scholars are in the business of discovering it (e.g., Wendt 1999: 109–10). Others (e.g., Gofas and Hay 2010) try to straddle the divide between materialism and constructivism through 'critical realism' (Bhashkar [1979] 1998), worried that if there is no 'objective' reality then there is no way to protect contextualized (social) 'scientific' explanation from the radical relativism of 'anything goes,' in which power and subjectivity could trump truth and objectivity. Yet others sit on the constructivist side of the divide, assuming that most of reality is constructed by the actors themselves beyond a very basic level, but they do not deny the 'materiality' of that most basic level.

To ask if material reality exists (correspondence vs. non-correspondence) is the wrong question, however. We do better to ask what is material and 'real' and what is real even if it is not 'material.' The latter is particularly the case of institutions that may be 'real' because they constitute interests and cause things to happen even though they are socially constructed or 'social facts' and thus not material in a visible, 'put your hand or rest your eyes on it' kind of concrete sense, which constitute what Searle (1995) calls 'brute facts.'

Wittgenstein in *On Certainty* (1972) suggests further answers to our questions by differentiating between different kinds of knowledge and certainty based in different 'forms of life,' as expressed through 'language-games' (see discussions in Schmidt 2008, 2010b, 2012: 97–100). He makes a little-noticed but important distinction between language-games based on our experience in the world and those based on our pictures of the world. Language-games based on everyday experience are ones for which radical uncertainties rarely occur, such as knowledge of one's own name and history, the numbers of hands and toes one has, the meaning of the words one uses. The kind of certainty is one in which we don't doubt that the mountain will disappear if we look away, such that anyone expressing such uncertainty would be assumed not to know the meaning of the words themselves, or be not rational.

By contrast, language-games based on our pictures of the world tend to involve knowledge closer to the kind found in (social) science, which can involve radical uncertainty akin to shifts in 'paradigms' and 'cosmologies.' Belief in the existence of the earth one hundred years ago, in the events of history, in the temperature at which water boils – always allow for doubts, mistakes, and even gestalt switches, although much less often for those at the 'foundation' of our picture of the world, which 'stand fast' because they are part of the very 'scaffolding' of our thoughts (Wittgenstein 1972: 211, 234).

The experience games of everyday life, in other words, are so certain as not to be doubted; but picture games may always be doubted, although some may be more uncertain than others depending upon their place in the overall system of picture games. Radical relativism, as a result, could be much more of a danger for picture games, in particular if they are far removed from the 'scaffolding' of our own pictures of the world, than for experience games, which tend to be more universal. As Wittgenstein has noted elsewhere: 'The common behavior of mankind is the system of reference by means of which we interpret an unknown language' (1968, I: 206). And although this need not mean that we will have words for everything, such as the Hopi Indian's understanding of time or the Eskimo's many words for snow (see Whorf [1956] 1997), we can translate these into our own language and experience. This ensures a high degree of certainty not only for common behavior (knowing one's name) but also commonly experienced material realities – what we see, like mountains and buildings – even if their significance may be more uncertain for us depending upon where they fit against our pictures of the world. One could even argue that there are certain bases to human rationality that allow for universalism, as illustrated in Wittgenstein's (1968, II, xi: 223) famous observation: 'if a lion could talk, we would not understand him.' And it is also the case that if all ideas are 'constructed,' it is possible, although not easy, to construct international ideas about interests and norms – what is the modern notion of human rights about, after all, if not that (see Risse et al. 1999)?

The distinction between matters of experience and pictures of the world, thus, is a crucial one for our discussion of epistemological questions related to knowledge and certainty, since it helps us avoid the risks of radical relativism. It suggests that social scientists' explanations have varying degrees of certainty, depending on their objects of knowledge and explanation. It demonstrates that social agents in any given culture and time can generally understand other cultures and times based on common experiences through translation and interpretation, even if they may have greater difficulty with their pictures of the world. Finally, with regard to sentient agents, it shows that knowledge and certainty are collectively constructed within given institutional contexts. And for such collective construction, we need to examine more closely the range of discursive actions in which sentient agents engage.

INTERACTIVE PROCESSES OF DISCOURSE

Discursive interactions generally fall into one of two domains in the public sphere: the policy sphere characterized by a 'coordinative' discourse among policy actors engaged in creating, deliberating, arguing, bargaining, and reaching agreement on policies; and the political sphere characterized by a 'communicative' discourse between political actors and the public engaged in presenting, deliberating, arguing over, contesting, and legitimating those policy ideas (see Schmidt 2002a, Chapter 5; 2006, Chapter 5; 2008).

The agents in the coordinative discourse are generally the actors involved in the policy process, including 'policymakers' or government officials, policy consultants, experts, lobbyists, business and union leaders, and others. They generate policy ideas and arguments with different degrees and kinds of influence. And they organize themselves in a variety of groupings as discursive communities in order to influence the generation, shaping, and adoption of policies, often activated by entrepreneurial or mediating actors and informed by experts.

'Discourse coalition' is arguably the most general way of conceiving of such discursive communities. Maarten Hajer (1993: 45) uses the concept to elucidate the 'discursive production of reality' by groups of policy actors who construct the new social idea or narratives, as in the case of acid rain policy in the country. Discourse coalitions are also used by Gerhard Lehmbruch (2001) to identify the policy actors who share ideas across extended periods of time, as in the rise of ordo-liberalism in Germany as well as the idea of a social market economy. Notably, the members of the discourse coalitions themselves need not share all the same ideas, beliefs, goals, or interests in order to promote a common policy program (see Jobert 2003). Rather, discourse coalitions may be engaged in constant argumentation in their efforts to develop the ideas that they hope policy actors will ultimately take as their own as they generate policies.

When discourse coalitions are conceived of mainly as linking actors on the basis of their shared ideas, they have also been called 'epistemic communities' to call attention to the loosely connected transnational actors who hold the same cognitive and normative ideas about a common policy enterprise that they seek to promote (Haas 1992). Another subset of discourse coalitions are 'advocacy coalitions,' a term that tends to be used for more closely connected individuals who don't just share ideas but also have access to policymaking (Sabatier 1993). In addition, particular agents in discourse coalitions may themselves be cast as policy 'entrepreneurs' (Kingdon 1984) or 'mediators' (Jobert 1989; Muller 1995) who serve as catalysts for change as they articulate the ideas of the various discourse coalitions or of discursive communities more generally.

Discursive communities, including discourse coalitions, often generate their own information, although increasingly the technical experts to whom they turn are organized in think-tanks, often separate from the discursive communities. Fischer (1993), for example, notes that in the

United States, while the Democratic Party first used policy analysts in think-tanks as a way to legitimize their 'new class liberal arguments' by disguising them as technocratic discourse, the Republican discourse coalition bested them by politicizing expertise via the conservative, politically engaged think-tanks that had been proliferating since the 1970s. Rich (2004) updates this with his own study of Washington-based think-tanks, in which conservative think-tanks that produce unabashedly political and value-laden research have gotten a much bigger bang for their buck than more progressive think-tanks, which seek to be (or at least to appear to be) more value-neutral and objective. Campbell and Pedersen (2014) have recently shown that a similar phenomenon has been developing in Europe, in which only in the past five years or so have think-tanks proliferated in national capitals and Brussels. Most importantly, however, national differences remain paramount, with the production and diffusion of policy ideas following from nationally specific modes of organization, cooperation or competition, and partisanship.

In the communicative discourse, the agents of change consist not only of the usual suspects: political leaders, elected officials, party members, policymakers, spin-doctors, and the like who act as 'political entrepreneurs' as they attempt to form mass public opinion (Zaller 1992), engage the public in debates about the policies they favor (Mutz et al. 1996), and win elections. They also include the media, interest groups acting in the specialized 'policy forums' of organized interests (e.g., Rein and Schön 1994), public intellectuals, opinion makers, social movements, and even ordinary people through their everyday talk and argumentation, which can play an important role not just in the forum of 'opinion-formation' but also in that of 'will-formation' (Mansbridge 2009). In other words, all manner of discursive publics engaged in 'communicative action' (Habermas 1989) may be involved, with communication going not only from the top down but also from the bottom up.

The spheres of coordinative policy construction and communicative policy legitimation are of course interconnected in terms of both the substantive content as well as the interactive process. To begin with, the policy ideas in the coordinative discourse – often more heavily weighted toward cognitive justification – are generally translated by political actors into language and arguments accessible to the general public as part of a communicative discourse that also adds normative legitimation, to ensure that the policy and programmatic ideas resonate with the philosophical frames of the polity (see Schmidt 2006: 255–7). The process itself is one in which the coordinative discourse can be seen to prepare the ground for the communicative. In the United Kingdom, for example, the ground was prepared for Margaret Thatcher's monetarist paradigm-change before her election, by the ideas developed in a coordinative discourse consisting of a small group of the 'converted' from the Conservative party, financial elites, and the financial press (Hall 1993). But Thatcher herself was the political entrepreneur who put these ideas into more accessible language through a communicative discourse to the general public (Schmidt 2002a Chapter 6).

This said, the coordinative and communicative discourses don't always connect with one another. Policy ideas may remain in the policy sphere, either because the public might not approve, as has sometimes been the case of more progressive policies, or because the public is not interested, as in the case of highly technical reforms of banking and finance. But there may also be cases where politicians argue for one thing in the coordinative policy sphere, another in the communicative political sphere. This has often been the case with the European Union, where the perceived democratic deficit is due in part to the blame-shifting of national political leaders who agree to one thing in the coordinative discourse of the Council of Ministers but, fearful of negative public reaction, say something very different in the communicative discourse to the general public (see Schmidt 2006 Chapter 1, 2008).

We still have a problem, however, because this discussion remains focused primarily on the discourse of elites, whether in a top-to-top coordinative discourse or in a top-down communicative discourse. Mostly, however, in addition to any formalized, elite processes of coordinative consultation and whatever the elite-led processes of communicative deliberation, the public has a whole range of ways of arguing about and responding to elite-produced policies. The media, for example, are often key to framing the terms of the communicative discourse, creating narratives, arguments, and images that become determinants of interpretations of a given set of events. In the case of the financial market crises, the framing has generally been personalized in terms of a rogue player rather than generalized as a deeper critique of the international banking system, as in the case of the Barings bank debacle (Hudson and Martin 2010), or when Martha Stewart became the poster child for the early 2000s financial crisis and Bernie Madoff for the 2008 crisis.

Social movements are also significant forces in a 'bottom-up' communicative discourse. Scholars who focus on 'contentious politics' demonstrate the many ways in which leaders, social movement activists, along with everyday actors spur change through ideas that contest the status quo, conveyed by discourse that persuades others to join in protest, which in turn generates debate and argumentation (e.g., Aminzade et al. 2001; Della Porta 2009). Charlotte Epstein's (2008) account of how 'Moby Dick' became 'Moby Doll' is a clear demonstration of the way in which social movements were able to change ideas through a communicative discourse that led to radically altered policies negotiated in the transnational coordinative sphere.

Social movements are best categorized as part of the communicative discourse because they are at least initially removed from the policy world, and rely on pressure from the outside, through media coverage of their protests and actions, rather than from the inside, through policy influence. But often, as social movements develop, the outside communicative practices are accompanied by inside coordinative ones. In some cases, as social movements become institutionalized, as is the case particularly with regard to the environment or women's issues, the coordinative discourse with policy actors becomes predominant, and the kind of activity engaged in makes the social movement one in name only except for the moments when a mobilizing issue comes up, and the social movement returns to protest and argumentation in the streets.

Finally, the general public of citizens and voters to whom this communicative discourse is directed also contribute to it and, thereby, spur policy change. They do this as members of civil society, not just through grass-roots organizing, social mobilization, and demonstrations, but also as members of 'mini-publics' in citizen juries, issues forums, deliberative polls, and the like (see Goodin and Dryzek 2006) as well as more simply as members of the electorate, whose voice is heard as the subjects of opinion polls, surveys, focus groups, as well as, of course, as voters – where actions speak even louder than verbal arguments. Not to be neglected in this, however, are also the everyday practices of ordinary people, even in cases where ideas are unarticulated, and change is individual, subtle, and slow, as they articulate their protest through sanctioning politicians in votes or by not voting at all (Seabrooke 2007).

THE CONTEXT OF IDEAS AND DISCOURSE

Institutional context also matters. If sentient (thinking and speaking) agents are the drivers of change, and their ideas (what they think and argue about what to do) and discourse (what they say about what to do) are the vehicles of change, then the institutional context is the setting within which their ideas have meaning, their discourses have communicative force, and their collective actions make a difference (if they do what they say they think about what to do).

Three elements – ideas, discourse, and institutions – all need to be considered in terms of the institutional context. That context is first of all the 'meaning context' in which ideas and discourse make sense, such that speakers 'get it right' in terms of the ideational rules or rationality of a given setting, by addressing their remarks to the 'right' audiences at the 'right' times in the 'right' ways. This is why even where a term may be disseminated internationally, when it is taken up nationally, it is likely to be used very differently, given differences in meaning context and all that that entails in terms of culture – economic, political, and social.

The context, however, may also refer to the 'forum' within which the discourse proceeds, following a particular logic of communication. Thus, for example, Stephen Toulmin (1958) shows that in any given 'forum of argumentation' or discourse, the procedural rules create a common set of understandings even when speakers lack trust or consensus, as in the adversarial arguments that take place in a courtroom. Moreover, in international negotiations where the rules are not preestablished and the 'forum' is an ad hoc creation dependent upon the players and the circumstances, prenegotiations are the context within which the rules of discursive interaction are set, even though the actual process involves other kinds of discursive interactions outside the negotiating context, such as with domestic constituencies and other international actors (Stein 1989).

Finally, formal institutions – as elaborated in historical institutionalist explanation – also constitute the institutional context and give shape to discursive interactions. Formal arrangements affect *where* discourse matters, by establishing who talks to whom about what, where and when. For example, although all countries have both coordinative and communicative discourses, one or the other tends to be more important due to the configuration of the political institutions. Political institutional setting helps explain why simple polities like France and the United Kingdom, where authority tends to be concentrated in the executive and reform agendas are generally decided by a restricted elite, tend to have more elaborate communicative discourses to the public – so as to legitimate those reforms – than in compound polities like Germany and Italy, where authority tends to be more dispersed, and their coordinative discourses among policy actors are necessarily more elaborate, given the wide range of actors involved (Schmidt 2000, 2002a, 2006).

The formal institutional context, however, is not neutral with regard to its effect on politics. But one cannot therefore simply map power onto position, as is often done in rationalist and historical institutionalist analyses that assume we know an agent's interests and power to serve those interests if we know their position (Schmidt 2010a). In discursive institutionalism, by contrast, there is always the recognition that ideas and discourse can also provide power, as actors gain power from their ideas at the same time they give power to their ideas (see also Wodak 2009: 35–6). This results, for example, when agents are able to 'set the agenda' as 'policy entrepreneurs' who build coalitions for reform or as 'political entrepreneurs' who gain public support for reform (Kingdon 1984; Baumgartner and Jones 1993). Moreover, actors can gain power from their ideas even where they may lack the power of position, whether they are part of discourse coalitions, as in the case of acid rain (Hajer 1993) or of social movements, as in the case of the whales (Epstein 2008).

Ideational power can also come from a position *qua* position, however, since ideas and values infuse the exercise of power and perceptions of position (Lukes 2005). Theories about the structures and practices of elite ideational domination abound among continental philosophers and macro-sociologists (e.g., Gramsci 1971; Bourdieu 1994; Foucault 2000). But the importance of discourse means that regardless of the power of the background ideational context, in which people may very well be socialized into a certain manner of thinking through elite-dominated ideas, foreground discursive abilities enable those self-same people to reason about and critique those ideational structures. But this is not to suggest therefore that simply recognizing, contesting, and thereby seeking to delegitimize the power of elites' ideas necessarily changes the structures of power and the power of position or coercion. Structural power is also the power not to listen, and to impose.

The different ways of thinking about the discursive power of ideas can be systematized in three basic ways: power *through* ideas, power *over* ideas, and power *in* ideas (Carstensen and Schmidt forthcoming). First, and perhaps most commonly analyzed within discursive institutionalism, ideational power *through* ideas occurs when actors have the capacity to persuade other actors of the cognitive validity and/or normative value of their worldview through the use of ideational elements. Second, ideational power *over* ideas is manifested as the capacity of actors to control and dominate the meaning of ideas. This may occur both directly, say, by elite actors' coercive power to impose their ideas, and indirectly, by actors shaming opponents into conformity – as when social movements' activism pushes elites to adopt their ideas – or resisting alternative interpretations – as in the power of neo-liberal economic experts to shut out neo-Keynesian alternatives. Third, and finally, ideational power shows itself when certain ideas enjoy authority in structuring thought or institutionalizing certain ideas at the expense of other ideas – as in analyses following Foucault, Bourdieu, or Gramsci. Here ideational power concerns the ways that historically specific structures of meaning or the institutional set-up of a polity or a policy area enhances or diminishes the ability of actors to promote their ideas. This also fits with historical or sociological institutionalist approaches to ideas.

CONCLUSION

In discursive institutionalism, then, we focus attention not only on the content of the ideas and discourse, which comes in a wide variety of forms and types at different levels and different rates of change, but also on the interactive processes of discourse. The 'sentient' agents in such processes engage in coordinative policy discourses and communicative political discourses that may go in many directions, whether from top to bottom, bottom to top, or that may even stay at the bottom. The institutional context in which they interact is also important. It is constituted not only by the meaning-based logics of communication in any given setting that agents navigate through their background ideational abilities, and that they maintain or change through their foreground discursive abilities. That context is also defined by their (in)formal institutions, since power and position also matter in terms of ideas and discourse as well as structural constraints.

NOTE

1. Rational choice institutionalism focuses on rational actors who pursue their preferences following a 'logic of calculation' within political institutions, defined as structures of incentives. Historical institutionalism details the development of political institutions, described as regularized patterns and routinized practices subject to a 'logic of path-dependence.' Sociological institutionalism concentrates on social agents who act according to a 'logic of appropriateness' within political institutions, defined as socially constituted and culturally framed rules and norms. See Schmidt (2010a).

REFERENCES

Aminzade, Ronald R., Jack A. Goldstone, Doug McAdam, Elizabeth J. Perry, William H. Sewell Jr., Sidney Tarry, and Charles Tilly (2001) *Silence and Voice in the Study of Contentious Politics*, New York: Cambridge University Press.

Baumgartner, Frank R. and Bryan D. Jones (1993) *Agendas and Instability in American Politics*, Chicago: University of Chicago Press.

Berman, Sheri (1998) *The Social Democratic Movement: Ideas and Politics in the Making of Interwar Europe*, Cambridge, MA: Harvard University Press.

Bevir, Mark (2010) *Democratic Governance*, Princeton: Princeton University Press.

Bevir, Mark, and R.A.W. Rhodes (2003) *Interpreting British Governance*, London: Routledge.

Bhashkar, Roy ([1979] 1998) *The Possibility of Naturalism*, 3rd edn, London: Routledge.

Blyth, Mark M. (1997) '"Any More Bright Ideas?" The Ideational Turn in Comparative Political Economy', *Comparative Politics* **29** (2), 229–50.

Blyth, Mark M. (2002) *Great Transformations: Economic Ideas and Institutional Change in the Twentieth Century*, New York: Cambridge University Press.

Bourdieu, Pierre (1990) *In Other Words: Essays towards a Reflexive Sociology*, Stanford, CA: Stanford University Press.

Bourdieu, Pierre (1994) *Raisons Pratiques*, Paris: Le Seuil.

Campbell, John L. and Ove Pedersen (2014) *The National Origins of Policy Ideas: Knowledge Regimes in the United States, France, Germany, and Denmark*, Princeton: Princeton University Press.

Carstensen, Martin B. and Vivien A. Schmidt (forthcoming) 'Power Through, Over and In Ideas: Conceptualizing Ideational Power in Discursive Institutionalism', *Journal of European Public Policy*.

Della Porta, Donatella (ed.) (2009) *Democracy in Social Movements*, Basingstoke, UK: Palgrave Macmillan.

Dobbin, Frank, Beth Simmons and Geoffrey Garrett (2007) 'The Global Diffusion of Public Policies: Social Construction, Coercion, Competition or Learning?', *Annual Review of Sociology* **33**, 449–72.

Dryzek, John (2000) *Deliberative Democracy and Beyond*, Oxford: Oxford University Press.

Epstein, Charlotte (2008) *The Power of Words in International Relations: Birth of an Anti-Whaling Discourse*, Cambridge, MA: The MIT Press.

Finnemore, Martha (1996) 'Norms, Culture, and World Politics: Insights from Sociology's Institutionalism', *International Organization* **50** (2), 325–47.

Fischer, Frank (1993) 'Policy Discourse and the Politics of Washington Think Tanks', in *The Argumentative Turn in Policy Analysis and Planning*, edited by Frank Fischer and John Forester, Durham, NC: Duke University Press.

Fischer, Frank and John Forester (eds) (1993) *The Argumentative Turn in Policy Analysis and Planning*, Durham, NC: Duke University Press.

Forester, John (1993) 'Learning from Practice Stories: The Priority of Practical Judgment', in *The Argumentative Turn in Policy Analysis and Planning*, edited by Frank Fischer and John Forester, Durham, NC: Duke University Press.

Foucault, Michel (2000) *Power*. Volume 3 of *Essential Works of Foucault, 1954–1984*, edited by J.D. Faubion, New York: New Press.

Freeden, Michael (2003) *Ideology: A Very Short Introduction*, Oxford: Oxford University Press.

Gofas, Andreas and Colin Hay (2010) 'The Ideas Debate in Political Analysis: Towards a Cartography and Critical Assessment', in *The Role of Ideas in Political Analysis*, edited by Andreas Gofas and Colin Hay, London: Routledge.

Goodin, Robert and Tilly Charles (eds) (2006) *Oxford Handbook of Contextual Political Analysis*, Oxford: Oxford University Press.

Goodin Robert and John Dryzek (2006) 'Deliberative Impacts: The Macro-Political Uptake of Mini-Publics', *Politics and Society* **34** (2), 219–44.

Gramsci, Antonio (1971) *Selections from the Prison Notebooks*, New York: International Publishing.

Haas, Peter M. (1992) 'Introduction: Epistemic Communities and International Policy Coordination', *International Organization* **46**, 1–35.

Habermas, Jürgen (1989) *The Structural Transformation of the Public Sphere*, translated by T. Burger and F. Lawrence, Cambridge, MA: The MIT Press.

Hajer, Maarten (1993) 'Discourse Coalitions in Practice: The Case of Acid Rain in Great Britain', in *The Argumentative Turn in Policy Analysis and Planning*, edited by Frank Fischer and John Forester, Durham, NC: Duke University Press.

Hall, Peter (1993) 'Policy Paradigms, Social Learning and the State: The Case of Economic Policy-Making in Britain', *Comparative Politics* **25**, 275–96.

Harmon-Jones, Eddie and Judson Mills (1999) *Cognitive Dissonance: Progress on a Pivotal Theory in Social Psychology*, Washington, DC: American Psychological Association.

Hay, Colin (2006) 'Constructivist Institutionalism', in *The Oxford Handbook of Political Institutions*, edited by R.A.W. Rhodes, S. Binder and B. Rockman, Oxford: Oxford University Press.

Howarth, David, Aletta J. Norval and Yannis Stavrakakis (eds) (2000) *Discourse Theory and Political Analysis*, Manchester: Manchester University Press.

Hudson, David and Mary Martin (2010) 'Narratives of Neoliberalism', in *The Role of Ideas in Political Analysis*, edited by Andreas Gofas and Colin Hay, London: Routledge.

Hunt, Lynn (1984) *Politics, Culture, and Class in the French Revolution*, Berkeley: University of California Press.

Jobert Bruno (1989) 'The Normative Frameworks of Public Policy', *Political Studies* **37**, 376–86.

Jobert, Bruno (2003) 'Europe and the Recomposition of National Forums', *Journal of European Public Policy* **10** (3), 463–77.

Kingdon, John (1984) *Agendas, Alternatives and Public Policies*, New York: Longman.

Kuhn, Thomas (1970) *The Structure of Scientific Revolutions*, 2nd edn, Chicago: University of Chicago Press.

Laclau, Ernesto and Chantal Mouffe (1985) *Hegemony and Socialist Strategy: Towards a Radical Democratic Politics*, Oxford: Blackwell.

Lehmbruch, G. (2001) 'Institutional Embedding of Market Economies: The German Model and Its Impact on Japan', in *The Origins of Nonliberal Capitalism*, edited by W. Streeck and K. Yamamura, Ithaca, NY: Cornell University Press.

Lukes, Stephen (2005) *Power: A Radical View Second Edition*, Basingstoke, UK: Palgrave Macmillan.

Mansbridge, Jane (2009) 'Deliberative and Non-Deliberative Negotiations', Harvard Kennedy School Working Papers, HKS Working Paper No. RWP09-010, http://papers.ssrn.com/sol3/papers.cfm?abstract_id=1380433#%23.

March, James G. and Johan P. Olsen (1989) *Rediscovering Institutions*, New York: Free Press.

Muller, P. (1995) 'Les politiques publiques comme construction d'un rapport au monde', in *La Construction du Sens dans les Politiques Publiques*, edited by Alain Faure, Gielles Pollet and Philippe Warin, Paris: L'Harmattan, pp.153–79.

Mutz, Diana C., Paul M. Sniderman and Richard A. Brody (1996) *Political Persuasion and Attitude Change*, Ann Arbor, MI: University of Michigan Press.

Nora, Pierre (1989) 'Between Memory and History', *Representations* **26**, 11–12.

Parsons, Craig (2003) *A Certain Idea of Europe*, Ithaca, NY: Cornell

Pedersen, Ove (2011) 'Discourse Analysis', *Encyclopaedia of Political Science*, edited by Bertrand Badie, Dirk Berg-Schlosser and Leonardo Morlino, Thousand Oaks, CA: Sage.

Rein, Martin and Donald A. Schön (1994) *Frame Reflection Toward the Resolution of Intractable Policy Controversies*, New York: Basic Books.

Rich, Andrew (2004) *Think Tanks, Public Policy, and the Politics of Expertise*, New York: Cambridge University Press.

Risse, Thomas, Stephen Ropp and Kathryn Sikkink (1999) *The Power of Human Rights: International Norms and Domestic Change*, Cambridge: Cambridge University Press.

Risse-Kappen, Thomas (1994) 'Ideas Do Not Float Freely: Transnational Coalitions, Domestic Structures, and the End of the Cold War', *International Organization* **48** (2), 185–214.

Roe, Emery (1994) *Narrative Policy Analysis*, Durham, NC: Duke University Press.

Rothstein, Bo (2005) *Social Traps and the Problem of Trust*, Cambridge: Cambridge University Press.

Sabatier, Paul (1993) 'Policy Change over a Decade or More', in *Policy Change and Learning: An Advocacy Coalition Approach*, edited by H.C. Jenkins-Smith, Boulder, CO: Westview Press.

Schimmelfennig, Frank (2001) 'The Community Trap: Liberal Norms, Rhetorical Action, and the Eastern Enlargement of the European Union', *International Organization* **55** (1), Winter, 47–80.

Schmidt, Vivien A. (2000) 'Values and Discourse in the Politics of Adjustment', in *Welfare and Work in the Open Economy*, Volume 1, edited by Fritz W. Scharpf and Vivien A. Schmidt, Oxford: Oxford University Press, pp.229–309.

Schmidt, Vivien A. (2002a) *The Futures of European Capitalism*, Oxford: Oxford University Press.

Schmidt, Vivien A. (2002b) 'Does Discourse Matter in the Politics of Welfare State Adjustment?', *Comparative Political Studies* **35** (2), 168–93.

Schmidt, Vivien A. (2006) *Democracy in Europe: The EU and National Polities*, Oxford: Oxford University Press.

Schmidt, Vivien A. (2008) 'Discursive Institutionalism: The Explanatory Power of Ideas *and* Discourse', *Annual Review of Political Science* **11**, 303–26.

Schmidt, Vivien A. (2010a) 'Taking Ideas *and* Discourse Seriously: Explaining Change through Discursive Institutionalism as the Fourth New Institutionalism', *European Political Science Review* **2** (1), 1–25.

Schmidt, Vivien A. (2010b) 'On Putting Ideas into Perspective: Schmidt on Kessler, Martin and Hudson, and Smith', in *The Role of Ideas in Political Analysis: A Portrait of Contemporary Debates*, edited by Andreas Gofas and Colin Hay, London: Routledge.

Schmidt, Vivien A. (2012) 'Discursive Institutionalism: Scope, Dynamics, and Philosophical Underpinnings', in *The Argumentative Turn Revised: Public Policy as Communicative Practice*, edited by Frank Fischer and Herbert Gottweis, Durham, NC: Duke University Press.

Schmidt, Vivien A. and Mark Thatcher (2013) 'Introduction: The Resilience of Neo-Liberal Ideas', in *Resilient Liberalism in Europe's Political Economy*, edited by Vivien Schmidt and Mark Thatcher, Cambridge: Cambridge University Press.

Seabrooke, Leonard (2007) 'The Everyday Social Sources of Economic Crises', *International Studies Quarterly* **51**, 795–810.

Searle, John (1995) *The Construction of Social Reality*, New York: Free Press.

Stein, Janice (1989) *Getting to the Table*, Baltimore, MD: Johns Hopkins University Press.

Stone, Deborah (1988) *Policy Paradox and Political Reason*, Glenview, IL: Scott Foresman.

Torfing, J. (1999) *New Theories of Discourse: Laclau, Mouffe and Zizek*, London: Blackwell.

Toulmin, Stephen (1958) *The Uses of Argument*, Cambridge: Cambridge University Press.

Weir, Margaret (1992) *Politics and Jobs*, Princeton, NJ: Princeton University Press.

Wendt, Alexander (1999) *Social Theory of International Politics*, Cambridge: Cambridge University Press.

Whorf, B.L. ([1956] 1997) *Language, Thought and Reality: Selected Writings of Benjamin Lee Whorf*, Cambridge, MA: The MIT Press.

Wittgenstein, Ludwig (1968) *Philosophical Investigations*, Oxford: Basil Blackwell.

Wittgenstein, Ludwig (1972) *On Certainty*, New York: Harper.

Wodak, Ruth (2009) *The Discourse of Politics in Action*, Houndmills, Basingstoke, UK: Palgrave.

Zaller, John (1992) *The Nature and Origins of Mass Opinion*, New York: Cambridge University Press.

10 Social justice and urban policy deliberation: balancing the discourses of democracy, diversity and equity

Susan S. Fainstein

Critical urban analysis is a recent form of scholarly inquiry, having developed in the West during the urban uprisings of the 1960s and 1970s, although it has antecedents at the turn of the twentieth century.[1] In the first part of that century the study of urban phenomena was within the disciplines of public administration, urban planning, and sociology. These largely assumed the existence of a unified public interest, technical methods of problem solving, and lack of conflict. Beginning mostly in the 1920s and extending through the postwar period, students of public administration concerned themselves with municipal governance; urban planning dealt with the physical form of cities; and urban sociology posited an ecological view of urban development. After the 1960s, interdisciplinary investigations of the political economy and of interacting socio-spatial phenomena within cities broke with past approaches (inter alia, Harvey 1973; Castells 1977; Soja 1980). By starting with the city rather than a discipline, urban scholars were inclined to connect processes with outcomes, see social divisions, and identify hierarchies of power. Much of this critical urban literature had as a subtext the identification of injustice and a normative standard on which it based its stance; nevertheless the criteria for determining just policy were rarely specified. This began to change during the 1990s when urban scholars started to address the topic of justice explicitly, and considerable effort has been made since the beginning of the new millennium to define justice and prescribe approaches to realizing it within the urban context (Marcuse et al. 2009; Hayward and Swanstrom 2011; Carmon and Fainstein 2013).[2]

In this chapter I outline a mode of policy analysis that takes justice into account.[3] Although the examples I provide here refer to efforts to restructure the built environment, the template described can also be used in reference to other policy areas like education or social services. Based on a theoretical argument that I developed elsewhere (Fainstein 2010), I use the three general principles of democracy, diversity, and equity as the hallmarks of justice. From them can be derived more specific metrics by which to judge the process and outcomes of particular policies. As in the case of environmental impacts, we cannot expect policies which perfectly fulfill all criteria, but we can compare alternatives in order to decide which most maximizes the principles of justice.

My approach conforms to the argument presented by Rainer Forst (2002, p. 238) in *Contexts of Justice*, where he comments: 'The principle of general justification is context-transcending not in the sense that it violates contexts of individual and collective self-determination but insofar as it designates minimal standards within which self-determination is "reiterated" . . . '. Forst's assertion echoes Nussbaum's (2000, p. 6) contention that there is a threshold level of capabilities (i.e., the potential to 'live as a dignified free human being who shapes his or her own life' (p. 72)) below which justice is sacrificed, and that it is incumbent on government to provide the social basis for its availability although not for its actual realization.

Choosing justice as the norm for urban policy reacts to the growing inequality and social exclusion resulting from the application of neoliberalism to public policy (Brenner and Theodore 2002; Fainstein 2014). Within this ideological framework, competitiveness has become the chief justification for policy choice. Policies to reduce inequality and provide advantages to minority groups, in the neoliberal view, hinder the workings of the market's invisible hand, produce moral hazards, and cause the economy to perform at a suboptimal level. By this logic efficiency becomes the single criterion for evaluating public policy, and cost/benefit analysis constitutes the tool for its realization. The counter-argument is that using justice as the yardstick for measuring public policy effectiveness does not negate efficiency as a goal but instead requires that the policy maker ask to what end efficiency applies. If a policy serves the goal of assisting the most disadvantaged without wasting resources, then the policy is efficient even if it does not maximize an aggregate benefit/cost ratio. Of course, for those who view the only measure of efficiency as maximizing utility in the aggregate, and if a policy succeeds in increasing overall growth more by subsidizing the already advantaged than would occur with a more redistributive program, then assisting the disadvantaged wastes resources.

The defense of justice as a principal goal for urban policy requires both moral and practical arguments. If one does not argue that people should take actions because they are right, then one has no way to counter self-interest. The moral argument comes from a commitment to fairness rather than selfishness. Rational choice theorists expect that everyone is going to act in his or her individual interest and rationalize selfishness through the mechanism of the invisible hand. Orthodox Marxists start with class rather than the individual and interpret action as the consequence of class interests. For Marxists justice is achievable only through transforming the relations of production. Interests, however, are subject to interpretation. How do you know what your individual or class interest actually is? There is an assumption that your material interest if you are a businessperson is to exploit your workforce as much as possible, while your class interest, if you are a worker, is to resist as much as possible. But in fact both individual and class interests encompass a broad spectrum of possibility, and part of everyone's interest is living in a decent society. Moreover, even from a practical standpoint, restricting the definition of interest to economic outcomes, business owners can benefit from a happier and more stable workforce and from customers with more disposable income. Similarly willingness to be open to difference also arises out of both a moral and a practical viewpoint. People have multiple identities and do not have to define themselves singularly by race, ethnicity, gender, or religion. Thus, morally inclusion derives from the recognition of a common humanity, while practically it results from recognition that intolerance easily leads to violence.

Moral philosophy offers a guide to discovering what constitutes a decent society. The problem with abstract philosophy, however, is that it establishes goals without providing a means to proceed toward them. What are the policies? What are the immediate aims of social movements? How do we move toward achieving the goal of a more just city?

HISTORICAL BACKGROUND

After the Second World War the development of the field of policy analysis as well as of urban planning focused on the creation of rational methodologies for determining appropriate policy measures. Deriving their approach from the scientific method, analysts separated the procedure for choosing among alternative policies from the formulation of the goals that the measures were supposed to maximize (Lazarsfeld and Rosenberg 1955; Dror 1983; Faludi 1983). Influenced by the use of Planning Programming Budget (PPB) in the US Department of Defense, policy makers applied the rational model, as it had been adopted by economists and refined into cost–benefit analysis and computer modeling, and sought to apply it broadly to all policy areas. Although users of these techniques did not assume that one could derive general goals scientifically, the very refusal to develop a means for deriving those goals resulted in the sharp separation of process from outcome. Within democracies it was vaguely supposed that politicians would reflect the public will and provide the values that the process would seek to maximize. The pressure to quantify results caused the maximization of benefits over costs to become the purpose of policy, in line with the utilitarian premise of the greatest happiness of the greatest number (Campbell and Marshall 2002). Since only certain kinds of benefits were easily quantified and measured (e.g., number of slum dwellings demolished; number of vehicle-miles attained; test scores raised), achieving high numerical outputs, usually expressed in monetary units, became ends in themselves with little regard for the consequences to those bearing the costs. Even those who supported satisficing and incrementalism rather than maximizing results did not examine the distributive issues involved (Lindblom 1959; Simon 1972).

Political rebellion in the 1960s and 1970s stimulated an intellectual response that critiqued the philosophical and scientific bases on which the rational model proceeded. The view that governing values were simply there to be applied rather than the product of dialogue was attacked (Fischer 1980; Fischer and Forester 1993). Critics exposed the negative results of programs like urban renewal and highway building, which destroyed communities, left slum dwellers in worse circumstances than previously, and created unpleasant environments (Jacobs 1961; Gans 1968). Scrutiny of power relations in cities demonstrated that the alleged scientific calculation of costs and benefits acted as just window dressing to justify programs in the interests of downtown businesses and real estate developers (Mollenkopf 1983; Fainstein et al. 1986; Logan and Molotch 1987; Stone 1989). Eventually the various critiques gave rise to an alternative stream of scholarship that called for other values than efficiency to guide policy analysis and which particularly emphasized democratic rather than expert-based decision making. Nevertheless, even while radical approaches arose out of a critique of the substantive outcomes of earlier methods, the separation of process from outcome continued (Fainstein 2005a). Now, however, the process was to be democratic participation rather than scientific calculation (Arnstein 1969). The underlying assumption became that if you had good processes that included the affected publics, you would have good outcomes (Innes 1996). It implied a role for the policy professional of facilitator and mediator rather than of someone who pressed for particular kinds of outcomes. Advocates of citizen participation professed skepticism regarding the ability of experts to be reformers. They thus gave up on the ideals of nineteenth-century progressives, who pressed for independent leadership by professionals within governmental bureaucracies, and also of twentieth-century welfare state advocates, who regarded state officials as progenitors of enlightened planning (Mannheim 1949).

In *The Just City* (2010) I argue that moving to an analysis that prioritizes justice requires an understanding of the socio-political contest, an examination of the policy making process, a discussion of the types of policies that will achieve these values, and an evaluation of the distributional outcomes of policies. Although the application of such criteria is context dependent and requires balancing conflicting objectives, it is nevertheless possible to develop a scorecard upon which the formulation and impacts of policies can be measured. The analogy would be to environmental impact statements. As in the case of environmental impacts we cannot expect perfect outcomes, but we can compare alternatives in order to decide which most maximizes the principles of justice.

Establishing principles of justice and calling on policy makers to realize them is subject to dismissal as utopian. Nevertheless, utopian goals, despite being unrealizable, have important functions in relation to people's consciousness (Harvey 2003; Friedmann 2011). Right now, in most parts of the world, the dominant ideology extols the superiority of the market as decision maker, growth rather than equity as the mark of achievement, and limits on government. To the extent that justice becomes intrinsic to policy evaluation, then the content of policy can change. If justice is considered to refer not only to outcomes but also to inclusion in discussion, then it incorporates the communicative viewpoint as well. Justice, however, requires more than participation; it also encompasses, at least minimally, a deontological reference to norms transcending the particular, as will be discussed below.

IS THE CITY THE APPROPRIATE UNIT FOR EXAMINING JUSTICE?

For theories of both deliberative democracy and social justice, scale presents an important problem. In terms of democratic participation, any deliberation that excludes people who will be affected by a decision is not fair. Yet, as a matter of practicality, inclusion of everyone affected, even with the potential offered by telecommunications and information technology, would make decision making either impossibly tedious or simply untenable. Questions of scale are particularly salient to urban policy, as the presence of jurisdictional boundaries typically limits planning decisions to relatively small places. A decision by the occupants of a gated community to lobby against construction of recreational facilities by the municipality to which they belong may be perfectly democratic and equitable within the community's boundaries while being undemocratic and unjust within the larger entity. Likewise competitive bidding among cities for industry can fulfill democratic and egalitarian norms within each city but undermine both on the scale of the nation. And, most glaringly, barriers to immigration and subsidies to enterprises by wealthy national governments are exclusionary and unjust in relation to inhabitants of other, poorer countries. Yet, in regard to social justice, the elimination of protective tariffs, subsidies, and restrictions on immigration can result in impoverishing everyone, as a completely unhindered flow of labor and capital exacerbates the race to the bottom already underway. Thus borders both exclude and protect. Moreover, the specific production of plans and policies must occur within formal institutions with delimited boundaries in a restricted time period.

Municipalities are usually the smallest units of public administration and depend on higher levels of government for their authority and resources. Typically, however, they have jurisdiction over a number of policy areas intrinsic to the well-being of their users. As a rule municipalities usually have at least some control over taxation, public safety, planning and zoning, incentive packages to developers, housing prices, social services, recreation, public health, and transportation access. In the United States considerable variation exists in the amount of home rule extended to municipalities by state governments; more centralized national governments produce greater uniformity but nevertheless generally allow considerable local decision making, particularly in relation to planning. Thus, if we look at cities within wealthy European countries we see some places with public land ownership, much social housing, and substantial amenities open to all, while others practice exclusion and privatization. Within poor nations some municipalities allow the informal economy to flourish and ensure access to electricity and water, while others carry out large-scale demolitions and push residents and markets to the periphery. Thus, even if meaningful income redistribution is not within the power of localities (Peterson 1981), much can be done at the urban level to improve the quality of life for the relatively disadvantaged. For progressive policy makers the chore becomes both to critique approaches that rationalize benefits to the best off on the basis of trickle down and to propose policies that will increase justice in the city.

POLICY MAKING FOR THE JUST CITY

The modern approach to the question of justice usually starts with John Rawls's (1971) argument concerning the distribution of values that people would pick in the 'original position,' wherein, 'behind a veil of ignorance,' they do not know their ultimate attributes and social standing. Rawls, using a model of rational choice, concludes that individuals would choose a system of equal opportunity, which, he says in his most recent formulation, involves 'a framework of political and legal institutions that adjust the long-run trend of economic forces so as to prevent excessive concentrations of property and wealth, especially those likely to lead to political domination' (Rawls 2001, p. 44). The metric for equality of opportunity is share of primary goods, which Rawls defines to include self-respect as well as wealth. If Rawls's conception of justice is applied to the city, public policy should aim at a fair distribution of benefits and the mitigation of disadvantage.

The philosophical literature contains innumerable discussions of the meaning of primary goods and the relationship between equality of opportunity and equality of condition. Rawls's use of the phrase 'prevent excessive concentrations of property and wealth' implies a realistic utopianism – the expectation is not of eliminating material inequality but rather of lessening it. Thus, the criterion for evaluating policy measures, according to Rawlsian logic, is to ensure that they most benefit the least well-off. This principle, however, exists in tension with a democratic norm under the circumstances of illiberal majorities. Democratic theory recognizes this issue by calling for protection of the rights of minorities, but this qualification does not overcome the inherent dilemma of divergent interests in a context where wealth and status (indicated by, inter alia, skin color, gender, and ethnicity) translate into political power.

Rawls's discussion is in relation to the nation-state and does not address the problem of spatial inequality. The French philosopher Henri Lefebvre, by introducing the concept of the right to the city, incorporates spatial relations within an egalitarian argument. Lefebvre alerts us to the way in which space and society are mutually constituted: 'Space and the politics of space "express" social relationships but [also] react against them' (Lefebvre 2003, p. 15). In delineating a right to the city, Lefebvre (1996, p. 147) is referring both to an individual right in relation to equal access to space and also to a joint aim: a city providing for individual human needs that are satisfied through social relationships developed in lived space. He thus goes beyond the liberal individualism of Rawls and his successors, pointing to qualities immanent in the collectivity.

Feminist and multiculturalist critics of Rawls contend that his definition of primary goods deals insufficiently with 'recognition' of difference (Young 2000; Benhabib 2002). Whether or not this concept can be subsumed under what Rawls calls self-respect (see Fraser 1997, p. 33, n.4), its salience for developing a model of the just city requires attention in an age of identity politics, ethnic conflict, and immigration. Within the vocabulary of urban planning and policy, the term diversity refers to such recognition and is the quality that writers like Richard Sennett (1992) and Jane Jacobs (1961) argue should characterize city life. The embodiment of diversity ranges from mixed use to mixed income, racial and ethnic integration, gender equality, and widely accessible public space (Fainstein 2005b). Nancy Fraser (1997, p. 16) points to the tension that exists between equality and diversity, or, as she terms it, redistribution and recognition:

> Recognition claims often take the form of calling attention to, if not performatively creating, the putative specificity of some group and then of affirming its value. Thus, they tend to promote group differentiation. Redistribution claims, in contrast, often call for abolishing economic arrangements that underpin group specificity . . . Thus, they tend to promote group dedifferentiation. The upshot is that the politics of recognition and the politics of redistribution often appear to have mutually contradictory aims.

Diversity and deliberation, like democracy and just outcomes, are in tension. If deliberation works best within a moral community under conditions of trust, then a heterogeneous public creates obstacles to its realization. Danielle Allen (2004), in her critique of Habermas's ideal speech situation, contends that the goal of consensus elides underlying difference; she distinguishes between notions of unanimity and wholeness, wherein unanimity reflects everyone's acceptance of the outcomes of a decision while wholeness only implies acceptance of the legitimacy of the decision making process. This occurs when participants expect that, if they bear the costs of one policy, they will be compensated by another – that is, they trust one another. Her position is intermediate to deliberative democrats on the one hand and theorists like Chantal Mouffe (2013) and Richard Sennett (1971), on the other. These latter regard conflict as salutary, although even they expect that there is an underlying commitment to peaceful resolution of disputes.

In cities, the issue of diversity is particularly sharp in relation to formal and informal drawing of boundaries. Does the much-decried division of US metropolitan areas into numerous separate jurisdictions only do harm or does it also serve to protect antagonistic groups from each other (Dreier et al. 2014)? Is racial and ethnic segregation inherently evil? In various parts of the world (Ethiopia/Eritrea, the Czech Republic/Slovakia, Serbia/Croatia, India/Pakistan, etc.), separation has been regarded as self-determination and perceived as a democratic solution. Iris Marion Young (2000, p. 216), whose work endorses a politics of difference, resists the ideal of integration, because it 'tends wrongly to focus on patterns of group clustering while ignoring more central issues of privilege and disadvantage.' She supports porous borders, widely accessible public spaces, and regional government but she also calls for a differentiated solidarity that would allow voluntary clustering of cultural groups.

Demanding that housing in any area encompass a broad income range and forbidding discrimination on the basis of race, ethnicity, or disability constitute standards conducive to justice. At the same time, housing provision and urban regeneration, two key areas of local public policy since the Second World War, are arenas in which the values of diversity, democracy, and equity are in tension. Individual aspirations for privacy and control of one's surroundings; communal sentiments toward preservation and membership in a group of likeminded people; housing shortages and lack of affordability; economic restructuring and consequent obsolescence of land uses; environmental hazards; aging of housing and infrastructure – all these make up the conditions through which framers of housing and redevelopment programs must work. Defining each dispute in terms of what constitutes the most just solution means that consequences for equity should always be spelled out and given priority, but depending on the context the appropriate strategy will differ.

For instance, requiring people to move against their will in order to achieve racial balance or dispersion of poverty infringes on liberty despite the inclusionary aim. The example of Chicago is instructive here. Beginning at the turn of this century the Chicago Housing Authority (CHA) embarked on a plan to demolish its large high-rise projects and disperse their occupants. It gave most of them housing vouchers to use in the private market and promised a minority the right to return to the mixed-income projects built on the vacated sites. The CHA had for years been under court orders (the *Gautreaux* decisions starting in 1966) to desegregate public housing and had made some effort toward relocating residents toward that end. It could point to (weak) evidence from studies of resulting moves to the suburbs that identified employment, housing, and educational improvements among African Americans who left voluntarily, using resources provided as remedies required by the court. In the 1980s, with public housing widely considered a failure, social science theories blamed geographical concentrations for the persistence of poverty over generations (Wilson 1987; Bennett et al. 2006). Referencing these theories,

> since the early 1990s CHA officials have sustained a strikingly consistent articulation of their main policy aims: to reduce the 'social isolation' of the 'distressed communities' that CHA developments had become; to employ the 'mixed-income model' of community development to save public housing; to humanize affordable housing through the use of new urbanist design techniques. (Bennett 2006, p. 293)

The CHA was accused of using its ostensibly beneficent policy as a subterfuge for encouraging gentrification. If we put aside the question of whether it was simply wholly cynical in its land-clearing efforts, in the name of diversity we can accept the goal of reducing social isolation and humanizing affordable housing. The effects of the policies intended to achieve this result, however, are at best mixed. The conclusions that Goetz (2005, p. 409) reaches concerning a similar program in Atlanta apply equally here: 'Against the modest set of benefits experienced by original residents, we must keep in mind the millions of dollars spent on the demolition and redevelopment of the sites, the disruption to households and social support networks by displacement and relocation, and the permanent loss of thousands of units of low-cost public housing' (see also Goetz 2003).

We see in this example, therefore, that the achievement of diversity may come at the cost of other values. If people are moved against their will, then democracy and equity are not served. If neighborhoods become diverse as a consequence of gentrification, then the remaining low-income residents may lose their sense of ownership of the area even if they receive improved services (Freeman 2006).

Thus, equity, diversity, and democracy are not automatically supportive of each other, and, in fact, in any particular situation, may well clash or require trade-offs. Moreover, internal to each of these norms are further contradictory elements (Campbell 1996). In addition to the hoary question of whether equality of opportunity can exist without prior equality of condition, there are the issues of whether equal treatment of those with differing abilities is fair or whether the disabled should get more, and conversely whether it is fair to deny rewards to those whose effort or ability make them seem more deserving (what philosophers refer to as the criterion of 'desert'). With reference to urban policies this raises the difficulty, for example, of whether, in terms of allocating public housing, the homeless should receive preference over those on waiting lists, or whether non-profit housing corporations should be able to select tenants so as to exclude families likely to be disruptive.

In regard to diversity the further issue arises of whether recognition of the other should extend to acceptance of groups that themselves are intolerant or authoritarian. Within cities this question has shown itself most intensely when groups impose their rules or lifestyles on others who share their spaces – Jews who discourage driving on the Sabbath, Muslims whose calls to prayer stop traffic and are heard by everyone in the vicinity, anarchists whose loud music and nighttime activities keep their neighbors awake.

WHAT POLICIES INCORPORATE THE VALUES OF THE JUST CITY?

In *The Just City* I provide a list of policies that would further social justice within the city. My list is probably too specific to be acceptable to rigorous deontological philosophers. Nevertheless, I believe that it offers a set of expectations that ought to form the basis for just urban planning and provides standards against which policy proposals can be critiqued. The contents of this list apply only to planning policies conducted at the local level; the components of a just national urban policy are more complex and will not be discussed here.[4] The list is as follows:

In Furtherance of Equity

1. All new housing development should provide units for households with incomes below the median, either on-site or elsewhere, with the goal of providing a decent home and suitable living environment for everyone. (One of the most vexing issues in relation to housing, however, is the extent to which tenant selection should limit access to people likely to be good neighbors. It is one of the areas where the criteria of equity and democracy are at odds with each other, and no general rule can apply.)
2. No household or business should be involuntarily relocated for the purpose of obtaining economic development or community balance.
3. Economic development programs should give priority to the interests of employees and small business owners. All new commercial development should provide space for public use and to the extent feasible should facilitate the livelihood of independent and cooperatively owned businesses.
4. Mega-projects should be subject to heightened scrutiny, be required to provide direct benefits to low-income people in the form of employment provisions, public amenities, and a living wage, and, if public subsidy is involved, should include public participation in the profits.
5. Transit fares should be kept very low.
6. Planners should take an active role in deliberative settings in pressing for solutions that improve the situation of disadvantaged groups and blocking ones that disproportionately benefit the already well-off.

In Furtherance of Diversity

1. Zoning should not be used to further discriminatory ends.
2. Boundaries between districts should be porous.
3. Ample public space should be widely accessible and varied but be designed so that groups with clashing lifestyles do not have to occupy the same location.
4. To the extent practical and desired by affected populations, uses should be mixed.

In Furtherance of Democracy

1. Plans should be developed in consultation with the target population if the area is already developed. The existing population, however, should not be the sole arbiter of the future of an area. City-wide considerations must also apply.
2. In planning for as yet uninhabited or sparsely occupied areas, there should be broad consultation that includes representatives of groups currently living outside the affected areas.

Adherence to this set of guidelines does not require that people who cannot get along live next door to each other. Indeed people have the right to protect themselves from others who do not respect their way of life. What is important is that people are not differentiated and excluded according to ascriptive characteristics like gender or ethnicity. But neither should people be required to tolerate disorderly conduct or anti-social behavior in the name of social justice.

The list can be extended to other policy realms besides planning. For example, within educational policy public funding should insure that schools in poor areas receive greater resources and staff than those in wealthy areas. In the area of public safety local police precincts ought to provide citizens with oversight powers and should pursue humane policies for dealing with infractions. Recreational facilities need to be provided free of charge and be available in neighborhoods where few can take advantage of privately owned health clubs.

Appointed public officials alone cannot realize these goals – the backing of a mobilized constituency and supportive politicians is necessary for the implementation of prescriptions for greater justice. Without pressure from beneath, without public participation and demands being made, people in the public sector are not going to show great concern about what happens to low-income people. Thus, it is critically important to have grassroots pressure. At the same time, ordinary citizens are often not very creative in their demands. Imaginative policy does require people who think about the issues full-time, and who have a commitment to values of equity and diversity. They may not be in government employment but instead may be the staff of labor unions or community organizations. There is a more significant role for such people to play than simply facilitating a process of public input.

Even in the absence of mobilization, planners and bureaucrats can continually press for a more just city, implement strategies that produce greater equity, and deploy principles of justice when evaluating decisions (Needleman and Needleman 1974). It is way too easy to follow the lead of developers, business owners, and politicians who make economic competitiveness the highest priority and give little or no consideration to questions of justice.

NOTES

1. American muckrakers, British Fabians, and Continental reformers launched attacks on municipal corruption and slums, while Marxists exposed the exploitation and misery of the poor.
2. See also the online journal *Justice Spatiale/Spatial Justice*.
3. This chapter is drawn from Fainstein 2009, 2010.
4. Markusen and Fainstein (1993) develop the elements of a national urban policy for the United States.

REFERENCES

Allen, Danielle (2004), *Talking to Strangers*, Chicago: University of Chicago Press.
Arnstein, Sherry R. (1969), 'A ladder of citizen participation', *Journal of the American Institute of Planners*, **35** (4), 216–224.
Benhabib, Seyla (2002), *The Claims of Culture*, Princeton, NJ: Princeton University Press.
Bennett, Larry (2006), 'Downtown restructuring and public housing in contemporary Chicago: fashioning a better world-class city', in Larry Bennett, Janet L. Smith and Patricia A. Wright (eds), *Where are Poor People to Live?*, Armonk, NY: M.E. Sharpe, pp. 282–300.
Bennett, Larry, Janet L. Smith and Patricia A. Wright (eds) (2006), *Where are Poor People to Live?*, Armonk, NY: M.E. Sharpe.
Brenner, Neil and Nikolas Theodore (eds) (2002), *Spaces of Neoliberalism*, Oxford: Blackwell.
Campbell, Heather and Robert Marshall (2002), 'Utilitarianism's bad breath? A re-evaluation of the public interest justification for planning', *Planning Theory*, **1** (2), 163–187.
Campbell, Scott (1996), 'Green cities, growing cities, just cities? Urban planning and the contradictions of sustainable development', *Journal of the American Planning Association*, **62** (3), 296–312.
Carmon, Naomi and Susan S. Fainstein (eds) (2013), *Policy, Planning and People*, Philadelphia: University of Pennsylvania Press.
Castells, Manuel (1977), *The Urban Question*, Cambridge, MA: The MIT Press.
Dreier, Peter, John H. Mollenkopf and Todd Swanstom (2014), *Place Matters*, 3rd edition, Lawrence, KS: University Press of Kansas.
Dror, Yehezkel (1983), *Public Policy Making Reexamined*, New Brunswick, NJ: Transaction Publishers.
Fainstein, Susan S. (2005a), 'Planning theory and the city', *Journal of Planning Education and Research*, **25** (2), 121–130.
Fainstein, Susan S. (2005b), 'Gender and planning: theoretical issues', in Susan S. Fainstein and Lisa Servon (eds), *Gender and Planning*, New Brunswick, NJ: Rutgers University Press, pp. 1–12.
Fainstein, Susan S. (2009), 'Planning and the just city', in Peter Marcuse, James Connolly, Ingrid Olivo Magana, Johannes Novy, Cuz Potter and Justin Steil (eds), *Searching for the Just City*, New York: Routledge, pp. 19–39.
Fainstein, Susan S. (2010), *The Just City*, Ithaca, NY: Cornell University Press.

Fainstein, Susan S. (2014), 'The resilience of neoliberalism and its urban effects', *Critical Policy Studies*, **8**, 356–358.
Fainstein, Susan S., Norman I. Fainstein, Richard Child Hill, Dennis Judd and Michael P. Smith (1986), *Restructuring the City: The Political Economy of Urban Redevelopment*, revised edition, New York: Longman.
Faludi, Andreas (1983), 'Critical rationalism and planning methodology', *Urban Studies*, **20**, 265–278.
Fischer, Frank (1980), *Politics, Values, and Public Policy*, Boulder, CO: Westview Press.
Fischer, Frank and John Forester (1993), *The Argumentative Turn in Policy Analysis and Planning*, Durham, NC: Duke University Press.
Forst, Rainer (2002), *Contexts of Justice*, Berkeley, CA: University of California Press.
Fraser, Nancy (1997), *Justus Interruptus*, New York: Routledge.
Freeman, Lance (2006), *There Goes the 'Hood*, Philadelphia, PA: Temple University Press.
Friedmann, John (2011), *Insurgencies: Essays in Planning Theory*, London: Routledge,
Gans, Herbert J. (1968), *People and Plans*, New York: Basic Books.
Goetz, Edward G. (2003), *Clearing the Way*, Washington, DC: Urban Institute Press.
Goetz, Edward G. (2005), 'Comment: public housing demolition and the benefits to low-income families', *Journal of the American Planning Association*, **71** (4), 407–410.
Harvey, David (1973), *Social Justice and the City*, Baltimore, MD: Johns Hopkins University Press.
Harvey, David (2003), 'The right to the city', *International Journal of Urban and Regional Research*, **27** (4), 939–941.
Hayward, Clarissa Rile and Todd Swanstrom (eds) (2011), *Justice and the American Metropolis*, Minneapolis, MN: University of Minnesota Press.
Innes, Judith E. (1996), 'Planning through consensus building: a new view of the comprehensive planning ideal', *Journal of the American Planning Association*, **62** (4), 460–472.
Jacobs, Jane (1961), *The Death and Life of Great American Cities*, New York: Random House.
Lazarsfeld, Paul Felix and Morris Rosenberg (eds) (1955), *The Language of Social Research*, New York: Free Press.
Lefebvre, Henri (1996), *Writings on Cities/Henri Lefebvre*, selected, translated and introduced by Eleonore Kofman and Elizabeth Lebas, Oxford: Blackwell.
Lefebvre, Henri (2003), *The Urban Revolution*, trans. by Robert Bononno, Minneapolis, MN: University of Minnesota Press.
Lindblom, Charles E. (1959), 'The science of "muddling through"', *Public Administration Review*, **19**, 79–88.
Logan, John R. and Harvey L. Molotch (1987), *Urban Fortunes*, Berkeley, CA: University of California Press.
Mannheim, Karl (1949), *Man and Society in an Age of Reconstruction*, New York: Harcourt, Brace, 1949.
Marcuse, Peter, James Connolly, Johannes Novy, Ingrid Olivo, Cuz Potter and Justin Steil (eds) (2009), *Searching for the Just City*, London: Routledge.
Markusen, Ann R. and Susan S. Fainstein (1993), 'Urban policy: bridging the social and economic development gap', *University of North Carolina Law Review*, **71**, 1463–1486.
Mollenkopf, John H. (1983), *The Contested City*, Princeton, NJ: Princeton University Press.
Mouffe, Chantal (2013), *Agonistics: Thinking the World Politically*, London: Verso.
Needleman, Martin L. and Carolyn E. Needleman (1974), *Guerrillas in the Bureaucracy*, New York: Wiley.
Nussbaum, Martha C. (2000), *Women and Human Development*, Cambridge: Cambridge University Press.
Peterson, Paul (1981), *City Limits*, Chicago: University of Chicago Press.
Rawls, John (1971), *A Theory of Justice*, Cambridge, MA: Harvard University Press.
Rawls, John (2001), *Justice as Fairness: A Restatement*, ed. Erin Kelly, Cambridge, MA: Harvard University Press.
Sennett, Richard (1971), *The Uses of Disorder*, New York: Vintage.

Sennett, Richard (1992), *The Conscience of the Eye*, New York: Norton.
Simon, Herbert A. (1972), 'Theories of bounded rationality', *Decision and Organization*, **1**, 161–176.
Soja, Edward S. (1980), 'The socio-spatial dialectic', *Annals of the Association of American Geographers*, **70** (2), 207–225.
Stone, Clarence Nathan (1989), *Regime Politics: Governing Atlanta, 1946–1988*, Lawrence, KS: University Press of Kansas.
Wilson, William Julius (1987), *The Truly Disadvantaged*, Chicago: University of Chicago Press.
Young, Iris Marion (2000), *Inclusion and Democracy*, Oxford: Oxford University Press.

11 Deliberation and protest: revealing the deliberative potential of protest movements in Turkey and Brazil*

Ricardo Fabrino Mendonça and Selen A. Ercan

An important event of the beginning of the 21st century has undoubtedly been the new emergence of protests that cross frontiers throughout the globe. From Iceland to Hong Kong – and including Tunisia, Egypt, Spain, Greece, the USA, Turkey and Brazil – the recent protest movements were widely noticed due to their size, their transnational dimension and their organizational logic. They have grasped the attention of scholars of various disciplines, journalists, politicians and, more fascinatingly, of many citizens who were not interested in politics otherwise. While some felt surprised by these huge and largely unexpected mobilizations, others saw them as natural consequences of decades of grassroots work.

The recent protests have also been at the heart of the scholarly debates on the theory and practice of democracy, social movements and political participation. They have challenged not only the conventional notions of 'collective action', 'political community' or 'political participation', but have also countered the mainstream diagnosis about political apathy in contemporary democracies. After all, millions of individuals were on the streets demonstrating, and placing what Claus Offe long ago defined as the 'meta question' of democracy at the centre of their action (Della Porta 2012, 37). Protesters were expressing their fatigue with traditional models of representative democracy and emphasizing the need to have a voice and be heard (Prentoulis and Thomassen 2013). While some interpreted these developments as a clear manifestation of the democratic crisis, others saw them as a potential cure to such a crisis (Chou 2015; Ercan and Gagnon 2014).

In this chapter, we are interested in offering an orientation to recent protests that speaks to concerns about democracy and social movements animating critical policy studies. In the context of contemporary democratic theory, we focus particularly on the contrast between deliberative democracy and agonism, seeking to belie the common notion that the two are mutually exclusive. Conventionally speaking, the framing of protests as the revival of agonistic politics would be seen as a proof of the passing of the age of deliberative democracy, given that agonistic politics and deliberative democracy are usually understood as mutually exclusive alternatives. Agonists would typically point out the anti-deliberative nature of the protests, claiming that protesters do not seek to achieve any kind of agreement with those they purport to challenge.

We problematize this reading of protests for relying on a false dichotomy between deliberation and conflict, whereby deliberation is presented as a pasteurized and consensus-driven dialogical exchange. We argue that the adversarial nature of the protests promote, rather than hinder, the prospects for deliberation. We see the recent protest movements as particularly well suited examples of the theoretical argument pointing out the adversarial nature of deliberation, and more broadly revealing the centrality of agonist politics in the context of deliberative democracy. We substantiate these points through a close examination of protests in Turkey and Brazil in 2013, focusing particularly on their similarities from a perspective of deliberative democracy. We reveal the deliberative potential of these protests by focusing on: (1) the way they were organized; (2) how they were carried out, especially in terms of the type of collective action they generated; and (3) their public consequences.

Overall, the chapter aims to advance the argument about the compatibility of deliberative democracy and agonism (see, for example, Knops 2007), by injecting some – and so far mostly missing – insights from empirical observation into this debate. This is relevant for the field of critical policy studies for several reasons. Firstly, the chapter shows that there is much more to deliberative policy making than what happens in relatively well designed, structured forums. Secondly, by bringing deliberative democracy in close connection with contentious politics, the chapter seeks to challenge the dominant assumption that a deliberative turn in politics would lead to a tamed society that either avoids or suppresses its intrinsic conflicts. On the contrary, we show that deliberation understood in discursive terms as a broad communication process that occurs within and around contentious politics is essential for a vitalized public and political life.

DELIBERATIVE DEMOCRACY

Deliberative democracy is a growing branch of contemporary democratic theory. Deliberative democrats suggest understanding democracy in terms of exchange of reasons rather than voting or aggregation of preferences. It has been developed as a response to the legitimation problems of representative democracies (Cohen 1989; Habermas 1996). Although deliberative democrats differ in the extent of their criticism of representative democracy, they often conceive of their view not as an alternative to liberal representative democracy but as an expansion of it. This means that while traditional tools of decision making (majoritarian voting, elections and legislatures) remain essential, the public deliberation of free and equal citizens becomes central in legitimating collective decisions. As Joshua Cohen (1989) puts it, on this account, democratic legitimacy is understood in terms of the 'right, capacity and opportunity' for those affected by collective decisions to participate in the making of those decisions.

Deliberation ideally involves a process of mutual justification where participants offer reasons for their positions, listen to the views of others and reconsider their preferences in the light of new information and arguments. This discursive process depends on the existence of publicity, which allows not only the actors' exposure to a diversity of perspectives, but also the establishment of normative boundaries for what can be accepted as a defensible argument (Bohman 1996). For deliberative democrats, it is the public exchange of reasons that pushes the best arguments forward, and makes collective decisions legitimate. Deliberative democrats advocate a collective process of opinion formation and preference construction, and place the need for discursive contestation at the heart of democratic theory and practice.

Over the last decade, the theory of deliberative democracy has gone through various iterations and has become increasingly diversified. The literature usually differentiates between two conceptions of deliberation: one focusing on its realization in structured forums (such as citizen juries, citizen assemblies, etc.) and another conceiving deliberation as a broad discursive process that occurs in the broader public sphere (Dryzek 2000). In recent years, scholars have been increasingly attracted to the idea of 'deliberative system' which offers a way of combining these two conceptions of deliberation and locates it on a spectrum of venues, from informal 'everyday talk' among citizens at one end, to formal decision making that takes place in public assemblies and parliament (Mansbridge et al. 2012).

This broad definition has made deliberative democracy one of the most productive fields of research in political theory (Dryzek 2007). The wide dissemination of deliberative ideals has, nevertheless, also strengthened the voice of its critics, who claim that deliberative democracy has become an approach so flexible and accommodating that it ends up supporting the status quo and the existing institutions of liberal democracies. In this context, as we discuss further below, deliberative democracy has also been conceived as eliminating ruptures and conflicts from the kernel of politics. This argument has usually been articulated to justify the opposition between deliberation and contentious politics.

IS CONFLICT AGAINST DELIBERATION?

Deliberative democrats are often criticized for advancing a conception of politics devoid of conflict. The critics of deliberative democracy, particularly agonists (such as Chantal Mouffe) and the difference democrats (such as Iris Young), have charged deliberative democrats with eradicating differences between conflicting groups in the name of achieving consensus. Despite their various differences, these scholars have argued that 'the force of a better argument' and consensus are not the best strategies to address the issues of domination and marginalization in contemporary societies. These issues, they noted, necessitate adopting contentious political strategies such as protests and demonstrations rather than structured, 'consensus-oriented' deliberative forums, as allegedly advocated by scholars of deliberative democracy.

Among deliberative democrats, this view is represented most notably by Iris Young (2003) who wrote an influential essay identifying the various challenges activists pose to the idea and practice of deliberation. She argues that activists are sceptical about deliberation because they believe that: 'democratic processes that appear to conform to norms of deliberation are usually biased toward more powerful agents' (Young 2003, 102). Peter Levine and Rose Nierras (2007) raise similar concerns, although they acknowledge that activists and deliberative democrats 'have much to learn from one another' (2007, 14). Similar to Young, they provide various reasons for activists to oppose the idea of deliberation, including embedded inequalities, the lack of representativeness in forums, the potential manipulation of deliberative forums by government agencies and the absence of actual consequences emanating from such forums. In addition to such reasons, some scholars have argued that activists often reject deliberation as they would prefer coercive actions, such as marches or sit-ins (Medearis 2004). Such actions are allegedly not considered by deliberative democrats as an appropriate way of articulating arguments in the public sphere.

Clearly, the distinction between protest and deliberation is not merely a conceptual one. It is also evident in the practice of deliberative democracy, most notably in the design of democratic innovations. The preference for random selection in citizen juries, planning cells, consensus conferences and deliberative polls elucidates the effort to promote dialogue among ordinary, un-mobilized citizens and not among activists who are considered to be too passionate or too certain of their own views to deliberate.

A more radical distinction between deliberation and contentious politics is drawn by Chantal Mouffe. According to Mouffe (2000, 13), the deliberative approach wrongly assumes the presence of a public sphere where power is eliminated and rational consensus is attainable. It thus fails to acknowledge the presence of irreconcilable values that generate antagonism. Mouffe argues that rather than aiming at eliminating antagonism caused by value pluralism, democratic politics should strive to transform antagonism into agonism, enabling a permanent battle between adversaries. For Mouffe, such understanding of democratic politics is unique because it does not try to eliminate passions from politics, or attempt to find permanent harmonious rational solutions. Jacques Rancière presents a similar approach when he criticizes the central place given to the objective of achieving consensus in contemporary political theory. According to him, consensus hides hegemonic interests, helping to sustain the status quo and existing power relations while forcing individuals to become partners in a dialogic relationship. Politics, for him, is grounded on dissensus, and consensus would amount to the exclusion of politics (Rancière 2007, 2010).

Contrary to those who view conflict and consensus in exclusionary terms, we argue that the alleged tension between conflict and consensus is mistaken for at least two reasons. First of all, and as many of the above-mentioned scholars would acknowledge, politics needs both of them. On the one hand, politics requires the moments of destabilization that emerge in conflicts, and entail the prospects of transformation that open new horizons for the future. On the other hand, and in the face of increasing pluralism, politics must also provide some type of (temporary and revisable) stabilization. To put it differently, stabilization always occurs through social practices, norms, values and decisions, although they may be ephemeral. Politics needs to reflect on these stabilizations and the way in which they are built.

When viewed from a deliberative democratic perspective, these stabilizations can be seen as some variants of consensus. This, however, is not to suggest that they are produced in a pure arena that is free from asymmetries, structural inequalities, or power relations. As a matter of fact, because the term consensus is usually associated with naïve connotations, we prefer to use 'mutual understanding' to capture the act of temporary stabilization in the common world. Furthermore, as noted by several scholars, deliberative democracy must not be based on a substantive idea of consensus (Dryzek and Niemeyer 2006). It is compatible with various forms of workable agreements provided that they are open to revisions (Dryzek 2000; Eriksen 2000). This understanding of deliberative democracy underpinned by the principle of workable and temporary agreement, rather than thick consensus, is actually in tune with Mouffe's understanding of politics, which is about creating some sort of 'unity in the context of conflict and diversity' (Mouffe 2000, 15).

Our second reason for rejecting as false the dichotomy between conflict and deliberation relates to the impossibility of distinguishing between contentious and deliberative politics in both theory and practice. The dichotomy between conflict and deliberation is reinforced by a mistaken definition of deliberation that reduces it to a direct (and oral) exchange of passionless arguments among political actors who agree to sit down together to resolve their disagreements. Yet, deliberation does not have to be understood in this way. As it has long been argued, deliberation is not opposed to disagreement or passionate articulations of individual viewpoints; on the contrary, deliberation necessarily involves disagreement and contestation (Dryzek 2000). Deliberative processes are discursive exchanges that allow different actors to engage with the task of defining the world in which they live together. Some arguments may be pervaded by outrage and anger. They can be presented through elaborate polite sentences, but also through incisive slogans as well as disruptive images or signs in a demonstration. In this sense, deliberation both requires and generates what Mouffe (2000, 16) has suggested with her agonistic account of democracy: 'a vibrant clash of democratic political positions'.

Recent articulations of deliberative democracy do acknowledge the role of conflict within deliberation and challenge the oversimplified conceptions of deliberation understood in terms of a consensus oriented process of public consultation (Chambers 2009; Della Porta 2009; Parkinson and Mansbridge 2012; Mendonça 2013). In fact, some scholars rightly note that it is a contentious civil society and a lively public sphere that stand at the heart of deliberative democracy (Dryzek et al. 2003). Besides sharpening the critical edge of deliberation, they thus also acknowledge that deliberation is necessarily a de-centered process that crosses several publics and multiple communicative networks (Bohman 2007, 5). Protests are obviously part of such communicative networks. They can potentially play a transformative role, and alter the existing codes through their statements, signs, marches and scenic disruptions (Melucci 1996). In doing so, they usually deal with the symbols that ground the shared understandings reproduced in everyday life. The broader point here is that there is always a discursive dimension in these strategies. And the contentious actions of protesters constitute an integral part of ongoing contestation of discourses in the public sphere. The displacement they generate seeks new forms of provisional stabilizations, making it quite unfruitful to establish a sharp distinction between conflict and consensus. In what follows, we seek to illustrate this argument by drawing on the recent protests in Turkey and Brazil.

WHAT IS DELIBERATIVE ABOUT THE 2013 PROTESTS IN TURKEY AND BRAZIL?

In 2013, both Turkey and Brazil witnessed massive public protests featuring similar patterns of organization and mobilization. The protests in Turkey started first, on 29 May 2013 in Istanbul, as a response to the government's decision to build a new shopping mall and residential complex on the grounds of an historically important public park (Gezi Park). What began as a peaceful environmentalist protest quickly exploded into massive resistance, spreading to many other cities, against the Justice and Development Party (AKP), and more specifically its leader Prime Minister Recep Tayyip Erdoğan. The brutal police reaction to peaceful demonstration transformed the protest within a couple of days from a local development issue to wider demonstrations across Turkey about a broad range of issues. By Friday 31 May, tens of thousands were clashing with police units in different districts of Istanbul and hundreds of protesters were in police custody.

Approximately one week later Brazil witnessed similar massive demonstrations, which had many similarities with those in Turkey.[1] In this case, the protests started in São Paulo, when the *Free Fare Movement* (*Movimento Passe Livre*) succeeded in mobilizing around four thousand people in a march against a 20-cent rise in public transportation fares. The dynamics triggering the massive protests in Brazil were associated with the broader agenda of the *right to the city* (Harvey 2012; Maricato 2013), which has acquired a new momentum with the organization of two '*mega-sports-events*' (the 2014 FIFA World Cup and the 2016 Summer Olympics) (Vainer 2013). The FIFA Confederations Cup (June 2013) was a window of opportunity to promote public claims about the injustices generated by these events. Similar to the Turkish case, police brutality played a role, turning public opinion in favour of the protesters. By 20 June 2013, more than 120 cities had risen and at least 1.4 million Brazilians were on the streets (Peschanski 2013, 59).

In both Turkey and Brazil, the massive protests brought together a variety of people with different ideological backgrounds and issues to voice. In Turkey, the protestors were primarily composed of young people, more specifically the generation born after 1990. Other visible groups, especially during the protests at Gezi Park, included a variety of left-wing organizations, environmentalists, Lesbian, Gay, Bisexual and Transgender (LGBT) groups, feminist groups and 'anti-capitalist Muslims', as well as many trade unions and professional organizations. The Kurdish organizations were at first reluctant to join, on the grounds that the protests might derail the peace process that was underway with the Turkish Government, but in the end they decided to enter the square. The main opposition Republican People's Party also welcomed the protests, and even individual members of the right-wing nationalist Action Party (MHP) joined in.

Similarly, in Brazil the protests brought together a variety of groups that were not necessarily on good terms with each other. Some demonstrations acquired a very nationalist tone, with the public exhibition of the Brazilian flag and its colours. Many citizens protested against corruption and many others claimed that they wanted schools or hospitals of the same quality as the stadiums delivered to FIFA. Political parties, congressional representatives, governors and the President were targeted in placards. Many demonstrators advocated same-sex marriage and the withdrawal of a bill that criminalizes homophobia, while others expressed the view that gay rights were immoral and that the mentioned bill would constrain freedom of speech.

In both Turkey and Brazil, protestors ignored political parties and distrusted the mainstream media and the institutions of representative democracy. They preferred the use of social media and local assemblies to keep informed about the events, to influence public opinion as well as to make collective decisions. As such, the protests entailed important deliberative elements, and helped to construct the meaning of legitimate political involvement as extending well beyond voting. In our view, the deliberative potential of the protests can be traced particularly in: (1) the way in which they were organized; (2) the way in which they were carried out; and (3) their public consequences. We discuss each of these dimensions in the context of the 2013 protests in Turkey and Brazil.

(1) Organizational Structure of the Protests

An important feature of the recent protest movements which had direct implications for their organizational structure is that they emerged as a challenge to 'politics as usual' as carried out by conventional actors, such as political parties, traditional associations and social movement organizations. The recent protests offered new arenas of debate, which were marked by more horizontal relations, diffuse leadership and inclusive participation (Della Porta 2009). Such organizational features help facilitate *prefigurative forms of politics*: 'expressed in the search for intrinsically rewarding forms of action, such as happenings' (Della Porta 2009, 89). These forms of politics are necessarily underpinned by the principles of inclusion and mutual understanding fostering the prospects for dialogue across differences.

To be clear, such dialogue does not necessarily require reaching consensus to generate collective action. In fact, contemporary protests illustrate how collective action is often performed by individuals with different logics, values, interests and purposes, without them having to reconcile their differences. In other words, what we observe is that individuals engage in protest not necessarily to achieve some sort of consensus with other protesters, but to express their personal views and demands. As such, they perform what Bennett and Segerberg (2012, 752) called 'an act of personal expression and recognition or self-validation achieved by sharing ideas and actions'.

Digital technology and social networks obviously play a crucial role in terms of enabling a 'flexible personalized communication' underpinned by 'coordinated adjustments and rapid action aimed at often shifting political targets' (Bennett and Segerberg 2012, 753). In this context, communication gains a structural importance; it enables collective action and bridges the plurality of individualities in temporary acts. In this context, communication weaves a reticular structure that can be marked by spontaneity, absence of clear leadership and a self-reflexivity that induces a deliberative form of politics (Castells 2013, 159–166).

When we consider the recent protests against this backdrop, it does not seem entirely correct to say that they were completely leaderless, spontaneous and horizontal. This however does not mean they were hierarchical social movements, in which all decisions were expected to be made by movement leaders. The overall picture in both countries was rather a result of the interaction between different layers of organizations. The organizational structure of the protests was neither a completely individualized spontaneous process without hierarchy, nor a structured conventional social movement, but a *sui generis* result of the combination of different layers of organized and spontaneous movements. In fact, what we observe in the context of the recent protests movements is that 'personalized connective action networks cross paths [. . .] with more conventional collective action networks' (Bennett and Segerberg 2012, 759). The way these two action networks were combined in the course of both Turkish and Brazilian protests depended, heavily, on the continuous public debate, which involved intense use of online platforms. Constant posts on Twitter, Facebook and various blogs brought new information about the protests. Unique humour and satire were regular resources, as well as emotional stories and touching images of protestors. Communication occurred across various venues and moments, connecting different publics in a massive discursive process.

Arguably, what is more important from a perspective of deliberative democracy is that this communication was characterized both by contestation of discourses and by reflexivity. The structure of the demonstrations was deeply discursive, as it was progressively rearranged through (and in) the public encounter of symbolic acts. Especially if deliberation is understood as a broader systemic process, rather than a forum-based communication, the deliberative logic behind the organizational structure of the protests becomes evident. The protests were forged within a comprehension of politics that is essentially communicative. Communication was not merely a tool for expression. It grounded the action throughout the process, creating the conditions for constant self-reflexivity. Even if there were leaders of specific groups, the broader picture of the demonstration was a snapshot of a horizontal encounter between individuals within a symbolic dispute that presented itself as a challenge to 'politics as usual'. As such, the way these protests were structured was not inimical to deliberation. In fact, the protests can be comprehended appropriately only with the aid of a deliberative conception of politics, which highlights the reflexive public clash of discourses, as well as the prospects for horizontally generated collective action.

(2) The Deliberative Dimension of the Protests in Terms of How They Were Carried Out

The relevance of the deliberative democratic approach for comprehending the recent protests becomes particularly clear when we consider the main demands advanced by the protesters and the way they have communicated these demands with each other. The protesters, both in Turkey and Brazil, emphasized the sense of not being heard. In order to challenge politics as usual, assemblies were established in both countries to deliberate about issues of common concern with respect to the ongoing protests and beyond.

These assemblies sought to be inclusive and visible, manifesting a different way to do politics. Although procedures varied significantly, some assemblies started with a draw to select who would chair that meeting. Following this, participants debated over basic procedures of discussion. The audience usually reacted through sign language. The process continued with exchanges of arguments. Filled with emotional narratives and individual stories of marginalization and exclusion, the communications carried out in the assemblies had an important role in terms of sustaining large mobilizations. Thematic committees allowed the deepening of topics. Some of them organized study groups and public lectures on certain topics.

It is important to highlight that these assemblies were not a paradise of respectful debate among equals. They were places of conflicts. They were not free of existing power relations, coercion or hierarchies. In one assembly in Brazil, for example, we witnessed a fight actually become physical between two participants who disagreed about the time slot that should be granted to each speaker. Such disagreements, however, did not destroy the deliberative potential of these practices. In both countries, the whole process of discussing procedures, debating issues, splitting the work of discussion into groups and producing collective decisions was in tune with the core ideas of deliberative democracy.

In his analysis of the New York Occupy General Assemblies, Seong-Jae Min (2014, 2) makes a similar point:

> The meetings were contentious and painfully slow. But they were drawn to the meetings; they were addicted to the procedural ideals of participatory democracy. It was as if they took a playbook from Jürgen Habermas's massive work in communicative action and deliberation, and put the demanding theory into real actions.

The assemblies in Turkey and Brazil were obviously not the only arenas where deliberation over the issues of common concern took place. There were multiple other arenas of debate and discussion providing a platform for the contestation of discourses. Creative banners assumed a reason-giving role and drew attention to the reasons behind the act of protesting. Arguments were presented through incisive slogans as well as disruptive images, signs or cartoons, thereby encouraging self-reflexivity. Some arguments were taken up and reproduced by the mass media, in social networks, in everyday conversations and in collective forums, thus feeding into systemic flows of communication across different arenas.

When seen from a deliberative perspective, another crucial aspect of the way protests were carried out in both Turkey and Brazil concerns the way protesters recognized and handled each other's differences, albeit in distinct ways. In Brazil, protests fostered an awareness of difference among different groups. Some groups could clearly see the strength of counter-discourses publicly expressed against the positions they have been advocating. This was clear in some of the discussions between LGBT activists and religious groups. In the symbolic battles of the protests, one Christian MP, who had just become the President of the Human Rights Commission, catalyzed religious conflicts that had remained silent in the history of the country. In the case of Turkey, there was already an awareness of differences, particularly along religious versus secular lines (Kanra and Ercan 2012). Here, rather than fostering an awareness of difference across different groups, the protests fostered dialogue and deliberation among those who have been traditionally hostile to each other. As Nilufer Gole (2013) rightly notes, in the heyday of the Turkish protests, Gezi Park in Istanbul turned into

... a scene for displaying the openness of the public space to all and its capacity to reassemble, in bringing together men and women, Muslims and non-religious, Alevis and Kurds, young and old, middle and lower classes. This has allowed a new critical imaginary to circulate, one which focuses on protecting public space in its physical sense, with its capacity for bringing people together in a convivial way.

The deliberative dimension of protests should now be clear. Our broader point here is that opposing conflict and deliberation as mutually exclusive alternatives is not helpful for the comprehension of these protests. The protesters' agonism had a strong deliberative dimension, which became evident in the context of the park assemblies, in the promotion of an awareness of difference, as well as in fostering deliberation across difference.

(3) The Deliberative Dimension of the Protests in Terms of What They Have Achieved

Finally, it is possible to observe the deliberative dimension of the protests in their public consequences. In both Turkey and Brazil, the protests had important institutional consequences as they made the political sphere more porous and responsive to public concerns and demands. The issues raised in the course of protests also were ultimately taken up in the policy processes of both countries.

In the case of Turkey, the most concrete policy outcome of the protests was that the government consented not to build the planned shopping mall. Yet, it would be a mistake to reduce the success of the protests to this particular outcome. If the actual goal of these protests is to raise awareness among citizens at large, to empower them through their participation in the movement and in a wide deliberation about their lives and their country, then the Turkish protests do qualify as successful. As one of the protestors put it, if anything, the protests highlighted for the Turkish Government the need to listen to ordinary citizens when making decisions that affect them directly.[2] One of the chief achievements of the recent Turkish protests was that: 'authorities lost their agenda-setting power, at least temporarily' (Bakiner 2014).

Similarly, the Brazilian protests yielded significant policy consequences. To start with the most manifest ones, the fare rises, which triggered the protests in the first place, were reversed in more than a hundred cities (MPL 2013, 17). Congress approved the allocation of 75% of Brazilian oil royalties to education and 25% to health. Senate passed a bill that declared corruption to be a heinous crime. A proposal for a constitutional amendment that reduced the power of the Public Prosecutor's Office and a bill that framed homosexuality as a disease were withdrawn, as many activists had demanded. These policy outcomes also had implications in terms of the self-understanding of citizens, who came to see that they could exert influence over representatives.

Obviously, and besides these institutional victories, a crucial consequence of the protests in both countries was the generation of deliberation on a variety of topics. Similarly to what Min (2014) observed in the Occupy movement in New York, in both Brazil and Turkey protests brought new debates into the public sphere, helping to set the public agenda. In addition, protests themselves have risen as a strong symbolic statement against established practices of liberal representative democracies.

In Turkey, many protesters began to realize how Kurdish rights had been violated by the state for decades, in the same way that their rights had been violated in the protests (Arat 2013, 808). In the case of Brazil, several topics around the *right to the city* were debated, including the possibility of free fare transportation, the consequences of mega-sports-events, homeless occupations, real estate speculation and security. Ordinary citizens, experts and political representatives debated technical issues, such as the demilitarization of the police and political reform. There was a broad discursive process in many arenas, and at different times.

When we consider the place of social media communications within this broad discursive process, it is true that online debates occurred usually among like-minded individuals who shared political positions and worldviews. These discussions, however, were important in terms of enhancing the overall quality of the protests: they strengthened the positions of the protesters and helped to clarify their aims, which could be taken up and advocated in other arenas, including the policy process (Lev-On and Manin, 2009). Overall, the public communications carried out during the protests helped to open up the public agenda to various issues while showing deliberation to be an integral part of contentious politics.

CONCLUSION

We have sought to identify the deliberative dimensions of recent protest movements, focusing on the 2013 protests in Turkey and Brazil. Our analysis shows that both protests followed a similar pattern of contentious politics entailing strong deliberative elements. We identified these elements in the horizontal and decentralized structure of the protests, in the type of collective action they generated, and in their public and policy consequences.

More broadly, our analysis suggests that it is misleading to take deliberation and agonism as mutually exclusive. Having said that, we are aware that there is no one standard way of synthesizing these two understandings of politics and democracy. The interplay between deliberation and agonism may manifest itself differently, depending on the particularities of the socio-political context.

In the case of Turkey, the interplay manifested itself through the establishment of horizontal alliances among groups that have been traditionally hostile to one another. Here, the agonistic, yet at the same time deliberative, nature of the protests opened up the possibilities of thinking and acting beyond the conventional dichotomies, such as Islam vs. secularism, Kemalism vs. the AKP, Kurds vs. Turks. The protests brought together people from a broad political spectrum, and consensus was neither the requirement – nor the outcome – of their collective action.

In the case of Brazil, agonistic politics showed that deliberation should not be restricted to formal participatory institutions, such as policy councils and participatory budgeting. Protests nurtured intense debates over, often invisible, issues, fostered the establishment of a new informal institution and stimulated the porosity of the political system. More interestingly, protests have generated an awareness of difference, exposing the existence of silenced controversial issues in a public sphere often inhospitable to disagreement. The strong polyphony of the streets compelled demonstrators to acknowledge the strength of dissensus over topics such as LGBT rights. The acknowledgement of this dissensus is an important step for an effective and broad clash of discourses.

In sum, in both Turkey and Brazil, recent protests showed that it is possible to experiment with different models of democracy, starting with deliberative democracy. In fact, the main alternative to 'politics as usual' was deliberation, although not the naïve deliberation as imagined by sceptics of this approach. Rather, deliberation and conflict can work together, and the recent protests offer striking examples of their compatibility in practice.

With the importance of democracy and social movements for critical policy studies, the emergence of recent protest movements is significant in understanding actual efforts at democratization that are being made in today's world. It is especially crucial to recognize that deliberative democracy – and deliberative forums in the policy process – should not be regarded as necessarily favouring consensus to the exclusion of the agonistic practices of contentious protest. Indeed, concrete efforts at democratization must combine stabilizations and ruptures, shaping the policy context through the vitalization of political life and the introduction of previously excluded issues onto the public agenda.

ACKNOWLEDGEMENTS

This article was written as part of the collaborative research project of the Federal University of Minas Gerais, and the University of Canberra, entitled Protests and Political Engagement, and funded by CNPq/Brazil (Process: 445955/2014-7 and Process: 305117/2014-9) and Fapemig (Process: PPM-00211-13). We would like to thank John Dryzek, Max Halupka, David Marsh, Marcus Abílio Pereira, and Peter Wagner for their insightful comments and suggestions on the previous version of this article. Previous versions of this article were presented at the 2014 American Political Studies Annual Conference in Washington DC and at the social movements workshop at the Institute for Governance and Policy Analysis, University of Canberra in 2014. We are also grateful to the participants of both occasions for their insightful suggestions, and critical engagements with this paper.

NOTES

* A previous and more developed version of this text was originally published by *Policy Studies* (Mendonça and Ercan, 2015, http://dx.doi.org/10.1080/01442872.2015.1065970).
1. It is important to highlight that the Brazilian demonstrations have acquired very different features and dynamics in different cities. This brief presentation outlines a broad overview of these singular processes.
2. Personal communication, September 2013.

REFERENCES

Arat, Yesim (2013) 'Violence, resistance and Gezi Park'. *International Journal of Middle East Studies*, **45**, 807–809.
Bakiner, Onur (2014) 'Gezi at one: Rethinking the legacy of the protests'. Jadaliyya, 6 June 2014. Available at: http://www.jadaliyya.com/pages/index/18023/gezi-at-one_rethinking-the-legacy-of-the-protests (last accessed on 25 June 2014).
Bennett, Lance and Alexandra Segerberg (2012) 'The logic of connective action – Digital media and the personalization of contentious politics'. *Information, Communication and Society*, **15** (5), 739–768.
Bohman, James (1996) *Public Deliberation: Pluralism, Complexity and Democracy*. Cambridge, MA: The MIT Press.
Bohman, James (2007) *Democracy Across Borders: From Dêmos to Dêmoi*. Cambridge, MA: The MIT Press.
Castells, Manuel (2013) *Redes de Indignação e esperança*. Rio de Janeiro: Zahar.

Chambers, Simone (2009) 'Rhetoric and the public sphere: has deliberative democracy abandoned mass democracy?' *Political Theory*, **37** (3), 323–350.
Chou, Mark (2015) 'From crisis to crisis: Democracy, crisis and the Occupy Movement'. *Political Studies Review*, **13** (1), 46–58.
Cohen, Joshua (1989) 'Deliberative democracy and democratic legitimacy'. In A. Hamlin and P. Pettit (eds), *The Good Polity*. Oxford: Blackwell, pp. 17–34.
Della Porta, Donatella (2009) 'Consensus in movements'. In Donatella Della Porta (ed.), *Democracy in Social Movements*. New York: Palgrave.
Della Porta, Donetella (2012) 'Critical trust: Social movements and democracy in times of crisis'. *Cambio Anno II*, **4** (Dicembre), 33–44.
Dryzek, John S. (2000) *Deliberative Democracy and Beyond: Liberals, Critics, Contestations*. Oxford: Oxford University Press.
Dryzek, John (2007) 'Theory, evidence, and the tasks of deliberation'. In S. Rosenberg (ed.), *Deliberation, Participation and Democracy: Can the People Govern?* New York: Palgrave Macmillan, pp. 237–250.
Dryzek, John S. and Simon Niemeyer (2006) 'Reconciling pluralism and consensus as political ideals'. *American Journal of Political Science*, **50** (3), 634–649.
Dryzek, John S., David Downes, Christian Hunold, David Schlosberg and Hans-Kristian Hernes (2003).*Green States and Social Movements*. New York: Oxford University Press.
Ercan, Selen A. and Jean-Paul Gagnon (2014) 'Crisis of democracy: Which crisis? Which democracy?', *Democratic Theory* **1** (2), 1–10.
Eriksen, Erik O. (2000) 'The European Union's democratic deficit – a deliberative perspective'. In Michael Saward (ed.), *Democratic Innovation – Deliberation, Representation and Association*. London: Routledge, pp. 53–65.
Göle, Nilüfer (2013) 'The Gezi Occupation: for a democracy of public spaces'. Open Democracy. Available at: https://www.opendemocracy.net/nilufer-gole/gezi-occupation-for-democracy-of-public-spaces (last accessed on 27 August 2015).
Habermas, Jürgen (1996) *Between Facts and Norms: Contributions to a Discourse Theory of Law and Democracy*. Cambridge, MA: The MIT Press.
Harvey, David (2012) *Rebel Cities: From the Right to the City to the Urban Revolution*. London and New York: Verso.
Kanra, Bora and Ercan, Selen A. (2012) 'Negotiating difference in a Muslim society: A longitudinal study of Islamic and secular discourses in the Turkish public sphere'. *Digest of Middle East Studies*, **21** (1), 69–88.
Knops, Andrew (2007) 'Agonism as deliberation – on Mouffe's theory of democracy'. *The Journal of Political Philosophy*, **15** (1), 115–126.
Levine, Peter and Rose Nierras (2007) 'Activists' view of deliberation'. *Journal of Public Deliberation*, **3** (1), 1–14.
Lev-On, Azi and Bernard Manin (2009) 'Happy accidents: Deliberation and online exposure to opposing views'. In Todd Davies and Seeta Gangadharan (eds), *Online Deliberation: Design, Research and Practice*, Chicago: Center for the Study of Language and Information, pp. 105–122.
Mansbridge, Jane, James Bohman and Simone Chambers et al. (2012) 'A systemic approach to deliberative democracy'. In John Parkinson and Jane Mansbridge (eds), *Deliberative Systems: Deliberative Democracy at the Large Scale*. Cambridge: Cambridge University Press, pp. 1–43.
Maricato, Ermínia (2013) 'É a questão urbana, estúpido!' In Ermínia Maricato et al. (eds), *Cidades rebeldes: passe livre e as manifestações que tomaram as ruas do Brasil*. São Paulo: Boitempo/Carta Maior, pp. 19–26.
Medearis, John (2004) 'Social movements and deliberative democratic theory'. *British Journal of Political Science*, **35**, 53–75.
Melucci, Alberto (1996) *Challenging Codes: Collective Action in the Information Age*. Cambridge: Cambridge University Press.
Mendonça, Ricardo Fabrino and Selen A. Ercan (2015), 'Deliberation and protest: strange

bedfellows? Revealing the deliberative potential of 2013 protests in Turkey and Brazil'. *Policy Studies*, **36** (3), 267–282.

Mendonça, Ricardo Fabrino (2013) 'The conditions and dilemmas of deliberative systems'. In APSA Annual Meeting, Chicago, 29 August–1 September. Social Science Research Network, pp. 1–31. Available at: http://papers.ssrn.com/sol3/papers.cfm?abstract_id=2303025.

Min, Seong-Jae (2014) 'Occupy Wall Street and deliberative decision-making: Translating theory to practice'. *Communication, Culture and Critique (early view)*, 1–17. Available at: http://onlinelibrary.wiley.com/doi/10.1111/cccr.12074/pdf.

Mouffe, Chantal (2000) 'Deliberative democracy or agonistic pluralism'. *Reihe Politikwissenschaft*, Institut für Höhere Studien (IHS). Available at: http://www.ihs.ac.at/publications/pol/pw_72.pdf.

Movimento Passe Livre (MPL) (2013) 'Não começou em Salvador, não vai terminar em São Paulo'. In Ermínia Maricato et al. (eds), *Cidades rebeldes: passe livre e as manifestações que tomaram as ruas do Brasil*. São Paulo: Boitempo/Carta Maior, pp. 13–18.

Parkinson, John and Jane Mansbridge (eds) (2012) *Deliberative Systems: Deliberative Democracy at the Large Scale*. Cambridge: Cambridge University Press.

Peschanski, João Alexandre (2013) 'O transporte público gratuito, uma utopia real'. In Ermínia Maricato et al. (eds), *Cidades rebeldes: passe livre e as manifestações que tomaram as ruas do Brasil*. São Paulo: Boitempo/Carta Maior, pp. 59–63.

Prentoulis, Marina and Lasse Thomassen (2013) 'Political theory in the square: Protests, representation and subjectification'. *Contemporary Political Theory*, **12** (3), 166–184.

Rancière, Jacques (2007) *On the Shores of Politics*. London: Verso.

Rancière, Jacques (2010) *Dissensus: On Politics and Aesthetics*. London: Bloomsbury Academic.

Vainer, Carlos (2013) 'Quando a cidade vai às ruas'. In Ermínia Maricato et al. (eds), *Cidades rebeldes: passe livre e as manifestações que tomaram as ruas do Brasil*. São Paulo: Boitempo and Carta Maior, pp. 35–40.

Young, Iris (2003) 'Activist challenges to deliberative democracy'. In James Fishkin and Peter Laslett (eds), *Debating Deliberative Democracy*, Malden: Blackwell, pp. 102–120.

12 Lost in translation: expressing emotions in policy deliberation

Anna Durnová

INTRODUCTION

Much of the research on discourse in political science has been predominantly shaped by discussion of how we analyze the meanings of policies (such as Keller 2005; Yanow 2006; Glynos and Howarth 2008; Howarth 2010). To a large extent, this discussion has been kept distinct from debates on the role of discourse as a tool for policy deliberation. In a nutshell, deliberation inquiry has been less concerned with methodological protocol, instead focusing on analyzing the process of achieving mutual understanding among actors (as suggest Fishkin 1991; Fischer and Forester 1993; Dryzek 2001; Gottweis 2003; Hajer and Wagenaar 2003; Fung 2006, 2007). These works did analyze arguments, assumptions, and positions of actors – all substantial components of discourse – but they did not always unpack the methodological reflection behind the analysis they were offering.

Both streams of research have emphasized that discourse is much more than a tool to say things, because it shapes our views on these things. By design, the critical policy analysis that uses discourse as the lens to explain policy making has elaborated an understanding of analysis of discourse as an enterprise, in which we must constantly and critically unfold our assumptions, truth claims, and analytical skills. This unfolding has been also one of the crucial moments of analysis in the deliberation inquiry (such as Fischer 2009 or Hajer 2009).

However, emotions were not considered in these reflections. One could even argue that evacuating emotions was the initial purpose of deliberation, especially when we bear in mind that deliberation was too often seen as a rationalizing instrument to achieve mutual understanding, to calm down controversies and conflicts – in fact, to calm down emotions (as argue Thompson and Hoggett 2001, or van Stokkom 2005 in their critiques of deliberation inquiry). This chapter suggests that what we miss in the deliberation inquiry is the translation of emotions into inherent structuring elements of deliberation.

If discourses are the products of power relations and the values and beliefs related to the policies discussed, as suggested by all these named approaches, then in turn we have to ask what role emotion plays in these discourses. How do power relations and values produce particular emotions and how are they reproduced by them? To investigate emotions in deliberation means to mount a challenge to the current criteria of determining what is rational and what is emotional and, with that, to propose a novel view of how deliberation is both thought of and performed.

This chapter reflects on the role of emotions in deliberation by drawing the analogy between emotions as they arise during fieldwork and emotions as deliberative tools. This has several implications. To begin with, the role of emotions in the course of fieldwork invites us to think further about the position of the researcher. In particular, it raises the issue of the interviewer's openness to acknowledge the emotional experience presented by the interviewee. Following this line of thought, respondents may also experience the tension between their individual experience and the collective validation of this experience. In this way, emotions lay the foundation for fieldwork strategies for the way the researcher gathers data as much as they reveal the tension between the individual and the collective dimension of emotional experiences.

These strategies do not disappear during deliberation but structure it from the outset. Looking at emotions in deliberation enables us to see the tension between the individual and the collective dimension of emotional experience, which becomes reflected both in how knowledge is produced and in what qualifies this knowledge as relevant. The same goes for the actors taking part in deliberation who are legitimized to take part in respective policy negotiations on the basis of that knowledge. In fact, both emotions and discourses reveal to us the tension between the individual part of knowledge (moment, feeling, point of view) and its collective validation (the cultural context, the habitus, the established practice, and the like). Integrating emotions in our analyses brings us more explicitly to the larger epistemological dimension, in which we think about policy deliberation with and through emotions.

By reviewing a number of empirical findings and results in recent studies on discourse in policy analysis, this chapter points out the analytical value emotions might have for critical policy deliberation. Emotions guide us through the main challenges of deliberation: the ambivalence of knowledge supporting the aims of deliberation, the institutional ambiguity that makes it challenging for actors to find their position in the deliberation process, and the modes of presentation and communication through which that deliberation is performed.

READING POLICIES WITH EMOTIONAL LENSES

A controversy over the creation of a new railway station in the city of Brno, Czech Republic, gave me the opportunity to study the intense emotional language employed by actors embroiled in that conflict. I augmented my investigation with extensive interviews, in which both sides – those who were for and those who were against the new railway station of the dispute – claimed that the other side was 'irrational' or not sufficiently qualified to put the proposition on the political table. The emotional situation was not the result of the two sides, after protracted negotiation, becoming frustrated with each other, resulting in a breakdown of negotiations. Instead, the emotional situation was entirely representative of how the two sides had interacted with each other from the beginning of the railway station planning process. They responded to each other in this way because they found their values, either for or against the new railway station, as irreconcilable (as I show in Durnová 2013).

In a similar manner, Maarten Hajer (2005) shows in his analysis of the planning negotiations for Ground Zero in New York that redesigning the almost-hallowed space after the 9/11 attacks was deeply emotional not because somebody might have offended someone during the design process, but because identifying someone as the legitimate speaker on this issue was linked, from the outset of the planning process, to grief about 9/11. The notion of grief became specific through the ways in which both public officials and citizens felt about the values and beliefs that were represented in the designs considered for the memorial.

That the emergence of emotions is mainly seen as evidence that something went wrong in the process is a commonly shared stereotype. This stereotype can be depicted also in the way that traditional approaches to policy analysis have established the so-called 'rationalizing' instruments in order to prevent policies from becoming wicked or loaded (see, e.g., Clemons and McBeth 2001, Jann and Wegrich 2003 or Schubert and Bandelow 2003). These approaches have consequently described policy making as a sequence of rational actions, causally following each other. The quest for a rationalizing structure can be seen also in the ways the roles of policy makers and policy analysts in the policy processes are designed to be figures without normative accounts, as someone having the technical ability to act without judging these actions. The notion of an objective, value-free actor formulating, evaluating, or implementing policies goes partly back to Weberian tradition, which conceives the administrator as the rational figure without evil passions that would prevent him/her from pursuing his/her worthy public goals (Weber 1926). If this figure displays emotions, then these are translated into some sort of 'productive emotions'

– ambition, charisma, or the like – whereas other sorts of emotions are seen to be 'disturbing.' We can follow the affinities of this development of such rationalizing actors through the history of the establishment of US or French public administrations marking an important development of public policy as a discipline based on rational models (as shown by, e.g., Fischer 2009 and 2013 for the United States and Zittoun 2014 for France).

Would it mean, then, that a smidgen of emotion is desirable but too much of it inhibits actors in their job of making policy? This is partly suggested by the literature on emotions in mainstream approaches to political science, since the inclusion of emotions in politics has always been wedded to a certain paradigmatic framing, making them the opposite of rationalized institutional procedures and scientific expertise. And yet, recent research on social movements (Goodwin 2001; Jasper 2011), psychosocial theorizing of emotions in social policies (Stenner and Taylor 2008; Barnes 2008), and analyses of the work of policy practitioners (Sullivan and Skelcher 2002; Newman 2012) suggest the contrary. These studies show that the separation between rationality and emotions is rather illusory because emotional accounts of knowledge production build the core of policy formulation and because emotions accompany actors' pursuance of goals and interests (see also Hunter 2003 or Jasper 2011). What is more, emotions point to values and beliefs that are shared among actors of a particular group. These groups distinguish themselves from others on the basis of this shared experience (see Jasper 2011; Cronin 2014).

While such framing of emotions as an inherent part of the rationality of actors is no longer new (see a more detailed review of these debates in Bondi 2005, 2014; Jasper 2011; Dixon 2012), the perception of some emotions as 'good' and others as 'disturbing' to the policy process seems to be pervasive in the policy literature. This aspect becomes particularly important when it comes to policy deliberations, where emotions are linked to the evaluation of actors as 'rational' or moderate while others are designated as 'radical,' 'too emotional,' and the like because the emotional lenses can lead us to the core of such evaluative judgment of actors.

A similar sort of separation between good and evil emotions for policy making suggests also the overview of recent studies of critical approaches to policy analysis.[1] Although these approaches contest the idea of linear and in that sense rational policy cycles and highlight the dynamic character of interactions among actors and their argumentation procedures that shape what counts as the 'valuable' knowledge or the 'pertinent' argument (see, e.g., Gottweis 2003; Hajer and Wagenaar 2003; Hajer 2005; Howarth 2010; Fischer and Gottweis 2012; Lejano and Leong 2012), their discussion of the criteria determining 'the valuable' and 'the pertinent' has not yet been extended to the issue of emotions. If some of these studies do evoke the issue of emotions (such as Gottweis 2007 or Fischer 2009), emotions are here thought of more in the performative sense of 'showing emotions.' In other studies, emotions are presented as a 'surplus' to the study of discourse by showing, for example, the heuristic values of fantasies (as do for example Glynos and Howarth 2008).[2] Works on policy planning have also raised the issue of emotions but framed it primarily as a kind of added value of strategies of policy practitioners who work with wicked problems (Sullivan and Skelcher 2002; Newman 2012).

In a more or less separate canon, feminist scholars have raised the issue of emotions in studying the layers of knowledge production and have contributed to the current debate of emotions as part of rationality (Fonow and Cook 1991; Martin 2001; Ahmed 2004).[3] However, feminist study of emotions was linked quite specifically to women's issues – largely understood – and raised the assumptions that emotions might be issue specific and need not be considered by researchers working on other issues. A comparable integration of emotions in the analysis was revealed in the field of health care innovation, or in care policies (Gottweis 2007; Orsini and Wiebe 2014), or in the field of minority rights – as Gould (2009) shows in the case of AIDS activists – where emotions were seen as related either to the threat projected in the technologies (fear, uncertainty, etc.) or to the value associated with persons having a minority status in the society (shame, pride, etc.).

Despite the indisputable explanatory value of all these studies for some aspects of emotions' role in public policy, research on discourse and deliberation would still seem to fall into the trap of traditional policy analysis approaches that have drawn the line between emotions and the rationalizing instruments of policy analysis. On the one hand, these studies give the impression of working with discourse as a kind of a rationalizing structure, as if both interaction and argumentation could be thought of in their purified manner of presenting knowledge without being shaped by emotions. Second, studies on planning conflicts, women's policies, or health care policies follow this bias by suggesting through their analyses that it is possible to separate policy issues into those that are 'emotional' and those that are 'rational' or 'technical.'

This chapter does not address where exactly emotions are to be settled (see Jasper 2011 for an extensive review on this) and whether they are more urges or motivation and the like. Examples such as those above should show that paying attention to how emotions are expressed in deliberation show us emotion's important relation to elements of discourses that create values and beliefs that become crucial for qualifying a policy issue as a 'relevant one' and that shape the constellation of actors. If emotions have in recent decades gained importance in this area of research, two important insights stand out: first, that emotions are both individual and collective occurrences, and, second, that they can be investigated in discourses that reveal this tension between individual and collective dimension of knowledge. Emotions are the result of both collective socio-political circumstances – which have labeled some emotions as appropriate and banned others as inappropriate – and of the individual interactive moments that can turn or at least reshape this distinction.

Reading policies with emotional lenses allows us to gain important insights into how to think of the role of discourses in policies, and how this might change once we get emotions on board consciously. Such an approach does not embrace the view that emotions would not hurt actions, would not cause negotiations to break down, and could not complicate policy making. This chapter offers a different take on this capacity of emotions by highlighting the analytic potential that emotions have in uncovering hidden values and underlying meanings because (a) the emotional lens reveals that some discourses are prioritized over others through the prioritization of some values and (b) it steers the identification of actors around a particular discourse. Unveiling these emotional accounts of discourses helps us see the boundary between the individual accounts of knowledge and its collective acknowledgment that emotions entail. Emotions affect the nature of the knowledge at stake in deliberation, they shape the repartition of actors who take part in the process, and they shape the way these actors take part in the process.

EMOTIONS AT THE INTERSECTION BETWEEN THE INDIVIDUAL AND THE COLLECTIVE

There are two particular sources of inspiration for applying emotional lenses. On the one hand, the recent reflection on the role of researcher in fieldwork and the eventual difficulties within which he/she deploys the research uncovers the tension between the individual and collective dimensions of knowledge production, inviting us to embrace a more complex notion of what we can know through discourses. On the other hand, recent works on public engagement strategies stress that conflicts must not be regarded as something bad, but that, indeed, conflicts can reveal hidden values and beliefs that build the opposition of the groups of actors and that structure their reciprocal judgments (see Thompson and Hoggett 2001; van Stokkom 2005; Barnes 2008). In both of these inspirations, emotions invite us to see the dynamic of ascribing some values and beliefs to some objects on the basis of a boundary between the individual experiences, which is self-interpreted and embedded in some kind of collective interpretations.

Let us start with the fieldwork side. In her studies of how researchers feel about their emotions during fieldwork, Virginia Dickinson-Swift and her team raise several interesting points for the role of emotions in the production of knowledge. First, research is an emotional labor in the way researchers show emotions during their investigations, 'signalling that the researcher had connected in a very personal and emotional way with the story' (Dickson-Swift et al. 2009: 65). Second, the Dickson-Swift study showed that many researchers did feel that showing emotions might be inappropriate, which alerts us to the already mentioned framing of emotions as something evil to research practices. Whereas the aim of the Dickson-Swift study is different – as it supports eventual programs for accompanying researchers whenever they need emotional support for the emotion work they are actually doing (as Hochschild 2003 conceptualizes) – we can take their investigation as the example of a tension where the researcher constantly reflects his/her surroundings either by affirmation or by distance, or by misunderstandings, paradoxes, and the like.

Critical approaches to fieldwork take us one step in that direction by refining the epistemological founding of research practices against the classical ethnography that has rather erased the subjective experience of the researcher in the field (as for example Shehata 2006 shows in his critique of the classical approaches). Analogous to what is described in the previous paragraph, fieldwork is then a challenging area of multiple tensions (Van Maanen 1988, 2011), a complicated venue, a 'swamp' for which the researcher has no map (as already depicted by Punch 1994). This tension of the possibilities of knowing has been discussed and investigated also by the participant epistemology (see mainly Fay 2005 and expansions of Fay in Wagenaar 2011) and critiques of mainstream research of public policy have framed this tension by partly adapting the language. Interpretive methods, for example, privilege in that sense 'hunches' over hypotheses (Schwartz-Sea and Yanow 2006) in order to reflect the dynamic character of fieldwork. Also, works on policy practices accentuate the 'unfolding character' of a practice (see mainly Cook and Wagenaar 2012). Studies in critical ethnography emphasize the multiple, and often conflicting, identities of the researcher, who is often outside the definitional margins; it is through this 'being outside while being there,' so to speak, that the researchers co-produce the knowledge of their fieldwork (as shown by Shehata 2006 or Dubois 2009).

In brief, these fieldwork discussions invite us to be constantly aware of the tension between the individual dimension of expression (verbal or nonverbal) and its collective interpretation (affirmation, opposition, support, etc.). Emotions then appear as a code for what is appropriate/ inappropriate to feel and to show what becomes negotiated according to the context and the actual interaction among actors. The tension between the individual and the collective is not exclusive to the analytic field. As the Dickson-Swift discussion of appropriateness of emotions already mentioned, this tension further teases out the implications for designing any analysis as a rational construct. Linda Finlay holds in support of even more conscious involvement of emotions in research:

> 'Coming out' through reflexive analysis is ultimately a political act. Done well, it has the potential to enliven, teach, and spur readers toward a more radical consciousness. Voicing the unspoken can empower both researcher and partici- pant. As more researchers grasp the nettle the research in the future can move in new creative directions. Are we ready to embrace the challenge? (Finlay 2002: 544)

One of such challenges is the field of deliberation where reflexivity has been one of the key tasks of actors aiming at achieving mutual understanding and solving conflicts.

DELIBERATING THE INDIVIDUAL AND THE COLLECTIVE

Policy deliberation is generally thought of as the interaction among actors in their attempt to arrive at a consensus. Widely shaped and inspired by Habermasian thought, the interaction is basically thought of as a dialogue of partners (see Dryzek 2001; Mendonça and Ercan 2015). Through the emphasis put on both partnership and dialogue, deliberative thinkers have simultaneously made the deliberation inquiry into an inquiry about democracy. For many of them, dialogue has adopted a status of a guaran- tee of democracy because all partners can interact in deliberative settings (see, e.g., Fung 2006). However, some studies on deliberation inquiry, inspired by the psychosocial tradition, have paid attention to the optic through which deliberation is regarded as a rationalizing tool, calming the disputes, solving conflicts, and, consequently, seeming to fit only in some policy issues or in some situations where actors are not too radical (see Thompson and Hoggett 2001; van Stokkom 2005; Newman 2012). In that sense, emotions structure deliberation as they unpack why some values are prioritized and reveal social relationships among actors, and especially why some values are qualified as trustworthy and others as disturbing.

I begin with the prioritization of values. Through appeals to certain emotions (such as shame, pride, fear, disgust), certain discourses become prioritized over others. This was the case, for example, in the Brno planning process, where activists against the new railway station linked the megalomaniac project of a new railway station with the pride of the city's public officials who do not want to listen to ordinary people. In the same vein, the public officials expressed their disgust toward dubious experts on the activist side and used this emotion to paint the opposing technical solution as dubious. In both cases, emotions are communicated experiences of values that actors want to emphasize in their proposition. And these values are collectively validated through the process.

Such prioritization of values goes hand in hand with the qualifying of actors. Let me stay with the example of the Brno railway station. The conflict emerging from the proposal to move Brno's main railway station to a new location approximately 800 meters south of the city center was launched in 2003. The mayor's office's unilateral decision to make the move became the catalyst for a group of experts and environmental activists to argue that modernization of the railway station was possible in its existing location and that the relocation project was therefore unnecessary. With this, the lines were drawn between the 'modernizing discourse' and the 'sustainability discourse,' leading to a local referendum in 2004. A clear majority, 85.78 per cent, of voters were against the moving project, but since only 24 per cent of Brno citizens voted on the issue, the mayor was not legally bound to the referendum decision. With that, a virtual tug of war between supporters of the moving project and its opponents persisted from 2006 until 2009. In early 2010, the mayor was forced to suspend planning and construction negotiations of the relocation project because the High Court of Administration, the Czech Republic's highest court for affairs of local government, canceled the current version of Brno's zoning plan by finding in favor of the activist initiative.

The fieldwork revealed to me that both the modernizing and the sustainability discourses are connected to how their adherents think about who is the actor entitled to speak, and how the process of formulating policy should be designed, who should take part in that process, and who should stay aside. The reciprocal expressive identification of both groups – either as 'fat cats' or as 'stupid activists' – that I have identified during the inquiry aptly illustrates the dynamic of the conflict. Both sides were unable to separate the arguments or data from how they felt about the other group. Their emotions were aroused not after the other side had done something specifically to provoke them, but from the context that they do not share common values and beliefs, not only about the location of the railway station, but, more importantly, about the nature of policies.

With this take we can also emphasize the evaluative potential that emotions have when entitling actors to deal with and to speak about an issue. This is apparent in Frank Fischer's discussion of the Goersdorfs' study of the Kerala project (2009), in which he suggests that such entitlements do not stem from emotional interactions directly, but rather that these entitlements are a co-production of both the interactive elements during respective communications and the sociocultural aspects on the basis of which the communication takes place. Returning to Hajer's example of Ground Zero designs (2005), we can follow how the planning process uses emotions by revolving around the definition of what is an 'appropriate memorial.' The values related to this were organized differently in the presentations of owners, mourners of victims, and stakeholders. Expanding on this, Rosie Anderson paints a complex picture of a policy practitioner working constantly within the realm of the emotional. She uses a figure of a 'fool' to illustrate the difficult position of a policy practitioner who works against sociocultural stereotypes and other discursive elements that want the stakeholder be a rational figure (Anderson 2014). Also, human geography has emphasized that emotions can be both interactions and contexts (Cronin 2014) and should be viewed intersubjectively (Bondi 2005).[4]

What I want to elucidate through these anecdotal examples is that emotions do not build the counterpart to discourse; instead, they co-produce discourse though their capacity to shape our perception and to evaluate discourse as 'good,' 'valuable,' 'important,' or the evoked 'emotional' and rational' (as shown by Tapolet 2000; Hochschild 2003; Ahmed 2004). Both emotions and discourse incorporate a code of perception and interpretation of the surrounding world. They are dependent on both the subject who observes the surrounding world and on the context in which he/she observes it. They are interdependent because they function as the context in which discourses emerge and through which they justify or deny practices.

With this duality, not only can we draw an analogical line between the explanatory role of discourses and the role of emotions, but, more importantly, we can depict that both enterprises bring us to the tension between the individual and the collective dimensions of the production of knowledge. If one of the central aims of critical approaches in policy studies has been to enhance our understanding of the complex development of policies – including their related misunderstandings, paradoxes, and contestations – it is central to move beyond framing emotions as symptoms of the situations when something gets worse, complicated, or 'too emotional.'

'AS GOOD AS IT GETS': EMOTIONS AS TRANSLATORS OF DELIBERATION

'And what if this is as good as it gets?,' goes the now-famous line from the Oscar-winning film of almost the same name (*As Good as It Gets*, 1997), asked by the main character, Melvin Udall, of the group of depressed patients waiting with him in the psychiatric office. While this quote becomes a positive turning point in the film, after which Melvin Udall applies a different take on his life, to ask 'and what if this is as good as it gets?' during policy negotiations is hardly imaginable for many of the cases we face in deliberation inquiry. But why is this so?

One answer leads us to the larger epistemological dimension in which we think of deliberation as a mutual consensus and in which we place our notion of policies as a solution to a problem. Emotions open for us the paradoxical arena in which deliberation inquiry has recently landed: while highlighting the ambivalence of knowledge, those of institutions and actors, and the ambivalent way of communication in policy making, policy analysts have still not surrendered the idea of the mutual consensus that will be found. How has this happened?

First, the complex character of many policy issues related to scientific knowledge (Irwin and Wynne 2003) – such as environmental policies or planning controversies (Gualini and Majoor 2007; Fischer 2009) – or policies related to health care innovations (Gottweis 2003, 2007) has been used to establish the ambivalence of knowledge and the protracted character of knowledge production. What counts as the relevant knowledge on which the measure should be developed is a matter of complicated negotiations among actors who search for the common ground to make it possible to define a particular knowledge as a relevant one. This ambivalence about knowledge has been, on the one hand, ascribed to the postmodern situation in policy making (Majone 1989; Gottweis 2003) and to the higher presence of the narrative of risk in Western democracies (Beck 1988). On the other hand, this ambivalence has been repeatedly stated because the common analytic instruments of policy analysis did not reveal what happens in protracted knowledge productions.

Emotions can be defined here as translators of this ambivalence because they enable us to see that all these negotiations count not just as arguments; rather, these arguments are co-produced by the negotiating actors' shared experiences. The sharing occurs on the basis of the collective validation of the individual emotional experience that an actor has brought to these negotiations. Such emotional experience is not only a commonly known reference to fear or anger but also the very relation to the issue from the individual's own perspective. Regardless of whether one is a regular citizen or a mayor, people do connect to the issue discussed because they have experienced something in a particular way. As we have seen earlier, because these experiences happen through emotions, emotions open to us the process of knowledge production and enable us to make sense of the ambivalence.

Second, analysts have characterized the actors taking part in policy making as possessing institutional ambiguity. In many aspects, governance has relaxed institutional rules because it has made the traditional institutional boundaries the subject of negotiations and, subsequently, of revisions. First, the actors now must establish their position in order to be recognized as actors and to take part in the negotiations. These ways of recognizing actors have often been explained through argumentation (Griggs and Howarth 2004; Fischer and Gottweis 2012), or through the way governance is being performed (Hajer and Versteeg 2005), in which actors build the trust of the surrounding collective on the basis of which they can then govern. However, how this trust becomes developed in the policy process too often has been ascribed to arguments and communication patterns without taking into account the role of emotions.

If we redirect our attention just slightly more toward emotions, we can see inside the trust-building process because we can explain why some arguments resonate among actors and other arguments do not. We have stated earlier that emotions reveal social relationships through the process of sharing the same sort of emotional experiences. That is how they build the groups of actors, and that is how they build trust. On that basis, they then also share communication patterns, because the latter stem from their values and experiences.

Third, these two ambivalences – in knowledge and in the position of the actor – lead us then to a number of protracted policy negotiations, such as the ones over the Brno railway station, where both sides continued engaging in the negotiations without arriving at a solution. Quite often, the policy analysts have stated that these difficult communication situations stem from the fact that the public seeks the advice of experts and institutions (see Bevir and Rhodes 2003 or Peters 2011) despite not necessarily trusting them (Blakely and Evans 2009 or Fischer 2009). A number of studies have thus suggested that we devise public engagement strategies that give people the opportunity to talk, and thereby that gain the people's trust through communication, such as in citizen conferences or citizen expert panels. Sometimes, however, these communicative strategies do not seem to help. Since emotions are able to show us the prioritization of values and the repartition of actors, they might then also reveal to us in the same manner that the values of the groups of actors are too contrary for any sort of consensus to be found. Some policies might be designed to fail, as there will be always two opposite experiences. To accept this tension between experiences, to make this misunderstanding between both parties legitimate, would mean reorienting the respective designs for deliberation, not toward a more refined concept of argumentation and communication, but toward offering the space for sharing these conflictual experiences without aiming at any other specific interest beyond this process of sharing.

CONCLUSION

In their long history in political science, emotions have been abundantly defined as rational actions, as evaluative judgments, and as a mode of conceiving the surrounding world. What is important for us when taking up the analytical role that emotions have in explaining deliberation is that, in all these reflections, emotions have been classified neither as surplus to political phenomena nor as *corpora delicti* indicating that something has gone wrong in the proceedings. Quite the contrary, as the review presented in this chapter illustrates, emotions can be identified as intrinsic parts of human interactions in which and through which discourses get articulated.

Although this canon of thought has been kept rather separate from the agenda of analyzing policy deliberation through discourse, this chapter shows how emotions can be taken up by critical scholars as elements gaining insight into the process of knowledge production and trust building. The chapter has also expanded on this role by showing that, if emotions do prioritize some values over others and build the repartition of actors, then some particularly complicated situations might have to stay as they are, indeed might remain unresolved, because that is the nature of the values and actors at stake. To get emotions on board can then save us from feeling that something went wrong in the deliberations, that something got lost in the translation into arguments, facts, and negotiation procedures. Emotions can, in this respect, provide us with some sort of positive turning point where we say 'this is as good as it gets,' so we should now try to coexist instead of feeling 'lost in translation.'

NOTES

1. These works consider themselves to be 'post-positivist,' 'interpretive,' or 'critical,' as I use them here (for an overview of these labels see, e.g., Durnová and Zittoun 2013).

Interestingly enough, mainstream policy analysts classify these approaches as 'irrational' (see, e.g., Clemons and McBeth 2001).

2. Also other traditions, such as the poststructuralist theory of emotions as acts of identification of actors around a discourse (Stavrakakis 2008: 6–7), Yannis Stavrakakis sees, together with Scott Lash, have affect as a part of discourses in which they are externalized. Discourses affect both: impulses and consequences (Stavrakakis 2008: 4–5).

3. Feminist approaches to both policy studies and political science in general also engage in studying emotions. These approaches have raised an important critique of the separation between rational and emotional (see Sauer 1997; Ahmed 2004; Ticineto-Clough 2007). Their heuristic potential has been focused mainly around the notion of body and bodily sensations. While important for the larger discussion on emotions, it nevertheless draws us away from the specific focus of policy analysis and the way in which public policy analysts downplay the role of emotions in the process.

4. Merleau-Ponty also suggests that emotions connect us to other people (see Combe 1991).

REFERENCES

Ahmed, Sarah (2004), *The Cultural Politics of Emotion*. New York: Routledge.

Anderson, R. (2014), 'Playing the fool: Activists' performances of emotion in policy making spaces'. *Emotion, Space and Society*. Doi: http://dx.doi.org/10.1016/j.emospa.2014.05.004.

Barnes, M. (2008), 'Passionate participation: Emotional experiences and expressions in deliberative forums'. *Critical Social Policy*, **28** (4), 461–481.

Beck, Ulrich (1988), *Risikogesellschaft auf dem Weg in eine andere Moderne*. Frankfurt am Main: Suhrkamp.

Bevir, Mark and Rod Rhodes (2003), *Interpreting British Governance*. London: Psychology Press.

Blakeley, G. and B. Evans (2009), 'Who participates, how and why in urban regeneration projects? The case of the new 'city' of East Manchester'. *Social Policy & Administration*, **43** (1), 15–32.

Bondi, Liz (2005), 'Making connections and thinking through emotions: Between geography and psychotherapy'. *Transactions of the Institute of British Geographers*, **30** (4), 433–448.

Bondi, Liz (2014), 'Understanding feelings: Engaging with unconscious communication and embodied knowledge'. *Emotion, Space and Society*, **10** (February), 44–54.

Clemons, R.S. and M.K. McBeth (2001), *Public Policy Praxis: Theory and Pragmatism: A Case Approach*. Upper Saddle River, NJ: Prentice Hall.

Combe, Dominique (1991), *La pensée et le style*. Paris: Gallimard.

Cook, N.S.D. and H. Wagenaar (2012), 'Navigating the eternally unfolding present: toward an epistemology of practice'. *The American Review of Public Administration*, **42** (1), 3–38.

Cronin, A.M. (2014), 'Between friends: Making emotions intersubjectively'. *Emotion, Space and Society*, **10** (February), 71–78.

Dickson-Swift, V., E.L. James, S. Kippen and P. Liamputtong (2009), 'Researching sensitive topics: Qualitative research as emotion work'. *Qualitative Research*, **9** (1), 61–79.

Dixon, T. (2012), '"Emotion": The history of a keyword in crisis'. *Emotion Review*, **4** (4), 338–344.

Dryzek, J.S. (2001), 'Legitimacy and economy in deliberative democracy'. *Political Theory*, **29** (5), 651–669.

Dubois, V. (2009), 'Towards a critical policy ethnography: lessons from fieldwork on welfare control in France'. *Critical Policy Studies*, **3** (2), 221–239.

Durnová, A. (2013), 'A tale of "fat cats" and "stupid activists": Contested values, governance and reflexivity in the Brno Railway Station controversy'. *Journal of Environmental Policy & Planning*, 1-17.

Durnová A. and P. Zittoun (2013), 'Discursive approaches to public policy'. *French Review of Political Science*, **63** (3–4), 85–93.

Fay, Brian (2005), *Contemporary Philosophy of Social Science*. Oxford: Blackwell.

Finlay, L. (2002), '"Outing"' the researcher: The provenance, process, and practice of reflexivity'. *Qualitative Health Research*, **2002** (12), 531–545.

Fischer, Frank (2009), *Democracy and Expertise: Reorienting Policy Inquiry*. Oxford: Oxford University Press.

Fischer, Frank (2013), 'L'expertise politique et le tournant argumentatif'. *Revue française de science politique*, **63** (3), 579–601.

Fischer, Frank and John Forester (eds) (1993), *The Argumentative Turn in Policy Analysis and Planning*. Durham, NC and London: Duke University Press.

Fischer, Frank and Herbert Gottweis (eds) (2012), *The Argumentative Turn Revisited: Public Policy as Communicative Practice*. Durham, NC and London: Duke University Press.

Fishkin, James S. (1991), *Democracy and Deliberation: New Directions for Democratic Reform*. Cambridge: Cambridge University Press.

Fonow, M.M. and J.A. Cook (eds) (1991), *Beyond Methodology: Feminist Scholarship as Lived Research*. Bloomington, IN Indiana University Press.

Fung, A. (2006), 'Varieties of participation in complex governance'. *Public Administration Review*, **66**, 66–75.

Fung, A. (2007), 'Democratic theory and political science: A pragmatic method of constructive engagement'. *American Political Science Review*, **101** (3), 443.

Glynos, J. and D. Howarth (2008), 'Structure, agency and power in political analysis: beyond contextualised self-interpretations'. *Political Studies Review*, **6**, 155–169.

Goodwin, James (2001), *Passionate Politics. Emotions and Social Movements*. Chicago: University of Chicago Press.

Gottweis, Herbert (2003), 'Theoretical strategies of poststructuralist policy analysis: Towards an analytics of government'. In Maarten Hajer and Hendrik Wagenaar (eds), *Deliberative Policy Analysis. Understanding Governance in the Network Society*. Cambridge: Cambridge University Press, pp. 247–265.

Gottweis, Herbert (2007), 'Rhetoric in policy making: Between logos, ethos, and pathos'. In F. Fischer and G.J. Miller (eds), *Handbook of Public Policy Analysis. Theory, Politics, and Methods*. Boca Raton, FL: Taylor and Francis.

Gould, D.B. (2009), *Moving Politics: Emotion and ACT UPs Fight Against AIDS*, Chicago: University of Chicago Press.

Griggs, S. and D. Howarth (2004), 'A transformative political campaign? The new rhetoric of protest against airport expansion in the UK'. *Journal of Political Ideologies*, **9** (2), 181–201.

Gualini, E. and S. Majoor (2007), 'Innovative practices in large urban development projects: Conflicting frames in the quest for "new urbanity"'. *Planning Theory and Practice*, **8** (3), 297–318.

Hajer, Maarten (2005), 'Re-building Ground Zero. The politics of performance'. *Planning Theory and Practice*, **6** (4), 445–464.

Hajer, Maarten (2009), *Authoritative Governance: Policy Making in the Age of Mediatization*. Oxford: Oxford University Press.

Hajer, Maarten and Wytske Versteeg (2005), 'Performing governance through networks'. *European Political Science*, **4**, 340–346.

Hajer, Maarten and Hendrik Wagenaar (eds) (2003), *Deliberative Policy Analysis. Understanding Governance in the Network Society*. Cambridge: Cambridge University Press.

Hochschild, Arlie (2003), *The Commercialization of Intimate Life. Notes from Home and Work*. Berkeley: University of California Press.

Howarth, D. (2010), 'Power, discourse, and policy: Articulating a hegemony approach to critical policy studies'. *Critical Policy Studies*, **3** (3–4), 309–335.

Hunter, S. (2003), 'A critical analysis of approaches to the concept of social identity in social policy'. *Critical Social Policy*, **23** (3), 322–344.

Irwin, Alan and Brian Wynne (2003), *Misunderstanding Science? The Public Reconstruction of Science and Technology*. Cambridge: Cambridge University Press.

Jann, W. and K. Wegrich (2003), 'Phasenmodelle und Politikprozesse: der policy cycle'. In Schubert Klaus and Niels Bandelow (eds), *Lehrbuch der Politikfeldanalyse*, Oldenbourg Verlag, pp. 71–104.

Jasper, J.M. (2011), 'Emotions and social movements: twenty years of theory and research'. *Annual Review of Sociology*, **37** (1), 285–303. Doi:10.1146/annurev-soc-081309-150015.

Keller, Reiner (ed.) (2005), *Die diskursive Konstruktion von Wirklichkeit. zum Verhältnis von Wissenssoziologie und Diskursforschung*. Konstanz: UVK.

Lejano, R.P. and Leong, C. (2012), 'A hermeneutic approach to explaining and understanding public controversies'. *Journal of Public Administration Research and Theory*, **22** (4), 793–814.

Majone, Giandomenico (1989), *Evidence, Argument and Persuasion in the Policy Process*, New Haven, CT: Yale University Press.

Martin, Emily (2001), *The Woman in the Body: A Cultural Analysis of Reproduction*. Boston: Beacon Press.

Mendonça, Ricardo Fabrino and Selen A. Ercan (2015), 'Deliberation and protest: Revealing the deliberative potential of protest movements in Turkey and Brazil'. In Frank Fischer, Douglas Torgerson, Michael Orsini and Anna Durnová (eds), *Handbook of Critical Policy Studies*. Cheltenham, UK and Northampton, MA, USA: Edward Elgar Publishing.

Newman, J. (2012), 'Beyond the deliberative subject? Problems of theory, method and critique in the turn to emotion and affect'. *Critical Policy Studies*, **6** (4), 465–479.

Orsini, M. and S.M. Wiebe (2014), '"Between hope and fear". Comparing the emotional landscapes of the autism movement in Canada and the United States'. In Luc Turgeon, Martin Papillon, Stephen White and Jennifer Wallner (eds), *Comparing Canada: Methods and Perspectives on Canadian Politics*, Toronto: University of Toronto Press, pp. 147–167.

Peters, B.G. (2011), 'Governance as political theory'. *Critical Policy Studies*, **5** (1), 63–72.

Punch, Maurice (1994), 'Politics and ethics in qualitative research'. In Norman K. Denzin, and Yvonna S. Lincoln (eds), *Handbook of Qualitative Research*. London: Sage Publications, pp. 83–97.

Sauer, Birgit (1997), *Geschlecht, Emotion und Politik*. Wien: Institut für Höhere Studien (IHS).

Schubert, Klaus and Niels Bandelow (2003), *Lehrbuch der Politikfeldanalyse*. Oldenbourg Verlag.

Schwartz-Sea, Peregrine and Dvora Yanow (eds) (2006), *Interpretation and Method. Empirical Research Methods and the Interpretive Turn*. New York: M.E. Sharpe.

Shehata, Samer (2006) 'Ethnography, identity and the production of knowledge'. In Dvora Yanow and Peregrine Schartz-Sea (eds), *Interpretation and Method, Empirical Research Methods and the Interpretive Turn*. New York: M.E. Sharpe, pp. 244–263.

Stavrakakis, Y. (2008), 'Peripheral vision: Subjectivity and the organized other: between symbolic authority and fantasmatic enjoyment'. *Organization Studies*, **29** (7), 1037–1059. Doi: 10.1177/0170840608094848.

Stenner, P. and D. Taylor (2008), 'Psychosocial welfare: Reflections on an emerging field'. *Critical Social Policy*, **28** (4), 415–437.

Sullivan, Helen and Chris Skelcher (2002), *Working across Boundaries: Collaboration in Public Services*. London: Palgrave Macmillan.

Tapolet, Christine (2000,) *Émotions et Valeur*. Paris: Presses Universitaires de France.

Thompson, S. and P. Hoggett (2001), 'The emotional dynamics of deliberative democracy'. *Policy and Politics*, **29** (3), 351–364.

Ticineto Clough, Patricia (ed.) (2007) *The Affective Turn. Theorizing the Social*. Durham, NC and London: Duke University Press.

Van Maanen, J. (1988), *Tales of the Field. On Writing Ethnography*. Chicago: University of Chicago Press.

Van Maanen, J. (2011), 'Ethnography as work: Some rules of engagement'. *Journal of Management Studies*, **48** (1), 218–234.

van Stokkom, B. (2005), 'Deliberative group dynamics: Power, status and affect in interactive policy making'. *Policy and Politics*, **33** (3), 387–409.

Wagenaar, Hendrik (*2011*). *Meaning in Action. Interpretation and Dialogue in Policy Analysis*, New York: M.E. Sharpe.

Weber, Max (1926), *Politik als Beruf*, 2nd edn, München/Leipzig: Duncker & Humblot.

Yanow, Dvora (2006), 'Philosophical presuppositions and the human sciences'. In Peregrine Schwartz-Sea and Dvora Yanow (eds), *Interpretation and Method. Empirical Research Methods and the Interpretive Turn*. New York: M.E. Sharpe, pp. 3–26.

Zittoun, Philippe (2014), *The Political Process of Policymaking: A Pragmatic Approach to Public Policy*. London: Palgrave Macmillan.

PART IV

POLICY PROCESSES: PROBLEM DEFINITIONS, EVIDENCE AND SOCIAL CONSTRUCTION

13 Problem definition and agenda-setting in critical perspective
Marlon Barbehön, Sybille Münch and Wolfram Lamping

INTRODUCTION

Public policy-making, as technocratically conceived, appears 'as a coherent process of solving known problems' (Colebatch 2005, p.15), culminating in a political decision that policy-makers think would maximize collective utility. This perspective on policy-making is also embedded in, and reflected by, the policy cycle model, which has become one of the core heuristics of policy analysis (May and Wildavsky 1979; Jann and Wegrich 2007). Policy-making and the policy cycle can together thus be understood as a linear process, following a clear, circular pattern and a predictable ordering of different stages: from the selection of allegedly objective policy problems as issues for active consideration, via policy formulation and decision-making, to implementation, evaluation as well as a feedback loop. The formation of a political *agenda* then appears to be 'a virtually automatic process occurring as a result of the stresses and strains placed on governments' (Howlett et al. 2009, p.94) by the mounting challenges resulting from economic and social modernization, while *problem definition* is at best a question of recognizing 'stresses and strains' and managing governmental capacities.

The simplicity and clarity of the way in which government is portrayed 'as a machinery for solving problems' (Colebatch 2005, p.17) partly explains the popularity of this heuristic concept among students of political science. However, the status and significance of this policy cycle framework for understanding contemporary policy processes is highly contested: it has been dismissed as inadequate for public policy making both as an inaccurate general *description* and as an impractical *normative model* (Howard 2005). Setting aside the question of whether and/or to what extent the policy cycle could actually serve as a normative ideal or 'policy cookbook' (Howard 2005, p.9) for improving policy-making, the theoretical assumptions and implications of this perspective are even more debatable: Policy cycle models tend to emphasize formal structures and procedures, generally adopt a legalistic governmental perspective – 'what governments do, why they do it and what difference it makes' (Dye 1976) – and usually conceptualize policy-making as rational problem-solving. These tendencies coalesce in supporting what Frank Fischer (1990) has called a distinct 'technocratic project'. The conventional policy cycle concept can, at times, even prevent students and scholars alike from better understanding what really happens in policy-making: it is a 'gateway drug' for those trying to understand the policy process, but the concept can do harm because 'it ignores the complex, value-laden nature of the policy process, as well as the primary role of political power in determining the direction of public policy' (Howard 2005, p. 3). The concept fosters the illusory image of a single issue moving from stage to stage, which ignores how governments must often cope simultaneously with a multitude of challenges and issues.

Against the background of this technocratic perspective on and conceptualization of the policy-making process, we develop a *critical perspective* on problem definition and agenda-setting by distinguishing between an *analytical* and a *conceptual* perspective on the presuppositions of mainstream policy analysis. From an analytical point of view, we draw attention to how a constructionist epistemology can help to denaturalize taken-for-granted policy assumptions and stress the role that power plays in policy-making. Despite (or, perhaps, because of) its framing of policy-making as problem-solving process, most mainstream approaches in policy analysis have paid little attention to practices of problem definition. However, problem definition is never simply a matter of recognizing objective stresses and strains since 'every description of a situation is a portrayal from only one of many points of view' (Stone 2002, p. 133) and therefore far from a universally objective definition. The possibility of influencing the dominant perception of a problem according to one's interests or preferences, or banning certain issues from the agenda, is an important source of power. Besides, problem definition and agenda-setting can together be regarded as a process affected by chance, fortune and political craft.

From a conceptual perspective, we address the fact that problem definition and agenda-setting are closely associated with the policy cycle metaphor and are therefore often conceptualized as distinct phases prior to policy formulation and implementation. However, as Paul Sabatier (1991) has argued, the stages metaphor or heuristic is misleading in that it emphasizes a sequential perspective of policy-making and suggests the stages as units of analysis that can be distinguished temporally and 'materially'. Therefore, we use the terms as analytical lenses and thus independently from any temporal-sequential implications. Instead, we argue for a more integrative approach. We suggest conceptualizing problem definition as a basic discursive process – part of the construction of a political world – and agenda-setting as a specific part of problem definition that attributes responsibility to a political actor or institution. From this perspective, problem definition and agenda-setting are not regarded as distinct phases but as constructions of reality that can be identified within the larger policy-making process.

In the discussion that follows, we develop these arguments by tracing how the technocratic assumptions underlying conventional works on problem definition and agenda-setting have been challenged from three different (at times overlapping) perspectives. In a first step, we introduce approaches that criticize the top-down and linear conceptualizations of policy-making as problem-solving and instead study *agenda-building* as a complex process of turning issues into political problems by bringing them onto the agenda. Secondly, we present a more fundamental epistemological challenge as constituted by post-positivist approaches and their recognition of the importance of problem definition. In contrast to the first line of thought, these approaches take a critical stance towards the alleged objectivity of social problems, thus focusing on the *discursive construction of policy problems* and the struggle over the definition of problems at various stages of the policy process. Lastly, we introduce approaches that emphasize the *role of power and political manipulation* in problem definition and agenda-setting. Taken together, these strands provide the basis for a critical perspective that is sensitive to the role of power in the social construction of allegedly objective problems while at the same time departing from the policy cycle metaphor and its linear composition of problem definition and agenda-setting.

FROM PROBLEM-SOLVING TO AGENDA-BUILDING

The view of policy-making as a virtually automatic process of problem-solving came under criticism in the early 1970s. Whereas, by that time, influential political theorists mainly posed the question of what alternatives are considered and put in place in concrete decision-making situations, Roger W. Cobb and Charles D. Elder (1971) were among the first to examine the processes of agenda-setting. Cobb and Elder (1971, p. 903) argued that 'pre-political, or at least pre-decisional, processes are often of the most critical importance in determining which issues and alternatives are to be considered by the polity and which choices will probably be made'. At the same time, the ability of actors to influence agenda-setting is unevenly distributed because resources and social rank within society vary among social groups. Therefore, Cobb and Elder maintain, the political process is a *politics of agenda-building* in which the formal institutional agenda reflects a pluralist struggle over problem recognition and selection. Another objection to the idea of policy-making as the solution of problems was put forward by Anthony Downs in his 1972 discussion of the *issue-attention cycle*. Downs argues that public and political awareness follow an up-and-down process that is relatively independent of pressure arising from the gravity of the problem. According to Downs, an issue gains salience due to extraordinary events and is debated in public and political arenas, until attention finally declines and other issues become more salient.

Building on these early considerations, a widely noted conceptualization of the agenda-setting process was elaborated by John W. Kingdon. With his *multiple streams*-approach, Kingdon ([1984] 2003, p. 172) opposes the problem-solving model by arguing that 'solutions float around in and near government, searching for problems to which to become attached or political events that increase their likelihood of adoption'. In his conceptualization, Kingdon differentiates between three distinct streams – a problem stream ('what is going on?'), a policy stream ('what can we do about it?') and a political stream ('what can we get support for?') (cf. Colebatch 2005, p. 16) – that may together offer a window of opportunity to put new issues on the agenda. Kingdon rejects the view of the policy process as a unidirectional procedure of identifying and politically reacting to a problem. He highlights temporary and occasionally unpredictable dynamics of political and societal developments – e.g. focusing events (Birkland 1998) – that increase the probability of an issue moving up the governmental agenda while marginalizing others. Rüb (2008, p. 99) has stressed how in the multiple streams approach problems and policy options are linked, not causally, but arbitrarily. This connection can be constituted only in hindsight through an act of 'retrospective sense-making' (Weick 1985 in Rüb 2008, p. 99). While the multiple streams approach departs from the rigid model of the policy cycle as problem-solving, the approach (and more recent advancements, such as by Zahariadis 2003) nevertheless adheres to an objectivist epistemology and is inspired by bounded rational choice theory. Under the condition of time pressure and ambiguous information, policy entrepreneurs engage strategically in coupling the streams to place their preferred alternatives onto the agenda (for the role of policy entrepreneurs see below). Although Kingdon ([1984] 2003, pp. 109–115) reflects on the importance of interpreting and politically defining 'what is going on' within the problem stream, problem definition as a process of collective sense-making is not at the heart of the approach.

Such a meta-theoretical foundation is also to be found in later theoretical approaches, particularly the *punctuated equilibrium* model of agenda change as elaborated mainly by Frank R. Baumgartner and Bryan D. Jones (1991). Baumgartner and Jones (1991, p. 1045) argue that agenda-setting processes and, ultimately, policy stability and change more generally can be explained with a focus on 'the interaction of beliefs and values concerning a particular policy, which we term the policy image, with the existing set of political institutions – the venues of policy action'. Using the example of civilian nuclear power in the US, the authors show how the public and political perceptions and the institutional venues of nuclear power changed during the 1960s and 1970s, culminating in the collapse of the institutionalized arrangements between governmental agencies and some of the nation's largest economic corporations. Therefore, the equilibrium model is able to capture agenda change even in the context of seemingly immovable organizations, institutions and procedures due to mutually reinforcing image and venue alterations (cf. Jones and Baumgartner 2005).

A general conclusion that can be drawn from these quick overviews of agenda-setting approaches is that they are critical of the idea of the policy process as a linear and incremental problem-solving procedure. However, these approaches do not focus on problem definition as socio-political practice, but analyze the roles that actors and structures play 'in sorting and advocating items for an agenda' (Peters 2005, p. 353). Agenda-setting is by and large conceptualized as an act of choosing and promoting an issue – it is about the '*selection* between diverse problems and issues' (Jann and Wegrich 2007, p. 46, italics in the original) rather than the construction of a problem through interpretation and discourse. The 'transformation of difficulties into problems', according to the literature so far considered, takes place within 'something of a black box prior to agenda formation' (Stone 1989, p. 281). In mainstream approaches, as Rochefort and Cobb (1993, p. 56) maintain, problem definition remains 'an immature analytic construct, productive of only a modest amount of scholarship that is lacking a coherent shared framework'.

FROM AGENDA-BUILDING TO THE SOCIAL CONSTRUCTION OF PROBLEMS

Since the early 1990s, the growing literature associated with the 'argumentative turn' (Fischer and Forester 1993; Fischer and Gottweis 2012a) or the 'interpretive turn' (Healy 1986; Yanow 1995) in policy studies has suggested a critical perspective by portraying policy-making as an 'ongoing discursive struggle over the definition and conceptual framing of problems, the public understanding of the issues, the shared meanings that motivate policy responses, and criteria for evaluation' (Fischer and Gottweis 2012b, p. 7). These approaches share a concern for the way in which language, discourse and rhetoric construct our knowledge of society and its problems and, therefore, question the basic assumption that problems are part of a pre-given 'neutral' reality.

Post-positivist approaches to problem definition generally sympathize with the *constructionist* assumption 'that there is nothing in the world whose meaning resides in the object itself' (Loseke 2003, p. 18). Accordingly, it is not the harm done by a phenomenon that turns it into a social problem; rather, 'the activities of parties external to the phenomenon give it a status of a social problem, and those activities must be understood in terms of their social structural context' (Heiner 2006, p. 6). Issues and problems are therefore both historically and culturally contingent. In contrast to approaches that stress the momentum of agenda-setting dynamics, the literature arising from a constructionist epistemology concentrates more on problem definition as structuring practice, which is inseparably inter-twined with the entire policy process. Because of these differences, Soroka (2007, p. 188) concludes that '[a]genda-setting and issue definition are in one sense unlikely bedfellows', with the study of agenda-setting being dominated by rational choice models, whereas the literature on problem definition finds its roots in a constructivist research tradition.

Whereas 'the ghost of positivism' (Dryzek 1993, p. 217) continued to haunt technocratic mainstream policy analysis for a long period of time, authors in the *labeling* tradition in the sociology of knowledge had decades earlier started to draw attention to interpretive procedures employed in 'recognizing' or 'constructing' deviance. Since the 1971 publication of Blumer's 'Social Problems as Collective Behavior', social construction-ism has emerged as a leading perspective in the sociology of knowledge. In one of the earliest and most influential contributions to this approach, Malcolm Spector and John I. Kitsuse ([1977] 2006) claim that the notion of social problems as a kind of undesirable condition should be aban-doned in favor of a view of them as a kind of activity:

> We have proposed to conceive all social problems to be the activities of individ-uals or groups making assertions about perceived social conditions which they consider unwanted, unjust, immoral, and thus about which something should be done. This definition proposes that any such claim may become a social problem, and focuses research on the process by which claims are assembled and asserted by the claimants. (Spector and Kitsuse [1977] 2006, p. xi)

It has therefore been suggested that it is more accurate to speak of 'prob-lematizations' rather than 'problems' in order to emphasize that problems acquire their shape and meaning through discursive processes (cf. Bacchi

1999, 2009; Howarth 2010; Fairclough 2013). This does not imply that they are merely constructions and do not really exist. On the contrary, these constructions have far-reaching consequences, as policies, interventions and institutions are built upon them.

Against the background of these epistemological foundations, over the past 20 years, post-positivist perspectives on problem definition and agenda-setting have gained prominence in the field of policy analysis (Torgerson 1996; Hoppe 2011; Soroka 2007). At the same time, as a range of new social movements have increasingly challenged the prevailing policy discourses and the dominant problem definitions they convey (Torgerson 2007), the technocratic 'speaking truth to power' of policy studies has been transformed into a reflexive policy analysis that tries to improve the quality of policy argumentation by 'making sense together' (Hoppe 2011, p.ix).

Deborah A. Stone (1989, 2002) was arguably one of the first who linked a post-positivist epistemology with problem definition and agenda-setting in a systematic way. Central to Stone's approach are *causal stories* that political actors employ in order to put an issue on the agenda:

> Problem definition is a process of image making, where the images have to do fundamentally with attributing cause, blame, and responsibility. Conditions, difficulties, or issues thus do not have inherent properties that make them more or less likely to be seen as problems or to be expanded. Rather, political actors *deliberately portray* them in ways calculated to gain support for their side. (Stone 1989, p.282, italics in the original)

According to Stone, whether an actor successfully influences the policy debate with his/her specific definition of a social problem does not depend primarily on his/her resources or institutional position but on his/her ability to put forward a persuasive story that portrays the specific view on a social phenomenon as the most adequate (cf. Hajer 1995, 2003, see below). Stone (2002, pp.138, 142) explores how definitions of policy problems have a narrative structure, with two broad storylines being particularly prevalent in policy-making: the story of decline and the story of helplessness and control. The former's dramatic tension is based on the implicit or explicit assumption that things were once better and that, without political action, the change for the worse causes – or will soon cause – suffering. This view is particularly common in the field of migration policy, for instance, when policy-makers warn of growing ethnic segregation or even 'ghettoization' and their story is challenged by urban researchers as 'myth' (cf. Münch 2010, p.250). Stories of control, on the other hand, come in different guises but have in common their assertion that there is choice. Whereas the conspiracy story ends with a call to the many to rise against the few, the common blame-the-victim story locates responsibility in the very people who suffer from the problem (Stone 2002, p. 144).

In a similar vein, Rochefort and Cobb (1993, 1994) draw attention to the anatomy of problem descriptions as reflected in problem-setting stories. In addition to the attribution of problem causes, they propose to analyze how the nature of the problem is being framed in terms of severity, incidence (whether growing, stable, declining), novelty, proximity (whether person-ally relevant or of general social concern), crisis and emergency. They also focus on how the possibility of a solution is interpreted as available or non-existent, acceptable or objectionable, affordable or unaffordable (Rochefort and Cobb 1993, p. 62). From this perspective, public policy-making as a complex process is understood 'as a function of the perceived nature of the problems being dealt with', but 'the qualities that define this nature are never incontestable (even though they may sometimes be taken for granted)' (Rochefort and Cobb 1994, p. 4).

Beyond single problem-setting stories, we encounter the concept of *frames*, which in the field of policy analysis has been associated with Martin Rein (1983) and Donald Schön (1983). In their collaborative work, Rein and Schön (1993, p. 146) define a frame as a comprehensive struc-ture that guides ways of 'selecting, organizing, interpreting, and making sense of a complex reality'. A policy controversy that builds on oppos-ing frames is thus not a dispute about the ends and means of policy but is based on fundamentally different constructions of 'what the problem really is' (cf. Healy 1986, pp. 383–384). Participants, in line with how they frame a problem, pay attention to certain aspects of reality while neglect-ing others. Frames, as Hubert Heinelt (2010, p. 22) points out, operate on a meta-level as they convey basic standards and assumptions about how the world functions and, on a micro-level, shape how 'a certain linguistic coding of problem definitions and patterns of action becomes binding for interactions'.

A recognition of complexity has led to the verdict that policy problems are 'complex', 'wicked' or 'squishy' (Dery 1984, p. 7). In particular, it has been argued that comparatively new issue areas, such as biomedicine or reprogenetics (the merging of reproductive and genetic technologies), are prone to produce 'wicked problems' and uncertainties, in the face of which we not only do not know the solution but are not even sure whether the conflict is between 'moral taboos and economic interests' or between 'individual rights and social consequences' (Herrmann 2009, p. 12). Frame conflicts are therefore hard to resolve because the frames themselves pre-reflexively determine what counts as evidence and how evidence is inter-preted (Rein and Schön 1993, p. 145). Accordingly, the frame approach shifts attention from single problematizations and agenda-setting practices to fundamental rationales in the construction of political problems. Because frames integrate facts, values, theories and interests, it makes a difference, for instance, whether drug addiction is framed in terms of a medical or legal discourse (Fischer 2003, p. 43) and whether riots are framed in terms of race relations, law and order, or a general decline in morals (Soroka 2007, p. 189).

Finally, what characterizes the literature on the social construction of policy problems, heterogeneous as it may be, is the importance accorded to *target populations* (Rochefort and Cobb 1993; Montpetit et al. 2005, p. 123). Helen Ingram and Anne Schneider (2005; Schneider and Ingram 1993) are committed to probing how problematizations construct target populations as deserving or undeserving. The authors distinguish four groups, differing both in terms of power and in terms of whether they are appraised positively or negatively. Therefore, Schneider and Ingram's approach gives a post-positivist answer to Harold Lasswell's question 'Who gets what, when, how?' In looking at the social constructions implicit in problem definitions and policies, the authors analyze how '[p]olicy sends messages about what government is supposed to do, which citizens are deserving (and which not), and what kinds of attitudes and participatory patterns are appropriate in a democratic society' (Schneider and Ingram 1993, p. 334).

FROM THE SOCIAL CONSTRUCTION OF PROBLEMS TO THE POWER OF DISCOURSE AND RHETORIC

As the discussion of the different post-positivist approaches has shown, sensitivity to power relations is at least implicit in all of them. However, some authors take it a step further. Instead of focusing on (the implications of) competing interpretations of reality, they integrate a conceptualization of power into their frameworks – either as deliberate manipulation or as an effect of discursive systems of knowledge. A concern with power relations can be traced back to the American political science debate on how to conceptualize power that began in the 1950s. In contrast to an understanding of power as the ability to dominate actual decisions (Dahl 1957), it was argued that power should be understood as the ability to create or reinforce 'barriers to the public airing of policy conflicts' (Bachrach and Baratz 1962, p. 949) or even to keep issues from being perceived as problems at all (Lukes [1974] 2005). More or less explicitly building on this line of thought, several critical approaches now veer away from the idea of the policy process as an act of deliberation and argumentation, instead critically addressing the power of discourse and rhetoric in the course of problem definition and agenda-setting (Zahariadis 2003, 2007; Gottweis 2006).

Herbert Gottweis (2006, p.476) stresses that policy-making cannot be reduced to communicative action but involves different forms of persuasion such as 'manipulation, the mobilization of fear, trust, and hope'. Policy-making, he argues, therefore is not only about constructing realities but also about questions of credibility, personal qualities and emotional states. The role of *emotions* in problem definition has been highlighted by post-structuralist inquiries into how discursive formations are more or less durable depending on how they mobilize Lacanian categories of fantasy and enjoyment. In analyzing fantasmatic narratives, Jason Glynos and his colleagues (2012) scrutinize the affective dimension of discursive practices, how key logics in media and policy responses have operated to narrow down public debate on causes and solutions for public problems such as the financial crisis. These fantasmatic narratives can take different forms: They can be beatific when the fullness of enjoyment is promised to follow the overcoming of an obstacle or the removal of a villain. The narratives can also be horrific, for instance by employing epidemiological metaphors such as 'toxic assets' or the 'contamination' of the financial system. The 'sacrifice of enjoyment' is routinely projected onto others and ascribed the status of 'stolen' in a manner that informs various types of scapegoating.

In a similar vein, Nikolaos Zahariadis (2007, p.70) argues that the social construction of meaning and identities is only a 'necessary condition', but is not 'sufficient' to explain agenda dynamics. In his analytical advancement of the multiple streams-approach (as discussed above), Zahariadis (2003) argues that *manipulation* – rather than argumentation – is the central mechanism to alter problem perceptions and political attention under the condition of ambiguity. Through 'systematic distortion, misrepresentation, or selective presentation of information', skilled policy entrepreneurs employ manipulating strategies to influence the relevant policy-makers (Zahariadis 2003, p.18). Zahariadis (2003, pp.9–16, 89–102) distinguishes three main strategies for entrepreneurs to put their favored issues onto the agenda: Firstly, actors in favor of risky options, e.g. those that will significantly change the status quo, will frame a problem as a threat of loss or danger. If, on the other hand, options represent only smaller deviations from the status quo, problems are framed as gains. Secondly, they may employ 'salami tactics' to split a larger issue into distinct aspects feasible for sequential decision-making. Thirdly, entrepreneurs may refer to collective high-order symbols to raise attention for, and emotional attachment with, a specific problem. Ultimately, whether entrepreneurs succeed in manipulating decision-makers depends upon their 'skills and resources' (Zahariadis 2003, p. 69), that is, their personal networks and their willingness to invest time, energy and money to employ these manipulating strategies. Proponents of this perspective on policy-making emphasize the multiple constraints policy-makers have to cope with, such as the shortages of time. 'Time' is a factor that sometimes explains why not every political problem actually ends up on the agenda and further complicates political decision-making that is already marked by complexity, contingency and ambiguity.

Taking these claims on the importance of manipulating symbols and emotions as a starting point, one could argue in favor of widening the perspective and including the analysis of cultural practices and dramaturgic techniques 'by which actors, individually or in concert, display for others the meaning of their social situation' (Alexander 2004, p. 529) and create the emotional connection of audience with an actor's *social performance*. Policy analysis is mainly preoccupied with policy documents or protocols while largely neglecting how meaning is conveyed through performative acts. Thus, the question of which problem constructions gain currency in specific contexts might be better understood by accounting for the staging of problematizations. Working on foreign policy, for example, Bliesemann de Guevara (2012) scrutinizes the practice of field and troop visits of high-ranking politicians and reveals how diverse actors with differing social roles, institutional interests and normative objectives 'enact' these journeys in different political arenas and for different audiences.

In contrast to these approaches that try to uncover the manipulative strategies of powerful actors, authors inspired by Foucault conceptualize power as a discursive condition that results from *systems of knowledge*. This approach challenges the notion of actor and departs from the interpretive-hermeneutical interest in how actors construct their knowledge of the world. Discourse as a historically specific system of signification is instead regarded as constitutive of identities (Gottweis 2006, p. 465). Among advocates of a Foucauldian notion of power in the context of problem definition and agenda-setting, Carol Bacchi (e.g., 1999, 2009) argues for studying *problematizations* 'to demonstrate how things which appear most evident are in fact fragile and [. . .] rest upon particular circumstances, and are often attributable to historical conjunctures which have nothing necessary or definitive about them' (2012b, p. 2, italics removed). Therefore, her analysis does not focus on policy problems but on the social practice of problematization that establishes a certain view on social phenomena as 'true' and 'real' (cf. Howarth 2010, pp. 324–326; from the perspective of critical discourse analysis, cf. Fairclough 2013, pp. 185–193).

In methodological terms, Bacchi (2009, p. 48) develops an approach that looks at policy documents and tries to reveal which implicit representations of what is considered to be 'the problem' are present. By applying a set of questions to the policy document, the researcher asks what limitations or gaps can be identified within the implicit problem representation and what alternative views are possible. Therefore, Bacchi's approach is a critical endeavor as it is interested in forms of power embedded in dominant problem representations. Furthermore, it is a call for 'critical reflexivity' (Bacchi 2012b, p. 7) as the approach encourages the researcher to reflect on his/her own presuppositions. With this argument, Bacchi stands in line with the post-positivist approaches discussed above. However, what makes her approach distinct is that she does not emphasize the strategic and deliberate character of constructing problems but, in the tradition of Foucault, the rather pre-reflexive way of seeing the world: 'the focus is not on intentional issue manipulation or strategic framing' but 'to understand policy better than policy makers by probing the unexamined assumptions and deep-seated conceptual logics within implicit problem representations' (Bacchi 2012a, p. 22).

Maarten Hajer's (2002, p. 62) contribution to what he has termed 'argumentative discourse analysis' (ADA) tries to reconcile these two conceptualizations of power: 'The real challenge for ADA is to find ways of combining analysis of the discursive production of reality with analysis of the socio-political practices from which social constructs emerge and in which actors are engaged'. According to Hajer, the argumentative turn not only concentrates on the argument as statement but on the verb 'to argue'. Therefore, he does not limit his discourse analysis to the analysis of talk, but also scrutinizes practices: whether a situation is perceived as a political problem depends on the narrative in which it is discussed. These narratives that symbolically condense the facts and values are called *storylines* and form the basis of *discourse coalitions* (Hajer 1995, pp. 52–72). Coalitions are successful if they not only dominate the discourse but have their definition of the problem implemented and institutionalized. Concrete policy vocabularies are 'consciously developed by policymakers' and hard and soft policy fields strategically linked (Hajer 2003, p. 105). Nevertheless, and this is where the post-structuralist inspiration comes back in, discourse coalitions act only 'within the confinements of the available discursive possibilities' (Gottweis 2006, p. 471).

CONCLUSION

What the conceptualizations of problem definition and agenda-setting presented here have in common is a challenge to the notion of policy-making as rational problem solving. In spite of their different epistemological foundations, they challenge both the tidy linearity of policy-making inherent in the policy cycle as well as the idea that certain decisions could be perceived as 'natural' responses. Each approach introduces particular aspects that, taken together, provide the basis of what we perceive to be a critical perspective on problem definition and agenda-setting.

Firstly, the literature on agenda-building stresses that policy-making should not be viewed as a virtually automatic reaction to 'known problems'. Instead, it highlights the formation of an agenda as political and as a decisive aspect of the policy process. The engagement of policy entrepreneurs, the reconfiguration of policy images and venues of political action, and unexpected social developments – all these influence which issues are selected for active political consideration. Therefore, the authors writing on agenda-setting discussed above provide a first facet for a critical perspective in that they (more or less explicitly) shed light on the role of *power* within agenda-setting processes. In this respect it is possible to distinguish among approaches that focus on the manipulating strategies of powerful actors, those that introduce a post-structuralist notion of power stemming from discourse theory, and those that try to reconcile these two understandings. However, agenda-setting is usually examined as a certain phase between problem definition and policy formulation, during which different actors use different forms of power to get certain issues onto the agenda. Although later works have widened the perspective on agenda-setting – and now include the media and informal coalitions outside of official decision-making bodies – the analysis still often assumes a neatly demarcated center of power where the agenda becomes visible. Moreover, agenda-setting remains conceived as an act of problem selection and thereby leaves the construction of collective problems in the dark.

Against this background, the research on problem definition provides two further aspects for a critical perspective. Empirical research on problem definition has, on the one hand, long left the cage of a neatly demarcated phase. It explores how certain policies, institutions and practices can be read as 'congealed ideas' about adequate solutions to undesirable social conditions – and thus as institutionally consolidated problem definitions (cf. Rüb 2006, p. 347). Dery (1984, pp. 92–93) was among the first authors to point out how the institutionalization of solutions carries with it the institutionalization of problem definition: 'Now, categories of understanding and meaning prevalent in a certain culture precede the rise of agencies that embody a certain conceptualization of public problems, which they, then, seek to guard.' Policies and interventions reflect specific interpretations of problem definitions and thereby provide opportunities for how and by whom new problems can be constructed. Accordingly, critical research on problem definition has been conducted within other 'stages' of the policy process as well – Bacchi (2009, 2012a) for instance shows how to reconstruct problem representations in documents of already established policy.

Much more explicitly than the literature on agenda-setting, studies of problem definition build on a *post-positivist epistemology* according to which language does not simply mirror the world, but serves to constitute it and can thus never be neutral. Despite differences between authors holding post-structuralist and interpretive-hermeneutical premises, these approaches are united in seeking to bury the idea of pre-political, innocent facts. The approaches both shed light on how problem definitions are embedded in the socio-political contexts and the power configurations in which they appear. The key point is that discourse and the language of claims do not exist independently of the social world, but are both a product of – and an influence upon – that world. Narrating problems is a medium for struggle and contestation in which socio-historical factors such as power relations and social norms play an important role. Hence, the analysis of problematization and agenda-setting involves the analysis of extra-discursive social practices from which social constructs emerge (Herrmann 2009, p. 29). This focus on social practices suggests an aim to deconstruct discourses which uphold iniquitous power relations and to demonstrate the way in which power is obscured – for example by pointing out that not all possible interpreters have the same resources to make their problem definitions heard (Herrmann 2009, p. 35).

How, based upon the diverse literature discussed here, might we develop a comprehensive critical perspective? On a *conceptual level*, we would argue that problem definition could be conceived as the basic discursive process for constructing and making sense of a political world, whereas agenda-setting could be seen as a specific part of problem definition. If we conceive of the 'agenda' as a snapshot of those collective problems a political community is dealing with and 'problems' as the contingent result of problem-setting stories, it follows that agenda-setting is itself a particular way of 'image making' (cf. Stone 1989, see above): it is not just about claiming a difference between 'is' and 'ought' but about constructing a problem as a matter for active political consideration. From this perspective, the question of whether attempts at agenda-setting succeed is basically a question of how a particular problem-setting story relates to others that likewise claim a political responsibility. Agenda-setting is a process that goes beyond problem definition in that it implies the recognition of problem constructions by government. However, this success of an argument in favor of political action can never be fixed but has to be constantly upheld in a continuous act of telling the story of what is to blame and who is in charge to solve the condition. In this sense, problem definition and agenda-setting should be uncoupled from the policy cycle in that they should not be understood as separate phases with agenda-setting as an act of selecting previously defined problems. Problem definition and agenda-setting are rather enduring and intimately intertwined aspects of the discursive construction of a socio-political reality. On an *analytical level*, 'denaturalization' and 'power' could be seen as the main anchors of a critical perspective on problem definition and agenda-setting, thereby allowing for a more comprehensive perspective on the policy process in general. Why is a phenomenon perceived as a problem (and accepted on the political agenda) and why are other potentially harmful phenomena not so perceived? Who are winners and losers in the context of certain problem definitions, agenda-setting processes and derived policies? These questions can help to challenge implicit commonsense perceptions, reveal policy 'truths' as contingent constructions, alert us to alternatives, and challenge us to explain why some 'problems' gain currency within specific settings while others do not.

REFERENCES

Alexander, Jeffrey C. (2004), 'Cultural Pragmatics: Social Performance between Ritual and Strategy', *Sociological Theory*, **22** (4), 527–573.
Bacchi, Carol (1999), *Women, Policy and Politics: The Construction of Policy Problems*, London, Thousand Oaks, CA and New Delhi: Sage Publications.
Bacchi, Carol (2009), *Analysing Policy: What's the Problem Represented to Be?*, Frenchs Forest, Australia: Pearson.
Bacchi, Carol (2012a), 'Introducing the "What's the Problem Represented to Be?" approach', in Angelique Bletsas and Chris Beasley (eds), *Engaging with Carol Bacchi: Strategic Interventions and Exchanges*, Adelaide: University of Adelaide Press, pp. 21–24.
Bacchi, Carol (2012b), 'Why Study Problematizations? Making Politics Visible', *Open Journal of Political Science*, **2** (1), 1–8.
Bachrach, Peter and Morton S. Baratz (1962), 'Two Faces of Power', *The American Political Science Review*, **56** (4), 947–952.
Baumgartner, Frank R. and Bryan D. Jones (1991), 'Agenda Dynamics and Policy Subsystems', *The Journal of Politics*, **53** (4), 1044–1074.
Birkland, Thomas A. (1998), 'Focusing Events, Mobilization, and Agenda Setting', *Journal of Public Policy*, **18** (1), 53–74.
Bliesemann de Guevara, Berit (2012), 'InterventionsTheater: Der Heimatdiskurs und die Truppen- und Feldbesuche deutscher Politiker – eine Forschungsskizze', in Michael Daxner and Hannah Neumann (eds), *Heimatdiskurs: Wie die Auslandseinsätze der Bundeswehr Deutschland verändern*, Bielefeld: transcript, pp. 273–302.
Blumer, Herbert (1971), 'Social Problems as Collective Behavior', *Social Problems*, **18** (3), 298–306.
Cobb, Roger W. and Charles D. Elder (1971), 'The Politics of Agenda-Building: An Alternative Perspective For Modern Democratic Theory', *The Journal of Politics*, **33** (4), 892–915.
Colebatch, Hal K. (2005), 'Policy Analysis, Policy Practice and Political Science', *Australian Journal of Public Administration*, **64** (3), 14–23.

Dahl, Robert A. (1957), 'The Concept of Power', *Behavioral Science*, **2** (3), 201–215.
Dery, David (1984), *Problem Definition in Policy Analysis*, Lawrence: University Press of Kansas.
Downs, Anthony (1972), 'Up and Down with Ecology – The "Issue-attention Cycle"', *Public Interest*, **28**, 38–50.
Dryzek, John S. (1993), 'Policy Analysis and Planning: From Science to Argument', in Frank Fischer and John Forester (eds), *The Argumentative Turn in Policy Analysis and Planning*, Durham, NC and London: Duke University Press, pp. 213–232.
Dye, Thomas R. (1976), *Policy Analysis: What Governments Do, Why They Do It and What Difference it Makes*, Tuscaloosa: University of Alabama Press.
Fairclough, Norman (2013), 'Critical Discourse Analysis and Critical Policy Studies', *Critical Policy Studies*, **7** (2), 177–197.
Fischer, Frank (1990), *Technocracy and the Politics of Expertise*, Newbury Park, CA: Sage Publications.
Fischer, Frank (2003), *Reframing Public Policy: Discursive Politics and Deliberative Practices*, Oxford: Oxford University Press.
Fischer, Frank and John Forester (eds) (1993), *The Argumentative Turn in Policy-Analysis and Planning*, Durham, NC and London: Duke University Press.
Fischer, Frank and Herbert Gottweis (eds) (2012a), *The Argumentative Turn Revisited: Public Policy as Communicative Practice*, Durham, NC and London: Duke University Press.
Fischer, Frank and Herbert Gottweis (2012b), 'Introduction. The Argumentative Turn Revisited', in Frank Fischer and Herbert Gottweis (eds), *The Argumentative Turn Revisited: Public Policy as Communicative Practice*, Durham, NC and London: Duke University Press, pp. 1–27.
Glynos, Jason, Robin Klimecki and Hugh Willmott (2012), 'Cooling Out the Marks: The Ideology and Politics of the Financial Crisis', *Journal of Cultural Economy*, **5** (3), 297–320.
Gottweis, Herbert (2006), 'Argumentative Policy Analysis', in B. Guy Peters and Jon Pierre (eds), *Handbook of Public Policy*, London, Thousand Oaks, CA and New Delhi: Sage Publications, pp. 461–479.
Hajer, Maarten A. (1995), *The Politics of Environmental Discourse: Ecological Modernization and the Policy Process*, Oxford: Oxford University Press.
Hajer, Maarten (2002), 'Discourse Analysis and the Study of Policy Making', *European Political Science*, **2** (1), 61–65.
Hajer, Maarten (2003), 'A Frame in the Fields: Policymaking and the Reinvention of Politics', in Maarten A. Hajer and Hendrik Wagenaar (eds), *Deliberative Policy Analysis: Understanding Governance in the Network Society*, Cambridge: Cambridge University Press, pp. 88–110.
Healy, Paul (1986), 'Interpretive Policy Inquiry: A Response to the Limitation of the Received View', *Policy Sciences*, **19** (4), 381–396.
Heinelt, Hubert (2010), *Governing Modern Societies: Towards Participatory Governance*, London and New York: Routledge.
Heiner, Robert (2006), *Social Problems. An Introduction to Critical Constructionism*, second edition, New York and Oxford: Oxford University Press.
Herrmann, Svea Luise (2009), *Policy Debates on Reprogenetics: The Problematisation of New Research in Great Britain and Germany*, Frankfurt and New York: Campus.
Hoppe, Robert (2011), *The Governance of Problems: Puzzling, Powering, and Participation*, Bristol: The Policy Press.
Howard, Cosmo (2005), 'The Policy Cycle: A Model of Post-Machiavellian Policy Making?', *Australian Journal of Public Administration*, **64** (3), 3–13.
Howarth, David (2010), 'Power, Discourse, and Policy: Articulating a Hegemony Approach to Critical Policy Studies', *Critical Policy Studies*, **3** (3–4), 309–335.
Howlett, Michael, M. Ramesh and Anthony Perl (2009), *Studying Public Policy: Policy Cycles & Policy Subsystems*, third edition, Ontario: Oxford University Press.
Ingram, Helen and Anne Schneider (2005), 'Introduction: Public Policy and the Social

Construction of Deservedness', in Anne Schneider and Helen Ingram (eds), *Deserving and Entitled: Social Constructions and Public Policy*, Albany, NY: State University of New York Press, pp. 1–34.

Jann, Werner and Kai Wegrich (2007), 'Theories of the Policy Cycle', in Frank Fischer, Gerald J. Miller and Mara S. Sidney (eds), *Handbook of Public Policy Analysis: Theory, Politics, and Methods*, Boca Raton, FL, London and New York: CRC Press, pp. 43–62.

Jones, Bryan D. and Frank R. Baumgartner (2005), *The Politics of Attention: How Government Prioritizes Problems*, Chicago: The University of Chicago Press.

Kingdon, John W. ([1984] 2003), *Agendas, Alternatives, and Public Policies*, second edition, New York: Longman.

Loseke, Donileen R. (2003), *Thinking about Social Problems: An Introduction to Constructionist Perspectives*, second edition, New Brunswick, NJ and London: Aldine Transaction.

Lukes, Steven ([1974] 2005), *Power: A Radical View*, second edition, Houndmills, Basingstoke, UK and London: Macmillan Education Ltd.

May, Judith V. and Aaron B. Wildavsky (eds) (1979), *The Policy Cycle*, Beverly Hills, CA and London: Sage Publications.

Montpetit, Éric, Christine Rothmayr and Frédéric Varone (2005), 'Institutional Vulnerability to Social Constructions: Federalism, Target Populations, and Policy Designs for Assisted Reproductive Technology in Six Democracies', *Comparative Political Studies*, **38** (2), 119–142.

Münch, Sybille (2010), *Integration durch Wohnungspolitik? Zum Umgang mit ethnischer Segregation im europäischen Vergleich*, Wiesbaden: VS Verlag.

Peters, Guy B. (2005), 'The Problem of Policy Problems', *Journal of Comparative Policy Analysis*, **7** (4), 349–370.

Rein, Martin (1983), 'Value-Critical Policy Analysis', in Daniel Callahan and Bruce Jennings (eds), *Ethics, the Social Sciences, and Policy Analysis*, New York and London: Plenum Press, pp. 83–111.

Rein, Martin and Donald Schön (1993), 'Reframing Policy Discourse', in Frank Fischer and John Forester (eds), *The Argumentative Turn in Policy Analysis and Planning*, Durham, NC and London: Duke University Press, pp. 145–166.

Rochefort, David A. and Roger W. Cobb (1993), 'Problem Definition, Agenda Access, and Policy Definition', *Policy Studies Journal*, **21** (1), 56–71.

Rochefort, David A. and Roger W. Cobb (1994), 'Problem Definition: An Emerging Perspective', in David A. Rochefort and Roger W. Cobb (eds), *The Politics of Problem Definition: Shaping the Policy Agenda*, Lawrence, KS: University Press of Kansas, pp. 1–31.

Rüb, Friedbert (2006), 'Wissenspolitologie', in Joachiam Behnke, Thomas Gschwend, Delia Schindler and Kai-Uwe Schnapp (eds), *Methoden der Politikwissenschaft: Neuere qualitative und quantitative Analyseverfahren*, Baden-Baden: Nomos, pp. 345–354.

Rüb, Friedbert (2008), 'Policy-Analyse unter den Bedingungen von Kontingenz. Konzeptionelle Überlegungen zu einer möglichen Neuorientierung', in Frank Janning and Katrin Toens (eds), *Die Zukunft der Policy-Forschung: Theorien, Methoden, Anwendungen*, Wiesbaden: VS Verlag, pp. 88–111.

Sabatier, Paul (1991), 'Towards Better Theories of the Policy Process', *Political Science and Politics*, **24** (2), 147–156.

Schneider, Anne and Helen Ingram (1993), 'Social Construction of Target Populations: Implications for Politics and Policy', *American Political Science Review*, **87** (2), 334–348.

Schön, Donald A. (1983), *The Reflective Practitioner: How Professionals Think in Action*, New York: Basic Books.

Soroka, Stuart N. (2007), 'Agenda-Setting and Issue Definition', in Michael Orsini and Miriam Smith (eds), *Critical Policy Studies*. Vancouver and Toronto: UBC Press, pp. 185–210.

Spector, Malcolm and John I. Kitsuse ([1977] 2006), *Constructing Social Problems*, second edition, New Brunswick, NJ and London: Transaction Publishers.

Stone, Deborah A. (1989), 'Causal Stories and the Formation of Policy Agendas', *Political Science Quarterly*, **104** (2), 281–300.

Stone, Deborah A. (2002), *Policy Paradox: The Art of Political Decision Making*, revised edition, New York and London: Norton & Company.

Torgerson, Douglas (1996), 'Power and Insight in Policy Discourse: Post-Positivism and Problem Definition', in Laurent Dobuzinskis, Michael Howlett and David Laycock (eds), *Policy Studies in Canada: The State of the Art*, Toronto, Buffalo and London: University of Toronto Press, pp. 266–298.

Torgerson, Douglas (2007), 'Policy Discourse as Dialogue: Emergent Publics and the Reflexive Turn', *Critical Policy Studies*, **1** (1), 1–17.

Yanow, Dvora (1995), 'Editorial. Practices of Policy Interpretation', *Policy Sciences*, **28** (2), 111–126.

Zahariadis, Nikolaos (2003), *Ambiguity and Choice in Public Policy: Political Decision Making in Modern Democracies*, Washington, DC: Georgetown University Press.

Zahariadis, Nikolaos (2007), 'The Multiple Streams Framework. Structure, Limitations, Prospects', in Paul A. Sabatier (ed.), *Theories of the Policy Process*. Boulder, CO: Westview Press, pp. 65–92.

14 Making distinctions: the social construction of target populations
Helen Ingram and Anne L. Schneider

INTRODUCTION

Deborah Stone has written that if social scientists ever discover the molecule of governance, surely it will be the 'category' because governance is conducted through rules, and rules are composed of categories (Stone, 2005). Establishing categories means drawing dividing lines and making distinctions. For critical policy studies no lines are more important than those drawn between people who are deserving and people who are undeserving of the benefits and burdens allocated through laws, regulations and other acts of government. Such determinations not only affect material welfare and social status but also identity, self-respect and citizenship.

In this chapter we explore the social construction of target populations, a subject that at first blush might appear of interest only to lawyers, legislative technicians, lobbyists and bureaucrats. A closer look quickly reveals that policies have a wide variety of pathways through which any public problem may be solved or purpose achieved (Ingram and Schneider, 1991). For instance, efforts to increase highway safety might focus on prohibiting texting while driving, more exacting licensing tests for everyone, punishing drunk drivers, raising the driving age for teenagers or requiring an adult in the car when drivers are under a certain age, mandating car manufacturers to include safety features, hiring more traffic police and/or changing the specifications road builders must follow, among many other potential targets. Often policy adopts quite roundabout courses of action, and devotes enormous effort and resources toward target groups that are only remotely connected to the actions that might plausibly lead to the desired goal. In other cases obvious targets are overlooked. Which target group is chosen reflects a political calculus that includes effectiveness, ease of implementation, availability of resources, and, importantly, elected legislators desire to align themselves positively with widely held public values of how different sorts of people should be treated.

In the sections that follow this chapter will argue that positive and negative images of groups too often trump rational analysis of which target groups should be treated in what way by public policy. We offer a useful

259

template for classifying target groups into four basic kinds – advantaged, disadvantaged, contenders and deviants – along with the policy tools and other policy characteristics that are likely to be associated with each grouping. The chapter then turns to the ways in which policies may redraw the lines between the categories of target groups to modify the distribution of benefits and burdens. It also considers by what means prevailing constructions of a target group may be changed and the impacts of social constructions on participation and democracy. The chapter concludes with a discussion of how social constructions provide a useful tool for critical policy scholars.

VALUES COME FIRST

Policies are about the allocation of values not just to obtain such putative public goals such as public safety, education and defence but also to provide good things to 'good' people and to punish those perceived as 'bad'. Bias, labeling, stereotyping and stigma are common human interactions, and public policies are only one of the many institutions and mechanisms that reflect and reinforce them (Schneider et al., 2014). Feelings of like and dislike emerge prior to any kind of mental processing, and according to psychologist and Nobel Prize winner Daniel Kahneman (2011) people rely upon what he calls 'fast thinking', 'affect' and 'availability' heuristics or subconscious scripts that guide judgments directly without deliberation or reasoning. Positive and negative reactions are part of peoples' associative memory where connections get made and depend upon familiar, often repeated images, with negative images frequently exerting the strongest sway (Tversky and Kahneman, 1973). Social constructions of target populations emerge from these emotional and intuitive reactions where rather than testing first impressions with facts, people collect data to justify and rationalize their positions using evidence selected to reinforce biases (Haidt, 2012).

Policy makers, especially elected politicians, respond to and in many cases encourage and manipulate such labeling and stereotyping in designing public policies. Looking to their political futures, elected politicians do not want to offend their constituents by providing benefits to bad people, and they look forward to the support they get for rewarding the well regarded. Moreover, treating good people well and bad people badly does not require complex explanations that may bore constituents who have already made up their minds and have short attention spans. As a consequence, policies reflect distinctions drawn to create categories of target groups not because such targets are best positioned to deliver policy purposes but instead to invoke positive and negative affect that serve political agendas. While this portrayal of the motivations of electoral politicians in designing policy seems fairly straightforward, it was not appreciated until the 1990s when we began writing about social constructions of target populations (Ingram and Schneider, 1990, 1991, 1993, 1995, 2005, 2006; Schneider and Ingram, 1990, 1993, 1997, 2005a, 2005b, 2007). Instead, explanations were more likely to be sought in the machinations of interest groups and governmental agencies and the absence of good policy advice.

POWER AND SOCIAL CONSTRUCTIONS OF TARGET GROUPS

Power is clearly related to how target groups get defined and treated. The greater the power, the bigger the influence is likely to be in establishing categories. The conventional measures of political power include among others: size of the group; its degree of mobilization and cohesion; its leadership and political skill; its position and access to governing institutions including academia, science and the press; its wealth and other material resources; and its propensity to vote and contact public officials. Many political scientists evaluate the strength of interest groups and social movements, and predict legislative success on the basis of such group attributes. The assumption is that the powerful are motivated by instrumental self-interest and mobilize to support public officials who serve their interests. In Figure 14.1 we portray the power dimension on the vertical axis of the matrix, and the most powerful groups are placed at the top of the box and less powerful groups are arranged towards the bottom.

Deservedness – that is, the positive and negative valence connected to groups through the value laden emotional formulations discussed above – is depicted on the horizontal axis of Figure 14.1. Groups associated with positive characteristics such as worthiness, virtue, contributions to the economy, loyalty, generosity, discipline, respectfulness, intelligence, attractiveness, creativity and the like are placed on the left side of the box. The groups who are thought to be undeserving are located on the right based on their images as lawless, unproductive, lazy, greedy, corrupt, immoral, ugly, impure, dangerous, disrespectful of authority and other negative stereotypes. These characterizations are not entirely unrelated to political power. After all, a great deal of wealth and power are regularly expended by groups to build more positive images, sometimes successfully. And, such virtues as contribution to economic productivity are likely to be accompanied by wealth. But, the two dimensions are not at all interchangeable and are only partially and indirectly translatable.

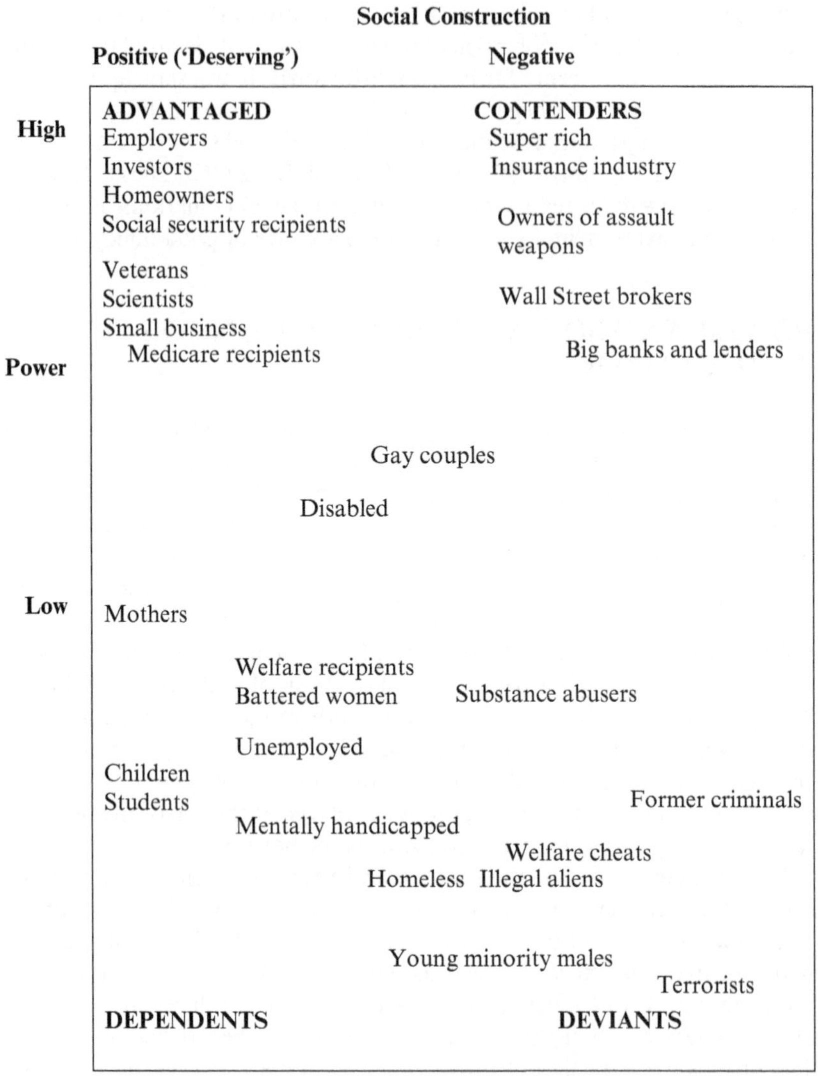

Social Construction

Positive ('Deserving')   Negative

High **ADVANTAGED**	**CONTENDERS**

ADVANTAGED
Employers
Investors
Homeowners
Social security recipients
Veterans
Scientists
Small business
   Medicare recipients

CONTENDERS
Super rich
Insurance industry
Owners of assault
  weapons
Wall Street brokers
Big banks and lenders

High

Power

Gay couples

Disabled

Low Mothers

Welfare recipients
Battered women   Substance abusers

Unemployed
Children
Students   Former criminals
Mentally handicapped
Welfare cheats
Homeless Illegal aliens

Young minority males
Terrorists

DEPENDENTS   **DEVIANTS**

Figure 14.1   Social construction and power typology

Figure 14.1 displays a matrix of how a number of target populations have been portrayed by researchers whose work directly employs or is closely related to the social constructions of target groups' frameworks (see Schneider and Ingram, 2005a, 2005b; Ingram, 2007; Pierce et al., 2014; Schneider et al., 2014). It is useful to provide labels for the groups that fall into the four distinct cells that emerge from the matrix. The exact placement of the groups among the four quadrants is imprecise and reflects our reading of research that was conducted at a particular time and probably changes. Of course, the list of groups in Figure 14.1 is highly selective among many pieces of research, the majority of which is concentrated on the lower half of the box and is too numerous and varied to be included (Pierce et al., 2014).

The *advantaged* have high levels of political power and enjoy positive constructions. Whenever possible the advantaged are chosen for benefits and are seldom the targets of policy mandated costs or punishments. It is unlikely that the public can be mobilized to protest benefits to well regarded, powerful target groups, while at the same time it is unlikely that costs directed towards them can be politically viable. Positive incentives such as entitlements, subsidies and grants are intended to coax behavior from the advantaged that is consistent with policy goals and wherever possible they are supplied with outreach information and training. One example of an advantaged group is veterans; who are numerous and well organized, but more importantly positively constructed as defenders of the nation. From the earliest years of the republic, the US Congress has directed pensions, land grants, educational support and other benefits to former members of the military (Mettler, 2002; Jensen, 2005). Veterans were targeted with special interest rates on home loans after World War II, and for decades they were given preference in the rules related to government employment.

Social security and Medicare beneficiaries are both positively constructed and powerful. Originally selected because of their positive social construction as older Americans deserving of a decent standard of living and health care in their old age, over time they have become a powerful force to protect their own interests (Mettler, 1998; Jacobs, 2007). Whenever the imperatives of policy make it unavoidable to levy costs on advantaged groups the tools selected often involve delayed enforcement that affects future rather than present qualifications, voluntary compliance and a minimum of coercion. Legislation to increase the age of eligibility for social security payments or lower the amount of veterans' payments, for instance, applies to people who would not be eligible for many years.

Dependents have little political power due to their lack of material resources and cohesion, inability to mobilize and lack of access to political arenas. While they may be viewed sympathetically, their inability to contribute to economic prosperity means that they do not attract much respect. Dependents are viewed as deserving because they did not create their problems, but they are also unable to solve them on their own.

Dependents are the targets of benefits, but less than might be expected considering the seriousness of their problems, and the benefits are typically insufficient to make much headway on resolving their difficulties. Rather than a public responsibility, the problems of the disadvantaged are often consigned to the private sector of churches and charities. Programs to help dependents, such as unemployment benefits and job training are usually short term and underfunded. While occasional disasters and news stories might highlight the plight of dependents and motivate an outpouring of concern, the attention does not last, and little headway is made. Further, paternalism has emerged in welfare policy that treats dependence as if its primary cause was lack of morality and personal responsibility. Typical for dependents, while they receive benefits, there are almost always strings, or costs, attached.

More than fifty years after President Lyndon Johnson declared war on poverty, 15 per cent of the residents of the United States continue to live below the poverty line. The Appalachia populations that were the subject of Walker Evans's depression photos and inspired Great Society Programs still struggle today. For instance, in McDowell County, West Virginia, where John F. Kennedy was shocked into consciousness about the poverty issue in the 1960 presidential primaries, the poverty rate for families with children is now 43 per cent and the median family income is only US$22 000. The political power briefly afforded Appalachia when John Kennedy needed to win a Democratic primary, quickly faded. Although nearly 47 per cent of personal income in the county is from social security, disability insurance, food stamps and other federal programs, allocations are neither sufficient nor directed at measures that might make a real difference (Gabriel, 2014). Moreover, the conditions under which the poor throughout the United States receive aid are often disempowering and demeaning. Welfare programs are rife with paternalism, and work promotion is accompanied by procedures for monitoring and documenting poor people's behavior. Aid recipients have been increasingly subjected to drug testing, finger printing and questioning regarding their sexual relations in order to establish paternity and pursue child support (Soss et al., 2011).

The *contender* target groups are those with considerable power who have a reputation for gaining it unfairly and/or abusing it. Contenders are only occasionally recipients of beneficial policy that is overt, because legislators do not want to risk doing good things for shady people. When they are allocated gains, it is normally because they are purportedly in the service of helping some advantaged or dependent group. Or, benefits are sub rosa, disguised and hard to trace. The more direct, targeted favors they get in policy come in ways not easily recognized by the public such as complicated tax relief or nearly invisible subsidies. When costs are allocated they tend to be more symbolic than real, and the power of contender groups is used to avoid implementation of penalties and other negative policy impacts. Contenders are able to employ their power and avoid the bite of penalties, charges and other costs even when there is wide public disapprobation.

Despite their negative reputation, the health insurance industry has been able to gain enormously in terms of expanding their client base through Medicaid and the Affordable Care Act, the object of which is to protect the poor and uninsured. And consider the treatment of another contender group, bankers, after the 2008–09 financial crisis for which they got much of the blame. While excessive bonuses and other perverse financial incentives were faulted for encouraging risk taking on real estate loans to unqualified borrowers, no real limits on executive pay have materialized. More importantly, the lack of adequate regulation continues to be problematic. Regulatory capture plays an important role (Laffont and Tirole, 1991). When regulators depend on the regulated for information essential to the regulatory role, and regulated groups have enormous resources to block the appointment of reformers to regulatory boards and to lobby and sue against regulations, then allocating effective costs to contender groups becomes very difficult. Also, it is not surprising that elected leaders failed to curb market bubbles and easy lending when faced with blowback from powerful groups (Grosse, 2012).

The *deviants* are powerless, negatively portrayed populations that are treated similarly in policy to advantaged groups, except that that they receive burdens rather than rewards. Deviants are targeted for punishments at a much higher level than justified by rationally designed policies aiming to efficiently pursue goals of public welfare and safety. One reason may be that elected leaders are constrained in their allocation of benefits to advantaged people because of budget constraints, and so have turned to doing bad things to bad people as a way to increase their public support. But implementing sanctions can often be very expensive. A critical critique would suggest that the democratic promise of equality and justice is becoming more and more difficult for capitalist democracies to justify, and deviants are a convenient way to deflect blame from themselves onto scapegoats. Being 'tough' on bad people has a long history in the United States, and recently has been shifting from 'tough on communists' to 'tough on crime' to 'tough on illegal aliens' to 'tough on terrorists'. In any case, coercive policies against deviants are high on the legislative agenda, especially during election campaigns. Among the sanctions directed at deviants are barring access to whatever benefits dependents get, suspension of civil rights, fines, incarceration, force and sometimes death.

Terrorists are the quintessential deviant group in society today, and legislators seem willing to make very large allocations of resources to capture and punish them in increasing numbers. In 2011, 171 prisoners remained at Guantánamo despite the international uproar over unfair judicial processes. To house each of such inmates costs over US$800 000 per year. The federal Bureau of Prisons was holding 362 people convicted of terrorism-related cases, 269 with what the bureau calls a connection to international terrorism – up from just 50 in 2000. An additional 93 inmates have a connection to domestic terrorism. Incarcerated terrorists are placed in special units that are more costly to administer and are subject to more strictly limited inmate phone calls and visits from outside (Shane, 2011).

Less negatively constructed, illegal aliens are also a large and growing deviant group. While in 2014 numbers of undocumented people coming across the southern border were down substantially from their peak in 2011, many members of Congress continued to clamor for greater inter-diction efforts. Congress has established a monthly quota for apprehensions by the border patrol that has to be met regardless of whether or not the overall numbers go down. Illegal immigrants were warned that even if immigration reform were to pass the legislature, if they entered the country without authorization they would be ineligible for citizenship. Race, youth and lack of education all feed into powerlessness and negative construction, spelling draconian treatment for another deviant group, young male high-school drop-outs. According to Guetzkow and Western (2007) the risk of imprisonment for Black men under the age of 30 was almost 60 per cent.

REDRAWING THE LINES OF TARGET GROUPS

The positioning of various groups in the matrix displayed in Figure 14.1 is not fixed: the power of a group may wax or wane and social constructions can become more or less positive. The designs embedded in public policy can play a role in changing the placement by expanding, contracting and redrawing the lines that create categories. The motivations of governmental officials for manipulating targeting to focus on more or less powerful groups and to modify images in more or less positive directions vary. Most agency officials and even elected leaders want to solve problems, and targeting greatly at odds with delivery on policy promise may prove problematic. Also, when too many well regarded, powerful people are swept into a target group branded as deviant, there is likely to be mobilization for change. For instance, the high rate of incarceration of people for minor drug offences was very expensive and became harder and harder to justify with rational arguments, and so small amounts of drugs like marijuana for personal use are being decriminalized. Target groups themselves have agency, and some members of various groups will distinguish themselves from others in their group in order to qualify for better treatment. For instance, immigrant groups and the Obama Administration have focused with some success on a newly carved out target group of illegal immigrants that has been relabeled as 'dreamers'. The members of this group were brought here as children, have excellent school records and no criminal records, and desire amnesty from deportation, in-state tuition at public colleges, driver licenses and other benefits available to their native born counterparts. Similarly, a subcategory of medical marijuana users has emerged from the larger category of illegal substance abusers, and has been awarded access to small amounts of the drug.

The history of juvenile justice is replete with examples of subdividing target populations to enable 'tough' punishment of some and more compassionate treatment of others. Early on, juveniles were separated from adult criminals precisely for that purpose and called 'delinquents' with less onerous punishments. Later, after runaways, truants and 'incorrigible' youth were being imprisoned, these youngsters were separated from the more serious delinquents and alternatives to imprisonment had to be found.

Redrawing of lines to make distinctions within target groups so that some are treated better than others is common, but not always objectively justifiable. Reichenbach (2002) found that the social construction differential between breast cancer and cervical cancer affected the higher priority given to those suffering from breast cancer in Ghana. Evidently, because cervical cancer is associated with a virus transmitted sexually, these victims are viewed as less deserving. Hogan (1997) found that the best protection against HIV/AIDS infection within a prison went to the health care workers and prison guards, and far less adequate protection was granted to the inmates who had the most deviant constructions.

Parsing definitions and boundaries of targets has real limitations as an avenue for changing social constructions. Whether or not redrawing of lines eventually results in expansion of target boundaries to make more people eligible for better treatment is uncertain and evidence is uneven. Many public officials oppose the softening of treatment to any illegal immigrants no matter how innocently and virtuously 'dreamers' are portrayed. Passage of medical marijuana laws in some states does seem to presage a more positive construction of all marijuana users and broader legalization, but the pattern remains unclear. It may be that 'creaming' the most positively constructed people from target populations renders those remaining in the group more negatively constructed and less likely to receive benefits. Up until the passage of the Affordable Care Act, it was extremely difficult to widen the net of those with government supported health insurance, at least in part because powerful, positively constructed older people were already receiving Medicare (Jacobs, 2007). Further, redrawing lines leads to only incremental changes in social construction, not a wholesale revision of images of deservedness, especially for those left behind.

FRAMING, DISCOURSES AND NARRATIVES

Social constructions are ubiquitous and can be found not just in policies but also frames, discourses and narratives where they must be consistent and fit comfortably or be forced to change. For substantial change in social constructions of a target group to take place, the frame, discourse and narrative also must change in a persuasive way. Baumgartner's work on the reframing of criminal justice such that 'punishment' is being replaced by 'justice' as the dominant frame is an example. Punishment requires a villain (deviant) who is mean, dangerous and threatening. 'Justice' as a frame shifts attention away from the perpetrator toward a more balanced view of fairness to victims and offenders alike (Baumgartner et al., 2008). On the other hand, attempts to change the social constructions of welfare recipients by requiring them to work failed to change public perceptions of them because the frame did not change the focus on people getting 'handouts' to more persistent causes of poverty (Soss and Schram, 2007). The fact that the policy *forced* welfare recipients to work did not change the welfare recipients' basic negative moral construction. Further, the negative perception of welfare recipients was multi-faceted and contained negative images not affected by being compelled to get a job. People using welfare were still constructed as lazy and not wanting to work, as drug users, as undisciplined, as willing to pursue educational opportunities only as a way of getting out of work, and as having too many children. The fact that policy resorted to forcing recipients to work and succumb to demeaning rules actually reinforced their negative construction.

Discourses often revolve around views of the 'other'. If the social construction of the target group doesn't fit the discourse of the other, then the social construction is not persuasive and will not be taken up by coalitions and other groups. The discourse of illegal aliens requires a construction of lawlessness, disrespect of authority, people who claim things that are not their birthright and who are inherently undisciplined. The central 'other' in this discourse is illegal border-crossers. The positive construction of the 'dreamers' as a young people brought here by parents through no fault of their own disregards that the central illegal act is the crossing of the border by lawless immigrants. The fact that the 'dreamers' were brought here against the law taints all their claims to American values such as working hard, going to school and staying out of trouble. For their social construction to change, the discourse has to evolve from the lawlessness of the parents' entry to a discourse about citizenship being earned by such things as long residence, paying taxes, working hard and earning an education. As long as the border and border-crossers dominate the discourse, attempts to reconstruct the dreamers will remain very difficult. Times change, however, and it would certainly seem possible to subdivide the 'illegal alien' population so that those who are here 'through no fault of their own' could be separated off for more compassionate treatment. Narratives are stories involving characters (Lejano et al., 2013). Characters are socially constructed to fit the story. The social construction of the character cannot change unless the narrative changes; but when it does, the social construction has to change with it. Miller (2012) argues that the narrative of the marijuana problem as the product of deviants involved characters that were Mexicans or other discriminated-against minorities leading to the criminalization of marijuana use. In the 1960s, the narrative changed to the social construction of marijuana users as characters who were long-haired, anti-war, hippies rioting in the streets and pursuing anti-American lifestyles. Both kinds of characterizations were negative. The character of a medical marijuana user seeking relief from chronic pain requires a very different story – of alternative medicine and scientific research that legitimates use. The story features doctors in white coats sitting across a table from elderly cancer patients in clinics that look exactly like doctors' offices with receptionists, sign-ins and waiting rooms.

MESSAGES, PARTICIPATION AND DEMOCRACY

In a democracy, all citizens are supposed to receive the same or similar messages from their experiences with public policy. When a democratic system is operating fairly each citizen receives benefits and sanctions depending upon the purposes of the policy and that citizen's association with policy goals. The process of specifying targets is constantly changing as new policies are made and others are modified. Our argument is that because the patterns of social constructions persist and are employed in many policies, policy treatment of citizens is not equal and democratic. Different target groups receive very different messages from public policy that impact their view of themselves as citizens, their orientation towards government, and their propensity to participate.

Advantaged groups receive mainly benefits justified on the grounds that they are deserving and their receipt of benefits is solving an important public policy problem. They are not only entitled, but their welfare is connected to public welfare. The message is that they are important, worthy citizens who are deserving of what they receive, and are contributing to the public interest even as they enjoy the benefits provided by others. They are encouraged to participate to protect their gains. Their participation is appropriate, and it is acceptable to pursue their self-interest.

Dependents receive very different messages. Benefits to dependents come because they are pitiable and other people are generous to them. They must be helped because they are unable to take care of themselves and be guided by regulations toward more productive use of their time. The messages that dependents receive are that they are not useful members of society because they do not contribute to the general economy. As a consequence the orientation of dependents toward government is that other people's interests are more important than theirs. The benefits they receive are almost always conditioned on actions that are restrictive of their liberty and demeaning. Research shows that when dependent groups are given agency, such as in Head Start programs (Soss, 2005), their participation increases to the same level as other groups. Older Americans had the lowest levels of participation of all groups until after social security sent different messages. Social security came from a trust fund into which everyone paid, and recipients earned their benefits. Their participation is now at the highest level of all age groups.

Deviants have the lowest levels of participation partly because access to voting is denied to many, but also because their experiences with government are predominately negative and the messages they receive are that they deserve only sanctions. Their modes of participation, if any, tend to be disruptive. Contenders also receive negative messages, but their participation is driven underground rather than being suppressed. Contenders get the message that politics is a game they can fix by lobbying, by campaign contributions and by deceitful advertising strategies. They are made to understand that government must be manipulated and the public must be fooled if they, contenders, are to receive what they believe is their due. Hence, their participation tends to be hidden: insider beltway politics, pressuring and suing regulators, and strategically placing campaign contributions.

The promise of American democracy is opportunity and equality. These are eroded when social constructions become entrenched and people receive very consistent messages across all of their experiences with policy. Participation becomes markedly uneven and those who might have the most to gain through government actually participate the least. Those who participate the most have little incentive to see beyond superficial constructions to underlying problems faced by the less fortunate. They are able to simply write people off because of the way they are constructed.

SOCIAL CONSTRUCTIONS AND CRITICAL POLICY STUDIES

The social constructions' typology provided in this article can be a powerful tool in the hands of critical policy scholars. The gap between the way target groups might be selected on the basis of accomplishing policy goals and what actually occurs when power and social constructions control targeting is often very great. Critical policy scholars can expose how inefficient and illogical much targeting actually is. Advantaged groups who are powerful and positively constructed as deserving receive far too many benefits, often threatening the public interest. For instance, home mortgage deductions reflect a huge public expenditure that can no longer be justified as the best means to promote home ownership and build stable communities. Yet policy makers treat the deduction as a birthright, afraid of the backlash that would occur not just from mortgage owners but the entire real estate and banking industry should the rules be changed. Dependents as a category are treated by welfare and other policies in ways that perpetuate their lack of power and construction as charity cases. If the purpose of policy were to raise people out of poverty, the payments would be more generous. If instilling pride, independence and political consciousness were the real aims of public policies directed to dependent populations, then policies would be designed to encourage participation, like Head Start programs. Instead policies are demeaning and disrespectful. Were the great public policy gains achieved by contender groups through devious means to be exposed, citizens would have greater respect for government, contenders' behavior would improve and unnecessary allocation of benefits to them would go down. Deviants as targets of public policies are attracting more and more policy attention, even though too many people are behind bars or on probation and the costs of the justice system are rising. Excessive policy burdens to growing numbers of people threaten the creation of a permanent underclass denied both political and economic participation. Policy analysts and political scientists are good at recognizing outside threats to democracy, such as terrorists, but not very good at recognizing the degenerative impact of negative portrayals of people for political gain.

Of course, social constructions will always be with us, but the historic role of public policy in democracy is supposed to solve problems, not simply generate and reproduce labels to ensure reelection. A worthy aim of critical research is to unmask the undemocratic values embedded in public policy.

REFERENCES

Baumgartner, Frank, Suzanna De Boef and Amber Boydstun (2008), *The Decline of the Death Penalty and the Discovery of Innocence*, Cambridge: Cambridge University Press.

Gabriel, Trip (2014), '50 Years into the War on Poverty, Hardship Hits Back', *New York Times*, 20 April.

Grosse, Robert (2012), 'Bank Regulation, Governance and the Crisis: A Behavioral Finance View', *Journal of Financial Regulation and Compliance*, **20** (1), 4–25.

Guetzkow, Joshua and Bruce Western (2007), 'The Political Consequences of Mass Imprisonment', in Joe Soss, Jacob Hacker and Suzanne Mettler (eds), *Remaking America: Democracy and Public Policy in an Age of Inequality*, New York: Russell Sage Foundation, pp. 228–242.

Haidt, Jonathan (2012), *The Righteous Mind: Why Good People Are Divided by Politics and Religion*, New York: Pantheon.

Hogan, Nancy (1997), 'The Social Construction of Target Populations and the Transformation of Prison-Based AIDS Policy: A Descriptive Case Study', *Journal of Homosexuality*, **32** (3/4), 77–114.

Ingram, Helen (2007), 'Poverty, Policy, and the Social Construction of Target Groups', in Joe Soss, Jacob Hacker and Suzanne Mettler (eds), *Remaking America: Democracy and Public Policy in an Age of Inequality*, New York: Russell Sage Foundation, pp. 245–253.

Ingram, Helen and Anne L. Schneider (1990), 'Improving Implementation through Framing Smarter Statutes', *Journal of Public Policy*, **10** (1), 66–87.

Ingram, Helen, and Anne L. Schneider (1991), 'The Choice of Target Populations', *Administration and Society*, **23** (3), 333–356.

Ingram, Helen, and Anne L. Schneider (1993), 'Constructing Citizenship', in Helen Ingram and Steven Smith (eds), *Public Policy and Democracy*, Washington, DC: Brookings Institution, pp. 68–94.

Ingram, Helen and Anne L. Schneider (1995), 'Social Construction (Continued)', *American Political Science Review*, **89** (2), 437–446.

Ingram, Helen and Anne L. Schneider (2005), 'How Public Policy Socially Constructs Deservedness', in Anne Schneider and Helen Ingram (eds), *Deserving and Entitled: Social Construction and Public Policy*, Albany, NY: State University of New York Press, pp. 1–34.

Ingram, Helen and Anne L. Schneider (2006), 'Policy Analysis for Democracy', in Michael Moran, Martin Rein and Robert E. Goodin (eds), *The Oxford Handbook of Public Policy*, Oxford: Oxford University Press, pp. 169–189.

Jacobs, Lawrence (2007), 'The Implementation and Evolution of Medicare', 'The Distributional Effects of "positive" Policy Feedbacks', in Joe Soss, Jacob S. Hacker and Suzanne Mettler (eds), *Remaking America*, New York: Russell Sage Foundation, pp. 77–98.

Jensen, Laura S. (2005), 'Constructing and Entitling America's Original Veterans', in Anne L. Schneider and Helen M. Ingram (eds), *Deserving and Entitled: Social Construction of Public Policy*, Albany, NY: State University of New York Press, pp. 35–62.

Kahneman, Daniel (2011), *Thinking, Fast and Slow*, New York: Farrar, Straus, and Giroux.

Laffont, Jean-Jacques and Jean Tirole (1991), 'The Politics of Government Decision Making: A Theory of Regulatory Capture', *Quarterly Journal of Economics*, **106** (4), 1089–1271.

Lejano, Raul, Mrill Ingram and Helen Ingram (2013), *The Power of Narrative in Environmental Networks*, Cambridge, MA: The MIT Press.

Mettler, Suzanne (1998), *Dividing Citizens: Gender and Federalism in New Deal Policy*, New York: Cornell University Press.

Mettler, Suzanne (2002), 'Bringing the State Back in to Civic Engagement: Policy Feedback Effects of the G.I. Bill for World War II Veterans', *American Political Science Review*, **96** (2), 351–365.

Miller, Hugh (2012), *Governing Narratives: Symbolic Politics and Policy Change*, Tuscaloosa, AL: University of Alabama Press.

Pierce, Jonathan, Saba Siddiki, Michael D. Jones, Kristin Schumacher, Andrew Pattison and Holly Peterson (2014), 'Social Construction and Policy Design: A Review of Past Applications', *Policy Studies Journal*, **42** (1), 1–29.

Reichenbach, Laura (2002), 'The Politics of Priority Setting for Reproductive Health: Breast and Cervical Cancer in Ghana', *Reproductive Health Matters*, **10** (20), 47–58.

Schneider, Anne and Helen Ingram (1990), 'Behavioral Assumptions of Policy Tools', *Journal of Politics*, **52** (2), 510–529.

Schneider, Anne and Helen Ingram (1993), 'The Social Construction of Target Populations', *American Political Science Review*, **87** (2), 334–346.

Schneider, Anne and Helen Ingram (1997), *Policy Design for Democracy*, Lawrence, KS: University Press of Kansas.

Schneider, Anne and Helen Ingram (eds) (2005a), *Deserving and Entitled: Social Construction and Public Policy*, Albany, NY: State University of New York Press.

Schneider, Anne and Helen Ingram (2005b), 'A Response to Peter deLeon', *Public Administration Review*, **65** (September/October), 631–633.

Schneider, Anne and Helen Ingram (2007), 'Social Constructions in the Study of Public Policy', in James Holstein and Jaber F. Gubrium (eds), *Handbook of Constructionist Research*, New York: Guilford Publications, pp.189–212.

Schneider, Anne, Helen Ingram and Peter deLeon (2014), 'Democratic Policy Design: Social Construction of Target Populations', in P. Sabatier and C.M. Weible (eds), *Theories of the Policy Process*, Boulder, CO: Westview Press pp.105–149.

Shane, Scott (2011), 'Beyond Guantanamo, a Web of Prisons for Terrorism Inmates', *New York Times*, 10 December. Retrieved 24 April 2014 from http://www.nytimes.com/2011/12/11/us/beyond-guantanamo-bay-a-web-of-federal-prisons.html?pagewanted=all&_r=1.

Soss, Joe (2005), 'Making Clients and Citizens: Welfare Policy as a Source of Status, Belief, and Action', in Anne L. Schneider and Helen M. Ingram (eds), *Deserving and Entitled: Social Construction of Public Policy*, Albany, NY: State University of New York Press, pp.291–328.

Soss, Joe and Sanford Schram (2007), 'A Public Transformed? Welfare Reform as Policy Feedback', *American Political Science Review*, **101** (1), 111–127.

Soss, Joe, Richard Fording and Sanford Schram (2011), *Disciplining the Poor*, Chicago: University of Chicago Press.

Stone, Deborah (2005), 'Foreword', in Anne Schneider and Helen Ingram (eds), *Deserving and Entitled: Social Constructions and Public Policy*, Albany, NY: State University of New York Press, pp.ix–xiii.

Tversky, Amos and Daniel Kahneman (1973), 'Availability: A Heuristic for Judging Frequency and Probability', *Cognitive Psychology*, **5** (2), 207–232.

15 The autopoietic text
Raul P. Lejano and Sung Jin Park

1. INTRODUCTION

Implementation research attempts to explain how policy outcomes can be affected by relationships between different policy actors, such as legislators and street-level bureaucrats. However, the literature has largely neglected the fact that these relationships are often mediated by policy texts. In this chapter, we problematize this fact and describe how implementation problems can derive from the nature and action of these texts. Strongly textualist notions of policy can further hegemonic policy milieus or, alternatively, confound even the best intentions of policymakers. The inherent textuality of policy can place inordinate focus on the production of texts in lieu of policy action. We will refer to an inordinate kind of textuality as *autopoiesis*. A deeper reading suggests a close relationship between textualism and ideology. After presenting the conceptual arguments, we illustrate them with a brief look at the example of information and communication technology (ICT) policies for international development. Problems that, in some way, trace back to the issue of textuality include predictably poor outcomes of these ICT projects and, in some cases, postcolonialist subjugation of recipient communities. We then end the discussion by sketching an alternative model of policy, one that revolves around narrativity rather than textuality.

From the earliest roots of implementation research in the 1970s, the literature has depicted the policy process as one involving activities at some locus of policy design and subsequent activities at the site of policy implementation (e.g., Bardach, 1977; Pressman and Wildavsky, 1979; Sabatier and Mazmanian, 1979). Notwithstanding recent attention to more diffused and networked models of the policy process, the portrayal of policy as a design/implementation dualism is still a powerful one and undoubtedly well describes many real policy situations. Much of the implementation research problematizes the relationship between the designers of policy (e.g., legislators) and its implementers (e.g., street-level bureaucrats). For instance, faulty communication between the two can lead to insufficient realization of policy objectives.

The early implementation research did already recognize problems with analytically separating policy formulation from policy implementation.

Rejecting the extreme views of, on the one hand, perfect correspondence between the two or, on the other, no correspondence at all, Majone and Wildavsky liken policy to general dispositions that create a range of possibilities that implementers would work out, primarily in material ways (1979). As we will attempt to show, this notion disregards the performative nature of mere words on paper, as Austin had said of speech (Austin, 1975). The inscription of policy, or what we will refer to as text, endows the latter with a kind of agency, whether in constructing a new field of policy, empowering or disempowering actors, or enacting processes in seemingly autonomous ways.[1]

We will focus on a little-studied aspect of the design/implementation relationship – the mediating action of text. More often than not, the relationship between the policy designers (or the design phase) and the policy implementers (or the implementation phase) is mediated by one or more key policy texts. As an example, an agency such as the US Environmental Protection Agency may formulate a new regulation (e.g., concerning emission controls from small drycleaners) as part of its regular rulemaking. The new rules would then be implemented by its delegated field agencies, such as local Air Quality Control Districts. These rules are transmitted through well-defined policy texts in the form of an item in the Federal Register and perhaps an official circular to all field agencies.

We problematize this otherwise simple feature of the policy process, which is the instrumentality and action of policy texts. We will argue that the manner in which these texts are inserted into the policy process, the mode by which they help construct relationships among policy actors, and the power-laden rationalities embedded in these instruments, are important in understanding a host of implementation problems. Policy texts exist not only for the obvious reasons (policymakers writing things down lest they forget), but because they structure the policy field, differentially positioning authors and readers and, within their narratives, emplotting policy actors in specific roles in the policy process. These texts can play more than a passive role in translating policy intents to policy actions, sometimes resulting in unintended effects. Later in the chapter, we examine how we might begin rethinking the role of policy texts by recognizing a more hybrid nature in them.

We first survey key issues in implementation research and, then, re-examine them in the light of the problem of textuality. As will be worked out in the ensuing discussion, the problems with textuality can be categorized in the following manner:

(i)   Policy texts, through inadequate or excessive *codification*, can confound implementation. In conjunction with high degrees of textualism, this can lead to 'shallow' rather than 'deep' implementation.

More generally, the textuality of policy can emphasize codification not action, and the communication of explicit, rather than tacit, information. A related problem is that through overspecification, textualization can produce hypostatized models of policy situations, sometimes amounting to an ideological system.

(ii)   Policy texts, by virtue of their capacity for *structuring* of the policy field, can further distance center from periphery, or bring them together, acknowledge and empower actors, or reject and disempower the same.

(iii) Policy texts, as a tool for *normalization*, can impose logics of domination upon recipient communities and, when these texts are strongly autopoietic, maintain rigid ideological socio-political systems.

At the end of the chapter, we describe an alternative model, one based on narrativity, which we counterpose against textuality and the latter's tendency to distinguish policy authors from policy implementers (whether the authorship is understood as strong prescription or general disposition). In the alternative model, we envision policymaking as a community of narrators, each employing different forms of capital to enact policy in all its material and semiotic dimensions. But before we turn to the alternative, we need to better work out the concept, and practice, of textuality.

2.   TEXTUALITY AND THE PROBLEM OF IMPLEMENTATION

How do we account for policies that, as they evolve, become institutions that their policymakers never expected or even start to regret? In 2001, in almost unanimous fashion, US Congress passed the Patriot Act which, among other provisions, gave the National Security Agency (NSA) new powers to access telephone metadata in its war against terror (Section 215). Years later, beginning with leakage of news concerning massive, routine collection of information from private citizens, many in Congress and the White House began questioning the NSA program.[2] How did the policy measure they imagined years ago lead to the errant agency actions they see today? As we discuss below, part of the problem lies in the power that policy texts have, enabling the restructuring of conventions, authorities, and practices almost with a kind of agency that enacts policy changes independent of whatever intents the policymakers may have had.

Periodic reviews of the literature on implementation show how some models persist over time (e.g., Matland, 1995; Barrett, 2004; Saetren, 2014). The most classic of these is the so-called top-down model of policy implementation. The basic model assumes a hierarchical process wherein policy is designed at some (often) centralized location or body and, then, passed on to field or local agents for implementation. Much of this literature employs a communication model, where the foremost issue is the ability of policy designers to communicate their intent with sufficient fidelity to implementers at other levels of the policy hierarchy (Pressman and Wildavsky, 1979). Implementation problems then stem from the inadequate or distorted transmission of policy intents from the designers or erroneous interpretation on the part of the implementers. Some of the most common sources of implementation problems in this strand of literature include:

(i)   problems of interpretation, stemming from unclear or inconsistent policy goals (Mazmanian and Sabatier, 1983);
(ii) overly complex chains of actors involved in policy implementation (Pressman and Wildavsky, 1979);
(iii) mismatches in priorities between policy designers and implementers (Van Meter and Van Horn, 1975); and others (see Matland, 1995 for a comprehensive review);
(iv) lack of capacity or resources for implementation – an example of this is the oft-decried issue of 'unfunded mandates' (Scheberle, 2004).

There is a second strand of literature that posits 'bottom-up' models of implementation, where non-local or macro-level institutional actors formulate policy goals, from which local or micro-level actors draw advice and then formulate the actual policy to be implemented with varying degrees of autonomy and discretion (e.g., Berman, 1980; Hjern and Hull, 1982). In addition to such problems in top-down models, this literature also points to these sources of implementation problems:

(i) insufficient flexibility to allow local actors to tailor a policy to the unique demands of the particular context (Maynard-Moody et al., 1990);
(ii) poorly adapted central policies and/or local actors who are not skilled in the task of local adaptation (Hull and Hjern, 1987).

There have also arisen models that integrate top-down and bottom-up modes of analysis (see Elmore, 1985; Goggin et al., 1990; Scott, 2001; Sabatier, 2008; Lejano and Shankar, 2013). Other efforts at a more integrative analysis include recent literature on network governance, in which policy design and implementation emerge from network relationships across a constellation of policy actors (O'Toole, 2000).

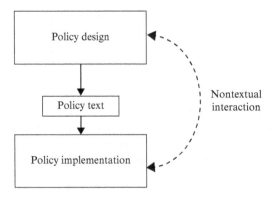

Figure 15.1   Classic design/implementation model as mediated by text

In this chapter, we study the implication of the fact that, invariably, actors at different levels of the policy process may not, or may only partly, directly interact – whether interpreted as top-down or bottom-up. Often, at least part of the relationship is mediated by the intervening presence of a policy text. Figure 15.1 depicts this for the case of the classic design/ implementation dichotomy – in this case, centrally located policy designers generate a policy text, which implementers then take up and act upon. The mediating action of such a text has not been examined in any depth, which we intend to begin doing herein. There may be significant effects from the lack of direct interaction between different sets of policy actors, precluding more deliberative forms of policymaking. Moreover, the policy text itself may affect policy processes in an autonomous manner, unintended by its authors.

At this point, we should clarify what we mean by the term *text*, which is related to but not to be conflated with the notion of a discourse. By *text*, we simply mean the codification of policy in literal form, whether on paper, digital, or other media. These texts may be formal and statutory, or informal and advisory – no matter, these are the ideas and prescriptions of one or more policy actors given objective form as text. In text, communication takes on a nominally objective form that endures through time and across place, though its meaning is always subject to interpretation (Ricoeur, 1981).

As such, the focus of our analysis is on the role and action of text in policy. Our focus is not on the larger discourse, both the general understanding of it as the whole communicative event and process of interaction among policy agents (Van Dijk, 1997) as well as the more specialized understanding of it as historically evolved language and associated practices producing particular socio-cultural fields of meaning (Foucault, 1981). While we place our attention on the smaller topic of text and textuality, we should be also cognizant of the larger discursive field within which the object of study is embedded (as suggested in Fischer, 2005).

Common connotations of the word *text* often associate it with authoritative documents. In the most extreme form, policy texts may be taken to be so authoritative that implementation is assumed to simply enact, absolutely and singularly, the prescriptions of the text, even when the latter may be deficient in this regard. *Textualism* is the condition of attaching absolute or near absolute authority to the literal text, constraining interpretation to the literal meaning of the text or, when these literal meanings are not sufficiently precise, referring back to the original meanings intended by its authors. For example, there has been a trend in judicial practice in the US to limit the latitude by which judges can depart from the most literal interpretations of constitutional text. As Scalia and Garner write, 'Textualism, in its purest form, begins and ends with what the text says and fairly implies' (Scalia and Garner, 2012, p. 16). To this, we formulate a related policy concept, referred to as *textuality*, which is the organization of policymaking around the production of texts.

Later in this chapter, we will refer to the closely related notion of *narrativity*. This term refers, first of all, to narrative or a plot consisting of a coherent system of events linked logically or temporally. Such plots are enacted or narrated by a set of particular characters. Unlike the idea of discourse, which structures what can be said and what meanings are privileged, narrative occurs within discursive fields (see also Lejano et al., 2013). Narrativity also refers to a second aspect, which is the act of narrating. Towards the end of the chapter, we consider the possibility of understanding policy not in terms of textuality but those of narrativity.

3.   THE MEDIATING ACTION OF POLICY TEXTS

Texts play important functions in policymaking, particularly those of codification, structuration, and normalization. These functions can be, at the same time, the source of implementation problems. We take each of these dimensions of policy textuality in turn.

3.1   Superscription

By *superscription*, we mean the over-textualizing of policy. In the description below, we introduce related issues incorporated into the term, superscription, which are the problems of *codification* and *autopoiesis*. In doing so, we point to a host of problems with policy texts that go beyond much of the literature's focus on interpretation problems.

To begin with, the implementation literature has well worked out problems with the interpretation of policy, particularly the reading of policy texts. This problem is most prominent in 'top-down' framings of policy implementation, the issue being misinterpretation of the original meaning embedded by policymakers into the policy text. There are two basic sources of misinterpretation. The first stems from the natural polysemy of text, which creates an inescapable need for some measure of interpretation on the reader's part. As Yanow writes, implementation can be understood as primarily an interpretive act (1993). This polysemy is exacerbated by deficiencies in the language and substance of the text itself – the problem of policy ambiguity (Hupe, 2011). Often, this reflects a tendency of policy texts to include broad, non-explicit language that allows a diverse coalition of policymakers to reach agreement. Another magnifier of these potential distortions is the length and complexity of the institutional pathways that the signal must travel before policy is finally and completely enacted, the issue being the accumulation of distortions generated each time the message crosses organizational or other boundaries (Pressman and Wildavsky, 1979).

Less recognized in the implementation literature is the inherent rigidity engendered by codification. Once written, a policy text assumes an objective nature that, to some extent, precludes deliberation. At issue is also what is codified, the problem being the gap between what the writers intuit from their centralized locations and the complex conditions experienced in multiple, possibly widely varying contexts. Policy texts, when they are too authoritative, create universalist prescriptions that may not match the needs of different specific locales. This was the case in the area of international development, when strong blanket prescriptions toward institutional reform (known as structural adjustment conditions) either proved ruinous or ineffective due to a mismatch between it and conditions in developing country contexts (Rapley, 1996). In the area of state and urban planning, policy texts created blueprints for placemaking that proved hostile to local community life (Jacobs, 1961). Implicit in this is the formal nature of the policy text, its inherent capacity to impose rigid logics and rationalities upon what policymakers might assume to be formless local contexts. It is the modernist urge to codify and to fix what, in reality, needs to be negotiated on the ground – that is, implicated.

One key characteristic of the policy text is its degree of *autopoiesis*, by which we mean the extent to which it is self-contained and complete. Autopoietic texts can contain authoritative blueprints for institutions, programs, and projects that need not refer to any other text outside themselves.[3] One might think of Le Corbusier's blueprint for La Ville Radieuse, which contains a detailed, comprehensive plan for the ideal city, from its panoramic logic to its intimate spaces for living and walking, all in itself. One key issue with autopoietic texts is the hypostatization of reality – i.e., essentially, over-specified texts (the products of superscription) can construct a complete system that readers may mistake as completely modeling the real world. As an example, the micro-economic model of the perfectly competitive market[4] can be mistaken to function as a faithful model of the real market, with sometimes very unfortunate results as the recession of 2008 suggests.[5] Some ideologies might be understood to be overspecified, hypostatized depictions of reality; in this sense, we might conceive of ideology as being a problem of superscription. As we work out below, in some cases, the autopoietic text can even be considered an ideology.

Codification problems are magnified in policy milieus that have a high degree of textualism, where policy meanings are subordinated to the literal text of the policy document. In these situations, implementation may consist of simple pro forma compliance with the most basic, often superficial, dictates of the policy text when, in reality, effective policy requires an active, interpretive readership. Textualism then leads to 'shallow' rather than 'deep' implementation, where the former refers to superficial compliance with the literal text of a policy, and the latter to creative practice that seeks to meet the overall intent of the policy (Park, 2013). That is, deep implementation requires going beyond what is contained in the policy text and adding to it in ways that further the goals of the policy.

The inherent textuality of policy can result in inordinate attention on the production of text, often treating the texts as primary outcomes of policy. In these cases, the production of text sometimes takes the place of policy action. As an example, Lejano describes how the mere production of hazard maps, rather than actual risk reduction, are taken to indicate project completion in the area of disaster risk prevention (2008), issues which have life-and-death implications. Essentially, policymakers can mistake the roadmap for the journey. Or consider the possibility that, just perhaps, part of the reason behind the stalemate of the Kyoto Protocol for climate change mitigation was textuality – i.e., structuring everything around the forging of a document in lieu of establishing new working relationships among countries and finding incrementally progressive ways to jointly act. As Prins and Rayner write: ' . . . the more parties there are to any negotiation, the lower the common denominator for agreement – as has been the case under Kyoto' (Prins and Rayner, 2007, p. 974).

Lastly, consider the potential of policy texts to preclude direct (e.g., verbal) communication between policy actors, constraining the possibility of interrogating, discussing, confiding, or other forms of mutual exchange.

This limitation can lead to the transmission only of explicit, not tacit, information. What is precluded is the kind of conversation where someone might ask, 'I know what the document says, but what do you *really* mean?' By virtue of codification, texts can prevent the exchange of tacit information. Of course, sometimes policy actors can 'talk past' the text, perhaps illicitly (as in state and federal governments violating legal treaties with native tribes in the 19th century).

3.2 Structuring

Policy texts have a structuring effect on the policy field. Most directly, they create a cognitive separation between the framers of policy and its recipients. This cognitive gap enables the previously discussed problem of what Scott refers to as high modernism in planning and policymaking (Scott, 1998). Policy texts also serve to identify who the winners and losers of a policy ostensibly are, and they construct the identities and characteristics of the targets of policy (Schneider and Ingram, 1997). These texts serve as markers of an institutional field, pointing out who hold key positions of power versus those who reside in the interstices of this field.

There is the distinct effect from the concrete production of policy texts. Aside from the power of the word, it is the power of the pen that we examine. The document is the material witness to the power of its author and to the institutional order it represents. Inscription can be a tool for conservatism, but it can also be a tool for change. The rush to commit words to paper is akin to the imperative to stake a claim on new territory. A new nation rushes to inscribe its new constitution. A new cult conspires to produce its sacred scripture. The invention of the printing press was said to usher in the Reformation and the modern era of nation-building (McLuhan, 1964, p. 161). Texts establish objective blueprints for new social orders, and these texts can then diffuse outwards and establish new actions in community after community, the result being the institutionalization of a new system.

Texts do not just create blueprints for (or against) change, they also position social actors differently – differentiating authors from readers. They also establish an order of literacy, distinguishing those who are judged to be able to read and interpret these texts from those who cannot. This is most obvious in the case of legal interpretations of law and in literary criticism, but it is found in other disciplines as well. In international development, for example, written blueprints such as the structural adjustment program not only create an imperial distance from their authors in their center of authority (e.g., in Washington, DC) and in the developing country recipients, but also establish an expert corps of field agents who are then sent to the latter to officially interpret these guidelines into actions on the ground. And, in a highly textualist policy field, instead of achieving the fusion of horizons of author and reader (Ricoeur, 1981), texts may simply separate them irrevocably.

But the issue is also the autonomous effect of the text, which structures in ways not intended or dreamt of by its authors. The power of the text has, over the ages, been used by political ideologues and zealots to take its words to extremes. Radical readings of the text have been used to do violence to both political subjects and the policy itself. For example, Fortune and Enger (2005) attribute historical violence toward women partly to the extremist readings of religious texts. It is precisely because of the objective, transcendent nature of texts that actions can be justified on their basis without recourse to dialogue – whereas the imagery of communicative rationality is that of oral communication, texts are the occasion for hegemony. And texts can communicate even in the absence or ignorance of their authors.

Texts distance writer from reader cognitively and temporally. Even when communication between author and reader is not hindered by texts, such communication is textually mediated. The resulting exchange between parties, when it occurs, is necessarily asynchronous. Akin to Bourdieu's description of gift exchange among the Kabyle (Bourdieu, 1977), the gap in time between the initial signal and subsequent responses can structure social relationships, positioning giver and receiver unequally. Even when the exchange of text can go in both directions (between sites of design and sites of implementation), the asynchronic nature of the exchange positions external and local actors unequally. A focus on structuring motivates us to recognize the performative aspects of text. We must appreciate its capacity for 'constructing' new policy frames, legitimizing policy actors that were hitherto marginalized, and creating new policy agendas that were hitherto invisible.

3.3 Normalization

Texts, by their partially objective nature, are instruments well suited for norm diffusion, which is the spreading of an institutional idea or policy design outwards from point of creation and into locales of implementation. The normalizing action of text may depend on the degree of textualism of a policy field. That is, the greater the tendency of policy meanings to be rigidly referenced back to the literal words of the key text, the greater (one presumes) the degree of normative purchase of such text. This points to a deeper problem underlying the textuality of policy models, which is an underlying conservatism.

It is easy to see the link between textualism and policy conservatism – after all, the latter stands opposed to legal or institutional activism that goes beyond the bare minima of policy that founding policy texts have set. For example, it is more difficult to make a case for a broader social safety net in the US when its constitution identifies only the most fundamental individual rights. One can rightly argue that founding policy texts merely set the broad outlines of real policy programs, which require further definition of policy in the field – but that goes against the spirit of textualism.

We immediately see the inherent link between textualism and ideology. Interpretive approaches to policy empower street-level agents to fashion programs to best fit their own contexts. But this is opposed to the shrinking of the state that conservative ideologues insist upon. To take conservative fundamentalism in the US as an example, it is driven perhaps less by an insistence upon the authority of the free market as the desire to remove any government encroachment into the private domain. As an example, diagnosing why it is that the US ranks alongside much poorer nations in health indices for obesity, infant mortality, and adult inactivity and, furthermore, fashioning effective interventions – requires the active presence of health experts in communities (Murray et al., 2013). This, in turn, requires comprehensive health reform and an interactive state, which conservative ideologues fight hard to overturn. As many argue (e.g., Berkes, 2007; Lejano and Ingram, 2007; Ostrom, 2008), policy texts can emerge from global discourses which can be hegemonic, denying local voices that speak to the needs and aspirations of communities and local ecologies.

Ironically, by elevating the power of the text (e.g., the Constitution), ideologues can reduce the power of the actor (e.g., the State). Ideologies can be understood as autopoietic texts that create complete, self-referential systems of truth-claims that are effectively isolated from other sources of knowledge (Lejano and Stokols, 2013). Logically, the degree of specificity of a text would increase with the degree of autopoiesis. As Valentinov writes, autopoietic systems 'build up their internal complexity at the cost of lowering their sensitivity to the complexity of their environment, both societal and ecological' (2014, p. 28).

Ideologies are ostensibly complete or self-contained systems of thought. But there are systems that might be thought of as open versus systems that are closed. It is best to use a narrative lens to understand the distinction. Ideologies are narratives that are self-contained and complete is. Ideologies are closed narrative schemes that contain, in themselves, a story of the world. In contrast, open systems are intertextual (Kristeva, 1980) – they are understood to draw their meaning from other texts in a universe of texts.[6] Conservative ideologies can be closed and autopoietic. An example of this is the narrative of climate science skepticism that insulates itself from acknowledging other, differing narratives such as the scientific. Ideological narratives can be low in textuality or, if they refer outside themselves, refer to texts that belong to the same corpus of texts within the same ideology.

What makes a text or system of texts autopoietic? What precludes interpretation on the part of the reader? First, there is the authority ascribed to text (i.e., textualism). Within the text itself, we can find closure, the lack of reference or what Barthes calls paradigmatic indices (1974) that point the reader away from the text at hand. Closure, which is a low degree of intertextuality, can be seen in the lack of acknowledgement of anything outside the text, whether textual or empirical. In fact, we might find, in ideological texts, an invariance that resists effects from other ideologies and from empirical reality altogether. Later in the chapter, we contrast autopoietic texts with more contextualist notions of policymaking (see also Lejano, 2006; Lejano and Shankar, 2013).

4.   ILLUSTRATION: ICT4D

We turn now to the policy field of Information and Communication Technology for Development (ICT4D) to illustrate our argument. ICT4D programs have embedded in their concept, organization, and practice a strong notion of textuality, with some adverse outcomes as a result.

ICT4D is a type of top-down development practice wherein lower-income communities are provided computer-based centers aimed at enabling locals to access digital and internet-based knowledge, with specific software packages for use in supporting local livelihood. A common form of ICT4D involves installation of telecenters in the community so that local farmers can sit at a computer terminal and use agricultural technology software packages that give them access to market prices, weather reports, and agricultural best practices. A range of telecenter franchise models promoted by public agencies or private companies – e.g., n-Logue's rural connectivity model (Howard et al., 2001) and Grameenphone's community information center model (Grameenphone, 2014) – constitutes some of the many ICT4D franchise models found today. The model guidelines aim to replicate development procedures in different regions. For instance, the Grameen Village Phone program model was adopted in 81,376 villages in Bangladesh as of 2010 and was then replicated in Uganda and Rwanda (Grameenphone, 2014).

ICT4D is a particularly appropriate area wherein to study the role of textuality in implementation. ICT4D implementation prioritizes text over action since these projects are often stand-alone, self-contained facilities that dictate the uses to be made of them. The idea is that, once deployed, the relocation of ICTs is either irrevocable or costly. Hence, the technical sufficiency of the ICT4D design is crucial, with primacy given to the design document. Another reason that ICT4D design follows a top-down process is that it is highly dependent on advanced technological knowledge, and the 'black boxes' of such technology are most often pre-packaged programs ready for field deployment (e.g., Johnson, 2007; Ackerman, 2012). In a more basic sense, the originary text might be thought of as the very code that makes up the embedded software. In the form of code, the text is the technology itself.

These texts originate in locales (e.g., Silicon Valley, Bangalore) far removed from their points of application in the developing world. Accordingly, the production of ICT4D design documents often takes place in those technologically advanced areas before being delivered into the hands of implementers in the project sites. As a result, implementing actors tend to be highly dependent on texts at the outset of the project.

4.1   Superscription

Fundamental imperfections of ICT4D policy documents have been tied to implementation problems (Fountain, 2001; Heeks, 2002; Anokwa et al., 2009; Bass and Heeks, 2011). The ICT4D literature refers to this problem as the 'design-reality gap' (Heeks, 2002) or the 'design blind spot' (Patterson et al., 2009). As a result of geographic and hierarchical separation between program design and implementation, local specificities such as regulatory environments (Gurumurthy and Singh, 2009) and telecommunication infrastructure conditions (Kaushik and Singh, 2004) are often not reflected in ICT4D design. In addition, project failure has been attributed to low quality of design, insufficient details (Keene, 2007), and faulty design assumptions (Patterson et al., 2009; Bass and Heeks, 2011). The general problem is the lack of fit between the specifications written into the policy texts by system designers and the widely divergent conditions in the many and differing contexts of application (Heeks, 2002; Gichoya, 2005).

Excessive textualism (i.e., an exclusive reliance on the written text) leads to problems of shallow implementation. In reality, adoption of ICT4D in a developing country situation requires the parallel development of basic capacities in the recipient community that the policy texts could not possibly specify. However, recipient communities often simply receive the ICT package as a black box (Latour, 1987) and deploy it without corollary actions such as training of a local corps of experts in running and maintaining the ICT systems, reducing the cultural barriers to use of technology by local residents, and tailoring some of the system applications to those needs particularly felt locally. It requires self-efficacy on the part of the text's reader to improvise other, unspecified capacities needed for a successful system. For example, Heeks describes an ICT4D project where needed system fine-tuning was missing because women participating from the local community tended to take the given technology as a fixed reality and did not feel empowered enough to critique the system.[7]

The lack of contextuality of ICT4D projects is embodied in rigid, pre-packaged texts that do not allow for local input. The actual telecenter or other facility that is built can be seen to be an extension of the text and takes on the same autopoietic character of the latter, neglecting active processes that need to occur at the local site (Toyama, 2010). The autopoiesis of the text is associated with the self-sufficiency of the ICT4D product. Rozendal discusses the lack of implementability of closed systems and associates this with the production of text such that 'the enclosed expectation about the project's future converge in the process of writing a plan' (Rozendal, 2003, p. 31).

4.2 Structuring

These self-contained ICT4D systems can have a structuring effect on the recipient communities. They can position their recipients as passive beneficiaries that need only accept the technology unquestioned. In this case, the policy text, which consists of the digital code and documentation, along with the media by which it is transmitted, make up the entire expert system. This is an example of an autopoietic text, which does not refer to any other text outside itself. It is perfectly autopoietic since the enabling code is embedded, entirely opaque and not amenable to the reader's interpretation.

These expert systems position recipient communities and developing country hosts as passive targets of technology. Ascribing no agency or autonomy to the recipients, ICT4D projects can be self-fulfilling prophecies in that the recipients learn to accept technology passively, assuming they transform the local contexts in automatic fashion. However, the reality is that recipient communities need to develop new capacities to adopt, utilize, and further develop technologies. In short, these countries need to create technology themselves (e.g., in the form of system operation and maintenance, knowledge use and development, and technology-community interface) but, failing to do so, fall into uneven terms of trade. Development theory refers to such a condition as dependency (Prebisch, 1950).

In the case at hand, dependency is deepened by the social construction of passive recipients of technology, reinforcing a world order in which technology flows only in one direction, deepening the recipient nation's subaltern status. This can occur, ironically, even in opposition to donors' best intentions to actually foster technology-driven development in the recipient communities.

4.3   Normalization

ICT4D packages transmit the norm of technology-driven development, which assumes that developing countries are deficient in knowledge capital and technology. This assumption fosters a knowledge-based economy, geared around digital empowerment.

These packages also accomplish what Adorno and Horkheimer referred to as equivalence (2002, pp. 81–2), which is the leveling of the entire field of development along a common plane of discourse – that of technology-driven development. Economies are increasingly equated with the global knowledge economy, and technology equated with digital technology. The end result is to transform recipient states into global consumers of digital commodities. Again, these results may well be completely unintended by ICT4D project proponents and emerge from the autonomous action of policy texts. Penetration of digital technology into developing country contexts creates conditions for the further penetration of digital commodities into the national economy.

These self-contained, independent packages are autopoietic texts that speak the ideology of technology. In a real sense, these knowledge systems are reified models of the physical world. An agricultural expert system may simulate an entire ecosystem and water/nutrient cycle and, in a real sense, they stand in for physical reality. But this ideological system has injurious effects on the recipient community because it deflects attention from social systems as multiple forms of capital (Bourdieu, 1986) while privileging technological capital to the exclusion of human, social, and other forms of capital. As black boxes, these packages tend to preclude necessary developments in these other forms of capital, since these autonomic expert systems assume no necessary adaptive changes on the part of the recipient – they are conservative and non-contextual. The literature speaks to ICT4D systems that are overly rigid, that overly circumscribe the allowable uses contemplated by its recipients, and that preclude adaptive actions on the part of the user (e.g., see Park, 2013).

Gurumurthy and Singh trace the history of ICT4D and argue that such systems serve to transform the poor into 'new channels of market penetration and control for global capital' (Gurumurthy and Singh, 2009, p. 5). By virtue of their often autopoietic nature, ICT4D systems can maintain an ideological approach to development that uses technology to construct passive consumers among the global poor. Through textual closure, recipient communities are prevented from taking on the capacity for technological development themselves. From the embedded code to the authoritative guidance documentation to the rigidly prescribed users' interfaces, these texts ensure that technology and technology-centered norms of development move only in one direction, from its center of authorship to its audience. Critics of ICT4D warn against the tendency to transform recipients into dependent consumers of commercial ICT products (Wade, 2002; Dillon, 2010; Díaz and Urquhart, 2012).

5.   CONCLUSION: FROM TEXTUALITY TO NARRATIVITY

Having problematized the textualist nature of policy, we now proceed to construct an alternative way of construing policy, which is to understand it as an everyday practice. This is not to be confused with an utter nontextuality, which finds policy to emerge out of completely informal processes. We need to depict policymaking in ways that do not privilege the production of policy texts. At the same time, we need to highlight the contextuality of effective policymaking (e.g., Lejano and Shankar, 2013).

   How do we conceive policy differently than a textualist system of codes authored for subsequent implementation? In this, we are helped by employing a dialectic, of sorts, wherein we identify policy elements that lie outside that of the policy text. We recall what the textualist model assumes (i.e., a set of encoded rules or plans of action and one or more authors) and ask what lies outside these. Apart from the crafters of policy, we have a host of other policy actors – implementors, funders, communicators, evaluators, recorders, the public, and the recipients of policy actions. Apart from the text of policy, there are innumerable other elements such as the material (infrastructure, funds, transportation) elements of the program being implemented; there are the means and processes of communicating; and there are the actual actions that constitute enactment of the policy. An alternative frame could be constructed by imagining a notion of policy creation that brings back in these other elements.

   The dialectic exercise is shown in Table 15.1. It seems to us that, as an alternative to the textuality of policy, we might better conceive of policy as narration.

   The model of narration exhibits the features listed on the right-hand side of Table 15.1. Unlike textualist models, which privilege an author over that of a reader, in a narrative model speakers and hearers all belong, at least potentially, to a community of narrators (Lyotard, 1984). Rather

Table 15.1   Contrasting features of the textualist and narrativist policy models

Elements of textuality	Elements of narrativity
Writing precedes speech	Speech precedes writing
Writers and readers	Community of narrators
Policy as design/implementation	Policy as performance
Design-implementation gap	Performative capacity

than policy as objective rules or facts to be realized in practice, policy is defined in varying fashion with each individual narration. Since policy texts are also associated with the word 'narrative', we use the word 'narrativity', which suggests the active sharing of story within a community of narrators (also see Lejano, 2012).

As depicted in Table 15.1, in contrast to the idea of an authoritative text (which presumes an author) and a readership, we instead have an ongoing narrative that is told and retold by each member of a narrative community. This may instill a sense of transitioning of development thinking away from technology, per se, towards the socio-technical. Lyotard, after all, contrasts narrative knowledge to the technical by describing the former as affording the right to speak and be heard to everyone in the community, as opposed to the unidirectional flow of communication in the technical model (Lyotard, 1984).

An important aspect of the narrativist model is its turning away from conservatism toward improvisation, and away from ideological stalemate toward collaboration. The thought that a good idea simply diffuses outward, away from its origin, to be wholly implanted into different contexts is problematic (Lejano, 2006). In many cases, the original text undergoes translation, modification, specification, and other alteration (Howlett and Rayner, 2008; Lejano and Shankar, 2013). Goldstein and Butler illustrate how policy can emerge from a collaborative process of narrative construction (2010). Prior work has illustrated how participatory governance almost invariably results in the blurring of formal rules and roles, including the boundaries between the creators of policy designs, implementors, and program recipients (Lejano, 2008). As Gerlak and Heikkila write 'in large collaborative settings . . . the lines between what is exogenous versus endogenous to the program become blurred' (2011, p. 20). In contrast, program rigidity and strong lines of authority inhibit collaboration (Munaretto and Huitema, 2012). The idea is to move away from the central design of blanket policy texts toward the adaptive fitting of policies to diverse local contexts (Young, 2002).

Understanding policy as narration weakens the strong notion of design (and implementation) and, instead, likens the process to one of performance (Goffman, 1950). Just as a rulemaking body performs symbolic work, field agents can be seen to perform policy in more material ways. The product of the policymaker cannot completely determine policy since his/her product may categorically differ from that of the agent in the field – but both act in concert to generate policy. To put it another way, the working institution comes into being through the interlocking action of different forms of capital (Bourdieu, 1986; see also Stokols et al., 2013). This approach focuses away from design-implementation gaps to performative capacities at each level of policymaking, thereby encouraging the empowerment of actors throughout a policy network.

This approach seems related to Majone and Wildavsky's notion of policy formulation as disposition, where policies are rough directional guides or tools that implementers then wield in producing outcomes that depend on the situation at hand and their improvisational strategies (Majone and Wildavsky, 1979). However, the narrative model diverges from their logic, which depicts policy outcomes as ostensibly emerging from a sequence beginning with authorship by policy designers and subsequent actions of the implementers. In the narrativist notion, policy is a phenomenon constituted by conjoint symbolic, material, cultural, and other actions assembled by a network of policy actors. So, while Majone and Wildavsky speak of faithfulness of implementation to policy mandates, their notion of implementation as evolution mainly understands the former as interpreting (or reshaping) original policy directives from a locus of policy design. Their concept understands policy design to subsist mainly in the world of policy ideas (which appear as policy texts), and implementation to subsist in translation (with some modification) into practice. While not linear, we find their notion of implementation to support the idea of a separation of domains, with the designers designing and implementers receiving and delivering/refashioning. 'Dispositions', in their terms, emerge from some locus of policy authority.

In our model, we seek to further eliminate necessary separations of domains and conceive of a network of policy actors, all combining differing forms of capital to enact a policy. Implementation is not so much an evolution, where, at some point in time, implementers take a thing and fashion it into a slightly (or considerably) different thing. Such a notion is very compatible with the strong mediation of policy texts between loci of policy design and implementation. In narrative, in all its plurivocity, a policy actor (say, a street-level bureaucrat) tells a story of a policy that does not need to modify that told by other policy actors (such as members of Congress). Consider, instead of a legislator from Washington,

DC, generating text, which a field agent in Boise, Idaho, subsequently receives and works and reworks, an assembly where all these policy actors congregate and exchange ideas about what the policy should be. Such a forum might not even reach a consensus around one, aggregate narrative that might subsequently be codified into a text. Rather, it is a collection of individual narratives, each an integral story of policy but, somehow, cohering and relating with each other.[8] If Majone and Wildavsky conceive of resultant policy as 'a' thing (albeit a thing reshaped by implementers), our model understands it in terms of an act of multiple narration somehow cohering together in a plurivocal manner.

To sum up, in this chapter we have sought to conceptualize the notion of textuality in policymaking and link the same to problems of policy implementation. We discuss these issues in terms of three issues related to textuality, namely superscription, structuring, and normalization. In response to the difficulties posed by a strongly textualist model of policy, we briefly sketch out an alternative model, one based on narration more than text. Future investigation should resolve to work out how such an alternative might be translated into practice.

NOTES

1. Ascribing agency to a nonhuman object, such as a text, coheres with Latour's notion of an actant as something that simply influences another actor (Latour, 2009, p. 75). But we trace our ideas about the agency of text to speech-act theory, especially Austin's idea of an utterance being performative and not simply declarative (Austin, 1975, p. 6).
2. See 'US senators rail against intelligence disclosures over NSA practices', downloaded on 18 August 2014 from http://www.theguardian.com/world/2013/jul/31/us-senate-intelligence-officials-nsa; and 'Obama decides to seek end of NSA phone records program, but many questions linger', downloaded on 18 August 2014 from http://www.huffingtonpost.com/2014/03/27/obama-nsa-phone-records_n_5044834.html.
3. The original notion of autopoiesis, deriving from biology, is that of the self-organizing, self-perpetuating system (such as a self-replicating cell). Use of the term for social systems derives from Luhmann, who describes autopoietic systems in terms of 'self-referential closure' (Luhmann, 1986), a notion we build on in the use of autopoiesis to describe systems of texts.
4. These models do appear as (scholarly) texts – e.g., Arrow and Debreu (1954).
5. Krugman, among others, points out how belief in the neoclassical model of the market economy led policymakers to attribute too high a degree of rationality to the market, thus failing to anticipate the real estate crisis and subsequent market meltdown of 2008 (Krugman, 2009).
6. Kristeva's idea of intertextuality draws much from Bakhtin's notion of dialogic works of literature, where dialogic refers to the way a literary work can inform and be informed by other works (Bakhtin, 1981). Kristeva's notion addresses semiotics more deeply and describes how meaning is not conveyed directly from author to reader but, instead, mediated by codes generated by other texts.
7. http://ict4dblog.wordpress.com/2009/01/23/participatory-design-problems-in-ict4d-the-low-self-efficacy-issue/.

8. In a model such as ours, policy directives from the legislator would not function as a necessary reference point, and the reader will see how weakening this referencing leads to a weakening of textuality in policy. We should also add that our model is not meant to supplant other models of the policy process, no more than Majone and Wildavsky's model supplants the stage model of policy, but, rather, exists in conversation with them.

REFERENCES

Ackerman, S. (2012). 'Cash, and time, runs out for Afghanistan's Wi-Fi City'. Wired.com, 14 May, http://www.wired.com/dangerroom/2012/05/jlink/all/1 (accessed 5 June 2012).

Adorno, T.W. and M. Horkheimer (2002). *Dialectic of Enlightenment*. Trans. Edmund Jephcott. Stanford, CA: Stanford University Press.

Anokwa, Y. et al. (2009). 'Open source data collection in the developing world'. *Computer*, **42** (10), 97–99.

Arrow, K.J. and G. Debreu (1954). 'Existence of an equilibrium for a competitive economy'. *Econometrica: Journal of the Econometric Society*, **22** (3), 265–290.

Austin, J.L. (1975). *How to Do Things with Words* (Vol. 1955). Oxford: Oxford University Press.

Bakhtin, M. (1981). *The Dialogic Imagination*. Trans. Caryl Emerson and Michael Holquist. Austin, TX: University of Texas Press.

Bardach, E. (1977). *The Implementation Game: What Happens after a Bill Becomes a Law*. Cambridge, MA: The MIT Press.

Barrett, S.M. (2004). 'Implementation studies: Time for a revival? Personal reflections on 20 years of implementation studies'. *Public Administration*, **82** (2), 249–262.

Barthes, Roland (1974). *S/Z*. Trans. Richard Miller. New York: Noonday.

Bass, Julian M. and Richard Heeks (2011). 'Changing computing curricular in African universities: Evaluating progress and challenges via design-reality gap analysis'. *Electronic Journal of Information Systems in Developing Countries*, **48** (5), 1–39.

Berkes, F. (2007). 'Community-based conservation in a globalized world'. *Proceedings of the National Academy of Sciences*, **104** (39), 15188–15193.

Berman, P. (1980). 'Thinking about programmed and adaptive implementation matching strategies to situations'. In H. Ingram and D. Mann (eds), *Why Policies Succeed or Fail*. Beverly Hills, CA: Sage.

Bourdieu, P. (1977). *Outline of a Theory of Practice*. Cambridge: Cambridge University Press.

Bourdieu, P. (1986). 'The forms of capital'. In J.G. Richardson (ed.), *Handbook of Theory and Research for the Sociology of Education*. New York: Greenwood Press, pp. 241–258.

Díaz Andrade, A. and C. Urquhart (2012). 'Unveiling the modernity bias: A critical examination of the politics of ICT4D'. *Information Technology for Development*, **18** (4), 281–292.

Dillon, R.S. (2010). 'Respect for persons, identity, and information technology'. *Ethics and Information Technology*, **12** (1), 17–28.

Elmore, R.F. (1985). *Forward and Backward Mapping: Reversible Logic in the Analysis of Public Policy*. The Netherlands: Springer, pp. 33–70.

Fischer, F. (2005). *Evaluating Public Policy*. Singapore: Wadsworth Publishing/Cengage.

Fortune, R.D.M.M. and R.C.G. Enger (2005). 'Violence against women and the role of religion'. VAWnet: The National Online Resource Center on Violence Against Women.

Foucault, M. (1981). 'The order of discourse'. In R. Young (ed.), *Untying the Text: A Poststructural Anthology*. Boston, MA: Routledge and Kegan Paul, pp. 48–78. Fountain, Jane E. (2001). *Building the Virtual State Information Technology and Institutional Change*. Washington, DC: Brookings Institution Press.

Gerlak, A. and T. Heikkila (2011). 'Building a theory of learning in collaboratives: Evidence from the Everglades Restoration Program'. *Journal of Public Administration Research and Theory*, **21** (4), 619–644.

Gichoya, D. (2005). 'Factors affecting the successful implementation of ICT projects in government'. *The Electronic Journal of e-Government*, **3** (4), 175–184, available online at www.ejeg.com.

Goffman, E. (1950). *The Presentation of Self in Everyday Life*. New York: Doubleday.

Goggin, M.L., A.O.M. Bowman, J.P. Lester and L. O'Toole (1990). *Implementation Theory and Practice: Toward a Third Generation*. Glenview, IL: Scott, Foresman/Little, Brown Higher Education.

Goldstein, B. and W. Butler (2010). 'The U.S. Fire Learning Network: Providing a narrative framework for restoring ecosystems, professions, and institutions'. *Society & Natural Resources*, **23**, 1–17.

Grameenphone (2014) http://www.grameenphone.com/, accessed 5 January 2014.

Gurumurthy, A. and P.J. Singh (2009). 'ICTD – is it a new species of development'. IT for Change Perspective Paper. Bangalore: IT for Change. Retrieved 27 April 2014 from http://www.itforchange.net/sites/default/files/ITfC/ICTD_Species_of_Devlp_Ed.pdf.

Heeks, R. (2002). 'Information systems and developing countries: Failure, success, and local improvisations'. *The Information Society: An International Journal*, **18** (2), 101–112.

Hjern, B. and C. Hull (1982). 'Implementation research as empirical constitutionalism'. *European Journal of Political Research*, **10** (2), 105–115.

Howard, J., C. Simms and E. Simanis (2001). 'What works: n-Logue's rural connectivity model'. A Digital Dividend Study by the World Resources Institute, pp. 1–25.

Howlett, M. and J. Rayner (2008). 'Third generation policy diffusion studies and the analysis of policy mixes: Two steps forward and one step back?' *Journal of Comparative Policy Analysis: Research and Practice*, **10** (4), 385–402.

Hull, C.J. and B. Hjern (1987). *Helping Small Firms Grow: An Implementation Approach*. London: Croom Helm.

Hupe, P.L. (2011). 'The thesis of incongruent implementation: Revisiting Pressman and Wildavsky'. *Public Policy and Administration*, **26**, 63–80.

Jacobs, J. (1961). *The Death and Life of Great American Cities*. New York: Random House.

Johnson, D. (2007). 'Evaluation of a single radio rural mesh network in South Africa'. In International Conference on Information and Communication Technologies and Development, Bangalore, India, 15–16 December, IEEE, pp. 1–9.

Kaushik, P.D. and N. Singh (2004). 'Information technology and broad-based development: Preliminary lessons from North India'. *World Development*, **32** (4), 591–607.

Keene, C. (2007). 'Development projects that didn't work: The perils of narrow approaches to complex situations'. Globalhood Paper, Globalhood, New York. Retrieved 7 June 2012 from http://globalhood.org/articles/briefingnotes/Development_Projects_That_Didnt_Work.pdf.

Kristeva, J. (1980). *Desire in Language: A Semiotic Approach to Literature and Art*. New York: Columbia University Press.

Krugman, P. (2009). 'How did economists get it so wrong?' *New York Times*, 2 September.

Latour, Bruno (1987). *Science in Action*. Cambridge, MA: Harvard University Press.

Latour, Bruno (2009). *Politics of Nature*. Cambridge, MA: Harvard University Press.

Lejano, Raul (2006). *Frameworks for Policy Analysis: Merging Text and Context*. New York: Routledge.

Lejano, Raul (2008). 'Technology and institutions: A critical appraisal of GIS in the planning domain'. *Science, Technology & Human Values*, **33**, 653–678.

Lejano, Raul (2012). 'Postpositivism and the policy process'. In E. Araral et al. (eds), *Routledge Handbook of Public Policy*, New York: Routledge, Chapter 8.

Lejano, R.P. and Ingram, H. (2007). 'Place-based conservation: Lessons from the Turtle Islands'. *Environment: Science and Policy for Sustainable Development*, **49** (9), 18–27.

Lejano, R. and S. Shankar (2013). 'The contextualist turn and schematics of institutional fit: Theory and a case study from Southern India'. *Policy Sciences*, **46** (1), 83–102.

Lejano, R.P. and D. Stokols (2013). 'Social ecology, sustainability, and economics'. *Ecological Economics*, **89**, 1–6.

Lejano, R., M. Ingram and H. Ingram (2013). *The Power of Narrative in Environmental Networks*. Cambridge, MA: The MIT Press.

Luhmann, N. (1986). 'The autopoiesis of social systems'. In F. Geyer and J. van der Zouwen (eds), *Sociocybernetic Paradoxes*. London: Sage, pp. 172–192.

Lyotard, J.F. (1984). *The Postmodern Condition: A Report on Knowledge* (Vol. 10). Minneapolis, MN: University of Minnesota Press.

Majone, G. and A. Wildavsky (1979). 'Implementation as evolution'. In J.L. Pressman and A. Wildavsky (eds), *Implementation* (3rd edition, expanded). Berkeley, CA: University of California Press, pp. 163–80.

Matland, R.E. (1995). 'Synthesizing the implementation literature: The ambiguity-conflict model of policy implementation'. *Journal of Public Administration Research and Theory*, **5**, 145–174.

Maynard-Moody, S., M. Musheno and D. Palumbo (1990). 'Street-wise social policy: Resolving the dilemma of street-level influence and successful implementation'. *The Western Political Quarterly*, 833–848.

Mazmanian, D.A. and P.A. Sabatier (1983). *Policy Implementation. The Encyclopedia of Policy Studies*. New York: Marcel Dekker, pp. 143–169.

McLuhan, Marshall (1964). *Understanding Media: The Extensions of Man*. New York: Signet Books.

Munaretto, S. and D. Huitema (2012). 'Adaptive comanagement in the Venice Lagoon? An analysis of current water and environmental management practices and prospects for change'. *Ecology and Society*, **17** (2), 19.

Murray, C.J., J. Abraham, M.K. Ali, M. Alvarado, C. Atkinson, L.M. Baddour and H.R. Gutierrez (2013). 'The state of US health, 1990–2010: Burden of diseases, injuries, and risk factors'. *Jama*, **310** (6), 591–606.

Ostrom, E. (2008). 'The challenge of common-pool resources'. *Environment*, **50** (4), 8–21.

O'Toole, L.J. (2000). 'Research on policy implementation: Assessment and prospects'. *Journal of Public Administration Research and Theory*, **10** (2), 263–288.

Park, S.J. (2013). 'Opening the Black Box of ICT4D: advancing our understanding of ICT4D partnerships'. Doctoral dissertation, University of California, Irvine.

Patterson, D.J., S.E. Sim and T. Aiyelokun (2009). 'Overcoming blind spots in interaction design: A case study in designing for African AIDS orphan care communities'. *Information Technologies and International Development*, **5** (4), 75–88.

Prebisch, R. (1950). 'The economic development of Latin America and its principal problems'. UN document no. E/CN.12/89/Rev.1. Lake Success, New York: United Nations.

Pressman, J. and A. Wildavsky (1979). *Implementation: How Great Expectations in Washington are Dashed in Oakland: Or, Why it's Amazing that Federal Programs Work at All, This Being a Saga of the Economic Development Administration as Told by Two Sympathetic Observers Who Seek to Build Morals on a Foundation of Ruined Hopes*. Berkeley, CA: University of California Press.

Prins, G. and S. Rayner (2007). 'Time to ditch Kyoto'. *Nature*, **449** (7165), 973–975.

Rapley, John (1996). *Understanding Development: Theory and Practice in the Third World*. Boulder, CO: Lynne Rienner.

Ricoeur, P. (1981). *Hermeneutics and the Human Sciences: Essays on Language, Action and Interpretation*. Cambridge: Cambridge University Press.

Rozendal, R. (2003). 'Cultural and political factors in the design of ICT4D projects in developing countries'. Research Report, International Institute for Communication and Development, The Netherlands.

Sabatier, P. (2008). 'Top-down and bottom-up approaches to implementation research: A critical analysis and suggested synthesis'. *Journal of Public Policy*, **6**, 21–48.

Sabatier P. and D.A. Mazmanian (1979). 'The conditions of effective implementation: A guide to accomplishing policy objectives'. *Policy Analysis*, **5** (4), 481–504.

Saetren, H. (2014). Implementing the third generation research paradigm in policy implementation research: An empirical assessment'. *Public Policy and Administration*, **29** (2), 84–105.

Scalia, A. and B.A. Garner (2012). *Reading Law: The Interpretation of Legal Texts*. St Paul, MN: Thomson/West.

Scheberle, D. (2004). *Federalism and Environmental Policy: Trust and the Politics of Implementation*. Washington, DC: Georgetown University Press.

Schneider, A. and H. Ingram (1997). *Policy Design for Democracy*. Lawrence, KS: University of Kansas.

Scott, J.C. (1998). *Seeing Like a State: How Certain Schemes to Improve the Human Condition Have Failed*. New Haven, CT: Yale University Press.

Scott, W.R. (2001). *Institutions and Organizations*. 2nd edn, Thousand Oaks, CA: Sage.

Stokols, D., R.P. Lejano and J. Hipp (2013). 'Enhancing the resilience of human-environment systems: A social ecological perspective'. *Ecology and Society*, **18** (1), 7.

Toyama, K. (2010). 'Can technology end poverty?' *New Boston Review*, November/December 2010. Downloaded on 27 April 2014 from http://new.bostonreview.net/BR35.6/toyama.php.

Valentinov, V. (2014). 'K. William Kapp's theory of social costs: A Luhmannian interpretation'. *Ecological Economics*, **97**, 28–33.

Van Dijk, T.A. (ed.) (1997). *Discourse Studies: A Multidisciplinary Introduction*. London: Sage.

Van Meter, D. and C. Van Horn (1975). 'The policy implementation process: A conceptual framework'. *Administration and Society*, **6**, 445–488.

Wade, R.H. (2002). 'Bridging the digital divide: New route to development or new form of dependency'. *Global Governance*, **8**, 443.

Yanow, D. (1993). 'The communication of policy meanings: Implementation as interpretation and text'. *Policy Sciences*, **26** (1), 41–61.

Young, O.R. (2002). *The Institutional Dimensions of Environmental Change: Fit, Interplay, and Scale*. Cambridge, MA: The MIT Press.

16 Co-production and public policy: evidence, uncertainty and socio-materiality
Heidrun Åm

INTRODUCTION

Considering the reliance of regulatory policy making on scientific knowledge and technocratic decision making, we can presume that policy making is in trouble when it faces 'wicked problems' that are in any way emerging and that are either encompassing and contested (such as climate change), morally loaded (such as embryo research), or uncertain and difficult to grasp (such as nanomaterials). For example, the regulation of technoscience is characterized by strong demands to avoid the failures of the past and to reestablish trust in public authorities. Consequently, efforts on the governance of new technoscientific developments, such as nanotechnology and synthetic biology, tend to occur early and proactively (Renn and Roco 2006; Murashov and Howard 2009; Zhang et al. 2011). The result is that regulatory discussions on emerging technologies take place in a dynamic governance landscape in which questions of definition are not yet settled and facts on environmental, safety, and health risks or socioeconomic consequences have not yet been established. How do governing bodies discuss and decide sociotechnical issues under such uncertain, controversial, or complex conditions?

In this chapter, I use nanotechnology regulations to illustrate the difficulties of policy making under conditions of uncertainty. In the case of nanotechnology, it is not even clear what the object of regulation is, which makes it difficult to determine what has to be regulated, or why. Nanotechnology has become an umbrella term for a whole range of scientific disciplines and technologies (Williams 2006), and because it has all along encompassed futuristic visions and promises, the term has essentially been over-filled (Wullweber 2008).[1] At this point in our world, in 2014, consumers constantly encounter nanotechnology products in their daily lives, be it in shoe sprays, paints, electric gadgets, or diverse coatings. Compared to their predecessors, these products can offer improved properties, such as dirt resistance, waterproofing, strength, or endurance. They may or may not be called nano. And they may or may not have adverse effects due to changed material properties at the nanoscale. Currently, the nanotechnology regulatory landscape is marked by anticipatory, flexible, open guidelines and recommendations, such as codes of conduct. Considering that it is uncertain whether there are risks at all, it is astounding that regulators and industry companies nonetheless have set in place these proactive, anticipatory regulatory frameworks. How can governance actors at multiple sites decide on regulating sociotechnical objects when they cannot predict their scope, let alone grasp or understand the full extent of the scope or the object, and why would they set out on such an endeavor?

Conventional approaches to policy analysis fall short in explaining such an emerging technoscientific issue that lacks stable reference points (Haddad et al. 2013: 108), such as actor interests or calculable risks, on which an analysis could hang. Also, risk assessment is not a straightforward, technical process that generates objective, neutral knowledge that is sought after; rather, it is a value-loaded and political enterprise that requires human decisions and interpretations both on input and output. In detailed sociological and anthropological studies of research practices, Science and Technology Studies (STS) has repeatedly shown that science is as much a sociocultural activity as a technical enterprise (Fischer 1998: 132). This is most true for regulatory science because regulatory decisions on sociotechnical issues are taken early, when consensus among scientists is often fragile (Jasanoff 1987: 197). Policy analysis that cannot account for this uncertainty has a problematic and consistent analytical deficit because policy making today takes place in a dynamic world in which new facts constantly arise. Therefore, policy making under conditions of uncertainty benefits from applying a critical, STS-informed approach to policy analysis.

Employing poststructuralist discourse theory, I argue in this chapter that a logic of pre-emption formed a condition of possibility for anticipatory regulations to emerge in the nanofield. But in order for us to understand how regulation came to take this particular form, analysis also must account for the role of technical practices (e.g., risk assessments) and material objects (e.g., nanomaterials) in subverting and shaping regulatory policy making. Thus, I will highlight that Critical Policy Studies (CPS) can benefit from combining their approaches with insights from STS. Hence, I put forward an argument for a co-productionist perspective to policy analysis. In this essay, I will show that the pre-emptive risk regime put in place for nanotechnology challenges regulatory policy making because nanotechnology dislocates evidence-based paradigms. The emerging solution for this emerging problem cannot be explained without taking into account nanotechnology's ambiguity. Methodologically, this chapter is based on empirical material from extensive interviews and document analyses conducted in 2007–2009 in the UK and Germany, with scientists, politicians, administrations, and NGOs.[2] I also draw on a secondary analysis of existing literature on nanotechnology regulation.

A CO-PRODUCTIONIST PERSPECTIVE TO POLICY ANALYSIS

Messy policy problems increasingly become the rule rather than the exception in policy making. For example, while environmental impact analysis into the 1970s basically consisted of simple indicators of environmental pollution (i.e., water tests and comparisons to the previous year or to neighboring rivers), environment agencies now deal with hundreds of widespread pollutants that do not have scientifically determinable safe levels of exposure (Jasanoff 1992). In addition, existing methods of comparing indicators do not necessarily work with technoscientific objects such as genetically modified crops, which might appear to be similar to natural crops grown from conventional seed (Waterton and Wynne 2006). Thus, regulatory policy making increasingly takes place in a context in which it is not clear who demands regulation, what the thing is that actually is to be regulated and why, and how and on what grounds regulations could be adopted. Obviously, 'wicked problems' of emerging technosciences, such as nanotechnology, challenge straightforward, scientific approaches to regulatory policy making and thus any straightforward analysis of these processes. Set against the multiplicities and uncertainties that mark today's governance landscape, we need theoretical approaches that make sense of uncertainty and acknowledge contingency and hegemony in the production of regulatory knowledge.

Generally, policy making is based on an ideal of evidence base in which 'science speaks truth to power' (Wildavsky 1979), but in this new context, evidence-based policy is no longer effective. Nevertheless, this ascendancy of evidence (Solesbury 2002) is an important contextualization particularly of the UK's nanotechnology politics where any policy debate was first and foremost marked by a strong demand for an evidence base in the Labour Government's modernization agenda (Parsons 2002). Regarding policy making, evidence is often seen as research-based knowledge that is available, true, and valid (Solesbury 2002: 94). Such evidence is considered constitutive to policy formulations. That is particularly true for regulatory sciences, a branch of public science purposed with conducting scientific research and analysis to regulate risk to health, safety, and the environment (Jasanoff 1987: 200ff, 1990, 1992: 196). In an idealized model of regulatory science, which is based on a linear model of policy making, representatives of 'the public' would articulate regulatory demands (Hood et al. 2001: 64). The government apparatus would subsequently launch a risk analysis and, depending on the scientific input generated, regulations would then be adopted (or not). However, such a perspective takes a shortcut concerning what counts as evidence and how this evidence is produced.

Regarding the production of knowledge, policy analysts can learn much from STS. Since Frank Fischer and Herbert Gottweis have been pointing this out since the 1990s, it is perhaps now time to explicate the mutually reinforcing explanatory power of CPS and STS more systematically. The notion of co-production can be a particular fruitful one for CPS. A co-productionist perspective makes available resources and concepts for thinking systematically about the processes of sense making through which human beings – and thus politicians, policy analysts, and lay publics alike – tackle a technoscientific world (Jasanoff 2006: 38). Co-productionist thinking acknowledges that 'the products of sciences, both cognitive and material, embody beliefs not only about how the world is, but also how it ought to be' (Jasanoff 2005: 19) and that 'natural and social orders, in short, are produced at one and the same time – or, more precisely, coproduced' (ibid.).

In fact, the notion of co-production has been successfully introduced to CPS in the last years (see, e.g., Elgert 2010; Grek 2014). These studies tend to focus on one important aspect of co-production, namely administrative, political institutions as sites of co-production that augment and cement their power by producing and deploying knowledge. Thus, these kinds of co-productionist studies point to the entanglement of knowledge and power and to the simultaneous making of political order and knowledge (see also Miller 2006; Waterton and Wynne 2006). While acknowledging the importance of these studies, STS approaches, gathered around the term 'co-production,' not only point to the social in the scientific, but they also regard the scientific in the social. Thus, they consider the agency of technoscientific objects and practices in the ways in which society is ordered (Jasanoff 2006). I suggest in this chapter that the latter also deserves more attention by CPS.

The role of the material is often disregarded in CPS (in the same way that STS tends to disregard questions of hegemony). Therefore, a co-productionist perspective is helpful in cases such as nanotechnology regulation because it helps CPS to bring 'the material' in. Co-production shows the mutually reinforcing interdependency of the production of scientific and other forms of knowledge, technical practices, and material objects in shaping, sustaining, subverting, or transforming (Jasanoff 2006: 4), for example, regulatory policies, *without positing unidirectional causal arrows from one domain to the other* (ibid.: 30). Hence, co-production is a necessary reminder for critical policy analysts of the role of matter in the midst of discourse. Co-productionist thinking investigates the connections between so-called technoscientific objects (such as synthetic nanoparticles) and social objects (e.g., experts or governments) (ibid.: 23) and makes explicit the connections between practices of science and those of politics and culture (ibid.: 18). From this perspective, policy actors (e.g., scientists, industry, or governmental agencies), policy ideas or culture, and nanotechnology itself (i.e., scientific practices, measurement techniques, or material objects) co-produce nanotechnology regulations.

In fact, CPS and STS have many commonalities. An important concept within a co-productionist perspective is 'boundary drawing,' which calls attention to

> the negotiable boundaries of many things whose hardness we ordinarily take for granted, such as facts, institutions, social roles, and even inanimate objects [. . .] showing that much of what we know through science or use as technology is produced and given solidity through socially accredited systems of rhetoric and practice. (Jasanoff 1995: xv)

In this respect, a focus on co-production allows the researcher to study not only the emergence of technoscientific objects but also their emergence as *political* objects similar to CPS's concept of demarcation. In other words, technoscientific phenomena such as nanotechnology or human embryonic stem cells are transformed into something 'politically signified' (Gottweis 2012: 230–231). This occurs through processes of boundary drawing or demarcation, and these processes of transformation merit the attention of policy analysts. In policy situations marked by uncertainty and mess, analysts need to focus attention on how order is established (Fischer and Gottweis 2012; Prainsack and Wahlberg 2013). For example, a critical approach to policy analysis can attend to how language and discourses endow scientific phenomena and social, political, and economic contexts with meaning (Gottweis 1998: 3). Discursive devices, such as metaphors, frames, narratives, and stories, can be powerful elements that bring order and stability into the complex, contradictory, and uncertain world of politics (ibid: 31–32), which earns them attention in both STS and CPS.

Nevertheless, to say that nanotechnology regulations are co-produced does not explain much. Poststructuralist discourse theory (one perspective within CPS) has drawn our attention to power struggles in the wider discursive context, hegemony, and existing regimes ('the normal way of doing things'). These are often disregarded in case studies of STS much similar to how CPS tends to disregard the material. Naturally, the social practices analyzed on the micro-level in case studies are intertwined with its discursive context. Social practices are largely repetitive, ongoing, routinized activities that we perform without much reflection but that nevertheless contribute to reproducing the wider systems of social relations (Glynos and Howarth 2007: 104). Normally, co-productive practices of ordering the messy realities of sociotechnical issues are neither reflected upon nor spelled out, so it falls to the critical policy analyst to shed light on them (Howarth 2000: 11–12). It is only when the normal way of doing things fails that the contingency of social practices comes to the fore and the logics informing the (re)production of a regime become questioned. Such a moment can be thought of as a dislocation, which occurs when something cannot be accommodated by pre-existing categories or ways of being. Thus, a moment of dislocation is a moment in which routines are disrupted (Howarth 2000: 111ff; Hajer 2009: 5). In such moments, political logics that make it possible to explain why social practices or regimes were instituted and contested (Glynos and Howarth 2007: 106) come into view. For the policy analyst, such moments can be a great advantage because they bring the contingencies and underlying struggles of hegemonic ways of policy making to the fore, opening our eyes to the fact that the normal way of doing things was not always, but once became, authoritative (Hajer 2009).[3]

In sum, the many similarities between CPS and STS need to be better recognized in the same way, as both can learn from their differences. In the remainder of the chapter, I examine nanotechnology regulations from a combination of the co-productionist perspective and poststructuralist discourse theory as outlined above. I begin in the following section with showing how nanotechnology became politically signified.

A PRE-EMPTIVE RISK REGIME

As mentioned earlier, proactive regulation taking the form of codes of conduct has been put in place for nanotechnology. A move to self-regulation and policing (e.g., by safety inspectors) has characterized the regulation of industries and technologies since the 1990s (Andersen and Sørensen 1992), but outstanding in nanotechnology regulation is the anticipatory aspect. Until the late 1970s, *reactive* regulations were most common. That is, regulations were formulated only after hazards were observed in a product. In contrast, attempts for proactive regulations attempt to predict previously unforeseen hazards (Tait and Levidow 1992). Particularly in the context of environmental policy, 'anticipatory policy making' signified the move in the late 1970s and early 1980s toward a 'more pro-active environmental policy regime' (O'Riordan 1989). The adoption of proactive, precautionary approaches is commonly justified on the grounds of complexity or uncertainty (Tait and Levidow 1992: 223). The Precautionary Principle was notably introduced in technology governance in Germany in 1976. In today's regulatory policies, we see a precautionary approach, for example in certain areas in the field of bio-technology around genetically modified organisms (GMOs).

However, debates on nanotechnology regulations are fundamentally different because with nanotechnology it is not even clear what the thing to be regulated actually is. Nanotechnology drew regulatory discussions 'from products and manufacturing processes to research or[,] even further upstream[,] to visionary declarations of the ambition to interfere with nature in novel ways' (Nordmann 2010: 32). Examples of such upstream regulatory discussions are attempts in the European Union to establish regulatory standards for nanofoods or discuss regulatory demands around nanomedicine that surpassed current technical capabilities (ibid.). How did this happen?

When it comes to nanotechnology, policy makers did not add risk to the agenda because they saw a 'real' threat by a certain product on the market or in a particular stream of research development; rather, nano-technology became linked with risks by policy makers drawing equiva-lences to past experiences (asbestos and diesel particulate as examples of late recognition of risk, and GMO protests as examples of early public resistance). So, the threat or risk to be contained was related not only to the science but also to the public. An important sociopolitical context for policy making in the nanotechnology field is the legacy of the controversy of science, technology, and risk, in particular in GMO and mad cow disease (Pidgeon and Rogers-Hayden 2007: 194). Specifically, promoters of nanotechnology were 'prone to project nano-phobia, and this projec-tion can become a phobia in itself, a nanophobia-phobia' (Rip 2006: 358). In other words, governance actors were scared off by the *prospect* of public protests against nanotechnology. For example, an interviewee from the Association of Chemical Engineers (VCI) in Germany recalled the social practices of how the VCI took strategic regulatory action on nanotechnology as follows:

> That nanotechnology became a big issue in the VCI originated from the com-munications department, which drew our attention to reports in the media occurring now and then in the year 2004 reporting that nanomaterials might be dangerous. The communications department pointed out that we might again have such a technology . . . like a cascade: nuclear technology, biotechnology, nanotechnology.
> So, we decided in the presidium that [. . .] we would coordinate the work,

attend stakeholder dialogues, participate in citizen conferences, and we decided to initiate regular roundtables to which we invited the press. This developed because we wanted to do it right this time with nanotechnology. (Interview material: VCI representative)

This central notion of getting it right was prevalent in both the UK and German cases and covers two dimensions. On the one hand, the potential for environmental catastrophes with nanotechnologies should be prevented, in contrast to previous failures with asbestos or accidents at nuclear plants. On the other hand, the notion of 'getting it right the first time' also refers to avoiding public resistance to new technologies. Globally, nanotechnology is largely regarded as offering an opportunity to apply 'learnt lessons' (see, e.g., Balbus et al. 2006; Einsiedel and Goldenberg 2006; Mehta 2006; David and Thompson 2008). With nanotechnologies, the goal was to act proactively.

That state elites were gripped by fears of public protests was a condition of possibility for anticipatory actions to occur. I suggest that efforts of anticipatory governance were driven by a political logic of pre-emption (Åm 2011). This political logic is carried by the assumptions that risks and conflicts, such as public resistance, shall be anticipated and settled before they even emerge. Although the logic of pre-emption has certain commonalities with precaution and preparedness (e.g., guiding action into the future) (Anderson 2010), pre-emption differs from anticipation and precaution in its focus on potential audiences, that is, in its attempts at *maintaining trust* and *pre-empting conflict*. At the same time, of course, this meant that a structure of vigilance (Gammel et al. 2010) was enacted that could react in the event that nanotechnology risks were identified. Thus, the anticipatory system pre-empts risks of accidents. Together, potential pitfalls should be pre-emptively met to guarantee the development of the technology, which was now recast as responsible development.

In the next section, I detail how governance actors approached this issue. In doing so, I focus for matters of feasibility on risk governance. Thus, I do not go into widespread efforts for public engagement that governments and stakeholders fostered early on. However, the reader should keep in mind that the regulatory discussion is a variant of a new adaptive governance regime that actually is supposed to be more about democratization of science policy making than about risk governance.

REGULATING NANOTECHNOLOGY? A 'WICKED PROBLEM'

Since the question of nanotechnology regulation has been raised, policy discussions have been primarily framed in terms of removing this scientific uncertainty. That is, demands for risk assessment and assessment techniques have been articulated (Bowman et al. 2013: 4), and the overarching demand became to close so-called knowledge gaps. Although enough is known to indicate some risk (Oberdörster et al. 2005; Maynard et al. 2006; Nel et al. 2006; Lin 2007: 106; Preston et al. 2010: 14) – for example, the element gold, which is yellow and inert as a bulk material, becomes red and toxic (Clift 2006: 49) in a certain particulate form – the precise nature and extent of these risks and the toxicology of most engineered nanomaterials remain unknown (Preston et al. 2010: 14; Reichow and Dorbech-Jung 2013: 85). Reacting within its dominant frame of evidence-based policy making, the actions set in place focused on collecting evidence. We can see this in the country cases already mentioned – both the UK and Germany commissioned studies on nanotechnology in 2003.

In the UK, the Royal Society (RS) and the Royal Academy of Engineering (RAEng) were commissioned to undertake such a study on nanotechnology. Such studies usually begin with a call for evidence. Indeed, the RS/RAEng received written evidence, organized oral evidence sessions, and held meetings and workshops in the process of producing its final nanoreport. Public engagement was part of RE/RAEng's evidence gathering. The final report problematized nanotechnology within risk governance and within a discourse of ethical, legal, and social aspects (ELSA) of technology development. From the first regulatory discussions on nanomaterials – such as the one that took the form of a workshop in the course of the RS/RAEng evidence gathering – 'filling the knowledge gap' became a central request in UK nanotechnology politics. For example, the government established a Nanotechnology Research Coordination Group (NRCG) to coordinate and plan risk research into nanotechnologies.

In Germany, the Office for Technology Assessment of the German Bundestag[4] (TAB) was commissioned with a task similar to that of the RS/RAEng. In the aftermath of this report, three governmental agencies[5] took the lead in driving nanotechnology regulatory policies in Germany by demanding a coherent strategy as well as funding risk research on nanoparticles. The main aim of such a strategy was to identify what kind of risk assessment on nanotechnology was needed from the perspective of the agencies. The three agencies stressed the uncertainties about nanomaterials' behavior and demanded that these knowledge gaps be closed. They articulated an urgent need to conduct risk research concerning measurement techniques of nanoparticles, exposure to nanomaterials, toxicology of nanomaterials via oral intake, and to determine accumulation and persistence of nanomaterials in the environment.

In both countries, nanomaterials – like any new materials – already fall under existing chemical regulations, waste doctrines, water directives, and occupational health and safety rules, to name a few existing regulatory frameworks. However, existing regulations face substantial challenges when confronted with nanotechnologies. Major existing regulatory schemes applying to nanomaterials, such as the EU's chemical regulation, known as REACH,[6] or the United States' Toxic Substances Control Act (TSCA), are good starting points for illustrating the prevalent issues. Both legislations require strict risk assessments for *novel* materials, whereas *existing* substances can be registered more quickly. For nanomaterials, the question emerges whether a smaller form, for example, of the element silver, is a new or an existing material. For a few nanomaterials, such as carbon nanotubes, the current regulatory approach is fine, but the vast majority of nanomaterials would not trigger regulatory demands and therefore would probably evade scrutiny because the molecular identity of nanochemicals is often the same as their macro counterparts (Preston et al. 2010: 16). Thus, current regulations ignore origins of novelty other than substance identity, but even if the materials are common, their manipulation at the nanoscale might create unexpected results (Lin 2007: 109).

How then to identify nanotechnology risk, if you cannot identify nanotechnology? Most conventional triggers for regulation fail. Most important, nanomaterials might not trigger regulation because of a lack of definition. For the reason of definition, it is also difficult to apply a precautionary approach. There is a wide gap between embracing precaution as a principle and applying it concretely: which products would precautionary regulations control if manufacturers themselves do not define their products as nano? Apart from that, the REACH and TSCA legislations operate with regulation triggers based on thresholds and exposure levels. But nanomaterials – due to their smallness – would not trigger regulation on the basis of weight or volume (Ludlow 2008: 188). In addition, regulators lack the risk information they need in order to define thresholds required to take regulatory action on nanomaterials (Marchant et al. 2008: 4). Thus, even if regulations may apply 'in principle' to nanotechnology, this would not necessarily occur 'in practice' (Ludlow 2008: 188).

NANOTECHNOLOGY DISLOCATES EVIDENCE-BASED REGULATORY PARADIGMS

We see that policy actors encountered difficulty when attempting to govern nanotechnologies. Their dominant way of sense-making of the problem was that there were knowledge gaps that remained to be filled. This policy story captured and ordered for them the uncertain, messy challenge of nanotechnology. Operating within this logic of evidence gathering, regulators perceived their only alternative to be postponing nano-specific restrictive regulatory action until sufficient evidence became available. In other words, because knowledge was seen as a prerequisite for acting, decision making on regulation was liable to be put on hold. To a great extent, this evidence-based thinking has persisted ever since (Bowman et al. 2013: 4). However, as I discuss below, this way of thinking has also become profoundly challenged.

The greatest problem is that these 'knowledge gaps' are destined to persist for some time. Often nanomaterials are defined as materials at the nanoscale, but the 100nm boundary is somewhat arbitrary: material properties might not differ very much between 98nm and 110nm. Besides, materials at the nanoscale can be naturally occurring (as opposed to them being technologically manufactured). In addition, material properties depend not only on size but also on form, function, and shape (Kermisch 2012: 34). The possible toxicity of nanomaterials depends on the size, shape, and route of exposure, as well as on manufacturing processes and facilities, and the connection between exposure and toxicity is uncertain (ibid: 35; Ludlow 2008: 184). But even today there exist few validated measurement techniques (Reichow and Dorbeck-Jung 2013: 88). Generally, one might say that current measurement techniques are not sensitive enough (Kermisch 2012: 35), so nanomaterials might defy such testing (Lin 2007: 17) or not be consistently picked up (Ludlow 2008: 184). In fact, the uncertainties are so comprehensive that researchers would not necessarily know that analytical techniques are inappropriate (Ludlow 2008: 189). Therefore, risk assessment has not yet produced sufficient data that could form the foundation for nanotechnology regulatory discussions, and it is by no means certain that generation of the required data will even be possible.

These technical details show how the construction of scientific evidence fails. Indeed, the uncertainties connected to intervening at the nanoscale are so pervasive that it is not even certain which questions to ask, which methods to develop, and in which context they might apply. Thus, *evidence-based regulatory policy making is confronted with a dislocation of its practices in the case of nanotechnology* because the consequences of human intervention at the nanoscale might as well be unimaginable, unthinkable, or impossible to predict (Nordmann 2010). Nanomaterials escape the practices of measurement and hence the practices of gathering the kind of evidence on which policies should be based. However, if technocratic rationality and scientific knowledge are considered the privileged ground on which to make decisions, where are we if they fail to deliver (Schön 1973 after Parsons 2002)?

AN EMERGING SOLUTION TO AN EMERGING PROBLEM

When policy paradigms are dislocated, policy actors have to learn in action and to try out new alternatives. After the TAB report in Germany or the RS/RAEng report in the UK, policy makers initiated public engagement exercises, drafted strategies for risk research, and established governance networks, such as the NanoCommission in Germany or, in the UK, the Nanotechnology Issue Dialogue Group (NIDG). As a way out of this stalemate, which was triggered by the impossibility of providing the evidence needed, some of these new governance actors challenged the necessity of an evidence base of policy making. Instead, policy actors and (regulatory) scholars voiced the idea that evidence does not necessarily need to support regulation, as one research participant explained in an interview:

> We just don't know what to do. We . . . rely on regulation . . . and . . . the trouble is that people don't understand [. . .] we don't have enough . . . we have lot of uncertainty because we don't have any data. We're going to commission programs of research which will inform the development of policy and regulation. We're also going to have voluntary reporting schemes that tell us about what people are making, and those two information strands come together, and on the basis of that you amend policy and regulation. That's the policy, that's the framework, that's the governance, it's evidence-based policy making, but because innovation *is* in its nature innovative, it doesn't fit the existing model [. . .] So, you have to go beyond regulation, and you have to accept that with nanotechnology we probably won't have a fit-for-purpose-method supporting regulation. (Interview material: Researcher and former policy actor UK)

Similarly, German policy makers suggested that an open, flexible, adaptive regulation should accompany technology development: 'An ideal suggestion would be to develop the potentials [. . .] and to support nanotechnology, while at the same time risk research is intensified and wherever necessary stopped; the entire thing as flexible and dynamic as possible' (Lahl[7] 2006: 50).

These two quotations by policy actors in the UK and Germany, respectively, illustrate how gradually the claim took hold that nanotechnology needs a rethinking of regulatory practices. While holding fast to the idea of evidence-based policy making, the painstakingly long evidence-gathering process worried policy makers, industry representatives, and scholars alike. They could not just sit on their hands and wait because the entire nanotechnology governance project was grounded by the wish to 'get it right the first time.' Thus, the demand to pre-empt potential risks and conflicts drove policy making. But nanotechnology's ambivalence rejected generic regulatory approaches that normally would be applied. There were always novel types of effects that would have to be taken into account (Swierstra and Rip 2007: 17) that made it impossible to determine once and for all the right criteria needed for assessing nanotechnologies' risks (Laurent 2010: 79, after Kermisch 2012: 35).

We see how the technological advances represented by nanotechnology made policy makers aware that they might have to dismiss the very idea that they *can know* (Hajer and Wagenaar 2003: 10). This move was underpinned by arguments, for example those about pace. In the face of rapid scientific developments, so it was said, the regulatory process with its lengthy development of appropriate risk assessments was lagging behind the pace at which nanomaterials are being brought to market (this is prevalent in my interview materials; see also secondary literature such as Bowman and Hodge 2008: 476; Marchant et al. 2008: 44; Dorbeck-Jung and Shelley-Egan 2013: 56). As a consequence, policy makers and (regulatory) scholars (e.g., Marchant et al. 2008: 53; Bowman et al. 2013; Dorbeck-Jung and Shelley-Egan 2013: 56) began to question whether regulating nanotechnologies would in fact not require a change of regulatory practices. The *pace argument* is underpinned by normative notions that 'policy-making in this area cannot be placed on hold until risk assessments are complete' (Corley et al. 2009: 1574).

Today, consensus is growing that nanotechnology needs 'a gradual, flexible, and evolutionary approach to nanotechnology regulation,' a '"soft law" approach' that is not just 'incremental, reflexive, and cooperative' (Marchant et al. 2008) but also 'adaptive, anticipatory, [and] open' (Cutcliffe et al. 2012), such as codes of conduct, 'incremental multi-actor oversight models' (Marchant et al. 2008) or a 'big regulatory toolbox' (Bowman and Hodge 2008). The regulations developed so far mostly fall under the category of 'soft regulation' and range from voluntary registration schemes, codes of conduct for researchers and health-and-safety guidelines for companies. These texts have been developed by the industry itself (e.g., BASF, Dupont), by stakeholder forums (e.g., the UK's Responsible NanoCode), and at the national level (e.g., Germany's

NanoCommission's report) or at a supranational level (e.g., the EU code of conduct for responsible nanosciences and nanotechnologies research).

CONCLUSION

In this chapter I present an approach that combines thoughts from STS and poststructuralist discourse theory for analyzing regulatory policy making. Particularly when it comes to wicked problems, I argue, we need to develop a discursive understanding of how issues are transformed into political objects and how policy makers order messy realities. I show how material objects, technics, and evidence-based, technocratic decision making themselves produce mess (the more we know about nanotechnology risk assessment, the more we realize that we do *not* know), and I suggest that discourses and discursive devices (such as stories, metaphors, and arguments) in the case of nanotechnology contribute to accomplishing a preliminary order through anticipatory regulation. A co-productionist approach attends to discourses, technical practices, and material objects in the shaping of policies. On the basis of this perspective, I set out to study the regulation of nanotechnologies and to examine how anticipatory, adaptive, flexible regulatory frameworks caught on.

I show that a logic of pre-emption constitutes a condition of possibility for transforming nanotechnology into a politically signified object. Against the sociopolitical context of public protests against GMO and a loss of trust in public authorities after the BSE crisis, governance actors sincerely endeavored to restore trust despite the lack of evidence for public mistrust or protests regarding nanotechnology. I argue that anticipatory regulations on nanotechnology were put in place to pre-empt the risk of public resistance. This strong demand to depoliticize is new in technology governance, and to be successful it had to manifest in policy action. Therefore, policy makers set out to govern nanotechnologies. One part of this adaptive governance regime was to query early on whether restrictions, in the form of regulations, on the production or use of nanomaterials were necessary. However, operating within a dominant social logic of evidence gathering, this endeavor soon reached its limits.

Knowledge production on invisible Lilliputian nanoparticles and other kinds of nanomaterials turned out to be a complicated, perhaps impossible, project. Traditionally, no knowledge means no regulation, no definition means no regulatory object, and no measurement tools means no monitoring. The technical practices and material objects dislocated evidence-based policy making. Therefore, 'adaption,' 'flexibility,' and 'openness' were terms accommodated in the anticipatory regulatory frameworks applied to nanotechnology. Thus, the technology itself, its ambiguity, was an important element in the co-production of existing nanotechnology regulatory frameworks. The uncertainty of the object 'nanotechnology' was mirrored in the flexible policy instruments adapted to nanotechnologies. The logic of pre-emption privileged or found a way out of what could be an endless boundary drawing conflict: a pre-emptive regime does not take a stance on whether nanotechnology is novel and how to define it. In so doing, uncertainty is acknowledged and the uncertainty promotes as a new way of regulation in form of adaptive, flexible, open guidelines as a solution.

To conclude, nanotechnology governance is also an interesting illustration of how to regulate post-normal science. In 1987, Sheila Jasanoff stated that a regulatory process in which science cannot provide definitive answers to questions about risks might threaten the legitimacy of political decision making because policy makers cannot resort to technical, and thus supposedly neutral and objective, justifications (Jasanoff 1987: 225). In nanotechnology, we see that the notion of responsibility can lend similar legitimacy even if the 'language of risk has failed' (McCarthy and Kelty 2010). Although anticipatory soft laws have obvious disadvantages, such as low compliance, distribution problems, and a lack of implementation (Kjølberg and Strand 2011; Dorbeck-Jung and Shelley-Egan 2013; Reichow and Dorbeck-Jung 2013), all the anticipatory actions (e.g., codes of conduct, stakeholder forums, public engagement) performed governance. Anticipatory soft regulation might have vague contents and little concrete impact, but governance actors at multiple sites (from research departments, to industry, to national and supranational public authorities) visibly enacted a governing style that can be seen as trustworthy (Hajer 2009: 21). Such performances that draw on the language of responsibility, foresight and anticipation, and that integrate different publics in engagement activities, contribute to boosting the perception of contemporary nanotechnology governance as persuasive and, thus, authoritative.

NOTES

1. Basically, nanotechnology products rely on the changed behaviors of materials created on the nanoscale, ranging from ca. 1nm to 100nm. This is incredibly small, with a human hair averaging a width of ca. 80000nm. At the 1–100nm level, mechanical physical laws might not apply, and the effects of quantum mechanics may be exhibited instead (Kulinowski 2006: 16).
2. This chapter is based on a dissertation project, see Åm 2011.
3. For more details on the analysis of hegemony and logics in poststructuralist discourse theory, see Howarth and Griggs, Chapter 6, this volume.
4. TAB – Büro für Technologie-Abschätzung beim Deutschen Bundestag.

5. The Federal Institute for Occupational Safety and Health (BfR) within the Consumer Protection Ministry, the Federal Environment Agency (UBA) within the Environment Ministry, and the Federal Institute for Occupational Safety and Health (BAuA) (working for the Labour Ministry).
6. Registration, Evaluation, Authorisation of Chemicals.
7. Director of the Department for Environment and Health of the German Federal Ministry for Environment from 2001 to 2009, Lahl is a former Green politician and the initiator of the German NanoDialogue event.

REFERENCES

Åm, H. (2011) 'Regulating the unknown. Governing nanotechnologies by a logic of pre-emption'. PhD thesis, University of Vienna.
Anderson, B. (2010) 'Preemption, precaution, preparedness: Anticipatory action and future geographies', *Progress in Human Geography* **34** (6), 777–798. DOI: 10.1177/0309 132510362600.
Andersen, B.H. and Sørensen, H.K. (1992 [1994]) *Frankensteins Dilemma. En bok om teknologi, miljø og verdier*. Oslo: Ad Notam Gyldendal.
Balbus, J., Denison, R., Florini, K. and Walsh, S. (2006) 'Getting nanotechnology right the first time'. In Hunt, G. and Mehta, M. (eds) *Nanotechnology. Risk, Ethics and Law*. Sterling, VA: Earthscan, pp. 130–139.
Bowman, D.M. and Hodge, G.A. (2008) '"Governing" nanotechnology without government?', *Science and Public Policy* **35** (7), 475–487. DOI: 10.3152/030234208X329121.
Bowman, D.M., Stokes, E. and Bennett, M.G. (2013) 'Anticipating the societal challenges of nanotechnologies', *Nanoethics* **7** (1), 1–5. DOI: 10.1007/s11569-013-0170-x.
Clift, R. (2006) 'Risk management and regulation in an emerging technology'. In Hunt, G. and Mehta, M. (eds) *Nanotechnology. Risk, Ethics and Law*. Sterling, VA: Earthscan, pp. 140–153.
Corley, E.A., Scheufele, D.A. and Hu, Q. (2009) 'Of risks and regulations: How leading U.S. nanoscientists form policy stances about nanotechnology', *Journal of Nanoparticle Research* **11** (7), 1573–1585. DOI: 10.1007/s11051-009-9671-5.
Cutcliffe, S.H., Pense, C.M. and Zvalaren, M. (2012) 'Framing the discussion: Nanotechnology and the social construction of technology – what STS scholars are saying', *Nanoethics* **6** (2), 81–99. DOI: 10.1007/s11569-012-0149-z.
David, K.H. and Thompson, P.B. (2008) *What Can Nanotechnology Learn from Biotechnology? Social and Ethical Lessons for Nanoscience from the Debate over Agrifood Biotechnology and GMOs*. 1st edn. Amsterdam, Boston: Elsevier, Academic.
Dorbeck-Jung, B. and Shelley-Egan, C. (2013) 'Meta-regulation and nanotechnologies: The challenge of responsibilisation within the European Commission's code of conduct for responsible nanosciences and nanotechnologies research', *Nanoethics* **7** (1), 55–68. DOI: 10.1007/s11569-013-0172-8.
Einsiedel, E. and Goldenberg, L. (2006) 'Dwarfing the social? Nanotechnology lessons from the biotechnology front'. In Hunt, G. and Mehta, M. (eds) *Nanotechnology. Risk, Ethics and Law*. Sterling, VA: Earthscan, pp. 213–221.
Elgert, L. (2010) 'Politicizing sustainable development: The co-production of globalized evidence-based policy', *Critical Policy Studies* **3** (3–4), 375–390. DOI: 10.1080/19460 171003619782.
Fischer, F. (1998) 'Beyond empiricism: Policy inquiry in post positivist perspective', *Policy Studies Journal* **26** (1), 129–146. DOI: 10.1111/j.1541-0072.1998.tb01929.x.
Fischer, F. and Gottweis, H. (2012) 'Introduction: The argumentative turn revisited'. In Fischer, F. and Gottweis, H. (eds) *The Argumentative Turn Revisited. Public Policy as Communicative Practice*. Durham, NC: Duke University Press, pp. 1–27.
Gammel, S., Lösch, A. and Nordmann, A. (2010) 'A "scanning probe agency" as an

institution of permanent vigilance'. In Goodwin, M., Koops, B.-J. and Leenes, R. (eds) *Dimensions of Technology Regulation*. Conference proceedings of TILTing perspectives on regulating technologies. Nijmegen: Wolf Legal Publishers – WLP, pp. 125–143.

Glynos, J. and Howarth, D. (2007) *Logics of Critical Explanation in Social and Political Theory*. London, New York: Routledge (Routledge Innovations in Political Theory).

Gottweis, H. (1998) *Governing Molecules. The Discursive Politics of Genetic Engineering in Europe and the United States*. Cambridge, MA: The MIT Press.

Gottweis, H. (2012) 'Political rhetoric and stem cell policy in the United States: Embodiments, scenographies, and emotions'. In Fischer, F. and Gottweis, H. (eds) *The Argumentative Turn Revisited. Public Policy as Communicative Practice*. Durham, NC: Duke University Press, pp. 211–235.

Grek, S. (2014) 'OECD as a site of coproduction: European education governance and the new politics of "policy mobilization"', *Critical Policy Studies* **8** (3), 266–281. DOI: 10.1080/19460171.2013.862503.

Haddad, C., Chen, H. and Gottweis, H. (2013) 'Unruly objects. Novel innovation paths and their regulatory challenge'. In Webster, A. (ed.) *The Global Dynamics of Regenerative Medicine. A Social Science Critique*. Basingstoke, UK: Palgrave Macmillan (Health, Technology and Society), pp. 88–117.

Hajer, M.A. (2009) *Authoritative Governance. Policy-making in the Age of Mediatization*. Oxford, New York: Oxford University Press.

Hajer, M.A. and Wagenaar, H. (eds) (2003) *Deliberative Policy Analysis. Understanding Governance in the Network Society*. Reprint. Cambridge: Cambridge University Press.

Hood, C., Rothstein, H. and Baldwin, R. (2001) *Government of Risk: Understanding Risk Regulation Regimes*. Oxford: Oxford University Press.

Howarth, D. (2000) *Discourse*. Buckingham, UK: Open University Press.

Jasanoff, S. (1987) 'Contested boundaries in policy-relevant science', *Social Studies of Science* **17** (2), 195–230. DOI: 10.1177/030631287017002001.

Jasanoff, S. (1990) *The Fifth Branch. Science Advisers as Policymakers*. Cambridge, MA: Harvard University Press.

Jasanoff, S. (1992) 'Science, politics, and the renegotiation of expertise at EPA', *Osiris* **7**, 194–217.

Jasanoff, S. (1995) *Science at the Bar. Law, Science, and Technology in America*. Cambridge, MA: Harvard University Press.

Jasanoff, S. (2005) *Designs on Nature. Science and Democracy in Europe and the United States*. Princeton, NJ: Princeton University Press.

Jasanoff, S. (2006 [2004]) 'Ordering knowledge, ordering society'. In Jasanoff, S. (ed.) *States of Knowledge. The Co-production of Science and Social Order*. London: Routledge, pp. 13–45.

Kermisch, C. (2012) 'Do new ethical issues arise at each stage of nanotechnological development?', *Nanoethics* **6** (1), 29–37. DOI: 10.1007/s11569-011-0137-8.

Kjølberg, K.L. and Strand, R. (2011) 'Conversations about responsible nanoresearch', *Nanoethics* **5** (1), 99–113. DOI: 10.1007/s11569-011-0114-2.

Kulinowski, K. (2006) 'Nanotechnology: From "wow" to "yuck"?' In Hunt, G. and Mehta, M. (eds) *Nanotechnology. Risk, Ethics and Law*. Sterling, VA: Earthscan, pp. 13–24.

Lahl, U. (2006) 'Innovationsräume mit einem Risikoradar orten', *Politische Ökologie*, **24**, 50–52. Available at: http://www.bmub.bund.de/fileadmin/bmu-import/files/chemikalien/nanotechnologie/nanodialog/application/pdf/vortrag_lahl_nano.pdf (last accessed 11 December 2014).

Lin, P. (2007) 'Nanotechnology bound: Evaluating the case for more regulation', *Nanoethics* **1** (2), 105–122. DOI: 10.1007/s11569-007-0012-9.

Ludlow, K. (2008) 'Nanoregulation – filtering out the small stuff', *Nanoethics* **2** (2), 183–191. DOI: 10.1007/s11569-008-0037-8.

Marchant, G.E., Sylvester, D.J. and Abbott, K.W. (2008) 'Risk management principles for nanotechnology', *Nanoethics* **2** (1), 43–60. DOI: 10.1007/s11569-008-0028-9.

Maynard, A.D., Aitken, R.J., Butz, T., Colvin, V., Donaldson, K., Oberdörster, G.

et al. (2006) 'Safe handling of nanotechnology', *Nature* **444** (7117), 267–269. DOI: 10.1038/444267a.

McCarthy, E. and Kelty, C. (2010) 'Responsibility and nanotechnology', *Social Studies of Science* **40** (3), 405–432. DOI: 10.1177/0306312709351762.

Mehta, M. (2006) 'From biotechnology to nanotechnology: What can we learn from earlier technologies?' In Hunt, G. and Mehta, M. (eds) *Nanotechnology. Risk, Ethics and Law.* Sterling, VA: Earthscan, pp. 121–129.

Miller, C.A. (2006 [2004]) 'Climate science and the making of global political order'. In Jasanoff, S. (ed.) *States of Knowledge. The Co-production of Science and Social Order.* London: Routledge, pp. 46–66.

Murashov, V. and Howard, J. (2009) 'Essential features for proactive risk management', *Nature Nanotechnology* **4** (8), 467–470. DOI: 10.1038/nnano.2009.205.

Nel, A., Xia, T., Mädler, L. and Li, N. (2006) 'Toxic potential of materials at the nanolevel', *Science* **311** (5761), 622–627. DOI: 10.1126/science.1114397.

Nordmann, A. (2010) 'Philosophy of technoscience in the regime of vigilance'. In Hodge, G.A., Bowman, D., and Maynard, A.D. (eds) *International Handbook on Regulating Nanotechnologies.* Cheltenham, UK and Northampton, MA, USA: Edward Elgar, pp. 25–45.

Oberdörster, G., Oberdörster, E. and Oberdörster, J. (2005) 'Nanotoxicology: An emerging discipline evolving from studies of ultrafine particles', *Environmental Health Perspectives* **113** (7), 823–839. DOI: 10.1289/ehp.7339.

O'Riordan, T. (1989) 'Anticipatory environmental policy impediments and opportunities', *Environmental Monitoring and Assessment* **12** (2), 115–125.

Parsons, W. (2002) 'From muddling through to muddling up – evidence based policy making and the modernisation of British Government', *Public Policy and Administration* **17** (3), 43–60.

Pidgeon, N. and Rogers-Hayden, T. (2007) 'Opening up nanotechnology dialogue with the publics: Risk communication or "upstream engagement"?', *Health, Risk & Society* **9** (2), 191–210.

Prainsack, B. and Wahlberg, A. (2013) 'Situated bio-regulation: Ethnographic sensibility at the interface of STS, policy studies and the social studies of medicine', *BioSocieties* **8** (3), 336–359. DOI: 10.1057/biosoc.2013.14.

Preston, C.J., Sheinin, M.Y., Sproat, D.J. and Swarup, V.P. (2010) 'The novelty of nano and the regulatory challenge of newness', *Nanoethics* **4** (1), 13–26. DOI: 10.1007/s11569-010-0083-x.

Reichow, A. and Dorbeck-Jung, B. (2013) 'Discovering specific conditions for compliance with soft regulation related to work with nanomaterials', *Nanoethics* **7** (1), 83–92. DOI: 10.1007/s11569-013-0165-7.

Renn, O. and Roco, M.C. (2006) 'Nanotechnology and the need for risk governance', *Journal of Nanoparticle Research* **8** (2), 153–191. DOI: 10.1007/s11051-006-9092-7.

Rip, A. (2006) 'Folk theories of nanotechnologists', *Science as Culture* **15**, 349–365.

Royal Society, Royal Academy of Engineering (2004) *Nanoscience and Nanotechnologies: Opportunities and Uncertainties.* London: Royal Society, Royal Academy of Engineering.

Solesbury, W. (2002) 'The ascendancy of evidence', *Planning Theory & Practice* **3** (1), 90–96. DOI: 10.1080/14649350220117834.

Swierstra, T. and Rip, A. (2007) 'Nano-ethics as NEST-ethics: Patterns of moral argumentation about new and emerging science and technology', *Nanoethics* **1** (1), 3–20. DOI: 10.1007/s11569-007-0005-8.

Tait, J. and Levidow, L. (1992) 'Proactive and reactive approaches to risk regulation', *Futures* **24** (3), 219–231.

Waterton, C. and Wynne, B. (2006 [2004]) 'Knowledge an political order in the European Environment Agency'. In Jasanoff, S. (ed.) *States of Knowledge. The Co-production of Science and Social Order.* London: Routledge, pp. 87–108.

Wildavsky, A.B. (1979 [1987]) *Speaking Truth to Power. The Art and Craft of Policy Analysis.* New Brunswick, NJ: Transaction Books.

Williams, R. (2006) 'Compressed foresight and narrative bias: Pitfalls in assessing high technology futures', *Science as Culture* **15**, 327–348.
Wullweber, J. (2008) 'Nanotechnology – an empty signifier à venir? A delineation of a techno-socio-economical innovation strategy', *Science, Technology & Innovation Studies* **4** (1), 28–45.
Zhang, J.Y., Marris, C. and Rose, N. (2011) 'The transnational governance of synthetic biology. Scientific uncertainty, cross-borderness and the 'art' of governance', BIOS Working Paper. London: BIOS, London School of Economics, pp. 1–36.

PART V

THE POLITICS OF POLICY EXPERTISE: KNOWLEDGE, THINK-TANKS AND ACTION RESEARCH

17 Politics and policy expertise: towards a political epistemology
Holger Strassheim

Public policies are sometimes very successful and do sometimes dramatically fail. In a highly complex world in which political actors (parties, governments, bureaucrats, experts and social movements) compete and fight for different policy options, failures are unavoidable. Introducing science-based knowledge into the political process seems to be a straight-forward way to improve policies beyond ideology. Following this idea, John Dewey argued that 'the operation of cooperative intelligence as displayed in science [is] a working model for the union of freedom and authority which is applicable to political as well as other spheres' (Dewey, 1939, p. 336). Today, more than 75 years later, we are not so sure anymore. Confronted with complex dynamics and 'wicked problems', such as global warming or worldwide food insecurities, decision-makers need to rely on the educated advice of specialists. At the same time, however, citizens question the role of expertise in society more than ever. While simulations and social experiments have become an indispensable basis for political decisions, the involvement of stakeholders and lay people in processes of policy advice and public deliberation has become an equally essential element of political legitimation. Both tendencies can be observed: the democratization of expertise and the 'expertization' of democracy.[1]

The aim of this chapter[2] is to critically explore the relationships among science, policy and society. In taking up the multiple problems and paradoxes of policy expertise, it addresses some key questions: How is policy expertise generated, communicated and justified in a given social context? How do these contexts shape and constrain the politics of policy expertise? Also, how can we describe and explain changes in the understanding of policy expertise across different social contexts? To answer these questions the view of 'political epistemology' is adopted linking both practices to validate and justify beliefs about the world and practices to collectively order and evaluate the world.

PROBLEMS AND PARADOXES OF POLICY EXPERTISE

What is the problem with expertise in politics and policy-making?[3] In the myriad decisions that have to be made – when setting the agenda, choosing among contested policy options, or assessing the effects of public policies – governments, parliaments and citizens alike would be lost without the facts provided by professionals. Without the expertise concentrated in government research agencies, advisory committees and academies the whole machinery of government would operate in such ignorance as to be ineffective. 'That the contours of any subject must be defined by the expert before the plain man can see its full significance', Harold Laski already argued in 1930, 'will be obvious to anyone who has reflected upon the social process in the modern world' (1930, p. 102).

Laski, however, was much more concerned about the limits of expertise: experts 'sacrifice the insight of common sense to intensity of experience' (102). By reason of their immersion in specific fields, experts tend to neglect evidence which does not come from their profession, are skeptical of novel views, and fail to see the scheme of values that is part of their judgment. Government by experts, he warns, would after a time inevitably lead to government in the interest of experts with either stagnation or social conflict as a result. Twenty years later, Alfred Schütz (1976 [1959], p. 130) describes the expert in a similar vein as someone whose frame of reference is rigidly limited and who ignores all those problems that are not evident in the expert's universe of discourse. Those outside this universe 'can expect from the expert's advice merely the indication of suitable means for attaining pregiven ends, but not the determination of the ends themselves'. Theodor W. Adorno (1972 [1965], p. 17) sums up this criticism in the dialectical style of the Frankfurt School by pointing out that, in turning his technical specialization against those he is supposed to advise, the expert actually figures as the rational *gestalt* of a deeply irrational society.[4]

Today, controversy about the role of expertise in society has not vanished. On the contrary: issues such as stem cell research, genetically modified organisms, food irradiation or nuclear waste disposal have become topics of contention. On the one hand, some argue that in a world faced with complexity, successful governing must be based on a sort of 'division of epistemic labor' whereby a subset of knowledge-intensive questions can only be answered by specialists while value-judgments remain to be solved by the general public in deliberative procedures (Kitcher 2001, 2011; Schudson 2006). From this point of view, only experts can speak 'truth to power'[5] because they are the only ones able to counter political power by the authority of a self-correcting community.

On the other hand, it is precisely this division between a seemingly apolitical sphere of scientific knowledge and a politically loaded sphere of values that is highly contested and can no longer be taken for granted. The 'modern consensus' dividing the representation of nature from the representation of people has come under pressure from different sides (Jasanoff 2004b; Latour 1993; Shapin and Schaffer 1985). From the normative viewpoint of political theory, the promotion of expertise is at odds with the democratic principle of equality. Because experts set the very standards by which their claims are to be evaluated, their knowledge is hardly questioned by the general public and is nearly beyond control by democratic procedures. This tendency poses problems for democracies in terms of both 'epistemic equality' in the sense of equal rights for everyone to be taken seriously when making knowledge claims and 'epistemic neutrality' in the sense of the impartiality of the state in ensuring open and fair discussion in the face of rival claims (Brown 2009b; Habermas 1968; Kitcher 2011; Longino 2002; Turner 2006). According to Ezrahi et al. (2008, p. 182), 'modern publics and policy making elites have come to realize, or at least intuit, that any social deployment of certified knowledge and technology has redistributive political effects, that it can be used to improve the symbolic, political and material resources of some groups while degrading the relative position of others'.

Moreover, since the 1960s the privileged position of experts has been countered by numerous efforts to democratize science and enhance public participation (Callon et al. 2011; Fischer 2009). This movement has promoted the spread and diversification of public engagement mechanisms, such as citizen juries and panels, stakeholder conferences and deliberative forums. Strengthening deliberative democracy is intended to help to legitimize decisions, put policy advisors under public scrutiny and foster a dialogue between experts and lay people – sometimes with the purpose of eliminating the boundaries between experts and lay people altogether. More recently, however, observers have described some of these deliberative mechanisms as technologies with a hidden purpose to 'domesticate' an increasingly skeptical public and shield experts against criticism (Rothstein 2013).

While expertise rapidly loses its credibility as an impartial source of objective truth, public policy seems to depend on it more than ever. The problem is being aggravated by the fact that today political decisions tend to be made under urgent pressures of time while the financial and human costs of those very decisions are dramatically increasing. It is a paradigmatic and well-known paradox of expertise that 'in the cases in which scientific advice is asked most urgently [. . .] the authority of science is questioned most thoroughly' (Bijker et al. 2009, p. 1; Limoges 1993).[6]

FROM OBJECTIVIST TO POLITICAL EPISTEMOLOGIES

Taking the problems and paradoxes of expertise as an opportunity, the chapter critically revisits research on the relationships among science, politics and the public. Policy analysis has treated the subject in contrasting ways. Two competing strands of argument can be distinguished – that of 'objectivist epistemologies' and that of 'political epistemologies'. From the perspective of 'objectivist epistemologies'[7] the erosion of expert authority calls for a more iterative and interactive policy process that works to monitor factual claims provided by experts and to evaluate them in terms of policy-principles. Here, the policy process itself is conceptualized in analogy to a scientific process of falsification and progressive problem-solving, allowing for policy-makers to learn from new evidence while keeping the core principles of policy programs intact. In rare cases, even the policy-principles themselves need to be modified, as when the unplanned consequences of policy decisions become visible. Since the 1960s, inspired by very similar ideas the 'policy analysis movement' has searched for ways to both minimize policy failures and maximize 'policy analytical capacity' by a more systematic application of evaluation methods, scientific expertise and evidence (Howlett 2009). Approaches such as 'evidence-based' or 'evidence-informed' policy-making are the latest expression of this movement, relying on the belief that the apparent certainties provided by sound science will lead to a more rational problem-solving process or, at least, to increased policy learning (Davies et al. 2000; Nutley et al. 2010).

In contrast, I propose an approach to analyzing the relationships among science, policy and the public in terms of what one could call 'political epistemologies'.[8] By this I refer to those research perspectives that focus on multiple practices both to validate and justify beliefs about the world and to collectively order and evaluate the world. While objectivist epistemologies insist upon separating knowledge and values, political epistemologies explicitly aim at reconstructing their interaction and mutual constitution. While objectivist epistemologies take the boundaries between science and policy for granted, political epistemologies focus on exactly this taken-for-grantedness of societal boundaries, asking for their construction in social processes of sense-making. Finally, while objectivist epistemologies tend to treat the rationalization of politics by science as their analytical vantage point, political epistemologies are more skeptical. Proponents assume that, depending on the institutional and cultural context, there are always multiple and potentially contested perceptions of how science and politics should interact and what rationalization could actually mean. In calling epistemologies political, a dual meaning of the term is employed: it refers both to an analytic angle (normative and cognitive claims are mutually constitutive) and to a (self-)critical stance (analyzing science and policy is always also a political endeavor in itself).

Thinking of expertise either in terms of objectivist epistemologies or political epistemologies makes a difference. Let us take the evidence-based policy movement again as an example. It has been especially strong in the UK, where in 1999 the Labour Government adopted evidence-based policy in its White Paper *Modernising Government* (Cabinet Office 1999). After nearly 15 years, assessing the effectiveness of public policies and making well-informed decisions on the basis of 'sound science' continues to be praised as one of the 'fundamental principles of good public services' (Cabinet Office 2013). At the same time, however, evidence-based policy as a mantra of modern government has been accompanied by public criticism. Some warn that there is 'a risk that "evidence-based policy" will become a means for policy elites to increase their strategic role over what constitutes a social problem in a way that devalues tacit forms of knowledge, practice based wisdom, professional judgment, and the voices of the ordinary citizens' (Marston and Watts 2003, p. 158). Because it tends to transform public debates into disputes involving only experts and to immunize policy decisions against counter arguments, evidence-based policy has been seen as a mode of 'stealth advocacy' (Pielke 2011). Some commentators even argue that the fixation on scientific certainty has led to an inversion of the original idea, turning evidence-based policy into 'policy-based evidence' (Sanderson 2011; Sharman and Holmes 2010; Straßheim and Kettunen 2014).

From the standpoint of an objectivist epistemology, this development calls for an even stronger standardization of evidence-based practices, for an intensified effort to ensure both scientific rigor and political rationality (Nutley et al. 2012). From the perspective of political epistemologies, however, evidence-based policy rests on political objectivity as a plausible fiction that tends to obscure many preliminary decisions that influence the production of numbers, indicators and standards. By uncovering the processes of politicization and de-politicization entrenched in evidence-based practices, political epistemologies in contrast contribute to the capability of political communities to critically re-examine normative issues and to redefine problems that have been framed in ways so far unquestioned in public debates (Adelle and Weiland 2013; Rüb and Straßheim 2012; Straßheim and Kettunen 2014).

CONVERSATIONS BETWEEN CRITICAL POLICY ANALYSIS AND STS

By outlining the basic principles of political epistemology, I hope to bring the argumentative and critical strand of public policy analysis (Colebatch et al. 2010; Fischer 2009; Fischer and Forrester 1993; Fischer and Gottweis 2012; Hoppe 2010) into conversation with studies on science, technology and society (STS) (Hilgartner et al. 2015; Jasanoff 2005a, 2012). Although these two fields differ considerably in terms of research foci, conceptual principles and methodologies, they share these basic views about the relationship between science and politics and the way it affects the role of expertise in society:

Firstly, both fields challenge the belief that science can be 'a value-free, technical project' (Fischer and Gottweis 2012, p.2), and that it is 'an autonomous 'republic' that can be separated from politics' (Beck 2015). Instead, they seek to 'understand the relationship between the empirical and the normative' (Fischer and Gottweis 2012, p.2) as they are configured in processes of 'the co-production of science and the social order' (Jasanoff 2004b): 'Briefly stated, co-production is shorthand for the proposition that the ways in which we know and represent the world (both nature and society) are inseparable from the ways we choose to live in it' (Jasanoff 2004b, p.2).

Secondly, the fields conceive of both expertise and scientific knowledge as embedding and being embedded 'in social practices, identities, norms, conventions, discourses, instruments and institutions' (Jasanoff 2004b, p.3). This approach follows a 'constitutive analysis of policy expertise' (Beck 2015; Long Martello and Jasanoff 2004)[9] that opens up venues for both comparing different cultural and discursive contexts of expertise and analyzing how these 'civic epistemologies' (Jasanoff 2005a) or 'policy epistemics' (Fischer and Gottweis 2012) shape the ways policy-relevant knowledge is produced, publicly justified and translated into policy-making. The focus of objectivist epistemologies on identifying general factors that could improve policy analytic capability is shifted towards international and intersectoral comparisons on multiple levels, highlighting 'local solutions to the political issue of expertise' (Miller 2005; Sismondo 2010, p.181).

> The goal would be to study the ways in which the members of these communities share background assumptions about the particular problem area, their ideas about the relations of particular scientific findings to decision-making, the role – if any – of citizen involvement, how they respond to criticism and opposition from outside their communities and more. (Fischer 2009, p.165)

WHO ARE THE EXPERTS?

In George Bernard Shaw's play, *The Doctor's Dilemma*, one of the pro-
tagonists famously argues that 'all professions are conspiracies against
the laity' (Shaw 1906, p. 36), assuming that experts and non-experts are
clearly separable. Until the 1950s and 1960s, studies of science in general
and policy analysis in particular shared this understanding. The authority
of expertise seemed to rest on basic principles and esoteric knowledge,
defining clear boundaries between scientific and ordinary knowledge.
Decision-making for the public interest would increasingly depend upon
the rationalizing force of science. By the end of the 1960s with the critique
of 'positivism' rising and Thomas Kuhn's work on scientific paradigms
becoming influential, science and expertise seemed more and more to be
questionable (Kuhn 1962). The 'Kuhnian revolution' (Sismondo 2010,
p. 12) challenged the assumption that scientific knowledge could be
traced back to firm foundations. According to Kuhn's view, science does
not accumulate knowledge over time, but moves from one paradigm
to another, each one being incommensurable with the other. With the
sociology of scientific knowledge and the 'strong programme' proposed
by the Edinburgh School (Bloor 1991 [1976]), philosophers, sociologists
and historians alike became even more agnostic about the foundations
of scientific truth, emphasizing such 'extra-scientific' factors as interests,
ideologies, cultures, discourse and practices, political pressures, and social
capital (Barnes et al. 1996). Epistemic authority, it has been argued since
the late 1970s, rests not on truth but on the successful mobilization of
norms, classifications, methodologies, technologies, rhetoric and other
resources to establish, maintain and defend the boundaries between those
knowledge claims that are scientifically accepted and those that are not
(Gieryn 1998; Shapin 1992; Sismondo 2010). This 'second wave of science
studies' (Collins and Evans 2006) coincided with a similar turn in policy
analysis, leading to an intensifying critique of positivism and to the foundation of a post-positivist school of policy analysis based on concepts
of interpretation, discourse and language (Torgerson 1986). From the
perspective of constructivist science studies and argumentative policy
analysis alike, experts and analysts are torn between the abstract rationalities of scientific research and the practical realities of political pressures
(Fischer and Forrester 1993; Gieryn 1995). Science and expertise, it is
argued, depend on the successful demarcation between scientifically valid
knowledge and politically tainted, somewhat subjective claims.

Since the 1970s, this process of demarcation has become more and
more difficult. As noted above, the push for a democratization of science
resulted in the international spread of public engagement mechanisms.

One of the most cited procedures of public deliberation, the 'consensus conference' established in the 1980s by the Danish Board of Technology, asked citizens to make recommendations to that country's parliament on specific technical issues. Experts were asked to advise the panel while citizens remained in control of the final report. This format was later exported to other countries, encouraging efforts to democratize technical decision-making and to develop alternative modes of lay involvement in science (Fischer 2009; Sismondo 2010, pp. 180–188). Along with 'citizen science' and 'participatory action research', an ambiguous figure has appeared: the 'lay expert' seems to cross a threshold, transforming expertise into a hybrid creature situated in the no-man's-land between science and politics (Epstein 2007; Jasanoff 2004a; Wynne 1996). Finally, one may argue, laity strikes back.

To save science, some have pointed to the necessity of developing a normative approach to expertise, identifying the genuine experts able to truly contribute to scientific endeavors, 'core scientists', who could not be questioned by lay people and whose expertise is thus generally acknowledged (Collins and Evans 2006, 2007; Turner 2006). The genuine experts are distinguished from people with 'interactional expertise' – including those able to interact with the specialists and carry out a sociological analysis of science – and people with 'no expertise' and thus unable to conduct either kind of interactive task (Collins and Evans 2007; for a critique see Wynne 2003). Instead, others propose to begin by recognizing the social complexity of expertise, which results from often controversial and culturally framed ways of attributing authority and reputation across different levels of social interaction (Hajer 2009; Jasanoff 2011b; Jung et al. 2014; Pielke 2011; Wynne 2003).

The frequent equation of expertise with science should be treated with caution. Experts are always already boundary workers. To accept someone as a policy expert means to attribute to that person both the competence to validate and justify knowledge claims ('epistemic authority') and the capability to make these knowledge claims relevant for collectively ordering and evaluating society ('political authority'). Experts may be peers in the context of science, colleagues in the context of professional organizations or citizens in the context of politics. As experts, however, they need to successfully employ both epistemic and political authority. This understanding serves to decouple the debate on the foundations of expertise from the debate on the foundations of science. The public skepticism about expertise and differences over the meaning of the term itself reflect changing views about how to bring together both epistemic and political modes of authority. That question is different from that of the foundation and boundary of science in society.[10]

It is thus proposed to conceptualize *expertise* as a nexus of political and epistemic authority attributions in terms of three interconnected dimensions of sense-making: the social, temporal and object dimensions:[11]

1. In the *social dimension* individual or collective actors are constituted and/or contested as experts when they become the object of, and struggle with, both competence attributions and role expectations. Social expectations determine the formal and informal rules of how to recruit experts, the practices by which experts gain credibility, the relationship between reputation and representation, the criteria of separating insiders from outsiders, the composition of commissions and advisory committees and the influence of reputation networks and alliances both within and between organizations. As connoisseurs, technical specialists, reputed scientists, representatives of societal interests, think-tank organizations, or global knowledge networks, different forms of expertise respond to and reproduce different discourses of objectivity. By acting as experts, actors have to cope with criteria of both scientific integrity and democratic representation (Brown 2009b; Daston and Galison 2007; Jasanoff 2011a). In addition, actors produce knowledge as contested bodies of expertise or counter-expertise.

2. In the *temporal dimension*, expertise becomes a matter of timing and opportunities. 'Scripts' – understood as compilations of procedural rules and routines – structure the practices of knowledge production, sorting them in a consecutive order. In committee rules and guidelines, such as those of the Federal Advisory Committees Act (FACA) in the US, the rhythm of procedural dynamics, together with the opening and closing of opportunity windows, influences which knowledge claims are perceived as politically relevant and scientifically valid (Brown 2009a; Brown et al. 2005; Jasanoff 1990). In the course of agenda setting and decision-making, potentially contested expertise might – once it has been entrenched in the proceedings and protocols of advisory processes – later emerge as an incontestable premise for further decisions (Zahariadis 2003).[12] In the long run, claims made by experts may be reinforced by positive feedback dynamics, triggered by bandwagon effects in public debates. However, such claims may abruptly lose public attention when policy failures and anomalies cumulate, with the possibility arising of sudden shifts from one paradigm of policy expertise to another (Baumgartner and Jones 2002; Blyth 2002; Hall 1993).

3. In the *object dimension*, the authority of expertise depends on objects of knowledge such as statistics, simulations or surveys. As configurations

of evidence, these tend to be regarded as the collectively visible and more or less unquestionable certainty of a fact. They fulfill an important function in stabilizing and legitimating the integrity of expertise applicable to very different contexts: 'It is through these processes that facts produced in one locality come to speak with authority to other questions even to other fields, times and places' (Morgan 2011, p. 7). Four different modes of objectivation can be distinguished (Rüb and Straßheim 2012): (1) social evidence by individual and collective judgments (e.g. connaisseurs, advisory boards, expert panels), (2) iconic-rhetorical evidence by visualizations and expressions (e.g. maps, metaphors, symbols), (3) calculative-axiomatic evidence by quantification and formalization (e.g. statistics, standards, indicators) and (4) mechanical evidence by automation and virtualization (e.g. models, simulations). By constituting 'boundary objects' (Star and Griesemer 1989), these modes of objectivation are able to gain attention across, and mediate among, science, politics and the public. Especially numbers and simulations enjoy authority by obscuring the many selections and valuations upon which they are based (Porter 1995). In her study on social policy in the US, for example, O'Connor has analyzed how the 'poverty research industry' in the 1970s started to change the very understanding of welfare by embedding hidden assumptions in micro-simulations and social experiments (O'Connor 2001).

The 'drama' of policy expertise lies precisely in the fact that experts have to perform across multiple audiences (for an analysis of expertise in the tradition of Goffman, see Hilgartner 2000). As medical professionals, engineers, climate experts or citizens enter the stage, they may be able to impress those who watch and listen. They also have to be prepared, however, to struggle for authority and acceptance, faced with changing and contradictory role expectations, temporal restrictions and the malice of objects. The many ways experts cope with this pressure depends, above all, on the values and norms, the administrative and political cultures and the epistemological premises that interpenetrate expertise in specific national and local contexts.

THE EMBEDDEDNESS OF EXPERTISE[13]

Historically, the early modern philosopher Gottfried Wilhelm Leibniz was one of the first to think systematically about policy expertise. In his political writings he proposed the installation of a 'theatrum naturae et artis', an experimental space provided by the state to encourage the public exchange of useful knowledge, the collaboration of experienced people and the initiation of inventions (Leibniz 1931a [1680]; Leibniz 1931b [1680]). The very representation of the state and its welfare would be localized in this archive, comprising all kinds of artefacts and data on population, education, trade and commerce, machines and engineering, health and poverty. This practical knowledge would, as Leibniz maintained, be highly valuable for political purposes. A system of cross references and tables could help to map the different sources of advice and data, ensure their political relevance, and thus be an 'instrument of self-governing'.[14]

In their seminal study on the role of social science in the history of the early welfare state, Wagner et al. (Wagner et al. 1991) have shown that the epistemic coordination between expertise and policy varies to a great extent over time and among different nations. Institutional and cultural legacies influence how social sciences are established, the relationship between the government and sciences, the organization of expertise, and its recruitment in decision-making processes. At certain times, science-policy relationships have been transformed dramatically and deeply, leading to new constellations and coalitions of expertise. While in the first half of the 20th century links between experts and political actors became more firmly established, there has been a pluralization of expertise and an 'epistemic drift' towards state programs and political purposes with the strengthening of the interventionist welfare state from the 1960s onwards (Elzinga 1985; Wittrock et al. 1991). Since then, research on policy advice has provided a great number of studies mapping the interactions among science, expertise and politics (see Craft and Howlett 2012; Fleischer 2012, p. 5). All in all, there have been relatively few comparative studies. One of the more influential was Renn's (1995) comparative analysis of styles of using expertise in Japan, the US, and Europe, showing that countries differ in the way they organize the coordination and collision between political values and expert knowledge. More recently, comparative approaches based on concepts of 'institutional logics' and 'organizational fields' have started to explore constellations of organizations, such as think-tanks and government research units, to compare differences in 'knowledge regimes' and their effect on political economies (Campbell and Pedersen 2014; Thornton et al. 2012).

There are, however, even fewer studies focusing specifically on the cultural, institutional and discursive forces shaping the public acceptance, (re)production and transformation of policy expertise (Jung et al. 2014). Most prominently, Jasanoff (2005a, 2011a) has presented a comparison of what she calls 'civic epistemologies'. Jasanoff shows that the very foundation of expertise rests on unquestioned and collectively shared commitments to specific styles of expertise. These 'institutionalized practices by which members of a given society test and deploy knowledge claims' (Jasanoff 2005a, p. 255) vary fundamentally among countries. The local specificity of particular cultures explains why – despite an international science system that is increasingly standardized and isomorphic – understandings and influences of policy expertise differ greatly among national contexts:

> [The] American system highlights the values of transparency and explicit public criticism while seeking to attain a view from nowhere in relation to scientific knowledge. British political culture is less concerned with specialized knowledge and more with the character of the experts who serve the public. British policy stresses experts' personal commitments to the public good and seek to ensure that experts will bring appropriate forms of experience to the issues before them. The German approach also implicitly embraces the idea of experts as society's delegates, but it does so by mapping the macrocosm of society onto the microcosm of committee structure. (Jasanoff 2011a, p. 32)

Jasanoff's conception appears relevant to different areas of concern: Studies on environmental policy have made use of it to explain crucial international and interregional differences in the adoption of standards and indicators of sustainability (Miller 2005). The transformative power of behavioral economics as a new approach to public policy seems to depend on differences in the responsiveness and innovative capability of expert cultures (Straßheim et al. 2015). Similarly, although the International Panel on Climate Change (IPCC) has been publicly criticized for its inability to coordinate diverging interests, one of its main difficulties seems to lie in the fact that, on the international and transnational level, there is no 'one-size-fits-all model of expertise' (Beck 2012, p. 9). Indeed, with the emergence of a 'global agora' of knowledge production, there is thus a growing need to rethink policy expertise and to find new modes to orchestrate political and epistemic authority on a transnational level (Beck 2015; Stone 2012; Quack 2013).

EPISTEMIC AND POLITICAL AUTHORITY IN THE 'POST-NATIONAL CONSTELLATION'

The emergence of a 'global agora' of policy expertise is triggered by at least three interdependent dynamics: Firstly, the multiplication of government research units, organizations of 'regulatory science' and other independent agencies on the national, international and transnational level has changed the balance between political and epistemic authority. These 'boundary organizations' (Guston 2000) are perfectly capable of switching between different audiences. With the 'rise of the unelected' (Vibert 2007)

– i.e. the expansion of unelected bodies on multiple levels of governing such as risk assessors, audit agencies, accounting standards boards or regulatory agencies – new questions about the problem-solving capacity of democratically elected bodies arise. Secondly, the increasing density and interconnectedness of knowledge networks among governments, private companies, researchers and civil society organizations change the ways evidence and expertise are translated into policy-making (Stone 2012). Globally active 'meta-organizations' (Ahrne and Brunsson 2008), such as the International Life Sciences Institute (ILSI), are influencing problem definition, risk regulation and standardization. ILSI is a paradigmatic example, providing a platform for the worldwide coordination, cooperation and collaboration among experts from industry, government and academia, and other civil society organizations. In policy areas such as food safety, nutrition, risk assessment and agriculture, ILSI has gained enormous influence by rapidly providing standards and guidelines, which later become the point of reference for all other regulatory bodies involved (Demortain 2009). Thirdly, tools and arrangements of worldwide comparison have been established, widening the horizon of mutual control and coordination. Benchmarkings and ratings translate the specificities of local contexts into globally communicable performance measurements (Miller 2008). Soft law mechanisms such as the European Union's Open Method of Coordination (OMC) rely on peer pressure, as well as naming and shaming, in order to enhance policy convergence across member states (Kröger, 2009).

Taken together, these dynamics help to constitute what has been called the 'post-national constellation' (Habermas, 2001). Agencification, global networking and international comparisons force nation states to open up to alternative modes and standards of expertise. As a consequence, so far unquestioned arrangements of policy-relevant knowledge production are no longer taken for granted. They are confronted by, and collide with, different norms of scientific integrity and political accountability. Due to the expansion of international communication, cultures of expertise come increasingly under pressure. The overall picture might be similar to the changes that some have observed on the national level:

> Rather than a grand transition from one mode of public expertise to another or some essential national style, driven by a handful of constitutional prime movers, we see multiple patterns in tension and competition with each other. These patterns conflict and vie for dominance, argue against each other, and hence partly develop in response to each other. Such is the make up of modern polities and the fact that we find similar tensions in the organization of expertise only shows how much expertise has become embedded in these politics. (Halffman and Hoppe 2005, p. 148)

These tensions result in 'first-order conflicts of acceptance', which may cumulate over time, triggering 'second-order conflicts of acceptance' (Zürn and Ecker-Ehrhardt 2012; Straßheim and Kettunen 2014). Second-order conflicts concern the basic principles of political expertise and the foundations of political and epistemic authority. Efforts such as the Transatlantic Trade and Investment Partnership (TTIP) to increase regulatory coherence and reduce trade barriers are not only controversial because of underlying economic interests; they also incorporate certain worldviews on how to harmonize fundamental principles of expertise and public knowledge production. The consequences of such global knowledge politics are not yet clear. They might involve 'epistemic fragmentation' (Blassime 2014) and a gradual disembedding of expertise from cultural contexts.

The possibility of disembedded expertise poses challenging questions for future research on expertise and democracy – and on how their relationship might develop under the conditions of the post-national constellation:

First and foremost, we need more comparative studies mapping shifts in epistemic and political authority across different levels of governing. Since policy expertise is rapidly changing, such studies should aim at identifying the mechanisms lending credibility to experts across different cultures. For example, with the rise of unelected agencies, a global mode of 'techno-corporatism' (Fischer 1988)[15] may take precedence over local values and worldviews: Inspired by behavioral economics some regulatory experts have started to argue that different understandings of regulatory principles among nations are basically expressions of behavioral biases common to decision-making under uncertainty (see also Jasanoff 2013). From this point of view, the precautionary principle[16] – today a statutory requirement in the EU – is not a political or ethical position. Rather, it is seen as a symptom of limited rationalities such as 'loss-aversion' and 'act-omission', resulting in 'real errors and significant confusion in thinking about risks' (Sunstein 2014, p. 154). By translating national understandings of risk into the language of behavioral economics and psychology, a global class of 'therapeutic authorities' (Miller and Rose 1994) has emerged, turning the epistemologies of nations into objects of collective de-biasing. Since behavioral insights provide perspectives for policy interventions beyond the model of the 'homo oeconomicus', they are vital for the future of political regulation. They need, however, to be carefully combined with insights from social sciences to avoid unintended side effects and to find ways to re-embed behavioral expertise in local contexts (Straßheim and Korinek 2015; World Bank 2015).

Secondly, research on expertise needs to focus more closely on the politics of participation. Public dialogue and stakeholder involvement seem to be omnipresent. From the local to the global level, various formats of deliberation and citizen empowerment have changed the landscape of collective decision-making (for an overview see Fischer 2009). There are, however, also critical voices, pointing to hidden consequences and controversies. As case studies in the field of food safety have shown, some regulatory agencies tend to organize 'frontstage' performances of consumer involvement; on the 'backstage', however, these performances are carefully orchestrated, shielding organizational purposes and practices from potential objections articulated by a wider audience (Rothstein 2013; Korinek 2014). In administrative procedures developed to realize biotechnical citizenship, the exchange between experts and citizens has been superseded by 'technoscientific norms' that, in contrast to the original purposes of participants, exclude political discussions and controversies (Bora 2010). Some even argue that these and other frustrating experiences have slowly undermined the trust in democratic deliberation. The politics of participation in areas such as climate change or biotechnology may result in what has been described as 'simulative democracy' – democratic participation is cultivated more than ever while its normative foundations are increasingly contested (Blühdorn 2013).

In the post-national constellation, the limits of policy expertise become visible. Scientists and policy advisors struggle for authority. As the late Ulrich Beck (1992)[17] has argued, these are the dynamics of 'reflexive politicization'. As a consequence, previously unquestioned arrangements become questionable. From the perspective of political epistemologies, the dynamics of reflexive politicization only mirror the deep intertwinement between cognitive and normative expectations. They open up opportunities for a critical re-examination and re-imagination of the multiple ways to produce publicly relevant knowledge. There is no need to worry about skepticism – the real problems begin with each attempt to reinstall science and expertise as rationalizing forces in society.

NOTES

1. This is not a new observation. See Weingart (1983) and Bader (2014) for a similar argument.
2. I would like to thank the editors for helpful comments and suggestions. I have profited greatly from discussions with Friedbert W. Rueb. Parts of this chapter are based on findings from the research project 'Studying the changing orders of political expertise', carried out at the WZB Berlin Social Science Center and funded by the Volkswagen Foundation.
3. For very different answers to this fundamental question see Schudson (2006) and Turner (2006).
4. On expertise as 'quasi-ideology' see also Habermas (1987).

5. On the contrasting ideas of 'speaking truth to power' and 'making sense together' see Hoppe (1999).
6. The early research on the utilization of knowledge in politico-administrative systems had already encountered several paradoxes and problems (Caplan et al. 1975; Weiss 1979, 1980). As Caplan et al. (1975) observed, political and administrative actors 'express an eagerness to get all the policy-relevant scientific information they can. Yet, paradoxically and for whatever reasons, they are not influenced by such information if they receive it' (p. 50). In a similar vein Nelkin (1987) has shown that 'ironically, the greater the utility of science in political affairs, the less it can maintain its image of objectivity that has been the very source of its political value' (p. 293).
7. Majone (1991) was one of the first to use this term in policy analysis, conceptualizing the policy process in analogy to a Popperian-Lakatosian understanding of science.
8. Understanding and use of the term differ (Fischer and Gottweis 2012; Friedman 2014; Latour 2004; Straßheim 2012). Latour (2004, p.241) defines political epistemology as 'the distribution of powers between sciences and politics'. Others have preferred the notion of a 'postpositivist epistemology' in order to denote those approaches that draw heavily on theories of discourse, deliberation, social constructivism and interpretive methods (Fischer and Gottweis 2012, p.1). In 2014, the American Political Science Association (APSA) approved an organized section on 'Political Epistemology' in order to study how people 'interpret either their own interests or the public interest; from what sources are these interpretations drawn; and how do these interpretations motivate political action' (www.apsanet.org/content.asp?contentid=258; 29 January 2015).
9. The term 'constitutive analysis' ('Konstitutionsanalyse') goes back to Schütz who uses it, following Husserl, to denote a type of analysis that aims at reconstructing the sedimentation of knowledge by processes of societal sense-making (Schütz 1974).
10. As Jasanoff (2011a) argues 'it is expertise, not science, that translates knowledge (or non-knowledge) into decisions, and expert legitimation is a different undertaking from securing the integrity of scientific studies and experiments' (p. 33).
11. Going back to Husserl's 'Phenomenology of the Lifeworld', these three dimensions of sense-making have been used in remarkably similar ways by different strands of social theory (Berger and Luckmann 1967; Luhmann 1995; Scott 1995). Jasanoff has suggested a different typology of expert dimensions, identifying 'three bodies of expertise' that are connected to the problems of expert legitimacy (Jasanoff 2005b). These include the 'bodies of knowledge' produced by experts, the advisory bodies and other collective bodies of expertise and the individual bodies of the experts themselves. However, the temporal dimension seems to be missing. Elliott (2011) has presented a fruitful application of Jasanoff's three body problem on environmental policy and research.
12. This is an argument originally made by Niklas Luhmann in his classical study on the different ways procedures generate public acceptance and political legitimacy by temporal sorting (Luhmann 1989 [1969]).
13. See Jung et al. (2014) and Jasanoff (2011a) for the concept of 'embeddedness'.
14. '. . . eines der beqvämsten instrumenten zu einer löblichen selbst-regierung . . .' (Leibniz 1931a [1680], pp.340–349). On the history of expertise see also Shapin and Schaffer (1985) and Daston and Galison (2007).
15. This would also mean to more carefully distinguish between 'technocratic strata of experts and specialized administrators' and 'a top echelon of political and economic elites' (Fischer 1988, p.27) and to analyze the relationship between them – something that is beyond the scope of this chapter. I would like to thank Doug Torgerson for pointing this out to me.
16. Basically, the precautionary principle supports taking protective action in face of risks, e.g. the withdrawal of a potentially hazardous product from the market, even before there is complete scientific proof of that risk (see Jasanoff 2013).
17. See also Strassheim and Kettunen (2014).

REFERENCES

Adelle, C. and Weiland, S., 2013, Policy assessment: The state of the art, *Impact assessment and Project Appraisal*, **30**, 1, 25–33.

Adorno, T.W., 1972 [1965], Gesellschaft, in R. Tiedemann (ed.) *Theodor W. Adorno: Soziologische Schriften I*, Frankfurt am Main: Suhrkamp, 9–19.

Ahrne, G. and Brunsson, N., 2008, *Meta-Organizations*, Cheltenham, UK and Northampton, MA, USA: Edward Elgar.

Bader, V., 2014, Sciences, politics, and associative democracy: Democratizing science and expertizing democracy, *Innovation: The European Journal of Social Sciences*, **27**, 4, 420–444.

Barnes, B., Bloor, D. and Henry, J., 1996, *Scientific Knowledge: A Sociological Analysis*, London: University of Chicago Press.

Baumgartner, F.R. and Jones, B.D. (eds), 2002, *Policy Dynamics*, Chicago: University of Chicago Press.

Beck, S., 2012, Between tribalism and trust: The IPCC under the 'public microscope', *Nature and Culture*, **7**, 2, 151–163.

Beck, S., 2015, Scientific experts, in E. Lövbrand and K. Bäckstrand (eds) *Research Handbook on Climate Governance*, Cheltenham, UK and Northampton, MA, USA: Edward Elgar (in print).

Beck, U., 1992, *Risk Society. Towards a New Modernity*, London/Thousand Oaks/New Delhi: Sage.

Berger, P. and Luckmann, T., 1967, *The Social Construction of Reality: A Treatise in the Sociology of Knowledge*, New York: Anchor Books.

Bijker, W.E., Bal, R. and Hendriks, R., 2009, *The Paradox of Scientific Authority. The Role of Scientific Advice in Democracies*, Cambridge/London: The MIT Press.

Blasimme, A., 2014, The politics of biomedical innovation: Institutional instability and epistemic fragmentation. Paper presented at the World Congress of the International Political Science Association (IPSA), Montreal, 19–24 July 2014.

Bloor, D., 1991 [1976], *Knowledge and Social Imagery (Second Edition)*, London: University of Chicago Press.

Blühdorn, I., 2013, The governance of unsustainability: Ecology and democracy after the post-democratic turn, *Environmental Politics*, **22**, 1, 16–36.

Blyth, M., 2002, *Great Transformations. Economic Ideas and Institutional Change in the Twentieth Century*, Cambridge, MA: Cambridge University Press.

Bora, A., 2010, Technoscientific normativity and the 'iron cage' of law, *Science Technology Human Values*, **35**, 1, 3–28.

Brown, M.B., 2009a, Federal advisory committees in the United States: A survey of the political and administrative landscape, in P. Weingart and J. Lentsch (eds) *Scientific Advice to Policy Making: International Comparison*, Opladen: Barbara Budrich, 17–39.

Brown, M.B., 2009b, *Science in Democracy. Expertise, Institutions, and Representations*, Cambridge, MA/London: The MIT Press.

Brown, M.B., Lentsch, J. and Weingart, P., 2005, Representation, expertise, and the German Parliament: A comparison of three advisory institutions, in S. Maasen and P. Weingart (eds) *Democratization of Expertise? Exploring Novel Forms of Scientific Advice in Political Decision-Making*, Berlin/Heidelberg/New York: Springer Verlag, 81–100.

Cabinet Office, 1999, *Modernising Government*, London: The Stationery Office.

Cabinet Office, 2013, *What Works: Evidence Centres for Social Policy*, London: Cabinet Office.

Callon, M., Lascoumes, P. and Barthe, Y., 2011, *Acting in an Uncertain World. An Essay on Technical Democracy*, Cambridge, MA/London: The MIT Press.

Campbell, A. and Pedersen, O.K., 2014, *The National Origins of Policy Ideas: Knowledge Regimes in the United States, France, Germany, and Denmark*, Princeton/Oxford: Princeton University Press.

Caplan, N., Morrison, A. and Stambaugh, R.J., 1975, *The Use of Social Science Knowledge in Policy Decision at the National Level. A Report to Respondents*, Ann Arbor, MI: Ann Arbor Center for Research on the Utilization of Scientific Knowledge.

Colebatch, H.K., Hoppe, R. and Nordegraaf, M. (eds), 2010, *Working for Policy*, Amsterdam: Amsterdam University Press.

Collins, H.M. and Evans, B., 2006, The third wave of science studies. Studies of expertise and experience, in E. Selinger and R.P. Crease (eds) *The Philosopie of Expertise*, New York: Columbia University Press, 39–110.

Collins, H.M. and Evans, R., 2007, *Rethinking Expertise*, Chicago/London: University of Chicago Press.

Craft, J. and Howlett, M., 2012, Policy formulation, governance shifts and policy influence: Location and content in policy advisory systems, *Journal of Public Policy*, **32**, 2, 79–98.

Daston, L.J. and Galison, P., 2007, *Objectivity*, New York: Zone Books.

Davies, H.T.O., Nutley, S.M. and Smith, P.C. (eds), 2000, *What Works? Evidence-based Policy and Practice in Public Services*, Bristol: The Policy Press.

Demortain, D., 2009, Legitimation by standards: Transnational experts, the European Commission and regulation of novel foods, *Sociologie du travail*, **51S**, e104–e116.

Dewey, John, 1939, *Theory of Value*, Chicago and London: University of Chicago Press.

Elliott, K.C., 2011, *Is a Little Pollution Good for You? Incorporating Societal Values in Environmental Research*, Oxford: Oxford University Press.

Elzinga, A., 1985, Research, bureaucracy and the drift of epistemic criteria, in B. Wittrock and A. Elzinga (eds) *The University Research System. The Public Policies of the Home of Scientists*, Stockholm: Almquist & Wiksell International, 191–220.

Epstein, S., 2007, *Inclusion: The Politics of Difference in Medical Research*, Chicago: University of Chicago Press.

Ezrahi, Y., Grove-Wright, R., Robins, R. and Jasanoff, S., 2008, Review symposion – controlling biotechnology: Science, democracy and 'civic epistemology', *Metascience*, **17**, 177–198.

Fischer, F., 1988, *Techno-corporatism in the United States: A Critique of Contemporary Technocratic Theory and Methods (Veröffentlichungsreihe der Abteilung Organisation und Technikgenese des Forschungsschwerpunkts Technik-Arbeit-Umwelt des Wissens chaftszentrums Berlin für Sozialforschung)*, Berlin: Wissenschaftszentrum Berlin für Sozialforschung.

Fischer, F., 2009, *Democracy & Expertise. Reorienting Policy Inquiry*, Oxford: Oxford University Press.

Fischer, F. and Forrester, J., 1993, *The Argumentative Turn in Policy Analysis and Planning*, Durham, NC: Duke University Press.

Fischer, F. and Gottweis, H. (eds), 2012, *The Argumentative Turn Revisited: Public Policy as Communicative Practice*, Durham, NC/London: Duke University Press.

Fleischer, J., 2012, *Policy Advice and Institutional Politics: A Comparative Analysis of Germany and Britain (Dissertation)*, Potsdam: Universität Potsdam.

Friedman, J., 2014, Political epistemology, *Critical Review*, **26**, 1–2, i–xiv.

Gieryn, T.F., 1995, Boundaries of science, in S. Jasanoff, G.E. Markle and J.C. Petersen (eds) *Handbook of Science and Technology Studies*, Thousand Oaks, CA: Sage, 393–443.

Gieryn, T.F., 1998, *Cultural Boundaries of Science. Credibility on the Line*, Chicago/London: University of Chicago Press.

Guston, D., 2000, *Between Politics and Science. Assessing the Integrity and Productivity of Research*, Cambridge: Cambridge University Press.

Habermas, J., 1968, *Technik und Wissenschaft als 'Ideologie'*, Frankfurt am Main: Suhrkamp.

Habermas, J., 1987, *Towards a Rational Society*, London: Policy Press.

Habermas, J., 2001, *The Postnational Constellation*, Cambridge, MA: The MIT Press.

Hajer, M.A, 2009, *Authoritative Governance. Policy-making in the Age of Mediatization*, Oxford: Oxford University Press.

Halffman, W. and Hoppe, R., 2005, Science/policy boundaries: A changing division of labour in Dutch expert policy advice, in S. Maasen and P. Weingart (eds) *Democratization of Expertise? Exploring Novel Forms of Scientific Advice in Political Decision-Making*, Berlin/Heidelberg/New York: Springer Verlag, 135–151.

Hall, P.A, 1993, Policy-paradigms, social learning and the state: The case of economic policy-making in Britain, *Comparative Politics*, **25**, 3, 275–296.

Hilgartner, S., 2000, *Science on Stage: Expert Advice as Public Drama*, Stanford, CA: Stanford University Press.

Hilgartner, S., Miller, C.A. and Hagendijk, R.P. (eds), 2015, *Science and Democracy: Making Knowledge and Making Power in the Biosciences and Beyond (Genetics and Society)*, London: Routledge.

Hoppe, R., 1999, Policy analysis, science, and politics: From 'speaking truth to power' to 'making sense together', *Science and Public Policy*, **26**, 3, 201–210.

Hoppe, R., 2010, *The Governance of Problems: Puzzling, Powering and Participation*, Bristol: The Policy Press.

Howlett, M., 2009, Policy analytical capacity and evidence-based policy-making: Lessons from Canada, *Canadian Public Administration*, **52**, 2, 153–175.

Jasanoff, S., 1990, *The Fifth Branch: Science Advisers as Policymakers*, Cambridge, MA/London: Harvard University Press.

Jasanoff, S., 2004a, Science and citizenship: A new synergy, *Science and Public Policy*, **31**, 2, 90–94.

Jasanoff, S., 2004b, The idiom of co-production, in S. Jasanoff (ed.) *States of Knowledge. The Co-production of Science and Social Order*, London/New York: Routledge, 1–12.

Jasanoff, S., 2005a, *Designs on Nature: Science and Democracy in Europe and the United States*, Princeton, NJ: Princeton University Press.

Jasanoff, S., 2005b, Judgement under Siege: The three-body problem of expert legitimacy, in S. Maasen and P. Weingart (eds) *Democratization of Expertise? Exploring Novel Forms of Scientific Advice in Political Decision-Making*, Berlin/Heidelberg/New York: Springer Verlag, 209–224.

Jasanoff, S., 2011a, Quality control and peer review in advisory science, in J. Lentsch and P. Weingart (eds) *The Politics of Scientific Advice. Institutional Design for Quality Assurance*, Cambridge/New York/Melbourne: Cambridge University Press, 19–35.

Jasanoff, S., 2011b, The practices of objectivity in regulatory science, in C. Camid, N. Gross and M. Lamont (eds) *Social Knowledge in the Making*, Chicago/London: University of Chicago Press, 307–338.

Jasanoff, S., 2012, *Science and Public Reason*, New York: Routledge.

Jasanoff, S., 2013, A world of experts. Science and global environmental constitutionalism, *Boston College Environmental Affairs Law Review*, **40**, 2.

Jung, A., Korinek, R.-L. and Straßheim, H., 2014, Embedded expertise: A conceptual framework for reconstructing knowledge orders, their transformation and local specificities, *Innovation: The European Journal of Social Sciences*, DOI: 10.1080/13511610.2014.892425.

Kitcher, P., 2001, *Science, Truth, and Democracy*, Oxford/New York: Oxford University Press.

Kitcher, P., 2011, *Science in a Democratic Society*, New York: Prometheus Books.

Korinek, R.-L., 2014, The construction of politico-epistemic authority. Comparing food safety agencies in Germany and in Britain. Paper presented at the ECPR General Conference, Glasgow, 2014.

Kröger, S., 2009, The open method of coordination: Underconceptualisation, overdetermination, de-politicisation and beyond, *European Integration Online Papers*, **13** (Special Issue 1, Art. 5).

Kuhn, T., 1962, *The Structure of Scientific Revolutions*, Chicago/London: University of Chicago Press.

Laski, H., 1930, The limitations of the expert, *Harper's Monthly Magazine*, **162**, 967, 101–110.

Latour, B., 1993, *We Have Never Been Modern*, Cambridge, MA: Harvard University Press.

Latour, B., 2004, *Politics of Nature. How to Bring the Sciences Into Democracy*, Cambridge, MA/London: Harvard University Press.

Leibniz, G.W., 1931a [1680], Entwürff gewisser Staats-Tafeln (Nr. 29), in Preussische Akademie der Wissenschaften/Akademie der Wissenschaften der DDR (ed.) *Leibniz: Sämtliche Schriften und Briefe (Akademie-Ausgabe, Vierte Reihe: Politische Schriften, Bd. 3)*, Berlin: Akademie Verlag, 340–349.

Leibniz, G.W., 1931b [1680], Von nützlicher Einrichtung eines Archivi (Nr. 28), in Preussische Akademie der Wissenschaften/Akademie der Wissenschaften der DDR (ed.) *Leibniz: Sämtliche Schriften und Briefe (Akademie-Ausgabe, Vierte Reihe: Politische Schriften, Bd. 3)*, Berlin: Akademie-Verlag, 332–340.

Limoges, C., 1993, Expert knowledge and decision-making in controversy contexts, *Public Understanding of Science*, **2**, 417–426.

Long Martello, M. and Jasanoff, S., 2004, Introduction: Globalization and environmental governance, in S. Jasanoff and M. Long Martello (eds) *Earthly Politics. Local and Global in Environmental Governance*, Cambridge, MA/London: The MIT Press, 1–29.

Longino, H., 2002, *The Fate of Knowledge*, Princeton, NJ: Princeton University Press.

Luhmann, N., 1989 [1969], *Legitimation durch Verfahren*, Frankfurt am Main: Suhrkamp.

Luhmann, N., 1995, *Social Systems*, Stanford, CA: Stanford University Press.

Majone, G., 1991, Research programmes and action programmes, or can policy research learn from the philosophy of science?, in P. Wagner, C. Hirschhorn Weiss, B. Wittrock and H. Wollmann (eds) *Social Sciences and Modern States. National Experiences and Theoretical Crossroads*, Cambridge: Cambridge University Press, 290–306.

Marston, G. and Watts, R., 2003, Tampering with the evidence: A critical appraisal of evidence-based policy-making, *The Drawing Board: An Australian Review of Public Affairs*, **3**, 143–63.

Miller, C.A., 2005, New civic epistemologies of quantification: Making sense of indicators of local and global sustainability, *Science, Technology, & Human Values*, **30**, 3, 403–432.

Miller, P., 2008, Calculating economic life, *Journal of Cultural Economy*, **1**, 1, 51–64.

Miller, P. and Rose, R., 1994, On therapeutic authority: Psychoanalytical expertise under advanced liberalism, *History of Human Science*, **7**, 3, 29–64.

Morgan, M.S., 2011, Travelling facts, in P. Howlett and M.S. Morgan (eds) *How Well do Facts Travel? The Dissimination of Reliable Knowledge*, Cambridge/New York/Melbourne: Cambridge University Press, 3–39.

Nelkin, D., 1987, *Selling Science: How the Press Covers Science and Technology*, New York: W.H. Freeman.

Nutley, S., Morto, S., Jung, T. and Boaz, A., 2010, Evidence and policy in six European countries: Diverse approaches and common challenges, *Evidence & Policy*, **6**, 2, 131–144.

Nutley, S., Levitt, M.R. and Solesbury, W., 2012, Scrutinizing performance: How assessors reach judgements about public services, *Public Administration*, **90**, 4, 869–885.

O'Connor, A., 2001, *Poverty Knowledge: Social Science, Social Policy, and the Poor in Twentieth-Century U.S. History*, Princeton, NJ: Princeton University Press.

Pielke, R.J., 2011, *The Honest Broker: Making Sense of Science in Policy and Politics*, Cambridge: Cambridge University Press.

Porter, T.M., 1995, *Trust in Numbers. The Pursuit of Objectivity in Science and Public Life*, Princeton, NJ: Princeton University Press.

Quack, S., 2013, Regime complexity and expertise in transnational governance: Strategizing in the face of regulatory uncertainty, *Oñati Socio-Legal Series*, **3**, 4, 647–678

Renn, O., 1995, Styles of using scientific expertise: A comparative framework, *Science and Public Policy*, **22**, 3, 147–156.

Rothstein, H., 2013, Domesticating participation: Participation and the institutional rationalities of science-based policy-making in the UK food standards agency, *Journal of Risk Research*, **16**, 6, 771–790.

Rüb, F. and Straßheim, H., 2012, Politische Evidenz. Rechtfertigung durch Verobjektivierung, in A. Geis, F. Nullmeier and C. Daase (eds) *Der Aufstieg der Legitimitätspolitik. Rechtfertigung und Kritik politisch-ökonomischer Ordnungen (Leviathan-Sonderband 27/2012)*, Baden-Baden: Nomos, 377–397.

Sanderson, I., 2011, Evidence-based policy or policy-based evidence? Reflections on Scottish experience, *Evidence & Policy*, **7**, 1, 59–76.

Schudson, M., 2006, The trouble with experts – and why democracies need them, *Theory and Society*, **35**, 491–506.

Schütz, A., 1974, *Der sinnhafte Aufbau der sozialen Welt. Eine Einleitung in die verstehende Soziologie*, Frankfurt am Main: Suhrkamp.

Schütz, A., 1976 [1959], The well-informed citizen. An essay on the social distribution of knowledge, in A. Schütz (ed.) *Collected Papers II: Studies in Social Theorie*, Den Haag: Martinus Nijhoff, 120–134.

Scott, W.R., 1995, *Institutions and Organizations*, London/Thousand Oaks/New Delhi: Sage.

Shapin, S., 1992, Discipline and bounding: The history and sociology of science as seen through the externalism-internalism debate, *History of Science*, **30**, 333–369.

Shapin, S. and Schaffer, S., 1985, *Leviathan and the Air-Pump. Hobbes, Boyle, and the Experimental Life*, Princeton, NJ: Princeton University Press.

Sharman, A. and Holmes, J., 2010, Evidence-based policy or policy-based evidence gathering? Biofuels, the EU and the 10% target, *Environmental Policy and Governance*, **20**, 5, 309–321.

Shaw, G.B., 1906, *The Doctor's Dilemma*, Stockbridge: Hard Press.

Sismondo, S., 2010, *An Introduction to Science and Technology Studies*, Malden, MA/ Oxford/West Sussex: Wiley-Blackwell.

Star, S.L. and Griesemer, J.R., 1989, Institutional ecology, 'translations' and boundary objects: Amateurs and professionals in Berkeley's Museum of Verterbrate Zoology, 1907–1939, *Social Studies of Science*, **19**, 3, 387–420.

Stone, D., 2012, *Knowledge Actors and Transnational Governance: The Private-Public Policy Nexus in the Global Agora*, London: Palgrave Macmillan.

Straßheim, H., 2012, Wissensordnungen. Theoretische Grundlagen und analytische Potentiale eines Grenzbegriffs, in J. Hofmann and A. Busch (eds) *Politik und die Regulierung von Informationen (Sonderheft der Politischen Vierteljahresschrift 46/2012)*, Wiesbaden: VS Verlag für Sozialwissenschaften, 48–84.

Straßheim, H. and Kettunen, P., 2014, When does evidence-based policy turn into policy-based evidence? Configurations, contexts and mechanisms, *Evidence & Policy*, **10**, 2, 259–277.

Straßheim, H. and Korinek, R.-L., 2015, Behavioural governance in Europe, in R. Doubleday and J. Wilsdon (eds) *Future Directions for Scientific Advice in Europe*, London: University of Cambridge/University of Sussex et al., 153–160.

Straßheim, H., Jung, A. and Korinek, R.-L., 2015, Reframing expertise: The rise of behavioural insights and interventions in public policy, in A. Berthoin Antal, M. Hutter and D. Stark (eds) *Moments of Valuation. Exploring Sites of Dissonance*, Oxford: Oxford University Press, 249–268.

Sunstein, C.R., 2014, *Valuing Life. Humanizing the Regulatory State*, Chicago/London: University of Chicago Press.

Thornton, P.H, Ocasio, W. and Lounsbury, M., 2012, *The Institutional Logics Perspective: Foundations, Research, and Theoretical Elaboration*, Oxford: Oxford University Press.

Torgerson, D., 1986, Between knowledge and politics. Three faces of policy analysis, *Policy Sciences*, **19**, 1, 33–59.

Turner, S., 2006, What is the problem with experts?, in E. Selinger and R.P. Crease (eds) *The Philosopie of Expertise*, New York: Columbia University Press, 159–186.

Vibert, F., 2007, *The Rise of the Unelected: Democracy and the New Separation of Powers*, Cambridge: Cambridge University Press.

Wagner, P., Hirschhorn Weiss, C., Wittrock, B. and Wollmann, H. (eds), 1991, *Social Sciences and Modern States. National Experiences and Theoretical Crossroads*, Cambridge: Cambridge University Press.

Weingart, P., 1983, Verwissenschaftlichung der Gesellschaft – Politisierung der Wissenschaft, *Zeitschrift für Soziologie*, **12**, 3, 225–241.

340 Handbook of critical policy studies

Weiss, C.H., 1979, The many meanings of research utilization, *Public Administration Review*, **39**, 5, 426–431.
Weiss, C.H., 1980, Knowledge creep and decision accretion, *Knowledge: Creation, Diffusion, Utilization*, **8**, 2, 381–404.
Wittrock, B., Wagner, P. and Wollmann, H., 1991, Social science and the modern state: Policy knowledge and political institutions in Western Europe and the United States, in P. Wagner, C. Hirschhorn Weiss, B. Wittrock and H. Wollmann (eds) *Social Sciences and Modern States. National Experiences and Theoretical Crossroads*, Cambridge: Cambridge University Press, 28–85.
World Bank, 2015, *Mind, Society and Behavior*, Washington, DC: World Bank.
Wynne, B., 1996, May the sheep safely graze? A reflexive view of the expert-lay knowledge divide, in B. Lash, B. Szerszynski and B. Wynne (eds) *Risk, Environment and Modernity*, London: Sage.
Wynne, B., 2003, Seasick on the third wave? Subverting the hegemony of propositionalism, *Social Studies of Science*, **33**, 401–418.
Zahariadis, N., 2003, *Ambiguity and Choice in Public Policy: Political Decision Making in Modern Democracies (American Governance and Public Policy)*, Washington, DC: Georgetown University Press.
Zürn, M., Binder, M. and Ecker-Ehrhardt, M., 2012, International authority and its politicization, *International Theory – A Journal of International Politics, Law and Philosophy*, **4**, 1, 69–106.

18 Global governance and sustainability indicators: the politics of expert knowledge
Laureen Elgert

THE INCREASING IMPORTANCE AND DOMINANCE OF INDICATORS IN GLOBAL ENVIRONMENTAL POLITICS

The increasing importance of indicators as authoritative and transparent representations of outcomes is evident in many policy domains. Nowhere, however, have discussions about policy indicators been more prolific than in recent debates about global sustainability policy. The growing importance of indicators of sustainability was recognized, for example, at several key sustainable development policy conferences in 2012, where they were promoted as necessary to measure, compare and direct environmental change (Biermann et al., 2012; Planet Under Pressure, 2012; UNCSD, 2012). These high-level policy discussions have tended to perpetuate the treatment of indicators as technical policy tools, emphasizing indicators as devices able to identify causal relationships between drivers of environmental change; the resultant environmental state; and the policy responses necessary to effect desirable changes. Although uncommon just two decades ago, sustainability indicator sets now exist in the hundreds at various scales of governance, all over the world, measuring the sustainability of products, processes and places.

While indicators have been generally accepted rather unproblematically into mainstream global environmental discourse (McCool and Stankey, 2004), the expansion of global indicators involves two main tensions in sustainability policy and the policy literature more generally. The first tension is between local and global governance. The growing importance of indicators is accompanied by a concurrent and sometimes conflictive emphasis both on local, decentralized decision making about the parameters of defining and measuring sustainability and on establishing sustainability norms and means of achieving and comparing sustainability on a global scale (Jasanoff and Martello, 2004). This tension is apparent, for example, in the recent plethora of roundtables that aggregate local stakeholder input into global standards for sustainable production (Cotula et al., 2008; Schouten and Glasbergen, 2011; Schouten et al., 2012). The second tension is between managerial and technocratic approaches to sustainability on the one hand and a focus on deepening democracy and environmental justice on the other (Paavola, 2007; Rayner, 2003). Although they are often heralded as means for the same goal of overall sustainability, the efficiency emphasized by managerialism and the equity emphasized by environmental justice often make strange bedfellows (Ford, 2003).

This chapter addresses these tensions by analyzing the knowledge-policy interface created by indicator projects, where indicators can be understood as both technologies of knowledge production and as technologies of governance (Davis et al., 2012b). Global indicators employ standardization and evidence as strategies for knowledge production that are widely accepted as objective means for measuring sustainability and directing policy in neutral and unbiased ways that promote both transparency and efficiency in sustainability governance. But social and political scientists engaged with critical policy analysis have shown that standardization and evidence are both socially embedded and politically contested processes of knowledge creation, that, when used in decision making for societies, have sometimes surprising consequences for sustainability governance. This chapter examines these complexities in the context of the global agricultural commodity chain of soybean.

In response to concerns about the environmental, economic and social impacts of soybean production, the Roundtable on Responsible Soy was convened in 2006 to develop indicators for 'responsible' soy production. These indicators embody the very definition of 'responsible soy'. They are also central to the soy industry's governance regime, as they provide the standards by which third-party verification differentiates producers that qualify for certification from producers that do not, thereby influencing behaviors and determining sanctions and rewards. This process of indicator development, however, has been deeply contested on a number of levels and has ramified problematic governance outcomes that have severely disadvantaged certain stakeholders in soy producing areas. This case provides insight into wider questions raised by two prominent tensions in the critical policy literature: (1) between the merits and ethics of local policy making at the global environmental scale; (2) between managerialist or technocratic approaches and calls for wider public participation in sustainability decision making.

INDICATORS: MODERN KNOWLEDGE FOR GLOBAL GOVERNANCE?

Conventional approaches to the relationship between knowledge and policy take indicators as a means of packaging and presenting knowledge in objective and universally valid ways for policy analysis (Shields et al., 2002) in order to create a vernacular of sustainability that is appropriate at the global level. This view of indicators has widespread appeal in light of growing concern about the global environmental crisis and demands of policy makers to 'get the politics out of policy making' – demands that emphasize an urgent need for impartiality in decision making and the direct transfer of knowledge to policy (Collins and Evans, 2007; Gardner, 2009; Leshner, 2002). These calls for 'modernized' governance provide the shorthand for institutionalizing methods that instrumentalize, rationalize and depoliticize policy processes (Fischer, 2003), thereby obscuring human intervention by letting the 'facts' drive policy making and rendering it 'more efficient and legitimate' (Solesbury, 2001). Such thinking underpins the widespread acceptance in global environmental governance of such features as a 'corporate form of thinking' (Davis et al., 2012a), 'audit culture' (Kipnis, 2008; Power, 1999; Shore, 2008) and 'evidence based policy' (Elgert, 2009; Hezri and Dovers, 2006; Marston and Watts, 2003; Solesbury, 2001). Critical policy analysts, in contrast, have criticized modernist approaches to governance for skewing power relations in environmental policy towards those individuals and entities who know how to create and communicate the 'right kind' of knowledge. They have also pointed out that modernist approaches misinterpret policy processes in linear terms of valid facts feeding good policy in an instrumentalist cycle of administrative efficiency (Dryzek, 1990, 2006). The critics argue instead for an understanding of policy in discursive terms as an outcome of political dynamics and struggles (Dryzek, 1990; Hajer, 1995).

The notions of standardization and evidence are key to understanding the uptake of indicators in conventional governance approaches. Here global organizations look to promote transparency, accountability and efficiency in efforts to direct, measure and compare progress towards sustainability – or in the anthemic words of the UNCSD – 'the future we want' (UNCSD, 2012). Standardization and evidence are key components of indicators that create and organize knowledge in an oft-assumed globally meaningful way. Constructivist studies, however, highlight the struggles, contingencies and politics of such maneuvers and emphasize the need for 'situating the technical in the social' (Fischer, 2009) by revealing and assessing social and political influences in indicators' development that are often muted or hidden. Far from being 'agreed upon', environments as represented by indicators are imbued with multiple and contested meanings and can therefore be only partially (as opposed to completely) understood by indicator sets. This observation points to the importance of examining not only finalized sets of indicators, but also the social and political processes of development that give rise to them (Astleithner and Hamedinger, 2003; Turnhout et al., 2007). While appearing to have a 'public' nature, standardization and evidence-making are two such processes. Furthermore, they can contribute to unexpected governance outcomes.

Standardization is central to modern life. In many respects, standards are seen as a benign characteristic of modern society (Lampland and Leigh Star, 2009), particularly in the realm of environmental regulation, where regulatory bodies are considered knowledgeable and protective. There are plenty of instances in which social movements have coalesced around imposing environmental standards. Nonetheless, there are many examples of resistance to standardization (Timmermans and Epstein, 2010) in areas such as education (Kohn, 2000), healthcare (Epstein, 2007), and environmental and sustainability policy (Rydin, 2007).

Behind many of these cases of resistance lies the issue that standardization, by its very definition, subsumes difference (Lampland and Leigh Star, 2009). Creating global standards sets benchmarks of performance and activity in a supposedly unitary global context. In order to develop global standards, diverse contexts are homogenized and knowledge is stripped of contingency. Unfettered by context, global indicators are seemingly imbued with a 'portability' that allows them to be transplanted from place to place with consistent meaning. Understanding indicators as neutral, factual representations of local realities suggests that the indicators can be smoothly and unproblematically mobilized at different levels of analysis. Such confidence in the validity and portability of indicators overlooks the way in which indicators represent particular world views – rather than some global consensus – about sustainability, and involve a 'refusal to recognize complexity and uncertainty in ecological affairs' (Dryzek, 2013, p. 71). Ideas about sustainability are not actually universal, but are bound up with complex socio-political meanings and dynamics that depend on dimensions of difference such as culture, class, gender and livelihoods (Adger et al., 2011; Elgert, 2009). Moreover, sustainability policies are likely to incur differential impacts on distinct socio-economic groups. Indicators that represent only aggregate income, for example, do not show how income is distributed, nor how alternative livelihoods – that may make a comparatively small but vital contribution to overall income and subsistence – might be impacted (Elgert, 2013). Standardization, through simplifying and homogenizing natural and social phenomena, enables the translation of complexity into conceptual maps that – though they are easily read and employed for purposes of intervention (Li, 2007; Scott, 1998) – often distort, misrepresent or overlook subtle but important details.

Indicators serve as 'snapshots' of a larger environmental and social story; they are employed to provide a truncated, summarized view of the bigger picture. Indicators rely on 'thin description' (Geertz, 1973) that is overly dependent on contested assumptions about environmental and social phenomena and that underestimates the field of meaning in context. Such simplified relationships are often portrayed as being natural and factual. But we need only look to the recent past in environmental debate to find examples of successful challenges to such assumptions. Population growth and environmental degradation, for example, were once portrayed as inextricably linked, thereby supporting predictions of catastrophic overpopulation, famine and war (Ehrlich, 1968). This relationship, however, has since been found to be uncertain and tenuous, being highly mediated by technological innovation and governance (Tiffen et al., 1994). More recently, research has questioned the modernist assumption that agriculture and biodiversity are incompatible, and has suggested that policies should encourage and incentivize agricultural intensification to increase production per land unit, 'sparing' more land for conservation in the form of parks and reserves. New ecological knowledge, changing debates about agriculture, and active and vocal rural social movements have successfully challenged the land sparing orthodoxy and have replaced it with a new understanding of the ways in which small-scale agriculture can promote biodiversity conservation (Perfecto and Vandermeer, 2010; Perfecto et al., 2009; Phalan et al., 2011). These examples show that facts are often contingent upon temporal, geographic and social limits of observation and debate. 'Facts' can, and often are, revised with the input of new participants in debates, changing physical environments and new understandings of socio-technical relationships (Forsyth, 2003, 2011). Indeed, we must be wary of a blind 'trust in facts' (Forsyth, 2011) and must regard cautiously and critically the indicators that are supposed to represent them.

In a discussion of the 'idiom of co-production,' Jasanoff (2004) suggests how knowledge of physical phenomena and understandings of power, culture and social structure are mutually affirming. In particular, processes of coproduction create representations of sustainability that are rooted not solely in the 'natural' nor in the 'social', but in socially and politically informed framings of biophysical objects and concepts (Forsyth, 2003; Latour, 1993). Studies that have examined processes of indicator development reveal negotiations, disagreements and contingencies in the debates about how and what indicators can be adequately and appropriately measured. Such debates cannot be simplistically assessed in terms of who is 'right' and 'wrong', but are be linked to environmental values, disciplinary norms, personal perspectives and technical limitations. Individual indicators might combine to create phenomena that did not previously exist, such as 'organic produce' (Guthman, 2004) and 'responsible soy' (Elgert, 2012). Even this process, however, is not without potential problems. The combination of particular indicators behind such phenomena may even themselves disappear from public view, as labels inspire new imaginaries that may bear little resemblance to empirical reality (Guthman, 2004). Even conscientious advocates, therefore, recognize that the contingencies and negotiations involved in the development of sustainability indicators are significant (Astleithner and Hamedinger, 2003), arguing that, 'the bases of, and rationale for, any indicator (should) be explicit and open to scrutiny. This would include such things as the assumptions underlying their selection, possible alternatives, liabilities and uncertainties . . . ' (McCool and Stankey, 2004, p. 295, parentheses added). In this light, indicators need to be understood as 'made' not 'found' (Turnhout, 2009).

Ultimately, however, in debates surrounding the development of indicator categories, criteria and methods of measurement most often become hidden, black-boxed and of secondary interest to all but the most curious and rigorous of observers. Indeed, 'indicators typically do not come with a discussion of such decisions or an analysis of the implications of the choice' (Merry, 2011, p. S86). At the same time, standardized and evidence-based indicators are held up as rational and efficient means of governing sustainability, an antidote to corruption and patronage in policy able not only to assess decision making outcomes, but also to assure transparency by holding them up for public scrutiny. The ultimate invisibility of the significant social influence in the development of indicators suggests serious problems for this link between indicators and transparency. Indeed,

> transparency can be superficial because the raw data used to construct indicators, and the methods used to simplify those data, are not necessarily easy to communicate and may in fact be treated as confidential. Even when such detailed information is provided, users may well not delve into the complexities and limitations of the underlying data and the analytic choices made in converting it into an indicator. (Davis et al., 2012a, p. 86)

Social scientists have identified attempts to increase transparency and accountability through standardized, evidence-based indicators not as technical improvements in governance, but as a cultural shift in civic epistemology. This shift is towards perceived objectivity and uniformity as 'the criteria by which members of that society systematically evaluate the validity of public knowledge' (Jasanoff, 2003, p. 394). Civic epistemologies, however, are not universal, and struggles for epistemological dominance in global governance are not fair fights. Asymmetries exist in the access different actors have to material, discursive and symbolic means to establish the baseline for discussion, including what 'counts' as evidence (Marston and Watts, 2003), and thereby influence the ways in which indicators take shape. The juxtaposition of so-called 'global' and 'local' knowledge provides a poignant example (Brown and Purcell, 2005; Jasanoff and Martello, 2004; Shiva, 1993). Science, understood in positivist terms, is thought to produce broad consensus and predictive power (Davies et al., 2000) and to have global validity. Meanwhile, knowledge termed 'local', 'folk', or 'traditional' is often assumed to be particular, unduly influenced by ignorance, superstition or politics (Jasanoff, 1998; Jasanoff and Martello, 2004). In this regard, 'local' knowledge can be valued for its normative contributions to environmental policy debates and further valued when it is congruent with more objective, observation-based knowledge. Unable to compete with the authority and credibility of scientific knowledge, however, such local knowledge becomes subsumed or reshaped by the 'facts'. Indeed, such science is typically authoritative: 'objective scientific expertise is generally valued more highly than other grounds for decision making . . . [such that] attacks on the scientific competence of regulatory agencies is a standard device for undermining their political legitimacy' (Jasanoff, 2000, p. 73). Similarly, 'people trying to make or influence policy often find the lack of scientific closure a potent weapon' (Taylor and Buttel, 1992, p. 406, quoting Jasanoff, 1992). Such is the case even though empirical work has shown how the production of so-called 'facts' rarely produces consensus and predictive capacity and often leads to greater uncertainty and contention in policy debates (Collingridge and Reeve, 1986).

Less subtle forms of power also exert tremendous influence on developing sustainability indicators and establishing norms in global environmental governance. Multinational corporations, for example, are increasingly involved in developing non-state, voluntary mechanisms to assert their own corporate social responsibility around sustainability issues, and these corporations have become significant actors in global environmental governance (Christmann, 2004; Elgert, 2011). Likewise, the power of wealthy nations to dictate global policy is not lost in the environmental realm. Global environmental norms, it is often noted, are 'made in the North, for the North' (Epstein, 2006, p. 32). Ultimately, indicators 'represent the perspectives and frameworks of those who produce them, as well as their political and financial power. What gets counted depends on which groups and organizations can afford to count' (Merry, 2011, p. S88). In recognition of these tendencies, there has been a growing emphasis on broadening public participation in indicators development through policy processes such as stakeholder roundtables as well as public and semi-public forums. Such processes, however, have often been unsuccessful in vanquishing the dramatic power asymmetries between diverse groups of participants (Elgert, 2011).

How indicators are defined, established and measured are not only decisions that are influenced *by* social factors. In turn, they are decisions that *constitute* the material and social world as indicator sets are used to evaluate policy outcomes, create rankings, invite comparison, create labels and distribute resources (Merry, 2011). Such functions often enable the explicit and implicit use of standardized policy sets to pressure or, even, force local sustainability policy making along distinct, 'globally' sanctioned directions. By incentivizing particular behaviors through punishments and rewards, global governance regimes can exert a 'coercive accountability' (Shore and Wright, 2000) by making even voluntary standards difficult to ignore. Once unleashed in the policy realm, indicators gain an 'inertia' (Bowker and Leigh Star, 1999, p. 14) such that for targeted stakeholders to change them or reject them can be difficult, time-consuming and costly (Thevenot, 2009). Even in cases where those subject to, or affected by, measurement and sanctions have had little input into emergent indicator systems, participation in the systems, or the consequences of non-participation, can be serious. Decline in market access, reduced attractiveness, or even punitive or legal action are potential outcomes of non-participation or poor performance. Incentive structures around participating in indicator systems, therefore, can be extremely powerful and effective, even in cases where the factual basis of indicators represent, for some stakeholders, conflicting values, lack of continuity or contingency. Even if participation in indicator systems is deemed 'voluntary', participation may imply valuable 'club membership', without which stakeholders forgo significant opportunity or suffer considerable loss.

THE STORY OF INDICATORS FOR RESPONSIBLE SOY

The expansion and globalization of industrial agriculture, particularly in developing countries, has had economic, environmental and social impacts that have generated considerable concern over the sustainability of production processes and structures. In response, governance regimes have emerged to develop indicators for sustainable production that enable third-party verification and certification that particular commodities have been produced under 'sustainable' conditions. The Roundtable on Responsible Soy (RTRS) is one such governance regime, developed in response to growing international attention to the impacts of the 'soy boom' in South America that range from deforestation (Altieri and Pengue, 2005) to the use of forced labor (Holland et al., 2008). These indicators, known as 'certification standards', are central to environmental governance:

> interventions aiming at changes in environment-related incentives, knowledge, institutions, decision-making . . . the set of regulatory processes, mechanisms and organizations through which political actors influence environmental actions and outcomes. (Lemos and Argrawal, 2006, p. 298)

Over the past three decades, Brazil and Paraguay have become two of the world's largest soybean producers, exporting most of their production to Europe as livestock feed. Soy production has been celebrated as an engine of growth in these countries. But growing soy production has been strongly associated with extensive deforestation in Amazonian and Interior Atlantic Forest Regions (Altieri and Pengue, 2006; Fearnside, 2001; Nepstad et al., 2006). Soy expansion is also closely linked to socio-economic and political problems adversely affecting the rural peasantry (Altieri and Pengue, 2006; ASEED, 2006; Elgert, 2012; Fogel and Riquelme, 2005). The list of grievances that the peasant groups have with the soy industry is an extensive one, holding the industry responsible for the concentration of land holdings at the expense of land for peasants, who are often forcefully expelled by politicians, foreign investors and hired guns (Fogel and Riquelme, 2005; Holland et al., 2008). Furthermore, fumigations on soy fields are routinely undertaken by airplane without regard for surrounding communities. Such pesticide use has resulted in hundreds of reports annually of illness and death (Holland et al., 2008). Finally, the highly mechanized nature of soy production excludes peasants, who are largely poor and in some cases landless, from employment opportunities and, more generally, from the economic benefits of soy production (Carter, 1994; Carter et al., 1996).

Such concerns have resonated throughout global commodity chains, inciting boycotts and protests in both Latin American and Europe that have targeted international soy markets. Organizers of the RTRS anticipated that the roundtable process would create consensus and cohesion among diverse factions within the soy debate. They thought this result would come from implementing a rigorous, science-based process for establishing responsible soy indicators. A 'technical meeting' was held in 2006, where

> Over 60 participants, including highly regarded international experts and key
> stakeholders from farmers associations, agribusiness, social and environmental
> NGOs participated in the science-based discussions over three days exchang-
> ing different regional experiences and perspectives related to soy production,
> processing and trade. (RTRS, 2008)

The aspiration of this meeting was to 'develop and perfect criteria and
indicators for sustainable soy production' (RTRS, 2008).

Developing and perfecting indicators for sustainable soy proved to
be an overambitious goal for one technical meeting, however, and even
eight years on, consensus among stakeholders remained elusive. Despite
early optimism, indicator development extended over the next several
years; by the end of 2008, iterations of the criteria were still being negotiated and revised. In addition to the debate among workshop participants,
stakeholders outside of the RTRS process began articulating their concerns
about the development of responsible soy indicators, further revealing considerably more social and political contention than anticipated. The final
version of the indicators for responsible soy was finally published in June of
2010. Nearly five years of indicator development for responsible soy, idealized as 'science-based' and driven by technical expertise, while aiming for
consensus and the achievement of a 'win-win' scenario, had not produced
a definitive, agreed-upon set of indicators for responsible soy production.
Questions concerning if, how and by whom 'responsible soy' is defined,
measured and monitored continue to be sources of controversy and debate.

Within the RTRS, problems associated with soy are framed as technical concerns, to be addressed through sustainable agricultural practices
and higher-level policies such as zoning and planning. For example, many
participants promote the usage of no-till cultivation as a sustainable
technique. No-till cultivation involves planting and cutting a cover crop
and then seeding directly into it, rather than into the soil. This eliminates
the need for any tillage. No-till cultivation hence is allegedly a sustainable practice because it prevents soil degradation and, further, carries the
potential of maintaining or even improving soil quality. Another technical
center of focus, particularly on behalf of governmental environmental and
agricultural agencies and NGOs, was higher-level policy space such as
zoning and planning. Zoning would involve such things as routing soy production away from ecologically 'high value' areas (WWF Canada, 2005).

These technical interventions tend to be accepted within the RTRS as
relatively uncontroversial ways of mitigating the impact of soy expansion.
But the sustainability of agricultural practices is shown to be dependent
on how sustainability is defined. No-tillage cultivation, used in conjunction with 'round-up ready' soy, has been shown to make significant contributions to the maintenance of soil quality over time. At the same time,

however, no-till requires the extensive use of pesticides for pest management, and many soy operations apply the 'mata-todo' (kills everything) approach by aerial spraying, which has little precision, and is linked to a host of peasant grievances from pollution to horrific accounts of pesticide-related illness and death. Likewise, systems of forest valuation have been controversial; the focus on 'high value' areas such as high bio-mass rainforest has been shown to accelerate the conversion of secondary forest and semi-deciduous forests to agriculture (Hecht, 2005). Other research has shown that this valuation system leads to less valued forests being considered as 'soy reserves' (Steward, 2007). Despite such challenging issues, technical arguments are featured as uncontroversial, rational and indisputable and have thus become privileged in the RTRS debate.

Internal deliberations only tell a small part of the story of responsible soy indicators. Some of the strongest contestation and debate came from outside the roundtable process. Almost as soon as the RTRS was convened, several NGOs and peasant associations organized an opposing 'counter conference'. The main message of the counter conference was clear: there is no such thing as 'responsible soy' (Holland et al., 2008). Indeed, the counter conference did not direct opposition at the specifics of the indicator development, and organizers had little to say about the technical details of the potential indicators in question. Their challenges to the RTRS took aim more broadly at the very discourse that assumed the possibility of sustainable soy (Elgert, 2012). The counter conference organizers drew attention to issues such as the rapid expansion of mechanized soy production that provides only miniscule job creation, the link between this expansion and the dramatic concentration of land holdings, and the predominance of genetically modified soy that is used in conjunction with glyphosate – a harsh chemical herbicide increasingly blamed for animal and human health problems in soy growing areas. At a broader level, the anti-soy discourse identified the soy industry as being part of a model of development – based on export crops, while necessitating economic globalization and global integration – that is synonymous with colonization and loss of local and national sovereignty (BASEIS, 2006). Inherent in the 'soy model' is a denial of true sustainability, based on democracy, participation and inclusion. Soy as an 'engine of growth' results in active underdevelopment, culminating in the actual exclusion of 'the people' (BASEIS, 2006; Holland et al., 2008). In the statements made by the counter conference, the concept of 'responsible soy' is impossible – always appearing in scare quotes – and the term itself is considered an oxymoron.

In the RTRS, some of the most controversial aspects of soy production such as land grabbing, the concentration of land and decreased rural employment were scarcely included as brief asides, and any detailed attention to how they might be addressed was notably (and perhaps predictably) absent. When one accounts for the dramatic inequalities among stakeholders, it is not difficult to understand how and why the RTRS agenda has thus emerged. The average Paraguayan peasant has around 10 hectares of land and an income of about US$3000 per year. Consider this in light of some of the RTRS members: Archer Daniels Midland Company, one of the largest agricultural processors in the world; Andre Maggi Group, the world's largest private producer of soybeans; and Cargill, an international food producer and marketer with over US$116 billion in sales in 2009. Early in 2009, agro-services giants Monsanto and Syngenta were admitted as members to the RTRS, sparking an outcry from the public and from other RTRS members. This move confirmed for some cautious observers of the RTRS that the roundtable was 'used to hide the interests of the business sector in alliance with transnational corporations' (ASEED, 2006). It seems to make sense that peasant groups have remained outside of a process in which they cannot possibly have any meaningful influence or voice. Yet their non-participation in discussions around technical indicators for sustainable soy has been met with criticism for 'refusing' to talk openly and instead, 'standing outside to demonstrate opposition' (RTRS member, personal communication).

Despite the profound influence of social and political dynamics on the construction of soy indicators, this influence may become obscured and of little interest to all but the most curious and rigorous of observers. Ultimately, the 'responsible soy' certification label that has emerged from the RTRS indicator development process might put the global consumers at ease as they see and interpret the RTRS branding. They might understand that the label implies presumably 'good' things like 'sustainable agricultural practices' and 'stakeholder participation'. But consumers are not likely to have the time, interest level or access to information to learn the story behind the development of responsible soy indicators. Even the overt struggles and contestations involved in the development of responsible soy indicators will, over time, fade from public consciousness. Once the criteria for sustainable soy have been finalized, soy producers will eventually begin to cultivate 'responsible soy', which will be promoted and most probably accepted as such in international markets. The political asymmetries and discursive struggles that have been an integral part of the story of 'responsible soy' indicators will become muted, hidden and of secondary concern.

CONCLUSION

The growing emphasis on global environmental governance means that an increasing number of people, places and products are being scrutinized for their contributions to, and detractions from, global sustainability. Under this scrutiny, there is a growing policy appetite for more and better knowledge and a general reticence towards policy seen to be 'unduly' influenced by politics. Standardized, evidence-based indicators have been a response, seen to 'depoliticize' sustainability governance by providing a transparent and efficient means of measuring and directing sustainable transformation. This trust in indicators, however, underestimates the role of socio-political influences in constructing in the standardized, factual basis for indicators (Forsyth, 2003) and in decision making processes at large (Fischer, 2009).

Once we delve into the stories behind indicators, as the case of 'responsible soy' shows, the social and political influences in their creation become apparent. The financial and political power of multinational corporations and international environmental organizations has dwarfed the potential for contributions of peasant groups to the responsible soy indicator development process. Debates have been dominated by technical concerns, despite the impossibility of reaching consensus on the technical parameters for sustainability, and these concerns have simultaneously marked political arguments as 'irrelevant' and 'unhelpful'. Assumptions that remain deeply contested remain unchallenged as 'facts'.

The way in which indicators are constructed, however, is not the end of their story. Even though social and political influences become muted as indicators are deployed in governance regimes, they continue to ramify in various unequal and potentially unjust governance outcomes. For example, as difference is subsumed in increasingly taken-for-granted ways, local actors become increasingly committed, either voluntarily or involuntarily, to homogenized understandings of sustainability. Such understandings represent particular (as opposed to 'global') cultural preferences, norms and values, albeit with a wider reach:

> The 'global' in the dominant discourse is the political space in which a particular local seeks global control and frees itself of local, national and international restraints. The global does not represent the universal human interest but it represents a particular local and parochial interest which has been globalized through the scope of its reach. (Shiva, 1993, p. 149)

In this sense, promoting standardization and evidence-making as 'global' technologies of knowledge must be understood as a way of disseminating the norms and values of a particular culture, not as simply making global governance more transparent and efficient.

REFERENCES

Adger, W.N., J. Barnett, F.S. Chapin III and H. Ellemor (2011), 'This must be the place: underrepresentation of identity and meaning in climate change decision-making', *Global Environmental Politics* (May).
Altieri, M. and M. Pengue (2005), 'Roundup ready soybean in Latin America: a machine of hunger, deforestation and socio-ecological devastation'. Retrieved 1 November 2010 from http://www.biosafety-info.net/article.php?aid=284.
Altieri, M. and M. Pengue (2006), 'GM soybean: Latin America's new coloniser', *Seedling* (January), 13–17.
ASEED (2006), 'Declaration: the development model for soy in Paraguay: irresponsible, unsustainable and anti-democratic'. Retrieved 6 September 2007 from http://www.aseed.net/index.php?option=com_content&task=view&id=285&Itemid=107.
Astleithner, F. and A. Hamedinger (2003), 'The analysis of sustainability indicators as socially constructed policy instruments: benefits and challenges of "interactive research"', *Local Environment*, **8** (6), 1–1. Doi: 10.1080/762742061.
BASEIS (2006), 'Acción contra el encuentro de la "soja responsable"' (email communication), 19 September.
Biermann, F., K. Abbott, S. Andresen, K. Backstrand, S. Bernstein, M. Betsill and R. Zondervan (2012), 'Navigating the Anthropocene: improving earth system governance', *Science*, **335**, 1306–1307.
Bowker, G.C. and S. Leigh Star (1999), *Sorting Things Out: Classification and its Consequences*. Cambridge, MA: The MIT Press.
Brown, C.J. and M. Purcell (2005), 'There's nothing inherent about scale: political ecology, the local trap, and the politics of development in the Brazilian Amazon', *Geoforum*, **36** (5), 607–624.
Carter, M.R. (1994), 'Sequencing capital and land-market reform for broadly based growth', Agricultural Economics Staff Paper, Madison: Department of Agricultural Economics, University of Wisconsin.
Carter, M.R., B.L. Barham and D. Mesbah (1996), 'Agricultural export booms and the rural poor in Chile, Guatemala, and Paraguay', *Latin American Research Review*, **31** (1), 33–65.
Christmann, P. (2004), 'Multinational comopanies and the natural environment: determinants of global environmental policy', *Academy of Management Journal*, **47** (5), 747–760.
Collingridge, D. and C. Reeve (1986), *Science Speaks to Power: The Role of Experts in Policy Making*. London: Frances Pinter Publishers.
Collins, H.M. and B. Evans (2007), *Rethinking Expertise*. Chicago: University of Chicago Press.
Cotula, L., N. Dyer and S. Vermeulen (2008), *Fuelling Exclusion? The Biofuels Boom and Poor People's Access to Land*. London: IIED.
Davies, H.T.O., S.M. Nutley and P.C. Smith (2000), *What Works? Evidence-Based Policy and Practice in Public Services*. Bristol: The Policy Press.
Davis, K.E., B. Kingsbury and S.E. Merry (2012a), 'Indicators as a technology of global governance', *Law & Society Review*, **46** (1), 71–104.
Davis, K.E., A. Fisher, B. Kingsbury and S.E. Merry (eds) (2012b), *Governance by Indicators: Global Power Through Classification and Rankings*. Oxford: Oxford University Press.
Dryzek, J.S. (1990), *Discursive Democracy: Politics, Policy and Political Science*. Cambridge: Cambridge University Press.
Dryzek, J.S. (2006), *Deliberative Global Politics*. Cambridge: Polity Press.
Dryzek, J.S. (2013), *The Politics of the Earth: Environmental Discourses* (3rd edition). Oxford: Oxford University Press.
Ehrlich, P. (1968), *The Population Bomb*. New York: Sierra Club/Ballantine Books.
Elgert, L. (2009), 'Politicizing sustainable development: the co-production of globalized evidence-based policy', *Critical Policy Studies*, **3** (3–4), 375–390.
Elgert, L. (2011), 'Certified community development? Local participation in corporate governance'. In J.P.R. Rothe, L.J.C. Carroll and D. Ozegovic (eds), *Deliberations in*

Community Development: Balancing on the Edge (pp. 277–288). Hauppauge: Nova Science Publishers.

Elgert, L. (2012), 'Certified discourse? The politics of developing soy certification standards', *Geoforum*, **43** (2), 295–304.

Elgert, L. (2013), 'Hard facts and software: the coproduction of indicators in a land-use planning model', *Environmental Values*, **22** (6), 765–786.

Epstein, C. (2006), 'The making of global environmental norms: endangered species protection', *Global Environmental Politics*, **6** (2), 32–54.

Epstein, S. (2007), *Inclusion: The Politics of Difference in Medical Research*. Chicago: University of Chicago Press.

Fearnside, P.M. (2001), 'Soybean cultivation as a threat to the environment in Brazil', *Environmental Conservation*, **28** (1), 23–38.

Fischer, F. (2003), *Reframing Public Policy: Discursive Politics and Deliberative Practices*. New York: Oxford University Press.

Fischer, F. (2009), *Democracy and Expertise: Reorienting Policy Inquiry*. New York: Oxford University Press.

Fogel, R. and M. Riquelme (2005), 'Introduction'. In R. Fogel and M. Riquelme (eds), *Enclave Sojero: Merma de Soberanía y Pobreza* (pp. 9–14). Asunción: Centro de Estudios Rurales Interdisciplinarios.

Ford, L.H. (2003), 'Challenging global environmental governance: social movement agency and global civil society', *Global Environmental Politics*, **3** (2), 120–134.

Forsyth, T. (2003), *Critical Political Ecology: The Politics of Environmental Science*. New York, London: Routledge.

Forsyth, T. (2011), 'Expertise needs transparency not blind trust: a deliberative approach to integrating science and social participation', *Critical Policy Studies*, **5** (3), 317–322.

Gardner, S. (2009), 'Developing environmental evidence-based policies', *Projects* (November), 24–25.

Geertz, C. (1973), *The Interpretation of Culture*. New York: Basic Books.

Guthman, J. (2004), *Agrarian Dreams: The Paradox of Organic Farming in California*. Berkeley and Los Angeles: University of California Press.

Hajer, M.A. (1995), *The Politics of Environmental Discourse*. Oxford: Clarendon Press.

Hecht, S. (2005), 'Soybeans, development and conservation on the Amazon frontier', *Development and Change*, **36** (2), 375–404.

Hezri, A.A. and S.R. Dovers (2006), 'Sustainability indicators, policy and governance: issues for ecological economics', *Ecological Economics*, **60** (1), 86–99.

Holland, N., L. Joensen, A. Maeyens, A. Samulon, S. Semino, R. Sonderegger and J. Rulli (2008), The round table on irresponsible soy: certifying soy expansion, GM soy and agrofuels: ASEED Europe, Base Investigaciones Sociales (BASEIS), Corporate Europe Observatory, Grupo de Reflexion Rural (GRR), Rain Forest Action Network.

Jasanoff, S. (1992), 'Science, politics, and the renegotiation of expertise at EPA', *Osiris*, 7, 194–217.

Jasanoff, S. (1998), 'The political science of risk perception', *Reliability Engineering and System Safety*, **59**, 91–99.

Jasanoff, S. (2000), 'Technological risk and cultures of rationality', *Proceedings of the National Academy of Sciences and Engineering*, Beckman Center, Irvine, CA, 25–27 January.

Jasanoff, S. (2003), 'Breaking the waves in science studies: comment on H.M. Collins and Robert Evans, "The Third Wave of Science Studies"', *Social Studies of Science*, **33** (3), 389–400.

Jasanoff, S. (2004), 'The idiom of co-production'. In S. Jasanoff (ed.), *States of Knowledge: The Co-production of Science and Social Order* (pp. 1–12). London: Routledge.

Jasanoff, S. and M.L. Martello (2004). 'Earthly politics: local and global in environmental governance'. In *Politics, Science, and the Environment* (pp. viii, 356). Cambridge, MA: The MIT Press.

Kipnis, A.B. (2008), 'Audit cultures: neoliberal governmentality, socialist legacy, or technologies of governing?', *American Ethnologist*, **35** (2), 275–289.

Kohn, A. (2000), *The Case Against Standardized Testing: Raising the Scores, Ruining the Schools*. Portsmouth, NH: Heinemann.

Lampland, M. and S. Leigh Star (eds) (2009), *Standards and Their Stories: How Quantifying, Classifying, and Formalizing Practices Shape Everyday Life*. Ithaca and London: Cornell University Press.

Latour, B. (1993), *We Have Never Been Modern*. Cambridge, MA: Harvard University Press.

Lemos, M.C. and A. Argrawal (2006), 'Environmental governance', *Annual Review of Environmental Resources*, **31**, 297–325.

Leshner, A. (2002), 'Science and Sustainability', *Science*, **297** (5583), 897.

Li, T.M. (2007), *The Will to Improve: Governmentality, Development and the Practice of Politics*. Durham, NC and London: Duke University Press.

Marston, G. and R. Watts (2003), 'Tampering with the evidence: a critical appraisal of evidence-based policy-making', *The Drawing Board: An Australian Review of Public Affairs*, **3** (3), 143–163.

McCool, S.F. and G.H. Stankey (2004), 'Indicators of sustainability: challenges and opportunities at the interface of science and policy', *Environmental Management*, **33** (3), 294–305. Doi: 10.1007/s00267-003-0084-4.

Merry, S.E. (2011), 'Measuring the world: indicators, human rights and global governance', *Current Anthropology*, **52** (3), 583–595.

Nepstad, D.C., C. Stickler and O. Almeida (2006), 'Globalization of the Amazon soya and beef insdustries: opportunities for conservation', *Conservation Biology*, **20** (6), 1595–1603.

Paavola, J. (2007), 'Institutions and environmental governance: a reconceptualization', *Ecological Economics*, **63** (1), 93–103.

Perfecto, I. and J. Vandermeer (2010), 'The agricultural matrix as an alternative to the land-sparing/agricultural intensification model: facing the food and biodiversity crises', *Proceedings of the National Academy of Science*, **107** (March), 5786–5791.

Perfecto, I., John H. Vandermeer and Angus Lindsay Wright (2009), *Nature's Matrix: Linking Agriculture, Conservation and Food Sovereignty*. London: Earthscan.

Phalan, B., M. Onial, A. Balmford and R.E. Green (2011), 'Reconciling food production and biodiversity conservation: land sharing and land sparing compared', *Science*, **333** (6047), 1289–1291.

Planet Under Pressure (2012), 'State of the Planet Declaration'. Retrieved 2 February 2014 from http://www.planetunderpressure2012.net/pdf/state_of_planet_declaration.pdf.

Power, M. (1999), *The Audit Society: Rituals of Verification*. Oxford: Oxford University Press.

Rayner, S. (2003), 'Democracy in the age of assessment: reflections on the roles of expertise and democracy in public-sector decision making', *Science and Public Policy*, **30** (3), 163–170.

RTRS (2008), 'Events: technical workshop key conclusions'. Retrieved 20 November 2010 from http://www.responsiblesoy.org/events_detail.php?id=8.

Rydin, Y. (2007), 'Indicators as a governmental technology? The lessons of community-based sustainability indicator projects', *Environment and Planning D: Society and Space*, **25** (4), 610–624.

Schouten, G. and P. Glasbergen (2011), 'Creating legitimacy in global private governance: the case of the Roundtable on Sustainable Palm Oil', *Ecological Economics*, **70** (11), 1891–1899.

Schouten, G., P. Leroy and P. Glasbergen (2012), 'On the delibeartive capactiy of private multi-stakeholder governance: the Roundtables on Responsible Soy and Sustainable Palm Oil', *Ecological Economics*, **83** (1), 42–50.

Scott, J.C. (1998), *Seeing Like a State: How Certain Schemes to Improve the Human Condition Have Failed*. New Haven and London: Yale University Press.

Shields, D.J., S.V. Šolar and W.E. Martin (2002), 'The role of values and objectives in communicating indicators of sustainability', *Ecological Indicators*, **2** (1), 149–160. Doi: 10.1016/s1470-160x(02)00042-0.

Shiva, V. (1993), 'The greening of the global reach'. In W. Sachs (ed.), *Global Ecology: A New Arena of Political Conflict* (pp. 149–156). London: Zed Books.

Shore, C. (2008), 'Audit culture and illiberal governance: universities and the politics of accountability', *Anthropological Theory*, **8** (3), 278–298. Doi: 10.1177/1463499608093815.

Shore, C. and S. Wright (2000), 'Coercive accountability: the rise of audit culture in higher education'. In M. Strathern (ed.), *Audit Cultures: Anthropological Studies in Accountability, Ethics and the Academy* (pp. 57–89). London: Routledge.

Solesbury, W. (2001), 'Evidence based policy: whence it came and where it's going'. ESRC UK Centre for Evidence Based Policy and Practice: Working Paper 1.

Steward, C. (2007), 'From colonization to "environmental soy": a case study of environmental and socio-economic valuation in the Amazon soy frontier', *Agriculture and Human Values*, **24** (1), 107–122.

Taylor, P.J. and F.H. Buttel (1992), 'How do we know we have global environmental problems? Science and the globalization of environmental discourse', *Geoforum*, **23** (3), 405–416.

Thevenot, L. (2009), 'Postscript to the special issue: Governing life by standards: a view from engagements', *Social Studies of Science*, **39** (5), 793–813.

Tiffen, M., M. Mortimore and F. Gichuki (1994), *More people Less Erosion: Environmental Recovery in Kenya*. Chichester: Wiley.

Timmermans, S. and S. Epstein (2010), 'A World of standards but not a standard world: toward a sociology of standards and standardization', *Annual Review of Sociology*, **36** (1), 69–89.

Turnhout, E. (2009), 'The effectiveness of boundary objects: the case of ecological indicators', *Science and Public Policy*, **36** (5), 403–412.

Turnhout, E., M. Hisschemöller and H. Eijsackers (2007), 'Ecological indicators: between the two fires of science and policy', *Ecological Indicators*, **7**, 215–228.

UNCSD (2012), 'The future we want: zero draft of the outcome document'. Retrieved 10 April 2013 from http://www.uncsd2012.org/content/documents/370The%20Future%20We%20Want%2010Jan%20clean%20_no%20brackets.pdf.

WWF Canada (2005), *High Conservation Value Forest Support Document* (Draft). Toronto: WWF – Canada.

19 The politics of policy think-tanks: organizing expertise, legitimacy and counter-expertise in policy networks
Dieter Plehwe

INTRODUCTION: EXPERTISE BETWEEN SCIENCE AND POLITICS

Policy research institutes, or think-tanks, have become prominent knowledge actors and agents in political processes at national and international levels. They have become subject to national, regional (e.g. European) and global surveys and rankings on a regular basis.[1] They are widely praised for their capacity to conduct policy relevant research, for their ability to innovate, and for reaching out to practical people involved in policy making (McGann and Weaver 2005). A recent promotion of the work of think-tanks in development politics by the British Overseas Development Institute, for example, underlines the need for 'evidence based' politics, which updates older versions of science-based policy making and technocratic governance (Sutcliff and Court 2005). The growing demand for evidence-based policy nurtures the growth of the think-tank population, and paradoxically contributes to the diversification of think-tank purposes.

Critiques have pointed out that many think-tanks do not contribute much in terms of original research, because they are mostly involved in editing and formatting tasks arranged by government institutions (Stone 2007). Diane Stone is also worried about the elitist character of most think-tanks, which contradicts apologetic claims to independence and pluralism. Think-tanks can additionally be observed to effectively undermine science-based policy making. A considerable number of think-tanks have been successfully used by tobacco and oil interests, for example, to cast doubt on public health and climate change scholarship, respectively (Oreskes and Conway 2010).

Although the affirmative and skeptical perspectives are clearly contradictory, a more comprehensive treatment of the politics of policy think-tanks can reconcile competing views by way of recognizing, firstly, different types of think-tanks, secondly, their diverse roles in the formation of policy communities and issue networks, and thirdly, their likewise diverse roles with regard to policy issues and subject matters at various stages of the policy process. Critical analysis of policy think-tanks at any rate has to go beyond the stereotypes and images manufactured and circulated by think-tank professionals who are dependent on an objective 'scientific' image as a major source of legitimacy and at the same time are constrained by the requirements of the tax code (e.g. meet 'not for profit', 'public interest' criteria). Thomas Medvetz (2012) has recently clarified the ways in which think-tanks in reality depend on four major fields that shape their existence: the scientific world, economic interests, media, and politics. While the four 'source fields' play a role for all policy related research organizations, each individual think-tank can be more dependent on one of these turfs than on the other. Think-tanks are therefore best studied as networks of individuals, organizations and ideas rather than 'erratic blocks', i.e. isolated organizations and instances of independent expertise – no matter if and to what extent a claim to independence (from government, private business or other interests etc.) can be legitimately made. Questions related to expertise and (in)dependence indeed are necessarily subject to closer investigation in all cases once we drop positivistic notions of pure science. Empirical research in turn is not easy in this area since many if not most think-tanks are best characterized by a near complete lack of transparency regarding their funding and financial practices.[2]

In the following section I will provide important background on the history of think-tank research and the origins of the use of the term. I will then revisit the efforts to define think-tanks and explain why this has proven to be a futile exercise unless we accept a sufficiently vague definition. A typology of think-tanks can point out important differences in terms of the focus of the work of think-tanks, which also implies different sets of major tasks. Real-world think-tanks do not necessary fall neatly into just one of the ideal type categories, of course, and it is imperative to take the linkages between say academic and advocacy or partisan think-tanks into due account. The next section is devoted to relating the work of think-tanks to the discussion of policy networks. Policy network configurations imply different roles and challenges for competing actors, frequently including think-tanks. Both constructive and destructive strategies in terms of research and consulting efforts of think-tanks – 'knowledge' creation and shaping – are described and further examined in the next section based on case studies in the area of deregulation, energy and the environment, and climate change. The concluding section summarizes the major results of our critical discussion of think-tank and policy community studies.

THINK-TANK RESEARCH TRAJECTORIES

While the United States was considered a unique polity with regard to the history and influence of policy think-tanks for a long time, US researchers have clarified that the term has become attached to policy-related research institutes during the 1960s only – after the work of the Rand Corporation became subject to severe criticism from anti-war protesters (Vietnam). Usage of the term became popular in the 1970s when the impact of the Heritage Foundation as an aggressive partisan and policy marketing think-tank made itself felt (Smith 1991, xiv f.). Previously, organizations involved in policy related research in the United States were simply considered research institutes much like they were in Europe and other world regions.

European scholarship in the meantime has pointed to the parallel rise of policy related research and think-tanks in many countries, albeit considerable differences in the national landscapes exist (Stone et al. 1998; Campbell and Pedersen 2014). Recent research has also pointed to the rise of transnational networks of (partisan) think-tanks, which are involved in policy research and consulting both within many different countries and across borders (Plehwe and Walpen 2006). A new generation of think-tank studies – additionally informed by post-positivist theory (Fischer and Forrester 1993) and science and technology studies (Jassanof 2005; Plehwe 2011a; Strassheim, Chapter 17, this volume) in particular – is now emerging.

The new generation of think-tank studies goes beyond the traditional national and comparative perspectives, which frequently took at face value think-tank claims to scientific truth, knowledge neutrality, independence and public interest. Scholars working in the spirit of critical think-tank studies agree that each of these claims raises important questions, which adds to the quest for empirical substance of think-tank research on the one hand, and to the theoretical fascination with the think-tank phenomenon on the other hand. Think-tanks are considered to be at the core of the (post-)modern condition of globalized capitalism (Harvey 1989), which generates far-reaching transformations of social relations, communication and public and private policy making discussed in the post-democracy debate (Crouch 2004; Mair 2013; Stone 2013). Circumventing traditional membership organizations like political parties or associations, think-tanks point to shadow elites and power brokerage (Wedel 2009), which requires dedicated capacities and creativity to generate storylines (Saloma III 1984).

In order to go beyond the traditional understanding of think-tanks, a historical and social network analytical approach offers promising opportunities at different, yet interrelated levels: firstly, to study individual policy think-tanks (networks of related intellectuals), secondly, to study networks of related organizations (think-tanks and other), and thirdly, to study networks of ideas (concepts, social constructs, storylines). Approaching think-tanks in this way allows scholars to clarify the social character of knowledge production (academic or not), to identify the political and ideological dimensions of interpretation and evidence supporting it, and to map the relevant dimensions of (transnational) *discourse coalitions* beyond narrow actor networks (Hajer 1993; Plehwe 2011b). An interpretative think-tank network approach combines structural and ideational dimensions, and thereby enables the researcher to integrate different, yet complementary approaches to think-tank studies needed to investigate the interplay of structure and agency in general, and of different types of academic, contract, partisan and party related organizations as well as interest groups, NGOs, media, and state institutions in particular. The focus of the research is not only the think-tank as an organization at the end, although it is certainly quite interesting to pay attention to the ongoing multiplication of the organizational form, but think-tank tasks and functions in policy processes (Pautz 2011). Such tasks and functions are not exclusive to think-tank organizations, of course. The rapidly increasing number of think-tanks across the world,[3] however, seems to suggest an increasing tendency for think-tanks to absorb and bundle together a number of tasks and functions important to policy making previously carried out elsewhere (e.g. interest groups, political parties, NGOs, corporations etc.).

THINK-TANK DEFINITIONS, FUTILITY OF NARROW DEFINITIONS, TYPOLOGY, NETWORKS

Even if a shift towards addressing think-tank functions can be considered a necessary step forward, scholars dealing with policy think-tanks cannot avoid questions of definition regarding the core subject. We will present a few efforts of significant researchers in the field to demonstrate why it is important to apply a sufficiently broad definition rather than missing some of the most important aspects of the subject matter.

In a conventional fashion Andrew Rich (2004, 11) defines think-tanks as '. . . *independent, non-interest-based, nonprofit organizations that produce and principally rely on expertise and ideas to obtain support and to influence the policymaking process*' [italics in the original]. Rich adds to his criteria legal status (US code 501(c)3) and the political character of aggressiveness in maximizing public credibility and political access to make their output relevant in policy making. He also excludes government and interest group-based research organizations. But definitional clarity is challenged immediately by his following admission: 'In truth, drawing irrefutable distinctions between think-tanks and other types of organizations is neither entirely possible nor desirable; rather, institutional boundaries are frequently amorphous and overlapping.' Rich nevertheless insists that 'products and objectives are central to any clarification of how think-tanks might be differentiated from other actors in their operations and influence', which in turn may need to be qualified again, however, if the background of products and objectives of think-tanks outside the organizational boundaries of the think-tank are taken into due consideration.

Diane Stone and Andrew Denham (2004, 2) recognize 'considerable difficulty in defining "think-tanks"' due to the diversity of organizations involved in policy related research. Anglo-American definitions insist on autonomy (from government, parties, interest groups etc.) they observe, but '. . . think-tanks are often in resource dependent relationships with these organizations'. Stone and Denham attempt a negative definition by way of observing a difference from universities (no students), from interest groups (no demonstration, no lobbying, usually not a single issue focus), from philanthropic foundations (no funds to finance others), no consultancy (no or limited role of charges for services). But the authors observe that operative foundations do maneuver like think-tanks in addition to funding others, and the degree to which think-tanks charge for services might matter less than she suggests, because think-tanks are frequently considered cheap consultancies. Lobbying has been recognized as an acceptable minor element of think-tank operations in the US code due to the notorious difficulty in drawing a clear line between 'educational' tasks and lobbying tasks. Each of the delimitations made by Stone and Denham can be challenged if we additionally consider the move of think-tanks towards offering fellowships to young professionals, and to teaching think-tank professionals, though the difference between think-tanks and universities is quite obvious. Universities can be observed to develop think-tank properties and outlets, however, which does muddy the water again.

There is no escape from these dilemmas of think-tank definitions. Because '. . . cultural understandings of independence, the degree of think-tank autonomy, and the extent of interest in policy and political issues vary dramatically not only from country to country but from one institute to another' (Stone and Denham 2004, 5), there simply is no satisfying and sufficiently distinguishing definition of a specific policy related research organization that can be exclusively referred to as a think-tank. In turn, this means we have to define think-tanks in a sufficiently broad way as organizations that are involved in policy related research and consulting efforts. This definition is broad enough to address the wide range and diversity of think-tanks without producing avoidable contradictions and without maintaining a naïve understanding of science and knowledge, which has helped to provide legitimacy to many different kinds of expertise.

A common and helpful approach to deal with the variegated think-tank phenomenon is to establish a typology of different kinds of think-tanks, which is certainly better than suggesting definitional clarity by way of selecting certain organizations (e.g. serious research, civil society, not for profit) and attributing to those an exclusive claim to the think-tank title. If a wide range of organizations refer to themselves as think-tanks, and are referred to as think-tanks, the 'wrong understanding' cannot be avoided by scholarly decision making, which itself is steeped in cultural prejudice. In this regard, the international comparison of think-tanks was an important step forward, taking the field beyond a specific Anglo-Saxon (narrow) understanding of issues and problems of organizations involved in policy related research. Typically think-tank experts distinguish academic think-tanks, contract research institutes, party related think-tanks, advocacy think-tanks (compare McGann and Weaver 2005, 6f.). But a number of additional types have been identified: for example, government and quango think-tanks, which recognize think-tanks as part of (devolved) government bureaucracy and contract research organizations that are fully dependent on government contracts (McGann and Johnson 2005, 14). Interestingly, the two authors at this point also distinguish independent think-tanks (the traditional American understanding of 'the' think-tank) from quasi-independent think-tanks, which are dependent on interest group and other financial agencies with considerable influence over a think-tank. If we look a little bit closer at the different types, we can learn more about important differences, but also about commonalities and interrelations. Table 19.1 provides an overview and attempts an assessment according to the major focus or tasks of the different (ideal) types of organizations.

Academic think-tanks or *universities without students* can be publicly or privately organized, much like universities themselves. If and to what extent they can be considered 'independent' is subject to closer examination (funding, governance structure, discourse). We would in any case expect to see ideological pluralism and diversity in the case of academic think-tanks on the one hand, and a high share of academic output on the other hand. Most if not all of the scholars working at academic think-tanks would be expected to be experts in their fields, though ranking obviously would inter alia depend on career stage or specialization.

Table 19.1   Types of think-tanks

Indicators / Type	Scientific research/ teaching	Applied policy research/ consulting	Policy orientation	Campaign research/ OpEd
Academic	X	X	(x)	(x)
Commercial	x	X	x	X
Advocacy		x	x	X
Political party	(x)	(x)	X	X
Partisan	(X)	x	X	(X)

Note: **X**: major share of work/output; x: minor share; (x): only common to part of the population or characteristic of the work of individual staff members.

Source: Own compilation.

Commercial or contract research organizations can also be expected to produce quality research, relying on recognized experts in a field. Contract research organizations frequently have no general funding, and are therefore more dependent on external direction (research subjects, scope etc.) than academic organizations no matter if securely financed by state budgets or by private endowment. Output furthermore can be expected to feature less in strictly academic publications since project funding usually does not extend to longer publication cycles like peer-reviewed journals, though this will depend on the organization and on the ambition of the individual researcher. Contract research think-tanks are typically involved in applied research work, which can also be carried out by specialized academic organizations (like Germany's Frauenhofer Institute) or by research staff of public agencies. Growth of contract research appears be partly a result of outsourcing of government services.

Advocacy think-tanks are expected to be quite obviously biased in support of a specific end. In contrast to the 'questioning' mode of research typical for academia, advocacy work refrains from asking many questions, unless it is considered a valuable strategy to support the answers supplied. Advocacy think-tanks typically make truth claims regardless of academic evidence, because owning a truth is a part of the proselytizing character of such organizations. Typically we associate human rights activists or environmental think-tanks with advocacy work even if many work on a single issue or a narrow range of objectives. In contrast to most typologies, which reserve a strong normative bent to advocacy think-tanks (and concede an ideological orientation to party related think-tanks), this author prefers another think-tank category to cluster ideological think-tanks that are neither related to specific political parties, nor to advocacy work in a specific policy area: partisan think-tanks (see below).

Political party related think-tanks would instead be expected to be normatively and ideologically closer to the political parties behind them. This would be expected to lead to publications in party related publishing venues, and programmatic output. Policy related research papers from such origins can vary greatly in academic quality, because individual researchers may or may not pursue a scholarly career. Expectations with regard to such papers in any case are not necessarily academic, although the work produced can improve the average policy discussion by way of devoting time and energy to substantiate a specific political perspective.

Last but not least, *partisan think-tanks* are normatively driven organizations like, or even more than, party think-tanks, and share a strong advocacy character with policy issue oriented think-tanks. Partisan think-tanks differ because they typically work across a broader spectrum of policy issues. They have been founded by interested actors to influence parties and other political actors (in business, media, academia and NGOs). They can be found in very different clusters in terms of output, both academic (like scientific research organizations) and non-academic. If academic in orientation, the difference is a much less diverse spectrum of scholars and publications. Partisan academic think-tanks concentrate a specific school of thought and perspective to influence the academic sphere. Partisan advocacy organizations direct energy to the political and the media worlds. But they all can be found devoting more energy to marketing knowledge than traditionally more complacent organizations in the academic world.

Each of the different types of think-tanks has something in common, setting them apart from the other types of think-tanks; however the different types can also share common characteristics – sometimes many characteristics. Scholars from academic think-tanks can be found to run contract, party related, advocacy and partisan think-tanks. It is quite normal for 'political', 'commercial', and 'partisan' think-tanks in particular to signal academic credibility by way of giving high-profile positions to renowned scholars who happen to share the normative orientation of a political think-tank or are otherwise in tune with the objectives of the less academic organization. Many academic think-tanks have become contract research organizations due to (partial) loss of funding, and due to a general process of commercialization in the scientific field. Due to the impact of aggressive partisan and advocacy organizations, traditional academic research think-tanks are also targeting media and general public audiences now in addition to the classical academic scene (Asher and Guilhot 2010).

If we single out specific types of think-tanks as the only or true 'think-tanks', or if we set different types of think-tanks too radically apart from each other, we can miss important interrelations that are characteristic of the social and political character of knowledge and of the politics of policy think-tanks. Think-tanks, therefore, are best understood as mixed or multi-professional organizations that carry out or otherwise play a role in policy related research and advisory functions, and are of particular importance with regard to transfer functions – from academic to political, media and business spheres, and vice versa. Think-tanks cannot but consider their work to play a political and intellectual role, which does not necessarily contradict or compromise academic quality, yet frequently does. Think-tanks in any case are involved in pushing policy communities, networks and processes in specific directions. They can frequently be found on either side of the battle lines, and help constituting discourses and movements as well as counter-discourses and counter-movements. We will consider the politics of policy think-tanks in some of the great battles and controversies in which they are prominently involved next. In order to make better sense of the roles of think-tanks, we will relate them to the policy network and community literature.

THINK-TANKS AND POLICY NETWORKS: FROM IRON TRIANGLES OR SUB-GOVERNMENTS TO POLICY COMMUNITIES AND NETWORKS, AND BACK?

Both the left and the right have been highly critical of the relationships between interest groups and the public sector in capitalist democracies after WWII. Oligopolistic industries (e.g. the automobile industry), regulated markets, public monopolies and high-level – corporatist – negotiations between employers and trade unions were held to generate and stabilize iron triangles, regulatory capture, or, more generally, organized or state monopoly capitalism. The sub-government or 'iron triangle' literature (Adams 1981) describes stable policy networks featuring industrial interests and their counterparts in congressional committees and government bureaucracies in the United States. The basic idea of the self-interested public servant conspiring with producer interests at the expense of consumers and the public at large features in the Chicago School's capture theory (developed by economists and legal scholars like George Stigler and Richard Posner, respectively; compare Novak 2013). Capture theory has been applied to the study of regulated industries like telecommunications, banking, or transportation. So-called 'independent' regulatory commissions (shielded to some extent from the political power relations in Congress) were held to pursue the interests of the companies they were designed to regulate in the public interest. Decision making in regulatory commissions also features a close coordination of producer, customer and trade union interests involved in the regulated industries concerned. Regulated companies and public enterprises in turn provided opportunities to blur the lines between material interests of public employees and elected officials on the one hand, and the official tasks set for the organizations (public service). Public enterprises additionally served to create close relations with supplier and service firms, which offered industrial policy opportunities.

Progressive critiques focused on the role of 'incumbent' big business in the case of collusion; right-wing and neoliberal critiques emphasized egoism of politicians and regulators as well as the workforce of regulated companies in addition to management. Both perspectives converged on an image of both stability and stagnation of aging capitalist democracies (Olson 1984). Iron triangle literature and a stable idea of policy communities in turn complement the resulting notion of path-dependent development and national diversity due to institutional configurations.

Economic and political developments which took place from the late 1970s onward were contradicting many collusion, social rigidity and monopolistic stability arguments. In the ensuing process of deregulation, (cross-border) liberalization and privatization, certain enterprises and trade unions failed to defend and maintain the established regulatory environment, and politicians gave up (or had to give up) their positions in quite a number of regulatory institutions and public enterprises. The 'iron law' of the ever expanding bureaucracy and uncontrolled hierarchy (Niskanen 1971) needed serious qualification in the face of dedicated public sector and regulatory reform. Sure, social regulation had increased due to environmental and welfare concerns, but economic regulation was on the decline.

If iron triangle and regulatory capture were synonymous with instances of institutional reproduction of prevailing order and (pathological) stability, the neo-pluralist policy network literature addressed a wider range of political configurations, albeit without denying instances of narrow forms of sub-government. Policy networks in any case were introduced to subject policy fields and issue areas to a more open comparative and empirical analysis (Heclo 1978). In line with the experience of the widening or softening of certain iron triangles due to deregulation and privatization, a greater number of policy actors and a greater variety of actor constellations needed due consideration, and a greater dynamic of (institutional) change at evidence in policy processes needed attention. Policy network research helped in gaining an understanding of policy communities no

Table 19.2 Types of policy networks and communities

Issue network constellation \ Policy community	Closed/narrow	Diverse/wide
Harmonious	Iron triangles/sub-government (e.g. military procurement)	
Adversarial		Contested community (e.g. climate change policy), contesting policy networks

Source: Own composition.

longer free of serious friction or overly harmonious. Correspondingly, experts and expertise were increasingly considered controversial rather than technocratic. A political perspective of think-tanks and policy related science emerged (Fischer and Forester 1993).

Dudley and Richardson (1996) coined the term of adversarial policy communities to explicitly address a change of policy over time. They thereby pointed to the need to examine endogenous agents of stability and change in policy fields in addition to exogenous shocks, which had been considered before in the institutional literature to explain sudden, yet far-reaching, change (compare Fligstein and McAdam 2011). Apart from a structural perspective on policy networks and policy outcome relations, an intentional explanation relies on characteristics of resource exchanges in networks (Marsh 1998). The following four field matrix presented above in Table 19.2 provides a quick typology of stylized cases with regard to narrow and broad policy communities on the one hand, and harmonious versus adversarial constellations on the other hand.

The neo-pluralist account moved the focus of the debate from cases in the upper left quadrant (iron triangles/sub-governments) to the lower right quadrant (contested community, contesting policy networks). In these cases, the policy outcome is likely to be less clearly or importantly related to the network structure(s) than to processes within the contested community and between contesting networks on the one hand, and the changing distribution of a range of resources (money, social capital, linkages, expertise etc.) on the other hand. Since policy making has become more strongly related to knowledge and expertise after WWII, knowledge related resources and capacities can be considered to be of particular relevance in conflict intensive policy networks and critical moments in policy processes. Agenda setting and decision making arguably are most sensitive to competition, though expertise can also play a role in implementation and evaluation stages if only to prepare for agenda modification.

In such knowledge intensive policy debates, think-tanks have become increasingly important and interesting policy actors in their own right, firstly, and, secondly, think-tanks have become critical agencies for many competing participating parties and interest groups. While technocracy and stabilizing expertise from think-tanks among other sources can be considered a strong element of sub-government closure, research on the role of science and knowledge in policy making has pointed to an emerging knowledge paradox. While science is supposed to help decision makers to have sound evidence in support of decision making, the increasing reliance on scientific support and policy related research in policy making has led to the politicization of science (Weingart 1983). While ensuing knowledge battles highlight the political character of knowledge, they can undermine the relevance of scientific knowledge, of sound method and evidence-based rationality, possibly reducing state of the art scientific knowledge to just another opinion. An important part of the story of the increasing numbers of policy actors in policy communities is precisely the growing number and diversity of knowledge actors. The number of think-tanks has grown extraordinarily fast during the past 20 years or so, during which about half the number of think-tanks existing worldwide has been created (McGann and Weaver 2005).

Knowledge actors in general and think-tanks in particular in turn are indeed less interesting in terms of their academic quality, which may or may not play a role, than due to their relationships with other actors in more or less adversarial networks or policy communities as a whole. In conflict intensive policy communities, competing groups promote expertise to back up their arguments. Usually there are strong links to recognized academics, if only in their function as advisory board members or in the references of think-tank policy papers. But then there also are strong links to business and other interests as well as to media and political organizations. Taken together, the resulting complex can be described as a discourse coalition (Hajer 1993) composed of agents and agencies operating beyond the narrow confines of advocacy coalitions in a policy field (Fischer 2003, 93f.).

Think-tanks are central to the formation of discourse coalitions. They provide crucial platforms for networks of individuals, organizations and ideas, which easily escapes scholars who deal with individual think-tanks as 'erratic blocks', i.e. isolated organizations and instances of independent expertise – no matter if and to what extent a claim to independence (from government, private business or other interests etc.) can be legitimately made. Concurring with the argumentative turn literature, the focus on think-tanks and policy communities can go a long way towards an adequately socialized understanding of knowledge and expertise instead of repeating positivist claims of objectivity and evidence. Even if evidence is solid indeed, experts and expertise cannot and indeed should not avoid acknowledging the political, economic and social character of knowledge and expertise in policy making. We will turn to a number of concrete cases of (large) policy controversies next in which think-tanks play a prominent role in order to observe multiple roles and functions of think-tanks in discourse coalitions, policy communities and policy processes.

THINK-TANKS AND DEREGULATION BATTLES: TURNING SUB-GOVERNMENTS INTO ADVERSARIAL POLICY COMMUNITIES

The transition from sub-governments to broader configurations of policy communities in transportation, telecommunication, or banking in the United States has been partly credited to participating think-tanks like the Brookings Institution or the American Enterprise Institute. Fortunately, an insider account of the process from one of the participating organizations does exist, namely from the Brookings Institution, which has also become a widely quoted academic standard history of deregulation. Martha Derthick and Paul Quirk's (1985) history of deregulation at the same time provides an outstanding example of the problems and many contradictions of traditional understandings of think-tanks and think-tank research.

The standard wisdom among political scientists has been that iron triangles operated among regulatory agencies, the regulated industries, and members of Congress, all presumably with a stake in preserving regulation that protected the industries, companies and their employees (and trade union representatives) from competition. Once created, structures like regulated industries are held to be reinforced by path-dependent developments despite almost unanimous agreement among economists that such regulation was inefficient. It seemed highly unlikely that deregulation could occur under these conditions because of the strength of the established protection. Yet from the late 1970s onward major deregulatory changes occurred that strongly favored competition, and dismantled regulatory regimes and eventually even independent regulatory agencies like the Federal Aviation Commission. The results are familiar to airline passengers, users of telephone services, long distance bus travelers, or rail and trucking customers, among others. Alfred Kahn, one of the academic architects of airline deregulation in the United States (Rose 2012), famously described radical and irreversible policy change with his sentence: 'You cannot unscramble the eggs.'

Martha Derthick and Paul J. Quirk ask why this deregulation happened. How did an allegedly diffuse public interest prevail over the powerful industry and union interests that sought to preserve regulation? Why did the regulatory commissions, which were expected to be a major obstacle to deregulation, instead take the initiative on behalf of it? And why did influential members of Congress push for even greater deregulation?

According to the authors, public interest and economic efficiency-oriented academic criticism was key to reform, although they also acknowledge (1) the proactive diffusion of academic work by think-tanks and foundations dedicated to develop political strategies in favor of reforms, (2) the entry of market oriented academics in government services, and (3) leadership of parts of the executive (Derthick and Quirk 1985, 36). Economists attacking regulatory politics were described as working quite isolated from the mainstream, attacking the most powerful legal cartel in US history (Seevers 1975 in a publication of the American Enterprise Institute, cited in Derthick and Quirk 1985, 9n). Derthick and Quirk to their credit observe that the loneliness of these economists was reduced by meeting at common conferences (1985, 9), though the authors refrain from closer examination of the linkages of capture theory made in Chicago, public choice theory made in Virginia and the new welfare economics literature based on the work of Ronald Coase and the subsequent generation of transaction cost economics. All the different scholars involved in the attack on regulatory interventionism were part of a broader neoliberal effort to counter the Keynesian revolution and welfare state capitalism. The American participants in this debate were tied into the global networks of the Mont Pèlerin Society and related think-tank networks, to which the American Enterprise Institute belonged, though not the Brookings Institution (compare Walpen 2004; Plehwe and Mirowski 2009; Plickert 2008; Burgin 2013).

The authors of the Brookings Institution concentrate on three cases: airlines, trucking, and telecommunications. Derthick and Quirk aim at claiming credit for the economic analysis carried out in their own think-tank, the Brookings Institution, possibly because major funding for deregulation related research was shifted from Brookings to the American Enterprise Institute in 1975, just when the political reform process gained steam (Canedo 2008). Previously, between 1967 and 1975, Brookings received US$1.8 million to support 22 books, 65 papers and

38 dissertations directed at the topic of state intervention and regula-
tory politics (Derthick and Quirk 1985, 36). Funding of the American
Enterprise Institute, far to the right of Brookings in general, grew from
US$879 000 in 1970 to US$10.4 million in 1980, partly due to major grants
from corporate foundations in support of deregulation oriented research
(Edsall 1984; Easterbrook 1986).

If deregulation scholarship rested on economic foundations steeped in
neoliberal norms and principled beliefs, and was disseminated by ideologically committed partisan think-tanks related to the university-based
intellectuals, what remains of Derthick and Quirk's claims to genuine
public interest advocacy? The authors of the history claim those powerful vested interests, established airlines, incumbent trucking companies,
and the Bell system, were defeated by the advocates of deregulation who
promoted the public interest. However, in each of the stories the authors
tell, some of the regulated corporations left the coalition of interests who
tried to defend the old regulatory structure, and joined the deregulation
bandwagon, which would make us wonder if they were suddenly acting
in the public interest, or if they simply conceived of their own interests
in a new way considering the shifting policy priorities. Secondly, in each
case the authors relate participation of customer firms who expected to
benefit from deregulation in addition to general consumers. Thirdly, the
authors refrain from speaking of the case of air freight deregulation, which
preceded air passenger deregulation. The air freight deregulation act of
1977 was dubbed the 'FedEx Bill' to acknowledge the profound impact of
the Federal Express corporation lobbying in favor of the new regulatory
regime, from which Fed Ex was expecting to benefit at the expense of the
previously established cargo airlines (Hamilton 1990). Even if Derthick
and Quirk firmly believe in the public interest character of the Brookings-
based research and the deregulation agenda, a more thorough reflection
reveals multiple links between expertise, experts, interests, media and
political functions. Public interest claims turn out to be naïve at best, or
purposefully hiding the fact that deregulation produces winners and losers
much like the preceding regulatory regime.

The think-tanks involved were important in many different ways:
Brookings was building up economic expertise challenging standard regulatory economics, financed by the Ford Foundation. Chicago and Virginia
School scholarship complemented and extended the economic debate by
way of integrating the state and public officials. Pro-market think-tanks
like the American Enterprise Institute closely related to the corporate –
anti-New Deal – sector aggressively pushed neoliberal scholarship, which
subsequently played a very prominent role in the public sphere. Way
beyond academic debates, think-tanks were prominent transfer agencies,

which helped to reconfigure entire policy communities in the fields of transportation, telecommunications and banking in favor of market advocates no matter if corporate, academic or think-tank professional, or public servant. While the big shift in the regulatory politics debate relied on established think-tanks, the environment and energy debates help us in shedding light on the founding of new think-tanks next.

NEW GENERATIONS OF ENVIRONMENTAL THINK-TANKS

The environmental (and energy) policy field is known to be extremely controversial. It was born during the 1970s following the building of major environmental policy institutions, both environmental ministries and regulatory commissions like EPA in the United States. Major battles occurred at the intersection of environmental and peace issues, namely the dual use of nuclear power (e.g. giving rise to the popular Greenpeace NGO). One such battle, the fight of local activists against a planned nuclear power facility took place in Whyl, Germany, close to the French border. Local activists adopted new social movement strategies like sit-down activism and other activities to block and delay construction. Confronted with a heavy police presence, German (and French) activists quickly needed legal support and arguments backing up their claims in the courtroom. To this end, a range of at the time marginal academic critics of nuclear energy, value conservative circles of Social Democracy and protestant churches as well as radical activists founded the Öko-Institut in Freiburg in 1977 (Roose 2002).

The new ecological research institute galvanized critical knowledge at the intersection of academic and social movement expertise. Although critics of nuclear power were a minority in physics and engineering departments at German universities, their insights and perspectives suddenly were revalued. Backed by a formidable and ultimately successful social movement, Germany's energy political agenda was disrupted, and opened up to alternative perspectives beyond fossil and nuclear energy sources. Back in 1980, the Öko Institut published a first study titled 'Energy revolution – growth and prosperity without oil and uranium' (Energiewende – Wachstum und Wohlstand ohne Erdöl und Uran), which proposed a scenario under heavy reliance on renewable energy, solar and wind power in particular. Tracking and tracing of arguments and counterarguments shows the trajectory from the pioneer document to Germany's exit from nuclear power after the Fukushima disaster in 2011 (http://www.energiewende.de).

Over the course of the 1980s and 1990s, the former radical social movement think-tank had become a widely respected policy research and
advisory organization. Öko Institut mostly serves public customers in
Germany and the EU, although there is also a growing customer base in
the private sector. Together with a number of other environmental think-
tanks (e.g. Ecologic in Berlin), the Öko Institute has also pioneered interdisciplinary research and environmental policy studies. The group has
created the network Ecornet (http://www.ecornet.eu/) to push for a change
in funding politics considered inimical to interdisciplinary environmental
studies.[4]

While Öko Institut and other environmental think-tanks clearly played
a major role in the rise of new social movements and the Green parties,
and at the same time led the way to new professional and, last but not
least, academic disciplines, these environmental policy institutes also
triggered a new opposition in the discourse field.

Confronted with the challenges of ecological criticism, which moved
from specific issues like nuclear power to a more comprehensive challenge
of the economic growth paradigm, corporate and ideological counter-
movements emerged with a new focus on environmental economics. So-
called 'new resource economics' was conceived by neoliberal academic
economists who helped in building up a case against ecological critiques.
Since academic space was hostile, the counter-movement had to rely on
private think-tanks backed by major corporations. John Baden's Political
Economy Research Center (PERC) was founded in 1978 in Montana, for
example, followed by the Foundation for Research on Economics and the
Environment (FREE) in 1985. Institutes like PERC and FREE quickly
became a central part of the neoliberal counter-movement, which challenged ecological interventionism advanced since the 1970s. Baden joined
forces with the neo-Malthusian theorist of the 'tragedy of the commons',
Garret Hardin. Together, the two men edited a volume suggestively titled
Managing the Commons in 1977. While this volume also united a number
of respectable critics of bureaucratic environmentalism like the Ostroms,
we also find a contribution from Gordon Tullock, the close colleague and,
with James Buchanan, co-founder of public choice theory. Tullock was
not known as an environmental policy expert. His contribution was about
the cost of regulation.

State failure theory in the field of environmental politics of course
paved the way for so-called 'free market environmentalism' (Eckersley
1993; Beder 2001). While few environmental policy experts think highly
of this branch of environmental economics, think-tanks promoting this
counter-movement are numerous and carry influence in highly publicized
debates around climate change, for example. The bulk of publications that

are critical of precautionary (= interventionist) climate change policies in the United States emanate from neoliberal and neo-conservative think-tanks (Jacques et al. 2008). Apart from the common message, think-tanks involved in climate change policy skepticism share membership in organized neoliberal networks. The full dimension of cross-border networking, funding and campaigning needs yet to be fully understood (Plehwe 2014).

If think-tanks contributed to the building up of expertise for policy reform in the case of transportation deregulation and the move towards renewable energy, the objective of the work of free market think-tanks in the field of climate change has been primarily destructive, aimed at undermining or delaying the case for policy reform. While there is continuing debate about the academic quality of the constructive knowledge base for deregulation, there is hardly any doubt about the non-academic character of the destructive knowledge base against climate change policies. Yet it would be difficult to deny the relevance of think-tank knowledge in both cases. Think-tanks are critical agencies in relevance making. If, when and why academic knowledge criteria do play a role is but one interesting question in think-tank and policy community research.

CONCLUSIONS: TOWARDS A MORE COMPREHENSIVE UNDERSTANDING OF KNOWLEDGE CREATION AND KNOWLEDGE SHAPING

In terms of the role of think-tanks in general and in the concrete policy struggles of deregulation, energy and climate change, we can clearly recognize the need to situate policy related research in wider webs of influence. With regard to deregulation agendas in academic and political arenas, attention needs to be paid to neoliberal intellectuals at universities on whom the work of think-tank-based researchers could draw, and the money from Ford and other corporate foundations that pushed research in particular directions, but also contributed to the popularization of deregulation in the wider public, and promoted deregulation politically by way of shifting resources from moderate to more radical deregulation advocates in the critical moment of the mid-1970s. The old regulatory policy community was subject to considerable change in the 1970s, which preceded the policy shift from the late 1970s onward. Similarly, the outsider expertise of the anti-nuclear power movement of the 1970s provided a formidable challenge to the established sub-governments reigning the energy and environmental fields. First based in social movement related think-tanks like the Öko-Institut in Freiburg, the critique of nuclear power formed the basis of Germany's shift from nuclear energy to renewable energies dubbed 'Energiewende' (energy shift).

Did the policy field and the character of expertise remain contested in the aftermath of deregulation and energy shift? Arguably not in the case of deregulation, although a fair amount of criticism of deregulation was expressed in the academic world and in think-tanks related to trade unions, for example. In the case of energy politics the record is mixed since pro-nuclear forces claim a need to rely on nuclear power to achieve climate change policy goals, for example. But unlike before, those anti-deregulation and pro-nuclear power pockets of expertise in the United States and Germany, respectively, were no longer considered to be central to the economic and social policy community visible in the transportation and energy and environment fields.

In climate change politics, knowledge-shaping activities (Bonds 2011) of Exxon Mobile and other climate change (policy) denial forces have yielded more limited results. But in this case as well, think-tanks are critical agents charged with the mobilization of counter-expertise against some of the most highly respected academic institutions. If a necessarily political and social character of knowledge has to be recognized, it becomes all the more important to recognize and to critically assess the socially distributed agency involved in knowledge production and shaping processes. The organizational space of think-tanks can hardly be overestimated in this regard. It can be considered a result of specialization and professionalization of policy knowledge processing at odds with other functions carried out in organizations that spin off or otherwise found think-tanks, an example of conflicting goals, or ambidexterity (Puhan 2008). By way of specializing and integrating knowledge and service functions, think-tanks and think-tank networks in turn grow into the role of a more or less diversified policy and transfer agency, operating in both public and private spheres, offering tool boxes akin to the multifunctional 'Swiss Army knife'.

NOTES

1. Compare overview provided here: http://onthinktanks.org/2011/04/03/think-tank-directories-and-lists/, last accessed 23 January 2015.
2. Although considerable differences exist with regard to think-tank rules between the United States (high public requirements) and Germany (low public requirements), complaints about the lack of transparency are common to both countries since funding sources can be easily concealed in the United States by using third parties.
3. Although the rate of growth of think-tanks is held to have declined during the last decade, half of the think-tanks in the United States have been launched after 1980 (McGann 2015). Similar observations have been made in Europe, where the collapse

of socialism and deeper European integration provided particularly ample opportunities for new think-tanks and strategies (Plehwe 2010). According to McGann's global survey, about 60 per cent of think-tanks are located in North America and Europe, though we need to think of this percentage as a very rough indicator due to selection problems and the limited resources available to this global survey effort (compare McGann 2015).
4. A similar shift has been explored by Tom Medvetz (2012), who demonstrates paradigm shift in the field of welfare state research in the United States based on the work of think-tanks. Social equality norms were replaced by dependency concerns as a guiding principle, requiring new and different research programs and strategies.

REFERENCES

Adams, Gordon (1981), The *Iron Triangle: The Politics of Defense Contracting, Council on Economic Priorities*, New York: Council on Economic Priorities.
Asher, Thomas and Nicolas Guilhot (2010), 'The collapsing space between universities and think-tanks', in *World Social Science Report*, Paris: UNESCO, pp. 338–344.
Beder, Sharon (2001), 'Neoliberal think-tanks and free market environmentalism', *Environmental Politics* **10** (2), 128–133.
Bonds, E. (2011), 'The knowledge-shaping process: elite mobilization and environmental policy', *Critical Sociology* **37** (4), 429–446.
Burgin, A. (2013), *The Great Persuasion: Reinventing Free Markets Since The Depression*, Cambridge, MA: Harvard University Press.
Campbell, John L. and Ove K. Pedersen (2014), *The National Origins of Policy Ideas: Knowledge Regimes in the United States, France, Germany, and Denmark*, Princeton, NJ: Princeton University Press.
Canedo, Eduardo (2008), *The Rise of the Deregulation Movement in Modern America, 1957–1980*, New York: Columbia University.
Crouch, C. (2004), *Post-Democracy*, Frankfurt am Main: Suhrkamp.
Derthick, Martha and Paul Quirk (1985), *The Politics of Deregulation*, Washington, DC: Brookings Institution Press.
Dudley, G. and J. Richardson (1996), 'Why does policy change over time? Adversarial policy communities, alternative policy arenas, and British trunk road policy 1945–1995', *Journal of European Public Policy* **4** (1), 63–83.
Easterbrook, G. (1986), 'Ideas move nations', *Atlantic Monthly* **1** (1986), 66–88.
Eckersley, Robyn (1993), 'Free market environmentalism. Friend or foe?', *Environmental Politics* **2** (1), 1–19.
Edsall, Thomas B. (1984), *The New Politics of Inequality*, New York and London: W.W. Norton & Company.
Fischer, Frank (1993), 'Policy discourse and the politics of Washington think tanks', in Frank Fischer and John Forester (eds), *The Argumentative Turn in Policy Analysis and Planning*, Durham, NC: Duke University Press, pp. 21–42.
Fischer, Frank (2003), *Reframing Public Policy: Discursive Politics and Deliberative Practices*, Oxford: Oxford University Press.
Fischer, Frank and John Forrester (eds) (1993), *The Argumentative Turn in Policy Analysis and Planning*, Durham, NC: Duke University Press.
Fligstein, N. and D. McAdam (2011), 'Toward a general theory of strategic action fields', *Sociological Theory* **29** (1), 1–26.
Hajer, Maarten A. (1993), 'Discourse coalitions and the institutionalization of practice: the case of Acid rain in Britain', in Frank Fischer and John Forrester (eds), *The Argumentative Turn in Policy Analysis and Planning*, Durham, NC: Duke University Press, pp. 43–76.
Hamilton, Geoffrey W. (1990), 'Federal Express – L'IBM des messageries exprès', in Philip Bowyer (ed.), *I.P.T.T Etudes 60*, Geneva: IPTT, pp. 1–37.

Hardin, Garrett and John Baden (eds) (1977), *Managing the Commons*, San Francisco: W.H. Freeman.

Harvey, David (1989), *The Condition of Postmodernity*, Oxford: Blackwell.

Heclo, H. (1978), 'Issue networks and the executive establishment', in A. King (ed.), *The New American Political System*, Washington, DC: American Enterprise Institute for Public Policy Research, pp. 87–124.

Jacques, Peter J., Riley E. Dunlap and Mark Freeman (2008), 'The organisation of denial: conservative think-tanks and environmental scepticism', *Environmental Politics* **17** (3), 349–385.

Jasanoff, Sheila (2005), *Designs on Nature: Science and Democracy in Europe and the United States*, Princeton, NJ: Princeton University Press.

Mair, Peter (2013), *Ruling The Void: The Hollowing Of Western Democracy*, New York and London: Verso Books.

Marsh, D. (1998), 'The development of the policy network approach', in D. Marsh (ed.), *Comparing Policy Networks*, Buckingham, UK: Open University Press, pp. 3–20.

McGann, James G. (2015), '2014 global go to think-tank report', Philadelphia: University of Pennsylvania. Available at: http://repository.upenn.edu/cgi/viewcontent. cgi?article=1008&context=think_tanks.

McGann, James G. and Erik C. Johnson (2005), *Comparative Think Tanks, Politics and Public Policy*, Cheltenham, UK and Northampton, MA, USA: Edward Elgar.

McGann, James G. and R. Kent Weaver (eds) (2005), *Think-tanks and Civil Societies. Catalysts for Ideas and Action*, Piscataway, NJ: Transaction Publishers.

Medvetz, Thomas (2012), *Think-tanks in America*, Chicago: University of Chicago Press.

Niskanen, William A. (1971), *Bureaucracy and Public Economics*, Aldershot, UK and Brookfield, VT, USA: Edward Elgar.

Novak, William (2013), 'A revisionist history of regulatory capture', in Daniel Carpenter and David Moss (eds), *Preventing Regulatory Capture. Special Interest Influence and How to Limit it*, Cambridge: Cambridge University Press, pp. 25–48.

Olson, Mancur (1984), *The Rise and Decline of Nations: Economic Growth, Stagflation, and Social Rigidities*, Yale, CT: Yale University Press.

Oreskes, N. And E.M. Conway (2010), *Merchants of Doubt: How a Handful of Scientists Obscured the Truth on Issues from Tobacco Smoke to Global Warming*, London: Bloomsbury Press.

Pautz, Hartwig (2011), 'Revisiting the think-tank phenomenon', *Public Policy and Administration* **26**, 419–435.

Plehwe, Dieter (2010), 'Im Dickicht der Beratung. Es mangelt nicht an EuropaThink Tanks, wohl aber an Transparenz', *WZB-Mitteilungen* **130**, S. 22–25. Available at: http://www. wzb.eu/publikation/pdf/wm130/22-25.pdf.

Plehwe, Dieter (2011a), 'Transnational discourse coalitions and monetary policy: Argentina and the limited powers of the "Washington Consensus"', *Critical Policy Studies* **5** (02), 127–148.

Plehwe, Dieter (2011b), 'Who cares about excellence? Commercialization, competition, and the transnational promotion of neoliberal expertise', in Tor Halvorsen and Atle Nyhagen (eds), *Academic Identities – Academic Challenges? American and European Experiences of the Transformation of Higher Education and Research*, Newcastle upon Tyne, UK: Cambridge Scholars Press, pp. 159–193.

Plehwe, Dieter (2014), 'Think-tank networks and the knowledge-interest nexus. The case of climate change', *Critical Policy Studies* **8** (01), 101–115.

Plehwe, Dieter and Philip Mirowski (2009), *The Road from Mont Pèlerin: The Making of the Neoliberal Thought Collective*, Cambridge, MA: Harvard University Press.

Plehwe, Dieter and Bernhard Walpen (2006), 'Between network and complex organization: the making of neoliberal knowledge and hegemony', in Dieter Plehwe, Bernhard Walpen and Gisela Neunhöffer (eds), *Neoliberal Hegemony. A Global Critique*, London: Routledge, pp. 27–50.

Plickert, P. (2008), *Wandlungen des Neoliberalismus. Eine Studie zu Entwicklung und Ausstrahlung der 'Mont Pèlerin Society'*, Stuttgart: Lucius und Lucius.

Puhan, Tatjana-Xenia (2008), *Balancing Exploration and Exploitation by Creating Organizational Think-tanks*, Wiesbaden: Gabler Edition Wissenschaft.

Roose, J. (2002), *Made by Öko-Institut. Wissenschaft in einer bewegten Umwelt*, Freiburg im Breisgau: Verlag Öko-Institut.

Rose, Nancy L. (2012), 'After airline deregulation and Alfred E. Kahn', *American Economic Review* **102** (3), 376–380.

Rich, Andrew (2004), *Think Tanks, Public Policy, and the Politics of Expertise*, Cambridge: Cambridge University Press.

Saloma III, John S. (1984), '*Ominous Politics. The New Conservative Labyrinth*, New York: Hill and Wang.

Smith, James A. (1991), *The Idea Brokers. Think Tanks and the Rise of the New Policy Elite*, New York: The Free Press.

Stone, Diane (2007), 'Garbage cans, recycling bins or think-tanks? Three myths about policy institutes', *Public Administration* **85** (2), 259–278.

Stone, Diane (2013), *Knowledge Actors and Transnational Governance. The Private-Public Policy Nexus in the Global Agora*, Houndmills, UK: Palgrave Macmillan.

Stone, Diane and Andrew Denham (eds) (2004), *Think Tank Traditions. Policy Research and the Politics of Ideas*, Manchester: Manchester University Press.

Stone, Diane, Andrew Denham and Mark Garnett (eds) (1998), *Think-tanks Across Nations*, Manchester: Manchester University Press.

Sutcliffe, Sophie and Julius Court (2005), *Evidence-Based Policymaking: What is it? How Does it Work? What Relevance for Developing Countries?*, London: ODI. Available at: http://www.odi.org/sites/odi.org.uk/files/odi-assets/publications-opinion-files/3683.pdf.

Walpen, B. (2004), *Die offenen Feinde und ihre Gesellschaft. Eine hegemonietheoretische Studie zur Mont Pèlerin Society*, Hamburg: VSA.

Wedel, Jeanine R. (2009), *Shadow Elite: How the World's New Power Brokers Undermine Democracy, Government, and the Free Market*, New York: Basic Books.

Weingart, Peter (1983), 'Verwissenschaftlichung der Gesellschaft – Politisierung der Wissenschaft', *Zeitschrift für Soziologie* **12**, 225–241.

20 Critical action research and social movements: revitalizing participation and deliberation for democratic empowerment
Hemant R. Ojha, Mani R. Banjade and Krishna K. Shrestha

1. INTRODUCTION

Critical scholars recognize a crisis in the promise of participatory development policy and practice (Kothari and Cooke, 2001). After a history of more than four decades, the participatory policy paradigm faces increasing concerns as citizens are without control of the policy politics affecting their choices and positions (Sassen, 1996).[1] The participatory approach emerged as a critique of top-down and techno-centric research and development that often ignored community values, local culture and indigenous knowledge (Shrestha and Mahjabeen, 2011). In many situations, however, even heavy investment in participatory projects has failed to foster effective deliberation, to promote the empowerment of communities, and to enhance the equitable allocation of resources (Mosse, 2005).

We argue that the Critical Action Research (CAR) approach has the potential to go beyond the dominant understandings advanced in conventional participatory research, which has a long tradition (Gaventa, 2004; Görsdorf, 2006; Mansuri and Rao, 2013). CAR seeks to enhance the interplay between research and social movement practices, an interplay we regard as crucial in improving the democratic quality of policy processes. Pre-existing power relations particularly undermine the democratic potential of participation and deliberation, and we focus here on how hegemonic forms of power relations might be engaged, to a certain degree at least, in order to democratize practices of participation and deliberation.

We conceptualize democratic policy making as a practice to address the concerns of affected people in a fair and equitable manner (Dryzek, 2000; Papadopoulos and Warin, 2007). Attempts have been made to revitalize the potential of participation by drawing on the ideas of citizenship (Mohan and Hickey, 2004), deliberative practices (Fischer, 2006), and community empowerment (Gaventa, 2004). However, evidence suggests that there have been limited improvements in actual policy processes and development practices (Mansuri and Rao 2004, 2013; Agarwal, 2009). By advancing CAR, we want to contribute to conceptual inquiry into the practice of policy research that might enhance both democratic practice and practical discourses concerning policy.

Critical inquiry into policy is not new, and there is indeed a long heritage of scholarship to challenge the positivist paradigm, advancing post-empiricist research strategies (Fischer, 1998). These efforts include the Habermasian notion of emancipatory reason, emphasizing the role of critical research in progressive policy decisions (Habermas, 1984), as well as a whole range of interpretive strategies and discourse analysis (Yanow, 2007). However, such endeavors are often constrained by what Bourdieu has called 'scholastic reason' (Bourdieu, 2009). When conventional research practice is confined within the scholastic domain, critical scholars can be effective in showing why a certain practice does not work, yet often fail to offer the nuanced understanding of practice needed to address practical challenges in the real world. Some have thus argued for a more engaged role of activist intellectuals to contribute to policy and practice (Hale, 2008). In our view, explaining why policies do not work is different from acting to explore how policies can work (Ojha, 2013). As Kurt Lewin argues: 'You cannot understand a system, unless you try to change it.' In a related, more radical approach, Paulo Freire has demonstrated ways to conscientize the oppressed through critical pedagogies (Freire, 1970 [2000]). Fals-Borda and Rahman have similarly emphasized the emancipatory potential of participatory action research by advancing an approach for critical researchers to work with the exploited groups (Fals-Borda, 1987; Fals-Borda and Rahman, 1991). However, we have yet to see anything more than limited attempts to blend critical inquiry, action orientation, and participatory research to achieve a better understanding, together with a transformation, of policy practices.

This chapter draws upon our long-term research practice as CAR oriented researchers who have worked closely with various social movement actors. In the course of our discussion, we present cases from three countries: Nepal, India, and Australia. In the case of Nepal (where Ojha and Banjade were involved), we recount a practice of linking research with a community forestry movement as part of influencing policy. With respect to India, we review the role of an activist NGO[2] in catalyzing inclusive urban development. In the case of Australia (where Shrestha was involved), we examine practices linking expert contributions to a landcare program. Drawing on these case studies, we explore how practices of critical inquiry and community participation emerged in different contexts to advance specific ideas of democratic governance seeking to enhance participation and deliberation in public policy processes.

In the sections to follow, we recall aspects of these cases in identifying four key elements of CAR that are relevant in its interplay with community participation and social movements. First, we demonstrate that CAR strives to achieve an empowering mode of interaction between researchers and local communities. Second, CAR intellectuals consider action as an integral element of learning process contributing to policy improvement. Third, CAR involves a dialectical epistemology in which both researchers and practitioners educate one another. Fourth, in an age of mediatization and glocalization (Robertson, 1995), CAR seeks to be active across multiple levels of governance in order to enhance the quality of democratic deliberation in policy making.

2.   CRITICAL ACTION RESEARCH AS COMMUNITY EMPOWERMENT

As techno-scientific approaches to understanding policy challenges are facing trenchant critique, the whole enterprise of research is under pressure to demonstrate its relevance in fostering constructive policy dialogues (Fischer, 1998). A key response to this pressure has been to advance a participatory approach to blend science and commonsensical knowledge, but this response has its limits. For the most part, the idea of participation usually presupposes the primacy of the knowledge of external scientists or professionals, who act as the leaders, while the communities are invited to perform certain roles, often framed by the external actors. Indeed, professionals or scientists working with communities often model the interaction as the one between expert and clients. Although the 'clients' may be conscious of the weakness in this approach, its proponents fail to offer a critical and transformative view of researcher-community interactions. The question of how researchers position themselves in the context of research and in relation to participating communities is thus a key concern.

A more engaged approach to such interactions was suggested long ago with the Deweyan idea of 'transactional inquiry' (Dewey and Bentley, 1949). Here, researchers and participants co-create themselves in and through the dialogues between them. Taking up this Deweyan view, we believe critical action researchers should have a deep appreciation of, and commitment to, transactional inquiry. This can come from working with people in particular contexts not only to generate critical evidence, but also to help people both critically analyze problems and act to influence the policy processes. That means finding ways to empower marginalized groups and to develop an active communicative interface with social movements involving the marginalized actors themselves. The goal is to carry forward and mobilize critical evidence in actual policy deliberations (Ojha, 2013).

In practice, the mode of interaction between CAR intellectuals and social movements must be understood in specific contexts. In that regard, Ojha (2013) identifies two challenges facing the CAR actors. First, how and to what extent does their work become legitimate in the eyes of not only the disadvantaged actors, but also of the dominant policy actors? This means that the context of power in which the CAR work is pursued becomes crucial. Second, the extent to which the CAR actors are prepared to throw into question their own 'mental models' (Argyris and Schön, 1996) is key to the conduct of inquiry. We turn now to three contexts: the cases involving Nepal, India, and Australia.

The case of Nepal illustrates how researchers interacted with the actors of a community forestry movement in producing critical knowledge as well as enhancing the empowerment of local communities. Although the Nepal government ceded some power to local communities through forest legislation in 1993, the policy process remained largely controlled by technocratic power of the government forest service (Ojha et al., 2014). In such a situation, a community of critical action researchers worked with an evolving social movement to influence public policy towards the devolution and decentralization of forest authority. This was evident from 2000 to 2010 in the collaborative work between a research NGO called ForestAction Nepal (consisting of CAR intellectuals) and the Federation of Community Forestry Users, Nepal (FECOFUN) (Ojha, 2013). Researchers at ForestAction worked with FECOFUN to define the scope of research and used the research outputs primarily to enhance FECOFUN's policy advocacy. ForestAction also engaged with other social movements in issues related to natural resources – such as land rights, access to irrigation, local governance and food sovereignty – using strategies similar to those used in the community forestry movement.

The CAR work of ForestAction also included an active engagement with multi-stakeholder deliberations at national and district levels, linking social movements with policy makers and practitioners. CAR social movement work also involved linkages from local to national scales, as local communities formed FECOFUN at the local, sub-national (meso), and national levels to articulate their rights during forest policy processes. While FECOFUN remained active on the ground demanding rights, the CAR actors created essential discursive forums at different governance levels and across scales, bringing actors to exchange their ideas, and share the results of the research around ongoing policy issues. Over the course of several years, FECOFUN became influential in terms of amplifying community voices in policy discourses. It also faced issues of internal representation and accountability to its own member communities – which became the subject of critical inquiry for the ForestAction researchers (Ojha, 2009).

The case of the Indian NGO – the Society for the Promotion of Area Resource Centers (SPARC) – demonstrates an empowering interaction between professional researchers and the marginalized slum communities in the urban social context. India is perhaps the country where the global challenge of social exclusion is most severe in the context of rapid urbanization. India's poverty is now manifest in cities where more than 40 per cent of people are slum dwellers, with limited access to basic services. In Mumbai alone, over 54 per cent of the population lives in informal or slum settlements without access to basic services.[3] India has also recognized the issues of urban poverty and inclusion, and has formulated various programs, such as *Rajiv Awas Yojana*, which aims to provide access to housing for people living in slums and also to address the underlying factors that create slums in the first place. How exactly such issues can be addressed in policy and practice has become one of the key challenges in India. Much planning and policy effort in the past has failed (Roy, 2009), mainly due to the continuation of top-down approaches to urban development that often ignore the role and rights of the poor and slum dwellers.

Recognizing these challenges, SPARC has championed a process to catalyze inclusive urban development and planning in several cities in India. Most notably in Mumbai, its principal strategy has been to work with networks and alliances of urban poor to enhance land tenurial security, to help people fight evictions by the government, and to demand at least relocation or access to affordable housing options and sanitation services (Patel, 2014). SPARC did not work for the poor – it worked with the poor – thus attempting to go beyond the instrumental framing of participatory development that usually involves an external agency setting the course of the development.

The institutional setting of SPARC's critical action research involves four different organizations: a professional group (SPARC itself); an association of women called Mahila Milan (MM); an association of slum dwellers called the National Slum Dwellers Association (NSDF), and a non-profit company led by SPARC and the other two alliance partners. The SPARC leader has indicated that 'the relationship with NSDF and MM is symbiotic and all strategies, risks and explorations emerge from a consensus to explore solutions and face challenges together' (Patel, 2014, p. 178). This approach demonstrates a deep commitment to an empowering interplay between researchers and communities – the kind of approach emphasized in CAR.

In the case of Australia, the landcare movement demonstrates diverse forms of interaction between researchers and communities affecting land-care policy and practice. It also shows that a technocratic resurgence occurred when CAR-oriented researchers encountered diminishing space for their engagement due to funding restrictions. The case is not a success story, but convincingly demonstrates the need for CAR in enhancing land-care policy and practice. Landcare is a grassroots movement in which individuals and groups seek to protect, restore and manage natural resources and their productivity. More than 6000 groups across the country joined the landcare movement. Many have worked closely with researchers interested in community participation, sustainable agriculture and river management. Interaction usually takes the form of participation in community workshops, field-days, tree planting, community rallies, and short trips to allied landcare groups to gain and share knowledge and experience. While the landcare movement emerged in relation to the parallel growth of research about land sustainability issues, government support and growing environmental challenges – such as salinity, drought, water shortages and floods – there is a gap in critical action research to advance truly decentralized and community-centric land governance. In particular, lack of efforts to expose the concerns of local people in policy discourses resulted in a number of laws, such as the Natural Heritage Trust Act, primarily crafted by technical experts[4] with little or no input from local communities.

Under the prevailing institutional environment, most researchers working with the Australian landcare movement have chosen to interact with people as 'advisors' or technical experts. Their work has also been heavily dependent on research funding from the government, whose priority has been shifting away from the landcare movement. As one of the actively engaged landcare researchers remarked: 'I have been forced to stop doing research on [the] landcare movement as government funding agencies find [it] irrelevant to fund such work.'[5] Moreover, university based researchers are also constrained by the pressures of academic award, which hardly encourages sustained and active policy engagement with particular public issues. The landcare movement in Australia thus demonstrates the need for more critical action research where researchers are willing to work with local communities and local governments.

3.   ACTION LEARNING AND THE MORAL DIMENSION

Policy research is not just an epistemic project, but also one involving engagement and relationship to prepare the ground for social learning and political negotiations (Hall, 1993). The action aspect has both moral and epistemological dimensions. First, it reflects a genuine effort to tackle or change the problematic situation in the context. Second, the action is a means for the validation of new knowledge through expanding the definition of evidence (to include action-reflection dynamics), which will otherwise not be adequately robust. While conventional policy analysis has focused on producing 'facts' for decision makers, the participatory shift has emphasized learning from practice. CAR actors take practice as a source for critical reflection and learning, as they aim for research results that build on action. The idea is that action-based evidence is more contextually grounded, containing the perspectives of the various social groups. The participatory inquiry project has oscillated between an action focus and a research focus, and CAR has evolved out of a need to develop a more thorough and integrated view of action as a form of critical research, reconciling both moral and epistemological dimensions. In CAR, we highlight maximizing both the immediate moral outcomes and the knowledge that can contribute to fair development through improved policy decisions.

Nepal's social movement for community forestry evolved over the last two decades largely because of the concerted efforts of local communities, critical action researchers, secondary associations, government forest service, NGOs and donors. The CAR offered opportunities for these actors by challenging the technocratic worldview and offering an alternative knowledge system produced through social action in partnership with the community forestry movement. Partly as a result of CAR, policy processes in Nepal exhibit some degree of commitment to the engagement necessary for inclusive and equitable development.

In India, SPARC created *SPARC Samudaik Nirman Sahayak* (SSNS) in 1998 to take charge of the works related to the development of tools, technologies, and the provisioning of financing. This name is translated in English as SPARC Community Construction Assistant. As the 2011–2012 annual report claims, 'SSNS acts as a learning lab to develop technical and financial tools, often emerging from processes of the urban poor, to support the work of Mahila Milan and NSDF to access finance, basic amenities and housing for the poorest of the poor . . . ' (SSNS, 2012). The emergence and continuing engagement of SPARC, as well as its gradual expansion, was based on the need to act at multiple scales – from household, through local communities and state government to national government and beyond.

4. CRITICAL ACTION RESEARCH THROUGH DIALECTICAL EPISTEMOLOGY

What forms of knowledge are most relevant to democratic empowerment in the policy process? That question has remained a key research challenge. Critical inquirers have emphasized adopting a 'dialectical epistemology' in which critical knowledge is generated not through the empirical-analytic exercise of the researcher, but through critically engaged dialogues or a 'dialectical clash' (Fischer, 1998) with the actors affected by policy. This also allows one to go beyond one-dimensional reliance on analytical logic, and engage in the creative processes of insight, interpretation and judgment (Fischer, 1998). As a critical project, it has to be 'directed at an audience of sufferers in order to make plain to them the causes of their suffering' (Dryzek, 2006a, p. 192). It is validated through 'reflective acceptance on the part of the audience' (Dryzek, 2006a, p. 192). In other words, critical policy research remains sensitive to particular contexts of a policy problem, and aims for a capacity to identify positive changes (Dryzek, 1987). Through demonstrating concerns with people and their issues, not only is crucial evidence generated, but marginalized human agents are empowered to carry forward the evidence in the process of political deliberation. We consider expanding deliberative space as a key intermediate outcome of critical inquiry practice. By deliberative space, we mean the prospect of approximating a context of undistorted communication in a Habermasian sense, thereby shaping discursive space as suggested by John Dryzek and Frank Fischer.

The work of ForestAction Nepal demonstrates the emergence of CAR activity in recognition of the clear need to forge a critical dialogue between the researchers and forestry stakeholders. Although the national-level policies and regulations were in favor of community rights over Nepal's forests, implementation of these regulatory instruments were fraught with several shortcomings due in large part to the continued resistance of techno-bureaucratic authority (Ojha, 2006; Sunam et al., 2013). Moreover, insufficient links between the local practices and national and sub-national-level policy deliberations, together with a lack of feedback loops in program planning and implementation, were also identified as reasons for the limited success of the community forestry programs in addressing the problems of exclusion, inequity, restricted political space, and meager benefits to the marginalized groups (Banjade, 2013).

During 2000–2009, CAR on behalf of ForestAction in Nepal (including co-authors Ojha and Banjade) involved action research at the local level, followed by workshops at district level (meso level), and finally taking the community and meso-level research into the national-level policy debates.

The work focused on generating evidence about emerging and ongoing policy issues, usually as a first step to engage in the process, so that we could understand the roles that different forms of hegemonic power play in deliberative practices. We formulated specific actions to test ideas in practice, to see how they work in the real world. This testing in practice entailed, for instance, working with local disadvantaged groups to explore more equitable arrangements in forest management while identifying possible public policy arrangements to enable such equity-oritented innovations. The key strategies used in facilitating CAR within the community groups included situation analysis, identifying key gaps in governance, resource management and benefit distribution, and developing indicators and action plans in order to improve institutions and practices. By institutionalizing collective learning and mechanisms for improved linkages with external actors and the market, the groups could resolve many shortcomings arising from local resource shortages, social hierarchies, culture and attitudes. Through CAR, many of the marginalized groups started challenging the established power of particular groups and individuals.

After working to empower partnerships with communities at the local level, the CAR team engaged with community federations and citizen networks in the mutual learning process. They focused on helping them understand the complexity of problems and possible ways forward. In several situations, communities were already undertaking resistance to dominant policy proposals, and our critical inquiry was oriented to sharpen their position and strengthen their political articulation (Chhatre, 2008). As they accumulated evidence and insights, they spent more effort in translating this knowledge into various forms of readable products and in circulating this material to wider networks and coalitions within and outside the country. They also created new discussion forums to strengthen face-to-face deliberation among state and non-state policy actors.

In the Indian case, SPARC leaders admitted at the beginning that they did not have a firm idea of how things could be changed, but they were committed to the organization's strategy of engaging in trial and error, while building learning networks among men, women, the poor and professionals (Patel, 2014). Unlike conventional advocacy campaigns, SPARC emphasizes generation of alternative knowledge, as demonstrated in its effort to generate alternative facts and figures through community profiling, as well as household survey and mapping exercises. Such concrete forms of knowledge and data did not only enable the urban poor to negotiate urban policies and programs, but also helped them to act better collectively. As SPARC leaders write, 'Mapping the settlement gives residents a sense of the area they occupy and its value, and also helps them plan future redevelopment options. This information allows a settlement to look at itself as a collective rather than a set of individual households' (Patel et al., 2012).

As Patel et al. (2012) further argue, 'With this data, as well as the strength and size of the communities it represents, the federation has the basis for negotiation, a better way of communicating a point than demonstrating for rights on the street outside city offices.' Presenting alternative data is important as city officials often see the work of poor communities as only delaying an action or project (Arputham and Patel, 2010). Community-based surveys enabled communities and cities to understand crucial aspects of urban poverty, including the condition of pavement dwellers, most of whom came from the poorest districts of Maharashtra and other parts of India, who worked for very low wages and who had no assets in the village when they left (Patel, 2014).

Like community forestry federation in Nepal and slum dwellers' associations in the Indian case, landcare groups have also formed networks at the state and national levels in Australia. Such landcare networks have also created a platform to engage critical research groups and the media on policy issues related to the rights of local communities. Such partnership offered some legitimacy and power to the landcare groups for pursuing their interests, while the researchers also found their research being politically mobilized, without the need for them to act politically. A specific form of partnership between landcare researchers and landcare groups was the joint survey of landcare groups to find out the characteristics and problems of local communities, an endeavor in which one of the co-authors of this paper was involved (Shreshtha). The survey generated several important forms of evidence, which contrasted with the government data,[6] and hence opened up new avenues for landcare groups to engage in meaningful dialogue with the relevant government agencies.

5. CRITICAL ACTION RESEARCH AS MULTI-SCALAR ENGAGEMENT

In an increasingly networked world with multi-level drivers of change, it is hard for critical researchers to influence policy by acting only at the local level and within arbitrarily delineated domains of formal institutions (Hajer, 2003). For example, local forest governance in Nepal is shaped by global processes related to knowledge, power, money and strategic interests (Ojha, 2014). Several United Nations resolutions have begun to supersede national legislation. Likewise, international development aid has emerged as a strong political force in shaping the policy systems in the developing world. Clearly, the policy process has come to include multi-scale elements of a contested deliberative system (Mansbridge, 1999; Mansbridge et al., 2012), where not just the citizens of sovereign states but a wide variety of actors have become legitimate players in the national policy field. More importantly, it is not just the number or the type of actors that make a policy system politically complicated, it is, in the language of Bourdieu (1989), the social field of practices with their own history, culture and power relations that influence policy in the increasingly networked society. This means that the task of a critical policy inquiry is not complete simply by looking at the interactions among individuals; it also needs to examine how the wider political economy of knowledge is produced and legitimated in the policy process.

In a globalizing world, natural resources are increasingly contested by a growing number of actors (Leach et al., 1999). In such contexts, as post-structural social sciences have revealed (Rosenau, 1991), meta-institutional categories of state, market and civil society do not suffice in understanding how things operate or change. We have a much more complex array of actors and interest groups within each of these categories (Dryzek, 2006; Rose and Miller, 2010). An example of the multi-scale nature of policy process is found in the case of natural resource governance systems, which are multi-scalar and interlinked economic, ecological and political systems (Holling, 2001; Mwangi and Wardell, 2012). This means that local-level governance of natural resources, however sovereign or autonomous legally, has to respond to (and hence engage with) the forces, drivers and actors operating at the higher levels (Armitage, 2008). In such contexts, critical researchers can choose the spheres of engagement in relation to discourses – ranging from local policy arenas to global policy fields, and from direct engagement to theoretical discourse. Critical action researchers emphasize mapping the context of influence over practical policy issues, then locating dominant waves of discourses affecting the policy process in defining the domains of engagement (Ojha, 2013).

In Nepal, the CAR work involved significant engagements at the district level, such as fostering interactions among community leaders, forest officials, civil society organizations, forestry project staff, and forest entrepreneurs. Such 'meso-level' work usually followed community-level engagement. A clear advantage of working with and observing the district-level process was an opportunity to understand the politics of policy implementation. This understanding helped to explore ways to facilitate a more progressive reinterpretation of existing policies, and subsequently used as an effective reason for challenging the predominant instrumental and technocratic modes of interaction. As a result of engagement in such processes, some District Forest Officers (DFOs) became more enthusiastic in supporting communities in forest management than they were earlier. In Nawalparasi District, for example, a DFO worked with our team during 2007–2008 to reinterpret a policy provision regarding the establishment of community forestry, which resulted in more communities being allowed to exercise their rights over forests.[7]

At the national level, CAR researchers promoted multi-stakeholder policy learning forums among the key actors – including senior government officials, community movement leaders, NGOs, academics and independent experts (Ojha et al., 2012). Participants identified key issues of the time, discussed and agreed upon the procedure for analyzing the current status of the identified themes, and formed an action group to do desk review and conduct field-level interviews. They also agreed to organize joint interaction programs with different stakeholders at district and community levels to understand local complexities; and through formal and informal channels they provided inputs to the policy process. Further, ForestAction also organized the production of the *Journal of Forest and Livelihoods* and a Nepali language journal called *Hamro Ban Sampada* (literally meaning 'our forest resources'), which widened the network of scholars, writers, editors and reviewers who have been engaged in the research produced by the CAR researchers, within and outside ForestAction.

In India, SPARC believed that the problems of exclusion that slum communities faced came from higher levels, so that communities alone could not effectively participate in policy development. A milestone in developing an alternative project emerged in the second year of SPARC, when it produced a report called 'We the invisible' in association with MM. That came about when pavement dwelling women requested the support of SPARC staff to seek dialogue and negotiation with the municipal authority of Mumbai. They had approached SPARC rather than take a confrontational approach when facing demolitions (Patel, 2014). Together, SPARC activists and slum dwellers have been able to forge active dialogue with city, provincial and national governments.

SPARC activists emphasize that there is a need to rethink what a 'participatory' process entails. These activists do value the role of external professionals and technical stakeholders, but are concerned about the way external stakeholders often use communities for purposes that are not those of the communities. Whether what results can be called a participatory inquiry or CAR is not clear. The word participatory is so misused and critical practices are so often undercut that even the most radical version is easily rendered deficient. Nonetheless, the needed processes involve capacity building, and solutions require development through contestation that engages formal, external and professionally conducted research practices.

The communities and their organizations offer possible means for the urban poor to become partners in development. The work of the alliances indicates how breakthroughs come about and how these practices are taken up in city-level development activities.

The work of SPARC was not confined to just acting on the ground – much of its reflections and experiences have been featured in a well-known, peer-reviewed journal called *Environment and Urbanization*. Since the late 1990s, nine articles have been published by that journal, through special invitation to the SPARC leader, Sheela Patel. This means that SPARC has remained active both on the ground and in the world of critical social science discourse. The number of citations[8] indicates that the work has been read and referred to widely, and this attests to the need to engage with science and discourse critically by sharing the empowering knowledge and stories from the field.

SPARC actors believe that in order to be effective in the context of Indian cities, it is important to form alliances beyond the country. Thus, their interventions are also linked to the international processes involving the network of like-minded researchers and community leaders from multiple countries. The Indian Alliance became a founding member of Slum/Shack Dwellers International, a transnational network of the urban poor that currently operates in over 30 countries. The work of SPARC thus demonstrates the need to empower disadvantaged groups, and assist them in mobilizing evidence, forging effective interactions among professionals and community networks, and engaging with multiple arenas of discourse and governance. Yet the continuing challenge of achieving a desired level of inclusion in the Indian cities in which SPARC has worked means that achieving inclusive public policy remains a daunting task. The project of exploring the possibilities and spaces for transformation needs to be a continual focus of inquiry in policy development fields.

In the Australian landcare case, in contrast with the cases of Nepal and India, there has been an erosion of the positive relationships and trust that local groups had established with state government agencies in previous partnerships. The frustrations these groups have experienced have been further exacerbated by the complex arrangements for accessing funding resources needed to implement 'on the ground' programs. And while landcare and other community groups are keen to participate in the entire range of decision-making processes, they are restricted to narrow involvement in the implementation of the programs on the ground. This situation is the result of key decisions on policies and plans being the exclusive domain of state-level ministers and senior bureaucrats. In this context of power relations, government agencies tend to use community participation primarily as a cheap and effective implementation instrument. The space for CAR to emerge and influence policy depends very much on how processes within the government policy and research community and their institutions remain conducive to the practice of critical action research on the ground. Alliance of the CAR team with social movement helps strengthen the confidence of the citizenry and increases the legitimacy (the credibility and relevance) of research in changing policies and practices.

6. CONCLUSION

Democratic empowerment through the interplay of CAR and social movements promises to revitalize the policy potential of participation and deliberation that conventional approaches have been unable to sustain. The three cases of Nepal, India and Australia indicate how the potential of that interplay has worked – or could work – in different contexts, while also identifying challenges that CAR practice faces. In order to understand the promise of CAR, we have demonstrated that four aspects are crucial: (1) how critical researchers and social actors interact for community empowerment, (2) the use of action as a basis of learning with a moral dimension, (3) the role of interactive learning based upon a dialectical epistemology, and (4) the importance of multi-scalar engagement. What is clear in all three cases is that there is enormous scope for advancing the CAR approach further by strengthening the ways in which researchers interact across scales with communities and policy actors while balancing epistemic and action objectives in the specific contexts.

The Nepal case of community forestry, in which critical researchers and community activists have worked together to advance participatory forest policy and practice, demonstrates the strong role of context in the production and mobilization of critical inquiry practices. In the unfolding democratic environment, researchers and communities could increasingly claim greater space and achieve greater agency to influence the policies and practices. The Indian case of NGO work on slum dwellers' groups further reinforces the point that producing alternative facts and forging alliances between critical researchers and the poor are crucial elements in critical inquiry practices. In contrast, the Australian landcare movement demonstrates that, when critical inquiry wanes, the participatory and community-based orientation of policy politics is also subjected to regressive bureaucratic pressure, thus compromising the democratic potential of policy making. A key message from this analysis is that attempts to deepen democratic policy processes require going beyond the focus on localized, participatory research to include cross-scale processes involving both local transformative action and critical engagement at the level of policy discourse. It is thus possible to advance the critical project for enhancing reflective learning activity among a wide range of actors participating in the regimes of governance and pathways of innovations. In practice, however, there are challenges in achieving the critical ideal.

A critical inquiry project should be seen as a situated practice in two senses: first, in relation to specific forms of power influencing policy in a given context, and second, to the social identity and positionality of the critical action researchers themselves. How CAR actors, local communities and policy actors interact depends on the construction of deliberative space defined within the context of power relationships and other contextual factors. The extent to which CAR researchers are able to address the limits imposed on them by context and history depends, in part, on how they are related with other policy actors in the policy field, and on what sort of knowledge is mobilized in the process. The ability of CAR actors to reflect and transcend limits of the institutional boundaries is also contingent upon the extent to which such research practices are funded or supported. While international funding in the cases of Nepal and India has, to some extent, enabled a more open engagement of critical researchers, the space has remained limited due to the reliance of critical researchers on the funding provided by their own government in Australia.

The CAR approach also signals a fundamental conceptual shift from participatory and demand driven research and development approaches. In standard participatory approaches, the association between scientists and local elites may tend to reinforce the existing social inequality among the different groups of local people (Vernooy and McDougall, 2003), and thus reduce the possibility for deliberative governance. CAR projects can rarely start simply by waiting for 'clients' or 'beneficiaries' to ask for a 'research service' (Ojha, 2013). In all three cases, there is significant space for researchers to work proactively.

The impact of CAR can be enhanced only if researchers actively find a space to do their work, even in highly restrictive political environments. This is why the notion of 'critical' is particularly important here, although it has been left out in many strands of action research and policy inquiry. However, being critical in action research and policy inquiry also involves a disposition to engage, not to simply dismiss or reject, the hegemonic power (Ojha, 2013). That said, the critical and action-oriented approaches face imposing challenges, including the asymmetry of power relations grounded in deep social structures that are often reinforced by unfolding political and economic drivers. What this means is that CAR is needed more, not less, to empower communities with critical knowledge and to guide policy actors in concrete, specific and contextually relevant ways.

NOTES

1. Critics have branded participation as a 'tyranny', which dominates development discourses and yet delivers little on the ground (Kothari and Cooke, 2001). 'Community participation' paradoxically contributes to the exclusion of women and disadvantaged groups in some settings (Agarwal, 2009). Problems also abound, as promoters tend to focus narrowly at the local level, ignoring politics outside of communities themselves (Mohan and Stokke, 2000). Alongside these failures, others see the project of participation as an extension of neo-colonial development ideology and a discursive weapon of Western development agencies (Escobar, 1995; Li, 1996; Blaikie, 2006). Even the World Bank, which has promoted participation as a key strategy for social capital-building (Woolcock and Narayan, 2000; Mansuri and Rao, 2004) has demonstrated that community participation has remained 'supply driven', usually reinforcing the status quo. Thus, despite years of research, policy experiments and practice, there remains a need to revisit the most basic questions such as: who is participating, how and in what ways, and for whose benefit (Cornwall, 2008) as well as interrogating the paradoxes underlying the idea of participation (Dill, 2009).
2. The work of an NGO called Society for the Promotion of Area Resource Centers (SPARC) based in the Indian city of Mumbai illustrates the trajectories, innovations and challenges associated with critical inquiry and participatory policy development in India. We came across the work of SPARC through a conference involving a Global Studio of urban professionals, teachers and activities which was organized by the University of Sydney in association with the India-based Maulan Azad National Institute of Technology (MANIT). As co-organizer of the conference called 'Inclusive Urbanization', we closely followed and reviewed the work of SPARC leader Sheela Patel who was invited to present the SPARC experiences in inclusive urbanization. At the same conference, one of us (Ojha) also presented the CAR work in Nepal's community forestry movement, and hence the conference became an important basis to forge dialogue between the two cases, later adding the Australian Landcare case which also had the substantial experience of one of the co-authors (Shrestha). SPARC was set up in 1984, with the mission of the founders being to create an institutional platform 'for professionals who wanted to work in partnership with communities of the urban poor to seek citizenship and equity' (Patel, 2014). By 2012, the organization had extended its activities in 70 cities and nine states in India.
3. See http://infochangeindia.org/poverty/news/54-of-mumbai-lives-in-slums-world-bank. html, accessed 12 July 2014.
4. Two items of legislation that affected the landcare movement were the Catchment Management Authority (CMA) Act 2003 – which established CMAs and outline aims, functions and purposes in terms of devolving power and involving communities in each CMA region, including the provision of financial assistance and incentives to landholders – and the Natural Resource Commission (NRC) Act 2003, which provides a framework and targets for all CMA activities based on scientific advice from experts; such expert commissioners are appointed by the minister on the basis of their technical expertise.
5. Interview with a professor based at Charles Sturt University, and working on the landcare movement.
6. One of the examples of such a discrepancy in the data set of critical researchers and the government was found in the number of landcare groups in state of New South Wales. While the government data had a record of 500 groups, the survey found out that there were 4200 groups. Likewise, government data on funding to landcare group was also several times higher than the data gathered by the researchers.
7. Personal communication with Kamal Bhandari, June 2014, Kathmandu, Nepal.
8. For example, one of the articles Patel et al. (2002) published in *Environment and Urbanization* was cited 116 times in Google Scholar on 5 March 2015.

REFERENCES

Agarwal, B. 2009. Rule making in community forestry institutions: The difference women make. *Ecological Economics*, **68**, 2296–2308.

Argyris, C. and Schön, D. 1996. *Organizational Learning II: Theory, Method and Practice*, Reading, MA: Addison Wesley.

Armitage, D. 2008. Governance and the commons in a multi-level world. *International Journal of the Commons*, **2**, 7–32.

Arputham, J. and Patel, S. 2010. Recent developments in plans for Dharavi and for the airport slums in Mumbai. *Environment and Urbanization*, **22**, 501–504.

Banjade, M.R. 2013. Learning to improve livelihoods: Applying an adaptive collaborative approach to forest governance in Nepal. In Ojha, H., Hall, A. and Sulaiman, V.R. (eds) *Adaptive Collaborative Approaches in Natural Resource Governance: Rethinking Participation, Learning and Innovation*, London and New York: Routledge.

Blaikie, P. 2006. Is small really beautiful? Community-based natural resource management in Malawi and Botswana. *World Development*, **34**, 1942–1957.

Bourdieu, P. 1989. Social space and symbolic power. *Sociological Theory*, **7**, 14–25.

Bourdieu, P. 2009. The scholastic point of view. *Cultural Anthropology*, **5** (4), 380–391.

Chhatre, A. 2008. Political articulation and accountability in decentralisation: Theory and evidence from India. *Conservation and Society*, **6** (1), 12–23.

Cornwall, A. 2008. Unpacking 'participation': Models, meanings and practices. *Community Development Journal*, **43**, 269–283.

Dewey, J. and Bentley, A.F. 1949. *Knowing and the Known*, Westport, CT: Greenwood Press.

Dill, B. 2009. The paradoxes of community-based participation in Dar es Salaam. *Development and Change*, **40**, 717–743.

Dryzek, J.S. 1987. *Rational Ecology: Environment and Political Economy*, New York: Basil Blackwell.

Dryzek, J.S. 2000. *Deliberative Democracy and Beyond: Liberals, Critics, Contestations*, Oxford: Oxford University Press.

Dryzek, J.S. 2006. Transnational democracy in an insecure world. *International Political Science Review/Revue internationale de science politique*, **27**, 101–119.

Dryzek, J.S. 2006. Policy analysis as critique. In Moran, M., Rein, M. and Goodin, R. (eds) *The Oxford Handbook of Public Policy*, Oxford: Oxford University Press, pp. 190–203.

Escobar, A. 1995. *Encountering Development: The Making and Unmaking of the Third World*, Princeton, NJ: Princeton University Press.

Fals-Borda, O. 1987. The application of participatory action-research in Latin America. *International Sociology*, **2**, 329–347.

Fals-Borda, O. and Rahman, M.A. 1991. *Action and Knowledge: Breaking the Monopoly with Participatory Action Research*, London: Intermediate Technology Publications, The Apex Press.

Fischer, F. 1998. Beyond empiricism: Policy inquiry in post posivist perspective. *Policy Studies*, **26**, 129–146.

Fischer, F. 2006. Participatory governance as deliberative empowerment. *The American Review of Public Administration*, **36**, 19.

Freire, P. 1970 [2000]. *Pedagogy of the Oppressed*, New York: Continuum.

Gaventa, J. 2004. Towards participatory governance: Assessing the transformative possibilities. In Hickey, S. and Mohan, G. (eds) *Participation – From Tyranny to Transformation? Exploring New approaches to Participation in Development*. London and New York: Zed Books.

Görsdorf, A. 2006. Inside deliberative experiments: Dynamics of subjectivity in science policy deliberations. *Policy and Society*, **25**, 177–206.

Habermas, J. 1984. *The Theory of Communicative Action, Volume I*, Boston, MA: Beacon.

Hajer, M. 2003. Policy without polity? Policy analysis and the institutional void. *Policy Sciences*, **36**, 175–195.

Hale, C.R. (ed.) 2008. *Engaging Contradictions: Theory, Politics, and Methods of Activist Scholarship*, Berkeley, CA: University of California Press.

Hall, P.A. 1993. Policy paradigms, social learning, and the state: The case of economic policy making in Britain. *Comparative Politics*, **25**, 275–296.

Holling, C.S. 2001. Understanding the complexity of economic, ecological, and social systems. *Ecosystems*, **4**, 390–405.

Kothari, U. and Cooke, B. 2001. Power, knowledge and social control in participatory development. In Kothari, U. and Cooke, B. (eds) *Participation: The New Tyranny?*, London: Zed Books, pp. 139–152.

Leach, M., Mearns, R. and Scoones, I. 1999. Environmental entitlements: Dynamics and institutions in community-based natural resource management. *World Development*, **27**, 225–247.

Li, T.M. 1996. Images of community: Discourse and strategy in property relations. *Development and Change*, **27**, 501–527.

Mansbridge, J. 1999. Everyday talk in the deliberative system. In Macedo, S. (ed.) *Deliberative Politics: Essays on Democracy and Disagreement*, New York and Oxford: Oxford University Press, pp. 211–239.

Mansbridge, J., Bohman, J., Chambers, S., Christiano, T., Fung, A., Parkinson, J., Thompson, D.F. and Warren, M.E. 2012. A systemic approach to deliberative democracy. *Deliberative Systems*, Cambridge: Cambridge University Press, pp. 1–26.

Mansuri, G. and Rao, V. 2004. Community-based and-driven development: A critical review. *The World Bank Research Observer*, **19**, 1.

Mansuri, G. and Rao, V. 2013. *Localizing Development: Does Participation Work?*, Washington, DC: World Bank.

Mohan, G. and Hickey, S. 2004. Relocating participation within a radical politics of development: Critical moderninsm and citizenship. In Hickey, S. and Mohan, G. (eds) *Participation – From Tyranny to Transformation? Exploring New Approaches to Participation in Development*, London and New York: Zed Books.

Mohan, G. and Stokke, K. 2000. Participatory development and empowerment: The dangers of localism. *Third World Quarterly*, **21**, 247–268.

Mosse, D. 2005. *Cultivating Development: An Ethnography of Aid Policy and Practice*, New Delhi: Vistaar Publications.

Mwangi, E. and Wardell, A. 2012. Multi-level governance of forest resources. *International Journal of the Commons*, **6**, 79–103.

Ojha, H.R. 2006. Techno-bureuacratic doxa and the challenges of deliebrative governance: The case of community forestry policy and practice in Nepal. *Policy and Society*, **25**, 131–175.

Ojha, H. 2009. Civic engagement and deliberative governance: The case of Community Forest Users' Federation, Nepal. *Studies in Nepalese History and Society (SINHAS)*, **14**, 303–334.

Ojha, H. 2013. Counteracting hegemonic powers in the policy process: Critical action research on Nepal's forest governance. *Critical Policy Studies*, **7**, 242–262.

Ojha, H. 2014. Beyond the 'local community': The evolution of multi-scalepolitics in Nepal's community forestry regimes. *International Forestry Review*, **16**, 339–353.

Ojha, H.R., Paudel, N., Khatri, D. and Bk, D. 2012. Can policy learning be catalyzed? Ban Chautari experiment in Nepal's forest sector. *Journal of Forest and Livelihood*, **10**, 1–27.

Ojha, H.R., Banjade, M.R., Sunam, R.K., Bhattarai, B., Jana, S., Goutam, K.R. and Dhungana, S. 2014. Can authority change through deliberative politics? Lessons from the four decades of participatory forest policy reform in Nepal. *Forest Policy and Economics*, **46**, 1–9.

Papadopoulos, Y. and Warin, P. 2007. Are innovative, participatory and deliberative procedures in policy making democratic and effective? *European Journal of Political Research*, **46**, 445–472.

Patel, S. 2014. Community driven solutions for inclusive urbanization: The experience of grassroots organizational alliances in India. In Shrestha, K., Ojha, H., McManus, P.,

Rubbo, A. and Dhote, K.K. (eds) *Inclusive Urbanization: Rethinking Policy and Practice in the Age of Climate Change*, London and New York: Taylor & Francis Group.

Patel, S., d'Cruz, C and Burra, S. 2002. Beyond evictions in a global city: People-managed resettlement in Mumbai. *Environment and Urbanization*, **14** (1), 159–172.

Patel, S., Baptist, C. and d'Cruz, C. 2012. Knowledge is power – informal communities assert their right to the city through SDI and community-led enumerations. *Environment and Urbanization*, **24**, 13–26.

Robertson, R. 1995. Glocalization: Time-space and homogeneity-heterogeneity. *Global Modernities*, 25–44.

Rose, N. and Miller, P. 2010. Political power beyond the state: Problematics of government. *The British Journal of Sociology*, **61**, 271–303.

Rosenau, P.M. 1991. *Post-modernism and the Social Sciences: Insights, Inroads, and Intrusions*, Princeton, NJ: Princeton University Press.

Roy, A. 2009. Why India cannot plan its cities: Informality, insurgence and the idiom of urbanization. *Planning Theory*, **8**, 76–87.

Sassen, S. 1996. *Losing Control? Sovereignty in an Age of Globalization*, New York: Columbia University Press.

Shrestha, K.K. and Mahjabeen, Z. 2011. Civic science, community participation and planning for knowledge based development: Analysis of Sydney Metropolitan Strategy. *International Journal of Knowledge-Based Development*, **2**, 412–432.

SSNS 2012. Annual Report. Mumbai: SSNS and SPARC.

Sunam, R.K., Paudel, N.S. and Paudel, G. 2013. Community forestry and the threat of recentralization in Nepal: Contesting the bureaucratic hegemony in policy process. *Society & Natural Resources*, **26**, 1407–1421.

Vernooy, R. and McDougall, C. 2003. Principles for good practice: Reflecting on Lessons from the Field. In Pound, B., Snapp, S., McDougall, C. and Braun, A. (eds) *Managing Natural Resources for Sustainable Livelihoods: Uniting Science and Participation*, London: EarthScan and IDRC.

Woolcock, M. and Narayan, D. 2000. Social capital: Implications for development theory, research and policy. *The World Bank Research Observer*, **15**, 225–249.

Yanow, D. 2007. Interpretation in policy analysis: On methods and practice. *Critical Policy Analysis*, **1**, 110–122.

PART VI

METHODOLOGICAL ISSUES: INTERPRETATION, FRAMING AND SOCIAL CONSTRUCTIONS

21 Making sense of policy practices: interpretation and meaning
Dvora Yanow

The modes of analysis established at the beginning of the policy studies 'movement' in North America – chief among them cost–benefit analysis and other forms that sought to evaluate policies in light of their planning objectives and budgetary allocations – might be said to have worked well enough for assessing policies whose goals could be unproblematically translated into measurable, quantitative terms. These evaluative tools rested on the assumption that social values, whether or not they were translatable into assessable measurements, could be separated out from the realm of facts, which were – so it was alleged – capable of being easily established. But when public policies entailed competing values that were not reconcilable in the passage of legislation; when debates and contention entailed complex political relationships; and, even more significantly, when the conceptual ground shifted concerning the possible separation of values from facts and the ghettoization of the former outside of the realm of policy analysis,[1] some researchers, both academic and practice-based, began to see that these tools did not always work well for assessing the central features of policy enactments and related practices. If these approaches and tools, based on notions of rational, economic 'man,' were experienced as inadequate, to what might one turn for a more adequate understanding of the successes or failures of public policies to achieve their intended and stated purposes? Moreover, might policy purposes include other than such explicitly stated intentions?

Here is where interpretive policy analysis began. It took its name from the interpretive turn in social sciences more broadly,[2] which had begun to develop at around the same time and which drew on ideas from a range of different sources. These included phenomenological and hermeneutic philosophies, along with critical theory's engagement with power; attention to symbols and their meanings within symbolic-cultural anthropology, semiotics, and literary studies; and pragmatism, symbolic interaction, and ethnomethodology's everyday action–meaning links. Interpretive policy analysis shifted the analytic focus in policy studies to meaning-making – its expression as well as its communication – as an alternative to instrumental rationality in explaining human action.[3] It also incorporated elements from various other 'turns' that became central to social scientific thinking in the latter part of the 20th century: the linguistic turn,[4] the historical turn,[5] the metaphoric turn,[6] the practice turn,[7] the pragmatist turn,[8] and so forth. While 'taking language seriously'[9] as one of the ways in which policy and implementing organizations' meanings are communicated, interpretive policy analysis also treats acts (Taylor's 'text analogues'[10]), such as nonverbal communication during meetings, policy evaluation,[11] and agency routines,[12] and objects (physical artifacts), such as programs and built spaces,[13] seeing these, too, as communicative 'media.'

Interpretive policy analysis draws, then, as much on participant-observer ethnographic methods[14] as it does on textual and other language-focused ones, and it may also include visual methods, including the analysis of built spaces.[15] 'Interpretation,' in this account, takes certain ideas from hermeneutics – mainly its focus on meaning, on epistemic (or interpretive) communities, on the recursiveness of the hermeneutic circle, and on the possibility for multiple meanings/interpretations of policy-related elements – without getting caught in its historically-situated insistence on a specific, and thereby limiting, set of rules for interpreting. Joined with phenomenology's insistence on the role of lived experience in shaping meaning-making/interpretation, these ideas have proved generative to the understanding of public policies, their processes and practices, from affirmative action to whaling.[16]

This chapter expounds on this background, highlighting the ontological and epistemological presuppositions that lie at the heart of interpretive policy analysis and their methodological implications, illustrated by an example from the author's research.

THE 'INTERPRETIVE TURN' IN POLICY STUDIES

The challenge to the top-down, instrumental-rational model of policy-making and implementation began to develop out of field-based studies of the work practices of implementers in various settings, including street-level bureaucrats.[17] These insights led Lipsky to argue – in a major critique of Weberian bureaucracy theory as applied to public policy processes – that the conceptualization of implementation needed to be inverted:[18] as experienced and observed, rather than as theorized absent empirical input, policies that were supposed to be being implemented in a-political administrative fashion were actually subject to local interpretation at the hands of street-level bureaucrats (given particular structural constraints), and through these acts the latter were understood by their clients as themselves *making* governmental policy. The whole conceptual apparatus, in other words, needed to be re-thought, including with respect to what bureau-cracy and other organizational theorists had argued were and should be a-political administrative practices.

Interpretive policy analysis grew out of these critiques that were grounded in theorizing about policy processes, supported by still another source, the so-called interpretive turn across the social sciences: concep-tual and philosophical works developing along parallel lines at the same time, some in other branches of political science,[19] some in anthropology and sociology,[20] others in philosophy, psychology, economics, and literary studies.[21] Several of these arguments were sounded by sequential editors of *Policy Sciences* or in articles on its and other journals' pages.[22] One of the points of critique centered on the potential for multiple possible interpretations of lived social realities, which emerges from a hermeneutic phenomenology. Subsequently, engaging Habermasian theorizing and theoretical developments in other fields, a significant section of interpre-tive policy analysis took a discursive, dialogical turn,[23] which, among other things, counters the denial of agency to those seen as 'targets' on the 'receiving end' of policies.[24] That move has, for several theorists, re-linked policy analysis to forms of governance that are more democratic and participatory,[25] especially in their discursive focuses.[26] In these approaches, policies may be viewed, for analytic purposes, as 'texts,' with implementers, clients, potential clients, and other policy-relevant publics, near and far, as 'readers' of these texts. Still, policy analysis – and especially implementation analysis – is grounded in action, and there is a strong desire on the part of many analysts to move beyond identification and description of communities of interpretation around specific policy issues and the understanding of what goes wrong (or right), to an explo-ration of communities of practitioners and the specific practices that are entailed in the communication of policy meanings.[27] Beyond seeing policy actions as 'text analogues,'[28] some theorists also look to establish grounds for intervention in order to improve the problems targeted by policies, which puts their work close to that of (participatory) action researchers.[29]

In their various approaches, interpretive policy analyses focus on meaning – both its expression and its communication. They seek to take into account the local knowledge of those for whom policies have been or are being designed in addition to that of policy-makers and implement-ers. This may include essaying to make what is known tacitly, in Michael Polanyi's sense, more explicit.[30] Interpretive policy analysis asks not only *what* a policy means – a context-specific question about a specific policy – but also *how* policies mean – questions about the processes by which meanings are communicated.[31] Interpretive policy analysts study various policy-relevant manifestations of the three broad categories of human artifacts that, through symbolic representation, give expression to their creators' meanings: language, clearly, but also acts and the objects drawn on and/or referenced in both language and acts. Borrowing a term from recent developments in cognitive linguistics, we might say that this focus on 'how' leads to a *multimodal* form of analysis, looking at various sources and genres of evidence and corresponding analytic modes.[32] In addition, interpretive forms of policy analysis have shifted attention from the search for (and belief in the promise of finding) one correct policy formulation (correct in its definition of the policy problem, a narrative which entails the seeds for problem resolution) to engage, instead, the possible multiplicities of problem definition resulting from different interpretive communities' experiences and perceptions. This includes exploring the possibility that conflicts among policy-relevant groups may reflect epistemological differences and not simply contests over facts: what is perceived and accepted as a relevant 'fact' is often part of the contestation, as Rein and Schön argued in respect of policy framing.[33] Language, objects, and acts that are symbolic – that is, which represent underlying meanings (values, beliefs, and/or feelings/sentiments) – enable multiplicities of (possible) meaning-making and a demarcation among communities of interpretation and of practice.

Recognizing the agency of those previously treated as 'targets' of public policies and, perhaps even more importantly, considering their local knowledge as itself an important source of expertise repositions the expertise of policy analysts from purely subject-matter knowledge to knowledge of inquiry processes. In this fashion, the practice of interpretive policy analysis intertwines its conceptual-theoretical approach with a set of methodological concerns that themselves engage and legitimize local knowledge. Associated methods generate data through the close reading of policy-relevant texts and other kinds of documents, formal and conversational interviewing, and participant-observer ethnography. To analyze those data, interpretive policy analysts draw on a range of meaning-focused methods, as appropriate to the character of the data.[34]

Data in the form of language predominate in interpretive policy analysis, in part due to the centrality of documents in legislative processes and organizational acts, and researchers' reliance on documentary and interview sources. Interpretive approaches recognize the requisite ambiguity of language – indeed, ambiguity in policy matters is often purposeful – and its centrality to multiple possible meanings. One stream of research investigates the work of metaphors in policy language, much of it building on theories from cognitive linguistics.[35] Other work looks at categories and at story-telling or other forms of narrative.[36] Framing is central to interpretive policy analysis, building on the work of Martin Rein and Donald

Schön, whose theorizing pointed to the extent to which 'intractable policy controversies' are often so not because of failures in policy design, but instead because of the particular way that the policy issue itself has been framed.[37] More recently, interpretive policy analysts have taken up discourse theories of various sorts.[38]

Language is not the only form of data generated or analyzed in interpretive policy analysis. To analyze policy-related acts, such as the act of choosing or declining to regulate EMF (electro-magnetic frequency) emissions, ethnographic analysis of the various groups involved might be drawn on, adding observational data to interview and/or documentary data. A meaning-focused approach to policy acts, for instance, leads to unsettling another assumption built in to positivist modes of policy analysis: it highlights the social reality that policy processes may also be an avenue for human expressiveness (of identity, of meaning), leading to the legislating of policies that are, in one way or another, unimplementable. To take one older, but clear, example, several city councils in the US – Santa Cruz, Hayward, Oakland, and Berkeley in California; Cambridge, Massachusetts; and others – passed legislation declaring themselves to be 'nuclear free zones.' Nuclear material, however, is trans-shipped over federal highways; and federal law, which regulates traffic on those roadways, takes precedence over local law. Whereas from the perspective of rational-instrumental policy-making, the bills are irrational (because they cannot be implemented), from an interpretive point of view, they can be understood as embodying stories each polity tells itself and other publics, near and far, about its identity – its values and beliefs, what is meaningful 'in private' and in public.[39]

Thirdly, language and acts also often refer to or use material objects. Examples might include particular programs – e.g., for housing policies enabling either purchase or rental, which pivot on the meaning of 'home,' whether in the context of ownership or occupancy – or the specific design of policy-relevant spaces, such as welfare department offices.[40] For such data, analysis might focus on the ways in which programmatic activities or built spaces communicate policy and wider societal meaning(s), and which meanings are being communicated and to what audiences, near and far. In addition, a wide range of visual materials – from paintings to photographs to videos – is increasingly becoming part of policy analysis, whether these are 'found objects' or generated by the researcher for use with participants in field research.[41]

All of these and other analytic devices would be used to try to elicit understandings of what specific policies might mean to various issue-relevant publics, as well as exploring how those meanings are developed, communicated, and (potentially) variously understood.[42] Through them analysts seek to 'map the architecture'[43] of policy arguments. The three categories of symbolic artifacts are useful for heuristic purposes, even though they are not always, in practice, distinct: language, acts, and objects are intertwined and mutually implicating, and whether one designates a bit of policy evidence as belonging in one rather than another category may at times make sense only from the perspective of the analysis one is trying to advance.

In these analytic treatments, the notion of policy, whether legislative document or state intention, as a single, authored text is implicitly or explicitly replaced by the 'constructed' texts of multiple 'readings' at the hands of various policy-relevant publics. The notion of a singular legislative 'author' is expanded by recognizing the possible existence of multiple discourse communities, whose members constitute collective 'readers,' literally and figuratively, of these texts (including 'text analogues'). Analyses emphasize the context-specificity of meaning. They are specific to events and times – the 'what' of a policy – and hew closely to the meanings made by policy-relevant actors – although an analysis may be, and often is, more broadly contextualized, whether by reference to multiple evidentiary sources or to the context of some theoretical literature to which the research question and analysis speak. Generalization relates to the 'how,' and it is a methodological or philosophical generalization: how legislators, implementers, clients, and other publics make policy meanings in thus and such ways; how some of these interpretations may conflict with each other; how analysts may make sense of those meanings and conflicts.

One final methodological point. Although phenomenology, in particular, has been criticized, especially by critical theorists, for being so involved with the individual 'Self' as to neglect power, this criticism, although perhaps holding at the philosophical level, seems not to obtain when phenomenological inquiry is directed toward policy matters. In such applications, interpretive policy analysts cannot help but include power dimensions, including of organizations and other institutions, especially when they consider voices that have been silent, by choice, or silenced, by forces beyond them.

A CASE EXAMPLE

One of the current public policy issues of great interest worldwide – and in some places, highly contested – is immigration, and specifically, in attractor states, policies to promote the integration of 'new' immigrants (some of whom may have been in residence for 20 or more years). As with other arenas of statecraft (e.g., education, employment, housing, welfare), in order to assess the achievement of policy goals, the state needs to be able to enumerate its population by the factors that are of interest; to do so, it needs to create categories, thereby naming the groups within its population who are understood to possess those features to be counted. Category structures (or taxonomies) give voice to and are supported by a social consensus that has been built up over time, including in and through state practices. Their intersubjectively constructed character, together with the policy issue's long-term intractability, makes them a realm for which interpretive policy analysis is, or can be, useful. We can ask of these categories: What meanings – values, beliefs, feelings – do they embody and convey? This section begins with a sketch of the theoretical and methodological bases for category analysis, before turning to a specific application drawn from my current research.[44]

Category analysis examines sets of terms and their structural relationships within a taxonomy. In assigning elements to one category or another, category-making structures highlight those dimensions that are deemed to be similar within the boundaries drawn and different from elements beyond those boundaries. Those samenesses of things within categories and differences between things in different categories constitute the organizing principles or logic around which categories are built: an element belongs in Category A because it shares 'A-ness' and is not 'not-A.' Classifying entails *an interpretive choice* on the basis of a decision about the relative importance of certain features over others, implicitly asserting that things belong together which, from another perspective, could be seen to be divergent. Moreover, the conceptual logic of category-making implies *sharp* differences between members of different categories which, from another viewpoint, may be only minor gradations of difference. And the features imputed to be important might, from some other perspective, be deemed insignificant, at the same time as the features occluded by that particular perspective are positioned as less important than they might be in another taxonomizing schema. Establishing the point of view from which the categories have been named, then, is an important part of analysis.

In general, categories appear to take one of two forms: slotting (think 'mailboxes'), in which boundaries are distinct; and prototyping (consider the central region in a 'normal distribution' Bell curve in statistical analysis), where lines of demarcation are less pronounced. From a slotting perspective, a set of categories implies two principles:

1.   nothing has been left out: the categories are exhaustive; everything in the taxonomic world has a place in one of the categories; and
2.   there is no overlap in category membership: the categories are discrete; no element fits into more than one category.

Slotting-type categories become problematic when either (or both) of these states is violated: when one or more elements do not fit the existing categories, or when one element fits into more than one category. These 'remainders' take on the aura of 'category errors' or 'mistakes.' The prototype approach is more forgiving: to the extent that they bear family resemblances with the prototype, outliers are still seen as belonging to the category. In policy discourse and practices, categories appear to start out as slotting-type entities; but over time, if lived experience increasingly no longer fits the boxes, they move towards a prototype character. The more the slots and prototypes break down and category mistakes become topics of public discourse, the greater the likely demand for policy change.

This is one way of understanding the drive for policy reform with respect to the taxonomy developed by the US Office of Management and Budget (OMB) in its 1977 Directive No. 15. Created for enumerating race-ethnic population groups for Affirmative Action/OEO purposes, it established the five categories that Americans come in, naming and defining them. Implemented in the 1980 decennial census (and in other policy practices), the utility of the categories began to unravel by the next census, in which the number of people marking 'some other race' grew by a rate of nearly 57 percent. In the terms of category-making and analysis, we can say that the number who no longer saw themselves as fitting clearly into one of the five categories – that is, the number of 'category errors' – grew geometrically, signaling the potential need for policy change. Ensuing Congressional hearings in the mid-1990s led the OMB to revise the taxonomy, dividing 'Asian and Pacific Islander' into two separate categories and making additional changes to category definitions, yielding a six-part taxonomy in Directive 15's 1997 revision.

One more conceptual-theoretical aspect of category-making is useful for analysis: the distinction (from linguistics) between marked and unmarked terms. The latter is, by linguistic and category logic, the 'normal' (or 'default') case: e.g., 'My *professor* is teaching this course.' The former conveys that what is being marked is somehow different, not usual, not expected, a deviation: e.g., 'The course is being taught by a *woman professor*' or 'by a *Nigerian professor*.' 'Professor' is the unmarked norm; 'woman' and 'Nigerian' mark 'professor' as having features other than the norm. In many cultures, marking renders the designated entity an inferior case of the unmarked norm.

Members of an interpretive (or epistemic or discourse) community have the ability to *and typically do* group objects into similarity sets without having to ask, or needing to make explicit an answer to, the question, '*Similar or different with respect to what?*' That, however, is precisely where analysis begins, seeking to explicate what those category terms and concepts mean in use, that is, as these meanings are reflected in and shaped by policy and administrative practices. Making these common-sense, taken-for-granted, everyday, tacitly known meanings more explicit requires thinking: How might things otherwise be? Or: As opposed to what? – examining these meanings not only as espoused, but even more so, as put into practice, reflecting the collective, social dimensions of category and concept construction, learning, and knowing.

Proceeding systematically in a policy context, category analysis aims to map the 'architecture of meaning' in the category structure by:

1. identifying the categories or category set (taxonomy) in use, looking at, e.g., poicy language in documents and debates, administrative language of implementing oranizations, and/or the language of general (political) discourse;
2. analyzing the elements of similarity (the features being highlighted) and difference (those to which we are being 'blinded'); i.e., engaging, and answering, the question, *'The same and different with respect to what?'*;
3. identifying the usually implicit point of view from which those similarities and differences are drawn; and
4. 'reading' them (e.g., as 'text analogues,' in Taylor's sense[45]) for their meanings.

Case Example: Categories in the Netherlands' Migrant Discourses

The policy and public discourse taxonomy concerning natives and immi-grants in the Netherlands is binary: one is either an *autochtoon* (autochthon in English; 'native') or an *allochtoon* (English: allochthon; foreign-born or of foreign heritage; I will continue to use the Dutch spelling for the sin-gular noun form). My analysis suggests that this taxonomy serves as a proxy for designating 'race,' a term whose use is prohibited by Article 1 of the Constitution (with exceptions made for certain medical and admini-strative actions). Language use focuses instead on 'ethnicity,' for which birthplace – the migrant's own, a parent's or a grandparent's – serves as surrogate. Examining the category-making aspects of these two terms as they are used by Statistics Netherlands (the English-language name for the *Centraal Bureau voor de Statistiek*) shows how the autochtoon–allochtoon taxonomy joins 'ethnicity'–birthplace with the unspoken 'race.'

In 1999 Statistics Netherlands standardized the definitions of autoch-toon and allochtoon. Dividing the latter between Western and non-Western and further dividing the non-Western category by generation – first and second then, more recently, adding third – introduced a more detailed

Table 21.1   Western versus non-Western allochtoons

Western	Non-Western
Europe (but not Turkey)	Turkey
	Africa [Morocco]
North America	Latin America
Oceania	
Japan	Asia
Indonesia (including former Dutch Indonesia)	[Suriname, Dutch Antilles/Aruba]

Note: Author's layout, arrayed to highlight the terminological oppositions, based on a 2000 linear (narrative) Statistics Netherlands document on the standardized definitions; bracketed words are from other sentences in that text which elaborate on the definitions.

Source: Yanow and van der Haar.[46]

taxonomic structure. Table 21.1 presents the distinctions between Western and non-Western allochtoon. Note the oppositions – e.g., of Europe and Turkey; of the respective locations of 'Western' and 'non-Western' entities (e.g., Japan is 'Western'; the non-Western states are predominantly in the southern hemisphere); and that 'Eastern' is not used as the opposite of 'Western.' These oppositions suggest the vantage point from which the categories are defined, and it implies the possible existence of another discourse embedded in this one. Specifically, the illogic of the 'category errors' – e.g., placing southern hemisphere states in the (differently-designated) 'east' – suggests that something other than an East-West orientation is operative.

Considering 'non-Western' as a marked term adds another analytic layer – that its members are somehow of 'lesser' status than those in the unmarked category (a claim supported by other aspects of the Netherlands' immigration-related policies and public discourse). Secondly, 'non-Western' and 'Western' are subcategories of allochtoon – non-native – whereas autochtoon is treated as a single, unified category, without subdivisions. Adding this point to Table 21.2 demonstrates a key feature of the taxonomy.

The autochthonous, 'native' Dutch are thereby treated as the unmarked, undifferentiated, 'normal' inhabitants of the Netherlands, whereas the marked, allochthonous residents of the Netherlands are constituted as a site of difference, otherness, and, by linguistic logic, inferiority. Following Mary Douglas (1966),[47] the taxonomy marks the allochthonous, 'hybrid' or 'hyphenated' 'rocks' – the metaphoric source of the allochtoon concept

Table 21.2   Unified autochtoon, divided allochtoon

Autochtoon	Allochtoon	
	Western	*Non-Western*
	Europe (but not Turkey)	Turkey
		Africa [Morocco]
	North America Oceania	Latin America
	Japan	Asia
	Indonesia (including former Dutch Indonesia)	[Suriname, Dutch Antilles/Aruba]

Source: Yanow and van der Haar.[48]

is geology – on the right side as 'matter out of place,' and hence, 'dirt,' thereby establishing a domain of 'pollution,' danger, and impurity on the right, distinguished from a unified domain of sanctification and 'purity' on the left. This attributed unity enacts a public amnesia concerning divisions among autochthonous Netherlanders – on the basis of religion or accent, for instance – which treats some as lesser than others.

Category analysis intertwines with other analytic approaches to support a policy-related inference that all the state and municipal immigrant 'integration' programs that might be imagined cannot change an allochtoon into an autochtoon. It is no wonder, from this perspective, that immigrant integration policies have been assessed as failures. It is not the program designs that are at fault, but, rather, the language of political discourse, reflected in state-defined categories and supported through their implementation. Analysis of the categories used in registration forms to obtain various kinds of services (e.g., educational, medical) leads to the same inference.

LOOKING FORWARD

Interpretive policy analysis seems at this point secure within the academy, at least outside of North America: 2015 marked a decade of annual meetings of the international conference, based (so far) in Europe and the UK, drawing attendance also from North America, South Africa, India, and Oceania; its associated journal is also thriving; a conference offshoot has begun in Australia, extending to New Zealand; and units engaging interpretive analysis have also been created within the UK's Political Studies Association and the European Consortium on Political Research. Within the American Anthropological Association, the equivalent of interpretive approaches to policy studies has been institutionalized in the recent creation of the Committee on Public Policy division, two of whose founders, Cris Shore and Susan Wright, co-edited two volumes on anthropology and public policy and are presently editing a book series on that topic at Stanford University Press.

As a way of knowing, interpretive policy analysis continues to enable a generative engagement with some of the problems that seem analytically intractable from a positivist perspective. It is also generative in theoretical terms, for instance with respect to the definitional problem found in policy studies textbooks. Is 'policy' the formal document that is the outcome of a legislative act? Is it a set of inclinations, as in 'The government's policy is . . .'? Is it a specific program? From an interpretive policy analytic perspective, the key question to ask may be not, 'What *is* a policy?' but instead, 'What *work* is a policy and/or its elements, including its legislation and implementation, attempted or achieved, doing, in this particular setting, situation or other context, at this particular time?' That kind of question, the sort of focus found in science studies, leads to a dynamic definition of policies as working 'to classify and organise people and ideas in new ways.'[49] It shifts analytic attention to the constructed character of concepts – such as 'policy,' in a broader, 'governance' discourse – or of specific terms in particular policy issues – such as 'integration' or 'housing decay' – and their potential for multiple interpretations.

The more interpretive policy analysis can engage and explore its own philosophical-theoretical grounding, perhaps in concert with interpretive methodologies and methods more broadly, the more it thereby stands on its own, clearly articulated, ontological and epistemological feet, and the less it has to adopt a defensive posture with respect to positivist-informed ways of knowing. Part of this grounding, currently attracting increasing attention, is an abductive logic of inquiry that is increasingly understood as lying at the heart of interpretive ways of knowing: analytic sense-making begins with a puzzle or surprise, often occasioned by the mismatch between the researcher-analyst's expectations and policy-specific lived realities, and looks for likely conditions that would 'normalize' it.[50]

Interpretive policy analysis scholars are increasingly drawing on methods that have not been widely used in recent years, and these still need a fuller accounting. Few researchers were engaging participant-observer ethnography at the time the approach was developing (although it had been fairly common in earlier policy and administrative research[51]); studies had privileged policy documents and elite or expert interviews.

For a field that wants to know about those living out others' policy decisions, methods that enable 'studying down' as well as 'studying-up,'[52] such as ethnography or participant observation, are key. Traditional policy analysis, as with nearly all political science, has largely engaged its subject matter 'at the top.' That is where power, the *leitmotif* of the discipline's work, is widely presumed to reside. This might partly explain the disinclination among interpretive policy studies scholars, until recently, to undertake ethnographic work, despite an orientation toward wanting to understand what is happening with policies 'on the ground.' But, as Cris Shore has argued, policies require not so much studying up as studying across and every which way in a network sort of fashion. This is what following a policy and its relevant actors, objects, acts, and language promises, 'teasing out connections and observing how policies bring together individuals, discourses and institutions . . . and the new kinds of networks, relations and subjects this process creates.'[53] The use of policy ethnography is growing, and interpretive ethnographic approaches could well be cultivated further.[54]

Following policy 'components' in these ways, another developing method in interpretive policy analysis – or, perhaps, a new way to talk about an older method – can lead analysts to trace the sites of agenda-setting, decision-making, and other sources of power and of silent and/or silenced voices without pressure to constrain the study to the borders of a specific physical setting. Tracing how a policy issue might be framed at one moment and reframed at another can transcend both physical boundaries and those of time. The policy itself is the site, not some geographically bounded entity, as is amply evident in, for instance, Charlotte Epstein's study of whaling (mentioned earlier). A similar sort of logic appears to provide a scientific rationale for comparative analysis from an interpretive perspective. When research is animated by a concern for situated meaning, 'most similar' or 'most different' logics of case selection – which require a priori designation of what is locally meaning-ful – seem an insufficient rationale. Instead, pursuing an abductive logic of inquiry, the policy analyst would follow policy issues to additional settings relevant to the policy element(s) being tracked, which might shed further light on the initial surprise.[55]

Such 'following' also brings physical artifacts back into analytic focus, alongside language and acts. Science studies and actor-network theoretic approaches such as these, which rematerialize the world of policy analysis, are appearing on the interpretive policy analytic horizon, perhaps joined by increasing attention to spatial domains.[56] A more systematic account needs to be made of these and other methods as they figure in interpretive policy analysis. By contrast, discourse analyses, increasingly central to the field's research, call for a different sort of attention. For one, researchers need to be clear about which among the several forms of discourse analysis they are engaging. Additionally, to the extent that treating language as the sole carrier of policy and implementing agency meanings, as many of these studies do, excludes an exploration of other forms of policy enactment, such as acts and attendant physical artifacts, analysis runs the risk of further removal from the world of practice. If our initial question was what and/or how policies mean, we must acknowledge that logocentrism, while a key characteristic of academic work, does not do justice to the panoply of meaning-communicative elements in policy practices: language is but one mode of meaning-making, and theoretical and analytic room must be created for acts and objects as well. As noted above, Taylor provides the philosophical grounds for considering not only literal texts but 'text analogues' – in his case, acts – as vehicles for the communication of meaning; the point holds as well for objects. Both have a place in interpretive policy analysis.

Moreover, an exclusive concern with written and spoken language constitutes a denial of the non-verbal, of the immediacy and accuracy of aesthetic and emotive responses, and of the fullest reality of tacit knowledge. It inclines us toward a privileging of explicit knowledge, and in particular the assumption that we cannot make sense of experience without converting it into verbal language. But in the world of practice, such reflection and conversion often halts, if not stymies, action, much like the centipede in response to being asked, 'What is your 37th leg doing when your 83rd is up?' Even more, in the world of practice there are many times when meanings are made, conveyed, and acted upon without such explicit, intentional, conscious reflection: we do communicate, through the symbolic representations of meaning in metaphors, stories, and so on, much that we know only tacitly. The emphasis on explicit language as the (only) way to communicate meaning privileges cognitive understandings over non-verbal and other visual ones, and explicitly communicable understandings over tacitly known ones.[57] Despite the fact that narrative and other language-focused turns create a space for tacit knowledge, they seem not to accord it the fullest weight and attention that it merits. An interpretive policy analysis that encompasses 'discursive spaces' in documents and policy talk without abandoning observed acts and/or material artifacts can enhance its analytic purchase.

Finally, on the methodological front, if interpretive policy analysts are serious about questions of knowledge and its power dimensions, they are going to have to take on board the methodological concerns raised by considerations of 'knowledge claims.' These have been addressed, in other arenas of inquiry, by attending to reflexivity and positionality: personal or demographic, physical or geographic, and/or theoretical situatedness.[58] Although increasingly *de rigueur* in interpretive methodologies broadly speaking, these are still very much contested methodological spaces in policy studies, where researchers are much more likely to consider the 'positionalities,' without using that term, of those researched than to explicitly reflect on their own. Aside from engaging matters of researcher subjectivity, reflexivity also links questions of knowledge directly with issues of power, especially concerning the relationships between researchers and those researched (a key concern, too, of research ethics). It should be central to interpretive policy analysis.

Interpretive policy analysis is increasingly growing beyond the field's original domestically-focused policy domain – welfare, housing, transportation, and so forth – to an engagement with regional and global policy concerns, such as foreign policy, European Union policies, terrorism and securitization studies, climate change and other environmental issues, and other arenas, many of which commonly have been the domain of international relations (IR). Such matters, after all, cross state lines, and policies – and, hence, their analyses – must do likewise. IR and comparative government scholars have to date largely worked in ignorance of the long-standing theoretical contributions of interpretive and other public policy analytic theorizing – and vice versa. Both sets of scholars stand to benefit from crossing such disciplinary boundaries, as European scholars have already been doing,[59] and resisting pressures to follow the US's four subfield disciplinary structure,[60] which could lead to re-balkanization of this analytic terrain. Interpretive understandings of policy processes are also proving generative for practitioners, as well, among them, in the US, Congressional Research Service analysts and staff at one of the Forest Service agencies. The challenge before us is to continue to explore and develop the several analytic practices that fall within this meaning-focused, context-specific domain, in ways that demonstrate its utility for both academic and practitioner concerns.

NOTES

1. Hawkesworth, M.E., *Theoretical Issues in Policy Analysis*, Albany, NY, SUNY Press, 1988; Rein, Martin, *Social Science and Public Policy*, New York, Penguin, 1976.
2. E.g., Geertz, Clifford, *The Interpretation of Cultures*, New York, Basic Books, 1973; Hiley, David R., Bohman, James F. and Shusterman, Richard (eds), *The Interpretive Turn: Philosophy, Science, Culture*, Ithaca, NY, Cornell University Press, 1991; Rabinow, Paul and William M. Sullivan (eds), *Interpretive Social Science*, Berkeley, University of California Press, 1979, 2nd edn, 1985. This paragraph and the next draw on Schmidt, Ron, Sr. and Yanow, Dvora, 'Introduction: Symposium: Interpretive methods and methodologies for studying migration and citizenship politics,' *Migration*

and Citizenship (Newsletter of the American Political Science Association Organized Section on Migration and Citizenship), Winter 2014–15, **3**/1, 4–5, 62, 67.

3. See Hawkesworth, loc. cit., for a detailed critique.
4. Fraser, Nancy, 'Pragmatism, feminism, and the linguistic turn,' in Seyla Benhabib, Judith Butler, Drucilla Cornell and Nancy Fraser (eds), *Feminist Contentions*, New York, Routledge, 1995, 157–72.
5. McDonald, Terrence J. (ed.), *The Historic Turn in the Human Sciences*, Ann Arbor, MI, University of Michigan, 1996.
6. Lorenz, Chris, 'Can histories be true? Narrativism, positivism, and the "metaphorical turn",' *History and Theory*, **37**, 1998, 309–30.
7. Schatzki, Theodore R., Knorr-Cetina, Karin and von Savigny, Eike (eds), *The Practice Turn in Contemporary Theory*, New York, Routledge, 2001.
8. White, Stephen K., 'The very idea of a critical social science: A pragmatist turn,' in Fred Rush (ed.), *The Cambridge Companion to Critical Theory*, New York, Cambridge University Press, 2004, 310–35.
9. White, Jay D., 'Taking language seriously: Toward a narrative theory of knowledge for administrative research,' *American Review of Public Administration*, **22**, 1992, 75–88.
10. Taylor, Charles, 'Interpretation and the sciences of man,' *Review of Metaphysics*, **25**, 1971, 3–51; see also Ricoeur, Paul, 'The model of the text,' *Social Research*, **38**, 1971, 529–62.
11. Colebatch, Hal K., 'Organizational meanings of program evaluation,' *Policy Sciences*, **18**/2, 1995, 149–64.
12. Freeman, Richard, 'Learning by meeting,' *Critical Policy Analysis*, **2**/1, 2008, 1–24; Yanow, Dvora, *How Does a Policy Mean? Interpreting Policy and Organizational Actions*, Washington, DC, Georgetown University Press, 1996, chapter 7.
13. Yanow, Dvora, 'Built space as story: The policy stories that buildings tell,' *Policy Studies Journal*, **23**/3, 1995a, 407–22.
14. Schatz, Edward (ed.), *Political Ethnography*, Chicago, University of Chicago Press, 2009; Dubois, Vincent, 'Towards a critical policy ethnography: Lessons from fieldwork on welfare control in France,' *Critical Policy Studies*, **3**/2, 2009, 221–39; van Hulst, Merlijn J., 'Quite an experience: Using ethnography to study local governance,' *Critical Policy Analysis*, **2**/2, 2008a, 143–59.
15. See, e.g., Yanow, Dvora, 'Methodological ways of seeing and knowing,' in Emma Bell, Samantha Warren and Jonathan Schroeder (eds), *The Routledge Companion to Visual Organization*, New York, Routledge, 2014a.
16. On the former, see Yanow, Dvora, *Constructing 'Race' and 'Ethnicity' in America: Category-making in Public Policy and Administration*, Armonk, NY, M.E. Sharpe, 2003; on the latter, Epstein, Charlotte, *Power of Words in International Relations: Birth of an Anti-whaling Discourse*, Cambridge, MIT Press, 2008. For additional discussion, sources, and examples of interpretive methodologies and methods, Yanow, Dvora and Peregrine Schwartz-Shea (eds), *Interpretation and Method: Empirical Research Methods and the Interpretive Turn*, 2nd edn, Armonk, NY: M.E. Sharpe, 2014.
17. Lipsky, Michael, *Street-level Bureaucracy*, New York, Russell Sage Foundation, 1980; Prottas, Jeffrey M., *People-processing*, Lexington, MA, D.C. Heath, 1979; Weatherley, Richard, *Reforming Special Education*, Cambridge, MIT Press, 1979. For two recent studies that extend the theorizing, see Maynard-Moody, Steven and Musheno, Michael, *Cops, Teachers, Counselors: Stories from the Front Lines of Public Service*, Ann Arbor, University of Michigan Press, 2003, and Dubois, Vincent, *La vie au guichet*, Paris, Economica, 1999 [English translation, *The Bureaucrat and the Poor*, London, Ashgate, 2010]. From a somewhat different angle, see Stein, Sandra J., *The Culture of Education Policy*, New York, Teachers College Press, 2004.
18. Lipsky, Michael, 'Standing the study of public policy implementation on its head,' in Walter Dean Burnham and Martha Weinberg (eds), *American Politics and Public Policy*, Cambridge, MA, MIT Press, 1978, 391–402.
19. In political theory, for instance, see Edelman, Murray, *The Symbolic Uses of Politics*,

Urbana, University of Illinois, 1964; Edelman, Murray, *Politics as Symbolic Action*, Chicago, Markham, 1971; Fay, Brian, *Social Theory and Political Practice*, Boston, George Allen & Unwin, 1975; Taylor, loc. cit.

20. Geertz, loc. cit.; Brown, Richard Harvey, 'Social theory as metaphor,' *Theory and Society*, **3**, 1976, 169–97; Gusfield, Joseph, 'The literary rhetoric of science,' *American Sociological Review*, **41**, 1, 1976, 16–34; Gusfield, Joseph R., *The Culture of Public Problems: Drinking-driving and the Symbolic Order*, Chicago, University of Chicago Press, 1981; Rabinow and Sullivan, loc. cit.

21. E.g., Bernstein, Richard J., *The Restructuring of Social and Political Theory*, Philadelphia, University of Pennsylvania Press, 1976; Bernstein, Richard J., *Beyond Objectivism and Relativism*, Philadelphia, University of Pennsylvania Press, 1983; Polkinghorne, Donald E., *Methodology for the Human Sciences*, Albany, NY, SUNY Press, 1983; Polkinghorne, Donald E., *Narrative Knowing and the Human Sciences*, Albany, NY, SUNY Press, 1988; McCloskey, Donald, *The Rhetoric of Economics*, Madison, University of Wisconsin Press, 1985; Fish, Stanley, *Is There a Text in this Class? The Authority of Interpretive Communities*, Cambridge, MA, Harvard University Press, 1983. An account of this intellectual genealogy would be remiss without mentioning two other works: Kuhn, Thomas S., *The Structure of Scientific Revolutions*, Chicago, University of Chicago Press, 2nd edn, 1970 [1962], which started many thinking about the ways in which scientific 'discoveries' are made and the role of epistemic communities in that – ideas that encapsulate the two meanings of paradigm in the work, parallel to understandings of the hermeneutic circle as both a way of knowing and the interpretive community that follows that logic of inquiry (see also 'Postscript – 1969' in the 2nd edn, 174–210, or Kuhn, Thomas S., 'Second thoughts on paradigms,' in *The Essential Tension: Selected Studies in Scientific Tradition and Change*, Chicago, University of Chicago Press, 1979); and Berger, Peter L. and Luckmann, Thomas, *The Social Construction of Reality*, New York, Doubleday, 1966, which introduced phenomenological ideas and the notion of social constructionism (or constructivism; the terms are used differently in different disciplines) to the English-reading academy.

22. In *Policy Sciences*: Ascher, William, 'Editorial,' *Policy Sciences*, **20**, 1987, 3–9; Brunner, Ronald D., 'The policy sciences as science,' *Policy Sciences*, **15**, 1982, 115–35; Brunner, Ronald D., 'Key political symbols,' *Policy Sciences*, **20**, 1987, 53–76; Dryzek, John S., 'Policy analysis as a hermeneutic activity,' *Policy Sciences*, **14**, 1982, 309–29; Healy, Paul, 'Interpretive policy inquiry,' *Policy Sciences*, **19**, 1986, 381–96; Torgerson, Douglas, 'Contextual orientation in policy analysis,' *Policy Sciences*, **18**, 1985, 241–61; Torgerson, Douglas, 'Between knowledge and politics,' *Policy Sciences*, **19**, 1986, 33–59; Torgerson, Douglas, 'Interpretive policy inquiry,' *Policy Sciences*, **19**, 1986, 307–405. Elsewhere, see DeHaven-Smith, Lance, *Philosophical Critiques of Policy Analysis*, Gainsville, University of Florida Press, 1988; Fox, Charles J., 'Biases in public policy implementation evaluation,' *Policy Studies Review*, **7/1**, 1987, 128–41; Fox, Charles J., 'Implementation research,' in Dennis J. Palumbo and Donald J. Calista (eds), *Implementation and the Policy Process*, New York, Greenwood, 1990, 199–212; Goodsell, Charles T., *The Social Meaning of Civic Space*, Lawrence, University Press of Kansas, 1988; Hawkesworth, loc. cit.; Jennings, Bruce, 'Interpretive social science and policy analysis,' in Daniel Callahan and Bruce Jennings (eds), *Ethics, the Social Sciences, and Policy Analysis*, New York, Plenum, 1983, 3–35; Jennings, Bruce, 'Interpretation and the practice of policy analysis,' in Frank Fischer and John Forester (eds), *Confronting Values in Policy Analysis*, Newbury Park, CA, Sage, 1987, 128–52; Maynard-Moody, Steven and Stull, Donald, 'The symbolic side of policy analysis,' in Frank Fischer and John Forester (eds), *Confronting Values in Policy Analysis*, Newbury Park, CA, Sage, 1987, 248–65; Rein, Martin and Schön, Donald A., 'Problem setting in policy research,' in Carol Weiss (ed.), *Using Social Research in Policy Making*, Lexington, MA, Lexington Books, 1977, 235–51; Yanow, Dvora, 'Toward a policy culture approach to implementation,' *Policy Studies Review*, **7/1**, 1987, 103–15.

23. See, e.g., Fischer, Frank and Forester, John (eds), *The Argumentative Turn in Policy*

Analysis and Planning, Durham, NC, Duke University Press, 1993; Hajer, Maarten A. and Wagenaar, Hendrik (eds), *Deliberative Policy Analysis*, New York, Cambridge University Press, 2003.

24. Such terminology was not uncommon even into the 1980s (and later, following these works) among both policy developers and academics. See, e.g., Sapolsky, Harvey M., *The Polaris System Development: Bureaucratic and Programmatic Success in Government*, Cambridge, Harvard University Press, 1972; Schneider, Anne and Ingram, Helen, 'Social construction of target populations,' *American Political Science Review*, **87**, 1983, 334–47.

25. Dryzek, John S., *Discursive Democracy*, Cambridge, Cambridge University Press, 1990; Schneider, Anne Larason and Ingram, Helen, *Policy Design for Democracy*, Lawrence, University Press of Kansas, 1997.

26. Fischer, Frank, *Reframing Public Policy: Discursive Politics and Deliberative Practices*, New York, Oxford University Press, 2003; Fischer, Frank, *Democracy and Expertise: Reorienting Policy Inquiry*, New York, Oxford University Press, 2009; Fischer and Forester, loc. cit.; Hajer and Wagenaar, loc. cit.

27. Hajer, Maarten, 'Discourse coalitions and the institutionalization of practice,' in Frank Fischer and John Forester (eds), *The Argumentative Turn in Policy Analysis and Planning*, Durham, NC, Duke University Press, 1993, 43–76; Yanow, Dvora (ed.) 'Practices of policy interpretation,' *Policy Sciences*, **29**, 1995b, 111–26; Freeman, Richard, Griggs, Steven and Boaz, Annette (eds), 'The practice of policy-making,' Special Issue, *Evidence & Policy*, 7/2, 2011, 127–227.

28. Taylor, loc. cit.; Yanow, Dvora, 'The communication of policy meanings: Implementation as interpretation and text,' *Policy Sciences*, **26**, 1993, 41–61.

29. For an extensive overview of this field, see Greenwood, Davydd and Levin, Morten, *Introduction to Action Research*, 2nd edn, Thousand Oaks, CA, Sage, 2006 [1998].

30. Polanyi, Michael, *The Tacit Dimension*, New York, Doubleday, 1966.

31. Yanow, op. cit., 1993; Yanow, op. cit., 1996.

32. On multimodality in cognitive linguistics, see Müller, Cornelia, *Metaphors Dead and Alive, Sleeping and Waking*, Chicago, University of Chicago Press, 2008. And tracing 'how things mean' leads further to the mapping for exposure and intertextuality that characterizes interpretive methodologies and methods more broadly; see Schwartz-Shea, Peregrine and Yanow, Dvora, *Interpretive Research Design: Concepts and Processes*, New York, Routledge, 2012.

33. Rein and Schön, loc. cit.; Schön, Donald A. and Rein, Martin, *Frame Reflection: Toward the Resolution of Intractable Policy Controversies*, New York, Basic Books, 1994.

34. For a suggestive, though not exhaustive, list of some two dozen analytic methods, see Yanow and Schwartz-Shea, loc. cit., xxiii.

35. For a cognitive linguistics approach, see Lakoff, George and Johnson, Mark, *Metaphors We Live By*, Chicago, University of Chicago Press, 1980; Lakoff, George, 'The contemporary theory of metaphor,' in Andrew Ortony (ed.), *Metaphor and Thought*, 2nd edn, New York, Cambridge University Press, 1993, 202–51. More recent work in this area looks at conceptual blending and multimodal metaphor; see Müller, loc. cit. For applications to policy, see Miller, Donald F., 'Social policy: An exercise in metaphor,' *Knowledge*, **7**, 1985, 191–215; Schön, Donald A., 'Generative metaphor,' in Andrew Ortony (ed.), *Metaphor and Thought*, Cambridge, Cambridge University Press, 1979, 254–83 (also in 2nd edn, 1993); Yanow, Dvora, 'Supermarkets and culture clash: The epistemological role of metaphors in administrative practice,' *American Review of Public Administration*, **22**, 1992, 89–109; see also Edelman, Murray, *Political Language*, New York, Academic Press, 1977; Carver, Terrell and Pikalo, Jernej (eds), *Political Language and Metaphor*, London, Routledge, 2008; and Cienki, Alan and Yanow, Dvora (eds), 'Linguistic approaches to analysing policies and the political,' Special Issue, *Journal of International Relations and Development*, **16**/2, 2013, 167–310.

36. On categories, see Keeler, Rebecca, 'Analysis of logic: Categories of people in U.S. HIV/AIDS policy,' *Administration & Society*, **39**/5, 2007, 612–30; Lakoff, George, *Women, Fire, and Dangerous Things*, Chicago, University of Chicago Press, 1987; Rasmussen, Amy Cabrera, 'Contraception as health? The framing of issue categories in contemporary policy making,' *Administration & Society*, **43**, 8, 2011, 930–53; Yanow, op. cit., 2003; Yanow, Dvora and van der Haar, Marleen, 'People out of place: Allochthony and autochthony in Netherlands identity discourse – metaphors and categories in action,' *Journal for International Relations and Development*, **16**/2, 2013, 227–61. On stories, see Forester, John, 'Learning from practice stories: The priority of practical judgment,' in Frank Fischer and John Forester (eds), *The Argumentative Turn in Policy Analysis and Planning*, Durham, NC, Duke University Press, 1993, 186–209; van Hulst, Merlijn, *Town Hall Tales: Culture as Storytelling in Local Government*, Delft, Eburon, 2008b; Yanow, Dvora, 'Public policies as identity stories: American race-ethnic discourse,' in Tineke Abma (ed.), *Telling Tales: On Narrative and Evaluation*, Stamford, CT, JAI Press, 1999, 29–52. On narrative, Kaplan, Thomas J., 'Reading policy narratives,' in Frank Fischer and John Forester (eds), *The Argumentative Turn in Policy Analysis and Planning*, Durham, NC, Duke University Press, 1993, 167–85; Roe, Emery, *Narrative Policy Analysis*, Durham, NC, Duke University Press, 1994; Shenhav, Shaul, *Analyzing social narratives*, New York: Routledge, 2015.
37. Rein and Schön, loc. cit.; Schön and Rein, loc. cit. See also Abolafia, Mitchel Y., 'Framing moves: Interpretive politics at the Federal Reserve,' *Journal of Public Administration Research and Theory*, **14**, 2004, 349–70; Bacchi, Carol, *Analysing Policy: What's the Problem Represented to Be?*, Frenchs Forest, Australia, Pearson Education, 2009; Linder, Steven H., 'Contending discourses in the electromagnetic fields controversy,' *Policy Sciences*, **18**/2, 1995, 209–30; Schmidt, Ronald, Sr., 'Value-critical policy analysis: The case of language policy in the United States,' in Dvora Yanow and Peregrine Schwartz-Shea (eds), *Interpretation and Method: Empirical Research Methods and the Interpretive Turn*, 2nd edn, Armonk, NY, M.E. Sharpe, 2014, 322–37; Swaffield, Simon, 'Contextual meanings in policy discourse: A case study of language use concerning resource policy in the New Zealand high country,' *Policy Sciences*, **31**, 1998, 199–224; van Hulst, Merlijn and Yanow, Dvora, 'From policy "frames" to "framing": Theorizing a more dynamic, political approach,' *American Review of Public Administration*, DOI: 10.1177/0275074014533142, 2014 (online 30 May); and Verloo, Mieke, 'Mainstreaming gender equality in Europe: A critical frame analysis approach,' *The Greek Review of Social Research*, 117B, 2005, 11–34.
38. See, e.g., Howarth, David J., *Discourse*, Buckingham, Open University Press, 2000; Epstein, loc. cit.; Wodak, Ruth, *The Discourse of Politics in Action*, Palgrave, 2011.
39. There is nothing to suggest that expressive acts cannot also be instrumental (or vice versa). Raymond Nairn (personal communication, July 1996) related the example of how a campaign that included hanging anti-nuclear signs on numerous homes, streets, schools, and offices across New Zealand influenced then-newly-elected Prime Minister David Lange's decision to change his stance on the matter, with a subsequent change in national policy.
40. Dubois, op. cit., 1999/2010. See also Goodsell, loc. cit.; Goodsell, Charles T. (ed.), 'Architecture as a setting for governance,' Special Issue, *Journal of Architectural and Planning Research*, **10**/4, 1993; Yanow, Dvora, op. cit., 1995a; Yanow, Dvora, 'How built spaces mean: A semiotics of space,' in Dvora Yanow and Peregrine Schwartz-Shea (eds), *Interpretation and Method: Empirical Research Methods and the Interpretive Turn*, 2nd edn, Armonk, NY, M.E. Sharpe, 2014b, 368–86.
41. See Yanow, op. cit., 2014a; Maher, Kristin Hill, 'Finding narratives through visual methods,' in Ron Schmidt, Sr. and Dvora Yanow (eds), Symposium: Interpretive methodologies and methods in studying migration and citizenship politics, *Migration and Citizenship* (Newsletter of the American Political Science Association Organized Section on Migration and Citizenship), Winter 2014–15, **3**/1, 32–6, 65–6, 67.
42. Yanow, Dvora, *Conducting Interpretive Policy Analysis*, Newbury Park, CA, Sage,

2000; Yanow, Dvora, 'Interpretation in policy analysis: On methods and practice,' *Critical Policy Analysis*, **1**, 2007, 109–21.
43. Pal, Leslie, 'Competing paradigms in policy discourse: The case of international human rights,' *Policy Sciences*, **18**/2, 1995, 185–207.
44. The methodological theorizing and methods discussion in this section draw on Yanow, op. cit., 2000, chapter 3, and 2003. The subsequent illustration draws on Yanow and van der Haar, loc. cit.; Yanow, Dvora, van der Haar, Marleen and Völke, Karlijn. 'Troubled taxonomies and the calculating state: "Everyday" categorizing and "race-ethnicity" – the Netherlands case' (manuscript, 2015); two Dutch-language articles; and Yanow, Dvora, 'Accounting for "natives" and strangers: The work of metaphors and categories,' in Ron Schmidt, Sr. and Dvora Yanow (eds), Symposium: Interpretive methodologies and methods in studying migration and citizenship politics, *Migration and Citizenship* (Newsletter of the American Political Science Association Organized Section on Migration and Citizenship), Winter 2014–15, **3**/1, 15–22, 64, 67.
45. Taylor, loc. cit.
46. Yanow and van der Haar, loc. cit., 240.
47. Douglas, Mary, *Purity and Danger*, London, Routledge & Kegan Paul, 1966.
48. Yanow and van der Haar, loc. cit., 248.
49. Shore, Cris and Wright, Susan, 'Conceptualising policy,' in Cris Shore, Susan Wright and Davide Peró (eds), *Policy Worlds*, Oxford, Berghahn, 2011, 1–25.
50. Schwartz-Shea and Yanow, loc. cit., chapter 2; see also Agar, Michael, 'On the ethnographic part of the mix: A multi-genre tale of the field,' *Organizational Research Methods*, **13**/2, 2010, 286–303; Locke, Karen, Golden-Biddle, Karen and Feldman, Martha S., 'Making doubt generative: Rethinking the role of doubt in the research process,' *Organization Science*, **19**/6, 2008, 907–18; Van Maanen, John, Sørensen, Jesper B. and Mitchell, Terence R., 'The interplay between theory and method,' *Academy of Management Review*, **32**/4, 2007, 1145–54. Cf. Glynos, Jason and Howarth, David, *Logics of Critical Explanation in Social and Political Theory*, New York, Routledge, 2007, on retroduction, which they say they use in the same sense. In a parallel field of study, see Friedrichs, Jörg and Kratochwil, Friedrich, 'On acting and knowing: How pragmatism can advance international relations research and methodology,' *International Organization*, **63**, 2009, 701–31.
51. E.g., Blau, Peter, *The Dynamics of Bureaucracy*, Chicago, University of Chicago Press, 1963 [orig. 1953]; Crozier, Michel, *The Bureaucratic Phenomenon*, Chicago, University of Chicago Press, 1964; Gouldner, Alvin W., *Patterns of Industrial Bureaucracy*, Glencoe, IL, Free Press, 1954; Kaufman, Herbert, *The Forest Ranger*, Baltimore, MD, published for Resources for the Future by Johns Hopkins University Press, 1954; Selznick, Philip, *TVA and the Grass Roots*, Berkeley, University of California Press, 1949; Selznick, Philip, *Leadership in Administration: A Sociological Interpretation*, New York, Harper & Row, 1957. See also Redman, Eric, *The Dance of Legislation: An Insider's account of the Workings of the United States Senate*, Seattle, University of Washington Press, 1973; Fenno, Richard F., Jr., 'Observation, context, and sequence in the study of politics,' *American Political Science Review*, **80**/1, 1986, 3–15.
52. Nader, Laura, 'Up the anthropologist: Perspectives gained from studying up,' in Dell Hymes (ed.), *Reinventing Anthropology*, New York, Pantheon, 1972, 284–311.
53. Cris Shore, 'Espionage, policy and the art of government: The British Secret Services and the war on Iraq,' in Cris Shore, Susan Wright and Divide Peró (eds), *Policy Worlds*, Oxford: Berghahn, 2011, 169–86.
54. See, e.g., Dubois, op. cit., 1999/2010; van Hulst, op. cit., 2008a. On political ethnography more broadly, see Schatz, Edward (ed.), loc. cit.
55. For further discussion, see Yanow, Dvora, 'Interpretive analysis and comparative research,' in Isabelle Engeli and Christine Rothmayr Allison (eds), *Comparative Policy Studies: Conceptual and Methodological Challenges*, Houndmills, Basingstoke, Palgrave Macmillan, 2014c, 131–59.
56. See, e.g., van Marrewijk, Alfons and Yanow, Dvora (eds), *Organizational Spaces:*

Rematerializing the Workaday World, Cheltenham, UK and Northampton, MA, USA, Edward Elgar, 2010.

57. See, e.g., Cook, Scott D.N. and Yanow, Dvora, 'Culture and organizational learning,' *Journal of Management Inquiry*, **20**/4, 2011 [1993], 362–79; Davide Nicolini, Silvia Gherardi and Dvora Yanow, 'Introduction: Toward a practice-based view of knowing and learning in organizations,' in Davide Nicolini, Silvia Gherardi, Dvora Yanow (eds), *Knowing in Organizations: A Practice-based Approach*, Armonk, NY, M.E Sharpe, 2003, 3–31; Yanow, Dvora and Tsoukas, Haridimos, 'What is reflection-in-action? A phenomenological account,' *Journal of Management Studies*, **46**/8, 2009, 1339–64.

58. See, e.g., Samer Shehata, 'Ethnography, identity, and the production of knowledge,' in Dvora Yanow and Peregrine Schwartz-Shea (eds), *Interpretation and Method: Empirical Research Methods and the Interpretive Turn*, 2nd edn, Armonk, NY, M.E. Sharpe, 2014, 209–27; Timothy Pachirat, *Every Twelve Seconds*, Yale University Press, 2011; and Zirakzadeh, Cyrus Ernesto, 'When nationalists are not separatists: Discarding and recovering academic theories while doing fieldwork in the Basque region of Spain,' in Edward Schatz (ed.), *Political ethnography*, Chicago, University of Chicago Press, 2009, 97–118.

59. See, e.g., Rowell, Jay, Campana, Aurélie and Henry, Emmanuel (eds), *La construction des problèmes publics en Europe*, Strasbourg, PUS, 2007; and on global political (and policy) ethnography, Steputtat, Finn, 'Knowledge production in the security–development nexus: An ethnographic reflection,' *Security Dialogue*, **43** (5), 2012, 439–55.

60. For a critique of the seeming normalcy of this political science structure, see Kaufman-Osborn, Timothy, 'Dividing the domain of political science: On the fetishism of subfields,' *Polity*, **38** (1), 2006, 41–71.

22 Transforming perspectives: the critical functions of interpretive policy analysis
Hendrik Wagenaar

1. INTRODUCTION

Interpretive policy analysis (IPA) presents the world with a radical epistemological claim: It is not merely a method, or family of methods, that differs in important respects from traditional empiricist social science. IPA is said to engender a *better* kind of knowledge, better in the sense that its methods, and the results these bring about, provide a better fit with the specific nature of the social world (Hajer and Wagenaar, 2003; Wagenaar, 2011), and enable the conditions for mutual understanding between social actors (Fay, 1975, 81). In this important sense IPA promises, both to its practitioners and its audience, an alternative to conventional empiricist policy analysis (EPA). By engaging in, for example, frame, discourse or poststructuralist analysis the analyst positions him-/herself with regard to his/her audience as critical. Likewise the audience knows that it can expect a different take on the conventional analysis of policy issues, a different kind of explanation that opens up aspects of the issue at hand that will assist ordinary citizens to emancipate themselves from hitherto unacknowledged oppressive conditions. However, as Fay has argued, IPA is not inherently critical. People may claim self-understanding while in actual practice they seem to be deceived about their motives or actions, or the way their motives and actions uphold repressive social arrangements (Fay, 1975, 87). Moreover, IPA harbors a potentially conservative tendency in that it doesn't acknowledge the possible threat to one's identity and the ensuing resistance that actors might have in engaging in unrestrained communication with actors with different beliefs or interests (Fay, 1975, 90). The question I will address therefore in this chapter is: To what extent and in what ways is the claim that IPA generates knowledge that is superior to the knowledge generated by EPA upheld in its theory and practice? How can IPA be called critical? Or, more precisely, in what ways can the characteristics intrinsic to the epistemic constitution of interpretive approaches help the analyst to be critical. In other words, I will, in a deliberate self-reflexive act, subject the alleged critical function of IPA to a critical analysis of its own.

In my 2011 book I have tried to bring some order to the varied and confusing field of IPA by dividing its central concern with meaning into three types: hermeneutic, discursive and dialogical meaning (Wagenaar, 2011, 40–41). *Hermeneutic meaning* focuses on the way that individual agents move about against a background of shared understandings and routines, on how they interpret themselves in the light of it. The task of the hermeneutic researcher is to make the actions of individual agents intelligible within this situated context. *Discursive meaning* focuses on the taken-for-granted linguistic-practical frameworks, largely unnoticed by individual agents, that constitute the categories and objects of our everyday world. These frameworks act both as grids of possibilities (making certain practices and beliefs possible, natural and self-evident) and conceptual horizons (by making other practices and beliefs incomprehensible, bizarre or illegitimate). The focus of the researcher is on clarifying how these unnoticed grids historically emerge and how they constrain and enable, often in surreptitious ways, the individual agent. *Dialogical meaning* focuses on the fundamentally social and practical nature of meaning. Individual agents become intelligible to themselves and to others by jointly engaging in practices, which themselves flow from an inarticulate background understanding; a shared life world that is 'always there' (Taylor, 1995a, 171). The analyst's focus is on how meaning is constructed in the interaction between agents and between agents and the world in everyday situations. Although the three types of meaning differ in the subject matter, scope of the research, preferences for certain research questions, methods used, the subject position of the researcher, and philosophical underpinnings (Wagenaar, 2011, 39), I do not claim that the distinction is hardwired into reality. In actual practice there is overlap and borrowing, and one could probably argue that in each act of practical judgment all three types of meaning come into play. For the purposes of this chapter it is important, however, to demonstrate what it means to be critical in each of these explanatory-empirical programs.

2. THE CRITICAL FUNCTIONS OF HERMENEUTIC POLICY ANALYSIS: CONFRONTING POLICY ABSTRACTIONS

Andrew Abbot argues that none of the main 'explanatory programs' in the social sciences is exhaustive in its analysis of social reality; they are always in a position to critique each other's inevitable limitations (2004, 27). IPA harbors a powerful critique of EPA, while, conversely, EPA contains a critique of the limits in comprehensiveness that are inherent to the small qualitative samples used in IPA. By reifying its key variables and concealing their grounding in, often strong, theoretical assumptions, EPA has two major limitations: it runs the risk of suggesting erroneous results, and, even when the results are valid and reliable, they have only limited explanatory value. In both cases hermeneutic IPA provides a critical alternative. Two examples will illustrate my point.

In an oft-quoted study Cho et al. (2013) claim to have demonstrated a statistical relationship between the legalization of prostitution and trafficking. Using data on human trafficking in 161 countries over the period 1996 to 2003, the authors 'show' that legalized policy regimes result in an increase in trafficking. Closer analysis reveals however that the data that Cho et al. have used are woefully deficient. As nations use different definitions of trafficking, the data on human trafficking are simply not comparable. Some countries lump human smuggling together with trafficking, some include labor trafficking, others don't, some countries use 'suspected' trafficking as a category, thereby inflating the numbers, while others use only 'officially identified' or 'certified' victims (personal communication Ron Weitzer). A simple hermeneutic inquiry in the meaning of the category of 'trafficking' reveals that the results of the study are definitely spurious and probably wrong.

Because EPA takes an unreflexive, realist view of the categories of analysis and is oblivious to the meaning of the data it analyzes, its conclusions about its object of study, while useful in describing quantitative trends, have a limited reach when it comes to explaining the determinants of the trends; information that is vital for properly diagnosing the problem and designing better policies. A study of government funding for technology transfer in Germany provides an example. The German government spends hundreds of millions of euros each year on basic research in its technical universities. The rationale for this spending is that the results of the research will cascade down into companies to be applied in product development. The links between science and business cannot be expected to emerge spontaneously, however, so the government stimulates and supports such links through a policy of technology transfer. Evaluation studies show that in terms of the creation of new businesses or the development of new products, technology transfer had little or no effect. What we see is that simple EPA has the critical effect of invalidating a number of generally accepted assumptions about technology transfer. The quantitative studies cannot explain however *why* technology transfer is largely ineffective. Hofmann's hermeneutic analysis reveals a world of business–university relationships that is shaped by mutual dependency; universities rely on business for research funds and up-to-date knowledge and businesses turn to universities for reasons of expediency and the avoidance of dead-end solutions to product development (Hofmann, 1995, 134). The critical power of hermeneutic analysis resides in its ability to provide explanations for puzzling phenomena in terms of the intentions of the actors (von Wright, 1971, 89), which can only be discovered through these actors' self-descriptions.

Abbot's argument about the circularity of methodological critique is persuasive, but it suffers from an important limitation. He assumes analytical symmetry between the five explanatory programs. Social science studies never operate in a politically neutral climate, however. Most policies are heavily contested, and can best be seen as protracted struggles over the interpretation and realization of key values (Stone, 1997). In such cases epistemology has political implications (Hajer and Wagenaar, 2003, 13). Cho et al.'s study, for example, is paraded by anti-prostitution activists as the definitive 'scientific' argument – with 'quantitative' being seen as synonymous with scientific – for prohibitionist policy measures. What is, or can be, the critical function of IPA in such contentious, antagonistic policy situations?

A common problem of policy making in contested domains is that the formulation of the policy problem, the 'image' of the social issue at hand that is shared by officials and sometimes the larger public, is overly schematic and/or distorted (Edelman, 1988). This is because of ideological simplification, of the social distance between the target group and the policy elite, or both. One obvious way forward in such situations is to critique such ideological distortion by restoring the voice of the vulnerable group in the policy debate.[1] By 'voice' I mean the free, unrestricted possibility of the target audience to articulate its experiences, needs, concerns, feelings, practices and aspirations. The methodological tool of choice is the unstructured qualitative interview; the elicitation of narratives of the respondent's life history or of visual representations of his/her life and environment (Weiss, 1994; Wagenaar, 2011, chapter 9). Surveys also allow respondents to express their point of view, but the weakness of surveys is that intentionally or unintentionally, in their choice of key categories and/ or omission of certain questions, they tend to reproduce received problem formulations. An example by way of illustration again.

In a comparative study of prostitution policy, Wagenaar et al. interviewed 130 sex workers, most of them migrants from Eastern Europe, about their entry into the sex market, their experiences with prostitution, their earnings, and their prospects and aspirations (Wagenaar et al., 2013). The interviewers were female (ex-)sex workers whom we had given interview training. In this way we attempted to capture as carefully and reliably as possible the lived experience of migrant sex workers. Giving voice to a vulnerable population in the debate over prostitution and trafficking had a number of powerful critical effects; critical, that is, in the sense of enlightenment. First, the number of women who said that they were or had been victims of exploitation was considerably smaller than the official debate suggested. Less than 10 per cent of our sample said that they had been in a situation of gross exploitation or dependency at one point in their career as a sex worker. Moreover, all of these sex workers said that they managed to extract themselves from this situation without much help from authorities. But perhaps more importantly, the interviews revealed that sex workers had many reasons to enter the sex trade. In fact, selling sex for money was one of the strategies with which migrants established themselves in the country of arrival, often supplemented by other jobs. In this they were assisted by friends, family members and others, who often received money for their support, or who temporarily shared an income with the sex worker. The interviews showed that the uniform policy category of 'trafficking' covered up a complex set of experiences of labor migrants, in which prostitution was only one, and often not even the most important, element. This example suggests one of the most common and powerful critical effects of interpretive research – its ability to redraw the boundaries of policy categories. In our case, the key policy category of 'trafficking', which shaped policy goals and design, was transformed into an issue of labor migration and the economic and sexual exploitation of marginal workers. This, subsequently, suggested a wholly different approach to prostitution policy, as part of a wider drive to fight labor exploitation of vulnerable social groups.

Hermeneutic IPA is critical in the sense of confronting one's assumptions of the world with the resistances that the world exerts on a policy intervention. The difference with EPA is in the type of 'data'. In the case of hermeneutic IPA they are meanings: the target group's narratives of the impact of the policy intervention on the lives of its members in the wider context of their life world and social-cultural milieu. Having one's sacred, taken-for-granted assumptions knocked over by the confrontation with a thick description of the lived experience of the target group is thus an elementary act of critique and enlightenment. Another important way in which hermeneutic IPA is critical is in disassembling what is assumed to be coherent. Policy makers hate this work of willful fragmentation. It undermines their quest for unity and control (Prainsack and Wahlberg, 2013). Its importance is that it acknowledges the complexity and pluralism of policy problems, features that everyone who intervenes in the world does well to respect. The strength of hermeneutic IPA lies in its emphasis on careful, patient fieldwork. The importance of fieldwork is in its ability to confront deeply held beliefs about the world. Good fieldwork creates the conditions for learning new things. Not just 'facts', but the explanations and conceptualizations that make sense of the 'facts'. Compared to field-work, theory leaves less space for learning. This is the deeper meaning of Austin's famous quote that facts are richer than diction.[2] You can't get more critical than this. Both camps often overlook how well EPA and hermeneutic IPA can work together in critically illuminating a complex policy problem. Again, an obvious point that needs occasional reaffirmation.

3.   THE CRITICAL FUNCTION OF DISCURSIVE POLICY ANALYSIS: OVERCOMING CAPTIVITY

In discursive forms of policy analysis the analyst tries to uncover the taken-for-granted ways that policy makers, the public, and often even the members of the target group themselves understand their situation. It is the task of the analyst, I argue, to clarify 'how these unnoticed grids historically emerge and how they constrain and enable, often in surreptitious ways, the individual agent' (Wagenaar, 2011, 40). The critical function of revealing hidden cognitive and behavioral frames seems so obvious, not least to the analysts who work in this vein themselves, that discursive analysis often brands itself as critical, as in Critical Discourse Analysis, or the 'critical study of language' (Fairclough, 2001).

Despite the self-professed critical credentials of discursive analysis, it is not easy to answer exactly *how* it is critical. Discursive analysis operates on a root image of captivity (Owen, 2003). Captivity is a term that originated with Wittgenstein. It refers to an integrated, more or less coherent, system of judgments that we pick up through a process of socialization. This system of judgments enables us to orient ourselves and move about in the world in an effective and meaningful way. It makes the world, and our place in it, intelligible (Owen, 2003, 84). In some instances, however, our judgments are off. Doubt sets in: about the rightness of things around us, or about our ability to understand these. In such cases a disjuncture has emerged 'between our ways of making sense of ourselves, on the one hand, and our cares and commitments, on the other' (Owen, 2003, 84). The obvious thing would be to adjust our system of judgments, but the problem is that, although we are unable to make sense of the world and our place in it, we are held captive by our world image. This may result in a situation that we call hegemony in which the captivity is so all-embracing and total that, although we have doubts or are critical about a particular aspect of the world, we are not even aware that we are locked up inside a particular world image that embraces both the aspect we criticize *and* our critique. Hegemony constrains imagination.

To understand the nature of captivity we need to make a distinction between 'aspectival captivity' and 'ideological captivity' (Owen 2003, 88). The distinction is important as both forms of captivity require different kinds of, and harbor different prospects for, critique. Ideological captivity 'refers to the condition of holding beliefs that are both false and compose a worldview that legitimates certain oppressive social institutions' (Owen, 2003, 89). Geuss, in his magisterial overview of critical theory, calls this type of ideology 'pejorative' and defines it on the basis of its epistemic, functional and genetic characteristics (1981, 13).[3] In epistemic terms a set of beliefs or form of consciousness is ideological when it considers value statements as statements of fact, when actors self-consciously and deliberately declare a belief or state of affairs to be natural instead of historically contingent, when they 'objectify' that state of affairs, when they mistakenly take a partial interest for a general interest, or when they take a self-fulfilling property for a non-self-fulfilling property (Geuss, 1981, 12–15). The functional characteristics of a belief or consciousness include those that support and/or legitimate certain kinds of social institutions and practices. Strictly speaking this involves all belief systems, but we apply the label ideology when it concerns unjust institutions and practices, those that constrain human flourishing: 'It is in virtue of the fact that it supports or justifies reprehensible social institutions, unjust social practices, relations of exploitation, hegemony or domination that a form of consciousness is an ideology' (Geuss, 1981, 15). Another functional element is that the beliefs serve to mask the support for unjust institutions (Geuss, 1981, 18–19). This should be taken, not in the sense of willful masquerading, but more in that of false consciousness. The actor is not aware that he holds certain oppressive beliefs, but if s/he were somehow made aware of it, s/he recognizes and, perhaps, no longer retains these beliefs (Geuss, 1981, 19). The third set of characteristics of ideological captivity refers to the origins of a set of beliefs, in the sense that the actor could not very well acknowledge these on pain of losing legitimacy (Geuss, 1981, 21). Ideology critique is, thus, explicitly tied to the falsity of the beliefs a person holds. Someone may be captive in that s/he is unable or unwilling to step out of her/his system of beliefs and judgments, but the analyst occupies a firm position in an alternative and more just or legitimate system of values and beliefs from which s/he is able to demonstrate the falsity of the actor's position.

Critical Discourse Analysis (CDA) is an example of ideology critique (Fairclough, 1992, 2001). The purpose of CDA is to reveal the common-sense frameworks in a text that disguise their ideological content but do so in a way that makes the text seem natural, self-evident. The analysis proceeds from an alternative position that enables the analyst to see the taken-for-granted position in the text in a contrasting light. An example will clarify my point. In our study of prostitution policy we analyzed media coverage of prostitution in the Netherlands (Goraj, 2012; Wagenaar et al., 2013). We analyzed all articles on prostitution in two major Dutch newspapers between 2000 and 2010. In practically all instances prostitution was described in negative terms. It was consistently associated with crime, described as out of control, while sex workers were depicted as victims of trafficking. What was interesting about the analysis were the mechanisms by which these images were naturalized. Goraj unearthed a number of such mechanisms: (1) vague quantifiers, such as 'mostly,' 'very big', 'often', 'large groups', or 'between 50 and 90 per cent' that conveyed that it was a large problem without having to report exact figures; (2) generalizing from single case descriptions (one horrific story of trafficking was described in graphic detail and generalized to the total population of sex workers); (3) the consistent use of negative terms to describe prostitution ('victims', 'slavery', 'addiction', 'serious crime', 'Sodom and Gomorrah'); and (4) mixing genres. Fairclough calls the latter *intertextuality*. Its function is to interpret and explain an issue by putting it into the context of a discourse that people are familiar with, or to increase the emotional intensity of the description. In newspaper reporting on prostitution we noticed that the genre of the news report was combined with that of the crime novel (with its graphic description of violence: 'Captive works for pittance in escort hell') and pornography (with its detailed description of sexual acts). By contrasting this image of prostitution as a problem of trafficking with the self-reports of sex workers, the low numbers of sex workers and victims, and the positive descriptions in some feminist literature, it was fairly straightforward to reveal the trafficking framework as a social construction.

According to Owen, aspectival captivity differs from ideological captivity in that it is independent of the falsity of the beliefs of the agents. Owen breaks this down in a number of characteristics. First, aspectival captivity refers to 'a system of judgments in terms of which our being-in-the-world takes on its intelligible character' (Owen, 2003, 89). This system of judgments, second, acts as a kind of necessary background to our moving about in the world (see also Taylor, 1995a; Cook and Wagenaar, 2012). It determines what can be considered true, or false, intelligible or unintelligible. It consists of tacit prejudgments that are integral to our acting in the world (Wagenaar, 2004). Third, the value of the world-picture is dependent upon its capacity to successfully guide our reflections and actions in ways that matter to us. Fourth, as so much of this is grounded in embodied practices and formed of tacit understanding and prejudgments that make more conscious judgment possible, we cannot easily reorient or even reflect on this form of captivity. These discernments reside in the background, they make certain actions and judgments possible, and they are activated when we feel compelled to act on the situation at hand (Wagenaar, 2004). Cook and Wagenaar call this 'ongoing business' which they describe as the intersubjective, embodied, experiential landscape in which actors who are engaged with a particular task move about. It is the 'stuff that is expected to be there' to make both the execution of the task as well as the sequence of judgments that precede and accompany the successful execution of the task, possible (Cook and Wagenaar, 2012). Owen does not spell this out, but in relation to ideological captivity, aspectival captivity has a more fundamental character as it is the 'mother code' that makes our effective functioning in society possible.

The distinction between aspectival and ideological captivity points towards different kinds of critical analysis. Contrary to ideology critique we cannot call our perspective into question so easily because we do not have ready access to an external, Archimedean point from which to assess this embodied life form. We are locked up, as it were, inside our system of judgments because it has colonized our collective consciousness. It has entrenched itself in our everyday language, imaginaries and practices, to the point that we are not even aware of the extent of our captivity. Our practices and judgments are so intertwined that it gives the whole aspectival edifice tremendous tenacity; to question one element has hardly any effect on the tangle of others that are implicated. Even if we harbor a sense of unease about some of our judgments or practices, we cannot very well question them because we cannot imagine a viable alternative that would help us to articulate our discomfort and dislodge our impaired judgments or practices – or, more precisely, to arrive at the point that we begin to recognize them as impaired. Alternative ways of talking, thinking and acting are effectively closed off. In a recent study of neoliberalism the historian Philip Mirowski illustrates the power of this kind of captivity. For many critics neoliberalism is a doctrine or ideology (Harvey, 2005) that is characterized by among other things a belief in a small state, the commodification of ever larger spheres of life, deregulation of financial markets, flexibilization of the labor market, and market exchange as an ethical system. However, by characterizing neoliberalism as a doctrine or political program we cannot very well explain why it has not been rejected wholesale by the public after the financial crash of 2008, or worse, that it has entrenched itself even more than before the meltdown as the major political-intellectual program for explaining and clearing the economic crisis. It also doesn't explain the hapless and futile efforts of Social-Democratic parties to gain any political advantage in the wake of the economic debacle. Mirowski argues that we need to see beyond the programmatic and doctrinaire aspects of neoliberalism and start to see it as a mentality that is deeply ingrained in our everyday life:

> The tenacity of neoliberal doctrines that might have otherwise been refuted at every turn since 2008 has to be rooted in the extent to which a kind of 'folk' or 'everyday' neoliberalism has sunk so deeply into the cultural consciousness that even a few rude shocks can't begin to bring it to the surface long enough to provoke discomfort. (Mirowski, 2013, 89)

Neoliberalism has now pervaded our culture to the point that it defines what it is to be a person or agent. Neoliberalism is the 'ongoing business' of our everyday life as employees, parents, citizens, children, spouses and leisure seekers (Cook and Wagenaar, 2012). It occupies our motivations, explanations, values, images, ambitions and justifications. Or, as Mirowski puts it:

> The fragmentation of the neoliberal self begins when the agent is brought face to face with the realization that she is not just an employee or student, but also simultaneously a product to be sold, a walking advertisement, a manager of her résumé, a biographer of her rationales, and an entrepreneur of her possibilities. She has to somehow manage to be simultaneously subject, object, and spectator. She is perforce *not* learning about who she really is, but rather, provisionally buying the person she must soon become. She is all at once the business, the raw material, the product, the clientele, and the customer of her own life. She is a jumble of assets to be invested, nurtured, managed and developed; but equally an offsetting inventory of liabilities to be pruned, outsourced, shorted, hedged, against, and minimized . . . This kind of everyday wisdom is so pervasive that one tends to notice it only in cases of extreme parody . . . (Mirowski, 2013, 108)

I cite Mirowsky at some length to give the reader a flavor of the sheer permeation of aspectival captivity. This goes far beyond the notion of an ideology or belief system. This is hegemony in its most advanced, beguiling form where even identity has been invaded and consciousness anesthetized. This is both a state of mind and a way of life that is so omnipresent that, even if we allowed ourselves a sense of unease to surface about where this all leads to, we would be at a loss to think of an alternative. We are deep inside Plato's cave of aspectival captivity. How, then, does one escape this kind of ubiquitous perspectivism? What does it mean to be critical in these instances in which, in the language of Foucault, the power relations that underlie the image are not disclosed by the image (Owen, 2003, 94)?

In philosophical terms the problem is one of non-foundationalism. Non-foundationalism is 'any epistemology that rejects appeals to a basic ground or foundation of knowledge in either pure experience or pure reason' (Bevir and Rhodes, 2010, 43). Instead, knowledge is always perspectivist. We don't have access to an immutable, preverbal or moral reality. Instead, whatever we perceive as facts are always facts under a particular description that selects and organizes our observations (Fay, 1996, 72–74). For this reason knowledge is also provisional; there is no final arbiter or external vantage point (brute facts, pure reason, superior values or perfect method) for determining the truth of a statement, and what is considered true today might require revision tomorrow. And while this is a widely accepted position in 20th-century philosophy, the social sciences have only just begun to grapple with its methodological consequences. To rephrase the question I put before: What does it mean to be critical in a perspectivist, non-foundational sense?

Non-foundational critical analysis is not unlike the methodological program of governmentality. The term 'governmentality' refers both to a theory of dispersed governing in liberal societies and a methodological program to study this type of governing. The governmentality literature has developed into two broad research agendas. The first concerns, what Rose and Miller call, 'political rationalities'. This line of inquiry focuses on the way that programs of government are formulated within broad discourses of collective truth, proper ruling and moral justification. Concretely, the approach inquires into the conceptualization of governmental power: how government officials determine how best to rule, and what concepts and legitimations they invent and deploy that make subjects governable. This is more or less straightforward discourse analysis. The second line of inquiry concerns not the mentalities of government but the technologies through which it tries to achieve its ends, the plethora of techniques that are deployed to put governmental rationalities into effect. Rose and Miller describe these technologies as the 'complex of mundane programmes, calculations, techniques, apparatuses, documents and procedures that act on the subjects of governance, to coerce, persuade, cajole, suggest, or goad them to behave in certain preferred ways' (1992, 175). These dispersed micro-practices then connect and aggregate in complex, only partly intentional, contingent, ways into formal state projects at the various levels of government (MacKinnon, 2000, 311).

However, this type of analysis, important as it is, merely lays the groundwork for a truly anti-foundational critical approach that is also aimed at transformation. The political theorist James Tully puts this point as follows:

> a genuinely critical political philosophy requires a second type of critique that enables participants to free themselves from the horizons of the practices and problematizations; to see them as one form of practice and one form of problematization that can be compared critically with others, and so to go on to consider the possibilities of thinking and acting differently. (2008, 31)

To get a perspective on viable alternatives to our aspectual captivity Tully suggests that we engage in historical and genealogical analysis: a historical survey of the emergence of our present political thought, and a genealogical survey of the emergence of our present political and economic institutions and practices. Polanyi's magisterial study of the emergence of the market and its subsequent imposition upon pre-market societies (Polanyi, 2001 [1944]), or Mirowski's historical analysis of the emergence of the 'Neoliberal Thought Collective' and its subsequent influence on all realms of collective and private life (2013, 73) are examples of the latter.

How is this double approach of discourse analysis and history of the present critical? The cognitive, moral and practical confinement that is intrinsic to aspectival captivity compromises our capacity for free, unfettered judgment and self-government. Genealogical analysis, as Owen puts it, 'motivates us, in terms of our commitment to self-government, to engage in the practical task of overcoming this condition of unfreedom. It does this through redirecting our political subjectivity towards experiments with altering our games of government to minimize the degree of domination within them' (2003, 95). In other words, genealogical analysis addresses, in a non-foundational way, both the question of how we sense that something is amiss and needs to be addressed, and the question of how to imagine, design and implement viable alternatives. I want to emphasize three aspects of non-foundational critical analysis that are central for its critical stance: it stretches beyond the academy in involving stakeholders and ordinary citizens, it is performative in that it proceeds though engaging in various practices, and it is thoroughly dialogical. The aim of non-foundational analysis is not just to analyze but also to change, to transform. Before I discuss these aspects of critical policy analysis I first need to introduce some of the basics of dialogical analysis.

4. THE CRITICAL FUNCTIONS OF DIALOGICAL POLICY ANALYSIS: TRANSFORMING PEOPLE AND SITUATIONS

Dialogical policy analysis is predicated on dialogical meaning. As Fay puts it: 'meaning arises out of the relationship between an act and those trying to understand it – it is the product of an interaction of two subjects' (1996, 142). Dialogical policy analysis is based on the philosophical hermeneutics of the German philosopher Hans-Georg Gadamer. Although it shares a noun with classical hermeneutics, philosophical hermeneutics is a different animal altogether. It differs in two respects from classical hermeneutics. First, it regards the act of understanding less as a form of reflection than an active achievement that involves more than one actor. Second, it sees the outcome of understanding not only as enlightenment and increased awareness, but above all as transformation, both of the actors and the situation at hand. In this sense policy analysis based on dialogical meaning transcends the analytic bias that characterizes the other two types of IPA. It would go beyond the purpose of this chapter to summarize Gadamer's remarkably sophisticated philosophy (see Fay, 1996, 142–147; Wagenaar, 2011, 195–208); for the purposes of exploring what it means to be critical in a dialogical sense I will focus on the key concepts of 'dialogue' and 'fusion of horizons'.

Gadamer develops his argument around the notion of distance. He sees distance, between people or between people and the world, as a kind of ontological starting point of the human situation. Think of people who have different perspectives on an issue, or who have different interests, who have an ideological conflict, or who are thoroughly puzzled by a natural or social phenomenon. Gadamer chooses historical distance and understanding as his example. Historical events that confound us enter our awareness and thus subtly broaden our horizon. But, at the same time, we understand things from our own point of view. By trying to understand something we inevitably 'add' something of our own to that that we attempt to grasp. Gadamer in fact extends the idea of ideographic knowledge to the person observing: what *I* perceive and understand will, inevitably, be different from what *you* perceive and understand. However this does not mean that we are locked into our own perspective and that our interpretations are wholly subjective. Not only do we add something to the object of our understanding; the reverse is also true. By engaging with an object that we attempt to understand we allow that object to reveal its significance for us (Fay, 1996, 143). Gadamer expresses this with his key concept of 'fusion of horizons'. Although both we and the object of our interpretations are locked inside a perspective or horizon, the act of understanding brings them together in a way in which the tensions between the two are maintained. Interpreters never simply read themselves into the object of interpretation. Instead:

> The interaction of the interpreter with the interpreted elicits from the interpreted various dimensions of meaning which become evident as it is placed in a new historical [or cultural] setting. Interpretation involves new reservoirs of (potential) meaning hidden from those in other historical moments ... In this it is the interpreted speaking to interpreters in their own tongue, not the interpreters speaking of themselves using the interpreted as a mere stimulus for their own self-enclosed conversation. (Fay, 1996, 144. See also Wagenaar, 2011, 204)

This is an accurate description of what happens in dialogue, but it can easily be misconstrued as overly intentional. When we set out to engage in a dialogue, we become aware of the limits of our perspective, and we broaden our perspective to embrace the formerly alien point of view of the other. But this is not what Gadamer wants to convey. His goal is both ontological and practical. His purpose is to formulate an ontology of ordinary understanding as a philosophical basis for the human sciences. For Gadamer understanding and dialogue are more possibilities of being than intentional, let alone instrumental, acts. Understanding/dialogue happens *to* us as much as we engage in it. Dialogue is as much a disposition as an act. Clearly, at all times we can engage in deliberate acts of systematic interpretation or carefully executed dialogues between contending parties, but Gadamer's point is that these intentional, methodical versions of understanding and dialogue are made possible, that is, they have a chance to succeed at all, because of the underlying process of understanding and dialogue as a mode of being.

Gadamer's philosophical hermeneutics suggests in what ways dialogical policy analysis is critical. First, understanding is always a shared enterprise. We do not understand, in the more encompassing sense of knowing who we are and what our role and position in the world is and should be, as detached autonomous minds but always in interaction with others. As Patsy Healey puts it:

> (T)he flow of life is not lived in the splendid isolation of the autonomous individual but in social contexts in which what it means to be a human individual and what it means to live in a 'polity' are in continuous formation. Facts and values, means and ends, analysis and ethics, problems and solutions, are as much discovered in these social contexts as they are preformed and a priori. (Healey, 2009, 3)

Second, we need dialogue when communication has broken down. Breakdown has many grounds: mutual distrust; the projection of misguided or mistaken ideas upon the other party; real grievances; conflict over uncertainty and ambiguity of knowledge; the arrogance and insensitivity of power. Such breakdowns function as moments of critical choice when simultaneously we become aware that the situation needs improvement (although we might have little idea what to do), of the limits of the situation, and of the perspectives of the actors involved, including ourselves. Third, this form of dialogue does not just happen through talk but also through acting on the situation at hand, through moving about in the world and learning from its 'backtalk' when we intervene (Pickering, 1995). Fourth, the performative nature of understanding in situations of communicative breakdown implies that this kind of 'conversation' is not only aimed at grasping a situation but also, and always, at transforming it, at finding accommodations, workable solutions and possibilities for change. In fact, the very notion of understanding in a dialogical situation implies that both parties have been able to find or design a better alternative that is grounded in their shared diagnosis of the problematic situation. All this is implicated for example in John Forester's notion of critical pragmatism:

> A 'critical pragmatism' . . . has to address actual possibilities – what we might really do – in situations characterized by deep distrust and suspicion, deep differences of interests and values, a good deal of fear and, often, anger, poor or poorly distributed information, and more. A critical pragmatism would not have to talk about 'power', but to explore power relations practically. (2013, 6–7)

Or, as Healey describes the pragmatist tradition in planning: '(D)ewey and Forester are both much more focused on the transformative potentials in practices, how to act in "little ways" to change perceptions, understandings, modes of practice, so that different outcomes become possible and different political cultures gather momentum' (2009, 8). The critical potential of dialogical policy analysis resides in the fostering of social hope and human potential (Healey, 2009, 2).

5.   INTERPRETIVE POLICY ANALYSIS AND DEMOCRACY

Interpretive policy analysis is not critical by default. Its critical function is as much an act of will as an epistemic property. To realize the different critical functions of interpretive policy analysis that are contained inside its unique epistemological DNA requires the patient, systematic and skilled application of the various interpretive approaches. It requires careful attention to the empirical world and the micropolitics of policy and planning, the acknowledgement of the practical experiences of a wide range of actors, the willingness to trace power by the way it realizes itself in shaping relationships, a tolerance for unfair and hostile criticism by power elites, and the hard work of synthesizing all this into a compelling account of the situation at hand and its possibilities for change. In actual practice this does not always happen. Too often we encounter articles in which the author 'explains' a policy controversy by organizing it into a number of 'frames' or 'story lines'. Or, in which the author presents a discourse analysis that is little more than a summary of the different positions in a national policy debate. Or when, under the banner of poststructuralist analysis, we are served yet another fiery analysis of the five or ten or 13 characteristics of neoliberalism, written from the safe position of a taken-for-granted emancipatory position. Like EPA, IPA can be inept and fatuous.

The purpose of this chapter, however, is to demonstrate the unique critical potential of IPA, to show that the epistemological properties of IPA allow it to be critical in different, important ways from traditional, empiricist policy analysis. In summary form, to be interpretively critical means (1) understanding actors from their own point of view, (2) uncovering the taken-for-granted frameworks of thinking, feeling and acting over which actors have little control but which influence their behavior, (3) to explore and transform our practical and cognitive horizons by engaging with our adversaries (see also Fay, 1975, 93–94). The ever-evolving association between interpretation, dialogue, knowledge and social practice suggests a convincing understanding of 'critical' in interpretivism in the real-world context of political strife and policy controversy. As we are aware, knowledge claims are rarely straightforwardly tied to the satisfaction of political purpose and human needs. For such claims to be authoritative, they need to be subjected to a process of deliberation. I therefore prefer to cast the term 'critical' as an epistemological and ethical relationship between interpretivism and democracy. I do not have in mind here traditional institutionalized liberal democracy where state actors initiate and implement public policy and to whose power policy analysis is meant to speak truth. Rather I refer to more decentered and participatory forms of governance.

For large classes of collective problems – wicked, complex, non-routine problems with a large potential for contingent spillover effects – states simply do not have the wherewithal to design and put through effective solutions. In such cases the challenge is to bring together and sustain over considerable periods of time coalitions of stakeholders, including grass-roots involvement (Stone, 1997, 315; de Souza Briggs, 2008). And, although the state plays an important role in such coalitions, more often than not the impetus for their formation originates in the civil sphere, outside the realm of government. Differently put, in decentered settings democratic inclusion has become intrinsic to effective governance. In fact, effective governance and public administration in complex, fragmented policy environments is seen to rest on four pillars: inclusive collaboration, democratic legitimacy ('meaningful and consequential participation in public life'), effectiveness (getting things done; having an impact) and accountability ('the need to rethink accountability relationships in the context of community leadership') (de Souza Briggs, 2008, 34; Forester, 2009, Ansell and Gash, 2007). In practice that means that democracy today consists of highly pluralistic and fluid ensembles of actors organized around concrete societal problems, often uncomfortably positioned in relation to the traditional institutional structures of liberal representative democracy. It is within these complex and shifting environments of democratic governance that the critical potential of IPA can best be realized.

The critical potential of IPA can be regarded as a philosophical argument for democracy. By being carefully attentive to rich empirical detail in the face of recalcitrant experience and argument, by restoring and giving voice to the lived experience of different actors affected by political decisions, in particular the disadvantaged and the powerless, and by being attentive to the ethical dimensions that are embedded in concrete choices, IPA can be seen as furthering collaborative forms of policy making; setting up dialogues of practice and argument that are as inclusive as possible. In this way IPA not only contributes to deepening democracy, but also lives up to its core ethical principle of changing societal conditions that exclude or prevent groups of people from flourishing.

NOTES

1. I deliberately use the language of critical theory here because I believe that standard hermeneutic analysis provides an important critical methodology. Interestingly, hermeneutic analysis never figured prominently in the methods that were recommended by critical theorists. On the contrary. Critical theorists such as Habermas were wary of hermeneutics, as they suspected it, as Habermas argued in his famous debate with Gadamer, of merely affirming unreflective tradition (Gadamer, 1975; McCarthy, 1978, 187–193). Habermas, who was deeply influenced by historical materialism, modeled critical theory after the social evolutionary theories that were the gold standard for explanation in Marxism. His form of critical theory was a diachronic, proto-genealogical analysis of oppressive ideological structures (McCarthy, 1978, 268). Habermas also saw a place for what he called a practical 'developmental-logical specification of the present level of social organization' (McCarthy, 1978, 266), but, apart from rather vague indications such as 'counterfactually projected reconstruction', he leaves that largely unspecified. Critical theory, thus, develops along lines of diachronic analysis at the expense of more empirically informed synchronic analysis of the meaning of social phenomena through the authentic voice of the 'oppressed' group.
2. The full quote is: '[H]owever well equipped our language, it can never be forearmed against all possible cases that may arise and call for description: fact is richer than diction' (John Austin's *Philosophical Papers*, 1970, 195). The quote was kindly suggested to me by John Forester.
3. The other types of ideology he distinguishes are 'ideology in the descriptive sense' and 'ideology in the positive sense'. The first refers to the beliefs, attitudes, values, rituals and so forth of a people. The second refers to a deliberately adopted set of goals, aspirations and desires to further the particular ends of a group. Both of these forms of ideology might lead to the exclusion or suppression of certain groups, and can thus be the subject of *Ideologiekritik*.

REFERENCES

Abbot, A. (2004). *Methods of Discovery. Heuristics for the Social Sciences.* New York: W.W. Norton & Company.

Ansell, C. and Gash, A. (2007). 'Collaborative governance in theory and practice', *Journal of Public Administration Research and Theory*, **18**, 543–571.

Austin, J.L. (1970). *Philosophical Papers*. Oxford: Oxford University Press.
Bevir, M. and Rhodes, R. (2010). *The State as Cultural Practice*. Oxford: Oxford University Press.
Cho, S.-Y., Dreher, A. and Neumayer, E. (2013). 'Does legalized prostitution increase human trafficking?', *World Development*, **41**, 67–82.
Cook, S.D.N. and Wagenaar, H. (2012). 'Navigating the eternally unfolding present; toward an epistemology of practice', *American Review of Public Administration*, **42** (1), 3–38
de Souza Briggs, X. (2008), *Democracy as Problem Solving: Civic Capacity in Communities Across the Globe*. Cambridge, MA: The MIT Press.
Edelman, M. (1988). *Constructing the Political Spectacle*. Chicago, IL: The University of Chicago Press.
Fairclough, N. (1992). *Discourse and Social Change*. Cambridge: Polity Press.
Fairclough, N. (2001). *Language and Power*, Harlow, UK: Pearson Education.
Fay, B. (1975). *Social Theory and Political Practice*. London: George Allen & Unwin.
Fay, B. (1996). *Contemporary Philosophy of Social Science*. Malden, MA: Blackwell Publishing.
Forester, J. (2009). *Dealing with Differences. Dramas of Mediating Public Disputes*. Oxford: Oxford University Press.
Forester, J. (2013). 'On the theory and practice of critical pragmatism: deliberative practice and creative negotiations', *Planning Theory*, **12** (1), 5–22.
Gadamer, H.G. (1975). *Truth and Method*. London: Continuum.
Geuss, R. (1981). *The Idea of a Critical Theory. Habermas and the Frankfurt School*. Cambridge: Cambridge University Press.
Goraj, J. (2012). 'The influence of media on society's perception of prostitution. Critical discourse analysis of the Dutch media on prostitution in the years 2011, 2009 and 2000'. Unpublished Masters thesis, University of Leiden, Department of Public Administration.
Hajer, M. and Wagenaar, H. (2003). 'Editors' introduction', in M. Hajer and H. Wagenaar (eds), *Deliberative Policy Analysis: Understanding Governance in the Network Society*, Cambridge: Cambridge University Press, pp. 1–30.
Harvey, D. (2005). *A Brief History of Neoliberalism*, Oxford: Oxford University Press.
Healey, P. (2009). 'The pragmatic tradition in planning thought', *Journal of Planning Education and Research*, **28**, 277–292.
Hofmann, J. (1995). 'Implicit theories in policy discourse; an inquiry into the interpretations of reality in German technology policy', *Policy Sciences*, **28** (2), 127–148.
MacKinnon, D. (2000). 'Managerialism, governmentality, and the state: a neo-Foucauldian approach to local economic governance', *Political Geography*, **19**, 293–314.
McCarthy, T. (1978). *The Critical Theory of Jürgen Habermas*, Cambridge, MA: The MIT Press.
Mirowski, P. (2013). *Never Let a Serious Crisis Go to Waste. How Neoliberalism Survived the Financial Meltdown*. London: Verso.
Owen, D. (2003). 'Genealogy as perspicuous representation', in C.J. Heyes (ed.), *The Grammar of Politics. Wittgenstein and Political Philosophy*. Ithaca, NY: Cornell University Press, pp. 82–99.
Pickering, A. (1995). *The Mangle of Practice. Time, Agency and Science*. Chicago, IL: The University Of Chicago Press.
Polanyi, K. (2001 [1944]). *The Great Transformation. The Political and Economic Origins of our Times*. Boston, MA: Beacon Press.
Prainsack B. and Wahlberg, A. (2013). 'Situated bio-regulation: ethnographic sensibility at the interface of STS, policy studies and the social studies of medicine', *BioSocieties*, **8**, 336–359.
Rose, N. and Miller, P. (1992). 'Political power beyond the state: problematics of government', *British Journal of Sociology*, **43** (2), 173–205.
Stone, D. (1997). *Policy Paradox. The Art of Political Decision Making*. New York: W.W. Norton & Company.
Taylor, C. (1995a). *To Follow a Rule . . . Philosophical Arguments*. Cambridge, MA: Harvard University Press, 165–181.

Taylor, C. (1995b). *Lichtung or Lebensform: Parallels between Heidegger and Wittgenstein. Philosophical Arguments.* Cambridge, MA: Harvard University Press, 61–79.

Tully, J. (2008). *Public Philosophy in a New Key, Volume 1: Democracy and Civic Freedom.* Cambridge: Cambridge University Press.

von Wright, G.H. (1971). *Explanation and Understanding.* Ithaca, NY: Cornell University Press.

Wagenaar, H. (2004). '"Knowing" the rules: administrative work as practice', *Public Administration Review,* **64** (6), 643–655.

Wagenaar, H. (2011). *Meaning in Action: Interpretation and Dialogue in Policy Analysis.* Armonk, NY: M.E. Sharpe.

Wagenaar, H., Altink, S. and Amesberger, H. (2013). *Final Report of the International Comparative study of Prostitution Policy,* The Hague: Platform 31.

Weiss, R.S. (1994). *Learning from Strangers. The Art and Method of Qualitative Interview Studies.* New York: Free Press.

23 Between representation and narration: analysing policy frames
Kathrin Braun

So, too, there are occasions when we must wait until things are almost over
before discovering what has been occurring and occasions of our own activity
when we can considerably put off deciding what to claim we have been doing.
(Erving Goffman)

INTRODUCTION

Frames and framing have become well-established concepts in the social
sciences, now referred to by an increasing number of papers, books and
articles. In policy studies particularly, frame analysis has been part of an
intellectual movement that set out in the early 1990s to challenge the dominant technocratic, empiricist orientation in the field. Critics contend that
empiricism neglects some of the most essential dimensions of politics and
policy making, namely language, values, normative judgements, ideas and
struggle over meaning, and thus misses the point of what politics is actually about (Fischer 2003; Hajer and Laws 2006; Wagenaar 2011; Braun
2014). So, some four decades since the publication of Erving Goffman's
Frame Analysis, from whence the introductory quotation is taken (1974,
2), it may be time to apply the invitation to frame analysis itself and consider 'what to claim we have been doing' when doing frame analysis.

This chapter argues that the concept of frame can be useful from a critical policy studies perspective in that it may serve to make visible dominant
policy frames that operate as part of larger patterns of domination. Frame
analysis, thus, may open up a space for exposing relations of inequality,
exclusion, domination and power, to reconstruct social movements' struggle for social justice and democratic participation and thereby contribute
to critical policy analysis in this sense. Yet, this chapter will argue, the
concept of frame is not 'critical' in and of itself. It can be used in different
ways, some of which remain within more empiricist or technocratic overall
frameworks. Whether approaches to frame and framing are critical in the
above-mentioned sense depends on how, to which end and within which
larger framework they are employed and which normative commitments
underlie these larger frameworks. In short, this chapter suggests, the value

of the frame concept for critical policy studies is a matter of interpretation; it hinges on how we interpret 'frame' and how we interpret 'critical'.

In policy studies, frame analysis received a major impetus from Donald Schön and Martin Rein's *Frame Reflection* (Schön and Rein 1994). To speak of frame analysis as one major approach in policy studies today, however, would be misleading as there is no single, definitive methodological approach involving the concepts of frame and framing but rather an array of approaches that use these concepts in different ways. Critical policy scholars, over the past two decades, tended to emphasize the commonalities among different uses of the frame concept and its distinctiveness in relation to empiricist approaches rather than the differences. Now that the concepts of frame and framing have become widely established in policy studies, however, it might be time to look into the varieties and differences concerning overall purposes, research objectives, methodology, and research practices. This chapter does not attempt to present a comprehensive overview of all work referring to the frame concept in policy studies; the literature is too vast to do so. Rather, it seeks to point out some divergences within the field. As with any critical concept in politics and the policy sciences, concepts of frame and framing have multiple meanings, and frame analysis, accordingly, may mean very different things. One of the divergences concerning the nature of research practices and possible outcomes is the divergence between a representational model that strives to yield a correct depiction of a segment of social reality and a participational model that strives to yield a plausible narration of what has been going on.

In terms of definitions, interestingly, these differences are not immediately evident. On the contrary, there seems to be quite a homogeneous answer to the question of what frames 'are'; scholars from different subject areas and disciplines have defined 'frame' in similar ways. An early definition by Todd Gitlin still sets the tone. For Gitlin, 'frames are principles of selection, emphasis and presentation composed of little tacit theories about what exists, what happens, and what matters' (Gitlin 1980, 6). Scholars in policy studies put the emphasis more strongly on the practical dimension; thus for Schön and Rein, frames are 'underlying structures of belief, perception, and appreciation' which 'select for attention a few salient features and relations from what would otherwise be an overwhelming complex reality' (Schön and Rein 1994, 23, 26).

Frames are understood to give a coherent organization to these features and relations, describe what is wrong about a certain situation as well as what needs fixing, and thereby hint at what is to be done. A frame is, in short, 'a perspective from which an amorphous, ill-defined, problematic situation can be made sense of and acted on' (Rein and Schön 1993, 146).

Concepts of frame have become increasingly popular in policy studies in recent years. Yet, while definitions of the concept converge widely, scholars do very different things when they do 'frame analysis'. Now, if it is the use of a word which actually gives the word its meaning, as Bevir and Rhodes (2010, 66) argue following Wittgenstein, a convergence of definition may well concur with a divergence of meaning. This chapter will look at four predominant ways of using the term in the literature, namely *frames as explanatory factor, frames as narrative, frames as resource,* and *frames as ideology.* In connection with these different understandings, I will make another distinction concerning the way frame analysis is actually done and what kind of results it may or may not yield. That is the distinction between representational and participational approaches. The former see frames basically as mental entities and aspire to arrive at as accurate as possible a representation of these entities through frame analysis. For the latter, frames are located in interaction, which inevitably takes place in time, and the purpose of frame analysis is to provide as plausible as possible an account of what has been going on. In order to understand the difference, it is worthwhile to take a fresh look at Erving Goffman's classic work, *Frame Analysis.*

'NOT MERELY A MATTER OF MIND': FRAMES IN GOFFMAN'S *FRAME ANALYSIS*

Most explications of the frame concept begin with a ritual reference to Goffman's 1974 *Frame Analysis* – and leave it there. It is worth noting though, that Goffman uses the frame concept in a manner different from most of the ensuing literature. Frames, for Goffman, are not conceived as cultural representations but as principles that organize experience and involvement. They are located in activity, not in text. They are of interest to sociologists because they determine the meaningfulness of an activity for the individual involved in it – not because they provide information about the individual's interests, preferences or identities 'behind' the frame. The key question for Goffman is: 'What is it that's going on here?' (Goffman 1974, 8). Importantly, that is first and foremost the key question for the individuals involved themselves, not only for the analyst. Put differently, the Goffmanian question is rooted in a participational perspective rather than one derived from representational epistemology.

Modern representational epistemology, as Taylor explains (Taylor 1995), starts from the notion of a disengaged, knowing subject who strives to provide a correct representation of an independent reality. In order to bridge the epistemological gap between the knowing subject and reality 'out there' and arrive at universally valid knowledge, the subject applies a neutral technique – a method – in order to see the object of study free from subjective distortions. Participational models, in contrast, start from the assumption that 'the mind participates in the being of the known object, rather than simply depicting it' (Taylor 1995, 3). The subject, conversely, is not taken for granted either but is taken as being affected, shaped, or defined by the interaction with social reality under study as well. Having a method may be helpful in allowing for recognition of what one is doing, but the quality and significance of outcomes does not hinge on the correct application of a neutral, formalized method since its neutralizing purpose is illusionary anyway.

Within the diverse field of frame analysis in social science and policy studies we find approaches that gravitate towards the representational model and approaches that gravitate towards the participational model. Both models have their merits and limitations, as will be argued here, but analysts should be clear which one they actually want to use. A problem arises when the participational model is judged against the standards of the representational model rather than on its own terms.

Goffman, as mentioned already, takes a participational perspective insofar as he locates frames, or frameworks (as he prefers to say) in interaction. Generally, frameworks are schemata of interpretation that are 'rendering what would otherwise be a meaningless aspect of the scene into something that is meaningful' (Goffman 1974, 21). Thus, ordinary citizens do perform frame analysis in everyday life. The analyst's mission is not to enlighten actors about the frameworks they find themselves in, but to systematize the different types of frameworks and how they operate in social life. Frameworks are about meaning and interpretation, which are firmly located in activity and involvement; they thus 'are not merely a matter of mind but correspond in some sense to the way in which an aspect of the activity itself is organized – especially activity directly involving social agents' (Goffman 1974, 247). In such a participational approach, the object of study is dynamic, not static or timeless. The relation of analyst and acting individuals is, moreover, not simply one between the knowing subject and the objects of study. Rather, both the analyst and the individuals studied are participants in a frame analysis community, albeit with different roles. All are trying to make out what is going on and what renders the activity meaningful. Such frame analysis does not hinge upon a formal method. It may be useful both for the analyst and for the individuals studied to vary perspectives: to look at things from a distance, or from different viewpoints, or in a more systematic way, and reflect on what one is doing. Since participants in interaction are engaged in frame analysis quite regularly, however, there is no need for a neutral intermediary instrument to bridge the gap between subject and object: there is no such gap.

From a policy studies perspective, the theoretical framework presented by Goffman does have its limitations, resulting largely from what Clifford Geertz called the game analogy (Geertz 1983, 33).[1] Based on a game analogy, Goffman's model focuses on face-to-face interactions in daily life. Fully-fledged, complex policy processes with aggregated interactions over long periods of time transcend the boundaries of this framework. Nonetheless, Goffman reminds us that frames are being *done* rather than being existent 'out there', that frames are not 'things' but activities. Goffman, therefore, is still highly relevant from a perspective of critical policy studies: his participation conception of frames may prevent us from reifying frames that had become dominant at some point in time. Additionally, it may invite us to engage with policy actors' perspectives, narratives and frame analytic capacities and treat them as participants in frame analysis rather than just passive objects of study.

FRAMING FRAMES: DIVERSIFICATION OF THE FRAME CONCEPT

Since the 1980s, the concepts of frame and framing have been employed across a range of disciplines and subject areas and have acquired a diversified set of meanings. In management and organizational studies, Kahneman and Tversky developed a behaviouralist, empiricist concept of framing as part of a formal decision theory they term prospect theory (Kahneman and Tversky 1979). Framing, here, denotes a phase of the decision process prior to and separate from valuation. Prospect theory holds that individuals' choices of action are strongly affected by the frame in which they were cast. The approach studies these effects under experimental conditions in order to establish empirical generalizations (Tversky and Kahneman 1992).

In linguistics and discourse analysis, in contrast, the concept of frame involves semiotics and social constructivism. Frames are construed as cognitive schemata that organize the way people perceive, interpret, organize and represent their knowledge of the world.[2] Frame analysis seeks to identify these hidden schemata by working its way from the surface of symbolic manifestations down to latent strata of texts and talk, employing what Wagenaar calls a representational epistemology of hermeneutic exegesis (Wagenaar 2011, 41). Frames are taken as cognitive entities that impact, if indirectly, people's thoughts, attitudes and behaviour. Hence, frames have an effect *on* action, they are not located *in* action.

In communication and media studies, the focus is more on framing *strategies* consciously exercised by media professionals (Gitlin 1980; Entman 1993; Scheufele 1999). In this vein, for Entman, '[t]o frame is to select some aspects of a perceived reality and make them more salient in a communicating text, in such a way as to promote a particular problem definition, causal interpretation, moral evaluation, and/or treatment recommendation' (Entman 1993, 52). Framing is a case of manipulative, strategic action deliberately deployed by actors. The task of frame analysis is to reconstruct the mechanisms and methods through which it is done and to detect the intentions, motives and purposes behind them. This is usually done through more or less formalized, qualitative or quantitative techniques of content analysis, applied to a well-defined selection of significant texts or text analogues.

A number of scholars in social movement studies have pursued a focus on selective representations (Gitlin 1980; Gamson and Modigliani 1989; Gamson 1995). For Gamson, media discourse produces selective representations of social issues, provides images and interpretations of what is at issue, obstructs and represses alternative views and so functions as a key site for the social construction of reality. To some extent, it may also form a site of framing competition, where social movements manage to challenge prevailing frames and offer alternative constructions. However, another approach to social movement theory, advanced by David Snow, Robert Benford and their associates, locates framing processes primarily in interaction, not in text or text analogues. Framing processes, they insist, should not be reduced to cognitive structures or mental schemata that would impact how individuals think or behave (Snow and Benford 2005, 207):

> Certainly, collective action frames are, in part, cognitive entities that aid interpretation and social action, but their essence, sociologically, resides in situated social interactions, that is, in the interpretive discussions and debates that social movement actors engage in among each other and in the framing contests that occur between movement actors and other parties . . .

Here, Snow and Benford also approach framing as strategic resource consciously deployed by actors.

Concepts of frames, framing or frame alignment – as developed in social movement theory – have proven increasingly useful in policy studies over the past 20 years. Policy scholars have applied these concepts to policy processes on the domestic, European, or international level. Research designs, however, vary greatly. A representational approach is, for instance, taken by Triandafyllidou and Foutio (1998) who studied the role of social movement organizations and institutional actors in

European environmental and transport policy. Their study aimed to show 'how social actors re-define policy options and promote solutions that are favourable to their interests and/or views through framing sustainability and sustainable mobility in different ways' (Triandafyllidou and Foutio 1998, 3.4). The authors used a formalized coding scheme to analyse interviews with key actors in these policy areas, scanning the interviews for occurrences of specific frames.

Frame analysis in this approach serves as a method that is supposed to guarantee rigour, reliability and validity of outcome. The privileged status of method here is indicative of a representational epistemology that strives to arrive at as accurate as possible a representation of social reality assumed to exist independently of the analyst. Johnston (1995) has pointedly argued this position. Confronting the accusation that too much loose interpretation was going on in frame analysis, as elsewhere in cultural analysis, he suggested micro-frame analysis as a systematic methodological strategy to determine mental structures of social movement participants within specific examples of written text or bounded speech. As with other calls for more systematic, rigorous techniques of frame analysis (Maher 2001; König 2005), his call bespeaks an equation of frame analysis and textual analysis that tends to reduce policy processes to authored texts (see also Lejano and Park, Chapter 15, this volume).

Systematic, formalized, micrological analysis of bounded speech or text may yield more reliable, intersubjectively valid results in terms of frame identification, measurement and validation. Yet, there is a price to pay: frame analysis becomes a rather static and microscopic affair and, additionally, brings about a methodological reiteration of what is already assumed to be known. König (2005), for instance, maintains that '[n]o matter which interpretative devices are used, the analyst should try to avoid creating a new set of frames for every study. Instead, interpretation should be guided by already established masterframes' (König 2005). Yet, if the relevant masterframes have been established already, why bother? Moreover, policy processes are moving targets, unfolding in time, demanding that the analyst be prepared to deal with puzzles s/he could not foresee and adjust her/his concepts, questions and categories as s/he goes. Although the adjustment may compromise the type of reliability to be gained from the application of preselected categories, the approach might enable us to find out something we did not already know.

Clearly, as suggested earlier, frame analysis cannot be reduced to one definitive approach or method in policy studies, but is rather a bundle of partly quite disparate approaches. For taxonomic purposes, I distinguish four main approaches to frame analysis in order to examine 'what the practitioners of it do' (Geertz 2000, 5), what kind of effort they undertake and to what end. I will now examine each of these four approaches in turn: frames as explanatory factors, frames as narratives, frames as resources and frames as ideology.

FRAMES AS EXPLANATORY FACTORS: EXPANDING EMPIRICIST FRAMEWORKS IN POLICY STUDIES

One approach uses concepts of frame and framing primarily as factors by which to explain policy outcomes. Studies along these lines seek to expand the empiricist epistemology to include cognitive factors such as frames, values and ideas, which are conceptualized as one set of factors among others (e.g. Daviter 2007). Drawing on literatures that emphasize the role of cognitive elements in social life, such as social constructivism, the new institutionalism(s), the advocacy coalition framework or social movement theory, a growing number of policy scholars have promoted such an ideational perspective on policy processes and policy outcomes over the past 20 years and have employed, among other concepts, those of frame and framing to examine how the definition of political issues affects agenda setting, policy formation or institution building. Although they do assign meaning a crucial role within the policy process, the approach does not fundamentally differ from empiricist enquiries in that it uses hypotheses, factors, variables and hypothesis-testing in attempting to establish causal explanations. The analyst is asked to take an observer's – not a participant's – point of view and to refrain from subjective judgements or practical intervention.

A growing number of studies in recent years have, for example, utilized concepts of frame and framing to investigate EU-level policy processes, arguing that policy framing is particularly relevant in contexts typified by ambiguity, complexity, crisis or uncertainty – as is often the case with EU structures. Conventional approaches such as rational choice theory, neo-functionalism, or neorealist intergovernmentalism, these authors argue, cannot sufficiently explain how institution-building or policy formation did, after all, occur in situations where the nature of the policy concern, the competence of institutions, or the institutional prospects of the whole polity were unclear or contested. Policy outcomes, such as the creation of a single market (Fligstein and Mara-Drita 1996), a particular market for electricity (Nylander 2001), a particular market for defence equipment (Mörth 2000), or a European direct tax policy (Radaelli 1999), did not result from political pressure exercised by the most powerful actors, as rational choice theory and neorealist intergovernmentalism would suggest, nor from increased levels of transnational activity as neofunction-alism would have it. Rather, these authors contend, it was a transforma-tion of policy frames that crucially affected the dynamics at play, making preference alignment and coalition formation more amenable to conflict management and agreement (Eberlein and Radaelli 2010). Policy frames are here taken as cognitive variables that serve to fill in explanatory gaps left by other theoretical approaches.

Studies that have examined policy frames from an advocacy coalition framework or a social movement theory perspective differ from a rational choice perspective in that they point out the changing structure of actors' preferences and how a frame perspective may illuminates these changes. Yet, they do not abandon the rational actor model altogether. They picture frames as resources that actors possess and utilize to advance their own agenda. The rational actor here precedes the processes of framing, which are assumed to be under the actor's control. What falls outside the scope of this perspective is the possibility that dominant frames may precede and shape actors' perceptions, self-understandings and identities in ways that are not wholly transparent to them.

Studies that build frames into a neoinstitutionalist framework tend to gravitate to the opposite pole, reifying the power of institutions rather than the sovereignty of the rational actor. Lenschow and Zito (1998), for instance, start from the assumption that the impact of policy frames on policy outcomes depends on the 'thickness' of their institutionaliza-tion. Studying the evolution of EU waste management and agricultural policies, they identify three major policy frames that have shaped policy evolution in these domains: the conditional environmental frame, the classical environmental frame, and the sustainability frame. They con-clude that due to the persisting influence of 'thick' institutions such as the Common Agricultural Policy, institutionalization of the sustainability frame, although increasingly prominent at the level of EU rhetoric, has largely failed to materialize in actuality (Lenschow and Zito 1998, 438).

One of the limitations characterizing the frames as explanatory factors orientation in this line of work is a focus on elites and elite strategies. Frame contests are studied as a largely intra-elite affair; efforts to chal-lenge dominant elite frames from beyond come into view only through attention to elite responses, if at all. Furthermore, this work tends to sub-scribe to a causal model of explanation – couched in terms of hypotheses, variables and causal factors – which takes causal forces as being external to, and independent from, the processes they supposedly explain. Applying a causal model to policy processes thus means positing the purported causal factors – whether conceptualized in terms of interests, events, ideas, preferences or institutions – as forces that are not constituted, shaped or transformed by and through the policy process itself, but that impact it from beyond. Hence, the approach posits the supposedly causal factors as stable and given, exempting them from further interrogation.

FRAMES AS NARRATIVES: THE ART OF REFRAMING POLICY CONTROVERSIES

The work by Schön and Rein (1994; cf. Rein and Schön 1993) has a different type of goal. Its main purpose is not to produce causal explanations of policy outcomes, but rather an interpretive exploration of pragmatic conflict resolution. Meaning is treated as a constitutive dimension of social life, not an additional factor among others. Furthermore, the approach is deliberately normative, clearly indicating its key value as being creative conflict resolution in liberal democracy. Framing and reframing are firmly located in interactions, not in cognitive structures manifest in text. For Rein and Schön, as Van Hulst and Yanow (2014) make clear, framing is a dynamic, situated interactional process through which actors seek to make sense of a certain situation through naming, selecting, categorizing and story-telling. Most notably, framing and reframing can display communicative – and not only instrumental – rationality.

Schön and Rein thus do not conceptualize framing as being essentially strategic. Policy practitioners, they insist, are capable not only of strategic action, but also of communicative action and practical reasoning. Framing – more exactly reframing and frame reflection – is one way of exercising these capacities. Occasionally, according to the authors, policy practitioners manage to creatively reframe contested policy issues, thereby making them amenable to pragmatic conflict resolution. Conflict resolution is ultimately the point of frame reflection. Similar to Goffman, but unlike most approaches discussed so far, Schön and Rein see frame analysis not as an activity monopolized by the analyst; policy practitioners are as capable as analysts of reflecting on how frames are structuring their interactions.

Schön and Rein indicate that conceptions of policy rationality are mainly derived from rational choice theory, the pluralist model, or more recently from models of mediated negotiation. All these approaches represent variants of instrumental rationality, resting on assumptions that take the interests of the actors in the policy process as given. As such, they are unable to account for both the existence and the resolution of intractable policy disputes. Such disputes are ones that cannot be solved by referring to the 'facts' or appealing to the contending parties' best interests, since actors hold conflicting frames which determine what counts as a fact and what the contenders see as being in their interests.

Frames, moreover, are usually tacit and not easily accessible to conscious reasoning. In order to study them in action, Schön and Rein suggest, it is useful to focus on stories. In policy controversies, actors will most likely present contesting stories about what it is that is going on, whether it is cast, for instance, as 'urban renewal' or 'gentrification'. A story about 'urban renewal' may refer to the same events as a story about 'gentrification' – while constructing the situation quite differently, pointing out different problems, identifying different culprits and suggesting a different course of action. Laws and Rein in later work clarify the connection between frames and stories; frames, they explain, are located in a particular kind of stories, namely normative-prescriptive stories, that 'wed fact and value into belief about how to act' (Laws and Rein 2003, 174). These stories mediate policy interaction and evolve over time. Note that a policy story, here, is not a stable piece of text that could be scanned for pre-given mental or cultural schemes. The task rather is to trace the redefinition of problems through the evolution of stories in policy interactions.

Writing in a US context, Schön and Rein view intractable policy conflicts – such as those on abortion, health care, or welfare reform – as a threat to liberal democracy, inasmuch as such conflicts strain intermediary democratic institutions and lead to stalemate or to the radicalization of positions (Schön and Rein 1994, 9). The point of *Frame Reflection*, however, is not so much to explain the persistence of policy controversies, but to demonstrate that even stubborn policy controversies can be, and in fact sometimes are, resolved through frame reflection on the part of policy practitioners. The analyst's task is to trace the trajectories of the different stories to see whether rapprochement has occurred over time and, if so, under what conditions. Frame analysis thus actually comes to mean frame reflection analysis. The eventual outcome is a story about stories.

Laws and Rein have taken this line of thought one step further by shifting 'from treating frames as stable objects or tools used by actors to command action and influence the distribution of resources to viewing frames as systems of belief that intertwine with identity and social action' (Laws and Rein 2003, 174). Neither frames, nor identities, they suggest, form stable entities. Rather, both frames and identities co-evolve within reframing processes. Combining Goffman with Bourdieu, they emphasize the critical dimension of practice for the dynamics of reframing. The evolution of the environmental justice frame in the US, for example, indicates that successful reframing requires not only a challenging of dominant beliefs and problem-definitions, but also the institutionalization of habits of thought and action in practices. Insofar as the environmental justice frame becomes more dominant from some point onwards, Laws and Rein may also draw our attention to the fact that the concept of 'dominant frames' should not be confused with the concept of 'frames as part of relations of domination'. Fortunately, sometimes frames that challenge existing relations of power, exclusion and domination become more dominant as a result of social movements' struggles – which is not to say that they eliminate power relations altogether.

Overall, reframing, for Schön, Rein and Laws, involves conflict resolution, learning and reflection, and they thus suggest that reframing contributes to an increase in policy rationality. Yet, is conflict resolution per se a good thing, regardless of what it is about? Could it not be that conflict resolution at times stabilizes unequal relations of power and domination, for instance through co-opting the forces that struggle for social change? Would frame reflection and reframing necessarily form an antipode to unequal power, so that the more frame reflection takes place, the more such power gets diminished? Or could frame reflection and reframing just be involved in alteration and reformation of unequal power relations? As suggested by Herrmann (2010), reframing and conflict resolution may well be enacted as part of established power operations, contributing to mere modifications within established relations of power and domination, rather than substantially destabilizing and altering them. Much like Habermas in his later work,[3] Schön and Rein are more concerned about demonstrating that communicative rationality is both necessary and possible than being concerned about actually existing relations of power and domination.

Issues of power and domination will come to the fore as we turn to consider, first, frames as resources and, after that, frames as ideology.

FRAMES AS RESOURCES: THE CASE OF WOMEN'S REPRODUCTIVE RIGHTS AND THE UN AGENDA

Policy scholars who have employed the frame concept as involving situated interaction in the manner of Snow and Benford (2005) have taken yet a different route. Their aim is to recount the evolution of a policy through frame contests and realignment within a specific institutional context. In this vein, Jutta Joachim (2007) for instance studied agenda formation on the international level. She particularly examined the evolution of the Cairo Programme of Action, adopted in 1994 at the UN International Conference on Population and Development (ICPD). The Cairo Programme established a reform agenda for international population policies that prominently featured the concept of women's reproductive rights and empowerment within the management of population growth. Joachim's study aimed at reconstructing how, and under what conditions, NGOs managed to achieve the unlikely result of redefining the agendas of UN organizations so as to include the issues of violence against women and women's health and reproductive rights. Strategic packaging of policy ideas, Joachim holds, was critical for the process. In line with social movement theory, she conceptualizes framing as a strategic activity, deliberately deployed by actors in order to advance their case.

In regard to women's health and reproductive rights, the process can be traced back to the First UN Population Conference, held in Bucharest in 1974. At the time, the agenda of the international population policy establishment was controlled by governments of the global North, particularly the US government. Population growth in the South was perceived as a source of political instability and thereby a threat to US national security. This concern left no room for issues of women's health or reproductive rights. Joachim shows how small shifts occurred in the opportunity structure in the early 1970s when a bloc of states in the global South, together with some Communist countries, promoted a new linkage between population policy and economic development – a linkage that proved compatible with US foreign policy at the time. Women's organizations successively used this shift to reframe population policy, managing to inscribe into the UN agenda the idea that 'socio-economic development would be curtailed without the active participation of women' (quoted in Joachim 2007, 146). In the course of the 1980s and 1990s, these organizations managed to introduce a quality of care framework into the programming activities of international population policy organizations which these had hitherto rejected for being 'unrealistic' (Joachim 2007, 144). The policy perspective of women's health activists differed from that of international population agencies. The activists prioritized women's health, well-being and control over their lives, rather than simply population reduction in the South. Consequently, user-controlled contraceptives such as condoms or diaphragms, which would not damage women's health, were preferred over long-term, provider-controlled measures such as sterilization, intrauterine devices (IUDs), hormone implants, or injectables (Joachim 2007, 143).

Issue framing, however, was also a matter of conflict within the global women's health movement, including the predominance of women from the global North at international meetings and conferences. A controversy over the appropriate action frame erupted in preparation of the 1994 Cairo Conference over the question of whether, for strategic or other reasons, women's organizations should align their struggles with the population policy frame at all (Joachim 2007, 150ff.). Radical critics of population policy objected that using the population frame, even as a strategic means to advance women's health and reproductive rights, would feed the dominant notion that major problems such as poverty or environmental degradation were caused by 'overpopulation' in the South. Framing the problem as a problem of overpopulation, so the critics argued, suggested an allegedly technical solution in the form of birth control for problems caused by power relations and inequality.[4] More liberal, pragmatic women's organizations contended that aligning with the population framework provided valuable strategic opportunities for introducing women's rights and health issues into the UN agenda.

The story Joachim recounts is a success story. In this story, radical and moderate organizations finally decided to work together and develop a division of labour; the moderates pushed for women's reproductive rights and health from inside the population establishment, the radicals built pressure from outside. Depending on your viewpoint, the Cairo Programme eventually reframed population policy either in terms of women's reproductive rights and health, or in terms of women's reproductive rights and health to the extent they are compatible with the goals of international population policy. However, whether Cairo was actually a success story remains a matter of contestation. For liberal and pragmatic feminists, it was a great achievement, but radical feminists denounced it as a case of instrumentalizing feminist struggles for purposes of domination and control because gender issues were disarticulated from issues of race, class, poverty and structural inequality (Schultz 2011).

Joachim presents a narrative version of frame analysis; she recounts the processes of framing and reframing as processes of conflict and interaction within specific historic and institutional contexts. The findings take the form of a story rather than a picture. Scanning a pre-delineated set of sources for pre-established schemes and categories makes little sense within a narrative research design. The analyst has to draw on a broad variety of data, complement it if necessary during the process, refine or adjust her/his categories, and assign differential weight to different data with regard to the context. Also, s/he is not merely an observer, but one who enters into interaction with the subject matter under study. There is no way of leaving subjectivity at the door when entering this type of research – even if there is a price to pay in terms of reliability and validation. Yet, as with any other approach, a narrative approach bears specific risks and limitations. A narrative approach faces a coherence requirement; in order to make a narrative, that is, the sequence of events has to have a beginning, an end, and a certain coherence – which might involve the temptation to straighten out discontinuity, ambiguity or loose ends. If the case is a success story, analysts may be tempted to play down or overlook ambiguity or failure. The reverse applies to stories of persistent failure or demise.

FRAMES AS IDEOLOGY: FRAME ANALYSIS AND TRANSFORMATIVE INTERVENTION

The approach that takes frames as ideology is primarily concerned with differential power relations, together with the possibility of intervening to change them. The focus here is not so much geared at explaining policy outcomes, illuminating the conditions of successful movement mobilization, or exploring the chance of policy conflict resolution. Instead, the point of the intellectual endeavour is to reveal the power dynamics obscured by the dominant discourses, not merely for analytical purposes but on the basis of a normative and political commitment. Frame analysis in this sense contributes to critical interventions into relations of power, dominance, exclusion and social inequality and thus can be considered a sort of critique of ideology. The concept of ideology here is taken from the Frankfurt School and does not simply denote false consciousness, nor a distinctive set of political ideas such as anarchism, socialism, or a stable, self-contained system of thought, but an inevitably contradictory effort to simultaneously legitimize and conceal relations of power and domination (Adorno 1974; Zizek 1994).

Critique of ideology, in this sense, presupposes a commitment to certain values such as political equality, social welfare or non-discrimination. It is the incoherence between the values proclaimed by those in power and actual policies and practices that makes critique of ideology possible. Ideology in this sense should not be mistaken for a merely ideational or mental phenomenon; it may be enacted in practices, policies and institutions and materialized in technologies and other artefacts. What distinguishes frame analysis as critique of ideology from the other strands of frame analysis discussed so far is its, more or less explicitly stated, purpose of destabilizing inequitable relations of power. The framing of policy problems, in this perspective, may be a crucial element of legitimating and thereby stabilizing power relations. At the same time, however, this perspective provides a point of entry for critique.

Many feminist scholars have pursued frame analysis in the manner of a critique of iedology.[5] A case in point is the feminist critique of development policy as formulated by Mary Hawkesworth (2012), who shows how framing the problem of global poverty in terms of development and under-development has reinforced hierarchical gender, race and class relations. Hawkesworth recounts the message of the development narrative and contrasts it with efforts by feminists and women's organizations to introduce alternative frames. 'Development', she argues, can be understood as a variant of the modern narrative of overcoming backwardness, ignorance, poverty and other evils by using science, technology and planning to transform 'traditional' agrarian subsistence economies into modern, industrialized, urbanized economies. The development frame dominated and shaped North–South relations for many decades. It offered a coherent account of the key problem – namely underdevelopment – and suggested a certain course of action, namely to foster economic growth. Moreover, the development narrative generated a host of practices and technologies, such as indicators, funding schemes, models and monitoring agencies, to tackle the global poverty problem. These practices and technologies regularly took the state as the unit of analysis – not gender, race or class relations within states – and they measured growth of the national economy in relation to other national economies, not in terms of the reduction of social inequality. In addition, indicators such as measures of earning or participation in the formal economy were largely drawn from the 'developed' world.

Casting the problem of global poverty in terms of development also defines what is *not* the problem and what does *not* require remedial relief – particularly dramatic inequalities of power and wealth. Within the development narrative, the poverty problem is construed as a technical one that requires technical expertise. It is not a political problem that would require redistribution of power and wealth. What gives coherence to the development frame as a whole is the assumption 'that factors internal to nations determined the stage of economic development' (Hawkesworth 2012, 123). Hence both problem and solution are located within the confines of the 'underdeveloped' state, and there is no need whatsoever for 'developed' countries to undergo transformation as part of the solution to global poverty.

A special narrative identified by Hawkesworth within the overarching development frame is that of overpopulation. Dating back to Thomas Robert Malthus's ideas of the late 18th and early 19th centuries, a focus on overpopulation further gained popularity through the eugenics movement in Western societies in the 1920s and 1930s (Briggs 2002) and then again in the late 1960s through Paul Ehrlich's book *The Population Bomb* (1968). Variations on the overpopulation theme can still be found today in international population policy discourse, its core message being that the poor have too many children in relation to their means of subsistence and that, therefore, poverty can be attributed to the behaviour of the poor themselves. Since the 1960s, concern mainly focused on population growth in the global South. Poverty, hunger, poor health – also political instability and the threat of communism – were attributed to uncontrolled fertility in the South (Hartmann 1995). Deforestation, environmental destruction and the subordination of women were added to the list (Hartmann 2002; Schultz 2006; Joachim 2007).

The overpopulation frame acts as an organizing principle that integrates a vast array of phenomena into a coherent whole and identifies the root of the problem and, consequently, a way to solve it: namely, through the reduction of women's birth rate in the global South. The overpopulation narrative also informed a series of material strategies and practices such as 'sterilization festivals' and the widespread distribution of long-term, provider-controlled contraceptives, such as hormone implants or hormone injections. The frame selectively highlights specific aspects of reality at the expense of others. What remains obscured are, among other things, patterns of consumption and energy use in industrialized countries, too few people monopolizing too many resources, food export demanded by 'structural adjustment', priority of military expenditure instead of health and education (Hartmann 1995, 2002).

Feminist critics of the development frame have pointed out that indicators were oriented towards standards of Northern modernization that privilege growth, labour participation and income generation in the formal sector of the economy, generally dominated by men. Within the development frame, the solution to the 'women question', as it was called, was women's integration into the formal economy and thus adaption to male and Northern, androcentric standards. Feminist scholars have questioned these standards and pointed out that they covertly reinforce asymmetrical power relations both between North and South and within the South itself.

An alternative feminist policy framework, the gender and development framework, defines the major policy problem as involving poverty, the subordination of disadvantaged groups such as women, and unequal power relations. Economic growth and income generation in the formal economy, feminists argue, are not suitable indicators to measure the reduction of poverty, inequality and social subordination. Framing the problem differently requires other indicators and instruments, including but not limited to, improvements in infrastructure and in services, such as facilities and programmes providing access to sanitation and clean water.

Feminist critiques of development may serve as a particular illustration of the critique of ideology in frame analysis. Such critique strives to expose hegemonic power relations inscribed into a policy frame while calling attention to the representational practices that mask the operation of power (Hawkesworth 2012, 116). It is worth noting, though, that this type of critique is contingent on certain conditions; it is not applicable to all kinds of dominant power; crude, violent, fundamentalist forms of repression are not amenable to critique of ideology in this sense. The notion of unmasking dominant power through the critique of ideology presupposes that such power is masked in the first place. It is thus development policy's illusory claim to reduce poverty and gender inequality that serves as a point of entry for feminist critique of ideology.

CONCLUSION

Framing approaches draw attention to the fact that defining policy problems is inevitably a selective and value-laden process. They can be extremely useful to shed light on underlying beliefs, values and assumptions that inform, structure and direct the way policy problems are tackled (or not) and thereby to refute technocratic claims that allegedly a certain course of action is without alternative or required by 'the facts'. However, doing frame analysis can mean very different things. Frame analysis can serve to make visible the contingent and political nature of constructing policy problems and their respective solutions and serve as a useful device for critical policy studies in that sense. Yet, this does not mean that frame analysis is critical of relations of power and domination per se. Concepts of frame and framing can only be as critical as the larger framework they are integrated into and they may be integrated into more or less empiricist frameworks as well as articulated to social critique and struggles for social change. Interpreting frames, for instance, as a set of factors among others assumes that one part of social reality is socially constructed and the other is not. The latter, then, is taken as given and excepted from critical inspection. Interpreting frames as a set of resources strategically employed by rational actors means to treat frames as means to an end while the ends as such as well as processes of subject formation are not examined any further. Interpreting reframing activities basically as a way to resolve policy controversies and increase policy rationality presupposes that resolving controversy is an end in itself without examining whether it stabilizes or destabilizes existing relations of inequality and domination. Even critics of ideology approaches, however committed to social critique, may have their blind spots in that they tend to compare social reality against official commitments to values largely derived from Western enlightenment without necessarily questioning these values as such. Unfortunately, or fortunately, a perfect methodological or epistemological approach does not exist and the lesson to draw from these insights is to reflect on these respective blind spots and consider whether and to what extent one wants to put up with them or not.

On a more fundamental level, critical policy scholars should consider whether they want to start from a representational or a participational model when embarking on frame analysis. In the literature, frame analysis is sometimes treated in terms of methodology, demanding a set of universally applicable techniques in order to safeguard intersubjective validity, reliability and rigour. These demands, I would argue, respond to a problem that arises from an underlying representational model of social sciences. Within a representational model frames are construed as mental entities to be detected through the application of a more or less formalized method in order to yield a correct depiction of a segment of social reality. In order to bridge the epistemological gap, the analyst needs a neutral, universally applicable instrument: the method. Once we conceive of social reality differently, however – namely as an ensemble of practices and interactions among participants seeking to make sense of what they are doing inter alia in form of narratives and frames – the epistemological gap vanishes. The analyst turns out to be a participant in interaction, interpreting interpretations in order to come up with a plausible account of what has been going on. This chapter has argued that due to its idea of static objectivity the representational model has serious limitations when it comes to analysing policy *processes*, struggles, interaction and changes over time. Hence, narrative approaches, derived from a participational model of social reality, should be judged on their own terms, not against the standards of the representational model – and the requirement of a formalized method is put into perspective.

After all, being critical is not a matter of definition or methodology, but a matter of commitment; hence the question is not so much *whether* I use the frame concept but *how* I use it and whether I articulate it to the critical analysis of larger patterns of power, exclusion and domination.

NOTES

1. Geertz identifies three prominent analogies in the social sciences: the game analogy ('life is a game'), the drama analogy ('life is a stage') and the text analogy ('life is a text'). He himself clearly subscribed to the text analogy (Geertz 2000, 452).
2. For an overview see Fisher (1997) and König (2005).
3. Unlike the Habermas of, for instance, *The Structural Transformation of the Public Sphere* (1962).
4. More on this controversy is found in Hartmann (1995) and Schultz (2006).
5. For a more representational variant of frame analysis as critique of ideology see for instance Verloo (2007) and Lombardo and Meier (2008).

REFERENCES

Adorno, T.W. (1974), *Soziologische Exkurse*, Frankfurt am Main: EVA.
Bevir, M. and R.A.W. Rhodes (2010), *The State as Cultural Practice*, Oxford: Oxford University Press.

Braun, K. (2014), 'Diskurs im Kampf um Bedeutung: Ansätze von Diskurstheorie und Diskursanalyse in der interpretativen Policy Analyse', *Zeitschrift für Diskursforschung/ Journal for Discourse Studies*, **1** (4), 77–101.

Briggs, L. (2002), *Reproducing Empire. Race, Sex, Science and U.S. Imperialism in Puerto Rico*, Berkeley, CA: University of California Press.

Daviter, F. (2007), 'Policy Framing in the European Union', *Journal of European Public Policy*, **14** (4), 654–666.

Eberlein, B. and C.M. Radaelli (2010), 'Mechanisms of Conflict Management in EU Regulatory Policy', *Public Administration*, **88** (3), 782–799.

Ehrlich, P.R. (1968), *The Population Bomb. Population Control or Race to Oblivion?*, New York: Ballantine Books.

Entman, R.M. (1993), 'Framing: Toward Clarification of a Fractured Paradigm', *Journal of Communication*, **43** (4), 51–58.

Fischer, F. (2003), *Reframing Public Policy. Discursive Politics and Deliberative Practices*, Oxford: Oxford University Press.

Fisher, K. (1997), 'Locating Frames in the Discursive Universe', *Sociological Research Online*, **2** (3), accessed 17 April 2014 at http://www.socresonline.org.uk/2/3/4.html.

Fligstein, N. and I. Mara-Drita (1996), 'How to Make a Market: Reflections on the Attempt to Create a Single Market in the European Union', *American Journal of Sociology*, **102** (1), 1–33.

Gamson, W.A. (1995), 'Constructing Social Protest', in H. Johnston and B. Klandermans (eds), *Social Movements, Protest and Contention*, Minneapolis, MN: Minnesota Press, pp. 85–107.

Gamson, W.A. and A. Modigliani (1989), 'Media Discourse and Public Opinion on Nuclear Power: A Constructionist Approach', *American Journal of Sociology*, **95** (1), 1–37.

Geertz, C. (1983), *Local Knowledge*, New York: Basic Books.

Geertz, C. (2000), *The Interpretation of Cultures: Selected Essays by Clifford Geertz*, New York: Basic Books.

Gitlin, T. (1980), *The Whole World Is Watching: Mass Media in the Making and Unmaking of the New Left*, Berkeley, CA: University of California Press.

Goffman, E. (1974), *Frame Analysis: An Essay on the Organization of Experience*, Cambridge, MA: Harvard University Press.

Habermas, J. (1962), *The Structural Transformation of the Public Sphere: An Inquiry into a Category of Bourgeois Society*, Cambridge: Polity Press.

Hajer, M. and D. Laws (2006), 'Ordering through Discourse', in M. Moran, M. Rein and R.E. Goodin (eds), *The Oxford Handbook of Public Policy*, Oxford: Oxford University Press, pp. 251–268.

Hartmann, B. (1995), *Reproductive Rights and Wrongs. The Global Politics of Population Control*, revised edition, Boston, MA: South End Press.

Hartmann, B. (2002), 'The Changing Faces of Population Control', in J. Silliman and A. Battacharjee (eds), *Policing the National Body. Race, Gender, and Criminalization*, Cambridge, MA: South End Press, pp. 259–289.

Hawkesworth, M. (2012), 'From Policy Frames to Discursive Politics', in F. Fischer and H. Gottweis (eds), *The Argumentative Turn Revisited*, Durham, NC: Duke University Press, pp. 114–146.

Herrmann, S.L. (2010), 'A Speaking Cure for Conflicts: Problematization, Discourse Stimulation and the Ongoing of Scientific "Progress"', *Critical Policy Studies*, **4** (3), 278–296.

Joachim, J.M. (2007), *Agenda Setting, the UN, and NGOs. Gender Violence and Reproductive Rights*, Washington, DC: Georgetown University Press.

Johnston, H. (1995), 'A Methodology for Frame Analysis: From Discourse to Cognitive Schemata', in H. Johnston and B. Klandermans (eds), *Social Movements and Culture*, London: UCL Press, pp. 217–246.

Kahneman, D. and A. Tversky (1979), 'Prospect Theory: An Analysis of Decision under Risk', *Econometrica*, **47** (2), 263–291.

König, T. (2005), 'Frame Analysis', accessed 17 April 2014 at www.ccsr.ac.uk/methods/pub
lications/frameanalysis/index.html.

Laws, D. and M. Rein (2003), 'Reframing Practice', in M. Hajer and H. Wagenaar
(eds), *Deliberative Policy Analysis. Understanding Governance in the Network Society*,
Cambridge: Cambridge University Press, pp. 172–206.

Lenschow, A. and T. Zito (1998), 'Blurring or Shifting Policy Frames? Institutionalization of
the Economic-Environmental Policy Linkage in the European Community', *Governance*,
11 (4), 415–441.

Lombardo, E. and P. Meier (2008), 'Framing Gender Equality in the European Union
Political Discourse', *Social Politics*, **15** (1), 101–129.

Maher, T.M. (2001), 'Framing: An Emerging Paradigm or a Phase of Agenda Setting',
in S.D. Stephen, O.H. Gandy and A.E. Grant (eds), *Framing Public Life: Perspectives
on Media and our Understanding of the Social World*, Mahwah, NJ: Lawrence Erlbaum
Associates, pp. 83–94.

Mörth, U. (2000), 'Competing Frames in the European Commission – the Case of the
Defence Industry and Equipment Issue', *Journal of European Public Policy*, **7** (2), 173–189.

Nylander, J. (2001), 'The Construction of a Market. A Frame Analysis of the Liberalization
of the Electricity Market in the European Union', *European Societies*, **3** (3), 289–314.

Radaelli, C.M. (1999), 'Harmful Tax Competition in the European Union: Policy Narratives
and Advocacy Coalitions', *Journal of Common Market Studies*, **37** (4), 661–682.

Rein, M. and D.A. Schön (1993), 'Reframing Policy Discourse', in F. Fischer and J. Forester
(eds), *The Argumentative Turn in Policy Analysis and Planning*, London: UCL Press,
pp. 145–166.

Scheufele, D.A. (1999), 'Framing as a Theory of Media Effects', *Journal of Communication*,
49 (4), 103–122.

Schön, D.A. and M. Rein (1994), *Frame Reflection*, New York: Basic Books.

Schultz, S. (2006), *Hegemonie, Gouvernementalität, Biomacht. Reproduktive Risiken und die
Transformation internationaler Bevölkerungspolitik*, Münster: Westfälisches Dampfboot.

Schultz, S. (2011), 'New Biopolitics? The Articulation of Demographic Aims and Gender
Policies in International Population Policy Programs', in K. Braun (ed.), *Between Self-
Determination and Social Technology. Medicine, Biopolitics and the New Techniques of
Management*, Bielefeld: transcript, pp. 219–269.

Snow, D.A. and R.D. Benford (2005), 'Clarifying the Relationship between Framing and
Ideology', in H. Johnston and J.A. Noakes (eds), *Frames of Protest: Social Movements and
the Framing Perspective*, Lanham, MD: Rowman & Littlefield, pp. 205–212.

Taylor, C. (1995), 'Overcoming Epistemology', in C. Taylor (ed.), *Philosophical Arguments*,
Cambridge, MA: Harvard University Press, pp. 1–19.

Triandafyllidou, A. and A. Foutio (1998), 'Sustainability and Modernity in the European
Union: A Frame Theory Approach to Policy-Making', *Sociological Research*, **3** (1),
accessed 17 April 2014 at www.socresonline.org.uk/3/1/2.html.

Tversky, A. and D. Kahneman (1992), 'Advances in Prospect Theory: Cumulative
Representation of Uncertainty', *Journal of Risk and Uncertainty*, **5** (4), 297–323.

Van Hulst, M. and D. Yanow (2014), 'From Policy "Frames" to "Framing" Theorizing a
More Dynamic, Political Approach', *The American Review of Public Administration*, DOI:
0275074014533142.

Verloo, M. (ed.) (2007), *Multiple Meanings of Gender Equality in Europe. A Critical Frame
Analysis of Gender Policies in Europe*, Budapest and New York: CPS Books.

Wagenaar, H. (2011), *Meaning in Action. Interpretation and Dialogue in Policy Analysis*,
Armonk, NY: M.E. Sharpe.

Zizek, S. (1994), 'The Spectre of Ideology', in S. Zizek (ed.), *Mapping Ideology*, London and
New York: Verso, pp. 1–33.

24 Critical policy ethnography

Vincent Dubois

Although policy is not commonly a central concern of ethnographers and ethnography is not an approach common among conventional policy analysts, ethnography and policy do share a deep common history. Ethnographers have been collaborating with policy makers for decades, as ancillaries of government agents. They also have publicly engaged in policy debates, accounting for situations and problems from the point of view of people who experience them, and sometimes advocating on this basis for grass-roots alternatives to government programs. Policy ethnography, however, must not be reduced to the ethnographic study of people subjected to policy. It consists more specifically in the ethnography of policy settings, agents, practices, organizations and processes. The number of studies that meet this definition has increased in recent years, along with qualitative and interpretive approaches to policy studies. These various encounters between ethnography and policy raise issues about ethnography itself and about the social and political role of the ethnographer. Policy ethnography is indeed at the intersection of a series of tensions: applied vs. fundamental ethnography, application for policy makers vs. application for people subjected to policies, ethnography for policy vs. ethnography of policy, people-centered vs. policy-centered ethnography. Here we may pose the question of when and how policy ethnography can be critical.

To address this question and illustrate critical epistemology, I will undertake the preliminary task of critical social scientists – reflexivity – which makes scholarship itself a focus of research (Bourdieu 2004). This is why this chapter includes a reflection on the history and current tensions in the positions, practices and orientations of scholars at the intersection between policy and ethnography. We will see that a critical approach is only one among numerous possible uses of ethnography related to policy matters. Therefore the question is to specify the features defining critical policy ethnography as such. I will single out four of them. First, from a methodological and analytic point of view, the critical potential of ethnography lies in its capacity to challenge mainstream positivist approaches to public policy. Second, ethnography is critical insofar as it effectively confronts the commonsense views at work in policy making, and the commonsense views of policy making itself. Third, whereas ethnography is most often associated with micro-level approaches, critical policy ethnography endeavors at setting its observations in the broader context of macro-structures of power and inequality. Lastly, thanks to this wider perspective, policy ethnography is critical as it serves to unveil social, economic, symbolic and political domination at work in policy processes.

I will first examine how ethnography and policy meet. This will be the occasion to address the question of the political role of policy ethnographers, from instrumentalization and manipulation by government agencies to protest activism, together with the question of the various theoretical orientations policy ethnographers adopt as scholars. After exploring these various positions and the conditions under which policy ethnography can be 'critical', I will consider the diverse research objects on which policy ethnographers focus their attention: from social groups targeted by policy programs to the multiple sites of policy processes and policy making. This will provide an opportunity to reflect on how to conduct critical policy ethnography. Lastly, I will synthesize the main contributions of this approach, contrasting them with the dominant views on public policies and underlining how policy ethnography can be 'critical'.

HOW DO ETHNOGRAPHY AND POLICY MEET?

Although policy ethnography can hardly claim the status of a clearly identified, distinct research domain, ethnography and policy do share a long history of exchanges. In my effort to show how policy ethnography can be 'critical', I will start by considering this shared history and the contemporary relationship between policy and ethnography. Inspired by Bourdieu's notion of reflexivity as a necessary step for critical knowledge (Bourdieu 2004), this reflection will consist of raising the questions about the position of policy ethnographers, their relation to their subject matter, the possible social and political uses of their work, and, more generally, the political implications of ethnographic research (on critical reflexivity, see also in a complementary way Schwartz-Shea and Yanow 2012, pp. 101–103).

One could be tempted to address these questions both in terms of political neutrality and of 'policy relevance'. That, however, would be far too simple. As Katz writes, 'to characterize a piece of ethnographic research as apolitical is a political statement' (Katz 2004, p. 280). 'Neutrality' is all the more impossible to achieve in the case of policy ethnography as, in addition to being involved on the field, policy ethnographers deal with power relationships, public problems and political ideologies. Therefore '"policy relevance" is an indirect way of demanding that political priority be given here and now to those with at least a foothold in institutions of power'

(Katz 2004, p. 281). 'Policy relevance' is indeed only the dominant official way of looking at the political implications and possible uses of policy ethnography. The fact that policy ethnography cannot escape its political implications does not mean that it inevitably serves as an ancillary to government agents. To paraphrase Howard Becker's famous statement, the question is therefore not whether policy ethnographers should take sides, but rather whose side they are on (Becker 1967). Perspectives other than those focusing on 'policy relevance' exist – from activism in favor of the oppressed, to collaborative applied anthropology, and to participation in (re)framing the public debate. In the following sub-sections I explore these approaches, first by providing a retrospective account of the relationship between policy and ethnography, then by sketching the current tensions in this relationship.

From Colonialist Anthropology to Policy Ethnography

In his conceptual and ideological history of applied and action anthropology, John Bennett proposes an interesting overview of the varied and sometimes contradictory ways in which British and American anthropologists have considered policy issues (Bennett 1996). Although based on the history of anthropology as a discipline, his overview gives a broader introduction to the complex relationship between policy and ethnography, both theoretically and in practice. The introduction of applied anthropology in policy making was a first historical stage. In the British case, this gave birth to 'colonialist anthropology', which fulfilled 'a humanitarian advisory function for colonial administration in Africa' under the British empire (Bennett 1996, p. S24). Anthropologists provided 'useful knowledge' enabling administrators to better govern colonized people and even collaborated in colonial government. The 'application of anthropology to current statecraft' promoted during the 1920s was not, however, without difficulties and misunderstandings (Belshaw 1976).

In contrast to the British paternalist orientation, applied anthropology in the United States appeared as 'a mixture of New Deal humanitarian liberalism and progressive industrial management ideology' (Bennett 1996, p. S23). Bennett here identifies three main origins. First, anthropologists took part in the public programs aimed at Native American reservations. Second, they participated in the multidisciplinary management-oriented research programs on industrial organization during the 1940s and the 1950s, together with sociologists and psychologists – as in the Department of Social Relations at Harvard or in the American Association for Applied Anthropology and its journal *Human Organization*. While not specific to public policy and administration, this 'anthropological engineering' was used in these domains. Lastly, anthropology was also directly employed in the New Deal agricultural community program for 'rural rehabilitation', as implemented by the Bureau of Agricultural Economics and Rural Welfare in the Roosevelt Administration's Department of Agriculture. Anthropologists analyzed the impact of socio-economic changes on rural communities and the conditions for development. This New Deal experience served as a milestone for the later involvement of anthropologists in policy programs.

In both the British and the American cases, 'the anthropologist was there to answer questions but not to pose them' (Bennett 1996, p. S28). The fieldwork researcher was mostly defined as a subordinate neutral adviser, 'leaving to statesmen (and journalists) the final decision of how to apply the results' (Malinowski 1929, p. 23; quoted in Bennett 1996, p. S29).

Despite national differences in orientation, the tradition of applied anthropology has three general characteristics that are directly opposed to what we could define as 'critical policy ethnography'. First, in applied anthropology, researchers depend on policy makers and administrators not only financially or for access in their fieldwork, but in the definition of the intellectual frame in which they conduct their research. Conversely, intellectual autonomy is a basic requirement for critical social science. Second, the intervention of applied anthropology is legitimized by its claim to neutrality. Conversely, critical scholars acknowledge their moral or political orientations, and at least reflect on the role of possible biases in the orientation of their work. Lastly, conventional applied anthropologists stood by the side of dominant policy makers and powerful administrations. Conversely, critical policy ethnographers generally strive against dominant ideas, to unveil power relationships or to propose alternative views.

Criticism of the applied tradition during the 1960s and 1970s can be regarded as a step toward a distinct critical policy ethnography. To name but one instance in the American case, Sol Tax criticized the employment of ethnographic practitioners by governments, arguing in favor of self-funded independent research in community-based development projects. In this perspective, scholars would directly intervene to help people solve their problems. This time, ethnographers would stand on the other side, the side of people facing social, economic or political domination. The populism of 'action anthropology' would replace the paternalism of traditional applied anthropology (Tax 1975).

Despite these strong oppositions, however, applied and action anthropology share a common problem-solving orientation in which the utility of ethnography is viewed in a direct and practical way. In both cases, ethnographic research focuses on problems and on the people who experience them, and is conducted *for* policy and reform, even when action anthropology proposes grass-roots alternatives to government programs. This focus on problems contrasts with the definition of policy ethnography as ethnography *of* public policy, focused on policy processes and practices primarily in order to better understand them.

Remaining Tensions

The range of contemporary ways for ethnographers to deal with policy remains impressively diversified. As a review of the terrains of policy anthropology shows (Okongwu and Mencher 2000), ethnographers dealing with policy issues still mainly focus on populations and on problems more than they study public policy itself, as in the ethnography *of* policy. Wedel et al. acknowledge this discrepancy when they contrast the involvement of anthropologists in policy with what they call the 'anthropology of public policy [. . .] devoted to research into policy issues and processes and the critical analysis of those processes' (Wedel et al. 2005, p. 31).

Thus the difference between ethnography *for* and ethnography *of* public policy accompanies the opposition between 'applied' and 'critical' research in current debates on the relationship between policy and ethnography. This point is clear when it comes to the question of the utility of ethnographic research regarding policy issues. If the notion that ethnography is useful in this domain is widely shared, ethnographers have different views regarding whom they should be useful for and how. A first type of response to these questions is formulated in terms of efficiency in policy making by the promoters of new forms of applied anthropology from the 1970s onwards. Before political or ethical preferences, there are professional reasons for this orientation, such as the defense of anthropology as a (useful) discipline. This is clear when anthropologists urge their colleagues to turn to applied research for policy, redefining anthropology as a policy science (Kimball 1978), and positing policy at the center of the renewal of the discipline. As Erve Chambers expressed it, 'the idea of policy is as central to the development of applied anthropology as the concept of culture has been to the anthropological profession as a whole' (Chambers 1985, pp. 37–38, quoted in Shore and Wright 1997, p. 7). In turn, the purpose of anthropology as a policy science is 'to provide information to decision makers in support of the rational formulation, implementation, and evaluation of policy' (see also van Willigen and DeWalt 1985; Fetterman 1993; van Willigen 2002, p. 161). Belshaw has defined this approach to policy as 'social engineering', or one that does not challenge the rational frameworks of the idea of policy making (Belshaw 1976).

In this approach, anthropologists would contribute to public policy by isolating 'variables that can be manipulated by public policy and with the identification of the point at which the cost of changing inputs outweighs the expected benefits' (Sanday 1976, p.xvii, quoted in Wedel et al. 2005, p.48). Government agencies share similar orientations when they call for ethnography to fill the gaps in information about target populations of their programs (United States General Accounting Office 2003).

Social engineering is not, however, the only response. Reflecting on applied anthropology, Shelton Davis and Robert Matthews ask: for whose benefit is anthropology being applied? Instead of providing data for decisions made by those in power, these authors propose to focus applied anthropology on the structures of power, in the interest of the power-less, and to communicate the results of their work to citizens (Shelton and Matthews 1999). In a similar way, Katherine Newman agrees on the usefulness of ethnography, but refuses to reduce usefulness to policy advisory (Becker et al. 2004, p.271). In this perspective, the usefulness of ethnography comes from its contribution to general knowledge and to the public debate, and not only because its results provide information to help policy makers in doing their job. It is 'by bringing ethnographic data into the resources of public reasoning' that ethnographers may 'hope to shift the character of the policy debate' (Stack 1997, p.191). Here, utility has more to do with social sciences as 'public' disciplines (Borofsky 1999; Burawoy 2005). This concern moves closer to what I call critical policy ethnography.

WHAT DO POLICY ETHNOGRAPHERS OBSERVE?

We now come to the problem of what policy ethnographers concretely observe and how they circumscribe their field of research. Even though the two can overlap, here, the question is not so much 'which side are policy ethnographers on' as 'which side are they looking at'. I will address this issue by contrasting people-centered approaches with policy-centered approaches, showing how both of them can contribute to critical analysis.

People-centered Policy Ethnography

The most common ethnographic method is the in-depth monograph, describing the living conditions, social organization, distinctive practices, values and beliefs of a social group. Ethnographers generally focus on the dominated classes, say, from the colonized peoples to the urban poor. Such a people-centered approach can prove an interesting, even if indirect, way to do policy ethnography, oriented towards how people experience policies they are subjected to, and how these policies impact their lives. Again, this approach raises the questions of whom ethnography is intended for.

Somewhat provocatively, Herbert Gans states that 'ethnography has always studied the underdog and the victim, partly because of how sociologists think and partly because that is funded by government and the foundations' (Gans, in Becker et al. 2004, p. 265). Beyond the (crucial) issue of funding, studying the underdog is what gives ethnography its social value and can make it useful (Gans, in Becker et al. 2004, pp. 265, 271). While promoting this idea of 'usefulness' does not equal reducing ethnography to 'social engineering', it amounts to defining policy makers as the addressees of relevant ethnographic knowledge, ethnographers advising or trying to influence them in order to make better policies.

In this perspective, ethnography focusing on people proves helpful to demonstrate and criticize what policies do to them. It can provide 'an important corrective to decontextualized and universalizing approaches to public policy analysis' which 'too often is narrated in a top-down discourse that fails to account for how people affected by policy experience it' (Schram et al. 2013, p. 255). Field research on welfare clients has revealed the often tragic consequences of welfare reforms in the United States, and shed light on the resulting deterioration of living standards, as in the case of isolated mothers (Edin and Lein 1997; Hays 2002). Even if they do not define their research as policy ethnography, American ethnographers specialized in poverty provide such a 'corrective' when they include welfare reform and its effects on people depending on welfare benefits in their research scope (Morgen and Maskovsky 2003). This is a major contribution to the debate on evaluating the social impacts of public policy (Lichter and Jayakody 2002), which possibly helps 'to create social policies that respect the variety of human experiences' (Stack 1997, p. 191).

In addition to providing a critical view on policies by assessing their actual consequences on human lives, people-centered ethnography goes a step further towards a critical approach when the claim of significance for this respectful account of human lives 'rests most firmly on the juxtaposition between the social realities documented by the ethnographer and those held to be true by people in power' (Katz 2004, p. 287). The critical power of ethnography then consists in the accuracy of its empirical descriptions, which can be used to contradict representations of the social world based on dominant socio-political beliefs and ideologies. This is what Biehl and Petryna do when they envision global health problems from the point of view of the people who face them: 'these peopled accounts – stories that are so often hidden from view, obscured by more abstract and bureaucratic considerations of public policy – are the very fabric of alternative social theorizing' (Biehl and Petryna 2013, p. 2).

When they speak of people in relation to policy, ethnographers either do it for them, on their behalf, or alongside them. Exploring these various postures is a new occasion to address the question of how policy ethnography can be critical. Jim Thomas contrasts 'conventional ethnographers', who, according to him, speak *for* their subjects, with 'critical ethnographers', whom he describes as speaking *on behalf* of their subjects, as a means for empowering them (Thomas 1993). This is an important opposition, but, in my view, the main distinction is that between the posture of autonomy, in which ethnographers' legitimacy rests on their ability to account for people's lives in their own words, and the posture of populist activism, in which legitimacy rests in the ethnographer's involvement as a political spokesperson. An ethnographer who adopts the first posture can, as we have seen, build on this basis alternative views and theories, or can 'communicate for the victims in opposition to the perpetrators', as Herbert Gans names the disenfranchised and those responsible for their disenfranchisement (Gans, in Becker et al. 2004, p. 265). Conversely, ethnographers who adopt the second posture are not necessarily 'critical', in the sense that their advocacy work may simply reflect commonsense views instead of challenging them.

A third posture deserves special attention. Instead of contrasting ethnographers detached from their subjects with those who depend on them, some authors have experienced and called for exchanges between researchers and the people they study or activists who mobilize for them, in an advocacy orientation which, in turn, serves scientific purposes. According to Schensul, a strong link between researchers and the activities of the group they study 'would reduce the false dichotomy between applied and basic research', to the benefit of both research and the concrete impact of its results (Schensul 1980, p. 312). Schram et al. recently followed a similar orientation, which they call Participatory Action-Research.[1] In PAR, researchers collaborate with the people being studied 'to help frame, constitute, and interpret the facts that the research produces'. In addition to being 'critical' in the sense of being politically engaged in democratizing the policy process by including 'the voices of those traditionally left out of that process', PAR offers the accountability which can provide better scientific results 'since researchers open their work to be checked against the understandings of the people on the bottom of the policy process' (Schram et al. 2013, p. 258). Here the focus on people subjected to policy and the study of policy processes can be complementary.

Ethnographying Policy Makers and Policy Processes

By diverting the ethnographers' attention from the study of public policy itself, priority given to 'those at the bottom' is conducive to overlooking the elite, institutions and the political and bureaucratic mechanisms impacting the lives of ordinary people. As a consequence, people-centered ethnography runs the risk of limiting itself to a partial view of power and domination relationships, therefore losing the political implications that consist in giving the knowledge about domination processes to the dominated groups in order to help them cope with domination. In my view, policy ethnography needs to fully account for these processes in order to be really 'critical', in both the scientific and the political senses of the term.

Providing a comprehensive view of domination by including the dominants in the analysis echoes the call to 'study up' formulated by Laura Nader some four decades ago. Nader put an emphasis on the political aspect (empowering the powerless thanks to a better knowledge of power relationships), urging fieldworkers to 'study powerful institutions and bureaucratic organizations [. . .], for such institutions and their network systems affect our lives' and since 'most members of complex societies [. . .] do not know enough about, nor do they know how to cope with, the people, institutions, and organizations which most affect their lives' (Nader 1972, pp. 292–293). Schensul argues more specifically that 'any good ethnography of a subordinated group must study, from the people's perspective, institutions which contribute to their subordination' (Schensul 1980, p. 311).

Studying policies from the people's perspective is, however, only one possibility among others for conducting policy ethnography critically. A wide range of studies using in-depth qualitative research methods have opted for observation at the level of officials, bureaucrats or professionals working in institutions. Studies focused on 'entities charged with putting policy into practice' (Yanow et al. 2012, pp. 340–341) give a critical view on policy, be it implicitly, shedding light on bureaucratic arbitrariness, power relationships or on the undesirable impacts policy organizations can have on the situations and populations they are supposed to take care of. They have powerfully accounted for their practices within institutional units such as mental hospitals (Goffman 1961), police squads (Fassin 2013) or bureaucracies dealing with the poor (Gupta 2012).

Since the implementation of public policies involves organizations, organization studies contribute more explicitly to policy ethnography. Some of the most classic analyses have used fieldwork methods and are therefore still major references for organization/policy ethnography even if their authors did not define themselves as ethnographers (see for instance Blau 1955). By revealing the actual relationships, the bureaucratic routines, the dilemmas and contradictions of agents in public services, such ethnographically informed organization studies have long been contributing to the understanding of how policies are concretely made on a daily basis. Organization ethnography is at the crossroads between this qualitative fieldwork method used by organization theorists and the choice of organizations as a subject matter or as an observation unit by proper ethnographers (Yanow et al. 2012).

Ethnographers can observe policy being made concrete in organizations by focusing on various aspects. Documents are a crucial objectification of policies as well as a major aspect of bureaucratic work. Ethnographers trace their writing, circulation, interpretation and uses (Yanow 2009, p. 34). When the fieldworker can access them, meetings in organization are a fascinating occasion for direct observation, enabling researchers to look concretely at leadership issues, internal power relationships, negotiations, and, sometimes, decision making (Schwartzman 1993, p. 39).

Fieldwork research on organizations has contributed to critical policy studies by drawing on the 'street-level bureaucracy' (SLB) approach initiated by Lipsky, who argues that policy implementation comes down to low-ranking public employees (Lipsky 1980). He coined the phrase 'street-level bureaucrats' to designate those who actually make policy real through their everyday routines, decisions and discretion – such as teachers, the police, or caseworkers. The SLB approach focuses on 'informal organizational routines that effectively constitute policy on the ground' (Brodkin 2011, p.i199). Street-level-bureaucrats do not mechanically enforce pre-existing rules. They use discretion to decide to apply them or not, to interpret them and to orient their application. In that sense, street-level bureaucrats are also decision makers who are part of the policy community. This approach has obvious affinities with policy ethnography since it views policies from the field and rests on long and detailed mainly qualitative observations. SLB theory supports critical approaches to public policy, since it contradicts the official, hierarchical and rational presentation of policy programs by governments while challenging the common top-down approaches of policy analysis. The approach reveals the complex mechanisms of actual policy making and its frequently poor democratic control.

Although diverse, street-level bureaucrats have in common their direct interaction with the public of public policy, pupils and their parents, delinquents and victims, or welfare clients. Observation of these interactions is therefore central in the SLB approach, and connects it with ethnographic methods – what I propose, for instance, in my work on encounters between bureaucrats and their clients at the desks of welfare agencies (Dubois 2010). My ethnographic approach reveals the asymmetric structure of these interactions, and the way they sometimes add bureaucratic alienation to the socio-economic domination of the poor. It also shows the various uses of these encounters by clients, including their resistance strategies, and the way these uses can in turn impact the routines of welfare bureaucracy.

Limiting the ethnography of policy making to the ethnography of organizations, generally at the bottom of bureaucratic hierarchy, would, however, be misleading. First, policy ethnographers can and should also observe the top level of policy making, since, from an ethnographic perspective, 'what happens in the executive boardroom, the cabinet meeting, or the shareholders' annual general meeting is no less important than that which occurs at the level of the factory floor or locality' (Wedel et al. 2005, p. 34; Yanow 2009, p. 34). This is illustrated by Rhodes's observation of British ministers and permanent secretaries (Rhodes 2011). Observing the daily practices and beliefs of government elites and elected officials usefully contributes to the ethnography of policy making, as research at the national, local and European level has shown (on the European Parliament, see Abélès 1993; Rhodes et al. 2007).

Second, policy ethnography can comprehensively include various levels of policy making, incorporating 'the full realm of processes and relations involved in the production of policy' (Wedel et al. 2005, p. 34). This is what Belorgey did in his multi-situated ethnography of public hospital reform in France. He was a participant observer of the production of expert knowledge in an audit agency which defined 'quality norms' and managerial indicators. For several months, he later conducted local ethnographies of hospitals, scrutinized the role of intermediate levels in the appropriation and in the implementation of reforms, and eventually analyzed their impact on clients in an emergency unit (Belorgey 2012). This example shows that taking various levels into account is not just about juxtaposing them, but is a matter of providing a comprehensive view of policy processes.

What we call 'the field' is, thus, no longer defined by an organization or by a group of actors, or even by a set of organizations and groups, but by the policy process itself which includes various levels and locations – 'from legislative chambers to legislators' offices, from the latter to implementers' offices, from there to the on-site locations where street-level bureaucrats meet "clients," and beyond' (Yanow 2009, p. 34). In his study of local governance, van Hulst crossed the institutional borders in order to account for the experience of the various categories of people involved in local governance (van Hulst 2008). To a certain extent, we may think of a de-localized policy ethnography, in which the object delimits the field, not the other way around. Feldman gives an example for this 'non-local ethnography'. Located in an office concerned with EU migration management policy, he did not aim to study day-to-day organizational culture and practice, but at following the processes by which four policy domains (security, development, employment and human rights) are brought into alignment through various intergovernmental meetings (Feldman 2011).

HOW CAN POLICY ETHNOGRAPHY BE 'CRITICAL'?

Up to now, I have examined how ethnographic fieldwork can contribute to critical policy studies. To do so, I explored a series of oppositions regarding the orientations of ethnography, the public it is intended for, and the objects of ethnographic study. In this concluding section, I will turn to the question of how policy ethnography can be critical, and will show how ethnography can provide a critical contribution (i.e. of decisive importance) to policy studies.

What Does 'Critical' Mean?

'Critical' is a generic term that can refer to various approaches. First, it can be used as a synonym for 'politically engaged', or at least politically conscious. This is what Jim Thomas proposes when he describes critical ethnography as 'conventional ethnography with a political purpose' (Thomas 1993, p. 4). According to this notion, critical ethnographers 'celebrate their normative and political position' and take on 'making value-laden judgments' (Thomas 1993, p. 4), as opposed to traditional scholars whose legitimacy rests on their claim to neutrality. This definition may appear too straightforward and narrow, as critical ethnography must not be viewed predominantly as a form of activism or partisanship to the detriment of its scientific contribution. This conception, however, draws our attention to the questioning of neutrality and to the political implications (even if indirect or implicit) at work in critical approaches in a broader sense. Second, the term 'critical' refers to non-positivist, interpretive and constructionist methodologies based on the idea that social reality is plural, and interpretively co-constructed (Schwartz-Shea and Yanow 2012, p. 4). I would add to this defining feature of critical research, however, that the various 'truths' on the social world may be equally valuable from a methodological or ethical point of view, but that they are not equivalent in the real world. Some of these 'truths' are made more 'true' than others through power relationships that promote them as unquestionable truths, shared principles of visions of the social world. Third, a critical approach could be defined by its ability to question the taken-for-grantedness of the social world as an outcome of social and symbolic domination. Policy and the state play a central part here, and ethnography proves an effective tool in revealing it. Unveiling their role in domination is what, in my view, delineates the political significance of critical policy ethnography.

Challenging Dominant Views

In various ways, ethnography provides a useful complement to the history and sociology of the construction of public problems and, more generally, to the critique of generally accepted views of the social world. This is what Katherine Newman means when she states that 'the special mission of ethnography [. . .] lies in its capacity to redefine the social landscape, to explode received categories [. . .] to develop different ways of thinking about a social universe' too often taken for granted (Becker et al. 2004, p. 271). The special advantage of ethnography, Newman explains, is to explore the subjective experiences of people and, therefore, to expose views on the problems they experience that may differ from the accepted, official view of these problems. In other words, a critical use of ethnography in policy studies consists in not only understanding, but also accounting for subjective points of view – seeing like a citizen or a client of the state, or like any person exposed to its policy – as a means of deconstructing the official vision – what James Scott terms as 'seeing like a state' (Scott 1988). This change of perspective also enables us to identify issues that do not generally attact attention because they '[contradict] cultural expectations about what kind of society we live in' (Becker et al. 2004, p. 269).

Doing critical policy ethnography can also consist of juxtaposing the observation of the ethnographers to the beliefs of policy makers (Katz 2004). We can think here of how welfare ethnography, which gives an insight into the real situations of the poor, allowed for a break with government and media rhetoric. As Morgen and Maskovsky explain: 'Ethnographers have deconstructed the hegemonic discourse on welfare restructuring, juxtaposing dominant ideologies with the so-called realities of impoverishment' (Morgen and Maskovsky 2003, p. 325). This critique went beyond the borders of academia, and enabled scholars to participate in the public discussions about welfare. Such analyses can be viewed as critical, not only because of their contents, but also because they are the occasion for ethnographers to intervene in the public debate, insofar as they lead researchers to study questions central to contemporary societies, which have furthermore been fiercely debated. Here again, critical ethnography meets public ethnography.

In his ethnographic research on 1960s colonial and rural Algeria, Bourdieu similarly showed that the concepts of work or income that are taken for granted in modern capitalist economies can prove unfamiliar and irrelevant to traditional forms of economy (Bourdieu 1979). He demonstrated that colonial domination partly consisted of imposing these ideas in order to reform and 'modernize' an economy described as archaic. Bourdieu's ethnographic approach has shown how colonial and economic domination went hand in hand with symbolic domination – in the sense of the imposition of categories of thought upon dominated social agents.

In my research, I have drawn on Bourdieu's framework to consider the enforcement of recent welfare program changes as the imposition of categories of perception and norms of behavior portrayed as universally legitimate, on people whose socio-economic attitudes have been delegitimized and corrected. I show that economic concepts that have set the tone of welfare reforms, such as the neo-classic theory of unemployment and the 'inactivity trap' model, for instance, fail to account for the actual attitudes of welfare clients as they are revealed by ethnographic fieldwork. This critical ethnography further consists in showing how, no matter whether true or false, these concepts are applied to the clients, thus eventually impacting their lives (Dubois 2014a).

How Does Policy Really Work?

Deconstructing taken-for-granted and dominant visions in policy processes breaks with the positivistic paradigm of policy as a reified entity and an unanalyzed given. We can go further in this critical reasoning by exploring what policy concretely is, and how it operates, in a way that may challenge the official image policy makers promote of their programs.

Ethnography accounts for the practical accomplishments of abstractions, such as 'the state' and 'policy'. Here we can follow Bourdieu when he focuses on 'state acts' by which agents vested with the power of the state define situations, classify people, and control access to resources. It is through these acts that the state comes into being (Bourdieu 2014). By accounting for these relations and for these acts, ethnography provides a critical view of the state – i.e. a view of what the state concretely consists of, as opposed to an abstract and ideal image. The same reasoning can be applied to policy. Studying it as a concrete set of relationships and practices, critical ethnography can debunk the ideal, abstract vision produced by official discourse and mainstream rationalistic theory, particularly when dealing with problem solving and top-down programming. In my work on anti-welfare fraud policies, for instance, I show that control practices aimed at ensuring 'the right payment to the right persons' and at identifying possible fraudsters, actually consist of a legal *bricolage* by investigators who apply ill-defined rules to complex and changing situations, thereby contradicting the appeal to legal rigor as the rationale for welfare control (Dubois 2014b). I argue that this arbitrariness is consistent with policy goals. It is a by-product of the individualization process of European welfare policies over the last decades. By making recipients 'less comfortable', it also serves policies aimed at making people prefer work to welfare. Conceived in this manner, the ethnographic observation of policy practices on the ground not only gives us a better understanding of the realities of public policy, it is also a powerful way of revealing the structural characteristics and current transformations of policy processes (Dubois 2009).

What Does a Policy Perform? Classification and Symbolic Power

By studying the meaning-making practices, relationships and concrete acts by which a policy comes into being, critical policy ethnography accounts for realization and performance of a policy and offers a path to escape the conventional way of viewing 'policy implementation' as the application of the pre-defined decisions of a program. Critical policy ethnography also accounts for what a policy realizes and performs, and avoids a restricted view of policy effects in terms of 'evaluation', understood as the final step of the policy process. Combining the two questions of how a policy is performed and of what it performs enables us to provide a consistent comprehensive view of policy, which invalidates the mainstream notion of a policy as a systematic process or cycle composed of well-organized stages. Since policy commonly operates by defining the categories through which people and problems are perceived and dealt with, the analysis of classification processes is an essential part of a comprehensive critical perspective.

As a first step, critical policy ethnographers question the conventional policy categories, showing their social and political roots and, by doing so, their non-natural, non-necessary character. This follows an anthropological tradition, initiated by Durkheim and Mauss in their seminal work on primitive classifications, that Douglas built on in her work on institutional thinking (Durkheim and Mauss 1963; Douglas 1986). Dvora Yanow beautifully illustrates the possible use of this research program in critical policy studies in her book on the construction of 'race' and 'ethnicity' in the United States (Yanow 2003).

In a second step, studying policy categories is about observing how policy makers and administrations use them and concretely apply them to people and problems. This is what Yanow does in her chapter on

'Making race-ethnicity through administrative practices' (Yanow 2003, pp. 113–180). This is also what I do in my observations of the way welfare agents relate their definition of the situations of the poor they meet to standard criteria and categories, translating the lives of their clients into the language of bureaucratic files (Dubois 2010, 2014b).

In a third step, the ethnography of classification processes identifies impacts on classified problems and people. One of the most effective ways of addressing this question is to evaluate to what extent individuals categorized by policy in turn refer to these categories to define their situation or their identity. Ian Hacking– in his work on scientific categories – has coined the phrase 'looping effect' to designate how 'invented' or constructed categories become 'real', in the sense that they create new groups – a process he terms 'making up people' (Hacking 2006).[2]

These three steps form a critical policy ethnography research program on categorization and classification processes: first, unveiling the construction of official categories; second, analyzing their mobilization in unequal power relationships by policy agents who process people and handle public problems; and third, identifying the impact of official categories on people who come to internalize them. This is a way for ethnographic research to contribute to critical policy studies, understood as the analysis of social and symbolic domination exerted throughout the policy processes.

CONCLUSION

Policy ethnography includes a wide range of research practices, from applied anthropology in development programs to the use of qualitative fieldwork methods by political scientists studying policy processes. This work generally stands apart from mainstream positivist policy analysis, but not always. Policy ethnography includes explicit political purposes in defense of the disenfranchised, but also embraces so-called 'neutral' practice-driven research providing 'useful knowledge' to those in power – the collaboration of anthropologists with colonial administrators being the most obvious example. Consequently, policy ethnography can neither in the epistemological nor in the political sense of the term be identified as 'critical' per se.

A critical approach needs to reflect on the social and political contexts, practices and uses of social science research. Critical policy ethnography should thus be regarded in relation to tensions between applied and basic ethnography, as well as between ethnography for policy makers and ethnography for the disenfranchised. We have seen how these oppositions could combine in complex ways with distinctions regarding the research objects, such as between people-centered vs. policy-centered ethnography. In this context, we can recognize four defining features of critical policy ethnography: challenging mainstream positivist approaches to public policy; confronting commonsense and official views on policy; setting individual experiences and micro-observations in the broader perspective of power and inequality structures; and unveiling social, economic, symbolic and political domination processes operating in and through policy processes. When policy ethnography succeeds in reaching these four objectives, and is thus fully 'critical', it marks a decisive advance in policy studies.

ACKNOWLEDGEMENTS

I want to thank Didier Fassin, Sanford Schram and the editors of this volume for their comments on a previous version of this chapter, and Jean-Yves Bart for his linguistic revisions. Jean-Yves is supported by the Excellence Initiative of the University of Strasbourg funded by the French government's Future Investments program.

NOTES

1. For an example of PAR in service of a critical policy ethnography that actually produced policy change, see Marianna Chilton's 'Witnesses to Hunger' project and its impact on food stamps, available at: http://www.centerforhungerfreecommunities.org/our-projects/witnesses-hunger.
2. Whereas Hacking mainly focuses on scientific categories, a similar approach can be adopted in the case of policy categories, by analogy, or because scientific constructions of populations and problems often inform their apprehension in policy programs.

REFERENCES

Abélès, M. (1993) 'Political Anthropology of a Transnational Institution : The European Parliament', *French Politics and Society*, **11** (1), 1–19.
Becker, H.S. (1967) 'Whose Side Are We On?', *Social Problems*, **14** (3), 239–247.
Becker, H.S., Gans, H.J., Newman, K.S. and Vaughan, D. (2004) 'On the Value of Ethnography: Sociology and Public Policy, a Dialogue', *Annals of the American Academy of Political and Social Science*, **595**, 264–276.
Belorgey, N. (2012) 'De l'hôpital à l'Etat: le regard ethnographique au chevet de l'action publique', *Gouvernement et action publique*, **2** (2), 9–40.
Belshaw, C.S. (1976) *The Sorcerer's Apprentice: An Anthropology of Public Policy*, Pergamon Press: New York.
Bennett, J.W. (1996) 'Applied and Action Anthropology: Ideological and Conceptual Aspects', *Current Anthropology*, **37** (1), S23–S53.

Biehl, J. and Petryna, A. (2013) *When People Come First. Critical Studies in Global Health*, Princeton University Press: Princeton, NJ.

Blau, P.M. (1955) *The Dynamics of Bureaucracy*, University of Chicago Press: Chicago.

Borofsky, R. (1999) 'Public Anthropology', *Anthropology News*, **40** (1), 6–7.

Bourdieu, P. (1979) *Algeria 1960*, Cambridge University Press: Cambridge.

Bourdieu, P. (2004) *Science of Science and Reflexivity*, Polity: Oxford.

Bourdieu, P. (2014) *On the State*, Polity: Oxford.

Brodkin, E.Z. (2011) 'Putting Street-Level Organizations First: New Directions for Social Policy and Management Research', *Journal of Public Administration Research and Theory*, **21** (Supplement 2), i199–i201.

Burawoy, M. (2005) 'For Public Sociology', *American Sociological Review*, **70** (1), 4–28.

Chambers, E. (1985) *Applied Anthropology: A Practical Guide*, Prentice Hall: Upper Saddle River, NJ.

Douglas, M. (1986) *How Institutions Think*, Syracuse University Press: Syracuse, NY.

Dubois, V. (2009) 'Towards a Critical Policy Ethnography: Lessons from Fieldwork on Welfare Control in France', *Critical Policy Studies*, **3** (2), 221–239.

Dubois, V. (2010) *The Bureaucrat and the Poor. Encounters in French Welfare Offices*, Ashgate: Aldershot, UK.

Dubois, V. (2014a) 'The Economic Vulgate of Welfare Reform: Elements for a Socioanthropological Critique', *Current Anthropology*, **55** (S9), 138–146.

Dubois, V. (2014b) 'The State, Legal Rigor and the Poor: The Daily Practice of Welfare Control', *Social Analysis*, **58** (2), 38–55.

Durkheim, E. and Mauss, M. (1963) *Primitive Classification*, University of Chicago Press: Chicago.

Edin, K. and Lein, L. (1997) *Making Ends Meet: How Single Mothers Survive Welfare and Low-Wage Work*, Russell Sage Foundation: New York.

Fassin, D. (2013) *Enforcing Order: An Ethnography of Urban Policing*, Polity: Cambridge.

Feldman, G. (2011) 'Illuminating the Apparatus: Steps toward a Nonlocal Ethnography of Global Governance', in Shore, C., Wright, S. and Però, D. (eds), *Policy Worlds: Anthropology and the Analysis of Contemporary Power*, Berghahn Books: New York and Oxford, pp. 32–49.

Fetterman, D.M. (ed.) (1993) *Speaking the Language of Power: Communication, Collaboration, and Advocacy. Translating Ethnography into Action*, Social Research and Educational Studies Series, Falmer Press: London and Washington, DC.

Goffman, E. (1961) *Asylums; Essays on the Social Situation of Mental Patients and Other Inmates*, Anchor Books: Garden City, NY.

Gupta, A. (2012) *Red Tape: Bureaucracy, Structural Violence, and Poverty in India*, Duke University Press: Durham, NC.

Hacking, I. (2006) 'Making Up People', *London Review of Books*, 17 August, 23–26.

Hays, S. (2002) *Flat Broke With Children: Women in the Age of Welfare Reform*, Oxford University Press: Oxford.

van Hulst, M.J. (2008) 'Quite an Experience: Using Ethnography to Study Local Governance', *Critical Policy Studies*, **2** (2), 143–159.

Katz, J. (2004) 'On the Rhetoric and Politics of Ethnographic Methodology', *The Annals of the American Academy of Political and Social Science*, **595** (1), 280–308.

Kimball, S. (1978) 'Anthropology as a Policy Science', in Partridge, W.L. and Eddy, E.M. (eds), *Applied Anthropology in America*, Columbia University Press: New York, pp. 277–291.

Lichter, D.T. and Jayakody, R. (2002) 'Welfare Reform: How Do We Measure Success?', *Annual Review of Sociology*, **28** (1), 117–141.

Lipsky, M. (1980) *Street-Level Bureaucracy: Dilemmas of the Individual in Public Services*, Russell Sage Foundation: New York.

Malinowski, B. (1929) 'Practical Anthropology', *Africa*, **2** (1), 22–38.

Morgen, S. and Maskovsky, J. (2003) 'The Anthropology of Welfare "Reform"', *Annual Review of Anthropology*, **32**, 315–338.

Nader, L. (1972) 'Up the Anthropologist. Perspectives Gained from Studying Up', in Hymes, D.H. (ed.), *Reinventing Anthropology*, Pantheon Books: New York, pp. 284–311.

Okongwu, A.F. and Mencher, J.P. (2000) 'The Anthropology of Public Policy. Shifting Terrains', *Annual Review of Anthropology*, **29**, 107–124.

Rhodes, R.A.W. (2011) *Everyday Life in British Government*, Oxford University Press: Oxford and New York.

Rhodes, R.A.W., Hart, P. 't and Noordegraaf, M. (eds) (2007) *Observing Government Elites: Up Close and Personal*, Palgrave Macmillan: Houndmills, Basingstoke, UK.

Sanday, P.R. (1976) *Anthropology and the Public Interest*, Academic Press: New York.

Schensul, S.L. (1980) 'Anthropological Fieldwork and Sociopolitical Change', *Social Problems*, **27** (3), 309–319.

Schram, S.F., Shdaimah, C. and Stahl, R. (2013) 'When You Can See the Sky through Your Roof: Policy Analysis from the Bottom Up', in Schatz, E. (ed.), *Political Ethnography: What Immersion Contributes to the Study of Power*, University of Chicago Press: Chicago, pp. 255–274.

Schwartzman, H.B. (1993) *Ethnography in Organizations*, Qualitative Research Methods Series, SAGE: Newbury Park, CA, London and New Delhi..

Schwartz-Shea, P. and Yanow, D. (2012) *Interpretive Research Design: Concepts and Processes*, Routledge Series on Interpretive Methods, Routledge: New York.

Scott, J. (1988) *Seeing Like a State. How Certain Schemes to Improve the Human Condition Have Failed*, Yale University Press: New Haven, CT.

Shelton, D. and Matthews, R.O. (1999) 'Public Interest Anthropology: Beyond the Bureaucratic Ethos', in Higgins, P.J. and Paredes, A. (eds), *Classics of Practicing Anthropology*, Society for Applied Anthropology: Oklahoma City.

Shore, C. and Wright, S. (1997) 'Policy: A New Field of Anthropology', in Shore, C. and Wright, S. (eds), *Anthropology of Policy. Critical Perspectives on Governance and Power*, Routledge: London and New York, pp. 3–39.

Stack, C.B. (1997) 'What are Given as Givens: Ethnography and Critical Policy Studies', *Ethos*, **25** (2), 191–207.

Tax, S. (1975) 'Action Anthropology', *Current Anthropology*, **16** (4), 514–517.

Thomas, J. (1993) *Doing Critical Ethnography*, Qualitative Research Methods Series, SAGE: Newbury Park, CA, London and New Delhi.

United States General Accounting Office (2003) *Ethnographic Studies Can Inform Agencies' Actions*, Washington, DC.

Van Willigen, J. (2002) 'Anthropology as Policy Research', in *Applied Anthropology: An Introduction*, Westport, CT: Greenwood Publishing Group, pp. 161–174.

Van Willigen, J. and DeWalt, B.R. (1985) *Training Manual in Policy Ethnography*, American Anthropological Association: Washington, DC.

Wedel, J.R., Shore, C., Feldman, G., Lathrop, S. (2005) 'Toward an Anthropology of Public Policy', *The Annals of the American Academy of Political and Social Science*, **600** (1), 30–51.

Yanow, D. (2003) *Constructing 'Race' and 'Ethnicity' in America: Category-Making in Public Policy and Administration*, M.E. Sharpe: Armonk, NY.

Yanow, D. (2009) 'What's Political About Political Ethnography? Abducting Our Way Toward Reason and Meaning', *Qualitative & Multi-Method Research*, **7** (2), 33–37.

Yanow, D., Ybema, S. and van Hulst, M. (2012) 'Practicing Organizational Ethnography', in Symon, G. and Cassell, C. (eds), *Qualitative Organizational Research: Core Methods and Current Challenges*, SAGE: London, pp. 331–350.

25 Making gender visible: exploring feminist perspectives through the case of anti-smoking policy
Stephanie Paterson and Francesca Scala

INTRODUCTION

Feminist politics has changed dramatically over the past few decades, particularly with respect to bureaucratic politics. Where questions of gender were previously conceptualized across Western states as those concerning 'special measures', they are now increasingly 'mainstreamed'. That is, gender is now built into the very fabric of policymaking architecture across more than 160 states. The goal of gender mainstreaming as bureaucratic practice is to make gender visible, even in those policy areas not typically conceptualized as gendered, such as transportation, taxation, and emergency-preparedness.[1] This key insight builds on the vast array of feminist policy scholarship that has exposed the ubiquity of gender politics and outcomes. But gender mainstreaming itself has not paid enough attention of the issues of hierarchy, power differentials and domination, which is the task of a critical feminist policy perspective as we show below. This chapter will provide an overview of the contributions made by feminist policy scholars and present a case study in which the gender implications are not obvious: tobacco control.

Despite the power of the tobacco industry, the anti-tobacco movement is arguably one of the most successful public health movements of the 21st century, resulting in the World Health Organization Framework Convention on Tobacco Control, adopted by more than 160 countries worldwide. As an international policy framework, states are required, among other things, to implement measures designed to address both supply and demand, raise awareness, and address issues of addiction and other health-related harms. While tobacco control is an issue with obvious economic, social and health dimensions, its gendered implications are less clear. How is smoking a gendered phenomenon? How do anti-smoking policies reflect and shape our understandings of gender and systems of penalty and privilege?

We will address these questions following an overview of key contributions to feminist policy studies. In doing so, we examine the critical dimensions of feminist policy studies to show where it can supplement critical approaches more generally. To develop our case study, we analyze several policy approaches to show the unique insights and contributions of feminist analysis. In our comparison, we discuss the value of each approach and highlight theoretical, epistemological and methodological considerations they bring to bear in policy deliberations and analysis. The chapter concludes with a brief discussion of the challenges of feminist policy studies and reflects on possible future developments in the field.

WHAT'S *FEMINIST* ABOUT FEMINIST POLICY STUDIES?

Feminist contributions to policy studies span several decades; however, it has only been since the 1990s that feminist policy studies has come into its own. Early works exposed androcentric biases in particular policy fields, such as economic policy (e.g. Waring 1988), development (e.g. Boserup 1970 [1989]), and social policy (e.g. Jenson 1986; Fraser 1987; Gordon 1990). In an important paper in the mid-1990s, Phillips (1996) summarized these contributions as attention to discourse, identity and voice (see also Hawkesworth 1994).

At this time, however, feminist scholars began engaging public policy scholarship more directly, calling for explicitly feminist policy theory and method (e.g. Burt 1995; Hawkesworth 1994). In an early overview of feminist policy studies appearing in a special issue of *Policy Sciences*, Hawkesworth (1994, p.110) notes,

> By fostering critical examination of the role of social values in framing research questions, characterizing objects of inquiry, accrediting forms of explanation, demarcating credible evidence, and structuring modes of argument, feminist scholarship offers traditional disciplines a means to increase sensitivity to error and to purge androcentrism from disciplinary paradigms. These goals structure the field of feminist policy studies.

Feminist policy studies has since shaped debates on all facets of policy scholarship, including policy 'problems' (e.g. Bacchi 1999), agenda setting and policy change (e.g. Abrar et al. 2000; Kenney 2003), policy design and implementation (e.g. Rixecker 1994), policy and program evaluation (e.g. Bustelo and Verloo 2009; Bacchi and Eveline 2010), policy networks (e.g. Boles 1994; Woodward 2004; Beckwith 2007; Holli 2008) and policy structures and processes (Squires 2007; Kantola and Squires 2012; McBride and Mazur 2012). Borrowing heavily from, but also challenging critical policy studies, feminist policy studies has resulted in an impressive range of theoretical and methodological frameworks designed to expose the ubiquity of gender in policy processes and outcomes (e.g. Marshall 1997; Bacchi 1999, 2009b; McPhail 2003; Verloo and Lombardo 2007; Hankivsky 2012a; McBride and Mazur 2012; see also Fonow and Cook 2005; McCall 2005; Manuel 2006).

In effect, what is now considered feminist policy studies is a broad field, ranging from analyses of substantive issue areas to those addressing the micro-dimensions of policy processes and outcomes. Indeed, as noted by Lombardo et al. (2013), the breadth and novelty of the field means that scholars do not necessarily label their work as such. In attempts to bring this work together, there have been a number of excellent recent overviews of the field (Mazur 2009; Mazur and Pollack 2009; Orloff and Palier 2009; Hawkesworth 2012; Lombardo et al. 2013; for earlier overviews, see Ackelsberg 1992; Hawkesworth 1994; Phillips 1996).

Characterized by a rich epistemological and methodological diversity, feminist policy studies include empiricist, interpretive, critical and post-structuralist approaches. These approaches, however, share a number of characteristics. First, despite a variety of feminist orientations, as well as varying conceptions of terms such as 'equality' and 'gender', feminist policy scholarship is united in its opposition to domination and marginalization. And while most privilege gender as the primary axis of oppression, recent scholarship challenges this focus, calling instead for intersectional analyses that expose complex structures of penalty and privilege (see, for examples, Manuel 2006; Hankivsky 2012a). Second, but in relation to the previous point, despite the variety of approaches, feminist policy scholarship is committed to exposing and remedying gender inequality. For some, this has resulted in process-focused analyses that illuminate the roles of political institutions, actors and policy processes that make woman-friendly, though not explicitly feminist,[2] policies possible (e.g. McBride and Mazur 1995, 2012; Mazur 2001, 2002; McBride 2001; Outshoorn 2004; Woodward 2004; Haussman and Sauer 2007; Strid et al. 2013). For others, this has resulted in content-focused analyses, which assess the degree to which policies, woman-friendly or not, sustain or challenge gender inequality and marginalization more generally (e.g. Bacchi 1999; McPhail 2003; Verloo 2007; Verloo and Lombardo 2007; Lombardo et al. 2009; Lombardo and Rolandsen Agustin 2011).

Third, although feminist policy scholars encourage methodological diversity, with few exceptions they tend to encourage research methods that nurture experiential knowledge and challenge the hierarchy of orthodox scientific methods (e.g. Hawkesworth 1994, 2010; Marshall 1997). Thus, feminist policy scholars have taken seriously the claims of feminist standpoint theorists in recognizing that individuals, and therefore knowledge, are socially located (e.g. Hill Collins 1990; Harding 1987). By including the 'situated knowledges' of marginalized groups, feminist perspectives help widen the theoretical underpinnings and evidential base of policy inquiry.

Finally, reflexivity is encouraged, directing researchers to interrogate and address their own assumptions and presuppositions regarding policy problems and social groups (e.g. Bacchi 2009). This has also required close attention to the social location of both researchers and participants and a heightened call for intersectional approaches that enable deep understanding of social contexts (e.g. Fonow and Cook 2005; Manuel 2006; Hankivsky 2012a; Walby et al. 2012; Hancock 2013; Strid et al. 2013). In sum, feminist approaches, like critical perspectives, are explicitly committed to emancipatory politics and social justice.

These features of feminist policy scholarship align nicely with those of critical policy studies. Attention to power and marginalization, transformative politics and social justice ensures that feminist policy scholars are also *critical* scholars. Bridging the work of critical and feminist scholars remains key, however, to fostering a mutually enriching dialogue that uncovers theoretical and methodological blind spots (e.g. Beland 2009; Orloff and Palier 2009). For example, as noted by Orloff and Palier (2009: 408) in the introduction to a special issue of *Social Politics*, feminist work on the roles of 'ideas, culture, discourse' in shaping institutional and policy processes and outcomes has often been neglected, even among critical scholars. Moreover, critical perspectives are not always cognizant of the gendered and gendering dimensions of their work, as early work by Rixecker (1994) revealed. In particular, insights from feminist and post-colonial interrogations of the 'public sphere' can supplement critical scholarship with respect to the theory and method of deliberative processes to transform relations of ruling (see, for example, Meehan 1995; see also Ahmed 2012). Feminist scholars have also shown how women's voices and experiences come to be marginalized in participatory research practices that routinely include women under the general categories of the 'oppressed' or the 'people' (Reid 2004). By bringing these issues to light, feminist scholarship contributes to the theory and praxis of policy studies.

FEMINIST CONTRIBUTIONS TO POLICY STUDIES

As noted above, there is a long tradition of exposing androcentric biases in policy fields, processes and outcomes. As the field developed, studies began to engage more explicitly with policy studies and analysis, calling attention to both theory and method (e.g. Hawkesworth 1994; Burt 1995;

Phillips 1996). These contributions can be summarized by two broad questions, and tend to focus on either policy processes or content (Lombardo et al. 2013): First, how do feminist (or woman-friendly policies) come to *be*? Second, how do policies come to *mean*? These areas will be discussed in turn, followed by a brief discussion of how the literature on gender mainstreaming, an approach to policy analysis that requires analysts to apply a gender lens to all policies and programs, effectively bridges these questions.

How Do Feminist Policies Come to Be?

One of the key goals of feminist policy research is to determine how feminist, or at least woman-friendly, policies develop. Early work in this area focused on the potential influence, or lack thereof, of women's movements (e.g. Boneparth 1982; Gelb 1987) and the roles of bureaucrats and policy elites in shaping public policy (see, for example, Ferguson 1984; Lovenduski 1986; Stivers 1993, 2002; Eisenstein 1995; McBride and Mazur 1995; Burnier 2003; for an early overview, see Hawkesworth 1994). More recently, however, literature addressing this area typically emphasizes the complex confluence of factors that give rise to feminist policy, including institutions, ideas and actors within both state and non-state organizations and within global, national and local contexts (see, for example, Squires 2007; Walby 2011; see also Kantola and Squires 2012). Indeed, as Walby (2011, p. 150) notes, 'The combination, achieved through alliances and coalitions, between grassroots NGOs and governmental bodies produces more substantial change than an exclusive development of activities either in specialized organizations or in the mainstream.'

This work has led to a number of interesting approaches with which to assess and understand gender equality architecture within and across states. Most notable is, of course, the state feminism literature, as represented by the Research Network on Gender Politics and the State (RNGS). As an empiricist approach to feminist policy studies, state feminist approaches adhere to positivist methods to trace policy debate and subsequent state responses as a function of characteristics of the women's movement, the policy environment, and women's policy agency characteristics and activities, leading to a number of testable hypotheses (Haussman and Sauer 2007, p. 6; for a summary, see McBride and Mazur 2012, pp. 13–16).

The RNGS framework has been foundational in feminist policy studies, leading to important national and comparative work on gender equality policy machinery (e.g. Mazur 2001, 2002; McBride and Mazur 2012, 1995; McBride 2001; Outshoorn 2004; Haussman and Sauer 2007). Indeed, a number of significant findings concerning the conditions for feminist policy success have emerged from this literature, including the importance of a cohesive women's movement, high-priority issues, left-of-center governments, and fit between activists and policymakers (Kantola and Squires 2012: 384). Less clear, however, are the characteristics of women's policy agencies and their relationship to success (e.g. McBride and Mazur 2012). As Kantola and Squires (2012: 384) note, success is more likely determined by 'external factors, namely the characteristics of the women's movement and the policy environment, than on internal factors, namely the features of the women's policy agency itself'.

This finding echoes the conclusions of other approaches working within this area, which point to the importance of synergistic relationships, so called 'strategic partnerships' or 'triangles of empowerment', between women's policy agencies, activists and elected officials (e.g. Squires 2007). For example, feminist network theory (e.g. Boles 1994; Halsaa 1998; Vargas and Wieringa 1998; Woodward 2004; Holli 2008), as well as feminist adaptations of the advocacy coalitions framework (e.g. Abrar et al. 2000) emphasize the necessity of cooperation and coalition building among actors alternatively positioned in the policymaking context. Adopting a political process model, Roggeband and Verloo (2006) reveal the importance of the 'needle's eye' in developing and implementing feminist policies, which includes structures, processes, actors and policy frames (see also Lombardo et al. 2013 for a discussion).

The collective works in this area expose the complexity of creating and implementing woman-friendly policy. However, this work tends to pay less attention to what actually constitutes feminist policy (Squires 2008), often adopting a minimalist approach where policies need be only 'nominally' feminist or woman-friendly (see McBride and Mazur 2012 for a discussion). Thus, policies that are oriented towards 'integrationist' or 'reversalist' approaches that seek accommodation in existing frameworks by either 'leveling the playing field' or re-valuing the 'gender-specific' contributions of men and women, respectively, are treated the same as 'transformational' approaches that attempt to trouble the very structures and systems that give rise to gender identity and domination.[3] Therefore, a focus on how policies come to mean fills an important gap in this work.

How Do Policies Come to Mean?[4]

Although the orienting question identified above implies on some level an attention to policy discourse and discursive politics, not all of the approaches discussed here are focused on these factors. Rather, the approaches discussed here illuminate the ways in which policies, feminist or otherwise, structure inequality and marginalization. Towards this end, a number of approaches have been developed to analyze policies in an attempt to shed light on the ways in which public policy is both gender*ed* and gender*ing*. We focus here on critical, discursive and intersectional approaches.

Much of the literature concerned with content exposes the ways in which policies structure lived experience and (re)produce or transform social hierarchies. Feminist political economists, for instance, made important contributions to this discussion long before we had a name for feminist policy studies (see, for examples, McIntosh 1978; Jenson 1986; Ng 1987; more recently, see Neysmith et al. 2005).

Picking up on the critical dimension of these works and speaking more directly to policy studies, feminist critical scholars have nurtured frameworks for policy analysis that encourage reflexivity, participation and deliberation. Marshall's (1997, 1999; see also Bensimon and Marshall 2003) work in the area of education has been particularly insightful:

> We need theories and methods that integrate gender issues with the realities of power and politics. The master's tools must be cast aside, by bringing into question all things that were common sense, structured and assumed, from male–female difference to male norms of leadership and power. Integrating feminist and critical theory into policy analysis will add critical issues and ways of framing questions about power, justice and the state. (Marshall 1997, p. 2, 1999)

From this perspective, the empiricist approaches associated with state feminism are limited in their ability to expose and remedy gender inequality. In contrast, much of the work in this field adopts critically oriented theoretical approaches and reflexive methodologies that aim to transform how we do policy analysis and its effects. By interrogating and scrutinizing ideas such as expertise and authoritative knowledge, this work is explicitly political in its objectives, seeking to transform social relations. Often the approaches are guided by sensitizing questions that attempt to reveal the gender*ed* and gender*ing* dimensions of policy texts. For example, McPhail's (2003) feminist policy analysis framework contains a list of questions that orient researchers and analysts to the gendered and intersectional dimensions of policies. Specifically, the framework calls attention to the voice of the policy text, the role of power, and the structuring of difference and diversity.

One of the most influential works in this vein is Bacchi's (1999 [2005]) *What's the Problem Represented to Be?* approach (WTP), or problem representation (see also Bacchi 2009a, 2010). Inspired by Foucault's work on discursive formations, Bacchi troubles the taken-for-grantedness of policy problems and invites researchers to interrogate underlying presuppositions and silences to determine how problems sustain or transform social locations. Instead of assuming 'problem definitions', the approach scrutinizes 'problem representations', or problematizations, which import particular understandings of gender and equality into policy texts and open or restrict the spaces for transformative politics. The approach aims at exposing the discursive, subjectivization and lived effects of policies, asking, for example, who is speaking and for whom, about what and to what effect, as well as asking who and what is missing or rendered invisible by dominant understandings of the problem.

More recent frameworks, such as Critical Frame Analysis (CFA) and Intersectionality-Based Policy Analysis (IBPA), have built on this work, offering innovative approaches for comparative and intersectional work. CFA, developed by Verloo and Lombardo (2007), integrates insights from frame theory, feminist policy analysis and feminist theory. CFA begins with the assumptions that policy issues are open to multiple and often contradictory interpretations and that all policy discourse is gender*ed* and gender*ing*. As an approach to policy analysis, CFA focuses on several dimensions of policy frames, including the diagnosis/prognosis of the 'problem'; the ways in which gender and intersectionality are represented therein; voice; roles and responsibilities; location of and mechanisms for sustaining the problem and its solution (see Verloo and Lombardo 2007 and Lombardo et al. 2013 for discussions). CFA is also concerned with the balance between diagnoses and prognoses. Diagnostic discourse implicates particular solutions (Bacchi 1999 [2005]); however, policy incoherence can arise where prognosis and diagnosis are incompatible. For example, diagnosing gender inequality as a problem of an unequal distribution of caring labor is not compatible with a perspective that acknowledges only market-oriented solutions.

These dimensions of policy frames help us to untangle and trouble the underlying and often implicit assumptions in policy texts and discourse. As such, CFA can expose the ways in which gender is reproduced or challenged by and through policies. This approach has contributed to a significant body of research, largely focused on Europe, that documents competing visions of equality, and contradictions, tensions and inconsistencies within and across policy texts (see Verloo 2007 and Lombardo et al. 2009 as examples). From this perspective, with an emphasis on discursive politics, the ways in which even expressly feminist policies might contribute to the oppression and marginalization of women are made visible.

Although CFA is attentive to intersectionality, IBPA, developed by Hankivsky (2012a), places social location at the center of analysis (see also Hankivsky and Cormier 2011). Inspired by Bacchi's work on problem representations and intersectionality theory and method (see Hankivsky 2012a: 48), the IBPA framework is designed to trouble the fixity of gender within mainstream feminist approaches. As a response to both academic and government approaches to policy analysis, IBPA attempts to make amenable social justice with applied policy analysis. It is organized around eight principles, such as an explicit commitment to social justice and reflexivity, and twelve substantive questions addressing reflexive, descriptive, prescriptive and transformative dimensions of analysis (see Hankivsky 2012a: 39–42). Moreover, it attempts to give voice to those who are often marginalized by mainstream policy analysis (see also Jordan-Zachery 2012).

All of the approaches discussed here, in examining how policies *come to mean*, examine the ways in which policy structures inequality. They attempt to make visible the ways in which policies might produce and sustain inequality. In so doing, they have exposed the complex role of policy discourse and content in shaping inequality. On the one hand, this work has revealed the ubiquity of gender by interrogating policy fields that seemingly have no gender dimensions. On the other hand, they have demonstrated that even expressly feminist policy might potentially reinforce systems of inequality. Moreover, they each problematize our understandings of gender and challenge its primacy as an analytic category in feminist policy analysis. Thus, approaches in this area take seriously the need for intersectionality, reflexivity, and an explicit commitment to exposing and challenging social hierarchies in both theory and method. All of these approaches are explicitly committed to transformative politics, which problematize both femininities and masculinities, seeking to transform the very meanings and lived experiences of social categories. However, these approaches tend to be silent on policy processes and the relationships between process and content. Thus, there is little insight on questions concerning access to policy processes, for example.

A subset of literature that in many ways bridges these two loci is the work on gender mainstreaming (GM). Since its adoption by more than 160 countries following the UN Fourth World Conference on Women held in Beijing in 1995, GM has been subject to intense academic scrutiny.[5] Although GM is a contested concept, and one that is varyingly defined, interpreted and implemented, at a minimum it requires analysts to apply a gender lens to (ideally) all policies and programs. While a detailed overview of this literature is beyond the scope of this chapter, it is worth noting that one of the central debates has centered on the transformative potential of mainstreaming (e.g. Squires 2005; Hankivsky 2005), which has illuminated, among other things, the ways in which processes and content are intricately intertwined. For example, Osborne et al. (2008) examine the role of femocrats and women's policy agencies in fostering participatory processes that in turn shape policy content. In addition, Meier and Celis (2011) suggest that the assumptions of rationality and intentionality underlying GM, which often give rise to procedural rather than substantive mechanisms, can be potentially offset where there is consensus for and clear goals regarding GM's role as a tool for gender equality.

This brief look at how gender mainstreaming literature has bridged analyses of process and content represents fruitful ground for further analysis and for feminist policy studies more generally. Indeed, as critical scholars remind us, participatory and deliberative processes figure prominently in any social justice agenda.

In the following section, we demonstrate some of the central insights of feminist policy analysis through a comparison of three broad epistemological approaches to policy studies, including instrumental rationality, critical inquiry and feminist analysis. Using the case of tobacco policy, we elucidate the power of feminist analysis to expose and remedy the potential analytical blindspots of mainstream and critical approaches.

WHAT'S GENDER GOT TO DO WITH IT? ANALYZING TOBACCO CONTROL POLICY THROUGH A FEMINIST LENS

In recent decades, smoking has become a pressing public health issue in most advanced industrialized societies. In the 1950s, studies began reporting the health risks associated with cigarette smoking and its link to certain forms of cancer. Once regarded as an innocuous social pastime, cigarette smoking soon became the target of government intervention. Today, governments have implemented a number of different strategies to prevent or reduce cigarette smoking, including: increasing the price of tobacco products; sales taxes; restrictions on the promotion and sale of tobacco products; anti-smoking media campaigns; smoking bans in public spaces and workplaces; and anti-smoking curricula in schools. All of these interventions aim to denormalize smoking behavior in an effort to reduce the rate of smoking among the general population. When evaluating smoking intervention strategies, policy analysts have been interested primarily in assessing the effectiveness of anti-smoking interventions in achieving their stated objectives, i.e. reducing smoking prevalence and smoking-related illnesses and morbidity. Less attention has been paid to the political, social and economic contexts in which smoking takes place or the link between gender, gender disparities and smoking.

At first glance, choosing the case of anti-tobacco policy for feminist policy inquiry seems counter-intuitive since it does not appear to have anything at all to do with gender or gender politics. While the centrality of gender is readily apparent in policy areas that directly implicate women, such as childcare, parental leave and reproductive health, this is not the case with policy domains that outwardly appear to be gender-neutral and not directly relevant to feminist activism. Taxation, national security, regional development and industry policy are but a few examples of policy domains where gender is seldom considered an evaluative or analytical priority. As a policy issue, anti-smoking interventions have often been framed in gender-neutral terms: the individual smoker is often constructed as a rational, individual actor who, when armed with the right information and the right incentives, will choose to give up smoking. More recently, critical scholarship in public health has rightfully challenged the conceptualization of smoking as an individual problem by illuminating smoking's link to poverty and income inequalities. However, with a few notable exceptions (e.g. Waldron 1991; Oaks 2001), the gendered and gendering effects of anti-smoking policy remain under-explored. Using anti-smoking interventions as an analytical entry point, we illuminate key differences between mainstream, critical and feminist approaches to policy analysis and highlight the benefits of adopting a feminist perspective.

Smoking as a Health Behavior Problem

Governed by the rationalist model of policymaking, conventional policy analysis is an exercise dominated by 'hard' facts and formal proofs. As Stark explains (1992, p. 519), this model utilizes 'the basic categories of microeconomics and the logic of choice – decision-making, objectives, alternatives, preferences, criteria, and trade-offs'. Policy analysis is primarily concerned with evaluating the effects of each alternative course of action for a particular problem and ultimately choosing that policy which will maximize total benefits. Ignoring the historical and social contexts of our knowledge and being, policy analysis becomes an insular activity confined to experts and social engineers. Ordinary citizens are relegated to the passive role of client or onlooker rather than participant in the policy process.

Conventional policy analysis's rationalistic assumptions of individual behavior are inscribed in many anti-smoking interventions. Governments impose taxes on cigarettes in order to provide economic disincentives to smoking. Smoking-related policies in most advanced industrialized countries also aim to 'denormalize' smoking by changing perceptions and practices at the individual and societal levels. Anti-smoking campaigns, which focus on disseminating information on the health risks of tobacco use to the public, construct the 'problem' of smoking as one of individual choice and responsibility. Underpinning these campaigns is an economic perspective that views the individual as a rational actor and smoking as a costly and 'potentially hazardous consumption activity' (Viscusi 1992, p. 120). The underlying assumption of policy interventions is that smokers are rational actors who once presented with information regarding the economic costs and health risks of smoking will 'respond appropriately' (Macnaughton et al. 2012, p. 457). These assumptions inform many health promotion policies that focus on changing the beliefs and behaviors of individual smokers and equipping them with the behavioral tools to make healthier lifestyle choices.

Critics contend that health promotion models, which target the decontextualized individual smoker and his or her behavior, do not take into account the broader structural forces that shape the social and material realities of smokers and their ability to alter their behavior. While these models do bring into their analysis social characteristics, such as sex, class, ethnicity, etc., they are treated as fixed individual attributes that mitigate individual beliefs and behavior rather than health status determinants. As Kelly (2006) explains: '[T]he key differences between social classes, men and women, ethnic groups, young and old, and residential circumstances are treated as background or contextual factors, rather than important determining factors in their own right.' Moreover, by focusing on the health-related risks of smoking, these health promotion strategies target individual lifestyle and behavior change rather than living conditions that shape health status and general well-being. Another important limitation of rationalistic health promotion models is that they view smoking as a reasoned action and not as an addiction. By constructing the act of smoking and smoking cessation as an individual choice, these models fail to take into account the role of the tobacco industry in producing and promoting a highly addictive and dangerous consumer product (Balbach et al. 2006).

Smoking as a Social Justice Issue

Whereas conventional policy analysis is primarily interested in 'solving' problems and achieving measurable outcome, i.e. lower smoking rates, critical policy scholars view public policy in terms of its relationship to power, social justice and self-realization. It brings to the foreground the socio-economic conditions that give rise to smoking and to higher rates of smoking-related diseases in certain segments of the population. Consistent with the social determinants' approach to public health (see Solar and Irwin 2010), critical policy scholars investigate smoking within the broader context of health equity and social justice. The prevailing view of smoking as primarily a biomedical or behavioral issue is rejected in favor of a perspective aimed at uncovering the underlying social, political and economic conditions that lead to differences in smoking and health status across groups in society.

Public health research on smoking in high-income countries has shown that while government policy has been successful in reducing smoking rates in general, smoking initiation, continuation and prevalence remain higher among groups with lower socio-economic status (Corsi 2013). Critical policy scholars attribute these disparities to intervention strategies that ignore how smoking and health behavior in general are deeply grounded in diverse cultural and socio-economic contexts. Like many health promotion and prevention programs, anti-smoking campaigns are built on a rationalist and individualistic conception of health behavior, thus ignoring socio-economic differences in attitudes and beliefs about healthy lifestyles. Messages about individual responsibility and disease prevention are less effective among disadvantaged groups that generally have lower expectancy of longevity and tend to attribute health status to chance (Wardle and Steptoe 2003). Disadvantaged groups are also less likely to benefit from public media campaigns than the more affluent due to lower levels of education, and unequal access to information and health-related services (Weiss and Tschirhart 1993). Instead, with smoking prevalence higher in low-income communities, the stigma of smoking is disproportionately borne by disadvantaged smokers (Kim and Shanahan 2003; Powers and Faden 2006: Voigt 2010). Burdened with negative stereotypes about smokers (i.e. ignorant, of low class, irresponsible) poorer smokers are less likely to seek out treatments and related health services thus further exacerbating health disparities and social exclusion (Powers and Faden 2006; also Bell et al. 2010; Voigt 2010).

Other anti-smoking strategies, such as smoke-free public spaces, also ignore the spatial distribution of poverty and the economic and social realities of low-income neighborhoods. For example, the higher-density housing that characterizes low-income neighborhoods along with the lack of private outdoor spaces often make it more difficult for individuals in those communities to physically avoid second-hand smoke as well as the social pressure to continue smoking. 'Women and men living on a low income are more likely to live in more crowded areas, with more smokers and less safe, open spaces. These physical constraints limit opportunities to avoid SHS exposure in spite of increasing restrictions' (Hemsing et al. 2012, p. 8). The marketing and availability of tobacco products is also greater in poorer neighborhoods. In North America, studies have shown that tobacco products are more readily available in economically disadvantaged neighborhoods, characterized by lower incomes, a higher percentage of social assistance and lone parent families, and lower levels of university or college degrees (Chaiton et al. 2014). With mass media tobacco advertising banned in most countries, tobacco companies have disproportionately used other marketing techniques, such as point of sale advertisements and price promotions, in disadvantaged communities to attract new smokers. The tobacco industry is therefore directly implicated in the emergence and maintenance of class differences in rates of smoking and related diseases (Barbeau et al. 2004).

In terms of praxis, critical policy analysis stresses the need for greater reflexivity on the part of the policy researcher to address the existing disconnect between 'the assumptions that tobacco control practitioners take as self-evident (e.g. the pre-eminent importance of health, the value of knowledge as a determinant of health) . . . and how smokers view their smoking and health' (Frohlich et al. 2010, p.43). Critical policy analysts also call for tailored intervention strategies aimed at the community level that reflect the needs of smokers in disadvantaged communities but in ways that are not stigmatizing. The active participation of poorer smokers and community-based organizations is key in the development of effective tobacco control campaigns and programs. The tobacco industry also becomes a target for government action. In the United States and Canada, governments have launched lawsuits against the tobacco industry to recover health costs related to smoking-related diseases. While the results of these lawsuits have been mixed, they work to expose the tobacco industry's culpability for smoking and smokers' deaths and diseases.

Smoking as a Gendered Phenomenon

In analyzing anti-smoking policy, feminist policy analysis shares the critical perspective's focus on marginalized or disempowered populations as well as a commitment to social justice goals. Rejecting the methodological individualism of conventional policy analysis, feminist policy analysis situates smoking in the social, political and cultural contexts in which it is experienced. Focusing on gender and gender oppression, feminist policy analysis interrogates the ways in which anti-smoking policy, both in terms of process and content, often ignores or marginalizes women's voices and experiences. Working from the premise that men and women are placed differentially vis-à-vis state policies, feminist policy analysis aims to uncover the gendered assumptions that underpin anti-smoking interventions and how they disadvantage women not only in terms of health status but also in terms of social and economic status. It is also attentive to how gender intersects with other forms of oppression (i.e. race, class, sexual orientation, etc.) to shape women's experience with smoking and related state interventions.

From the perspective of feminist policy analysis, smoking, like all other social, cultural or health experiences, is primarily viewed as a gendered phenomenon (Courteney 2000) best understood in its social, political and historical context. In their analysis of smoking, feminist historians have illuminated the central role played by gender constructions in the evolving discourses of smoking and smoker identities. Historically, the representation of women smokers in society and in policy texts has changed dramatically. In the late 1800s and early 1900s, cigarette smoking was generally associated with men and regarded as a symbol of masculinity. By the 1920s, with the development of 'milder' cigarettes, a female consumer base for smoking was born. Cigarette advertisement campaigns began targeting women with images that represented smoking as a symbol of female confidence and elite social status. One of the earliest media campaigns directed at women in the 1920s also marketed cigarette smoking as an appetite suppressant for women wanting to maintain a slim figure required for the 'flapper' style fashion of the day (Cook 2012). In the 1960s and 1970s, emerging against the backdrop of the women's rights movement, female smoking became represented as an act of political and sexual liberation. By the 1990s, with smoking increasingly stigmatized, the marketing campaigns that once glamorized female smoking would be replaced by government campaigns that portrayed women smokers, especially mothers, as deviants and dangers to their children.

Today, governments continue to direct anti-smoking media campaigns towards young women and mothers, often overburdening them with smoking-associated stigma. Pregnant and childrearing women are most susceptible to the stigmatizing effects of anti-smoking campaigns that often focus on the dangers posed by maternal smoking for fetal development and infant health. Rather than being value-neutral, anti-smoking strategies are inscribed with dominant cultural ideals of femininity and motherhood that work to contribute to the social control of women's behavior. Depicted as 'bad mothers', women who smoke while pregnant and childrearing are often the target of negative moral judgment. Due to the greater stigma attached to maternal smoking, women smokers are also less likely to report their smoking status in research studies and to seek medical advice or treatment (Wigginton and Lee 2012). In comparison, campaigns targeting paternal smoking lack similar moralistic judgments. This difference, according to Oaks (2001, p. 17), 'reflects not only the relative newness of the topic of the fetal health effects of men's smoking but also the different social expectations faced by mothers- and fathers-to-be regarding their responsibilities to ensure fetal health'. These anti-smoking campaigns serve to justify the moral policing of pregnant smokers and fetal protection initiatives, putting at risk women's reproductive rights (Oaks 2001; Abrahamsson et al. 2005; McDermott et al. 2006; Wigginton and Lee 2012).

While women and girls tend to be the subjects of anti-smoking media campaigns, other intervention strategies rely on androcentric assumptions that obfuscate the different ways gender influences all aspects of the smoking experience, including smoking patterns, health beliefs and help-seeking behavior (Waldron 1991; Gritz et al. 1996). The narrow, individualistic focus on health that underpins most intervention strategies renders invisible the social and cultural meanings women attach to smoking. For example, smoking among young women is often prompted by issues related to body image and weight (Napolitano et al. 2011). Studies have shown that young women are more likely than young men to use smoking as an appetite suppressant in an effort to control their weight (Copeland et al. 2006). Moreover, the use of smoking as a strategy for weight control was shown to be more prevalent among young white women (Camp et al. 1993). For feminist researchers, the motivation and behavior of women smokers cannot be understood without considering the greater social pressure exerted on women to adhere to the culturally prescribed thin female body ideal. By situating women's smoking behavior in its broader social context, feminist policy analysis re-problematizes (Bacchi 1999 [2005]) smoking among young women as a product of society's objectification of the female body (Fiissel and Lafreniere 2006).

Feminist policy analysis also problematizes the public-private distinction that informs both mainstream and critical perspectives on anti-smoking policy. For feminists, smoking as a policy issue cannot be understood outside of the *gender division* of labor in the home that continues to disadvantage women. The meanings women attach to smoking in their everyday lives are also linked to the primacy of women's role in the so-called private or domestic sphere. Several studies show how the experiences of women smokers are situated in the context of care work. For women smokers, smoking is associated with carving out a space for themselves – a break from daily domestic responsibilities and a mechanism to cope with isolation, boredom and stress. As Graham explains, smoking represents a time when 'anticipated breaks can be temporarily put to one side and the mother can enter a social world which is not exclusively focused on childcare' (1994, p. 117). While knowledgeable of the negative health effects of smoking, women often continue to smoke as a coping mechanism for the stress in their daily lives. Studies on gender differences in smoking addiction confirm that factors other than nicotine dependence make it more difficult for women to give up smoking (Perkins

1996). Sensory and situational cues, such as the sight and smell of smoke, the hand-to-mouth sensation and the people and locations associated with smoking often trigger relapses in women smokers. Instead of nicotine-replacement therapies and information campaigns that focus exclusively on the health-related dangers of smoking, feminist policy analysis advocates anti-smoking strategies that openly recognize the pleasure and empowerment (Cook 2012) women derive from smoking and the emotional and psychological needs it fulfills in their lives.

Smoking bans and smoke-free spaces also implicate women more than men due to women's position vis-à-vis the public and private spheres. These strategies, which have been adopted in many North American and European cities, are actively (re)shaping the social interactions between smokers and non-smokers both in the public and private spheres. With smoking increasingly being practiced and negotiated in the private domain, women smokers are more vulnerable to social isolation given that they generally perform most household-related chores. The movement of smoking from public spaces to the private domain also increases women's exposure to secondhand smoke. Other studies (Hemsing et al. 2012) show that gender-based power inequalities in the home often made it difficult for women to limit their exposure to the secondhand smoke of their male partners. 'Due to sex segregation of both paid and domestic work, women may have more responsibilities within the domestic sphere but a limited ability to participate in decision making on SHS policies' (Hemsing et al. 2012, p. 7). Smoking bans are even less beneficial for women smokers in poorer neighborhoods whose social lives are more housebound, thus limiting their access to smoke-free spaces (Robinson et al. 2010). For feminist policy analysts, relegating smoking to the domestic sphere not only increases women's exposure to smoking and related health risks but limits their ability to participate in the public sphere as active members of their communities.

Recognizing differences among women is a central component of feminist policy analysis. Using intersectionality as a theory and practice, a feminist perspective on smoking uncovers how gender interacts with other categories of marginalization such as race and class to produce and maintain inequalities. Income level is an important determinant of women's smoking and giving up behavior. The lack of social support and economic resources, rather than lack of knowledge, often determines whether a woman will continue to smoke (Oakley 1989). As noted earlier, poorer women also face greater social isolation and exposure to second-hand smoke due to the lack of smoke-free spaces in disadvantaged neighborhoods. The stigma of smoking is also imposed disproportionately on already disadvantaged women, such as the poor, youth and, in the case of Canada, Aboriginals. Feminist policy analysis calls upon researchers to pay attention to such power and social inequalities in the design and evaluation of anti-smoking policy. Not doing so will result in policies that perpetuate existing inequalities not only between men and women, but also among women themselves.

Like critical policy analysis, feminist policy analysis calls for greater reflexivity on the part of policy researchers to ensure that their privileged position and knowledge does not influence or guide the research agenda. Participatory research practices are also encouraged in order to ensure that women's voices, in all their diversity, are included during all stages of the research process and policy development. Adopting a feminist-informed research agenda requires analysts not only to uncover the impact of policy on gender equality and women's rights but also to identify opportunities for collaboration among feminist researchers, activists and women's groups. While the state remains a key target of feminist activism and advocacy, community engagement and empowerment become key elements of smoking cessation programs and health promotion strategies directed at women. Top-down strategies developed by policy elites and experts are eschewed in favor of programs informed by the diverse needs of women and their communities. Policy messages that perpetuate self-responsibility and victim blaming are deconstructed and replaced by policies that target the socio-economic forces that shape women's smoking in their everyday lives (Crawford 1977; Logan and Spencer 1996).

CONCLUSION

As part of a broader feminist project, feminist policy analysis makes social location, including intersecting factors such as gender, race, class, ability, sexuality and gender identity and expression, relevant and central to policy theory, inquiry and practice. The case of anti-smoking policy presented in this chapter illustrates how social location is a core factor in the unequal distribution of a policy's risks, burdens and benefits within society. It also underscores the importance of making gender visible in policies that at first glance do not seem to directly implicate women. While policy issues such as childcare and reproductive health have long been considered 'women's issues', others, such as smoking, are often not regarded as particularly salient for feminist theorizing or activism. Feminist policy analysis troubles the traditional boundaries of 'women's issues' by shedding light on how policies typically considered gender-neutral are, in fact, highly gender specific and lead to different outcomes for men and women. Making gender visible in the analysis of smoke-free public spaces, for example, illustrates how the relegation of smoking to the private realm, i.e. the home, was not only detrimental to women's health but also impacted their status as active members of their community. It also shows how smoking-related policies worked to stigmatize already vulnerable women, thereby exacerbating existing systems of inequalities based on race/ethnicity and class.

The case of anti-smoking policy highlights the benefits of feminist policy analysis but also some of the challenges that remain. First, the research on women and smoking tells us much about the gendered and gendering effects of the design of smoking-related policies. Less is known, however, about the processes in which these 'gendered' designs materialize. As noted by Lombardo et al. (2013), developing approaches that bridge both process and content is crucial if we are to better understand the role policy plays in both political and social life. Second, despite the emergence of several feminist 'models' in both academic and advocacy arenas, there is still much work to be done to encourage state actors to use them. As in the case of anti-smoking policy, much of the gender-based analysis that is conducted by governments has been limited to gender statistics and analysis. If feminist policy analysis can transform social relations, it will be through the adoption of approaches that are sensitive to social locations and power relations. Third, intersectionality has had significant implications on the study and practice of feminist policy analysis, with the debate often centering on the place of gender in intersectional theory and its potential appropriation by white feminist researchers (e.g. Bilge 2013; Strid et al. 2013). As a result, it has been a challenge to advance and maintain an explicitly feminist agenda while adopting an intersectional lens that does not prioritize gender (see also Walby 2011 for a recent discussion).

Moving forward, these challenges represent potential sites for feminist scholarship to further advance the study of public policy. As they reflect on their own ways of 'doing policy analysis', feminist analysts will continue to emphasize alliances between academics, practitioners and activists in their efforts to bring forward women's voices in the theories and practices of policy analysis. By structuring their analysis around questions of power and difference, feminist perspectives join forces with other critical approaches to achieve the emancipatory potential of policy analysis.

NOTES

1. Despite its presence in state bureaucracies across the globe, there remain serious concerns about how successful gender mainstreaming has been in transforming gender relations. See Squires (2005), Hankivsky (2005), Meier and Celis (2011) and Prügl (2011) for discussions.

2. The state feminism literature distinguishes between woman-friendly and feminist movements and policies. The latter is distinguished from the former by the explicit recognition of and challenge to patriarchy. See McBride and Mazur (2012, p. 5) for a discussion.
3. See Fraser (1997) for a theoretical discussion and Verloo and Lombardo (2007) for an application. This concern has been recently addressed by RNGS scholars through the inclusion of 'transformative state feminism'. See McBride and Mazur (2012) for a discussion.
4. This question was inspired by Yanow (1996).
5. See Hawkesworth (2012) for a detailed discussion of the ways in which gender equality has been reconceptualized through development studies. See also Jahan (1995).

REFERENCES

Abrahamsson, A., J. Springett, L. Karlsson and T. Ottosson (eds) (2005), 'Making Sense of the Challenge of Smoking Cessation During Pregnancy: A Phenomenographic Approach', *Health Education Research*, **20**, 367–378.
Abrar, Stefania, Joni Lovenduski and Helen Margetts (eds) (2000), 'Feminist Ideas and Domestic Violence Policy Change', *Political Studies*, **48** (2), 239–262.
Ackelsberg, M. (1992), 'Feminist Analyses of Public Policy', *Comparative Politics*, **24** (4), 477–493.
Ahmed, Sara (2012), *On Being Included: Racism and Diversity in Institutional Life*, Durham, NC and London: Duke University Press.
Bacchi, Carol Lee (1999 [2005]), *Women, Policy, and Politics: The Construction of Policy Problems*, London and Thousand Oaks, CA: Sage Publications.
Bacchi, Carol Lee (2009), *Analysing Policy: What's the Problem Represented to Be?*, Frenchs Forest, NSW: Pearson.
Bacchi, Carol (2009), 'The Issue of Intentionality in Frame Theory: The Need for Reflexive Framing', in E. Lombardo, P. Meier and M. Verloo (eds), *The Discursive Politics of Gender Equality Stretching, Bending and Policymaking*, London: Routledge, pp. 19–35.
Bacchi, Carol (2010) 'Post-Structuralism, Discourse, and Problematization: Implications for Gender Mainstreaming', *Kvinder, Køn & Forskning*, **4**, 62–72.
Bacchi, Carol and Joan Eveline (2010), *Mainstreaming Politics Gendering Practices and Feminist Theory*, Adelaide: University of Adelaide Press.
Balbach, E.D., E.A. Smith and R.E. Malone (2006), 'How the Health Belief Model Helps the Tobacco Industry: Individuals, Choice, and "Information"', *Tobacco Control*, **15** (Suppl 4), iv37–iv43.
Barbeau, E.M., N. Krieger and M.-J. Soobader (2004), 'Working Class Matters: Socioeconomic Disadvantage, Race/Ethnicity, Gender, and Smoking in NHIS 2000', *American Journal of Public Health*, **94**, 269–278.
Beckwith, Karen (2007), 'Mapping Strategic Engagements: Women's Movements and the State', *International Feminist Journal of Politics*, **9** (3), 312–338.
Beland, Daniel (2009), 'Gender, Ideational Analysis, and Social Policy', *Social Politics: International Studies in Gender, State & Society*, **16** (4), 558–581.
Bell, Kirsten, Lucy McCullough, Amy Salmon and Jennifer Bell (2010), '"Every space is claimed": Smokers' experiences of tobacco denormalisation', *Sociology of Health & Illness*, **32** (6), 914–929.
Bensimon, E.M. and C. Marshall (2003), 'Like it or Not: Feminist Critical Policy Analysis Matters', *Journal of Higher Education*, **74** (3), 337–349.
Bilge, S. (2013), 'Intersectionality Undone: Saving Intersectionality from Feminist Intersectionality Studies', *Du Bois Review*, **10** (2), 405–424.
Boles, Janet K. (1994), 'Local Feminist Policy Networks in the Contemporary American Interest Group System', *Policy Sciences*, **27** (2–3), 161–178.
Boneparth, Ellen (ed.) (1982), *Women, Power, and Policy*, New York: Pergamon Press.

Boserup, Ester (1970 [1989]), *Woman's Role in Economic Development*, London: Earthscan.
Burnier, D. (2003), 'Other Voices/Other Rooms: Towards a Care-Centered Public Administration', *Administrative Theory & Praxis*, **25** (4), 529–544.
Burt, S. (1995), 'The Several Worlds of Policy Analysis: Traditional Approaches and Feminist Critiques', in S. Burt and Lorraine Code (eds), *Changing Methods: Feminists Transforming Practice*, Peterborough, Ontario: Broadview Press, pp. 357–378.
Bustelo, María and Mieke Verloo (2009), 'Grounding Policy Evaluation in a Discursive Understanding of Politics', in E. Lombardo, P. Meier and M. Verloo (eds), *The Discursive Politics of Gender Equality Stretching, Bending and Policymaking*, London: Routledge, pp. 153–168.
Camp, D.E., R.C. Klesges, G. Relyea (1993), 'The relationship between body weight concerns and adolescent smoking', *Health Psychology*, **12** (1), 24–32.
Chaiton, Michael, Graham Mecredy, Jürgen Rehm, Andriy V Samokhvalov (2014), 'Tobacco Retail Availability and Smoking Behaviours Among Patients Seeking Treatment at a Nicotine Dependence Treatment Clinic', *Tobacco Induced Diseases*, **12** (19) (2 December). Online.
Cook, Sharon Anne (2012), *Sex, Lies, and Cigarettes: Canadian Women, Smoking, and Visual Culture, 1880–2000*, Montreal: McGill-Queen's University Press.
Copeland, A.L., P.D. Martin, P.J. Geiselman, C.J. Rash and D.E. Kendzor (2006), 'Smoking Cessation for Weight-concerned Women: Group vs. Individually Tailored, Dietary, and Weight-control Follow-up Sessions', *Addictive Behaviors*, **31**, 115–127.
Corsi, D.J., S.A. Lear, C.K. Chow, S.V. Subramanian, M.H. Boyle et al. (2013), 'Socioeconomic and Geographic Patterning of Smoking Behaviour in Canada: A Cross-Sectional Multilevel Analysis', *PLoS ONE*, **8** (2), e57646. Doi: 10.1371/journal.pone.0057646.
Courtenay, W. (2000), 'Constructions of masculinity and their influence on men's well-being: a theory of gender and health', *Social Science and Medicine*, **50**, 1385–1401.
Crawford, R. (1977), 'You are dangerous to your health: the ideology and politics of victim-blaming', *International Journal of Health Services*, **7** (4), 663–680.
Eisenstein, E. (1995), 'The Australian Femocratice Experiment: A Feminist Case for Bureaucracy', in Myra Marx Ferree and Patricia Yancey Martin (eds), *Feminist Organizations: Harvest of the New Women's Movement*, Philadelphia, PA: Temple University Press, pp. 69–83.
Ferguson, Kathy E. (1984), *The Feminist Case against Bureaucracy: Women in the Political Economy*, Philadelphia, PA: Temple University Press.
Fiissel, D.L. and K.L. Lafreniere (2006), 'Weight Control Motives for Cigarette Smoking: Further Consequences of the Sexual Objectification of Women?', *Feminism and Psychology*, **16**, 327–344.
Fonow, M. and J. Cook (2005), 'Feminist Methodology: New Applications in the Academy and Public Policy', *Signs*, **30** (4), 2211–2236.
Frohlich, K.L., B. Poland, E. Mykhalovskiy, S. Alexander and C. Maule (2010), 'Tobacco Control and the Inequitable Socio-economic Distribution of Smoking: Smokers' Discourses and Implications for Tobacco Control', *Critical Public Health*, **20** (1), 35–46.
Fraser, Nancy (1987), 'Women, Welfare and The Politics of Need Interpretation', *Hypatia*, **2** (1), 103–121.
Fraser, Nancy (1997), *Justice Interruptus: Critical Reflections on the 'Postsocialist' Condition*, New York: Routledge.
Gelb, Joyce (1987), *Women and Public Policies*. Revised and expanded edition, Princeton, NJ: Princeton University Press.
Gordon, Linda (ed.) (1990), *Women, the State, and Welfare*, Madison, WI: University of Wisconsin Press.
Graham, H. (1994), 'Surviving by Smoking', in S. Wilkinson and C. Kitzinger (eds), *Women and Health: Feminist Perspectives*, London: Taylor & Francis, pp. 102–123.
Gritz, E.R., I.R. Nielsen and L.A. Brooks (1996), 'Smoking Cessation and Gender:

The Influence of Physiological, Psychological, and Behavioral Factors', *Journal of the American Medical Women's Association*, **51** (1–2), 35–42.

Halsaa, B. (1998), 'A Strategic Partnership for Women's Policies in Norway', *Women's Movements and Public Policy in Europe, Latin America, and the Caribbean*, New York: Garland, pp. 167–187.

Hancock, Ange-Marie (2013), *Solidarity Politics for Millennials: A Guide to Ending the Oppression Olympics* [S.l.], New York: Palgrave Macmillan.

Hankivsky, Olena (2005), 'Gender vs. Diversity Mainstreaming: A Preliminary Examination of the Role and Transformative Potential of Feminist Theory', *Canadian Journal of Political Science/Revue Canadienne de Science Politique*, **38** (4), 977–1001.

Hankivsky, Olena (ed.) (2012a), *An Intersectionality-Based Policy Framework*, Vancouver, BC: Institute for Intersectionality Research and Policy.

Hankivsky, Olena (2012b) 'The Lexicon of Mainstreaming Equality: Gender Based Analysis (GBA), Gender and Diversity Analysis (GDA) and Intersectionality Based Analysis (IBA)', *Canadian Political Science Review*, **6** (2/3), 171–183.

Hankivsky, Olena and Renee Cormier (2011), 'Intersectionality and Public Policy: Some Lessons from Existing Models', *Political Research Quarterly*, **64** (1), 217–229.

Harding, S. (1987) *Feminism and Methodology: Social Science Issues*, Bloomington, IN: Indiana University Press.

Haussman, Melissa and Birgit Sauer (eds) (2007), *Gendering the State in the Age of Globalization: Women's Movements and State Feminism in Postindustrial Democracies*, Lanham, MD: Rowman & Littlefield Publishers.

Hawkesworth, Mary (1994), 'Policy Studies within a Feminist Frame', *Policy Sciences*, **27** (2–3), 97–118.

Hawkesworth, Mary (2010), 'Policy Discourse as Sanctioned Ignorance: Theorizing the Erasure of Feminist Knowledge', *Critical Policy Studies*, **3** (3–4), 268–289.

Hawkesworth, Mary (2012), 'From Policy Frames to Discursive Politics: Feminist Approaches to Development Policy and Planning in an Era of Globalization', in Frank Fischer and Herbert Gottweis (eds), *The Argumentative Turn Revisited: Public Policy as Communicative Practice*, Durham, NC: Duke University Press, pp. 114–148.

Hemsing, Natalie, Lorraine Greaves, Nancy Poole and Joan Bottorff (2012), 'Reshuffling and Relocating: The Gendered and Income-Related Differential Effects of Restricting Smoking Locations', *Journal of Environmental and Public Health*. Doi: 10.1155/2012/907832.

Hill Collins, P. (1990), *Black Feminist Thought: Knowledge, Consciousness, and the Politics of Empowerment*, Boston, MA: Unwin Hyman.

Holli, Anne Maria (2008), 'Feminist Triangles: A Conceptual Analysis', *Representation*, **44** (2), 169–185.

Jahan, Rounaq (1995), *The Elusive Agenda: Mainstreaming Women in Development*, Dhaka, Bangladesh/London/Atlantic Highlands, NJ: University Press and Zed Books.

Jenson, J. (1986), 'Gender and Reproduction, or Babies and the State', *Studies in Political Economy*, **20** (2), 9–46.

Jordan-Zachery, J. (2012), 'An Intersectionality-Based Policy Analysis of How U.S. HIV/ AIDS Policy fails to "Rescue" Black Orphans', paper presented at the First International Conference on Public Policy in Grenoble, France, June 2012.

Kantola, J. and J. Squires (2012), 'From State Feminism to Market Feminism?', *International Political Science Review*, **33** (4), 382–400.

Kelly, Michael P. (2006), 'The Challenge of Changing Patient Behaviour', in Kiran C.R. Patel and Ajay M. Shah (eds), *Prevention, Treatment and Rehabilitation of Cardiovascular Disease in South Asians*, Birmingham, UK: South Asian Health Foundation, pp. 7–20.

Kenney, Sally J. (2003), 'Where is Gender in Agenda Setting?', *Women & Politics*, **25** (1–2), 179–207. Doi: 10.1300/J014v25n01_07.

Kim, S.-H. and J. Shanahan (2003), 'Stigmatizing Smokers: Public Sentiment toward Cigarette Smoking', *Journal of Health Communication*, **8**, 343–367.

Logan, S. and N. Spencer (1996), 'Smoking and Other Health Related Behaviours in the Social and Environmental Context', *Archives of Disease in Childhood*, **74**, 176–179.

Lombardo, E. and L. Rolandsen Agustin (2011), 'Framing Gender Intersections in the European Union: What Implications for the Quality of Intersectionality in Policies?', *Social Politics: International Studies in Gender, State & Society*, **19** (4), 482–512.

Lombardo, Emanuela, Petra Meier and Mieke Verloo (eds) (2009), *The Discursive Politics of Gender Equality: Stretching, Bending, and Policy-Making*, Routledge/ECPR Studies in European Political Science 59, Abingdon, UK and New York: Routledge.

Lombardo, E., P. Meier and M. Verloo (2013), 'Policy Making', in G. Waylen, K. Celis, J. Kantola and L. Weldon (eds), *The Oxford Handbook of Gender and Politics*, New York: Oxford University Press, pp. 679–702.

Lovenduski, J. (1986), *Women and European Politics: Contemporary Feminism and Public Policy*, Amherst, MA: University of Massachusetts Press.

Macnaughton, Jane, Susana Carro-Ripalda and Andrew Russell (2012), '"Risking Enchantment": How Are We to View the Smoking Person?', *Critical Public Health*, **22** (4), 455–469.

Manuel, Tiffany (2006), 'Envisioning the Possibilities for a Good Life: Exploring the Public Policy Implications of Intersectionality Theory', *Journal of Women, Politics & Policy*, **28** (3–4), 173–203.

Marshall, C. (1997), 'Dismantling and Reconstructing Policy Analysis', in C. Marshall (ed.), *Feminist Critical Policy Analysis I*, London: Taylor & Francis, pp. 1–41.

Marshall, C. (1999), 'Researching the Margins: Feminist Critical Policy Analysis', *Educational Policy*, **13** (1), 59–76.

Mazur, Amy (ed.) (2001), *State Feminism, Women's Movements, and Job Training: Making Democracies Work in the Global Economy*, Women and Politics in Democratic States, New York: Routledge.

Mazur, Amy G. (2002), *Theorizing Feminist Theory*, Oxford: Oxford University Press.

Mazur, Amy G. and Mark A. Pollack (2009), 'Gender and Public Policy in Europe: An Introduction', *Comparative European Politics*, **7** (1), 1–11.

McBride, Dorothy E. (ed.) (2001), *Abortion Politics, Women's Movements, and the Democratic State: A Comparative Study of State Feminism*, Gender and Politics, Oxford and New York: Oxford University Press.

McBride, Dorothy E. and Amy Mazur (eds) (1995), *Comparative State Feminism*, Thousand Oaks, CA: Sage Publications.

McBride, Dorothy E. and Amy Mazur (2012), *The Politics of State Feminism: Innovation in Comparative Research*, Philadelphia, PA: Temple University Press.

McCall, L. (2005), 'The Complexity of Intersectionality', *Signs*, **30** (31), 1771–1802.

McDermott, L.J., A.J. Dobson and N. Owen (2006), 'From Partying to Parenthood: Young Women's Perceptions of Cigarette Smoking Across Life Transitions', *Health Education Research*, **21**, 428–439.

McIntosh, M. (1978), 'The State and the Oppression of Women', *Feminism and Materialism*, London: RKP.

McPhail, Beverly A. (2003), 'A Feminist Policy Analysis Framework: Through a Gendered Lens', *The Social Policy Journal*, **2** (2–3), 39–61.

Meehan, J. (ed.) (1995), *Feminists Read Habermas: Gendering the Subject of Discourse*, London and New York: Routledge.

Meier, P. and K. Celis (2011), 'Sowing the Seeds of its Own Failure: Implementing the Concept of Gender Mainstreaming', *Social Politics: International Studies in Gender, State & Society*, **18** (4), 469–489.

Napolitano, M.A., E.E. Lloyd-Richardson, J.L. Fava and B.H. Marcus (2011), 'Targeting Body Image Schema for Smoking Cessation among College Females: Rationale, Program Description, and Pilot Study Results', *Behavior Modification*, **35** (4), 323–346.

Neysmith, S., K. Bezanson and A. O'Connell (2005), *Telling Tales: Living the Effects of Public Policy*, Halifax, Nova Scotia: Fernwood.

Ng, R. (1987), 'Gendering Policy Research on Immigration', in R. Ng (ed.), *Gendering Immigration: Integration Policy Research Workshop Proceedings and a Selective Review of Policy Research Literature 1987–1996*, Ottawa: Status of Women Canada, pp. 13–22.

Handbook of critical policy studies

Oakley, Ann (1989), 'Smoking in Pregnancy: Smokescreen or Risk Factor? Towards a materialist Analysis', *Sociology of Health and Illness*, **11** (4), 311–335.

Oaks, Laury (2001), *Smoking and Pregnancy: The Politics of Fetal Protection*, New Brunswisk, NJ: Rutgers University Press.

Orloff, A.S. and B. Palier (2009), 'The Power of Gender Perspectives: Feminist Influence on Policy Paradigms, Social Science, and Social Politics', *Social Politics: International Studies in Gender, State & Society*, **16** (4), 405–412.

Osborne, K., C. Bacchi and C. Mackenzie (2008), 'Gender Analysis and Community Consultation: The Role of Women's Policy Units', *Australian Journal of Public Administration*, **67** (2), 149–160.

Outshoorn, Joyce (ed.) (2004), *The Politics of Prostitution: Women's Movements, Democratic States, and the Globalisation of Sex Commerce*, Cambridge and New York: Cambridge University Press.

Perkins, K.A. (1996), 'Sex Differences in Nicotine Versus Nonnicotine Reinforcement as Determinants of Tobacco Smoking', *Experimental and Clinical Psychopharmacology*, **4** (2), 166–177.

Phillips, Susan (1996), 'Discourse, Identity and Voice: Feminist Contributions to Policy Studies', in Laurent Dobuzinskis, Michael Howlett and David H. Laycock (eds), *Policy Studies in Canada: The State of the Art*, Toronto: University of Toronto Press, pp. 242–265.

Powers, Madison and Ruth Faden (2006), *Social Justice: The Moral Foundations of Public Health and Health Policy*, New York: Oxford University Press.

Prügl, Elisabeth (2011), 'Diversity Management and Gender Mainstreaming as Technologies of Government', *Politics & Gender*, **7** (1), 71–89.

Reid, C.J. (2004), 'Advancing Women's Social Justice Agendas: A Feminist Action Research Framework', *International Journal of Qualitative Methods*, **3** (3), 1–15.

Rixecker, Stefanie S. (1994), 'Expanding the Discursive Context of Policy Design: A Matter of Feminist Standpoint Epistemology', *Policy Sciences*, **27** (2–3), 119–142.

Robinson, J., R. Deborah, A. Amos, S. Cunningham-Burley, D. Ritchie, L. Greaves et al. (2010), 'Waiting Until they Got Home: Gender, Smoking and Tobacco in Households in Scotland', *Social Science & Medicine*, **71**, 884–890.

Roggeband, C. and M. Verloo (2006), 'Evaluating Gender Impact Assessment in the Netherlands (1994–2004): A Political Process Approach', *Policy & Politics*, **34** (4), 615–632.

Solar, O. and A. Irwin (2006), 'Social Determinants, Political Contexts and Civil Society Action: A Historical Perspective on the Commission on Social Determinants of Health', *Health Promotion Journal of Australia*, **17** (3), 180–185.

Squires, J. (2005), 'Is Mainstreaming Transformative? Theorizing Mainstreaming in the Context of Diversity and Deliberation', *Social Politics: International Studies in Gender, State & Society*, **12** (3), 366–388.

Squires, Judith (2007), *The New Politics of Gender Equality*, Houndmills, Basingstoke, UK and New York: Palgrave.

Squires, Judith (2008), 'The Constitutive Representation of Gender: Extra-Parliamentary Re-Presentations of Gender Relations', *Representation*, **44** (2), 187–204.

Stark, Andrew (1992), '"Political-Discourse" Analysis and the Debate Over Canada's Lobbying Legislation', *Canadian Journal of Political Science*, **XXV** (3), September, 513–534.

Stivers, C. (1993) *Gender Images in Public Administration: Legitimacy and the Administrative State*, Newbury Park, CA: Sage Publications.

Stivers, Camilla (2002), *Gender Images in Public Administration: Legitimacy and the Administrative State*, 2nd edn, Thousand Oaks, CA: Sage Publications.

Strid, S., S. Walby and J. Armstrong (2013), 'Intersectionality and Multiple Inequalities: Visibility in British Discourse on Violence Against Women', *Social Politics: International Studies in Gender, State & Society*, **20** (4), 558–581.

Vargas, V. and S. Wieringa (1998), 'The Triangle of Empowerment: Processes and Actors in the Making of Public Policy for Women', in Geertje Lycklama a Nijeholt, Virginia Vargas and Saskia Wieringa (eds), *Women's Movements and Public Policy in Europe, Latin America, and the Caribbean*, New York: Garland, pp. 3–48.

Verloo, Mieke (ed.) (2007), *Multiple Meanings of Gender Equality: A Critical Frame Analysis of Gender Policies in Europe*, English edition, CPS Books, Budapest and New York: CEU Press.

Verloo, Mieke and Emanuela Lombardo (2007), 'Contested Gender Equality and Policy Variety in Europe: Introducing a Critical Frame Analysis Approach', in Mieke Verloo (ed.), *Multiple Meanings of Gender Equality: A Critical Frame Analysis on Gender Policies in Europe*, Budapest: Central European University, pp. 201–244.

Viscusi, W. Kip (1992), *Smoking: Making the Risky Decision*, New York: Oxford University Press.

Voigt, Kristin (2010), 'Smoking and Social Justice Public Health Ethics', first published online 16 April 2010. Doi: 10.1093/phe/phq006.

Walby, Sylvia (2011), *The Future of Feminism*, Cambridge and Malden, MA: Polity Press.

Walby, Sylvia, Jo Armstrong and Sofia Strid (2012), 'Intersectionality: Multiple Inequalities in Social Theory', *Sociology*, **46** (2), 224–240.

Waldron, I. (1991), 'Patterns and Causes of Gender Differences in Smoking', *Social Science and Medicine*, **32** (9), 989–1005.

Wardle J. and A. Steptoe (2003), 'Socioeconomic Differences in Attitudes and Beliefs about Healthy Lifestyles', *Journal of Epidemiology and Community Health*, **57**, 440–443.

Weiss, J.A. and M. Tschirhart (2103), 'Public Information Campaigns as Policy Instruments', *Journal of Policy Analysis and Management*, **13** (1), 82–138.

Waring, Marilyn (1988), *Counting for Nothing: What Men Value & What Women Are Worth*, Wellington, NZ: Allen & Unwin and Port Nicholson Press.

Wigginton, B. and C. Lee (2012), 'A Story of Stigma: Australian Women's Accounts of Smoking during Pregnancy', *Critical Public Health*, **23**, 466–481.

Woodward, A. (2004), 'Building Velvet Triangles: Gender and Informal Governance', in T. Christiansen and S. Piattoni (eds), *Informal Governance and the European Union*, Cheltenham, UK and Northampton, MA, USA: Edward Elgar, pp. 76–93.

Yanow, Dvora (1996), *How Does a Policy Mean? Interpreting Policy and Organizational Actions*, Washington, DC: Georgetown University Press.

Index